Entrepreneurship

THIRD EDITION

Entrepreneurship

Strategies and Resources

Marc J. Dollinger

Indiana University

Prentice
Hall

Upper Saddle River, New Jersey 07458

Library of Congress Cataloging-in-Publication Data

Dollinger, Marc J.
   Entrepreneurship: strategies and resources/ Marc J. Dollinger.—3rd ed.
     p. cm.
   Includes bibliographical references and indexes.
   ISBN 0-13-090995-5
   1. New business enterprises.   2. Entrepreneurship.
HD62.5 .D65 2002
658.4′21—dc21

                                              2001056124

Acquisitions Editor: Melissa Steffens
Editor-in-Chief: Jeff Shelstad
Editorial Assistant: Kevin Glynn
Senior Marketing Manager: Shannon Moore
Marketing Assistant: Christine Genneken
Managing Editor (Production): John Roberts
Production Editor: Kelly Warsak
Permissions Coordinator: Suzanne Grappi
Associate Director, Manufacturing: Vincent Scelta
Production Manager: Arnold Vila
Manufacturing Buyer: Michellé Klein
Cover Designer: Jayne Conte
Composition: BookMasters, Inc.
Full-Service Project Management: BookMasters, Inc.
Printer/Binder: Von Hoffman Graphics
Cover Printer: Coral Graphics

Credits and acknowledgments borrowed from other sources and reproduced, with permission, in this textbook appear on appropriate page within text.

Pearson Education LTD.
Pearson Education Australia PTY, Limited
Pearson Education Singapore, Pte. Ltd
Pearson Education North Asia Ltd
Pearson Education, Canada, Ltd
Pearson Educación de Mexico, S.A. de C.V.
Pearson Education—Japan
Pearson Education Malaysia, Pte. Ltd

                                      10 9 8 7 6 5 4 3 2 1
                                      ISBN 0-13-090995-5

Brief Contents

Contents

Preface

Since the publication of the first edition of *Entrepreneurship: Strategies and Resources*, the field of entrepreneurship has grown even faster than I would have predicted. There are more courses and schools teaching entrepreneurship than ever. The major business periodicals, *Business Week, Fortune,* and *The Wall Street Journal* continue expanding their coverage of entrepreneurs and their companies. *Success* magazine has begun a ranking of top business school entrepreneurship programs. Business plan competitions at the graduate and undergraduate level continue to proliferate and the prizes get larger and larger. International interest in new venture creation has grown exponentially and some of this has been delivered through the Internet in distance learning formats. I personally participated in one such effort between Indiana University and City University of Hong Kong. The technology enabled us to form joint ventures between students in the United States and Hong Kong for the purpose of starting businesses. It was marvelous.

In this third edition of *Entrepreneurship: Strategies and Resources*, I have tried to improve upon the foundation set in the first and second editions. This book is designed to be friendlier to the user, beginning with its new design and softcover. A number of new features will help make the text easier to read and understand. Dozens of new examples and minicases, called "Street Story," have been added. International examples and applications are integrated throughout the book.

ORGANIZATION OF THE BOOK

Entrepreneurship: Strategies and Resources is organized into three parts. Part I introduces the major themes and theory of the book. Chapter 1 describes the roles that new venture creation plays in the international economy, defines entrepreneurship, and shows how three factors—individuals, environments, and organizations—come together to create the entrepreneurial event.

Chapter 2 sets this textbook apart from others because it casts entrepreneurial phenomena in terms of the predictive theory of the resource-based framework. In this chapter, we present the basic concepts and model of the resource-based theory. There are six types of resources in our theory: financial, physical, technological, human, organizational, and reputational. The theory says that entrepreneurs can create sustainable competitive advantage for their ventures when they possess or can acquire and control resources that are rare, valuable, hard to duplicate, and nonsubstitutable. Here we emphasize the importance of human resources, especially the entrepreneur. We then explain how these resources are a source of profit and rent for the entrepreneur and how the new venture needs to protect these rents and profits through isolating mechanisms and first-mover advantages. Last, we offer a model of resource-based feasibility analysis to guide the student throughout the rest of the book.

Part II of *Entrepreneurship: Strategies and Resources* describes the environment for entrepreneurship. It presents the tools and techniques for analyzing business and competitive conditions and evaluating entrepreneurial opportunities. It is comparable to the strategy formulation phase of corporate strategic management. The purpose of this section is to show how the environment affects, directs, and impinges on the strategy formulation problem in new venture creation. It does this in two ways that can be expressed by the resource-based model: The environment helps determine what is rare, valuable, imitable, and substitutable *and* it is the source of resources that possess these four attributes. The strategy formulation problem in new venture creation can be stated as follows: What configuration of resources will provide the new firm with the best chances of achieving a competitive advantage?

Chapter 3 covers the aspects of the macro- and microenvironment that affect entrepreneurship and new venture creation. We present a process model for environmental analysis and then describe a five-element model of the macroenvironment: political, economic, technological, sociodemographic, and ecological factors. Next we offer the elements of the competitive environment. We incorporate the Porter model (5-forces model) into the analysis. We begin by asking two questions of utmost importance to the entrepreneur in the early stages of new venture creation:

1. Is the industry the entrepreneur is about to enter an attractive one?
2. What are the best ways to compete to increase the chances of creating a high profitability venture?

To address the first question, the chapter depicts an industry's profitability as a function of buyer and supplier power, the threat of substitutes, entry barriers, and the state of interfirm rivalry. Students are shown how to do this analysis in sufficient depth and with limited data by resorting to the basics of microeconomic theory. To address the second question, we discuss the ways that the possession and acquisition of the four-attribute resource base provides the entrepreneur with tools to overcome strong industry forces and exploit weak industry forces. The resource-based model is incorporated into this discussion by demonstrating its applicability as a screening device for new venture ideas. We create and describe a resource-based implementation matrix — the four attributes of sustainable competitive advantage by the six types of resources: financial, physical, technological, reputational, human, and organizational resources.

Chapter 4 presents types of new venture strategies and examines different positions that entrepreneurs take regarding the resources required for their firms. We present the basic entry wedges available to the new venture and develop the set of resource-based strategies. We look at how the industry life cycle influences strategy choice. New ventures can be created successfully across the life cycle, but each poses its special challenges. The chapter concludes with an overview of strategic postures and orientations that entrepreneurs can take.

Chapter 5 presents the major tool for formulating and creating new ventures: the business plan. We offer an in-depth outline for a business plan, including all the key sections and tips on how to structure the plan and the financial proposal for maximum effectiveness. The chapter continues with a discussion of the criteria and techniques for evaluating business plans. At the end of the chapter, we offer proven tips for the format and presentation, writing, and editing of successful business plans. A complete business plan follows the chapters.

Part III of *Entrepreneurship: Strategies and Resources* makes the transition from the formulation of entrepreneurial strategy to the implementation stage. The section covers strategic choice, implementation issues, and the problems of securing resources.

Chapter 6 is an entirely new chapter called "The E-Entrepreneur." It explores the special nature of electronic entrepreneurship and the impact the Internet has had on entrepreneurs and start-ups everywhere. We examine who is likely to be an e-entrepreneur and what makes Internet start-ups likely to succeed. Within the framework of the resource-based theory, we conclude that you must be able to do something that provides you with a competitive advantage. We then take a look at the underlying strategies that e-entrepreneurs can employ for their firms. Finally, we evaluate a number of e-commerce models that have been tried during the e-commerce boom.

Chapter 6 in the first and second editions covered entrepreneurship and marketing. We still think there is important information in this chapter, but it will be included in the auxiliary material for the instructor.

Chapter 7 introduces the elements of entrepreneurial finance. We discuss how financial resources can and cannot be a source of advantage for the new venture. Then we show how the venture can determine its financial and cash flow needs. After reviewing the types and sources of potential financing, we present three methods of new venture valuation. The chapter has an appendix: a brief introduction into the process of going public.

Chapter 8 shows how entrepreneurs actually obtain investors and structure the financial deal. We look at the characteristics of various types of investors and how to appeal to their needs. The basic elements of the deal structure are presented, and then more advanced elements, such as phased financing and the use of options, are introduced. The chapter concludes with a review of the legal and tax issues raised by seeking outside investors. This chapter has two appendices: an outline of a typical investment agreement and a description of the negotiable terms to a financial agreement .

Chapter 9 examines the creation and development of the organization. We begin with a discussion of the top management team and provide guidelines for effective top management processes. We do the same for boards of directors. Then we discuss the design of the new venture. Two new sections have been included in Chapter 9. The first is a summary of the research from Collins and Porras's *Built to Last*. We feel that the time to begin to think about building an enduring organization is right at the start of the venture, and the *Built to Last* concepts have great insight into the entrepreneurial problem. The second is an introduction to the dimensions of the *balanced scorecard*. We explore these in the context of entrepreneurial performance and show that performance is not just financial, but a set of indicators across four dimensions. The *balanced scorecard* can be a system of management for the entrepreneurial TMT. Last we offer a vision of the entrepreneurial workplace. We discuss how culture, ethics, and personnel practices can help make organizations unique and, therefore, provide a competitive advantage.

Chapter 10 discusses corporate entrepreneurship (intrapreneurship) and the factors that lead to successful intrapreneurship and those that hinder large corporations from being entrepreneurial. The second section discusses the possible networking and alliance formation that entrepreneurs can use to enhance their strategies, resources, and market position. The third section discusses franchising. We discuss what elements make a business concept a legitimate franchise opportunity, and what factors potential franchisees should evaluate before buying a franchise. For both sections, we offer guidelines for effective decision making.

PEDAGOGIC FEATURES

The third edition of *Entrepreneurship: Strategies and Resources* provides several features that are designed to aid the learning process:

- **Chapter outlines** at the beginning of each chapter inform the students about what they should know about entrepreneurship when they complete the reading.
- **Chapter objectives** blueprint concepts the student should understand upon completion of the chapter.
- **E-Notes** capsulize important entrepreneurship concepts for the student in a boxed format throughout each chapter.
- **Theory-based text** enables the student to analyze, evaluate, and predict the prospects for various business concepts and plans and make recommendations that increase the venture's chances.
- **Practical applications and guidelines** are offered in all the chapters to show the student how to deal with the real world of entrepreneurs, markets, and competitors.
- **Street Story** is the name of our boxed series of minicases. Each chapter contains these real-life examples drawn from the pages of the business press. Each Street Story illustrates the application of good theory to everyday new venture creation.
- **Tables and figures** throughout the book help illustrate difficult points and summarize the material for the student.
- **Extensive references** at the end of each chapter provide documentation for all of the arguments offered and enable the student to follow up with additional reading.
- **End-of-chapter case and questions** provide the basis for stimulating discussion. Adapted from real situations described in the business press, these short cases are provocative illustrations of what can go right and what can go wrong in the process of new venture creation.
- **Key terms** are listed at the end of each chapter so that the student can be familiar with the language in use of entrepreneurship.
- **Chapter discussion questions** can provide the basis of classroom debate as well as be used for written assignments.
- **Chapter exercises** are designed for two purposes. The first is to aid the student in the development of his or her own business plan. The exercises guide the students to complete the portion of their plan covered in the chapter. Chapter exercises can also be used to complement the classroom experience by having the student go out into the business community to observe entrepreneurship first hand.

- **End-of-text cases** provide an in-depth learning exercise for the student. We have prepared 10 cases for analysis. The cases deal with the problems and opportunities of new venture creation, of securing resources, of building reputations, and of operating in a competitive market. The instructor's manual offers a comprehensive teaching note for each case.
- **Name and subject indexes** at the end of the book aid in finding topics and key people and companies.
- **State-of-the-art design** makes the book more readable and enhances learning.

ACKNOWLEDGMENTS

As with the first and second edition, I would like to thank all the people at Prentice Hall, especially my editor Melissa Steffens and the production editor Kelly Warsak.

I have been fortunate to work for a very understanding dean, Dan Dalton, and department chair, Patricia McDougall, who have supported my efforts. I would like to thank Larry Glaubinger, who has inspired me through his own entrepreneurial activity and supported this work most generously.

A special thank you to my wife and partner Mimi, who helped with the organizing, writing, editing, and proofreading and who had great enthusiasm for the project.

Finally, I would like to thank the many reviewers and adopters of this edition and past editions. I have tried to incorporate all of your many helpful suggestions and comments. All errors of commission and omission are mine alone.

Dr. Kellye Jones—University of Texas–San Antonio
Prof. Roy Serpa—Texas A&M University
Prof. Lindle Hatton—California State University–Sacramento
Dr. George Norman—Tufts University
Dr. Michael Evanchik—University of Maryland
Dr. Eugene Fregetto—University of Illinois–Chicago
Dr. George H. (Jody) Tompson—University of Tampa

Marc Dollinger
Indiana University

About the Author

Dr. Marc J. Dollinger is the Glaubinger Professor of Business Administration in the Management Department at the Kelley School of Business, Indiana University. He received his MBA and Ph.D. from Lehigh University (1978, 1982) in Pennsylvania and spent 5 years at the University of Kentucky before his appointment to Indiana. He is also a visiting professor in the International Management Department of the International University of Japan. Prior to receiving his doctorate, he was the program administrator for Lehigh's Small Business Development Center.

Currently, he is the chairman of the Kelley School of Business's Undergraduate Program. Marc is also a member of the editorial board of *Entrepreneurship: Theory and Practice* and a former board member of the *Academy of Management Review.* His 1990 paper, "The Evolution of Collective Strategies in Fragmented Industries," was awarded the Best Paper Award by the *Academy of Management Review.*

The focus of Marc's career has been teaching and researching and consulting entrepreneurship and small business issues. He has published articles in the *Academy of Management Journal, Academy of Management Review, Strategic Management Journal, Entrepreneurship: Theory and Practice, Journal of Small Business Management,* and *Journal of Small Business Strategy.* He is currently working on the consortium of the Panel Study of Entrepreneurial Development.

Dr. Dollinger teaches both undergraduate and MBA entrepreneurship courses at Indiana University's School of Business and has conducted workshops for many small business groups, including manufacturer's representatives of a major medical products company, minority business owners, and owners of small firms in the retail music business. He also conducts workshops for executives, most recently for the Asian–Pacific Management Development Consortium, ALCOA-CSI, and Otis Elevator, North American Operations.

CHAPTER

A Framework for Entrepreneurship

In school, getting one right out of one is an A, whereas getting two right out of twenty is an F. In business, two for twenty is an A, whereas one for one is probably luck.

—CARY ROSEN
executive director of the National Center for Employee Ownership, Oakland, California

Outline

Entrepreneurship and Your Future
    How Does This All Add Up?
What Is Entrepreneurship?
    Creation
    Economic Organization
    Risk and Uncertainty
Where Is Entrepreneurship?
    Economic Growth and Freedom
The New Entrepreneur
Dimensions of Entrepreneurship
    New Venture Creation
    Resources, Capabilities, and Strategies
    Individuals
    Environment
    Organizations
Organization of the Book
A Final Word
Summary

Learning Objectives

After reading this chapter, you will understand:

■ How to define *entrepreneurship*
■ How entrepreneurship may affect *your future,* whether you're an employee, a venture creator, or a consumer
■ How to define the *resource-based theory* of sustained competitive advantage

1

- The *paradoxes* of entrepreneurship
- The basics of *quality* in entrepreneurial firms
- The components of an entrepreneur's *economic organization*

ENTREPRENEURSHIP AND YOUR FUTURE

As we begin the new millennium, the ideas, talents, skills, and knowledge that promote entrepreneurship are evident in young people all around the world. This is a change from previous times when the forces for economic creativity tended to favor the older and more established businesspersons. The face of the world economy has shifted, however, and the youth of today seem especially well suited for entrepreneurial activity. For instance,

- The youth of today are technologically precocious. They are comfortable with new technologies and are not fearful of change and the radical shifts that new technology can bring. Younger people are at home with computers. Over 60 percent of homes with children have computers and access to the Internet. A Carnegie Mellon study found that children and young adults are the authority on computer technology in the home.[1] Adults take a backseat to the kids. Even beyond the technical competency, young people are immersed in technology and have internalized its power.
- This generation is passionate, inquisitive, and challenging. They welcome change and embrace the idea of progress. Their lives have seen the improvement of information technology, medical and biotech processes and products, and radical changes in the way people communicate and work. They believe that continued improvement and even revolutionary change is awaiting them in the future.
- They think differently. As *Fast Company* puts it, "Forget the experience curve. The most powerful force in business today is the inexperience curve. Young companies, born on the right side of the digital divide, are running circles around their older, richer, and slower rivals. If you want your company to think outside the box, why not learn by working with people who don't know there is a box?"[2]
- They are independent. More and more "twentysomethings" consider themselves free agents. They have portable skills and will take them to wherever they can do the most good or make the most money. These workers consider themselves free agents and show little loyalty to companies that continue to make strategic mistakes or fall behind the market.

How Does This All Add Up?

The sum of these trends is more entrepreneurship and business startups for younger people. Many new ventures will be technology based. The traditional career path may become a rarity.

- The youth of today are more entrepreneurial than any previous generation. More and more people are striking out on their own. According to the Opinion Research Council, 54 percent of 18- to 24-year-olds are highly interested in starting a business, compared with 36 percent of 35- to 64-year-olds.[3] A *US News* survey found that "entrepreneur" was the preferred career of Generation X.[4] A *Newsweek* poll asked millenials (people who have come of age within a few years of the millennium) to name their hero, and more than half named Bill Gates, the founder of Microsoft.[5]

In fact, most teenagers entering college know more about business than their parents ever did. Many more teenagers work today than their parents did as teenagers. According to the Bureau of Labor Statistics, more than half the teens in the United States have jobs and over 90 percent have summer jobs.[6] Many high school students belong to investment clubs and Junior Achievement and help raise money for charities through a variety of business-like activities. Ever buy a Girl Scout cookie? Harvard University recently struck down a long-standing ban on operating businesses out of dorm rooms because they feared losing student entrepreneurs to Stanford or Columbia. *Vanity Fair* magazine has coined a new word—"enfantrepreneurs."[7]

You and your peers (entrepreneurs or enfantrepreneurs) will bring us the future. It is only a matter of time before this entrepreneurial activity brings the innovations that will shape the new millennium. The spirit of entrepreneurship—the notion of human progress, development, achievement, and change—motivates and energizes people.

Innovations in the way we work and play, travel and eat, and start our families and raise our children all create opportunities for entrepreneurs to build businesses and organizations that will exploit new technology and trends. You can also say that entrepreneurship is a self-perpetuating phenomenon: If a society has it, it is likely to get more. In the United States, we have vast and growing entrepreneurial resources and as Street Story 1-1 illustrates we have another enfantrepreneur in the making.

A best-selling book, *Workplace 2000*, argues that entrepreneurship not only affects our lives through innovation but also represents the working future for many of us.[8] As large corporations continue to lay off middle managers to realize their goals of flatter, more responsive organizations, these middle managers must "go"—and the place that they will go is into business for themselves. What will they do? They will fill the niches and markets of servicing their former employers—providing consulting, aftermarket service, and other support functions. These former middle managers will operate small entrepreneurial firms that provide high quality and value to their customers in a way that working inside the bureaucracy of a large corporation made impossible.

There are other entrepreneurial alternatives as well. In a business environment where large corporations try to stay flat, lean, and responsive, there will be a burst of growth in "micro-business" firms—firms with four or fewer employees. Some of these will be started by former middle managers and executives who have been let go. Some will be started by current managers trying to beat the clock to the next wave of layoffs. Many will be started by people who have never and will never work for *Fortune* 1000 companies.

In addition to micro businesses, there will be more corporate-backed ventures: spin-offs, joint ventures, intrapreneurial units, and partnering arrangements. Although these organizations originate in larger corporations, they are being formed specifically to stay small and entrepreneurial, to avoid bureaucracy, and to maintain their innovative edge.

"Throughout the 1990s, companies will be looking for business opportunities. Many companies will provide financial backing for innovative employees who are willing to take a risk and develop an idea for a new product or service . . . [people with] the greatest chance of developing an idea that can turn

It's a "Brand" New Game

"I'm a risk taker," says 22-year-old Jessica Nam, "but not to the point where I'd do this on my own."

Nam is doing more than starting her own small business. After graduating from Brown University, she originally planned to open a bakery to produce the banana bread and mocha brownies her college friends adored. Now, however, it looks like Jessica Nam is headed toward becoming a CEO instead of a baker. With the help of an experienced business mentor and $750,000 in seed money, Nam hopes to distribute single servings of her delicious breads, cakes, and cookies to coffee shops and convenience stores throughout New England.

Nam is a true collegiate entrepreneur. She started baking in her dorm room at night after class. She developed her business, now known as Jessica's Wonders, during an independent study course for college credit. Nam invented the flavors and recipes and gave her products zany titles based on the names of her friends. She created labels using Magic Markers and colored paper. She made good money, earning as much as $10 per loaf when she peddled her baked goods to local stores in Providence, Rhode Island.

Of course Jessica's Wonders are not just baked goods. In her business plan, Jessica described her signature product as "Bursting ripe bananas freshly baked in a moist bread with an oozing strawberry river running through it, and slices of real banana hidden in every bite. Topped with the perfect amount of cinnamon streusel crunch, this will leave you speechless!" That description helped her win second place in Brown University's first annual business plan competition.

Nam's business plan then attracted the attention of Steve Massarsky. A former entertainment lawyer and experienced promoter, Massarsky signed Nam to be the first start-up company for his new Business Incubation Group (BIG). Companies like BIG create a nurturing environment for new businesses by providing office space, marketing, accounting, personnel assistance, and mentoring advice in exchange for a percentage of the eventual profits. Massarsky also arranged for Nam to polish her own promotion skills through a summer internship at a New York City advertising agency and helped her raise funding from "angel" investors (angels are wealthy, individual investors). He believes that together they can build Jessica's Wonders into a $13 million dollar company over the next 3 years.

If they are successful, a lot of the credit will go to marketing. Massarsky transformed Jessica Nam from a baker into a brand name. Now she is not just selling banana bread, she is selling a product with a homemade feel that was created by a bright and fresh-faced young woman who competed in the Miss Rhode Island pageant and also volunteered at a homeless shelter. "She understands that she's the product," Massarsky says about Nam. "She has to be a marketer, and we're selling Jessica to a large extent."

Jessica Nam's name and face will appear on the label of every product she sells. Massarsky is also working hard to convince Nam to dress in a banana suit for the promotional photos. "If you

(continued)

(continued)

walk into a store and see an attractive woman's face staring out of a banana suit, you're going to pick up the package," he theorizes.

Nam isn't entirely comfortable with either the banana suit or the self-promotion, but she feels good about her entrepreneurial transformation out of the kitchen. "I just knew I loved coming up with ideas and creating the names and the way I want people to think of it," she says. "I also like baking, but it's true—I get sick of baking the same thing over and over."

Source: Adapted from Emily Barker, "Bananas, My Brand, and Me," *Inc.*, October 1, 2000. This article can be found online at www.inc.com/articles/details/0,,CID20435_REG3,00.html, accessed November 2001.

into a growth business will be those who get wide exposure . . . [and this exposure] will greatly increase the chance that they will identify an emerging trend or market niche that can be filled with a start-up business."[9]

You really do not need to be a futurist, however, to see that entrepreneurship will play a large and increasing role in the future of our nation's and our individual working lives. The nature of organizations, work, and employment is changing, and individuals who recognize these changes and prepare for them will be best able to succeed in the new environment. Therefore, most people will encounter entrepreneurship through the marketplace, in new products, services, or technologies, or through their own employment. The better they understand the marketplace, the better they will be able to survive and thrive in the new entrepreneurial environment.

WHAT IS ENTREPRENEURSHIP?

There have been as many definitions of entrepreneurship as there have been writers on the subject. It has been suggested that trying to define entrepreneurship may be fruitless because the term is too vague and imprecise to be useful.[10] Table 1-1 provides a short selection of definitions that have been offered.

If we examine the common elements in these definitions, we might find the following characteristics:

- Creativity and innovation
- Resource gathering and the founding of an economic organization
- The chance for gain (or increase) under risk and uncertainty

Entrepreneurship, then, is the creation of an innovative economic organization (or network of organizations) for the purpose of gain or growth under conditions of risk and uncertainty.[11] What are the implications of this definition?

Creation

The term **creation** implies a founding and an origin. Therefore, technically speaking, the purchase of an existing firm or its transfer to new owners does not represent

TABLE 1-1 Definitions of Entrepreneurship	
Source	*Definition*
Knight (1921)	Profits from bearing uncertainty and risk
Schumpeter (1934)	Carrying out of new combinations of firm organization—new products, new services, new sources of raw material, new methods of production, new markets, new forms of organization
Hoselitz (1952)	Uncertainty bearing . . . coordination of productive resources . . . introduction of innovations and the provision of capital
Cole (1959)	Purposeful activity to initiate and develop a profit-oriented business
McClelland (1961)	Moderate risk taking
Casson (1982)	Decisions and judgments about the coordination of scarce resources
Gartner (1985)	Creation of new organizations
Stevenson, Roberts, & Grousbeck (1989)	The pursuit of opportunity without regard to resources currently controlled
Hart, Stevenson, & Dial (1995)	The pursuit of opportunity without regard to resources currently controlled, but constrained by the founders' previous choices and industry-related experience

Sources: Knight, F. *Risk, Uncertainty and Profit.* Boston: Houghton Mifflin, 1921; Schumpeter, J. *The Theory of Economic Development.* Cambridge, MA: Harvard University Press, 1934; Hoselitz, B. "Entrepreneurship and Economic Growth." *American Journal of Economic Sociology,* 1952; Cole, A. *Business Enterprise in its Social Setting.* Cambridge, MA: Harvard University, 1959; McClelland, D. *The Achieving Society,* New York: John Wiley, 1961; Casson, M. *The Entrepreneur.* Totowa, NJ: Barnes and Noble, 1982; Gartner, W. "A Conceptual Framework for Describing the Phenomenon of New Venture Creation." *Academy of Management Review* 10 (1985): 696–706; Stevenson, H., M. Roberts, and H. Grousbeck. *New Business Venture and the Entrepreneur,* Homewood, IL: Irwin, 1989; Hart, M., H. Stevenson, and J. Dial. "Entrepreneurship: A Definition Revisited." Babson Frontiers of Entrepreneurship Research, 1995.

entrepreneurship. As one group of authors point out, if founding were the only criterion for entrepreneurship, then neither Watson of IBM nor Kroc of McDonald's would qualify.[12] It is rare for an organization to change ownership without a change in its management and resource configuration; however, the degree of change and innovation determines whether entrepreneurship is present. To see how large a change is needed, we can rely on Schumpeter's categories of "new combinations." Is:

- A new product or service offered?
- A new method or technology employed?
- A new market targeted and opened?
- A new source of supply of raw materials and resources used?
- A new form of industrial organization created? (This is, perhaps, the rarest of all innovations.)

Now we can see how Watson and Kroc can reapply for membership in the entrepreneur's club.

Economic Organization

The term **economic organization** means an organization whose purpose is to allocate scarce resources. This can be a firm, a business unit within a firm, a network of independent organizations, or a not-for-profit organization (NPO).[13] In what may seem paradoxical to many people, even governments can create entrepreneurial organizations under the right conditions. The business organization can, of course, pursue gain and growth as its motivations. In fact, some firms use both profit and size as their main objectives.[14] Other businesses do not seek growth, which distinguishes entrepreneurial firms from small businesses.[15] Do NPOs seek gain and growth? You bet they do. Although NPOs may be prohibited by law from making profits for stockholders, they are allowed to accumulate surpluses in their accounts. NPOs certainly seek growth: More members, more services performed, more clients served—the list may be endless.

Risk and Uncertainty

Entrepreneurship exists under conditions of risk and uncertainty. The two terms are not the same. **Risk** refers to the variability of outcomes (or returns). If there is no risk, the returns are certain. A firm operating in a risk-free environment would continue to expand forever, because a negative outcome could not occur. Therefore, risk is a limit to ever-expanding entrepreneurship.[16] **Uncertainty** refers to the confidence entrepreneurs have in their estimates of how the world works; their understanding of the causes and effects in the environment. If there is no uncertainty, then the environment can be perfectly known. If this is true, then everyone can know it (at least for a price), and it could be a source of lasting profit for anyone. Uncertainty is what makes markets and poker games. Who would continue to place bets on a hand if all the cards were face up?

E-NOTES 1-1

Entrepreneurship

A definition of entrepreneurship includes:

- innovation
- economic organization
- growth during risk and/or uncertainty

WHERE IS ENTREPRENEURSHIP?

Two conditions must exist in order for entrepreneurship to flourish. First, there must be freedom: freedom to establish an economic venture, and freedom to be creative and innovative with that enterprise. Second, there must be prosperity: favorable economic conditions that give an entrepreneurial organization the opportunity to gain and grow.

Economic Growth and Freedom

The Heritage Foundation and the *Wall Street Journal* publish an annual Index of Economic Freedom. The index examines the trade policies, taxation levels, government intervention and regulation, monetary policies, and six other categories of over 150 countries. Data from the seven years that these rankings have been made are available online at www.index.heritage.org. The 2001 rankings show that once again Hong Kong is number one. This is despite the 1997 return of Hong Kong to the People's

Republic of China under the "one country–two systems" formula. Other countries in the top of the rankings of "free" economies are (in order): Singapore, Ireland, New Zealand, Luxembourg, United States, United Kingdom, Netherlands, Australia, Bahrain, Switzerland, and El Salvador. The seven countries with the lowest rankings and categorized as "repressed" were: North Korea, Angola, Burundi, Congo, Sierra Leone, Somalia, and Sudan. Data collected by the index supports several conclusions that are important for entrepreneurs and the study of entrepreneurship. First, the study indicates the high correlation between a high level of economic and political freedom and a high standard of living. Second, a comparison of data over several years indicates that as wealthy countries become richer, they often impose fiscal restrictions that reduce economic freedom, such as higher taxation and social welfare programs. This is why the relatively well-off countries of Scandinavia and Western Europe are mostly missing from the top 10 list. The poorest countries are poor because of the lack of economic freedom, not because of a lack of aid from richer countries or a lack of natural resources.[17]

Two examples from formerly communist economies illustrate how important economic freedom can be to entrepreneurship. After years of exile in France, Anoa Dussol-Perran returned to her native Vietnam to open a passenger-helicopter service in Hanoi. To avoid a possible 3-year wait for government approval, Ms. Dussol-Perran attempted to smuggle her first helicopter into Vietnam without filing the proper paperwork. The helicopter was discovered and impounded by the Vietnamese government. It was released to Ms. Dussol-Perran only after a long wait, followed by a grueling 6-hour interview. When the time came to add a second helicopter to her service, Ms. Dussol-Perran elected to fly the new equipment from Paris to Hanoi herself rather than risk importing another machine.[18]

In contrast Jake Weinstock and his two partners have enjoyed relatively smooth sailing as they set up a Gold's Gym franchise in Moscow. Although Russia is still ranked as mostly unfree in the Index of Economic Freedom, it did place 14 slots above Vietnam in the 2001 survey. Weinstock was able to avoid customs problems with his imported equipment—reportedly the toughest hurdle for new businesses in Russia—by letting his Russian partner, a former athlete and sporting goods trader, handle those negotiations. He has also been able to avoid the organized crime threats that plague other foreign businesses. "We built up many relationships and alliances, which meant we were less susceptible to shakedowns," explains Weinstock. "We made sure important people were interested in our success."[19]

Yet even in the "free" United States entrepreneurs can run into problems concerning the economic freedom of entrepreneurs. Consider the case of Andrew Beebee. Mr. Beebee is an Internet entrepreneur who started his dot.com in the largely Hispanic Mission district of San Francisco. He signed a 5-year lease for five floors of a nine-story building when his business began to skyrocket. When he moved in, his landlord told many of the other tenants that they would not have their leases renewed because they would be removing asbestos and the building was going high-tech. These tenants, however, have their freedoms too. Over the next several months there were sit-ins, acts of civil disobedience, and picketing to protest what the neighbors and tenants saw as the gentrification of the area. Mr. Beebee was stymied and his company hemmed in by political activity and zoning ordinances. "*Aqui estamos, y no vamos*" ("Here we are, and we are not going.") chant the demonstrators.[20]

THE NEW ENTREPRENEUR

Ask any group of businesspeople today if they consider themselves to be entrepreneurs. According to Bill Sahlman, professor and senior associate dean at the Harvard Business School, "most of them will raise their hands. That doesn't mean that they are entrepreneurial, but they would certainly not like you to think they aren't."[21]

If entrepreneurship is one of the hot labels today, it is because the concept of being an entrepreneur has changed. Fifteen years ago an entrepreneur might have been described as a business version of a John Wayne cowboy (tough, gutsy, and significantly male) who steered his business through the rodeo of commerce without the help of training or education and without the assistance of bankers or other experts. Entrepreneurs were once seen as small business founders with a strong independent streak and maybe a flair for the dramatic. Entrepreneurs were once born, not made.

Things are different now (see Table 1-2). What is emerging today is a class of *professional entrepreneurs* who rely more upon their brains than their guts—and who have been trained to use both methods and technology to analyze the business environment.

TABLE 1-2 **Entrepreneurs**	
Then	*Now*
Small-business founder	True entrepreneur
Boss	Leader
Lone Ranger	Networker
Secretive	Open
Self-reliant	Inquisitive
Seat of the pants	Business plan
Snap decisions	Consensus
Male ownership	Mixed ownership
	In 1993, women owned one-third of all sole proprietorships, up from one-quarter in 1980.
Idea	*Execution*
In 1982, 80% of the CEOs of the *Inc.* 500 companies believed their companies' success was based on novel, unique, or proprietary ideas.	1992, 80% of the CEOs of *Inc.* 500 companies said that the ideas for their companies were ordinary, and that they owed their success to superior execution.
Knows the Trade	*Knows the Business*
Eastern, one of the first airlines in the United States, was founded by pilot Eddie Rickenbacker.	Federal Express, an overnight delivery service utilizing airplanes, was developed from a business plan written by Fred Smith while he was studying for his MBA at Yale.
Automation	*Innovation*
Technology lets business automate the work people had always done.	Technology lets people do things never done before.

Source: Adapted from Tom Richman, "The Evolution of the Professional Entrepreneur," *Inc.'s The State of Small Business Special Issue*, 1997, pp. 50–53.

According to Bill Wetzel, professor at the University of New Hampshire, the difference is like night and day. Wetzel says that the old-style entrepreneur of business founders was thought primarily to be about earning a living, while today's entrepreneur "has the intention of building a significant company that can create wealth for the entrepreneur and investors."[22]

The new entrepreneurs come from different sources, too. Many of them are corporate-track dropouts, pushed out by downsizing or lured out by the quest for status, big money, or control of their personal lives. Globalization has promoted an entrepreneurial spirit in both big and small companies, while information technology now enables many small start-ups to compete against big business.

Academia has contributed to the creation of this new professional entrepreneur class, too. Harvard Business School, which once had 3 or 4 professors teaching courses about small business, now has 17 full-time faculty in its entrepreneurial-studies program. Staffing at other colleges and universities reflects the same trend. The content of many finance, marketing, and other business courses has also been adjusted to reflect new venture concerns and development methods. The new class of entrepreneurs don't just do, they understand what they're doing.[23]

Entrepreneurial activity often leads to more of the same. In Street Story 1-2 we see how academia can spawn a new company for one of the new class of entrepreneurs.

DIMENSIONS OF ENTREPRENEURSHIP

New Venture Creation

This book is concerned with entrepreneurship as the formation of a new business enterprise. This is most often called simply **new venture creation.** It contains theory and research about, and descriptions of, practice and techniques of entrepreneurship. We take an economic and managerial perspective on entrepreneurship and new venture creation, although at times we borrow important material from other disciplines. Much has been written about the phenomenon of entrepreneurship and new venture creation from the economic and managerial perspectives. There have been numerous descriptive studies and some valuable empirical research, but no textbook, including this one, can offer prospective entrepreneurs advice that will ensure their success. As the introductory quote illustrates, not enough is known about entrepreneurship (or business in general) for it to be considered a "sure thing." In fact, any guidance obtained from a book is probably of little long-term value to a potential entrepreneur.[24] However, the insights a reader gains by comparing personal experience with the material in this book may be invaluable.

Resources, Capabilities, and Strategies

The foundation for this book is the **resource-based theory** of sustained competitive advantage.[25] The resource-based theory is the most appropriate to understand new venture creation because it best describes how entrepreneurs themselves build their businesses from the resources and capabilities they currently possess or can realistically acquire. Successful entrepreneurship is not simply an analytical exercise. Industry and competitor analysis—the application of the theory of industrial organization economics—alone is insufficient. The resource-based theory argues that the choice of which industry to enter and what business to be in is not enough to ensure success. The theory says that the nature and quality of the resources, capabilities, and strategies the entrepreneur possesses and can acquire can lead to long-term success.

Dot.Com Shopper

He certainly doesn't look like he knows anything at all about shopping. He wears tattered jeans and torn sweatshirts and refuses to wear a suit and tie for interviews or business meetings. His long hair is loosely gathered into a bun at the back of his head. He has a nice house, but there is no furniture in the living room. He claims that his hobby is reading and writing poetry and describes himself as a "quirky, unique person."

But despite his appearance, 31-year-old Farhad Mohit is a shopping expert. He is the co-founder of BizRate.com, an "infomediary" Web site that helps guide consumers through the sometimes bewildering array of products and services available on the World Wide Web. Shoppers can visit BizRate to search for products ranging from candy to electronics, get a listing of the vendors who carry those products, and then access feedback from other customers and BizRate research to rate those vendors.

For example, a recent search for "digital cameras" on the BizRate site produced a listing of 10 models and provided a brief description for each camera along with a low and high price. A click on one camera model produced a listing of 20 different Internet vendors. In-stock availability and price of the camera was listed for each vendor, along with a notation that this information had been updated the previous day. Each of the vendors was then rated in a variety of categories including ease of ordering, customer support, on-time delivery, and Web site performance. Another click on the vendor's name either led shoppers to a description of the vendor including physical address, phone, and the credit cards accepted, or connected them directly to the ordering site.

Farhad Mohit was born in Iran, which he fled with his family during the revolution in 1978. He has degrees in math, computer science, and economics from UCLA. By 1995, he was on his way to becoming a college professor, pursuing an MBA in entrepreneurial management at the Wharton School, when a classmate introduced him to the Internet. "Suddenly there was a way for all the world's vendors to compete," he realized. He also realized that there was a niche opportunity for an entrepreneur to help consumers find the best Internet retailers.

Mohit wrote BizRate's 80-page business plan for one of his MBA courses. He then enlisted fellow student Henri Asseily and marketing professor Dave Reibstein to start the company in June 1996. They raised $260,000 in start-up funding from family and friends, and then worked out of Mohit's family home in Los Angeles for two years to develop the Web site and secure $4.5 million in venture capital funding.

By its fourth year of operation, BizRate was attracting 4 million visitors a month, and signed more than 3,600 e-shops as its partners. Sources estimate that BizRate may be currently valued as

(continued)

(continued)

high as $500 million. "No one has established this level of credibility and depth of adoption among vendors," say John Hagel, former McKinsey & Co. partner and author of a book about infomediaries.

Mohit's company makes money by earning between 1 percent and 20 percent of every sale that is referred to a retailer from the BizRate site. It compiles customer feedback into monthly reports and sells them for $20,000 each per year to approximately 200 merchants. BizRate also sells some of its data to magazines and other research sites, including *Consumer Reports Online.* Although the company is not yet profitable, it anticipates earnings of $10 million this year.

Mohit is now dreaming about taking the company public. However, some ex-

perts think that BizRate services will be less valuable as the e-commerce market tightens. "As retailers fall out, and consumers become comfortable shopping online, they'll just go back to the retailers they like. That's where the BizRate model starts to fall apart," says David Cooperstein, market analyst for Forrester Research, Inc.

Mohit responds by noting that BizRate is adding more than 400 merchants each month. He adds, "The more consumers that come in, the more BizRate becomes a perfect marketplace." Mohit is then quick to share the company slogan with both critics and consumers: "Don't get e-screwed."

Source: Adapted from Arlene Weintraub, "E-commerce Crusader," *Business Week E.Biz,* June 5, 2000, pp. EB77–82.

Using resources that are rare, valuable, hard to copy, and have no good substitutes[26] in favorable industry conditions provides sustainable competitive advantage. Choosing the appropriate resources is ultimately a matter of entrepreneurial vision and intuition. The creative act underlying such vision is a subject that has so far not been a central focus of resource-based theory. This book extends the theory and views of entrepreneurship within the context of the resource-based theory of the firm.[27]

E-NOTES 1-2

Resource-Based Theory

The resource-based theory utilized in this book states that an entrepreneur uses resources that are:

- rare
- valuable
- hard to copy
- have no good substitutes to obtain a sustainable competitive advantage

Intelligence Versus Business Success   The resource-based theory of entrepreneurship also helps explain two of the paradoxes of entrepreneurship in ways that other theories cannot. The first paradox is often stated as, "If you are so smart, why aren't you rich?" Certainly professors and researchers can testify that there are a great many more smart people than rich people. A good theory of entrepreneurship needs to explain why intelligence does not always lead to success in business. Common logic seems to dictate that the better we understand a phenomenon such as new venture creation, the more likely we are to be successful in its practice. Textbook presentations of entrepreneurship that provide facts without examining cause and effect may make the student smarter (in some narrow sense), but these approaches are unlikely to make anyone (except the authors) richer.

The resource-based approach acknowledges that keen analysis (strategy formulation) and fact accumulation are necessary but insufficient tasks for entrepreneurs. Also, the resource-based theory follows the reality that some aspects of entrepreneurship cannot be analyzed; they are hard to copy because no one, including the founders, quite understands how or why they work. This inability to be duplicated or explained is actually a business advantage because competitors cannot copy the entrepreneur's strategy if they can't understand it. In simple language, what is known (or knowable) to all is an advantage to none. You can get smarter without getting richer if the knowledge you possess lacks any of the four characteristics (rare, valuable, hard to copy, or no substitutes).[28]

Barriers to Entry   The second paradox is summed up by the old line, "You wouldn't want to belong to any club that would have you as a member." The parallel application of this saying to new venture creation is that "you wouldn't want to enter any industry that would have you" (low-entry barriers) because if you could get in, then anyone could. Therefore, the opportunity will appear unattractive. This is the traditional economic analysis that examines the height of the entry barriers and weighs the cost of entry against the profit potential (margins) of firms in the industry and the probability of retaliation by incumbents.[29] One implication of this analysis is that, for the vast majority of economic organizations, the existing firms have the edge. Yet, experience indicates that certain individuals create businesses in industries with seemingly insurmountable barriers, and these individuals achieve superior and sometimes spectacular results. Analysis of industry structure fails to explain this because it cannot explain why everyone cannot follow. The resource-based theory can explain the likes of Sam Walton, founder of Wal-Mart (see Street Story 1-3), Ted Turner of Turner Broadcasting, and Dave Thomas of Wendy's as individuals with unique personal resources. They were able to enter industries that appeared to have powerful predatory competitors and go against the odds to build major influential organizations.

There are three significant dimensions used to study entrepreneurship: individuals, environments, and organizations. These are required to flesh out the arguments and examples.[30] The interactions among individuals, environments, and organizations make each new venture unique and must be considered.

Individuals

The role that individuals play in entrepreneurship is undeniable. Each person's psychological, sociological, and demographic characteristics contribute to or detract from his or her abilities to be an entrepreneur. Personal experience, knowledge, education, and training are the accumulated human resources that the founder contributes to the enterprise. The

Sam Walton's 10 Best Rules

Sam Walton was born in 1918 and died in 1992. In between he built the largest, most successful retail organization in the world and became America's richest person. His chosen path to empire was either "overlooked or underestimated by his rivals."

He began his life in humble beginnings but graduated from the University of Missouri and went right to work for J.C. Penney in 1940 for $75 per month. He loved retailing and the competitiveness of it. He bought his own store, a Ben Franklin, when he was mustered out of the Army in 1945. However, it was not until 1962 that the first Wal-Mart was opened.

In between, "Mr. Sam" developed many of the habits and garnered the experience that was to serve him so well later. He says his big lesson came early when he found that if he "bought an item for 80 cents . . . and priced it at a dollar, [he] could sell three times more of it than by pricing it at $1.20. I might have made only half the profit per item but because I was selling three times as many, the overall profit was much greater."

In the early 1960s, Mr. Sam discovered that others were beginning to develop large discount stores and chains. He did his homework and spent many nights on the road visiting these other merchants' stores. He admits that he "borrowed" quite a bit from Sol Price, founder of Fedmart. He finally decided that the future was discounting, and the first Wal-Mart was opened in 1962. In that year the first Kmart, Target, and Woolco stores were also opened.

Ten years after the opening of the first Wal-Mart, the scoreboard read: Kmart, 500 stores and $3 billion sales; Wal-Mart, 50 stores and $80 million sales. In addition, the four leading retailers of the first half of the century—Sears, J.C. Penney, Woolworth, and Montgomery Ward—were still flourishing, and every urban area had a regional department store or chain with which to compete. Many had resources far in excess of Walton's. So how did Mr. Sam become number one?

In a book written shortly before his death in 1992, Mr. Sam was asked about this. He said that the keys were (1) going head to head with Kmart, because the pressure of the competition made everyone a better retailer and encouraged innovation and change; (2) going small town (under 50,000 people), because it was an underserved niche; (3) employee profit sharing, because it made everyone an owner directed toward the same goal; and (4) communication and sharing information with all people inside the organization, because it empowered people and pushed responsibility for decision making down. Sam wouldn't say it, but a fifth factor was his tireless and unceasing dedication to keeping costs down and spirits up. His leadership was unparalleled by any of his competitors.

So it is clear that Mr. Sam possessed personal experience, values, vision, and dedication in heroic proportions, unequaled by any of his rivals. But were his business decisions so unique that they cannot or could not be duplicated by another firm? When asked this question, Mr. Sam came up with his 10 rules to follow, rules that worked for him. If you follow these rules, can you be the next Sam Walton?

(*continued*)

(continued)

Rule 1: Commit to your business and believe in it.

Rule 2: Share your profits with your partners (employees).

Rule 3: Motivate your partners, challenge them, and keep score.

Rule 4: Communicate everything.

Rule 5: Appreciate your associates with well-chosen words.

Rule 6: Celebrate your successes.

Rule 7: Listen to everyone and get them talking.

Rule 8: Exceed your customers' expectations.

Rule 9: Control your expenses.

Rule 10: BREAK ALL THE RULES. Swim upstream. Go the other way.

Rule 10 is a doozy (as well as a paradox). It suggests that rules 1 through 9 may not be for everyone. It also suggests that Mr. Sam himself knew that if you followed everyone's advice on everything, you could never achieve much more than everyone else did. Just as Mr. Sam visited as many Kmarts as he could, everyone who paid attention could have visited all the Wal-Marts and copied what they did. You could easily duplicate rules 1 through 9, but you could never duplicate precisely the decisions that were made following rule 10. This is the unique and idiosyncratic aspect that made Mr. Sam the world's greatest merchant.

Source: Fortune, March 23, 1992, pp. 113–114, and June 29, 1992, pp. 98–106.

personal integrity of the entrepreneur and the way the entrepreneur and the new venture are viewed by others is captured in the reputation of the firm. The risk profile of the entrepreneur determines the initial configuration of the venture — for example, financing, product offerings, and staffing. Although we speak now of the individual entrepreneur, frequently the entrepreneur is not alone. Entrepreneurs rely on a network of other people, other businesspeople, and other entrepreneurs. These contacts are personal resources that help them acquire additional resources and start their business. It is true that "who you know" and "who knows you" are sometimes very valuable resources in new venture creation.

One of the most important responsibilities of the entrepreneur as an individual is the establishment of the ethical climate for the new venture.

Business **ethics** has been defined in many ways by many people. One definition of ethical behavior is: any business decision that creates value for the customer by matching quality and price. Why is this so? Ethical decisions (1) provide the customer with valid data about the product and service, (2) enable the customer to make a free and informed choice, and (3) generate customer commitment to the product and the organization that provides it. Violations of these three rules produce unethical behavior — invalid and false data, coerced and manipulated decisions, and low integrity and poor reputation for the firm.[31]

How important are ethics and a good reputation? According to one advertising executive, "The only sustainable competitive advantage any business has is its reputation."[32] Entrepreneurs are sometimes placed in situations where ethical decision making appears hard. It is tempting to cut corners, look for the edge by shading the truth, and adopt a *caveat emptor* (let the buyer beware) attitude. If entrepreneurs see themselves as outsiders, underdogs, overworked, and underappreciated, they may make decisions employing the premise that the ends justify the means. Caution is advised. The means will become known, and if the means fail the tests for ethical conduct, the fine reputation of the product and the entrepreneurial team will be irreparably tarnished.

Environment

The environment poses both opportunities and threats for new venture creation. The opportunities come mostly in the form of resources—money, people, technology. The entrepreneurial challenge is to acquire resources from the environment, combine them with other resources already possessed, and configure the new venture into a successful organization. The threats, or constraints, imposed by the environment are those inherent in any competitive marketplace. The entrepreneur can overcome these constraints, or protect against their worst effects, by developing strategies that exploit the firm's resources. The key elements of the environment are the government and politics, the economy, technology (i.e., innovation and invention), sociodemographics, and the ecosystem. Because the environment is characterized by change, uncertainty, and complexity, entrepreneurs must continually monitor events and trends and make adjustments to their organizations and strategies.

Organizations

The result of nearly all entrepreneurial start-ups is the creation of a new organization. The organization has a form and structure. It has a strategy that enables it to penetrate or create a market (entry wedges) and protect its position (isolating mechanisms). It possesses resources that it transforms into value for its customers.

However, an organization can be even more than this. An organization is made up of people who have skills and talents, values and beliefs, and maybe a recognition that by working together they can create something special. The organization can have a culture that supports high performance and high quality.

Quality is a difficult concept to grasp, yet it is critical to success. Garvin identified five different approaches to the concept of **quality:** transcendent, product based, user based, manufacturing based, and value based.[33]

The Transcendent Approach   The transcendent approach to quality is philosophical and asks questions about the nature of things. From this viewpoint, quality is concerned with "innate excellence."[34] Some experts dismiss this approach as being of little practical value for the businessperson, but we believe it can offer some guidance. A product's or service's quality concerns the function that it is intended to serve. Anything that inhibits that function detracts from quality. For example, consider quality in terms of a restaurant meal. Its quality includes its nutritional value, premium ingredients, taste, aroma, presentation, and timeliness. A poor-quality meal lacks what is necessary and also has other qualities attached, such as slow service, foreign ingredients, poor presentation, and careless preparation. The high-quality meal is distinguished from the poor-quality meal because it has only the elements it should and none of the detracting elements.

Product-Based Approach   The product-based concept of quality focuses on an attribute of the product that is held in high regard—for example, the high butterfat content in ice cream, the tightness and intensity of evenness (consistency) of stitches in a garment, or the durability of a washing machine. Quality of this sort can be ranked because it lends itself to quantitative measurement. Because the assessment of these attributes can be made independently of the user, product-based quality is sometimes referred to as "objective" quality.[35]

User-Based Approach   User-based quality is "subjective"—it exists in the eye of the beholder. Customers have different preferences, wants, and needs and therefore judge a product's quality by its usefulness to them. Are producers who meet these needs, but do so in nonquantitative ways (perhaps through advertising or superior product distribution), producing quality products? And when "subjective" quality competes with "objective" quality, is "good enough" really enough?

Manufacturing-Based Approach   Manufacturing-based quality, or process quality, concerns the attention to detail in the construction and delivery of the product or service. It is linked to customer wants and needs and to objective quality because it presumes that someone defined "conformance standards" for the product or service. *Quality* is defined as the degree to which the product conforms to set standards or the service to set levels and times. In other words, high reliability and zero manufacturing defects are important. The problem with this definition is that the link between standards and customer preferences was established in the past, perhaps long ago, and is not responsive to changes in the environment. Manufacturing-based quality shifts attention internally, on how things are done. At its worst, it leads to doing the wrong things but doing them very well.

Garvin's last category of quality is value based. This approach takes the concept of quality farther than the previous definitions. **Value** evaluates quality in terms of price. This is what customers consider when they decide whether to buy a product or service. If money were not scarce, nothing would be valuable, not even quality, because everyone could buy anything—but this is, of course, not true. Therefore, in business where prices are signals and money is scarce, value, not pure quality, is critical.

Which is the correct perspective on quality and value for the entrepreneur? We believe that entrepreneurs should understand all these perspectives and be able to make decisions based on their current situations. The ability to understand many facets of quality improves the entrepreneur's decision making. It enables an entrepreneur to meet the challenges posed by complex problems. Figure 1-1 illustrates the dimensions of entrepreneurship and new venture creation.

Organizations

An economic organization has:

- something of value to offer customers (generic strategies)
- form and structure (functional-level strategies)
- entry wedges (to penetrate or create a market)
- isolating mechanisms (to protect its position)
- a culture that determines performance and quality

ORGANIZATION OF THE BOOK

Chapter 1 provides the framework for the study of entrepreneurship, beginning with the theme that entrepreneurs succeed because of the resources that they possess and acquire and the strategies they employ. This resource-based theory is described in greater detail in Chapter 2, where we also examine different types of resources and capabilities, and explore the relative importance of each.

Chapter 3 portrays the environment for entrepreneurship as two interrelated components: first, a remote environment that cannot be controlled by the entrepreneur, and second, a competitive environment in which the entrepreneur executes his or her strategies and plans. The importance of environmental scanning and a model for scanning are also presented in this chapter. Chapter 4 details exactly how entrepreneurs go into business by looking at the strategies they pursue. We will also cover many of the marketing, sales, and pricing strategies that are critical for the new venture. Chapter 5 explains the basics of writing the business plan. The plan is required for all new ventures and it is the transition from planning to implementation.

Chapter 6 examines e-entrepreneurship. The advent of electronic commerce and the Internet has changed forever the nature of starting a business for those who incorporate technology into their operations and products. We will focus on information-related businesses and see how the combination of possessing rare, valuable, and hard-to-copy information and the Internet provide new opportunities for entrepreneurs.

Chapter 7 describes the foundations of entrepreneurial financing, including debt, equity, and cash flow. Chapter 8 continues the discussion of financial issues by looking at how investors and entrepreneurs view each other, and describes how they are likely to want to structure a financial deal. The chapter also covers legal and tax issues.

Chapter 9 explores the new venture's organization. We will look at how some organizations are strong from the start and have characteristics that enable them to persevere through many business cycles. Our discussion is based on Collins and Porras's book, *Built to Last*. Chapter 10 describes corporate venturing and intrapreneurship. We see how large organizations try to keep fresh so they can stay innovative and entrepreneurial.

The 10 chapters are followed by a selection of cases drawn from real situations and business plans. These cases illustrate the possibilities and opportunities facing entrepreneurs—many who were once students just like you.

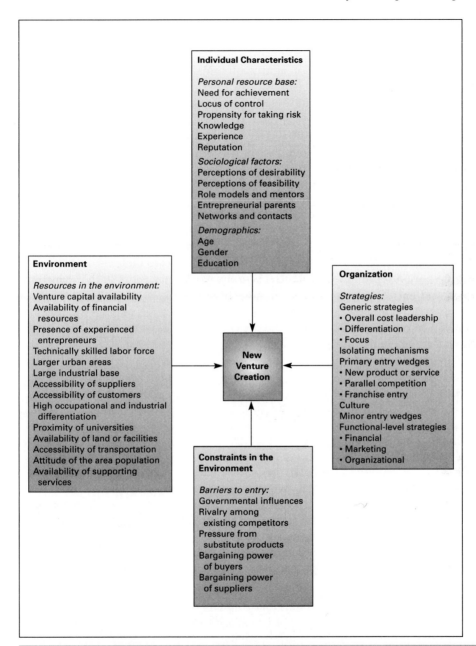

FIGURE 1-1   Dimensions of New Venture Creation

Source: Adapted from W. Gartner, "The Conceptual Framework for Describing the Phenomenon of New Venture Creation," *Academy of Management Review* 10 (1985): 696–706.

A FINAL WORD

Not everyone will succeed as an entrepreneur, and sometimes the people who do succeed do so only after a number of painful attempts. As the introductory quote illustrates, studying entrepreneurship and being an entrepreneur are two different things. The odds of success are quite different in these two endeavors, and the outcomes are evaluated by different criteria. However, the student of entrepreneurship should realize that he or she can be a successful entrepreneur. Previous academic achievement is not a requirement. Many of the students who excel in accounting, marketing, or finance will spend most of their careers working for entrepreneurs—people who were better at seizing opportunity than taking classroom examinations.

Try not to be too concerned about the grades you receive in this class. Consider the story of Fred Smith, founder of Federal Express. It is said that when he took the entrepreneurship course in which he proposed a nationwide delivery system for packages that would compete with the U.S. Post Office, he received the grade of C for his efforts. Sometimes the teachers of entrepreneurship have limits to their vision as well. The true test of your entrepreneurial potential is in the marketplace, not in the classroom.

Summary

The future is full of entrepreneurial opportunities, and new venture creation and entrepreneurship are changing the face of the world's businesses and economies. Historically, entrepreneurship has taken many different turns. In today's market-based economies, new venture creation is the key to technological and economic progress. Through entrepreneurship, people will continue to live better, longer, and more rewarding lives.

We have defined entrepreneurship as the creation of an innovative economic organization (or network of organizations) for the purpose of gain or growth under conditions of risk and uncertainty. This definition enables us to make distinctions between entrepreneurship and other wealth- and income-generating activities.

Although entrepreneurs and entrepreneurship have been studied from many different perspectives, we take an economic and managerial perspective in this book. The guiding framework for our discussion and analysis of entrepreneurial opportunities is the resource-based theory of sustainable competitive advantage. This theory enables us to understand what is unique about the new venture and how the new enterprise will create value for its customers and subsequently its founders. The managerial dimensions of entrepreneurship are individuals, environments, and organizations. These dimensions provide us with a useful organizing framework to view the complex forces and interactions that produce entrepreneurial activity.

Key Terms

- Creation
- Economic organization
- Entrepreneurship
- Ethics

- New venture creation
- Quality
- Resource-based theory
- Risk

- Uncertainty
- Value

Discussion Questions

1. What would it be like to work for an entrepreneurial firm? A micro business? Compare this to working for a *Fortune* 500 firm.
2. What are Schumpeter's definitions for an entrepreneurial new venture? Give examples of businesses you know that meet these criteria.
3. What can modern societies that have little or no history of entrepreneurship (like Russia) do to encourage and sustain it?
4. What kind of changes might have to occur in a country like Vietnam or Cuba to make them more accessible to entrepreneurs?
5. What kind of American-style ventures do you think would prosper abroad, especially in those countries with a low level of economic freedom?
6. Do you think entrepreneurs are *born* or *made?*
7. Why doesn't "being smart" easily translate into "being rich?"
8. How do entrepreneurial dimensions of individuals, environments, and organizations interact to produce new ventures?
9. Discuss the different forms of quality. Why is quality important for an entrepreneur?
10. What is value? How is it created?

Exercises

1. Search the business press (*Business Week, Fortune, Wall Street Journal,* and others) to identify future entrepreneurial opportunities. These could fulfill any of Schumpeter's criteria. What different options would an entrepreneur have in developing these opportunities? Could you develop these?
2. Take any of the future entrepreneurship examples at the beginning of the chapter and describe what kinds of businesses could be created from these opportunities. How would these businesses be developed? Could you develop these?
3. Interview an entrepreneur. Find out what "rules" he or she followed to become a successful entrepreneur. Ask your entrepreneur if he or she agrees with Sam Walton's Rule 10.
4. Interview a government official in your city or county. How does this person view entrepreneurship? What does the government do to encourage or discourage entrepreneurship? Why do they do this?
5. Read a nonbusiness book or article about entrepreneurship. (Hint: Go to the library.) How is entrepreneurship treated in this material? How does it add to the economic and managerial approach we take in the business school?

DISCUSSION CASE

Invasion on the Internet

Once Web surfing became popular, it was only a matter of time until the Internet was transformed into a huge, thundering pipeline of . . . advertising! Billboard-style banner ads are spread across many Web pages, and you can purchase everything from astrological predictions to vacuum cleaners via the Internet. In case you're one of the many Web cruisers who have learned to tune out those bright but passive banner ads, some electronic entrepreneurs have now developed new interactive ways to deliver their commercial messages.

Ad robots are perhaps the most obnoxious—oops! advanced—new method of Internet advertising. If you like to spend some of your Internet time in chat rooms, be forewarned that what you type gives listeners information about you and your lifestyle. For example, if you enter a chat room sponsored by Planet Direct of Wilmington, Massachusetts, and you happen to type in a word like *dirty,* you may receive an on-screen visit from Dusty, a cartoon character that wants to tell you all about products made by Black & Decker. Dusty looks suspiciously like one of that company's dustbuster appliances, and because this ad robot has identified you as a neatness freak, Dusty is just full of cleaning tips and product pitches from his producer.

Less obtrusive but just as tricky is the advertising method known as push technology. An example of this is the Game Ticker developed by Yoyodyne, Inc., an Internet promotions and marketing company from Irvington, New York. Game Ticker is a kind of virtual slot machine that spins new matches every four minutes in a small window on a viewer's screen. You may not have to search for Game Ticker; thanks to computer technology, it may pop up unrequested on your PC as part of a screen saver or as a companion to weather information. Every time your eyes glance at the Game Ticker you can't help but notice the small box ads from sponsors such as Duracell and Tinactin directly beneath the slot window. If Game Ticker spins three symbols in a row while you're watching, you win a prize. The advertiser is the real winner, however, because you have to provide your e-mail address to claim the prize, guaranteeing that you'll also receive a lot more advertising sent directly to your computer address.

Of course you can't really get something for nothing, even on the Internet. In cyberspace you may be asked to pay in advance with your patience and undivided attention. "We didn't think the banner ads had much value" because they are easily ignored, says Michael Paolucci, CEO of Interactive Imaginations Inc. of New York. Paolucci's company produces Riddler, an Internet trivia and word game site that reports that it has about 65,000 visitors each day. While each visitor is waiting for Riddler's games to download onto their computer, they are forced to watch full-page computer screen ads from companies such as MasterCard and Snapple. Bingo Zone, an interactive bingo game site from nineCo Inc. of Boston, makes viewers sit through a succession of computer ads before they are allowed to play the game.

Innovative as these new electronic pitches may be, potential advertisers are

(continued)

(*continued*)

somewhat nervous about how consumers will react. "Publishers and advertisers have the real potential to ruin their brand if they're too over the top," says Evan Neufeld, an online advertising analyst for the media-tracking firm of Jupiter Communications LLC of New York. Black Sun Interactive Inc. of San Francisco, creator of the server that makes the ad robots possible, claims to have a "consumer bill of rights" that any advertiser using the robots must agree to uphold. These rights stipulate that a robot must identify itself as advertising as soon as it starts talking, and that viewers must have the ability to mute the robot. Even the advertising agency that arranged for the Black & Decker ad robots isn't completely comfortable with the concept. "My mind is far from made up," says Rob Goergen, supervisor at McCann-Erickson Worldwide in New York.

Both agencies and advertisers are keeping a close watch on how consumers respond to this new interactive technology. After all, there are some people who said that the public would never tolerate any advertising on the Internet . . . and some who said that TV advertising would never work, either.

For an update on Yoyodyne, go to www.cnet.com/news/0,10000,0-1003-200-334118,00.html.

CASE QUESTIONS

1. As a consumer, how do you feel about this new advertising technology?

2. To what ethical standards do you think Internet advertisers should adhere?

3. Would you predict that interactive computer advertising will become commonplace or not?

4. Do you think the creators of these new advertising methods are entrepreneurs? Why or why not?

Source: Adapted from Rebecca Quick, "Web Sites Start Using A Much Harder Sell," *Wall Street Journal,* April 24, 1997.

CHAPTER

2

Resources and Capabilities

There is nothing as practical as a good theory.
—KARL POPPER

Outline

Learning Objectives

After reading this chapter, you will understand:

■ Various approaches and theories about *entrepreneurship*
■ The *resource-based theory of entrepreneurship*, which explains how new firms can obtain and sustain competitive advantage
■ *Strategic resources*, and how these resources influence success
■ Some of the misconceptions about *personality traits* and the entrepreneurial personality

24

■ Why and how an entrepreneur is the primary *human resource* for a new venture

■ The components of the *entrepreneurial event,* which is the creation of a new venture

Why do entrepreneurs need a theory of entrepreneurship? Because it enables its user to be efficient. Efficiency for the entrepreneur means recognizing what kinds of information are helpful and knowing where it can be obtained. The efficient entrepreneur uses the theory to translate this raw information into usable data and process the data into categories and variables. A good theory tells the user how things and events are related—which are likely to be external causes and independent, and which are likely to be internal results and controllable. A good theory also tells us the probable direction of causality. Elements may vary in a positive direction (go up or down together), in a negative direction (move in opposite ways), or be unrelated. Finally, a theory tells the user the timing and sequencing of events. Some things occur before others, and these are leading variables; others occur after, and these lag. When events happen at the same time, they are concurrent.

Therefore, an entrepreneur with a good theory of how entrepreneurship works is practical and efficient. This is crucial because entrepreneurship can be expensive. Real-time failures cost money and the irreplaceable time of many people as well as their hopes and reputations. There are thousands of opportunities for entrepreneurship, but we cannot try them all. Which will we pursue? By employing a good theory, we can think about all of the problems and issues of new venture creation without having to start business after business to see what works and what does not.

A warning is in order. A theory is not a law. A theory does not pretend to explain precisely what will happen with absolute certainty in all cases. It deals with hypotheses and propositions—educated guesses about the chances that certain relationships exist and the strength and nature of these relationships. If there was a "law of entrepreneurship," then once it was known, everyone could apply it and experience unlimited success. This does not make sense in any market-based economy where competition is prevalent. Besides, if everyone could succeed, there would not be much profit in it. We should be pleased that we have a theory and not a law of entrepreneurship.

Some people say that there have been a great many successful entrepreneurs and most of them did not have a theory. How did they do it? One serious possibility (we will discuss it later in the chapter) is luck.[1] Another possibility is that they succeeded after many failures, an expensive and time-consuming method. But the most likely explanation is that their success was the result of a tacit, or unspoken, theory of how their businesses and industries operate. Like Sam Walton, the entrepreneur who created Wal-Mart and Sam's Club, and his rules in Chapter 1 (Street Story 1-3), a lifetime of experience can help to summarize the theory, but some pieces are still so complex and intuitive that they are unknown even to the theorist.

This chapter introduces the fundamentals of the resource-based theory of entrepreneurship. The resource-based theory is efficient and practical because it focuses on the strengths, assets, and capabilities of entrepreneurs and their ventures. It incorporates market opportunity and competition into the model, but it emphasizes resources. The entrepreneur may already control these resources or may be able to obtain them in the future. But without resources to exploit a situation, even the best situation cannot create an entrepreneur.[2] First, we present the basic terminology and concepts of the theory. Then we look at the relative importance of the different types of resources the entrepreneur will need to start the business. We then take a more in-depth look at how the entrepreneur is a key human resource for the new venture.[3]

E-NOTES 2-1

Theories

A good theory:

- identifies useful information and tells where it can be obtained
- explains how variables can be related
- forecasts what may happen (causality) when elements are positive or negative
- predicts timing and sequencing of events

IDENTIFYING ATTRIBUTES OF STRATEGIC RESOURCES

What is a resource? A **resource*** is any thing or quality that is useful.[4] No two entrepreneurs are alike, and no two new firms are identical. Our resource-based theory of entrepreneurship makes sense for the study of new venture creation because it focuses on the differences that characterize entrepreneurs and the founding of their companies. Entrepreneurs are individuals who are unique resources to the new firm, resources that money cannot buy. The theory says that firms have different starting points for resources (called "resource heterogeneity") and other firms cannot get them (called "resource immobility"). Our theory values creativity, uniqueness, entrepreneurial vision and intuition, and the initial conditions (history) under which new ventures are created.[5]

What are the origins of new firms? Economic organizations that have their origins in the resources of the entrepreneur and the assets that entrepreneurial team controls can potentially acquire and, finally, combine and assemble. Firms usually begin their history with a relatively small amount of strategically relevant resources and skills, and each company's uniqueness shows how these resources are expected to perform in the marketplace.[6] Our theory has a rather simple formula:

Buy (or acquire) resources and skills cheaply→
Transform (the resource or skill) into a product or service
Deploy and implement (the strategy)→
Sell dearly (for more than you paid)

However, this is only possible if cheap or undervalued resources and skills exist. Their availability depends on market imperfections and differences of opinion about

---

*To improve the readability of the text, at various times we will use the terms "resource," "capital," and "asset" interchangeably. Also, when we say resource we intend it to include "skill" and "capability." **Capability** and **skill** in this context mean the ability to do something useful.

prices and events. These are not limitations, because perfect agreement seldom exists, and the key to an entrepreneur's vision is insight into the future.[7]

Our resource-based theory holds that sustainable competitive advantage (SCA) is created when firms possess and employ resources and capabilities that are:

1. *Valuable* because they exploit some environmental opportunity
2. *Rare* in the sense that there are not enough for all competitors
3. *Hard to copy* so that competitors cannot merely duplicate them
4. *Nonsubstitutable* with other resources.

Why are these four characteristics so important? When a firm possesses and controls resources with these four characteristics, it can withstand competitive pressures. If the new enterprise can protect these resources and maintain these four qualities, it will have competitive advantage over the long term. New ventures that form with some of these characteristics but not others have short-term or minor advantages. Firms with all these qualities, but not in full measure and without a plan to protect the resources, will have a competitive advantage until other firms are able to copy and imitate them. If the entrepreneur's goal is to achieve SCA for the new venture, then he or she must create a venture that is forgiving, rewarding, and enduring.[8] If not, the entrepreneur fades into an also-ran whose bundle of resources and skills may soon be depleted by the forces of destructive capitalism and go out of business.[9]

What are strategic resources? Strategic resources create competitive advantage. There is a distinction between strategic and nonstrategic, or common, resources. Not all capital resources are strategically important for the entrepreneur. Many can be considered "common" because they are necessary for carrying out the firm's usual activities but provide no specific advantage. Ordinary desks, chairs, and office furniture are examples. Some resources may prevent the formulation and implementation of valuable strategies by their shoddiness, imperfections, and lack of quality. Still others may prevent beneficial strategies by blinding the entrepreneur to alternative possibilities because he or she focuses too narrowly on resources already controlled rather than resources potentially controllable.[10]

It is also important to distinguish between **competitive advantage** and **sustained competitive advantage.** Competitive advantage occurs when the entrepreneur "is implementing a value-creating strategy not simultaneously being implemented by any current or potential competitors."[11] "Value creating" in this definition refers to above-normal gain or growth. Sustained competitive advantage is competitive advantage with a very important addition: Current and potential firms are unable to duplicate the benefits of the strategy. Although SCA cannot be competed away by duplication, this does not mean that it can last forever. Changes in the environment or industry structure can make what once was SCA obsolete. Important strategic factors in one setting may be barriers to change in another or simple irrelevant.

Valuable Resources

What makes resources valuable? Resources are **valuable** when they help the organization implement its strategy effectively and efficiently. This means that in a "strengths, weaknesses, opportunities, and threats" model of firm performance, a valuable resource exploits opportunities or minimizes threats in the firm's environment. A valuable resource is useful for the operation of the venture.[12] Examples of valuable resources and capabilities are property, equipment, people, and skills such as marketing, financing, and accounting. All of these are fairly general, however, so we must look at other factors.

Rare Resources

Valuable resources shared by a large number of firms cannot be a source of competitive advantage or SCA. Because of their widespread availability, they are not rare. An example might be legal resources, either independent professionals on retainer or staff. Their major purpose is to minimize threats of lawsuits from a contentious environment. Clearly these are valuable resources in the sense that they neutralize a threat, but lawyers are not rare. Most, if not all, firms have access to approximately the same legal talent (at a price, of course). Retaining legal counsel or building a corporate legal staff cannot be the source of an advantage. Common resources like these may be necessary under certain conditions and may improve chances for survival, but they are not a source of SCA.

How rare does a resource need to be to generate a competitive advantage? A unique and valuable resource clearly gives the firm SCA, but does it need to be one of a kind? Probably not. A resource can be considered rare as long as it is not widely available to all competitors. If supply and demand are in equilibrium, and the market-clearing of the resource is generally affordable, it would cease to be rare. Examples of resources that may be considered rare are things like a good location, managers that are also considered good leaders, or the control of natural resources like oil reserves (if you are in the oil business).

Hard-to-Copy Resources

Firms with rare and valuable resources clearly have advantages over firms lacking such assets. Indeed, such strategic endowments often lead to innovation and market leadership.[13] However, at some price even rare resources can be obtained. If the price is so high that no profit is made, there is no SCA because the firm has spent its advantage on the resource. Where duplication is not possible at a price low enough to leave profits, the resource is said to be **hard to copy** (also called *imperfectly imitable*). There are three factors that make it difficult for firms to copy each other's skills and resources: unique historical conditions, causal ambiguity, and social complexity.

Unique Historical Conditions   The defining moment for many organizations is their founding. At birth, organizations are imprinted with the vision and purpose of their founders. The initial assets and resources that accompany the organization's origin are unique for that place and time. Firms founded at different times in other places cannot obtain these resources; thus, the resources cannot be duplicated. Examples of unique historical foundings abound, such as starting a company in a great location that was unrecognized by others at the time. Another example might be the creation of a new venture by scientists and engineers whose special knowledge represents human capital. Recently this has been true for companies in genetic engineering or software development.

Ambiguous Causes and Effects   Causal ambiguity exists when the relationship between cause and effect is not well understood or ambiguous.[14] In business, this means that there is doubt about what caused what and why things happened. When these things are imperfectly understood, it is difficult for other firms to duplicate them. Even though the pieces may look the same as in the original, the rules of congruence are unknown, so the imitator cannot make it work. Entrepreneurs themselves often cannot explain their own success, so how can imitators hope to duplicate their operations?

It may seem odd that a firm with high-performance skills and resources has no better idea why things work than the potential imitator. How is that possible? Economic organizations can be very complex. The relationships among product design, development, manufacturing, and marketing are not subject to complete quantitative analysis. They often depend on the complex interaction of social, psychological, economic, and technical factors. Even when organizations have all the information about their competitors, they often are unable to answer such questions as

- What makes one firm's sales force more effective?
- What makes its production more efficient?
- Why are its designs more appealing to the customer?

These are but a few of the areas that are ambiguous. Nobody can answer these questions.

What if there is no causal ambiguity? Consider a firm that understands the causes and effects between its resources and its performance. Can it keep that secret from its competitors? Not in the long run. Competitors have strategies to unearth the information they need. Among these are hiring workers and managers away from the advantaged organization and devising schemes to extract the needed information. It may take time and money, but in the long run the vital secrets will be known throughout the industry. The entrepreneur who started with an advantage will not be able to sustain it indefinitely.

Complex Social Relationships   Social complexity is the third reason a firm's capabilities and resources may not be easily duplicated. As long as a firm uses human and organizational resources, social complexity may serve as a barrier to imitation. Why? The interpersonal relationships of managers, customers, and suppliers are all complex. Someone, for example, could identify that our customers like our salespeople, but knowing this does not make it possible for competitors to copy the likability of our salespeople. The competitor could even hire away our whole sales force, but even this may not reproduce the original relationship: The sales force may now work under different conditions, with different managers, and for different incentives.

Perhaps the most complex social phenomenon is **organizational culture.**[15] The new venture's culture is a complex combination of the founder's values, habits, and beliefs and interaction of these elements with the newly created organization and the market. The culture might be, among other things, very supportive, highly authoritarian, very aggressive, extremely thrifty, or combinations of all these and additional factors. As organizations grow, subcultures form, adding additional complexity. Organizational cultures are difficult to "know" from the outside; they cannot be directly observed and resist quantitative measurement. That makes them almost impossible to copy. In Street Story 2-1, we see the kind of organizational culture that can be created by a very competitive former athlete as he tries his hand at starting a number of companies.

Playing the Competitive Edge

If you were an investor who had poured $40 million of your own money into an Internet incubator and funneled another $2 million into each of the 14 fledgling companies started in that incubator, who would you pick to run one of those companies?

If you are Scott Blum, CEO of the net incubator ThinkTank, you'd pick a former athlete and seasoned competitor. "Resumes aren't worth the paper they're printed on," explains Blum. "If someone excelled at sports, that's interesting to me."

Blum's faith in the way sports prepares people to compete in business comes from his own experience. Enrolled in a swimming class at the age of 5 to control his hyperactivity, Blum became a national junior champion swimmer at the age of 8. Dropping out of community college after just 1 year, Blum borrowed $17,000 from his father to launch a company called "MicroBanks" to sell memory modules for computers. Two years later, he scored when he sold MicroBanks to Sentron Technology for $2.5 million.

His next venture was Pinnacle Micro, a company that manufactured optical compact disc components. Blum fumbled there when the Securities and Exchange Commission charged the company with illegally reporting sales of products in one quarter that were not shipped until the following quarter. However, Blum rebounded in 1997 with buy.com, a Web superstore that attracted customers by selling everything below cost in the beginning, using lots of advertising to increase sales, and reducing costs by "virtual fulfillment." This was, in fact, a Scott Blum innovation: He was the first e-tailer to outsource the entire order fulfillment process to other companies.

Now Blum's focus has shifted to ThinkTank. "I have a passion for starting companies," he says. "Now I want to help other entrepreneurs get to the next level." At ThinkTank, entrepreneurs share a marketing department, human resources department, and other services. Start-up employees work in open cubicles instead of offices to facilitate the easy exchange of ideas. Most of the new ventures being hatched at ThinkTank were actually created by Blum. The start-up company eJets, which serves executives who charter jets, was born when Blum had problems leasing a plane to return from a surfing vacation. Within 24 hours, Blum had purchased the eJets domain name, and a couple of months later he hired a CEO and launched the site.

Blum will have to be a sharp competitor to win a gold medal with Think-Tank. Industry analysts say that there is an overload of Internet incubators; more than 350 new companies who want to help new ventures grow were created in the past year. "Some of them will succeed—especially those that are run by people with golden Rolodexes and a lot of experience raising good companies," predicts Dinah Adkins, executive director of the National Business Incubation Association. "Some won't." With so many dot-coms now in trouble and the market for initial public offerings in decline, many once highly regarded incubators are striking out.

Backed by his team of sports-seasoned employees, Scott Blum remains optimistic about the chances for Think-Tank. "We want to score home runs," he says, "but all I need is a single or a triple."

Source: Adapted from Arlene Weintraub, "In Search of the Perfect Wave," *Business Week E.Biz,* September 18, 2000, pp. EB 116–120.

Organizational cultures are the kinds of resources that are very hard to copy. It may not always be pretty, but it is informative.

Nonsubstitutable Resources

Nonsubstitutable resources are strategic resources that cannot be replaced by common resources. For example, let us say that there are two firms, A and B. A has a rare and valuable resources and employs this resource to implement its strategy. If B has a common resource that can be substituted for the valuable and rare resources of A, and these common resources do basically the same things, then the rare and valuable resources of A do not confer strategic advantage. In fact, if B can obtain common resources that threaten the competitive advantage of A, then so can many other firms, thereby ensuring that A has no advantage.

Very different resources can be substitutes for each other. An expert-system computer program may substitute for a manager. A charismatic leader may substitute for a well-designed strategic-planning system. A well-designed programmed-learning module may substitute for an inspirational teacher. Figure 2-1 summarizes the four resource attributes needed for competitive advantage.

FIGURE 2-1   Resource Attributes and Competitive Advantage

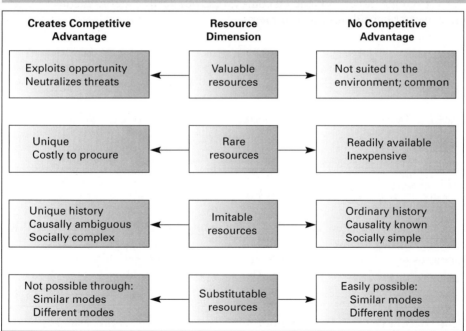

Source: Adapted from J. Barney, "Firm Resources and Sustained Competitive Advantage," *Journal of Management* 17 (1991): 99–120.

Resources

A resource is:

- any thing or quality that is useful

In our resource-based theory of entrepreneurship, a resource also:

- can help an organization implement its strategy (valuable)
- may not be available to all competitors (rare)
- may not be able to be duplicated easily or inexpensively (hard to copy)
- may not be the same as the resources of another firm (nonsubstitutable)

RESOURCE TYPES

Our resource-based theory recognizes six types of resources: **P**hysical, **R**eputational, **O**rganizational, **F**inancial, **I**ntellectual/human and **T**echnological. These can be called our **PROFIT** factors. These six types are broadly drawn and include all "assets, capabilities, organizational processes, firm attributes, information and knowledge."[16] We review these six types and note the special situations where these resources may confer particular advantage, or no advantage at all.

Types of Strategic Resources: The PROFIT Factors

We have identified six types of business resources:

- **P**hysical
- **R**eputational
- **O**rganizational
- **F**inancial
- **I**ntellectual and Human
- **T**echnological

Physical Resources

Physical resources are the tangible property the firm uses in production and administration. These include the firm's plant and equipment, its location, and the amenities available at that location. Some firms also have natural resources such as minerals, energy resources, or land. These natural resources can affect the quality of its physical inputs and raw materials.

Physical resources can be the source of SCA if they have the four attributes previously described. However, because most physical things can be manufactured and purchased, they are probably not rare or hard to copy. Only in special circumstances, like a unique historical situation, will physical resources be a source of SCA.

Reputational Resources

Reputational resources are the perceptions that people in the firm's environment have of the company. Reputation can exist at the product level as brand loyalty or at the corporate level as a global image. Although technological resources may be short-lived because of innovations and inventions, reputational capital may be relatively long-lived. Many organizations maintain high reputations over long periods of time. *Fortune* magazine's annual survey of corporate reputation indicates that 7 of the top 10 corporations in any given year have appeared in the top 10 many times. The *Fortune* survey uses eight different criteria for their rankings:

- The quality of management
- The use of corporate assets
- The firm's financial soundness
- The firm's value as an investment
- The quality of products and services
- Innovativeness
- The ability to attract, develop, and retain top people
- The extent of community and environmental responsibility

Our own research indicates that the most important of these are product quality, management integrity, and financial soundness.[17] The value of reputational relationships goes beyond personal relationships because these reputations continue even after the individuals originally responsible for them are no longer around (either in that job or with the firm).

Organizational Resources

Organizational resources include the firm's structure, routines, and systems.[18] The term ordinarily refers to the firm's formal reporting systems, its information-generation and decision-making systems, and formal or informal planning.

The organization's structure is an intangible resource that can make the difference between the organization and its competitors. A structure that promotes speed can be the entrepreneur's most valuable resource. In the postindustrial economy, organizations will be required to make decisions, innovate, and acquire and distribute information more quickly and more frequently than they have in the past.[19]

Organizational structures that separate the innovation from the production function speed innovation; those that separate marketing from production speed marketing. The appropriateness of designs depends on the complexity and turbulence in the environment.[20] Organizational resources also show up as the skills and capabilities of the people. Different combinations of resources can be associated with the age and life-cycle stage of a business. Depending on where the firm is in its life cycle, certain resources are more vital than others. For example, although human capital and experience are more important early on, organizational resources dominate later.[21]

For new ventures that have emerged from the embryonic stage or those that are a spin-off or business development effort of an ongoing firm, other intangible resources are available. Collective remembered history (myth) and recorded history (files and archives) may also be considered organizational resources. These are part of the organization's past and, to the extent that "past is prologue," organizational history will be incorporated into the culture of the new venture, providing a set of rules, norms, policies, and guides for current and future behavior.

Financial Resources

Financial resources represent money assets. Financial resources are generally the firm's borrowing capacity, the ability to raise new equity, and the amount of cash generated by internal operations.[22] Being able to raise money at below-average cost is an advantage attributable to the firm's credit rating and previous financial performance. Various indicators of a venture's financial resources and financial management skills are its debt-to-equity ratio, its cash-to-capital investment ratio, and its external credit rating. Although start-up entrepreneurs see that access to financial resources is the key to getting into business (it is certainly a necessary component), most agree that financial resources are seldom the source of sustainable competitive advantage. Why is it, then, that fledgling entrepreneurs see money and financial resources as the key to success but established businesses seldom do? Table 2-1 summarizes the results of a survey that compares high-tech and service industry entrepreneurs' perceptions of the sources of sustainable competitive advantage. Financial resources did not rank near the top. In fact, financial resources were named by just 16 percent of high-tech manufacturing firms

TABLE 2-1 Sources of Sustainable Competitive Advantage		
Factor	*High Tech[a]*	*Service*
Reputation for quality	38	44
Customer service/product support	34	35
Name recognition/profile	12	37
Good management	25	38
Low cost production	25	13
Financial resources	**16**	**23**
Customer orientation/market research	19	23
Product line depth	16	22
Technical superiority	44	6
Installed base of satisfied customers	28	19
Product innovation	22	18

[a]The numbers represent the frequency of mention by respondents. Numbers can add to more than 100 percent.

Source: Adapted from D. Aaker, "Managing Assets and Skills: The Key to Sustainable Competitive Advantage," *California Management Review* 31 (Winter 1989): 91–106. Abridged list of 20 factors from a study of 248 California businesses.

and 23 percent of service firms. Out of 20 different factors mentioned, financial resources were ranked 12th by manufacturers and 6th by the service firms.

Limitations of Financial Resources

Why do entrepreneurs think that financial resources are not the most important? To shed light on these findings, we can examine financial resources by the four attributes of resources.

Are Financial Resources Valuable?   No doubt about it. Valuable resources enable a firm to lower its costs, increase its revenue, and produce its product or service. Without financial resources—that is, money—no firm can get very far. Start-up incurs real financial costs even for micro businesses and home-based businesses. The axiom that you have to spend money to make money is true, and the entrepreneur who cannot acquire any financial resources may find that the dream never becomes reality.

Are Financial Resources Rare?   Sometimes yes and sometimes no. At various times in the business cycle, credit crunches deter banks and other lending institutions from making loans and extending credit. (However, because banks do not often finance pure start-ups, this rarity applies to going concerns.) Similarly, the economic climate that governs initial public offerings (the IPO market) sometimes favors new issues (when the stock market is high and climbing) and at other times discounts new issues heavily (when the market is low and falling). For firms that must spend money before collecting receipts, financial resources are rarer than for firms who can collect receipts and deposits before expenses are paid. However, overall financial resources are not rare. It is estimated that each year as much as $6 billion is available through formal investors and an additional $60 billion through informal investors, or angels. This does not include the money invested by the entrepreneur and the top management team themselves.[23]

Are Financial Resources Hard to Copy?   No. One person's money looks and spends the same as another's. It yields competitive advantage in trading markets only for large transactions.[24] For example, the leveraged buyout of RJR Nabisco required about $25 billion in financing. Only a few organizations had the connections and were capable of securing that much money: Shearson-American Express; Kohlberg, Kravis, and Roberts; and Forstmann Little. In such a situation, the absolute size of the financial resource is an advantage. Most deals, however, are settled at amounts below $25 billion, and on a strictly financial basis, money is a perfect copy of itself.[25]

Are Financial Resources Nonsubstitutable with Resources That Are Common? Once again, the technical answer is no. A few entrepreneurs succeed on the basis of sweat equity, and nothing is more common than sweat. This means that they start very small, on little capital other than their own hard work and effort. This is called "bootstrapping." Through frugality, efficient operations, and reinvestment, they are able to grow. Eventually they can cross the threshold that makes them attractive to investors. Under certain circumstances, hard work substitutes for outside financing. Another alternative is a relationship with another firm. Strategic alliances can replace financing because they enable the firm to meet its goals without additional investment by piggybacking on the investment of another firm.

To summarize: Financial resources are valuable and necessary, but because financial resources are not rare, hard to duplicate, or nonsubstitutable, they are insufficient (in most cases) to be a source of sustainable competitive advantage.

However, the *management* of financial resources—the firm's organization, processes, and routines that enable it to use its resources more effectively—*can be a source of SCA*. This is because capable financial management involves complexity and a human element that is valuable, rare, hard to copy, and nonsubstitutable. So although money as a resource is inert and static, the ability and skill to manage money is dynamic, complex, and creative.

Intellectual and Human Resources

Intellectual and human resources include the knowledge, training, and experience of the entrepreneur and his or her team of employees and managers. It includes the judgment, insight, creativity, vision, and intelligence of the individual members of an organization. It can even include the social skills of the entrepreneur.[26] Entrepreneurs often perceive great opportunities where others see only competition or chaos; therefore, entrepreneurial perception is a resource. The values of the entrepreneurs and their beliefs about cause and effect can form the initial imprint of the firm's culture. For example, entrepreneurs who believe in racial and cultural diversity and who can build a workforce around these values make out even better. A new study indicates that diversity interacts with strategy in three ways to improve performance: improved productivity, improved return on equity, and improved market performance.[27]

In addition, human capital includes **relationship capital** as a subset. Relationship capital refers not to *what* the organization's members know but rather to *who* the organization's members know and what information these people possess. Networking gives the entrepreneur access to resources without controlling them. This minimizes the potential risk of ownership and keeps overhead down. Entrepreneurial networking has become standard practice, and the old view of the "entrepreneur as the rugged individualist" has been modified to reflect the realities of today's complex business environment.[28] In fact, relationships can help you obtain financing. Even your mother can help you get financing, as Street Story 2-2 demonstrates.

Frequently, the most important and valuable resource that the new venture has is the founding entrepreneur. These are unique people with their own special characteristics, histories that cannot be duplicated, and complex social relationships. For the rest of this chapter we will focus on the entrepreneur as a human resource.

Technological Resources

Technological resources are made up of processes, systems, or physical transformations. These may include labs, research and development facilities, and testing and quality control technologies. Knowledge generated by research and development and then protected by patents is a resource, as are formulae, licenses, trademarks, and copyrights. Technological secrets and proprietary processes are resources as well. There is a distinction between technological capital and intellectual capital. Intellectual capital is embodied in a person or persons and is mobile. If the person or persons leave the firm, so does the capital. Technological resources are physical, intangible, or legal entities and are owned by the organization.

Can complex physical technology provide a basis for SCA? The answer in general must be no. Technological resources—machines, computer systems, equipment, machine tools, robots, complicated electronics, and so on—cannot be the basis for SCA because they can be duplicated and reproduced. There is enough mobile and capable

Getting By with a Little Help from Mom's Friends

Andrew Morris had almost everything he needed to start his Caribbean-flavored grocery store in a New York City suburb. He had an MBA from Columbia University, a business plan, and a $50,000 loan from the European American Bank.

However, after he negotiated the rent on a 1,600-square-foot retail space in Hempstead, New York, he found he did not have enough cash left for inventory, payroll, marketing, and licenses. Thanks to his mother—and her friends—he was able to secure an additional $15,000 in resources, which enabled him to stack his shelves with dozens of kinds of hot sauce, curry brands, and reggae music that the growing Caribbean community craves.

Morris got the money from his mother's *susu,* a kind of club or fund developed by West Indian housewives to provide rotating credit for big-ticket household purchases. A *susu,* which means "partner," typically has about 20 members, most of them either relatives or close friends. Each week, every member contributes a fixed sum, or *hand,* into the fund for a 20-week period. Any time during those 20 weeks, each member is entitled to borrow an amount or *draw* to use interest-free during that time. For example, if a 20-member susu has a set weekly contribution of $100, each member pays $100 into the fund every week, or pays a total of $2,000 over 20 weeks. Each member is then also able to draw $2,000 at any point during that period. Essentially the susu is a kind of planned savings program that pools money to help members of the group who need help with cash flow.

The Caribbean susu is not really a unique concept in the United States. Asian-Americans and other ethnic groups have also developed informal lending networks for their members. What is distinctive is the way the susu resources are now moving from the kitchen tables into the small business cash registers. Andrew Morris has dipped into his mother's susu a number of times to help his business grow. He used the money to pay a sales tax obligation, to purchase a commercial oven to bake Jamaican meat patties, to produce a special Easter promotion with traditional cheese-and-sweet-bread sandwiches, and to expand his inventory to include unusual but popular items, such as Jamaican Chinese soy sauce. "It's a cash flow boon," Morris says. After 7 years of ongoing susu support, Morris's store now has annual revenues of over $1 million.

The susu is gaining recognition from big business, too. Both Chase Manhattan and Fleet Boston now recognize susu deposits as a sign of creditworthiness in small business applications. Karl Rodney, publisher of a nationally distributed Caribbean-American newspaper, believes that susu support enabled the number of Caribbean businesses in the United States to grow about 15 percent during the past 5 years and allowed another 10 percent of those businesses to expand into prosperous operations like Andrew Morris's store.

Morris is now counting on susu support to help him expand into distributing coffee and developing a Web site. "It's no longer just a Christmas Club," he says. "It's a way of life."

Source: Adapted from Meera Louis, "Pooled Savings Help Jamaicans Build Businesses," *The Wall Street Journal,* October 17, 2000, B1–B2.

engineering and scientific human resources to take apart and put together any of this complex technology. A patent, however, might make it illegal for the competition to commercially develop an exact copy.

However, complex technology is not worthless as a source of competitive advantage. Although several firms can all have the same complex technology, one firm may be more adept at exploiting this technology through its human or organizational resources. If the method of exploiting the technology is not easy to copy (assuming it is valuable, rare, and difficult to substitute), then other resources can augment technology to provide SCA.[29] For example, even a company that was originally based on a physical

---

E-NOTES 2-4

Strategic Resources Outline

Resources	Valuable	Rare	Hard to Copy	Nonsubstitutable
Physical	yes	sometimes	not usually	sometimes
Reputational	yes	yes	yes	yes
Organizational	yes	yes	yes	yes
Financial	yes	sometimes	no	no
Intellectual	yes	yes	usually	sometimes
Technological	yes	sometimes	sometimes	sometimes

---

technological advantage, like Gateway 2000, now finds that the technology is no longer the only key to success. Gateway is transforming itself by using its customer base and reputation to sell Internet services. Street Story 2-3 provides the details.

A PSYCHOLOGICAL APPROACH

Personality Characteristics

Are there personality characteristics that help us predict who will be an entrepreneur and who will not? Who will be a successful entrepreneur and who will not? Over the past few decades, entrepreneurial research has identified a number of personality characteristics that differentiate entrepreneurs from others.[30] Among the most frequently discussed are the need for achievement, locus of control, and risk-taking propensity.

The Need for Achievement   The entrepreneurial need for achievement, or **n Ach,** was first identified as a personality trait by McClelland in his work on economic development.[31] People with high levels of n Ach have a strong desire to solve problems on their own, enjoy setting goals and achieving them through their own efforts, and like receiving feedback on how they are doing. They are moderate risk takers.

However, the link between n Ach and entrepreneurship has not always held up in empirical testing. Researchers who have attempted to replicate McClelland's findings or apply them in other settings have occasionally been disappointed. For example, n Ach is a weak predictor of a person's tendency to start a business, and people specially

Leapfrogging Toward the Information Superhighway

The chairman of the 6th largest manufacturer of personal computers claims he is ready to stop selling what he calls "the boxes." "I'd be totally happy if I didn't sell a PC 5 years from now," says Ted Waitt, the 37-year-old cofounder and current chairman of Gateway 2000. Waitt believes future growth in the computer industry will revolve around accessing the Web through information technology (IT), and he is building on Gateway's computing resources and capabilities to leapfrog the company toward the Internet Generation.

"Gateway is the flag bearer for the beyond-the-box strategy," says industry analyst Robert Cihra. "They've recognized that the value of PC sales is not just the box. The real value is where the PC becomes a platform for other revenue streams."

Waitt has made this kind of jump before. He quit college during his junior year to work in mail-order sales for a Des Moines company selling PCs and software. Nine months later, Waitt and a friend cloned that experience to establish the company that became Gateway 2000. Within a year, the company was assembling its own PCs. Gateway became the first PC manufacturer to sell its products on the Internet, to launch its own Internet service, and to sell computers on the installment plan.

Sales of computers, which Gateway markets primarily to individual consumers and small businesses, now account for just 25 percent of the company's operating income. Financing, including a program that bundles a computer with software and Internet access for one low monthly fee, is the next biggest source of income. Significantly, three new revenue streams for the company are programs that link directly to the Web: sales of software and peripherals, Internet-access service, and Web-based training courses. Gateway already complements its PC sales with three innovative Web-oriented products, including a desktop cruiser for e-mail and Net access, a wireless Web pad, and a kitchen countertop touch pad. Even the network of Gateway retail stores is geared towards the Web: The stores carry no inventory, and employees focus on training and demonstrating products, directing customers to purchase the Gateway product they want over the Internet. According to Michael Larson, a senior vice president at rival Compaq, "Gateway has executed a beyond-the-box strategy better than any other company."

Waitt foresees a future where PCs will be obsolete, replaced by Web-access devices that hook into Internet data centers with powerful megacomputers. Consumers will then pay a monthly technology fee of around $50 to obtain software, communicate, make purchases, and do a variety of other tasks—and they'll be able to do it all faster and easier than they can with their personal computer now. Waitt is eager to convert Gateway into a company that provides that kind of service and service appliances; he has calculated the potential market to be tens of millions of

(continued)

(continued)

of customers, and he has estimated the profit margin at 60 percent.

In addition to developing new hardware, Gateway is preparing for that next leap with two important steps. First, the company is working to maintain close ties with the largest customer base in the e-tailing industry, currently more than 22 million customers. Second, Gateway has entered into a partnership agreement with AOL Time Warner. They currently share the gateway.net Internet access service and have plans to start a variety of e-commerce sites in the near future. Although some experts have questioned the AOL Time Warner alliance, Waitt sounds positive. "We have a common view of how the world will develop with devices and how they'll be sold and how the whole solution will be packaged."

Waitt is making a personal leap, too, by selling large chunks of his Gateway stock and investing the money in music-related Internet start-ups, such as MP3. com, Listen.com, and Launch.com. He happens to be a dedicated rock-and-roll fan, but the move is also part of his vision of the computerized future. "Music over the Internet will be the first wave of convergence," the ponytailed computer mogul predicts.

Source: Adapted from Steven V. Brull, "Gateway's Big Gamble," *Business Week E. Biz,* June 5, 2000, pp. 26–36.

trained to have high n Ach sometimes perform no differently from a control group that receives no training. The causal link between n Ach and small business ownership has not been proven.[32]

Locus of Control   A second trait often associated with entrepreneurship is **locus of control.**[33] In locus-of-control theory, there are two types of people: (1) **externals,** those who believe that what happens to them is a result of fate, chance, luck, or forces beyond their control; and (2) **internals,** those who believe that for the most part the future is theirs to control through their own effort. Clearly, people who undertake a new business must believe that their efforts will have something to do with the business's future performance.

A logical prediction of this theory would be that internals are more entrepreneurial than externals. Evidence supporting this hypothesis, though, has been inconclusive.[34] Some studies have shown that there are more internals among entrepreneurs, but others show no difference between entrepreneurs and others. In fact, it could be argued that any good manager must also possess the qualities of an internal: a person who believes that efforts affect outcomes. So, although locus of control might distinguish people who believe in astrology from those who do not, it may not differentiate potential entrepreneurs from potential managers or just plain business students.

Risk-Taking Propensity   Related to the need for achievement is **risk-taking propensity.** Because the task of new venture creation is apparently fraught with risk and the financing of these ventures is often called "risk capital," researchers have tried to determine whether entrepreneurs take more risks than other businesspeople. That hypothesis has been tested in a number of ways, but the work by Brockhaus has been most incisive.[35]

In Brockhaus's research, the risk-taking propensities of entrepreneurs were tested objectively using a series of decision scenarios. The results obtained from the entrepreneurs were compared with those obtained from a sample of managers. The conclusion was that risk-taking propensity is not a distinguishing characteristic of entrepreneurs.

Inadequacy of the Trait Approach

Overall, the trait approach has failed to provide the decisive criteria for distinguishing entrepreneurs from others. What distinguishes entrepreneurs from nonentrepreneurs is that entrepreneurs start new businesses and others do not.[36]

One researcher described the search of the entrepreneurial trait this way: "My own personal experience was that for 10 years we ran a research center in entrepreneurial history, for 10 years we tried to define the entrepreneur. We never succeeded. Each of us had some notion of it—what he thought was, for his purposes, a useful definition. And I don't think you're going to get farther than that."[37]

The trait approach looks for similarity among entrepreneurs. However, as our resource-based theory suggests, if all entrepreneurs have a certain trait or characteristic, it is not an advantage to any of them, for it is neither rare nor hard to duplicate. To understand entrepreneurship, we must look for circumstances that produce differences, not similarities. For this we turn to a sociological framework that emphasizes personal history and the uniqueness of an individual's path to new venture creation.

A SOCIOLOGICAL APPROACH

How are entrepreneurs unique? Each has a unique background, history, and biography. The sociological approach tries to explain the social conditions from which entrepreneurs emerge and the social factors that influence the decision. A sociological model is presented in Figure 2-2.[38] It depicts the decision to become an entrepreneur as a function of two factors: the impetus factors and the situational factors. The model is multiplicative: A zero on either of the causes means a failure to produce the entrepreneurial event.

Impetus for Entrepreneurship

What propels entrepreneurs toward self-employment? There are four factors: negative displacement, being between things, positive push, and positive pull. A recent study proposed that pull entrepreneurs may perform better than push entrepreneurs, and those that can be classified as both push and pull may be the most motivated of all.[39]

Negative Displacement

Figure 2-2 begins with the notion that people who find themselves displaced in some negative way may become entrepreneurs. **Negative displacement** is the alienation of individuals or groups of individuals from the core of society. These individuals or groups may be seen as "not fitting in" to the main flow of social and economic life.

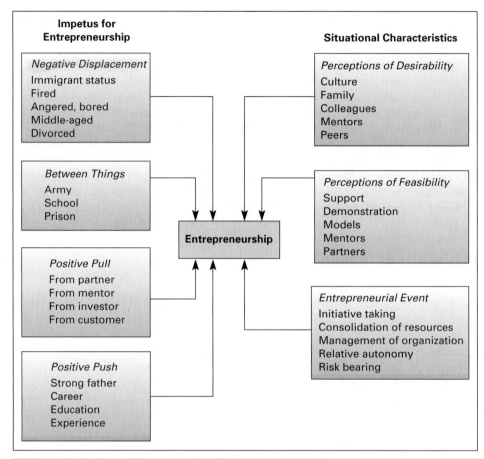

FIGURE 2-2   The Supply of Entrepreneurship

Source: Adapted from A. Shapero and L. Sokol, "The Social Dimensions of Entrepreneurship," in C. Kent, D. Sexton, and K. Vesper, eds., *Encyclopedia of Entrepreneurship* (Upper Saddle River, NJ: Prentice Hall, 1982), pp. 72–90.

Because they are on the outer fringes of the economy and of society, they are sensitive to the allure of self-employment; having no one to depend on, they depend on no one. An example of this phenomenon is the tendency of immigrants to become entrepreneurs. In societies where economic rights are more easily exercised than political rights, immigrants turn to entrepreneurship. Throughout the world, for example, Asian and Jewish immigrants, wherever they have settled, have gone into business for themselves. Recent trends in the United States demonstrate high levels of entrepreneurship in the Vietnamese and Korean populations. One statistical estimate of Korean immigrants in the New York City area concludes that 65 percent of Korean families own at least one business.[40] Take the example of Jung Pack, a Korean who emigrated to the United States in 1982. Jung works 16 hours a day in his own grocery business even though he has a college degree in business administration and was in construction management back in Korea. Jung says he left Korea because it was too rural and he wanted to live in a big "cosmopolitan" country. However, when he arrived in the United States, downward mobility forced him to give up thoughts of a white-collar career to become a self-employed shopkeeper. His career in the United States has been blocked by the language barrier and skepticism about the value of his academic degree. But Jung can probably expect his two children, who will be U.S. citizens, to pursue either professional careers or entrepreneurial opportunities in business services like data processing or management consulting. Meanwhile, Jung says he still dreams of "a better life."

Other negative displacements result from being fired from a job or being angered or bored by current employment. Many bored managers and stifled executives in large corporations are leaving their white-collar jobs and looking for challenges and autonomy. According to Harry Levinson, a Harvard psychologist who specializes in career and life-cycle issues, "The entrepreneur, psychologically speaking, has a lot more freedom than anybody in a big corporation."[41] To illustrate this, consider the case of Philip Schwartz, who was an executive with Olin Corporation and Airco Inc. He left his middle-level managerial career to start a business as a wholesaler of packaging materials and cleaning supplies and to find out "who and what I am." He reports that he enjoys the autonomy and action of drumming up business and interacting with customers. He enjoys putting his own personal stamp on his company. Having only four employees, he can create a family atmosphere, relaxed and friendly. He imprints his own values of honesty and dependability on the business, something that no middle-level corporate manager can do.[42]

Middle age or divorce can also provide the impetus for new venture creation. In an unusual example, one entrepreneur recreated his business because of a midlife crisis. Tom Chappell cofounded a personal-care and health-products business, Tom's of Maine Inc. A number of years ago, he realized that he was not happy running this business even though he was successful. He went back to school and obtained a master's degree from Harvard Divinity School. His studies there led him to examine his values and his motivation for managing his own firm. He changed the company's goals, setting its mission to "address community concerns, in Maine and around the globe, by devoting a portion of our time, talent and resources to the environment, human needs, the arts and education."[43]

"Between Things"

People who are **between things** are also more likely to seek entrepreneurial outlets than those who are in the "middle of things." Like immigrants, people who are between things are sometimes outsiders. Three examples are offered in the model in Figure 2-2: between military and civilian life, between student life and a career, and between prison and freedom.

Positive Pull

Positive influences also lead to the decision to investigate entrepreneurship, and these are called **positive pull** influences. They can come from a potential partner, a mentor, a parent, an investor, or a customer. The potential partner encourages the individual with the offer of sharing the experience, helping with the work, and spreading the risk. The mentor raises self-esteem and confidence. Mentors and partners can also introduce the entrepreneur to people inside the social and economic network for new venture activity.[44] There also appears to be a relationship between a parent's occupation and offspring entrepreneurship: Many entrepreneurs have a strong self-employed father figure in the family.[45] Investors that provide the initial financing can convince the individual that "there may be more where that came from." The prospect of a potential customer pulling the entrepreneur into business raises some difficult ethical and economic issues.[46] However, having a guaranteed market for the products or services is a temptation few can resist.

Positive Push

The final category of situations that provide impetus and momentum for entrepreneurship is termed **positive push.** Positive-push factors include such things as a career path that offers entrepreneurial opportunities or an education that gives the individual the appropriate knowledge and opportunity.

What types of career choices can people make that put them in good position to become entrepreneurs? Two types of career paths can lead to entrepreneurship. The first is the **industry path.** A person prepares himself for a job or career in a particular industry and learns everything there is to know about that industry. Because all industries display some sort of dynamics, or change, over time, entrepreneurial opportunities that exploit that change come and go. A person with a deep knowledge of the industry is in an excellent position to develop a business that fills a niche or gap created by industry change.

People taking the industry path to new venture creation emphasize that specialized knowledge is the key resource. That knowledge may be embodied in particular people, a technology, or a system or process. The new firm may be a head-to-head competitor, it may serve a new niche not served by the former employer, or it may be an upstream firm (a supplier) or a downstream firm (a distributor or retailer). Whatever its functional form, a spin-off is a knowledge-based business; its primary resources are the competencies and experiences and the networks and contacts being transferred to a new venture.[47] The challenge for these people is to procure the other resources, financial and physical, that will enable them to make their plan a reality.

A different approach, the **sentry path,** emphasizes the money and the deal. People with careers in sentry positions see many different opportunities in many different industries. They tend to be lawyers, accountants, consultants, bankers (especially business loan officers), and brokers. These people learn how to make deals and find money. They have contacts that enable them to raise money quickly when the right property comes along. The challenge for these people, because they are experts in the "art of the deal" and not part of any particular industry, is to locate and retain good managers.

Situational Characteristics

Once the individual's inclination for entrepreneurship has been activated, situational characteristics help determine if the new venture will take place. The two situational factors are perceptions of desirability and perceptions of feasibility.

Perceptions of the Situation

Perceptions of Desirability   Entrepreneurship must be seen as desirable in order to be pursued. The factors that affect the perceptions of desirability can come from the individual's culture, family, peers and colleagues, or mentors. For example, the Sikhs and Punjabis who dominate the service station business in New York City also dominate the transportation and mechanics business in their native country. Sometimes religion can spark entrepreneurship and legitimize the perception of desirability. For example, Zen Buddhist communities are historically self-sufficient economically and provide the background for the story of an unusual entrepreneur, Bernard Glassman.

Glassman was born the son of immigrant Jewish parents and trained as a systems engineer; now he is building a better world by combining Zen entrepreneurship with a mission to help people at the bottom of the economic ladder. After Glassman's introduction to Buddhism, he found that meditation alone could not meet his spiritual needs. So he chose the Way of Entrepreneurship. In 1983, he and his Zen community launched Greyston Bakery in Yonkers, New York, supplying high-priced pies and cakes to wealthy consumers. He received his early training as a baker from another Zen sect in San Francisco. Today his bakery grosses $1.2 million and employs 200 people, many previously considered unemployable. Many entrepreneurs say that they want to help the poor and needy, but Glassman has made it happen. Through Greyston's profits, he has been able to renovate buildings, provide counseling services, and open a day-care center. He still has to pay close attention to the bottom line, however; the bakery is his mandala and he must concentrate intensely to make it a success.[48]

Perceptions of Feasibility   Entrepreneurship must be seen as feasible if the process is to continue. Readiness and desirability are not enough. Potential entrepreneurs need models and examples of what can be accomplished. They require support from others—emotional, financial, and physical support. Again, ethnic and immigrant networks provide examples. Not only do the Koreans and Indians help train and employ each other in their businesses, but they demonstrate by their perseverance that it can be done.

E-NOTES 2-5

The Entrepreneur as a Human Resource

The sociological approach theorizes that an entrepreneur's inclinations are propelled by:

- negative displacement (losing a job, etc.)
- being between things (transition from school to career, etc.)
- positive pull (example made by parent, mentor, etc.)
- positive push (a job, education, etc.)

. . . and activated by situations that positively affect:

- perceptions of desirability (message from culture, peers, etc.)
- perceptions of feasibility (demonstration, etc.)

. . . and culminate in an entrepreneurial event.

So what happens next? At the end of the process depicted in Figure 2-2, the new venture creation process begins. The pre-entrepreneurial conditions described end in the entrepreneurial event, that is, in the creation and management of a new venture. One model of this process comprises five components:[49]

- *Initiative.* An individual or team, having been brought to the state of readiness by personal factors and by perceptions of desirability and feasibility, begins to act. Evidence of initiative usually includes scanning the environment for opportunities, searching for information, and doing research.
- *Consolidation of resources.* Levels of resource needs are estimated, alternatives for procurement are considered, and timing of resource arrival is charted and eventually consolidated into a pattern of business activity that could be called an organization.
- *Management of the organization.* The business's resource acquisition, transformation, and disposal are routinized and systemized. Those elements that are not easily systematized are managed separately.
- *Autonomous action.* The management of the new venture is characterized by free choice of strategy, structure, and processes.
- *Risk taking.* The initiators have put themselves at risk. They are personally affected by the variability of returns of the business and by its possible success or failure.

Another process-oriented model by Stevenson emphasizes entrepreneurial behavior toward resources. This model makes two valuable contributions to our understanding of the entrepreneurial process: (1) It recognizes that no entrepreneur behaves in an entrepreneurlike manner all the time. There are forces acting upon the individual that sometimes make entrepreneurial behavior appropriate and that at other times make administrative or managerial behavior appropriate. (2) It emphasizes that the commitment and control of resources are as important to the process as environmental scanning and opportunity recognition.[50] Each entrepreneur assesses the forces pushing for entrepreneurial action and those requiring administrative action and then makes the choice that is best for the new venture.

Summary

This chapter presents the basic concepts of the resource-based theory, including the four attributes of resources necessary to achieve sustainable competitive advantage: They must be rare, valuable, hard to copy, and nonsubstitutable. Our resource-based theory allows that certain aspects of entrepreneurship are not analyzable—they are causally ambiguous because no one, including the founders, quite understands how or why they work. New ventures created around the possession and controllability of resources with these characteristics have the potential to be rewarding, forgiving, and enduring.

The chapter also describes the six types of resources: physical, reputational, organizational, financial, intellectual/human, and technological. These are the basic profit factors to be used in assessing the potential of the new venture. All of the resources are important for the new venture, but the ones that are most likely to lead to competitive advantage are organizational, reputational, and human resources.

The entrepreneur is the primary human resource for the new venture. Although it is uncertain what, if any, personality traits make the best entrepreneurs, the entrepreneur's life history, experience, and knowledge make each founder a unique resource.

Key Terms

- "Between things"
- Bootstrapping
- Capability
- Competitive advantage
- Externals
- Financial resources
- Hard to copy
- Industry path
- Intellectual and human resources
- Internals

- Locus of control
- n Ach (Need for achievement)
- Negative displacement
- Nonsubstitutable
- Organizational culture
- Organizational resources
- Physical resources
- Positive pull
- Positive push
- Rare

- Relationship capital
- Reputational resources
- Resources
- Risk-taking propensity
- Sentry path
- Skill
- Sustained competitive advantage
- Technological resources
- Valuable

Discussion Questions

1. What are the characteristics of a good theory? What makes a theory practical? How can an entrepreneur use the resource-based theory for his or her advantage?
2. Explain the problems we would have if there was a "law of entrepreneurship."
3. How do each of the four attributes of resources contribute to SCA?
4. What is the difference between competitive advantage and sustainable competitive advantage?
5. How can an organization's culture be a source of SCA?
6. Describe how each of the six types of resources can be a source of SCA. What are the strengths and weaknesses of each type?
7. Why are personality traits not sufficient for evaluating and predicting successful entrepreneurship?
8. Describe the sociological approach to entrepreneurship. How can this approach be used to promote more entrepreneurship within the economy?
9. If immigrants are a major source of entrepreneurship in the economy, why do most countries limit the number of immigrants they allow in each year?
10. How are entrepreneurs behaviorally different from managers? When can we expect entrepreneurs to behave managerially? When can we expect managers to behave as entrepreneurs?

Exercises

1. Research a company and inventory its resource base by using the six types of resources discussed in the chapter. Evaluate these resources in terms of the four attributes of resources necessary for SCA. Does the company have a competitive advantage? A sustainable competitive advantage? What recommendations about resource procurement and development would you make for this company?
2. Interview an entrepreneur. Ask the entrepreneur to describe the "keys to successful entrepreneurship." Ask the entrepreneur to estimate how much of his or her success was the result of luck or unknown factors. Do the answers seem to fit the resource-based model?

3. Inventory your personal resource base by using the six types of resources described in the chapter. Evaluate these resources by employing the four criteria. Comment on your individual potential to start a business that has the prospect of achieving SCA.

4. If you are in a group with other students, inventory the group's resources and repeat exercise 3.

5. Assume you have access to your college's or university's resources. Redo your inventories (see exercises 3 and 4). How have you increased your potential for competitive advantage?

Exercises for Writing a Business Plan

Beginning with this chapter, the exercises are designed to prepare the student to develop and write a business plan. These exercises can be done either individually or in a group setting.

1. Exercise envisioning. Sit in a quiet and dark room and begin to think about what kind of business you would like to start. Close your eyes and let your mind's eye see yourself working in that business. What do you see? Is it a manufacturing business, a service or retail outlet, a construction site, or something else? Notice the physical setting and the people around. What are they doing? Which are employees and which are customers? Are the people happy? Busy? Confused?

2. Develop 20 ideas for a new business. Make the 20 ideas into 100 ideas, no matter how unusual or apparently strange. Sort the ideas into the 10 best, and make the concepts more original. At the end of the exercise you should have 20 to 30 truly creative new business ideas.

3. For each of the group's or individual's best ideas, do the following short assignment:
   a. Describe the business in 25 words or less. The description should include the product/service, the customer, and the technology employed.
   b. Describe the opportunity that you believe this business exploits. In other words, why do you think this is a great business idea?
   c. Describe the resources you believe you would need to execute this new venture idea. Use the six categories from Chapter 2. Which resource(s) will be the source of competitive advantage?
   d. Estimate how much money it would cost to actually get this business started. The estimate will be very rough, but try to make an educated guess.

> ## DISCUSSION CASE

Zara: Innovative and Devastating

Zara does things differently, and this difference has made Zara the "most innovative and devastating retailer in the world," according to fashion director Daniel Piette. Zara is a Spanish company, located in Galicia. Unlike traditional clothing stores, Zara can ship new products to over 400 stores every few days instead of once a season. Instead of making 200 or 300 new products a year, Zara can come out with more than 11,000 items. There are no overstocks at Zara; slow-selling merchandise is whisked off the shelves after just a week. (This means no sales and price-cutting to move this merchandise.) Most amazingly, the company takes just 10 to 15 days to go from designing an item to selling it. Of course, sometimes the design is a knock-off, but it is still amazingly fast.

How do they do it? By disregarding conventional wisdom (breaking some rules). While most retailers outsource production to Third World countries, Zara produces its own goods in fully automated, robotic-controlled factories. While most retailers have arms-length relationships with their subcontractors and frequently fire the least productive, Zara's goods are finished and assembled by a network of 300 or so small companies in Galicia and northern Portugal. These companies are more like partners than contractors. While most retailers produce large runs and enormous lots of skirts, dresses, and suits, Zara produces small lots so they can see if the clothing is selling before committing to larger orders.

The key to Zara's success is its two major capabilities: speed and control. In retailing, inventory is death. Why? Because it is merchandise that is not moving, not turning over, not earning a return. It is already paid for, but no cash is coming in. Eventually, it has to be sold at a deep discount or even a loss. Zara is three times more efficient at moving merchandise than Gap. It is fast and cheap and the toughest competitor out there.

Why doesn't everyone just copy Zara? Why not benchmark against the best and improve efficiency, margins, and profitability? Because they can't do it. Relationships with finishers in Galicia are not easily replicated. The skills of the designers are rare and valuable. The investment in technology is integrated into a system of production, and it is not quickly duplicated without an attempt to replicate the whole system. You cannot copy the parts and expect the same results. The business world is just not that simple.

CASE QUESTIONS

1. What appear to be the key resources and capabilities of Zara?

2. What kinds of mechanisms does Zara use to keep others from copying its methods?

3. If you were going to start a clothing company today, would you try to adopt Zara's approach, or use more traditional methods?

4. What can Zara do to make sure that it maintains its competitive advantage(s) for the future?

Source: Adapted from James Surowiecki, "The Most Devastating Retailer in the World," *The New Yorker,* September 18, 2000, p. 74.

CHAPTER

The Environment for Entrepreneurship

3

The central task facing an organization which has entrepreneurial aspirations is to take advantage of the opportunities from change that appear in its environment.

—S. OSTER

Outline

Learning Objectives

After reading this chapter, you will understand:

- The components of the *business environment*
- The *process* of business environment analysis
- The five segments of the *macroenvironment,* and the issues presented by each of them
- What changes in the macroenvironment can become *sources of opportunity* for the entrepreneur
- The seven elements of the *industry environment,* and the components that affect each of those segments

SCHEMATIC OF THE NEW VENTURE'S ENVIRONMENT

What does the world look like to the entrepreneur? What parts of that world are important for making entrepreneurial decisions and finding opportunities for the new venture? Figure 3-1 shows the business environment as it might appear to an entrepreneur as a series of concentric circles. The innermost circle represents the firm and its resources. This is the core of the entrepreneur's world. The next circle holds all the elements that are part of the firm's industry but not part of the firm itself. The largest circle represents everything that is not part of the firm's industry, but is still important for the new venture. This is the **macroenvironment** in which the firm operates. Five identifiable, though overlapping, segments are within the macroenvironment:

1. Politics and government
2. Macroeconomy
3. Technology
4. Sociodemography
5. Ecology

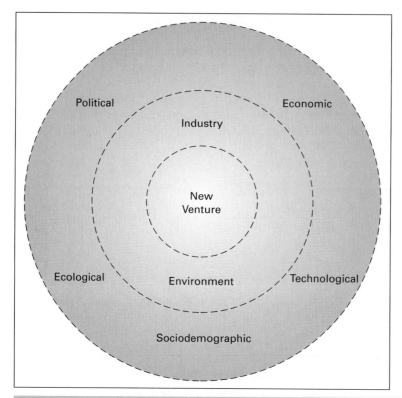

FIGURE 3-1   Schematic of the New Venture's Environment

In this chapter, we describe the characteristics and segments of the macroenvironment, and also the characteristics and segments for the industry or competitive environment. The distinction between the two environments is somewhat artificial because in the long run all the productive resources merge. That is, they are interchangeable between organizations and institutions. Indeed, the organizations and institutions themselves are also exchangeable. They come and go as society, technology, and the rules of law dictate. As new industries are created from new technologies or the desires of consumers, resources from deteriorating industries are converted for their use. The purchasing power of a declining industry's customers can be redirected either to a new industry or to another more stable industry. Thus, the concentric circles representing the business environment appear as broken lines to depict the permeability of environmental boundaries and the possibility, indeed the necessity, of flow and exchange.

In the second half of this chapter, we examine the competitive environment for entrepreneurship. To do this, we employ the model of competitive industry analysis popularized by Michael Porter of the Harvard Business School.[1] We conclude the chapter by discussing how competitor analysis based on our resource-based model can exploit industry opportunities and lessen the threats arising from unfavorable industry conditions.

PROCESSES OF BUSINESS ENVIRONMENT ANALYSIS

Most of the time, thinking and analyzing are done very quickly, and we are quite unaware that we are doing it. Sometimes, though, it is necessary to be more conscious of our thinking and to do our analyzing in systematic ways. This is true when we are thinking about the environment for entrepreneurship. We want to make sure we are being comprehensive and analytical. Four separate (although sequentially related) tasks are required for a comprehensive entrepreneurial analysis: scanning, monitoring, forecasting, and assessing.[2]

E-NOTES 3-1

Environmental Analysis

Analysis of the business environment includes:

- scanning to detect change
- monitoring to track development
- forecasting to project the future
- assessing to interpret data

Scanning

How does this comprehensive process begin? It begins by looking around. **Scanning** the environment is the process by which the entrepreneur first identifies the key elements and their characteristics. It is a surveillance system for early detection. The goal of scanning is to detect change that is already underway. Successful scanning catches important changes early, giving the new venture enough lead time to adapt.

The entrepreneur scans innumerable sources of data. *The Wall Street Journal, Business Week,* and *The Economist* are solid sources for the broad picture. Television provides a general and continuous source of data through Cable News Network (CNN), network news, special reports, and documentaries. More specialized business programming is becoming increasingly popular on cable channels like MSNBC. Surfing the Internet has become an important scanning activity. In addition, through "people-to-people" interactive scanning, entrepreneurs consult with a variety of professionals and experts outside their field of expertise. Accountants, lawyers, engineers, consultants, and, yes, even professors are available to the entrepreneur for information and advice. Scanning gives the entrepreneur a sensitivity to environmental conditions that sometimes looks like intuition.

Monitoring

Monitoring is the process of tracking the evolution, development, and sequence of critical events that affect the survival and profitability of the future new business. Data from the scanning process are input into the monitoring process. Specific trends and events identified for the new venture are monitored in real time to confirm or disprove predictions about how they will affect the firm. Monitoring is less general and, therefore, more focused than scanning. The entrepreneur follows specific periodicals, consults selected experts, and even convenes focus groups.[3] The outcome of the monitoring process is a detailed model of how various elements in the macroenvironment influence and affect the firm. The model, however, is not reality, but a workable version of cause and effect.

Forecasting

Forecasting enables the entrepreneur to develop plausible projections for the future. These can be projections for elements such as the level of prices, the direction of interest rates, or future scenarios for cause and effect; for example, a typical forecast might be—if the money supply grows at above-target rates, then inflation will occur. Thus inputs for forecasts are the data from monitoring.

Forecasting uses a series of techniques to provide insight into the future. The specific techniques chosen for a task should correspond to the type of data used as input and the nature of the desired forecast. When forecasting is used to help search for new business opportunities and to uncover potential macroenvironmental constraints on these opportunities, the following five-step process is suggested.[4]

1. *Choose* the macroenvironmental variables that are critical to the new venture. These will probably relate to the resource base of the firm.
2. *Select* the sources of data for the forecast. These will probably be those you have been monitoring.
3. *Evaluate* various forecasting techniques.
4. *Integrate* forecast results into your plan for the creation of the new venture. These will probably concern resource levels and availability and sales forecasts.
5. *Keep track* of the critical aspects of your forecast. This will mean comparing actual results with forecasted results. If and when a gap appears, it is time for another forecast, beginning at step 1.

Table 3-1 summarizes the costs and benefits of six quantitative and judgmental forecasting techniques.

Assessing

Assessing the environment is the most difficult and important of the four tasks of environmental analysis. Here the entrepreneur has to answer that most difficult of questions: "What does it all mean?" Interpretation is an art form, and so is assessment. In a poker game, players can agree on what cards are showing, the previous bets made, and the value of the cards they are holding. Some players hold, some fold, and others raise. Because their assessments are different, their behavior is different. So also, in assessing most entrepreneurial opportunities, there are few facts that people would agree can be generalized.

Although the four-part process we just described seems quite analytical, it actually takes place over time in a mode that would appear to be more intuitive than rational. This is what is sometimes called "entrepreneurial insight" or "vision." For example, in

TABLE 3-1	Quantitative and Judgmental Forecasting Methods for Emerging Industries, New Ventures, New Products		
Method	*Description*	*Cost*	*Complexity*
1. Sales force estimate	A bottom-up approach that aggregates unit demand	Low	Low
2. Juries of executive opinion	Forecasts jointly prepared by experts in a functional area	Low	Low
3. Customer surveys: market research focus groups	Learning about intentions of potential customers and final users	Medium	Medium
4. Scenario development	Effects of anticipated conditions imagined by forecasters	Medium	Low
5. Delphi method	Experts guided to consensus	Low	Medium
6. Brainstorming	Idea generation in a noncritical group situation	Low	Medium

Source: Adapted from J. Pearce and R. Robinson, *Strategic Management,* 4th ed. (Homewood, IL: Irwin, 1991).

Street Story 3-1, Luis Espinoza made a number of critical, insightful observations as he started and grew his business.

POLITICAL AND GOVERNMENTAL ANALYSIS

Politics is the art of the possible. You could say the same thing about entrepreneurship. Analyzing the political scene will give the entrepreneur a feeling for what is possible, what is probable, and what is unlikely. The political and governmental segment of the business environment is the arena where different interest groups compete for attention and resources to advance their own interests, establish their own values, and achieve their own goals. It is the arena in which particular individuals and groups exercise political power. To a large extent, the individual entrepreneur is forced to accept the current political environment of the new venture. Collectively and over time, however, an organized group of entrepreneurs can influence the political sector. One such group, the National Federation of Independent Business (NFIB), lobbies hard for issues that affect entrepreneurs and small businesses.

Stakeholder Analysis

How many different individuals, groups, and interests can influence the survival, development, and profitability of the new venture? Quite a few, and these are its **stakeholders**. Their influences can be both positive and negative. Not all stakeholders are alike. Stakeholders may vary along the following seven dimensions.[5]

- *Degree of organization:* The extent to which stakeholders are organized for collective action locally, regionally, and nationally. Some stakeholders are very well organized and influential. Others are disorganized or have their organization incompetently managed and are less of a threat.

A Taste for Analysis

At one time, it was not easy to buy Hispanic foods in northern Indiana. When Luis Espinoza first moved to South Bend in 1993, he had to drive into Chicago to pick up the spices and canned foods his family loved, the same way his father used to drive from Texas into Mexico to purchase authentic foods.

But Espinoza saw change when he scanned his South Bend environment. First, he saw a growing number of residents from Mexico, the Caribbean, and Central America moving into the area. Second, he saw many of those residents becoming more interested in Hispanic culture: Even his own adult children, who he insisted speak only English when they were growing up, were now learning to speak Spanish on their own. Third, through his involvement with the local Hispanic Chamber of Commerce, the League of United Latin American Citizens, and other community organizations, Espinoza began to develop a special knowledge of the kinds of foods Hispanic residents wanted but could not find.

Even though he already had a full-time job at I/N Tek, a local steel-finishing plant, in 1997 Espinoza decided to open the El Taco Tipico restaurant in South Bend. Espinoza's big break came when an assistant manager from the local Kroger supermarket dined in his restaurant one night. Chatting with this customer, Espinoza explained that he also had started Inca Quality Foods in a spare room above the restaurant to distribute canned goods and spices to area Hispanic-neighborhood markets. This customer arranged for Espinoza to make a presentation about Hispanic foods to his supermarket manager, who in turn agreed to let Espinoza install a display of spices near the meat counter on a trial basis.

Through monitoring, the supermarket manager discovered that not only did the Hispanic spices sell well, but they also attracted new customers who purchased produce, paper goods, and other products while they were in the store. He relayed that information to a Kroger district manager, who contracted with Inca Quality Foods to install Hispanic food display cases in 19 additional stores. This was an important step for Espinoza, who says, "The whole key to this business is volume." Revenues for Inca Quality Foods jumped from $60,000 to an estimated $500,000 in 2 years. A study conducted by two MBA students from Notre Dame confirmed that, overall, Kroger store sales increased when an Inca display went into a store.

Forecasting, the next step of analysis, has caused some dilemmas for Espinoza. Inca's prospects for growth are good. As Espinoza says, "To run a company growing that fast, you need passion." Not only that, you need time and hands-on involvement. Espinoza, however, is reluctant to leave his full-time job or walk away from the corporate pension he'll earn in a few years. Forecasting has also led Espinoza to consider that he might prefer to utilize his Hispanic food retailing knowledge as a consultant to national chains like Kroger and Kmart, instead of bearing the costs and burden of expanding his distribution business.

(continued)

(continued)

Forecasting has also led to some new demands from Kroger. The supermarket chain is eager to expand Inca's displays to 30 more stores, and Espinoza is not sure he can find the $250,000 he needs to do that. If he cannot, Kroger says they will find another Hispanic-foods vendor. Like many entrepreneurs, though, his scanning, monitoring, and forecasting have left Espinoza committed to pursuing his small business. "I would never let my business go," he says. "Never."

Source: Adapted from Nancy J. Lyons, "The Start-Up Diaries: Moonlight over Indiana," *Inc.* online, January 1, 2000; "The Forks in Their Roads," *Inc.* online, April 1, 2000; available at www.inc.com.

- *Resource capability:* The degree to which stakeholders have access to resources that help influence businesses or agencies and that can be categorized in the same way as described in Chapter 2 (financial, physical, technical, reputational, human, and organizational; rare, valuable, hard to copy, and nonsubstitutable).
- *Extent of influence:* The degree to which the interest group is able to promote its agenda. Some stakeholders are organized as lobbying groups and have enormous influence—for example, the National Rifle Association or Mothers Against Drunk Driving.[6]
- *Nature of interest:* The type of agenda the interest group has; a specific agenda (e.g., cleaning up toxic waste sites) or a general agenda (e.g., making business responsive to people's needs).
- *Duration:* The length of time the interest group has been active and its potential staying power. Sometimes stakeholders are interested in issues that prove to be fads or of passing interest. This is especially true in areas affecting consumer goods and travel and leisure industries.
- *Degree of manifestation:* The ability of the interest group to take its case directly to the public or to the media.
- *Bases of influence:* The extent to which an interest group can gain support from other interest groups that share an affinity for similar causes.

Stakeholder analysis helps the entrepreneur identify which groups and interests are friendly to the new venture and which are hostile. It enables the entrepreneur to see whether any groups have an immediate affinity for the product or service, and whether this affinity can be translated into a market. The analysis also reveals trends regarding consumer attitudes and behavior for the new venture's products, competing products, and complementary goods.

Global and International Issues

Although it may seem to the entrepreneur that her business is strictly local, in truth very few businesses are. We are all interconnected in a global economy, and events that occur thousands of miles away can influence our business. At the global level, the main issues are trade barriers, tariffs, political risks, and bilateral and multilateral relationships. All of these issues are interrelated.

Trade Barriers and Tariffs   Trade barriers and tariffs hinder the free flow of resources across national boundaries. They are the result of economic interest groups within a country attempting to prevent transnational competition. The trend is the reduction of trade barriers worldwide.

Trade Agreements   Since World War II and especially since the end of the cold war, the trend has been toward increased trade agreements. These country-to-country and regional agreements have set the economic rules businesses follow when they are interacting with businesses within the cosigning group of nations.

Political Risk   **Political risk** refers to the potential for instability, corruption, and violence in a country or region. It is an important variable because in areas where political risk is high, it is difficult and costly to procure, protect, and dispose of resources. There is always the risk of governmental nationalization and legal appropriation. Even in a stable democracy, people can vote to take away other people's money.

National Issues

Political and governmental analysis on the national level are concerned with taxation, regulation, antitrust legislation, government spending, and patent protection.

Taxation   At the national level, the primary political factor facing the entrepreneur is taxation. Governments require large amounts of money to promote the public good and to carry out the will of the people (stakeholders) who exercise political power. However, taxation reduces the cash available to the firm for reinvestment. Thus, the entrepreneur is able to invest or reinvest not the economically rational amount but an amount somewhat less than that, known as earnings after taxes. The outside investor is also left to calculate returns after taxes, which means that required rates of return must be high enough to cover the government's share. Some new ventures are not able to generate outside financing because their after-tax returns to investors will simply be too low to justify the investment.

Taxation affects not only each business individually but also the relationships between businesses, giving some firms advantages over others. Special tax breaks for certain industries, like depreciation and depletion allowances, work to the benefit of the firms that receive them. Capital intensive companies, like manufacturers, benefit disproportionately from the tax shield that depreciation affords, whereas service businesses with large investments in training and development cannot depreciate their employees. The differential tax treatment given to interest and dividends under the U.S. tax code favors firms that can obtain bank loans and other forms of debt over equity-financed firms that pay dividends and whose investors receive capital gains. Because "bankable" businesses—those to whom a loan is likely to be offered—are generally older firms that are likely to have physical assets than can serve as collateral, new ventures, especially service businesses, are disadvantaged by the current tax code.

There is a global perspective to taxation as well. Different countries treat dividends, interest, and capital gains in different ways. For example, Japanese firms pay very low dividends relative to their German and U.S. counterparts because dividends are more highly taxed in Japan. Thus, the Japanese investor prefers capital gains, which are not taxed at all. This enables Japanese firms to keep more of their cash for reinvestment.[7]

Regulation   The government controls the flow of resources to firms and the property rights of business owners through federal agency regulation. These agencies are created by government in response to some special-interest group or group of stakeholders to protect their interests, values, and goals. This is not an inherently bad thing because we all belong to some special-interest groups. For example, we all eat and take medicine at some time. The Food and Drug Administration helps protect our interests in these matters.

The effects of regulation on business, however, are sometimes negative. Regulatory agencies impose significant costs on firms in the form of paperwork, testing and monitoring, and compliance. These costs may or may not be recoverable through higher prices. If the industry being regulated has good substitutes for its products and the substitute industry is less regulated, the firms in the more highly regulated industry have to absorb the costs, and profitability suffers. This results in less reinvestment and overall lower output in the regulated industry. If higher prices can be charged, then the public eventually pays for the protection and services it receives from the regulations.

Antitrust Legislation   Each national government determines the level of antitrust activity it will enforce. The United States has the toughest antitrust laws in the world. The antitrust division of the United States Justice Department was a driving force in the breakup of AT&T and in IBM's change in strategy. As of this writing, Microsoft has been the focus of antitrust litigation by both the U.S. Department of Justice and the attorney generals of 18 states. A settlement has been reached at the federal level; however, local cases may continue to go forward. The outcomes of these cases is not yet known. Other countries, most notably Japan, have a different view of the antitrust problem. In these countries, the zeal of regulatory enforcement may be a function of national economic interests (such as balance of trade or currency exchange). When national interests collide with consumer or entrepreneurial interests, national interests have priority. Generally, it is unlikely that new ventures will be in danger of violating antitrust laws. New firms are more likely to be victims of lax antitrust enforcement.

Patent Protection   National governments grant patents and enforce patent laws. A patent is legal property that enables its holder to prevent others from employing this property for their own use for a specified period of time. There are three types of patents:

1. **Utility patents** for new articles, processes, machines, and techniques
2. **Design patents** covering new and original ornamental designs for manufactured products
3. **Plant patents** covering various forms of life and genetically engineered organisms

A patent is a resource and, therefore, can be analyzed using our resource-based model. In countries where patent enforcement is lax, the firm may need to consider the costs of publicly divulging the technology versus the benefits of the protection (such as it is) before applying for a patent. In many cases, small changes to a product or design erode the patent protection enough to make the patent worthless.

Government Spending   In most countries, the national government is the largest purchaser and consumer of goods and services. The government is, therefore, a large market, and it displays preferences for products, services, and suppliers. These preferences are influenced by pressures from the various interest groups, stakeholders, and political or-ganizations that constantly lobby the government. At times it appears that the political winds are favoring defense spending, and new entrants into defense and related indus-tries benefit. At other times, government priorities may be set on building infrastructure or developing social programs. Construction contractors, consultants, and related service industries would then benefit.

State, Regional, and Local Issues

State, regional, or local level tax policies can create opportunities or disadvantages for the entrepreneur. At the state level, three other areas affect business: licensing, securi-ties and incorporation laws, and economic development and incentives.

Licensing   Licenses are economic privileges granted to individuals and firms that enable them to legally conduct a business. Not all businesses require licenses, but many do. At one time, licenses were valuable franchises and a way of limiting entry and rais-ing quality within a particular industry. Today, however, state and local authorities of-ten consider licenses as a revenue source and do little to monitor the performance level of the licensees. The entrepreneur must still be watchful of current regulation and po-tential changes that would affect the new venture.

Securities and Incorporation Laws   Many security regulations and incorporation laws are written and enforced by the states. Because the U.S. Constitution does not specifically grant to the federal government the power to regulate business incorpora-tion, this is one of the major regulatory roles left to the states. Although the federal gov-ernment does have an important regulatory role under the Securities Act of 1934, which created the Securities and Exchange Commission, new incorporations are granted and monitored at the state level. Most early financing that the firm receives is covered by state securities regulations. Entrepreneurs need to employ lawyers and accountants to ensure that the firm complies with all state regulations.

Incentives   State and local authorities control the granting of economic develop-ment incentives and tax abatements to new businesses or to old businesses relocating within their jurisdiction. These incentives can be a powerful stimulus for new firms. They can include subsidized job-training programs, real estate improvements and favorable real estate tax treatment, and improved infrastructure (e.g., roads and interchanges, sidewalks, water and sewer improvements). Local governments also control zoning or-dinances and laws, which determine how property can be used and developed. Every firm has a local component. Entrepreneurs can scan and monitor these developments, especially when considering location.

At the municipal level, taxation again erodes the firm's ability to finance itself and reward its investors. Local taxes include income and property, sewer, water, and waste disposal. If local taxes can be allocated to particular services provided by local govern-ment for business use, they are not really taxes but fees for service.

To summarize, the entrepreneur must be knowledgeable about a variety of politi-cal issues, particularly those related to securing, protecting, and disposing of resources.

TABLE 3-2 Political and Governmental Issues			
Global	*National*	*State and Region*	*Local*
Trade barriers	Taxation	Taxation	Taxation
Trade agreements	Regulation	Securities law	Zoning
Tariffs and duties	Antitrust legislation	Licensing	
Political risk	Patent protection	Incentives	
	Government spending		

Of primary concern is the effect of political power on property rights. Table 3-2 presents the four levels at which political and governmental analysis should be performed.

MACROECONOMIC ANALYSIS

The macroeconomy is the total of all goods and services produced, distributed, sold, and consumed. Where does all of this activity take place? At the global, national, and local levels. Each level has its own macroeconomy, and the sum of all the lower levels is the global economy. These geographic distinctions are important to policy makers because policy makers usually have geographic limits to their power and influence. The geographic distinctions are also important to the entrepreneur because, to a greater or lesser degree, every business is entwined in all three macroeconomies. The entrepreneur should analyze all three macroeconomies, but the time spent on any one should be proportional to its potential impact on the firm's performance. Macroeconomic change can occur at any of the three geographic levels discussed previously.[8]

There are two types of macroeconomic change: structural change and cyclical change.

Structural Change

Structural changes in the macroeconomy are major, permanent shifts of resources and customers from one sector of the economy to another. As these shifts occur, the financial capital, physical resources, and employees diminish in an industry that is fading and flow to the emerging industry.

Cyclical Change

The second type of macroeconomic change is **cyclical change**. The macroeconomy enjoys periods of growth and then sustains periods of contraction. These alternating time periods form what is called the **business cycle**. Business cyclicality is the degree to which the new firm follows the trend of the business cycle. A venture that grows and contracts as the economy does is **procyclical**; one that runs against the business cycle is **countercyclical**. A venture that is unaffected by the business cycle is **acyclical**.

Understanding the new venture's relationship to the business cycle is crucial to the entrepreneur because it is difficult, if not impossible, for the new business to run counter to its natural cyclicality. Thus, if the firm is in a procyclical industry and current trends in the business cycle are downward, the firm will have a difficult time going against this trend and expanding. Clearly the entrepreneur needs to scan and monitor the economic variables that indicate the direction of economic trends.

E-NOTES 3-2

Economic Analysis

Analysis of the economic segment of the macroenvironment explores the impact of:

- structural change (major shifts of resources)
- cyclical changes, including:
  procyclical (mirrors the economy)
  countercyclical (runs against the economy)
  acyclical (unaffected by economy)

TECHNOLOGICAL ANALYSIS

What is technology? **Technology** can be defined as "the branch of knowledge that deals with industrial arts, applied science, and engineering," and "a process, an invention, or a method." The first part of the definition tells us that technological analysis is concerned with the "what" of science. Technological analysis, then, requires scanning and monitoring from the time of basic research through product development and commercialization. The second part of the definition implies that technology is also concerned with the "how" of science. Therefore, a complete technological analysis also includes scanning of operations and manufacturing techniques.[9] Technological change takes place in two ways: through pure invention (and scientific discovery) and through process innovation.

Pure Invention

Pure invention is the creation of something radically different from existing technologies or products. Because it is different, it has certain characteristics that are economically interesting. An invention may have no competitors at its birth, thereby giving a monopoly to the individuals who hold the legal rights to the invention. The disadvantage is that the invention also has no market at the time of its invention, and there may never be a market for the commercial version of the invention. The combination of the monopolist upside with the no-ready-market downside makes the economic aspect of invention risky because the outcomes are potentially so variable.

New inventions can create new industries. The invention of the semiconductor created the computer industry in all its forms. The scientific discoveries made by geneticists created the biotech industry with all of its niches and segments. In the initial phase of such technologies and discoveries—in the creation of products and markets—entrepreneurs play the most important role. Over the product's life cycle, large organizational units develop to exploit these products and markets as they mature.

Process Innovation

After the invention is successfully commercialized, the second type of technological change, **process innovation**, becomes dominant. Whereas invention is radical and revolutionary, carrying with it the potential to create new industries, process innovation is incremental and evolutionary. Its purpose is to make existing industries more efficient. Process innovation refers to the small changes in design, product formulation and manufacturing, materials, and service delivery that firms make to keep their product up-to-date and their costs down. Table 3-3 shows how technology and key related variables change over the course of the product life cycle. Scanning and monitoring the technological environment is difficult. Early in the life of a scientific discovery or breakthrough, much of the information relating to it is accessible only to highly trained scientists. Sometimes the information is purely conceptual, appearing only in scientific journals. Sometimes the information is simply private and not accessible to anyone but the research team. Aside from conferences and meetings of academicians and scientists, the most accessible sources of information are government databases such as those maintained by NASA or the National Technical Information Service (NTIS). Many of these are accessible on the Internet.

Frequently process innovation improvements are made by people working for large companies. If these companies are not the best place to fully exploit these improvements, the people who develop the changes may decide to become entrepreneurs. They literally spin themselves and their new product off into a new venture.

E-NOTES 3-3

Technological Analysis

Analysis of technology studies the changes that occur from:

- pure invention
- process invention

SOCIODEMOGRAPHIC ANALYSIS

The sociodemographic phase of business environment analysis has two highly related aspects: demographics and social trends (sometimes referred to as "lifestyle trends"). The interaction of these produce popular culture. Within a society's popular culture reside enormous business opportunities in consumer and durable goods, retailing and services, leisure and entertainment, and housing and construction.

Demographics

Demographic changes are a major source of long-term social change. **Demography** is the study of trends in human populations: the size of the population and its various subgroups; the population's age structure, geographic distribution, and ethnic and racial mix; and the distribution of income and wealth within the population. Demographic change refers to changes in any of these variables and changes in the relationships between them. Demography is destiny, because all of these factors form the essence of consumer demand, industrial capacities, and purchasing power. From demographic analysis markets are created.

TABLE 3-3 Forms of Technological Change over the Product Life-Cycle Stages

	Product Life-Cycle Stage			
	Introduction	*Shakeout*	*Growth*	*Maturity*
Type of Innovation	Major product innovation or invention	→	→ Incremental product/major process innovation	→ Incremental product/process innovation
Location of Innovation	Entrepreneur	→ Marketing/ R&D	→ Marketing/ production	→ Production
Bases of Competition	Product, performance, or novelty	→	→ Product differentiation price	→ Price, image, minor differences
Production Process	Job shop	→ Batch	→ Islands of automation	→ Assembly line → Continuous flow
Dominant Function	Entrepreneur	→ Marketing/ R&D	→ Marketing/ production	→ Production/ sales (promotion)
Management Role	Entrepreneur	→ Sophisticated market manager	→ Administrator/ integrator	→ Steward
Modes of Integration	Informal communication	→ Informal communication, task forces, teams	→ Informal communication, teams, project manager	→ Formal communication, senior management committees
Organizational Structure	Free form	→ Functional organic	→ Project/matrix	→ Functional/ bureaucratic

Source: Adapted from W. L. Moore and M. L. Tushman, "Managing Innovation over the Product Life Cycle," in M. L. Tushman and W. L. Moore, eds., *Readings in the Management of Innovation* (Boston: Pitman Press, 1982), 143.

Some of the best demographic data that we get is from the census. In the United States, a census is taken every 10 years, and the results for the most recent 10-year period (1990–1999) have recently been released. A number of important trends emerged from this study and from comparing this last 10-year period with the first 10-year period of the twentieth century.[10]

First, it is clear that we are living longer. The most important increases in life expectancy are occurring for older people. At the beginning of the twentieth century and for most of the next 75 years, increases in life expectancy occurred because of better health care for children. Fewer children died young. Now the increases are on the other end of the life cycle. Older people are living longer. During the second half of the twentieth century, life expectancy for people in their 70s grew by an additional 5 years, to age 82. Seniors are living substantially longer and more healthy lives.

At the beginning of the twentieth century, a wave of European immigration brought millions of new citizens to the United States. By midcentury, this wave had greatly diminished. In 1900, the percentage of foreign-born people in America was 14 percent. By 1970, it had dropped to 5 percent. It is now back at 10 percent, which represents about 27 million people. The major new groups of immigrants come from Korea, Haiti, Vietnam, and Mexico.

The population of the United States is moving south and west. California is our largest state with over 33.9 million people. Twenty-two percent of Americans live in the west; that figure would be higher except for the fact that the Census Bureau counts Texas as being in the south. This makes the south the largest region, with 36 percent of the total population. Arguably, this makes the most important invention in the history of U.S. demographics the air conditioner.

The total population of the United States is growing, too. In 1900, U.S. total population was half the combined totals of Britain, France, Germany, and Italy. Now we have more people than all of those countries combined. By 2050, we will be twice as populous as we are now; in Japan, there is negative population growth, and growth is flat in Western Europe. No wonder we have the most vibrant and dynamic marketplace in the global economy. We have the most customers, too.

Social Trends and Values

Social trends refer to the modes and manners in which people live their lives. Lifestyles reflect people's tastes and preferences in an economic sense. Lifestyle-related variables that affect new venture creation include household formation, work modes and labor force participation rates, education levels and attainments, patterns of consumption, and patterns of leisure.

Scanning and monitoring lifestyle changes is relatively easy because many diverse sources of data are available. Much of the data is aggregated and, therefore, suggests trends. There are both public and private sources for demographic data. The national government, through its agencies, bureaus, and regulatory bodies, collects vast amounts of data. Trade publications and specialist magazines and newspapers contribute demographic analysis. Consumer reports and the annual reports of corporations furnish additional details. One publication, *American Demographics,* is specifically designed to ferret out unusual and important trends.

Social values and social change together form an important component of sociodemographic analysis. "A **value** is a conception, explicit or implicit, distinctive of an individual or characteristic of a group of the desirable, which influences the selection of available means and ends of action."[11] This means, simply, that the choices we make reflect our values. The values that individuals and groups hold cluster around the dimensions of the macroenvironment discussed earlier in this chapter. People hold political values relating to the role of government, political participation, and distributive justice.[12] They hold regulatory values concerning issues like consumerism and energy policy. Their social values reflect their choices concerning work, the relationship between races, and gender. Economic values are reflected in the choices they make relating to growth and taxation. Some of these values are at the core of the individual's belief systems, and other values are on the periphery.

Sociodemographic Analysis

Analysis of the sociodemographic investigates the impact of changes in:

- demographics
- social trends and values

ECOLOGICAL ANALYSIS

Ecological analysis is the study of the current state of the ecology. The **ecology** pertains to such issues as pollution and waste disposal, recycling of usable materials, protection of wildlife and wilderness preserve areas, workplace safety and hazards, and the general quality of life. Ecological analysis cuts across all the other areas already discussed: politics and government, the macroeconomy, technology, and lifestyle values. Ecological issues are bottom-line issues, and the entrepreneur must be as accountable as any other businessperson or citizen. Ecological awareness goes beyond simply addressing the manufacturing issues of pollution and waste.

The entrepreneur is part of the world movement toward **sustainable development**, that is, meeting the needs of the current generation without compromising the needs of future generations.[13] Future economic progress must be guided by ecological conservation. The ecosystem and its protection enters into all major entrepreneurial and business development decisions. For example, product development and design issues take into account the rate of usage and transformation of natural resources and the disposal of waste products. These decisions should be made in the planning stage of a business, not at the crisis stage. Also, financial calculations should fully value natural resources for their current worth and their potential value to future generations. Undervaluation of natural resources causes waste and overdemand. The time when entrepreneurs could run the earth like a business in liquidation has long since passed.[14]

E-NOTES 3-5

Macroenvironment

The five segments of the business macroenvironment are:

- politics and government
- economy
- technology
- sociodemographics
- ecology

SOURCES OF OPPORTUNITY

What is the most important thing to notice about the business environment? Change. Changes in the business environment offer opportunities for entrepreneurs. Existing firms have their resources, strategy, and organization structure geared for the past or current macroenvironment. When a change occurs, it is frequently easier for the new firm to spot the change and configure a set of resources and an organization to meet the new needs and the new realities. There are seven sources of opportunity to look for in the macroenvironment.[15]

The Unexpected

When current businesses are surprised by an unanticipated event, they are often unable to adapt quickly enough to take advantage. The event can be an unexpected success (good news) or an unexpected failure (bad news). For example, if war breaks out where it is unexpected, it changes the economics and demand structure of the warring parties and their populations. This can provide opportunity if it is ethically pursued. Similarly, a breakthrough in a peace negotiation also provides opportunity, because it changes the economies of the former combatants. Sometimes the unexpected happens directly to the company, and the shock can be fatal or it can be the source of new opportunities. In Street Story 3-2, we see that the unexpected loss of a company's biggest customer provided a chance to break away from the old ways of doing business.

The Incongruous

Incongruity is dissonance, things that "ought to be" but are not. It creates instability and opportunity. For example, it is incongruous for a growing industry with increasing sales not to be profitable, but it happens and is happening now on the Internet. Some key to the industry's economics has yet to be discovered. When reality and conventional wisdom collide, incongruity exists. Listen for "expert old-timers" who use the words "never" and "always" to explain how things should be. These unexamined assumptions

Waking Up to Unexpected Opportunity

The whole world changed for 26-year-old entrepreneur Di-Ann Eisnor early one morning.

Eisnor, founder and CEO of a company that creates off-line publicity for online brands, thought her breakfast meeting with her company's major client was going well. When they sat down for coffee, this client was providing 80 percent of the revenues for the year-old Eisnor Interactive.

Between bites of fruit salad, however, the client's marketing manager unexpectedly told Eisnor that the parent company had decided to abandon its online bookstore venture, meaning they no longer needed the promotion services of Eisnor Interactive. Suddenly, Eisnor would have to scramble to pay the salaries for herself and seven other employees.

Eisnor expected her employees to desert her when she broke the news, but their reaction surprised her. "I thought it was a great opportunity," says Kevin Starace, now Eisnor's director of business development. "I would be able to help grow a company wtihout any of the limitations a large client brings."

After spending 5 frantic days cold-calling prospective new clients without success, Eisnor and her staff went on a retreat to develop a new approach and strategy document for the company. They decided to narrow their focus from general publicity to a unique product where they had been successful: attention-grabbing campaigns in places like airports and subways that publicized online brands through street stunts, guerilla marketing gimmicks, and giveaways in conjunction with print ads. Although in-person physical promotion may seem a bit incongruous for Internet businesses, Eisnor's approach gives her clients a unique marketing edge and allows them to target specific demographic groups. They also decided to hire a public relations firm to generate buzz about their company and scheduled a series of appearances at conferences where they could meet potential clients face to face to help change the perceptions of potential clients.

Eisnor Interactive landed its first new client at another breakfast meeting less than 5 weeks after the initial crisis. Two years later, the company has 19 clients, and billings have gone from $1 million to an estimated $36 million.

Eisnor now knows it was a big mistake to bask in the security of one big client, even initially when the dollars looked good. Constant promotion will be the key to her company's survival. "I was so against it," she says, reflecting on how the bad news that forced her company to transform itself into a self-promotion powerhouse was an unexpected opportunity in disguise. "But we needed to start building a name for ourselves. It was really a dangerous position for us to be in."

Source: Adapted from Hillary Stout, "After Its Biggest Client Abruptly Disappears, a Start-Up Scrambles," *The Wall Street Journal,* April 5, 2000, p. B1.

may have once been right but may now be wrong and, therefore, provide opportunities for the responsive entrepreneur.

The Process Need

This opportunity has its source in technology's inability to provide the "big break-through." Technicians often need to work out a way to get from point A to point B in some process. Currently, efforts are being made in the areas of superconductivity, fusion, interconnectivity, and the search for a treatment and cure for AIDS. Thomas Edison and others knew that in order to start the electric energy industry, they needed to solve a process need—to develop a lightbulb that worked. Process need opportunities are often addressed by program research projects, which are the systematic research and analysis efforts designed to solve a single problem, such as the effort against AIDS.

Industry and Market Structures

Changes in technology, both innovation and invention, change market and industry structures by altering costs, quality requirements, and volume capabilities. This alteration can potentially make existing firms obsolete if they are not attuned to it and are inflexible. Similarly, changes in social values and consumer tastes as well as demographics shift the economics of industries to new equilibria. The markets of firms that do not adapt are fair game for the entrepreneur.

Demographics

Demographic changes are changes in the population or subpopulations of society. They can be changes in the size, age, structure, employment, education, or incomes of these groups. Such changes influence all industries and firms by changing the mix of products and services demanded, the volume of products and services, and the buying power of customers. Some of these changes are predictable, because people who will be older are already alive, and birth and death rates stay fairly stable over time. Other changes are not predictable and are caused by natural disasters, war, social change, and immigration. Population statistics are available for assessment, but opportunities can be found before the data are published by observing what is happening in the street and being reported in the newspaper.

Changes in Perception

"Is the glass half full or half empty?" The two perceptions are logically equivalent but reflect significantly different attitudes and behaviors. People hold different perceptions of the same reality, and these differences affect the products and services they demand and the amounts they spend. Some groups feel powerful and rich; others, disenfranchised and poor. Some people think they are thin when they are not; others think they are too fat when they are not. The entrepreneur can sell power and status to the rich and powerful, and sell relief and comfort to the poor and oppressed. Whether people are rich or poor, if they perceive that they are middle class, they will demand education for their children, good housing for their family, and travel for their vacations.

New Knowledge

New knowledge is often seen as the "superstar" of entrepreneurial opportunity. However, it can be "temperamental, capricious, and hard to manage."[16] It is not enough to have new knowledge; there must also be a way to make products from it and to protect the profits of those products from competition as the knowledge is spread to others. In addition, timing is critical. It frequently takes the convergence of many pieces of new knowledge to make a product. For example,

> A number of knowledges came together to make possible the computer. The earliest was the binary theorem, a mathematical theory going back to the seventeenth century that enables all numbers to be expressed by two numbers only: one and zero. It was applied to a calculating machine by Charles Babbage in the first half of the nineteenth century. In 1890, Hermann Hollerith invented the punchcard, going back to the invention in the early nineteenth century by Frenchman J-M. Jacquard. The punchcard makes it possible to convert numbers into "instructions." In 1906 an American, Lee de Forest, invented the audion tube, and with it created electronics. Then, between 1910 and 1913, Bertrand Russell and Alfred North Whitehead, in the Principia Mathematica, created symbolic logic, which enables us to express all logical concepts as numbers. Finally, during World War I, the concepts of programming and feedback were developed, primarily for the purposes of antiaircraft gunnery. By 1918, in other words, all the knowledge needed to develop the computer was available. The first computer became operational in 1946.[17]

E-NOTES 3-6

Entrepreneurial Opportunities

Sources of opportunity in the macroenvironment can originate with:

- the unexpected
- the incongruous
- the process need
- industry and market structures
- demographics
- changes in perception
- new knowledge

COMPETITIVE ANALYSIS

The tools of competitive analysis are derived from economics, the so-called dismal science. Jokes are sometimes told to illustrate how deflating economics can be to entrepreneurs. So, let us begin with a joke.[18] A student and her economics professor, while walking together across campus, were engaged in a serious discussion concerning the price elasticity of demand for a college education. As they walked, the student's eyes fell on a piece of paper on the walk ahead of them. As they got closer, the student could see that the paper was a $20 bill. When they were upon the bill, the student bent down to pick it up. "What are you doing?" asked the economics professor. "There's a $20 bill on the walk," replied the student. "Nonsense," said the professor. "If there were a $20 bill on the ground, someone would have picked it up by now."

The joke demonstrates that a strong belief in the all-powerful, efficient-market model of economics can prevent a person from seeing an opportunity, even when it is right under his nose. The economics professor cannot believe that a $20 bill (an opportunity) would be lying on the walk, because under the assumptions of the efficient market, opportunities disappear instantly.[19] However, current reality and economic history show that there are truly many opportunities for individuals who follow their instincts and act on them intelligently.

We should not, though, dismiss the model of efficient markets too quickly. Although it is conceivable that the first mover, the initiator, or the innovator can earn the high returns of entrepreneurship by identifying and retrieving the $20 bill that no one else has seen, few business opportunities are of the once-and-done variety. Most ventures must be managed and operated over the foreseeable future, if not indefinitely. This is the point of our introductory quote. The key for the new venture is to find a measure of distinctiveness and develop a strategy to protect it. Therefore, the microeconomics of the firm and of that firm's industry are crucial to determining the venture's profit potential and the strategies most appropriate for realizing it.

INDUSTRY ANALYSIS

The purpose of industry analysis is to determine what makes an industry attractive and to decide which segments of the industry are most attractive. This analysis reveals appropriate strategies and resources to be procured or developed. Industry attractiveness is generally indicated either by above-normal profits or high growth. It depends on the resources and cost positions of the firms in the industry. For example, hard-to-replicate efficiency levels (resources) lead to high industry profitability, but they also make the industry less attractive for inefficient firms. On the other hand, high-growth industries are relatively more attractive for less-efficient firms than for efficient firms.[20] Research has shown that some industries are more profitable over the long run than others. Each year, *Fortune* surveys all major industry groups and publishes the data. The results are remarkably stable over time. One-year results might be spectacularly bad or good, but overall profitability within an industry is constrained by the industry's characteristics.

The firm's ultimate objective is to earn above-normal profits. It does this in one of two ways: (1) developing a product that is distinctive enough that the customer will be willing to pay a price high enough to produce attractive margins, or (2) if it has a product identical to the competition's, being able to produce it at a cost low enough to produce attractive margins and profitability. These two strategies are broadly referred to as **differentiation strategy** and **low-cost strategy**, respectively. When a firm pursues either the differentiation or the low-cost position for a subsegment of a market (as opposed to the general market), the strategy is called a **focus strategy**.[21]

A comprehensive analytical tool for determining the attractiveness of an industry is the *model of competitive analysis*.[22] This model describes five forces that determine the price/cost relationships within an industry and, therefore, define the industry's margins:

1. The **bargaining power of buyers**
2. The **bargaining power of suppliers**
3. The **threat of** relevant **substitutes**
4. The threat of new entrants into the industry (presence of **entry barriers**)
5. The **rivalry** among existing firms (influenced by the other four factors)

Figure 3-2 provides a schematic of the five forces at work. The industry under analysis is referred to as the **focal industry** to distinguish it from the buyer, supplier, and substitute industries that exert pressure on it.

BUYER POWER

In perfectly competitive markets, buyers or customers have no power other than to accept or reject the product offered. All products are the same, so there is no shopping around for quality, service, or other characteristics. All have the same price, so no haggling is possible. In fact, it is almost ironic that the model is known as the "competitive" model, because sellers do not actually compete directly for customers. Products are produced for the market and are either purchased or not purchased depending on the buyer's utility function (for a final consumer) or on the production function (for a producer).

When we relax this condition, we find that in a number of scenarios the buyer has a great deal of bargaining power. The two issues that are dearest to the buyer in bargaining situations are (1) decreases in price for the product, and (2) increases in the product's quality. Both of these buyer bargaining positions decrease the producer firm's margins. Price concessions squeeze margins from the revenue side; increases in quality squeeze margins by increasing the seller's costs.[23]

Once the conditions for perfect competition are relaxed, a buyer group can become powerful in several circumstances.

1. *Buyer Group Concentration.* If there are more sellers selling than there are buyers buying, the natural tendency is for the sellers to reduce prices to make a sale. Even if they do not reduce prices, they offer additional services to make quality improvements to their products, both of which have the same effect of squeezing margins. If the buying group makes large purchases, in an absolute as well as a relative sense, it will bargain for volume discounts. The bases for these discounts are (1) the threat to withhold the order and disrupt production, (2) lower per-unit costs of billing and shipping large orders, and (3) lower production costs resulting from long production runs.

2. *Buyer's Costs.* If the products represent a significant share of the buyer's total costs or total income, the buyer becomes extremely price sensitive. When purchases are large, small concessions in price produce large benefits for the buyer. Most consumers are familiar with this situation, because bargaining over the price of cars and homes is the primary consumer bargaining experience. The automobile and residential real estate industries allow people to bargain over the prices of these items because they know their customers are price sensitive owing to the size of the purchase. These industries have, of course, adapted to this sensitivity by hiding the true reservation prices (the lowest price the seller will take) of the products from the customer at all times. Consumers bargain a little, but they still pay enough to salvage the margins of the sellers.[24]

3. *Similar Products.* If the buyer is indifferent among sellers because the products available for purchase are basically alike, the buyer has power. If buyers can procure alternatives, they naturally look for a reason to buy from a particular seller, and one good reason is a lower price. The implication here is that the selling firm may believe it has a product that should command a premium price because of its high quality and special features. If these features are unimportant or not communicated to the buyer, the buyer will still shop on price.

FIGURE 3-2 Elements of Industry Structure

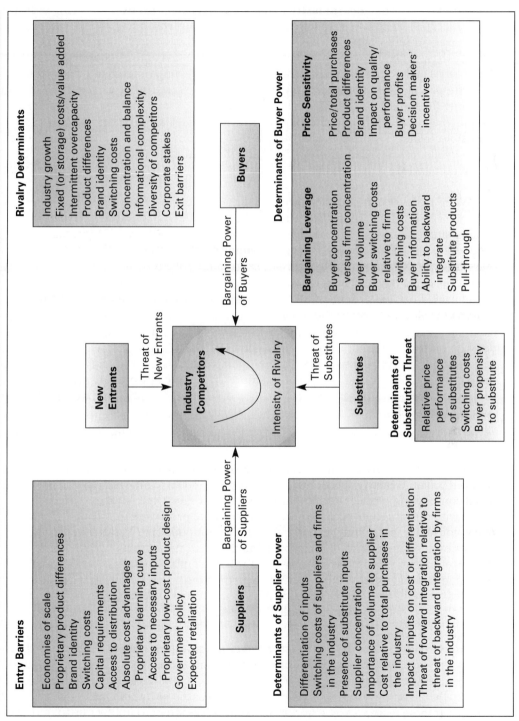

Source: Adapted from The Free Press, A Division of Simon & Schuster, from *Competitive Advantage: Creating and Sustaining Superior Performance* by Michael E. Porter. Copyright © 1985 by Michael E. Porter.

4. *Switching Costs.* If the buyer faces few switching costs and can shop for price or quality without incurring high transaction costs, the buyer is powerful. Switching costs are costs that lock the buyer into an ongoing relationship with the seller. An example is frequent-flyer miles. Travelers will fly higher-priced, less-convenient air routes to accumulate these miles. The cost of switching airlines is the loss of the frequent-flyer miles.[25] Sometimes high transaction costs also result from switching vendors or searching for information. Faced with these costs, the buyer remains passive in the current relationship, enabling the seller to maintain profitable margins.

5. *Buyer Income.* The buyer who earns low profits or has a low income is price sensitive. Sensitivity is increased when the buyer is short of funds, either personal income (for consumers) or profits from operations (for industrial buyers). Although rich people sometimes haggle over a price and purchasing agents of profitable companies search for a penny-saving agreement, more often, when the buyer has enough funds, the cost of negotiating a tough deal outweighs the minor savings.

6. *Threat of Integration.* If the buyer firm can make a credible threat to fabricate a product or provide a service itself if it chooses not to buy it on the open market, it increases its power by gaining bargaining leverage over the sellers in the industry. This factor brings into play the classic make-or-buy decision, and it does so on a strategic level. If it can provide all the product itself, it is a credible threat for full **backward integration**. If it can provide some of the input, the process is known as **tapered integration**. The reasons for increased buyer power are as follows: (1) The buyer can make a take-it-or-leave-it offer to the seller with the full knowledge that if the seller "leaves it," the firm can still supply itself; (2) the buyer knows the actual costs of producing the product or delivering the service and can negotiate more effectively down to the seller's reservation price. The major offsetting factor for the seller is the credibility of its threat of **forward integration**.

7. *Indifference to Quality.* If the products or services in an industry are not distinguished by quality, cost is a determining factor in consumer choice. In the presence of indifference to quality, the major reason for distinguishing between sellers is price. Increased price sensitivity causes buyers to shop around and will negatively affect the industry's margins.

8. *Full Information.* The more information the buyer group has about product prices, manufacturing costs, comparative product attributes, and the negotiating strategies of sellers, the more bargaining leverage it has. In young industries, where buyers and sellers are new at dealing with one another, certain cost and price data can be kept secret. This makes firms in young industries less likely to face pressure on margins. In mature industries, as firms build up long records and files of information on each other, they are more likely to have full information, causing downward pressure on prices.

Seldom do an industry's products have only one type of buyer. Certainly, for consumer products, market segmentation analysis demonstrates that there are many types of buyers. Each segment possesses its own utility functions and is, therefore, subject to strategic product-positioning tactics. The same is true in industrial marketing. This makes **buyer selection** a key strategic variable. Firms strive to hold a portfolio of buyers, each with a different degree of bargaining power. If a firm has only weak buyers, its short-term margins may be good, but the firm is not producing high-quality products and is probably not investing enough in the kind of product improvements and innovation that more powerful buyers demand. These deficiencies make the venture potentially vulnerable to an innovative competitor that produces high-quality products or services. If the venture has only strong buyers in its portfolio, it will have low margins and will always be a captive of its customers. Such a firm is vulnerable to the whims of its customers and to their desire to increase their own profits.

SUPPLIER POWER

Like buyers, suppliers exert bargaining power over an industry in two ways. Suppliers seek to (1) increase the prices they charge for the products and services they sell or (2) decrease the quality of those products and services for the current market-clearing prices. Either of these bargaining objectives has the net effect of squeezing the margins in the focal industry and, other things being equal, making the industry less attractive. If the supplier industry is successful in the use of these tactics, it shifts profits from the focal industry to its own industry, capturing the economic power that the focal industry may have with its own buyers and appropriating the gains for itself. Entrepreneurs who concentrate all their energy and analysis on their buyers and none on the supplier industry may well find that profits are quickly eroded by cost-squeeze pressures.

Supplier power is basically the other side of the buyer-power coin. The same principles apply, only this time the focal industry is the buyer. Suppliers can exert pressure on margins under several conditions.

1. *Supplier Concentration.* When the supplying industry is dominated by a few companies and is more concentrated than the focal industry, suppliers have power.

2. *Role of Substitutes.* Suppliers are powerful when there are few good substitutes for the supplying industry's products. Even large, powerful suppliers cannot maintain high prices and low quality if good substitutes for their products are available.

3. *Purchasing Power.* If the focal industry is not an important customer for the suppliers, the suppliers have power. If the total dollars spent by the focal industry is small relative to the supplying industry's total sales, it will be difficult for the focal industry to obtain price concessions, quality improvements, or extra services such as delivery, warranties, and on-site repair.

4. *Importance of Quality.* When the product or service being purchased is crucial to the success of the industry's product or service, this input must be high quality. Focal industry firms often pay dearly for this high quality. Without substitutes of similar quality, the focal industry can expect cost increases for the product or service, which could severely diminish its profitability.

5. *Switching Costs.* Switching costs prevent buyers from playing suppliers off against each other in an attempt to bargain for price concessions or improvements in quality. This is, of course, analogous to the buyer-power conditions mentioned in the preceding section.

6. *Threat of Integration.* Again, the analogy to the buyer-power situation is apparent. If suppliers can do for themselves what the focal industry does, the focal industry cannot

expect to exert much bargaining power. For suppliers, this is a use-or-sell decision. They have the option to either sell their input to another firm or use that input themselves to produce a final product. Also, tapered integration, where the supplier uses only some of the input internally, can be used to generate data on costs, which enhances the supplier's bargaining power.

Although it is natural to think of suppliers only as firms that sell the entrepreneur goods and services, other supplier industries may require analysis. For example, labor, capital, land, information, and business services are all suppliers. Each can be analyzed using the framework described previously. Every new venture has a portfolio of suppliers—some can be influenced by strategy and some are too powerful to be influenced. **Supplier selection strategy** minimizes the possibility that profits made in output markets will be lost in input decisions.

THE THREAT OF SUBSTITUTES

Every industry competes against other industries for customers. Sometimes the competition is fairly direct, such as with fiberglass insulation versus rock wool, cellulose, or plastic foam.[26] At other times, the substitute-product rivalry is indirect, though still real. For example, the "eat at home" food-processing industry and its distribution chain—the grocery stores and supermarkets—competes with the "meals away from home" restaurant industry and all its many segments. There are times when it is difficult to tell whether another industry is a factor. For example, does the motor home industry compete with other vehicles (cars, trucks, and boats), or does it compete with motels located along interstate highways and near campgrounds and parks? Clearly the substitute product is defined by its function, not by the way it looks, by how it is produced, or even by what it costs.

It is important for the entrepreneur to understand the nature of substitute products for three reasons. First, when the entrepreneurs are the first to market a new product or product type, they sometimes believe they have no competition because "we're the first ones doing this." However, competition often exists in function, and a competitive challenge from a substitute industry is likely to surface. Second, substitutes can limit the potential returns to the focal industry by placing a price ceiling on what the industry can charge. There is always a price so high that it will force customers to switch from one industry's product to another's. The more attractive the value of the substitute (its price/performance relationship), the lower the price ceiling.

Last, existing firms often disparage the threat of substitutes because of psychological factors that block quick action. For the entrepreneur, this can be an advantage. The entrepreneur usually has a period of time to maneuver before established firms recognize the threat.

ENTRY BARRIERS

Why is it that the professor of economics is so certain that the $20 bill (remember our little joke) is not there? It is because nothing prevents someone else from picking it up first. There are no entry barriers to the "found $20 opportunity." Entry barriers are a crucial factor for entrepreneurs in analyzing industry structure.[27] The entrepreneur must overcome entry barriers as they currently exist and later attempt to create entry barriers to prevent others from following and diminishing the found opportunity.

This is the **paradox of entrepreneurship**. If the entrepreneur can find an industry that is easy to enter, then it may be similarly easy for others to enter. This makes the opportunity a fleeting one, because low-entry barriers are a characteristic of unprofitable industries. If the entrepreneur finds an industry that is difficult to enter (and by implication profitable), all its profit potential might have to be expended in high initial start-up costs to overcome the barriers.[28] The conclusion might therefore be: No profit can be made in an industry with low-entry barriers, and no profit can be made in an industry with high-entry barriers (the conclusion is the same for intermediate situations). In other words, "What $20 bill?" The answer to the paradox is that new entrant resources and strategic differences between new firms and existing firms allow entry despite high barriers.

Table 3-4 presents the major entry barriers that face a new venture entering an existing industry. There are two general types: (1) **structural barriers**, which result from the industry's history, technology, and macroenvironment, and (2) **retaliatory barriers**, which are a function of current competitors' anticipated reactions.

Structural Barriers to Entry

The structural barriers prevent the entrepreneur from getting started, and that represents a lost opportunity. But more dangerous to the entrepreneur are the retaliating barriers, because these can destroy the entrepreneur's chances of success after a large investment of time, money, and resources.

Retaliatory Barriers to Entry

Usually, when a new firm, especially one that is relatively small, enters an industry, there is little response from that firm's large, well-established competitors. Sometimes, however, entry by a new venture provokes a strong response from larger and more powerful firms. Because retaliation becomes an immediate threat to the survival of the new

TABLE 3-4   Entry Barriers

Structural Barriers	*Retaliatory Barriers*
Economies of scale	Competitors' reputation
Excess capacity	Industry history
Product differentiation core	Attack on competitors' business
Specific assets	Slow industry growth rate
Capital requirements	Competitors with substantial resources
Switching costs	Price cutting
Access to distribution channels	Legal challenges
Cost disadvantages unrelated to size	

venture, the owners of new firms should understand when they may provoke retaliation. Large, established firms retaliate under the following three conditions:

1. *When they have a reputation to uphold and a history of retaliation.* Firms that are historically known as aggressive competitors do not want to lose that reputation, even if the competition is a new venture of small size. This is because that reputation is an asset (rare, valuable, imperfectly imitable, and nonsubstitutable) that helps protect the competitor from other aggressive strategies and tactics. If the reputation is tarnished, other firms may decide to attack.

2. *If the attack is at the core business.* When a newcomer attacks the core business of an established firm, that firm feels the greatest threat and will most likely retaliate.

3. *If the entry occurs in a slow-growth industry.* When an industry is growing slowly, in terms of total sales dollars and unit volume, each new entrant takes away a small percentage of sales that an established firm was counting on. The slow-growth industry has the elements of a zero-sum game: Sales garnered by one firm are forever lost to all other firms.

Price Cutting

Retaliation can be expected in two additional situations: when the product is commodity-like and when the industry has high fixed costs. Both are likely to cause price-cutting retaliation in an attempt to force the new firm out of business by driving the industry price level down to the entry-deterring price, the hypothetical price that will just balance the rewards and cost of entry. In other words, it is the product or service price that makes the entrepreneur forecast zero profits for the proposed new venture. When an industry's prices are above the entry-deterring level, no rational entrepreneur would start a new business in that industry. The existing firms will allow prices to rise again when the threat of entry has subsided. If the threat is persistent, these firms have to use other methods or concede that their industry imposes low-entry barriers and, therefore, other things being equal, is not an attractive industry to be in.

In some situations, the small, new venture is protected from entry-deterring price cuts. Table 3-5 lists the factors that both encourage and inhibit the use of price cutting as a competitive tactic. The table illustrates that when price cutting is not likely to work—when it is likely to cause major losses for the price cutter and probably provoke large, existing competitors to follow suit—the new firm can operate under the **price umbrella** of the existing competition without fear of price retaliation.

TABLE 3-5 Factors Affecting Retaliatory Pricing	
Encouraging Factors	*Discouraging Factors*
Elastic demand	Inelastic demand
Cost advantages	No cost advantages
Excess capacity	Tight capacity
Small competitors	Large competitors
New competitors	Long-time rivalry
Single-product markets	Market interdependency

Legal Challenges to New Ventures

The new firm can expect retaliation to take forms other than just price cutting, especially when price cutting is not advisable for the larger firms. Legal attacks have become common. The basis for a court battle could be patent, copyright, or trademark infringement, violation of a former-employee noncompete clause, claims of defective products, violation of environmental laws, or, in the case of a foreign new venture entrant, claims of dumping and unfair competition.

Let us conclude our discussion of entry barriers by returning to the anecdote of the economics professor and the $20 bill. The professor refuses to pick up the money because he cannot believe it is still there. Why? Because there are no entry barriers that would prevent somebody else from picking it up first. Because the professor is nothing if not rational, and the odds that he got there first minuscule, the bill cannot exist. This is a case of his assumptions preventing him from seeing the opportunity, but before we condemn the professor for his blindness, let us consider this: If he would look down and see the bill, so might others at approximately the same time. They might rush over and contest the ownership of that $20 bill. Some would be loud, and others might use force. A deal would then be struck giving each competitor for the money just enough to reward him or her for the trouble it took to strike the bargain. In some sense, they would all be even and the costs would equal the rewards. Thus, it is not only the professor's assumption but also the competitors' reactions that lead him to keep walking.

RIVALRY BETWEEN FIRMS

The effects of strong buyer power, strong supplier power, good substitutes, and low-entry barriers on an industry make the industry more competitive. Each force, by itself, can cause costs to rise or prices to fall, or both. This cost push or price squeeze reduces the operating margins of the firms in the industry. Reduced margins force less-efficient firms to go out of business (if exit barriers are low),[29] the modestly efficient firms to break even, and the most efficient firms to endure low profitability until industry conditions are altered.

The rivalry and competitiveness between firms increase when the other four forces in the model are negative. However, additional conditions lead to rivalry and low industry attractiveness. These conditions focus on the status of the existing firms. Rivalry among firms increases (and, other things being equal, margins and profitability decrease) when the following conditions prevail.

1. *Numerous and Balanced Competitors.* The more competitors there are, the more likely it is that some of them will "misbehave" by slashing prices and quality. This causes problems for everyone. When competitors are balanced and all are about the same size, there is no clear leader in the industry to whom the others can look for direction. An industry leader helps maintain price discipline and keeps the industry from engaging in destructive price wars.

2. *Slow Industry Growth.* When an industry is growing, there are enough customers to go around and fill most firms' capacity. Slow growth causes firms to compete for customers, either with price decreases or quality increases. Also, as growth slows, the need for advertising may increase, adding an additional expense and hurting margins.

3. *High Fixed Costs.* Firms with high fixed costs have high operating leverage. This means that they need high volumes to break even, but after the break-even point has been reached, each unit sold adds significantly to the bottom line. Therefore, industries with high fixed costs have strong incentives to fill capacity any way they can. This may lead to price cutting. Examples of this are the recent history of the airline and automobile industries.

4. *Commodity-Type Products.* When the product is a commodity, or is perceived by the public as a commodity because the industry cannot differentiate products, pressures for intense price and service competition grow. Related to this condition is the absence of switching costs and increased buyer power.[30] It is time to address the "all things being equal" assumption interspersed in our discussion. In this context, "all things being equal" refers to the firms' resource-based strategies. That is, industries are attractive or unattractive for entry without considering the resources the new entrant may bring to the venture. The type of resources and the extent to which they possess the four attributes of competitive advantage do make a difference. An unattractive industry might be a profitable opportunity for a firm with a winning configuration of resources. An attractive industry might produce mediocre results for a firm without any resource advantages.

One industry that might seem to have all four of these characteristics is the dry-cleaning industry. Numerous, balanced competitors, slow growth, and a commodity-type product have kept this industry a backwater for years. But change is afoot and something might be pressing, as Street Story 3-3 illustrates.

COMPETITOR ANALYSIS

So what is the new entrepreneur to do with all of this analysis? The new entrant in an industry must perform a detailed analysis of its competition. The industry analysis, discussed previously, precedes the competitor analysis and is more general. The data required for the industry analysis were aggregated; in their disaggregated (firm-level) form, these data provide the raw material needed to assess the strategy and resource base of the competition.

Identifying the Competition

The first step is to determine who the competition is. This is the equivalent of asking, "What business am I in?" and "What needs does my product/service fulfill for the customer?" The competition consists of firms that fulfill the same customer needs or have the potential to serve those customers. How can this competition be determined?

Current competitors can be identified in a number of ways. A direct method is to ask customers (of existing firms) or potential customers (of new ventures) where else they would consider procuring the product or service. Indirect methods include scanning trade and business directories, the *Yellow Pages,* and the Internet. To discover the larger competitors, the entrepreneur should check *Value Line, Standard & Poor's* classifications, and the *Disclosure* database that identifies firms by the U.S. government's four-digit Standard Industrial Classification code.[31]

The Pressing Rivalry of Dry Cleaners

No industry is more competitive—or less rewarding—than dry cleaning. In most communities, there is a dry-cleaning storefront at every major intersection. Industry growth is actually declining, thanks to more washable fabrics and home dry-cleaning kits, yet the fixed costs for real estate, labor, and machinery remain high. Until recently, dry cleaners had a tough time differentiating themselves from one another, because they all used the perchloroethylene ("perc") chemical process, and they all seemed to break buttons and lose customers' garments at about the same rate.

Change is on the way for the dirty laundry business now, thanks to three new start-ups: Hangers Cleaners, Zoots, and Purple Tie Inc. Each of these new ventures has enlisted big dollar backing from private investors to revolutionize the dry-cleaning industry.

The 40-plus Hangers Cleaners stores, operated by Micell Technologies, are perhaps the most innovative. Micell, founded by a professor from The University of North Carolina and two of his graduate students, uses liquid carbon dioxide to clean clothes. Liquid carbon dioxide is considered to be an eco-friendly process, unlike perc, which has been labeled a possible carcinogen by industry and government reports. Although liquid carbon dioxide is gentler to both the environment and delicate fabrics, the cost for the new technology's machines is three times the cost of the standard perc machines. That has not prevented Hangers Cleaners from enlisting the support of some deep-pocketed entrepreneurs, including Ken Langone, the cofounder of Home Depot.

Other cleaners are experimenting with replacing perc with petroleum-based solvents or improved water-and-detergent methods. Cleaners are eager to find an alternative, because the potential cost of cleaning up a perc spill or contamination has increased the cost of insurance premiums, eating into an industry profit margin that was never generous.

Zoots and Purple Tie are changing the industry through customer service. Both companies allow time-pressed customers to schedule laundry pick-up over the Internet, and then have the clean clothes delivered to their homes. San Francisco's Purple Tie has eliminated storefronts completely by using trucks and vans to pick up clothes, transport them for cleaning at a central facility, and then deliver them back to the customer. Zoots attracts customers by retaining the traditional stores but improving their service by offering drive-through windows and installing lockers in the foyers of their stores, which customers can access with a credit card to pick up laundry any time of the day or night. The founder of Staples Inc. is one of Zoots' prime investors, and they currently have more than 40 locations.

These innovations, which can change both the balance between competitors and the commodity-type nature of dry cleaning, are still more of a promise than a reality. "All the new start-ups promise top quality and great prices, but they have to deliver on that," notes Jay Calleja, vice president of the International Fabricare Institute, the industry's leading trade group.

Source: Adapted from Mike Hofman, "Upstarts: Dry Cleaning," *Inc.* online; January 1, 2001, available at www.inc.com.

Ranking Competitors

The next step is to evaluate a set of relevant current and potential competitors on the basis of the qualities of their resources. This analysis will give a picture of the competitors' relative strengths and weaknesses and will present a comparative framework enabling the entrepreneur to position the new venture. Weaker competitors may be attacked head-on. Competitors with characteristics similar to the new entrant's may be candidates for alliances that would strengthen both firms. Or the entrepreneur may be required to position the new venture around powerful competitors to avoid head-to-head conflict.

A useful tool for competitor analysis is the resource-based grid in Figure 3-3. The grid presents the six types of resources by attribute for each relevant competitor and requires the entrepreneur to assign a score for each dimension.[32] The entrepreneur's own venture is included in the analysis.

The initial information derived from the competitor analysis will rank the competitors on each type of resource, producing a grand ranking of all competitors. The next step is to examine how the competitors use their resource bases to confront industry forces. That is, how do the competitors' strategies influence buyer power, supplier power, threats of substitutes, entry barriers, and rivalry among firms? The competitors' strategies are revealed by studying their deployment of resources.[33] This examination enables the entrepreneur to answer the second question posed earlier in the chapter: What is the best way to compete in the industry for the highest profitability? The answer is: *Look for ways to employ your resource base that reduce the forces threatening firm profitability, and position your firm for leadership in that area.*

E-NOTES 3-7

Industry Environment

Analysis of the industry or competitive environment involves issues including:

- competitive analysis
- industry analysis
- buyer power
- supplier power
- the threat of substitutes
- entry barriers
- rivalry between firms

Summary

One way of looking at the business environment is as a stock of resources: financial, physical, technological, reputational, human, and organizational. The entrepreneur with an effective strategy for acquiring resources can control some of these resources,

Instructions On a scale of 1 through 7 evaluate the competition's resource base. A value of 1 indicates that the firm has absolutely no advantage in the resource area; a value of 4 indicates that the firm possesses about the same resource capabilities as other industry participants; a value of 7 indicates that the firm possesses an absolute advantage in the resource category.

Resource Type and Attribute	Own firm	Competitors #1	#2	#3	#4	#5
Financial resources						
Rare						
Valuable						
Imperfectly imitable						
Nonsubstitutable						
Physical resources						
Rare						
Valuable						
Imperfectly imitable						
Nonsubstitutable						
Human resources						
Rare						
Valuable						
Imperfectly imitable						
Nonsubstitutable						
Technical resources						
Rare						
Valuable						
Imperfectly imitable						
Nonsubstitutable						
Reputational resources						
Rare						
Valuable						
Imperfectly imitable						
Nonsubstitutable						
Organizational resources						
Rare						
Valuable						
Imperfectly imitable						
Nonsubstitutable						

Total Scores _____

Grand Mean _____

+/– from Mean _____

FIGURE 3-3   Resource-Based Competitive Analysis Grid

with others being controlled by competitors and potential competitors. No single entrepreneur can control all the resources. Larger forces are at work, and it is unlikely that the trends in the macroenvironment will be influenced by any single firm.

The entrepreneur must understand the macroenvironment, for it establishes the political, economic, technological, sociodemographic, and ecological rules under which the new firm is created and must operate. The entrepreneur must be able to scan and monitor the macroenvironment and to recognize the contingencies and constraints the macroenvironment imposes. This analysis, however, is not enough for the firm's success. The entrepreneur must be able to forecast and assess development, using as a knowledge resource the four attributes required for competitive advantage. Also required is the ability to marshal the resources necessary to overcome the constraints or effectively deal with the contingencies.

Understanding the elements and the processes of the competitive market enables us to discover the forces that make an industry attractive to the entrepreneur. These forces are power of buyers, the power of suppliers, the threat of substitutes, the height of the entry barriers, and the nature of the rivalry between competitors. When buyers and suppliers are powerful, when good substitutes exist for the firm's products, and when entry barriers are low and rivalry is intense, the industry is not attractive because profits are likely to be low.

However, the resource configuration of the entrepreneur occasionally enables entry into an unattractive industry. If an entrepreneur can configure his or her resource base and design a strategy that offsets the profit-reducing forces within an industry, the new venture can achieve a sustainable competitive advantage.

Attractive industries provide opportunities for profitability. The forces that determine rivalry in attractive industries are not strong forces, and the rivalry is not cutthroat. Firms compete on the level of product innovations, advertising and brand loyalty, and distribution channels, a level that enables firms to differentiate and position their products. There is little pressure on prices, and increased costs are passed along to the customer as increased value. Operating margins are generous and sufficient for reinvestment and shareholder distributions. An industry characterized by high profitability and good returns to investors is attractive for entry, all things being equal.

Key Terms

- Acyclical
- Assessing
- Backward integration
- Bargaining power of buyers
- Bargaining power of suppliers
- Business cycle
- Business selection
- Countercyclical
- Cyclical change
- Demography
- Design patents
- Differentiation strategy
- Ecology
- Entry barriers
- Focal industry
- Focus strategy
- Forecasting
- Forward integration
- Low-cost strategy
- Macroenvironment
- Monitoring
- Paradox of entrepreneurship
- Plant patents
- Political risk
- Price umbrella
- Process innovation
- Procyclical
- Pure invention
- Retaliatory barriers
- Rivalry
- Scanning
- Stakeholders
- Structural barriers
- Structural change
- Supplier selection strategy
- Sustainable development
- Tapered integration

- Technology
- Threat of substitutes
- Trade barriers
- Utility patents
- Values

Discussion Questions

1. Perform "thought experiments" on the following businesses using the five dimensions of the macroenvironment: politics, macroeconomy, technology, sociodemography, and ecology factors.
   a. Video game designer
   b. Pizza restaurant
   c. Manufacturer of women's sweaters
2. What are the costs and benefits of the process model of environmental analysis? How could an "ordinary" entrepreneur set up and manage such a process?
3. Discuss the primary factors in political and governmental analysis. Compare and contrast these factors for the following countries: United States, Russia, China, Nigeria.
4. Identify the stakeholders of the university or college that you attend. Which are the most powerful? Why and when? Which are the least powerful? Why and when?
5. Discuss how technological change creates entrepreneurial opportunities. What are some current changes underway and what opportunities do they create?
6. Discuss how demographic change creates entrepreneurial opportunities. What are some current changes underway and what opportunities do they create?
7. Discuss how ecological change creates entrepreneurial opportunities. What are some current changes underway and what opportunities do they create?
8. How does challenging old assumptions and traditions lead to entrepreneurial opportunities?
9. How can the entrepreneur influence the power of buyers and suppliers to make them more favorable or overcome them?
10. How do substitutes influence industry attractiveness and profitability?
11. How do entry barriers influence industry attractiveness and profitability?
12. Explain the paradox of entrepreneurship.
13. How can the entrepreneur employ resources to obtain a sustainable competitive advantage? Refer to the elements of the Porter model in your answer.

Exercises

1. Return to the business treatments and business ideas that you developed in the Chapter 2 exercises.
   a. Set up a system for analyzing the business environment for that business. Where does the information come from and how will you assess and evaluate it?
   b. Evaluate the five dimensions for your business:
      Political-governmental
      Macroeconomy
      Technology
      Sociodemographics
      Ecology
2. Return to the business treatments and ideas that you developed in the Chapter 2 exercises. In what ways do these ideas emerge from the business environment? How does the business environment support these ideas? What resources are available from the business environment that will support these business ideas?

3. Scan the business press. Identify the entrepreneurial opportunity from each of the seven sources described in the chapter.
4. Perform an analysis of the industry that you (and your team) are considering for your new venture. Use outside sources for data, such as the library, computer databases, and industry experts.
5. Perform an analysis of the competitors for your new venture. Use Figure 3-3 as a summary sheet to guide you in your research.

⟨ **DISCUSSION CASE** ⟩

Entrepreneurial E-Tailing: Competing with Clicks

Maurizio Zecchione knows all about rivalry between firms. The president of Internet clothing retailer StyleClick.com, Zecchione learned the hard way that relatively low entry costs in the dot-com industry, coupled with strong consumer power and increased availability of competing products, have made marketing on the Web very expensive. He says that the average Internet e-tailer spends $45 "to acquire a customer who generally spends $35 and never comes back." Zecchione responded by reducing his efforts to make direct sales through the Style Click.com Web site and then cutting deals with portals such as America Online Inc. and iVillage Inc., where he has to share revenues but can also reduce his up-front customer acquisition expense.

The high fixed costs for customer acquisition and customer service, along with a Web overflowing with competitors, are three of the big reasons why some e-tailers are biting the dust. Many analysts note, however, that the Internet has changed retailing forever and predict that e-tailers with good name recognition and enough cash will eventually prosper despite slow industry growth.

The first hurdle for Internet retailers remains competition from traditional stores. Ellen Neuborne, an analyst for *Business Week,* says three important factors give e-tailers an edge. The first advantage is speed, including speed of access, speed of transaction, and speed of delivery. Although many brick-and-mortar retailers design their stores for customers who spend more time and ramble through more departments,

e-tailers cater to consumers with busy lives who want to make a purchase with just a few clicks. Neuborne cites a survey by market researcher Dataquest Inc., which notes that 75 percent of online shoppers identify convenience as the reason they shop online.

Ironically, the convenience factor hurts some Web retailers. The Internet makes it easy for consumers to comparison shop for price and availability, meaning that e-tailers have to keep their prices low—often below cost—to attract shoppers. E-tailers who once hoped to reduce fixed costs by not having to build and staff costly stores now feel pressured to build more warehouses to speed delivery, provide more customer service representatives, and even absorb shipping costs. Advertising costs, both on the Web and in traditional media, eat into profit margins, too.

Neuborne says that smart e-tailers understand that shopping is often a community experience. Interacting with the community of shoppers can make products less commodity-like, too. That's why Delias.com, which markets clothing to young girls, sponsors a chat room where teens can talk about music and trends as part of its Web site. Lands End, the catalog retailer now making a big online push, offers shoppers the chance to chat with a human customer service rep via a toll-free telephone line while they are browsing at the site. Barnes & Noble sponsors free online enrichment courses on the Internet and then markets the books that complement the course to enrollees.

Developing a good product concept and sticking with it is one of the hallmarks

(continued)

(continued)

of a successful traditional retailer, but Neuborne notes that constant change is the sign of a successful Internet retailer. "Whatever is happening right now in cyberspace, it is guaranteed to be light-years different a year from now," observes Kurt Barnard, a veteran retailing consultant. "The pace of change, to meet new challenges, is incredibly fast."

Keeping up with changes in cyberspace is expensive, however, and almost all e-tailers are losing money. Amazon.com, one of the best known e-tailers, lost $720 million in 1999. Industry analyst Goldman Sachs predicts that half the e-tailers currently online will need to woo more capital investment from a stock market that has become disenchanted with dot-coms or investors who are now wary. Yet, few doubt that e-tailing is here to stay, if only because the fixed costs of establishing a quality Web site with good brand recognition still costs far less than setting up a chain of national stores.

Traditional retailers already backed by name recognition and the capital to keep their purchasing costs low—like Wal-Mart—may have a distinct advantage, but David Blohm, president of SmarterKids.com, believes that an entrepreneurial e-tailer can compete with traditional stores, e-tailers, and hybrids. SmarterKids.com invites parents to fill out a survey that describes their children's learning styles and academic interests, and then uses that information to sell them games and toys that are not only more unique than products available elsewhere, but also more profitable. According to Blohm, the list of e-tailers that survive the competitive shakeout "will be defined by those who can add value."

CASE QUESTIONS

1. What other low-cost strategies might Maurizio Zecchione employ to increase StyleClick.com's competitive edge?

2. What obstacles do you think might inhibit e-tailing growth?

3. What could a traditional brick-and-mortar retailer do to prepare for becoming an e-tailer?

4. What products other than toys could e-tailers market in an innovative way?

Source: Adapted from William M. Bulkeley and Jim Carlton, "E-Tail Gets Derailed: How Web Upstarts Misjudged the Game," *The Wall Street Journal,* April 5, 2000, A1, A6; Ellen Neuborne, "Why E-Tail Will Click," *Business Week E.Biz,* July 24, 2000, p. EB 14.

Entrepreneurial Strategies

Profits are not made by differential cleverness, but by differential stupidity.
—ATTRIBUTED TO DAVID RICARDO, ECONOMIST, BY PETER DRUCKER

Outline

Learning Objectives

After reading this chapter, you will understand:

■ How entrepreneurship is related to *strategic management*
■ Five different *hierarchies of strategy* that an entrepreneur can employ
■ What an *entry wedge* is, and the different major and minor entry wedges
■ Three *resource-based strategies* an entrepreneur can utilize to achieve sustainable competitive advantage
■ *First-mover advantage*
■ Five different *industry environments,* each with its own unique *life cycle*
■ How to evaluate *entrepreneurial strategies*

What is the most common criticism that entrepreneurs hear about their business ideas, and their new venture strategies? It is "If that's such a good idea, why hasn't someone else already done it?" The answer implied by David Ricardo in the introductory quote is that most people never have a good idea, and many who do lack the faintest clue what to do next. Human intelligence and energy are the scarce resources. There are countless strategies for creating and operating profitable enterprises, but most of them have not yet been conceived.

In this chapter, we examine some of the strategies entrepreneurs have already conceived to create and guide their new ventures. However, many entrepreneurs are unaware that they are following any strategy. Often the strategy is not written or spoken by the founders. For example, the founders of Cisco Systems, a computer networking firm with over $22 billion in sales, reported that they started their firm "without a particular business vision."[1] It certainly would not surprise the publishers of this book to find that many entrepreneurs had not read it before launching their enterprises. Further, this chapter cannot tell you what strategy to employ to become successful. If we really had that information, then (1) we would not be writing textbooks about it, and (2) by releasing the information, we would make the strategy easy to imitate and it would cease to be rare. Once everyone has the keys to success, the locks must be changed.

What this chapter *can* do is describe a wide range of entrepreneurial strategies called "entry wedges." Then we examine some of the strategic choices available to new ventures. Next, we introduce the industry life cycle and see how the different stages influence new venture strategy. We also look at the effects of fragmented environments. At the end of the chapter, we present a model for assessing entrepreneurial opportunities and evaluating the strategies chosen.

ENTREPRENEURSHIP AND STRATEGY

How is entrepreneurship like business strategy? Some of the concepts presented in this chapter are borrowed and adapted from the strategic management literature.[2] In this literature, **strategy** is defined as "the patterns of decisions that shape the venture's internal resource configuration and deployment and guide alignment with the environment."[3] This definition has two major implications. The first is that "patterns of decisions" means both **strategy formulation** and **strategy implementation**. Formulation includes planning and analysis. Implementation is the execution and evaluation of the activities that make up the strategy. The second implication is that the entrepreneur has to consider both internal factors such as the firm's resources and competencies, and external factors such as the market environment. That is what we did in Chapters 2 and 3.

One of the core assumptions of strategic management is that strategy exists on different levels within the firm. In descending order, these are the enterprise, corporate, business, functional, and subfunctional levels. Part of the environment for each level is the level above it; lower and higher levels must be aligned, with the higher levels leading the way. One result of this hierarchy is a cascading effect. Strategy formulation starts at the top of the hierarchy and flows down to each level. As it does, strategy formulation is increasingly replaced by implementation. The cascade effect contributes to consistency and helps hold together organizations that are sometimes large and far-flung.

E-NOTES 4-1

Strategic Management

Strategic management can be defined as patterns of decisions that:

- determine a business venture's internal resource structure and implementation
- influence its interaction with the macroenvironment

Strategic management includes:

- strategy formulation
- planning
- analysis
- strategy implementation
- execution
- evaluation

Enterprise-level strategy is at the top of the hierarchy. It is concerned with the relationships between the firm and society at large. The context for analyzing this strategy was presented in Chapter 3. **Corporate strategy** focuses on the problems of diversification and the management of a portfolio of business. Because the new venture is most often a single business, corporate strategy is not discussed in this book. **Business-level strategy** is oriented toward competing within a single industry. It deals with the acquisition, organization, and employment of resources. Industry analysis was examined in Chapter 3. The strategies that correspond to industry conditions are the subject of this chapter. In other words, this chapter is about business-level strategy. **Functional** and **subfunctional strategies** involve marketing, finance and accounting, and human resource policies, which will be examined in Chapters 6 through 9.

E-NOTES 4-2

Strategy Hierarchy

A business venture can employ five different levels of strategy:

- enterprise level—to relate to society
- corporate level—to manage diversification within the firm
- business level—to relate to competitors
- functional level—to manage marketing, finance, and accounting
- subfunctional level—to manage human resources

ENTRY WEDGES

Entry wedges are momentum factors.[4] They are not really full-blown strategies but are rather the methods the founders use to get their initial foothold in a business. Because the entry wedge becomes an important part of the firm's history, it may influence later strategic decisions. Because each founding is unique, the entry wedge can, therefore, be part of the firm's sustainable competitive advantage.

Major Wedges

All new ventures employ one or more of three major entry wedges: new product or service, parallel competition, and franchising.

New Product or Service   A new product or service is one of the most potent entry wedges. Truly new products and services are relatively rare. If they employ a new technology as well, they may be hard to imitate. Typically, new products have a lower failure rate than new services, primarily because most service organizations face lower entry barriers. Firms that do employ the new service wedge are likely to offer or introduce a related product if the firm gains a foothold in the industry. Ventures that initially offer a new product sometimes follow up with a related service, but this is less common.[5]

The new product or new service wedge is what Drucker has called the "being first with the most" strategy.[6] The strategy is aimed at achieving a permanent leadership position either within an existing industry or by creating a new industry. Success in this strategy requires a concentrated effort at being comprehensive and innovative. "Being first," like the first-mover advantage, gives the firm a head start and possibly an insurmountable lead in market share, in low-cost manufacture and supply, and in public awareness and recognition. This is the strategy that Intel employs in manufacturing microprocessors. "With the most" requires that the product or service be comprehensive. If it is missing something (for example, service, warranty, delivery, or functional components that customers require), the door is left open for competitors. This is the high-risk, high-reward entry wedge.

New technology can be the source of product innovation. In Street Story 4-1, the Web provides the entry wedge for a dot-com consulting firm.

Parallel Competition   Parallel competition is a "me too" strategy that introduces competitive duplications into the market. These duplications are parallel, not identical, to existing products or services. They represent an attempt to fill a niche, a small hole in the market. This can be done with a small innovation or variation in an already well-accepted and well-understood product line or service system. An entrepreneur who notes that the current customers of a firm are unhappy and conceives a strategy to make them happy would be entering with a parallel wedge strategy. Marginal firms always risk being replaced by others that do basically the same things but do them better.

Most retailing start-ups, for example, enter with the parallel competition wedge. The only difference between one retail operation and another might be location or minor variations in merchandising and marketing. The typical retail store carries the same or similar products from the same suppliers and charges approximately the same markups. This type of entry is fairly easy, because entry barriers are low. Firms of this type can produce stable income and profits over a long time if they possess some distinctive competence. More likely, though, these firms are low-sales/low-profit operations. For the entrepreneur, they are alternatives to other jobs and replace income from other employment. Without a distinctive competence, these small retailers quickly become marginal and risk being replaced by another firm using the parallel wedge strategy.

However, if used with creativity and vision, the parallel wedge can lead to superior payoffs. Drucker calls this form of the parallel strategy "creative imitation."[7] Creative imitation combines the common business configuration of the competition (the imitation part) with a new twist or variation (the creative part). Two types of competitors are susceptible to a new venture's creative imitation: those with weak spots and those with blind spots. Firms with weak spots may have the same resources as others but not employ them well. The new venture, without different assets but knowing how to use the assets it does have, has an advantage. Some entrepreneurs also have blind spots—things they do not see about the market, the competition, or themselves—that make them vulnerable to creative imitation. Examples include:

- The *"not invented here" syndrome*. Firms are sometimes slow to adapt innovations or are reluctant to change because they did not initiate the idea themselves. This makes them easy to target for the new venture that is quick to adopt the new standard.
- The *"skim the market" blind spot*. Firms that charge high prices and attempt to capture only the most profitable business are vulnerable. Other firms can operate under their price umbrella, gain market share, and become close to their customers. The creative imitators learn how to add value by serving the tougher customers.
- *Technological tunnel vision*. Firms that emphasize product- and manufacturing-based quality to the exclusion of user-based quality have technological tunnel vision. They are vulnerable as minor changes in customer needs and perceptions go unnoticed by them but are obvious to the imitator.
- *The maximizer complex*. Firms that try to do too much, that serve all types of customers with all types of products and services, are vulnerable because they

Winning by Doing What No One Wants to Do

Their business plan presentation was a little strange. The company's CEO and other employees appeared before the group dressed in hospital gowns, sitting in wheelchairs, with their faces burned and their heads wrapped in bandages. They were joined by two buxom women dressed in skin-tight nurse uniforms, who sang a company song written to the tune of *The Flintstones* theme song: "Village! Safety Village! We're your health and safety com-pa-ny! Help you! Let us help you! And most accidents won't come to be!"

Crazy as it was, the presentation helped start-up SafetyVillage.com beat 20 other new ventures to win the $10,000 prize in an "edutainment" competition for "the most commercially viable dot-com enterprise." The unconventional competition was hosted by 33-year-old San Diego entrepreneur Bob Bingham, who said, "I just wanted to do something that would have some edge." Other presentations featured a Marilyn Monroe impersonator, dancing chefs, and zany humorous skits, but the final selection for the best model Internet start-up plan was made on the basis of the business plan's content and commercial value.

Wacky humor is not the entry wedge that SafetyVillage.com plans use to launch its Internet business. Instead, the major wedge is an innovative service. SafetyVillage.com provides workplace safety consulting for small- and medium-sized businesses, delivering their analysis, training, and monitoring services entirely over the Web.

The company has developed a four-stage cycle where they use unique software to profile each customer's safety needs and then analyze that profile by matching it against the often bewildering array of state and federal government safety regulations. The third step is delivery of safety implementation tools, including downloadable checklists, Web-based training that employees can access from either home or work, and a wide array of safety products at discounted prices. The final step is a compliance function that will help customers virtually monitor their safety products inventory and keep clients abreast of any changes in workplace regulations. "I love businesses that do things that others have to do but don't want to do," says Stephen Tomlin, an entrepreneurial investor and one of the three main judges of the San Diego competition.

"Implementing and supporting a robust, company-wide safety program not only reduces employee injuries but improves company efficiency and employee effectiveness," says Steve Sullivan, founder and CEO of SafetyVillage.com. "These benefits are critical elements for a company successfully competing in today's global economy." In addition to marketing directly to small businesses, SafetyVillage.com hopes to convince insurance carriers to sponsor its service as a value-added product for their clients.

Although the San Diego presentation may have bordered on slapstick, SafetyVillage.com's imaginative and comprehensive development of its major entry wedge proves that this start-up's shot at sustaining competitive advantage will be much more than an accident.

Source: Adapted from D. M. Osborne, "Boing! Whiz! Bang! Dunk!" *Inc.* online, June 1, 2000; available at www.inc.com and www.safetyvillage.com.

may serve no customers particularly well. A parallel competitor who carves a niche to serve a specialized customer base can succeed here.

Franchising   The third major wedge is franchising. Franchising takes a proven formula for success and expands it. The entrepreneur may be either the franchisor or the franchisee. The **franchisor** is the seller of franchises. For the franchisor, franchising is a means of expanding by using other people's money, time, and energy to sell the product or service. These other people are the **franchisees**. In return for a franchise fee and royalties (usually based on sales), they gain the expertise, knowledge, support (training, marketing, operations), and experience of the franchisor. This reduces the risk of failure for the new entrepreneur.

The key to franchising's power is that it is a geographic expansion under a license agreement. Geographic expansion enables the franchise system to saturate markets. Saturation gives the franchise the benefits of visibility and recognition, logistical cost savings, volume buying power, lower employment and training costs, and the ability to use the mass media for advertising efficiently. The license agreement gives the franchise system a mechanism for standardizing its products or services, incentives for growth, and barriers to entry. All three parties to the franchise system (franchisor, franchisee, and customer) benefit, which explains why franchising has become the most prevalent form of new business start-up. We will return to franchising in Chapter 10.

Minor Wedges

A number of other entry wedges are designated as minor because they can be classified under the three major categories. Four categories of minor wedges, each with several variations, include exploiting partial momentum, customer sponsorship, parent company sponsorship, and government sponsorship. Table 4-1 cross-references the major entry wedges with the minor ones.

Exploiting Partial Momentum   Sometimes the entrepreneur already has market and product information that indicates the new venture will be successful. This information acts as the impetus for the launch. The entrepreneur can exploit this existing momentum in three ways: by geographic transfer, by filling a supply shortage, or by putting an underutilized resource to work. A **geographic transfer** occurs when a business that works in one area is started in another. For example, a restaurant concept that is successful in Los Angeles might be tried by a different entrepreneur in New York City. The New York City entrepreneur gains partial momentum by studying the Los Angeles venture. The major wedge that more fully exploits this factor is franchising.

Entrepreneurs can launch new ventures by filling market gaps such as **supply shortages**. Sometimes the product or service in short supply must be physically transferred from one area to another. In this case, filling the supply shortage resembles geographic transfer. A better example is the entrepreneur who organizes resources to fill a shortage within an area. For example, recent trends indicate that for various tasks at varying times of the year, many firms prefer to hire temporary workers rather than full-time employees. However, there is a shortage of people available for temporary positions, because most people prefer to work full-time if they can. New ventures have been developed that specialize in personnel services for temporaries. These firms organize the resource that is in short supply (temps) to meet market demand. They also meet the

TABLE 4-1 Major and Minor Entry Wedges

| | *Major Entry Wedges* | | |
Minor Entry Wedges	*New Product/ Service*	*Parallel Competition*	*Franchise System*
Exploiting Partial Momentum			
1. Geographic transfer			X
2. Supply shortage		X	
3. Tapping underutilized resources	X	X	
4. Creating or modifying existing distribution channels	X	X	
Customer Sponsorship			
5. Customer contract		X	
6. Second sourcing		X	
Parent Company Sponsorship			
7. Joint venture	X		
8. Licensing		X	
9. Market relinquishment		X	
10. Spin-off	X		
Government Sponsorship			
11. Favored purchasing		X	
12. Rule change	X		
13. Direct assistance	X	X	

Source: Adapted from K. Vesper, *New Venture Strategies* (Upper Saddle River, NJ: Prentice Hall, 1980).

demands of the temporary personnel by scheduling additional work after each temporary assignment expires. For the firm, the shortage is relieved; for the personnel, they have full-time work (in various temporary assignments).

An **underutilized resource** is one with an economic value that is not recognized or one that is not being employed in its best use. Many times people are the most underutilized resource, and entrepreneurs who can more fully realize their economic value are called "leaders." The underutilized resource can also be physical, financial, reputational, technological, or organizational. For example, entrepreneurs in the financial sector find ways to better use nonperforming financial assets, such as cash or bonds. Entrepreneurs have helped large organizations with strong positive reputations—for example, Disney and Coca-Cola—gain additional income by licensing their brand names, trademarks, and copyrights. Underutilized physical resources are often somebody's junk, waste, by-product, or worn-out product. These are the core of the recycling and remanufacturing industries. For example, entrepreneurs are building businesses by finding new uses for the mountains of worn-out tires dumped across the United States. Others are building vending machines that take in aluminum cans for recycling and dispense store and manufacturers' coupons.

By **creating or modifying existing distribution channels**, the new venture can take advantage of the momentum that already exists in the value chain. For example, if there are already strong production or in-bound logistical areas, finding new channels helps to reach new markets. Many longtime successful catalog sellers like Lands End now use their new Web sites as surrogate catalogs. They still do most of their business by mail order, but the Web is a new channel for them. Or consider the intrapreneurial efforts of Robin Burns. She was hired to break the stranglehold that department stores have over cosmetics distribution. Her goal is to form a new company that will sell single lines of cosmetics and fragrances in boutique-type stores. Her sponsor, The Limited, has helped by starting her with their Victoria's Secret line. Therefore, this is also a spin-off.[8]

Customer Sponsorship   A new venture's launch may depend on the momentum supplied by the firm's first customers. A customer can encourage an entrepreneur in either of two ways. A **customer contract** can guarantee the new firm sales and help it obtain its initial financing. Because the customer is not assumed to have altruistic motives, the entrepreneur should look to expand the customer base once the venture is up and running. Sometimes customers encourage entrepreneurs to become a **second source**. If the customer has previously had difficulty working with a single supplier, good purchasing practice would suggest that the customer rebid the contract. However, a good alternative for obtaining the product or service is not always available. When this is the case, the customer can encourage and even provide assistance (managerial, technical, financial) to an entrepreneur who can supply the customer's needs. Both customer-contract and second-source sponsorships generally lead the firm to employ parallel competition as the major wedge.

Parent Company Sponsorship   A parent company can help launch a new venture in four ways. Two of these require ongoing parent company relationships: **licensing** and **joint venturing**. The other two methods may continue the parent–new venture relationship, but it is optional. These are **market relinquishment** and the **spin-off**.

Under a licensing agreement, the entrepreneur contracts with the parent company to produce a product or service or to employ a system or technology. The connection between the entrepreneur and the parent provides momentum for the new venture because the founders have previous organizational experience with the parent and technical experience with the product or technology. The joint venture differs from the license in two significant ways: (1) Resources are commingled when the joint venture is formed, and (2) the ownership rights in a joint venture require negotiation. These differences make the joint venture more difficult to manage, but the benefits of having two (or more) organizational parents can outweigh the cost.

Market relinquishment means that the parent company decides to stop serving a market or producing a product. Although the parent's motivation for this can vary, usually it is because the parent is not cost-efficient. This is especially likely to be true if the product volume or market niche is small, for a large company's overhead can be high enough to make a small niche unprofitable. However, such a niche may be profitable for a small firm. The most likely candidates to start that small firm are the large firm's former managers of that product/market niche. So when the larger corporation relinquishes the market, the former managers may have the opportunity to purchase the larger firm's specialized assets and continue in their jobs, but this time as owner/ managers instead of just managers. This provides the new venture strong momentum: The change may not be visible to customers and suppliers, but the new firm can be much more profitable (and perhaps strategically more flexible) without the need to support the corporate bureaucracy.

E-NOTES 4-3

Major and Minor Entry Wedges

Major entry wedges include:

- new products or services
- parallel competition
- franchising

Minor entry wedges include:

- exploiting partial momentum
- customer sponsorship
- parent company sponsorship
- government sponsorship

One of the most common starting points for new venture creation based on previously acquired knowledge is the spin-off. A spin-off is a new firm created by a person or persons leaving an existing firm and starting a new firm in the same industry. The most frequent examples of spin-offs today are in high-tech businesses, biotechnology, semiconductors and computers, consulting, law, and medicine (and medical devices). What do these diverse industries have in common? Both emerging industries and growing industries are prime breeding grounds for spin-offs. In these industries, pockets of information possessed by employees can be disseminated throughout the market. This information is mobile; it is embodied not in a machine or particular location but in individuals, a process, or a technique. Both the knowledge and the individuals can be transferred at very low cost to just about any place on earth.

The knowledge assets transferred to the new firm in a spin-off have certain dimensions that can be analyzed to determine whether they possess the four attributes of competitive advantage. Table 4-2 displays the opposing poles of the dimensions of knowledge.[9] The characteristics on the right-hand side of the table are more difficult to

TABLE 4-2   Taxonomy of Knowledge Assets in the Resource-Based Theory

Easy to Copy		*Hard to Copy*
Articulated knowledge	⟵⟶	Tacit knowledge
Teachable knowledge	⟵⟶	Nonteachable knowledge
Skills observable in use	⟵⟶	Nonobservable in use
Simple and singular knowledge	⟵⟶	Complex and multidimensional knowledge
Independent skills	⟵⟶	Interdependent skills

Source: Adapted from S. Winter, "Knowledge and Competence as Strategic Assets," in D. Teece, ed., *The Competitive Challenge* (Cambridge, MA: Ballinger, 1988), pp. 159–184.

transfer, but if the new management team is able to successfully transfer them, the firm will gain momentum toward competitive advantage.

For example, tacit skills, knowledge, and competencies are based on rules and behaviors that are unknown to the person performing the tasks. Individual skills are often tacit; people cannot explain the process they go through in applying their skills. Evidence even suggests that there are different brain structures for procedural (process) knowledge and declarative (content) knowledge.[10] For the organization, tacit knowledge comes embedded in the people who work for the firm. Other members of the firm may have articulated knowledge of the kind reflected in: "Oh, yes, we have someone working here who knows how to do that." Much of the relational skill and knowledge in an organization is tacit; some people know some things about who can get things done under what conditions, but most company participants do not know the details of these relationships.

Knowledge that is not teachable is also difficult to transfer to the spin-off, but it is also rare and hard to duplicate if it comes with the new venture management team. Skills and competencies that are observable in use can be copied and transferred. Complex knowledge is more difficult to copy than simple knowledge; an independent skill is easier to transfer than one that requires cooperation, teamwork, or coordination.

When individuals leave one firm to start another in a related industry, they take with them the knowledge and competencies they acquired and developed. The most important elements for the new business are the hardest to transfer, yet they are also the most valuable, most rare, and hardest to duplicate.

We see, then, that knowledge and competencies that are widely available and easily taught and transferred cannot be the source of competitive advantage for a new venture. But this does not mean that entrepreneurship cannot be taught.

Government Sponsorship   In Chapter 3, we discussed the impediments and constraints that government often imposes on new ventures. However, the government can also act as a sponsor for new ventures and provide entrepreneurs with launch momentum. We saw this in Street Story 4-1. There are three mechanisms for this: direct assistance, favored purchasing, and rule changes.

Direct assistance   "They're from the government, how can they help you?" A number of local, state, and federally supported programs can aid the entrepreneur in starting or managing a new business. Most provide managerial or technical assistance; a few, like the Small Business Administration, may also on occasion provide financial assistance. One of the less well-known sources of technical assistance is the federal research laboratory system. At these labs, such as the Oak Ridge National Laboratory in Oak Ridge, Tennessee, scientists and engineers help businesses solve difficult technical problems. Other federal agencies have started programs to help small and medium-sized businesses. NASA offers free consulting advice in cooperation with state agencies in Tennessee, Mississippi, and Louisiana. The Sandia National Laboratory in Albuquerque, New Mexico, also has a program.[11]

Favored purchasing   Favored purchasing rules enable some firms to enter the marketplace with an edge. The federal government's own procurement policies often mandate set-asides and quotas for small businesses, minority and woman-owned firms, firms started and managed by physically disabled people, and Vietnam era veterans. Many of these favored purchasing rules have also been incorporated into procurement policies and practices at other government levels and throughout corporate America.

Rule changes   As government regulatory practices change and as new laws are implemented, opportunities for new firms arise. One of the most significant areas for changes in government policy of the last decade has been in the area of privatization. Over the years, governments frequently found themselves in the business of providing goods and services to people. These have ranged from the provision of rail service to the running of hotels on government-protected lands. Of course in former communist countries where the government owned all of the means of production, privatization has been the method to put these assets into the hands of entrepreneurs. Even as we begin the twenty-first century, privatization opportunities abound for the sharp-eyed and quick-moving entrepreneur.[12]

RESOURCE-BASED STRATEGIES

How can our resource-based theory help us to create entrepreneurial strategy? We have already discussed the fundamentals of competitive strategy in terms of our resource-based theory. Briefly, resource-based theory says that for firms to have a sustainable competitive advantage, they must possess resources and capabilities that are rare, valuable, hard to copy, and nonsubstitutable (with resources that are neither rare nor valuable). A recent study of the silicon crystal industry tested the importance of resources, capabilities, and competences on market-entry strategies and found that they are significant predictors.[13] There are three strategies that relate directly to the resources and capabilities of the new venture. These are rent-seeking, growth, and quality.

Rent-Seeking Strategies

Strategy in the resource-based framework is rent seeking.[14] There are four types of rents, and the strategies available to obtain them are different. Firms can attempt to capture more than one type of rent simultaneously. The four types of rents are:

- **Ricardian rent:** Rents derived from acquiring, owning, and controlling a scarce and valuable resource. These are most often derived from ownership of land or natural resources or from a preferred location. This type of rent can be collected as long as ownership and control exist, possibly in perpetuity.
- **Monopoly rent:** Rents collected from government protection, collusive agreements, or structural entry barriers. Examples of government protection include patents and copyrights, restrictive licenses, and government-granted franchises. Many collusive practices such as price-fixing and conspiracies in restraint of trade are illegal in the United States, but enforcement varies by time and place.
- **Entrepreneurial rent:** Rents accrued from risk-taking behavior or insights into complex and uncertain environments. This is also known as "Schumpeterian rent," and is the type most closely associated with new venture creation. Schumpeterian rents are not as long-lasting as Ricardian and monopoly rents because of the eventual diffusion of knowledge and entry by competing firms into the market.

- **Quasi-rent:** Rents earned by employing firm-specific assets in a manner that other firms cannot copy. These rents are often based on idiosyncratic capital and dedicated assets. They are derived from a distinctive competence in how to use the resource as opposed to mere control.

Resource-based strategies are geared toward rent-seeking behavior. The most prevalent of the four rent-seeking behaviors is the entrepreneurial strategy; a firm enters with a new resource configuration or implementation strategy and makes above-average profits until, through technological diffusion and increased knowledge, competitors are able to enter and compete away those profits. This describes the cycle of "destructive capitalism" that constantly redeploys capital to its most economic use.

Ventures that possess the four attributes required for sustainable competitive advantage are positioned to employ strategy to collect one or more of the four types of rents. The more types of rent the firm can accumulate, the better its overall long-term performance will be. Rents of any of the four types require ways for the firm to protect its advantage. These protective devices are called "isolating mechanisms." The absence of isolating mechanisms means that others (workers, investors, customers, competitors, governments) can work out strategies to claim the rents for their own.

ISOLATING MECHANISMS AND FIRST-MOVER ADVANTAGE

An entrepreneur who is fortunate enough to create a new venture must expect that competitors will attempt to retaliate and protect their own positions.[15] Therefore, it is important for the entrepreneur to find ways to increase these benefits and cash flows for either future investment or personal incentives. The methods the entrepreneur employs to prevent the rents generated from the new venture from leaking out are known as **isolating mechanisms**.

Types of Isolating Mechanisms

Isolating mechanisms can take a number of forms. Most obvious are **property rights**, which take the form of patents, trademarks, and copyrights. Any secrets, proprietary information, or proprietary technology also help isolate the firm from competitive attack. These mechanisms, though, will not last indefinitely; therefore, the entrepreneur must be prepared to move quickly and establish a strong position. This is known as **first-mover advantage**. First-mover advantage can also be a powerful isolating mechanism when combined with a government rule change that encourages privatization or industry deregulation.[16]

Sources of First-Mover Advantage

First-mover advantages are isolating mechanisms that prevent the erosion of the new venture's competitive advantage.[17] The first use of a technology, known as **technological leadership**, can provide first-mover advantages. The first mover in a particular technology can, of course, obtain the initial patents, but these are seldom decisive.[18] More importantly, the first mover builds up a research and development base that can lead to further innovations and improvement, keeping the venture ahead of the pack. As production (either *through* the new technology or *of* the new technology) increases, the learning curve is pushed ahead of competitors', often conferring cost advantages and economies of scale that can preempt or delay competition.

Being the first mover may mean obtaining valuable and scarce resources ahead of others. It may mean getting rights to natural resources, securing the best locations, or crowding distribution channels (distribution space is a valuable and rare resource).[19]

The final source of first-mover advantage is imposing switching costs on buyers.[20] **Switching costs** can be developed through marketing or contractual obligations. When a new venture creates brand loyalty through effective advertising, high buyer learning and evaluation costs, or complementary products, the firm makes it difficult for others to compete away the venture's profit.

First-mover advantages can also be a disadvantage in certain situations. In some cases, the first mover must reveal the underlying business concept, and others may copy this by using different resource combinations. The first mover invests in resolving the technological and production problems that go with any new venture. Other firms can then benefit from these investments. Also, being first once does not guarantee that you will always be first. Indeed, inertia can make the successful first mover resist abandoning a strategy when it is no longer effective. Later in the chapter, Figure 4-2 summarizes the entrepreneurial process of strategic choice.

E-NOTES 4-4

First-Mover Advantage

First-mover advantage is a rent-seeking strategy that operates as an isolating mechanism and may include:

- technological leadership
- obtaining resources more quickly than others
- switching costs

Street Story 4-2 gives us a great example of first-mover advantage. In the story, we see how a simple but powerful idea is protected and how royalties will flow to the first mover from all who adopt the new business method.

Growth Strategies

So far, we have seen how new ventures enter using their wedges and how they seek to collect rents based on their capabilities and resources. We can also use our resource-based model to account for the rate and direction of a venture's growth strategies. Firms grow in the direction of underutilized resources and toward their areas of expertise. The rate of growth is a step function, not a smooth path, because resources are usually employable only in bulky, discrete increments.[21] Basically, the limits to firm growth are limits to resources. Resources determine the industry the firm will enter and the levels of profit it can attain. For example, labor shortages and finance and technological barriers all limit growth.

Protecting the Rights to the Right Idea

The next time you order lunch at McDonald's or Kentucky Fried Chicken, the cashier may hesitate before handing you your change. Software loaded into the restaurant's computerized cash register may prompt the cashier to offer you a soft drink or a small food item instead of coins, even if items normally sell for less than the change you are owed. This practice, known as "up selling," allows the store to build profits by increasing its per customer sales. In fast-food restaurants where the program has been tested, retail sales have increased by as much as 4 percent.

Even if you take advantage of this offer, the restaurant will not get to keep all the extra profit. They'll have to pay a royalty to Retail DNA, a subsidiary of Walker Digital Corporation, who developed and patented this up-selling method. Walker Digital is a "think tank" company founded by Jay Walker, the billionaire entrepreneur who also created Priceline.com. The fact that Walker has decided to protect his property rights to this up-selling method with a patent has placed him in the middle of a growing controversy within the business community.

The number of patents granted for "business methods" have dramatically increased recently. Approximately 1,300 such patents were issued in 1999. Jay Walker claims that we have to look at information as the raw material of innovation today, just like steel or chemicals are often the raw material of more traditional patents. Opponents claim that these legal isolating mechanisms stifle creativity or permit cagey first movers to benefit unfairly from bright ideas. "What I find most offensive about business method patents is that fundamentally they allow somebody to patent an idea," says Tim O'Reilly, a publisher of technology books in California. "That is at odds with so much that we hold sacred."

A spokesperson for Microsoft adds, "We respect intellectual-property rights, but we don't respect some companies abusing the system." Priceline.com has sued Microsoft for copying its name-your-own-price business method on its Expedia travel Web site. Amazon.com also sued Barnes & Noble Inc. for copying its 1-Click shopping method. They lost the first round and are considering appeal. Despite the pending suit, Jeff Bezos, the founder of Amazon.com, has publicly stated that he believes business method patents should only last from 3 to 5 years, unlike other patents that last for 20 years.

A bill presented in the U.S. Congress would help level the playing field by requiring the U.S. Patent and Trademark Office to publish a list of business method patent applications and permit challengers to present arguments against the patent. This posting and hearing process is not required for other types of patents. In the meantime, Walker Digital has 50 inventors, including many marketing and business experts, who are hard at work thinking up new business methods and filing for patent applications to protect them.

Source: Adapted from Julia Angwin, "'Business-Method' Patents, Key to Priceline, Draw Growing Protest," *The Wall Street Journal,* October 3, 2000, p. B1.

In the long run, however, the most important limit of all may be the scarcity of management capacity. There are two demands on managerial capacity: (1) to run the firm at its current size, and (2) to expand and grow. Current managers recruit new managers to increase the growth potential of the venture. However, these new managers need to be trained and integrated into the firm's current activities, and this takes time away from existing managers. While ingesting these new managers, the firm's growth slows. When the new managers have been incorporated into the venture's structure and systems, growth begins again. This implies that "management is both the accelerator and brake for the growth process."[22] This rubber-band process, called the "Penrose effect" after the theorist who first proposed it, suggests that fast growth in one period will be followed by slow growth in the next period (that is, there is a negative correlation between period growth rates).[23]

Quality as a Strategy

Considerable thought, energy, and money have been devoted to making quality a source of sustainable competitive advantage. Hundreds of articles and books have been written on the subject. A prestigious national contest, the Malcolm Baldrige National Quality Award, is promoted each year. Sixteen states now have programs to help companies develop and improve their products' quality.[24] Total quality management (TQM) programs that emphasize customer satisfaction (user-based quality discussed in Chapter 1) as the number one priority for the firm have entered the language and curriculum of top-rated business schools. Companies that promote TQM programs are themselves a fast-growing industry. Consultants sell "off-the-shelf" TQM programs based on some simple ideas that can be understood by the analogy with playing golf:

- **Continuous improvement.** This is the process of setting higher standards for performance with each iteration of the quality cycle. In golf terms, yesterday you shot a score of 112, so today you try to shoot 111.
- **Benchmarking.** This means identifying and imitating the best in the world at specific tasks and functions. If you believe that Ben Hogan had the best swing, you try to swing like Ben.
- **Quality circle.** This is a loop of activities that includes planning, doing, checking, and acting. Keep your head down, keep your eye on the ball, don't press. Now, where did it go?
- **Outsourcing.** This means procuring the top quality from outside the organization if the firm cannot produce it inside. If you can't hit this shot, can somebody else hit it for you?[25]

TQM programs require a sure knowledge of the customer through highly developed market research. Once the knowledge base exists, the prescriptions often call for organization-wide commitment, top management involvement, training and team building, and empowering individual employees to be responsible for quality-related decisions.[26]

The resource-based approach calls into question the efficacy of these quality programs for long-term competitive advantage. If any firm can buy the principles of TQM off the street (so to speak), then they are not rare. Benchmarking, which is neither more nor less than copying, is by definition able to be copied. Outsourcing products from the best quality vendors is both substitutable by producing in-house or sourcing from other best quality vendors. Can TQM be an effective strategy for sustainable competitive advantage?

Research indicates that TQM programs are not magic formulas.[27] At best, they were termed a "partial success." Among the general conclusions were that:

- Copying other firms may expend time and money on the wrong things.
- Adoption of a TQM program, under certain conditions, can actually make things worse because the program is so disruptive.
- Companies often fail to link the TQM program with "bottom line" results.
- Benchmarking is not effective unless the company already has a comprehensive quality program.
- Lower-performing firms should adopt TQM programs gradually; middle performers are better able to begin full-scale adoption; and high performers benefit the most from TQM.

Because they are hard to implement and their contingencies are complex, TQM programs have value. Because successful quality programs depend on the firm's already having a well-developed resource base, the quality program enables the firm to add to that base. This means: *Quality can work as a strategy for sustainable competitive advantage because it is not easy to implement and everyone cannot master it.*

A successful TQM program has several requirements. First, it requires excellent market research. Market research is knowledge (one of those tacit, difficult-to-duplicate resources). Market research that is original and proprietary can be a source of sustainable competitive advantage. Next, TQM requires an organizational system capable of adapting to the new regime, incorporating its premises, and executing its policies. Organizational systems are incredibly complex because of social relationships, ambiguous cause and effect, and culture. This complexity can be a source of sustainable competitive advantage. Further, the highly capable human resources that the successful TQM program requires also possess the four attributes. Finally, the firm with a reputation for outstanding quality products and service is in a position to collect rent for the investment it has made.

E-NOTES 4-5

Resource-Based Strategies

An entrepreneur can utilize strategies including:

- rent-seeking strategies
- growth strategies
- quality strategies

STRATEGY AND INDUSTRY ENVIRONMENTS

But not all ventures enter the same industry. How much difference does the industry itself make in determining strategy? The answer is, "quite a lot." Entrepreneurs can significantly add to the success of their strategies by understanding the industry environment they are entering. A static description of industry structure was presented in Chapter 3. However, industry environments are static only in the short term; over a longer period of time, they evolve. This evolution is called the **industry life cycle**. The industry life cycle progresses through four stages: emerging, transitional, maturing, and declining.

The industry life-cycle progression is not the same for all industries. The length of each stage and the timing of the stages are highly variable and difficult to predict. The same is true for product and organizational life cycles. Entry and competition take on different forms, depending on which stage of the life cycle the industry is in.[28] Figure 4-1 presents a diagram of the industry life cycle. It follows the familiar S-curve of many economic phenomena.[29] The shape of the curve shows that emerging industries are characterized by increasing rates of growth. Transition occurs as growth continues at decreasing rates. In the mature stage, growth rates approach zero. A declining industry is characterized by no growth or negative growth rates, whether measured in total units of production or in dollars.

Emerging Industries

Emerging industries are the newly created networks of firms launched to exploit a new technology, a new market configuration or set of customer needs, or other changes in the macroenvironment.[30] Emerging industries experience high levels of uncertainty, rapid change, and a growing number of organizations (high rates of births). Recent ex-

FIGURE 4-1   The Industry Life-Cycle Curve

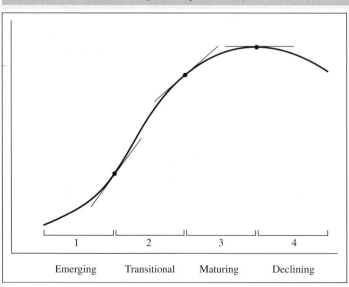

amples of emerging industries are biotechnology, the electric automobile industry, cellular telephones, and the interactive television industry.

Individual firms and entrepreneurs can create or reconfigure entire industries through vision, creativity, and innovation. An innovation strategy can create a customer where none previously existed.[31] How can this be done?

- *By creating utility.* The entrepreneur can change something that is hard for people to do into something that is easy for people to do. For example, there had been "mail" since Roman times, but the industry arose with the creation of a postal service in Great Britain, making it easier for people to pay for and send a letter.
- *By creating value.* The entrepreneur can change something that was expensive into something that is inexpensive and thereby create value through creative pricing. King Gillette did this when he unbundled the razor from the razor blade. Xerox did this when it realized it did not have to sell copiers, just the use of the copiers. It changed a relatively large capital investment decision into a small operating expense to gain acceptance.
- *By changing the customer's reality.* The entrepreneur can help customers buy products through creative distribution and financing, and help customers use products by simplifying operation and providing training. Entrepreneurs help customers solve problems by selling systems instead of products.

Structural Uncertainties   Even for ventures on the verge of revolutionizing the market, however, entry into emerging industries imposes certain structural conditions and constraints. The most imposing structural condition is uncertainty. There are no "traditional ways of doing things," "rules of thumb," "standard operating procedures," or "usual and customary practices." There are only the unknown future and the entrepreneur's will to succeed. Technological uncertainty means that the final configuration of resources, especially technological resources, is still unsettled. Firms are, as laboratories, trying new combinations of technology, human resources, and organizational systems to discover what works. Successful combinations are adopted by other firms as fundamental, and further experiments are conducted to refine the concepts and practices. Usually a single standard emerges for all firms. Occasionally, two competing standards reach the public at the same time as, for example, video technologies like Beta and VHS. But only one survives.

Strategic Uncertainty   Emerging firms also face a great deal of strategic uncertainty. New ventures in emerging industries are often unaware of who the competition is (or will be), what types of products and processes the competition is working on, and what posture the government will take toward the new industry. Because birth rates are high, new firms are starting all the time, and it is difficult to keep up on who and what they are. Government regulatory agencies at all levels are slow and bureaucratic. They are unlikely to have existing rules to help guide the new ventures.

Resource Uncertainty   Additional uncertainty looms in the firm's input markets. It is often difficult for the new venture to raise capital, because financial sources are unfamiliar with the new industry's risk/reward profile. Although some venture capital firms specialize in supporting investments in emerging industries, most financial institutions shy away from them. Labor is another input that is difficult to procure, especially managerial talent. Managers and executives face a great deal of career risk and economic uncertainty when joining firms in emerging industries. Turnover may be high in an unstable and turbulent industry. Managers and executives may need to be as entrepreneurial as the founders in order to meet the challenge of a new venture in a new industry.

The procurement of raw materials, supplies, and parts may also be difficult during the industry's emergence. If these inputs are also employed by other industries, there may be shortages until the vendors can adjust their capacity. If the inputs are newly created, developed, or engineered, they may be of uneven quality *and* in short supply. In either event, input costs are likely to be at their highest during the emergence stage.

Customer Uncertainty   Uncertainty also plagues the output (customer) market. To a large extent, the customer market is only vaguely understood: buyer needs and wants, income levels, demographic characteristics, psychographic profiles, and buyer behavior characteristics (knowledge of these is complete). Prices and the points where customers will resist high prices are uncertain, and there may be quite a bit of instability as firms, producing widely diverse and nonstandard products, come to market with diverse, nonstandard prices. The customer is also confused by the variety of product offerings, the lack of standardization, the perception of rapid obsolescence, and the erratic quality of some competitors. Street Story 4-3 shows us that it was customer uncertainty that led Sun Microsystems to look past its strategy of selling hardware and move into another emerging industry. Problems at eBay, an important customer, were the catalysts.

Controlling Uncertainty   In the face of difficult structural conditions and constraints, what must the new venture in an emerging industry do to be successful?

> *Look toward developing, generating, acquiring, and controlling resources that have the four attributes (rare, valuable, hard to copy, nonsubstitutable) needed for sustainable competitive advantage.*

The priority in an emerging industry is to acquire resources. Ventures that acquire resources early are more likely to set the rules and standards for industry competition, technological configuration, and product quality. Speeding up decision making, product development and introduction, and organizational systems and processes all have positive effects on firm survival and performance.[32] One industry that is attempting to speed itself up and that represents a typical emerging industry in its early stages is superconductive materials.

The next priority is to employ resources to gain a defendable foothold in the industry on which to build. The early acquisition of a core group of loyal customers is a major accomplishment. This enables the firm to develop experience in production and marketing, evaluate new products and alternative pricing schemes, and provide steady cash flow. From this base, expansion is possible.

Last, because knowledge and information can possess the four attributes of SCA, the new venture must move as quickly as possible to develop an intelligence network to forecast future environmental trends, competitive moves, and technological developments.[33] The initial turbulence and change that made the formation of a new industry possible are not likely to subside once a handful of early new entrants is formed. The turbulence continues unabated, often for years. While the new entrants sort out the standards, later entrants make their appearance and attempt to capitalize on the efforts

Firing Up an Emerging Industry:
Computer "Gun" Control

On the surface, Sun Microsystems Inc. does not look like a company in an emerging industry. Founded in 1982, Sun already dominates the computer industry by providing more than 40 percent of the servers that power current Internet Web sites. In addition, Sun is considered by many to be the most profitable computer company of all time.

But in 1999, Sun realized its sales success could be leading it to ruin. In June of that year, eBay Inc., the Internet auction site, suffered a series of server crashes, including one 22-hour service outage that was covered by media around the world. eBay, like many other fledgling dot-coms, uses a Sun Microsystems server. However, eBay did not understand how to maintain the Sun equipment; eBay's operations site did not have enough air-conditioning to keep the computer cool, and their technical people had neglected to install a preventative software patch that Sun had distributed months earlier. The mistakes were made by eBay, but Sun Microsystems was smart enough to realize that the problems reflected badly on their company. Suddenly, Sun management woke up to the fact that "selling computers to some of these dot-coms is like giving a gun to a 5-year-old."

That was when Sun changed its focus from producing hardware and moved into an emerging industry that would provide customers with an assortment of revolutionary e-business software, storage and backup products, and unprecedented consulting by Sun experts. Sun's goal is to make the Internet as reliable as the telephone system. As Sun Microsystems President Edward Zander describes the change, "I want to be the safe bet for companies that need the most innovative technology."

Sun foresees that, in the future, software will be distributed over the Internet by servers, instead of packaged on CDs to be installed on personal computers. They responded by bundling innovative software into an e-commerce suite that is guaranteed to run on their computer systems. They also combined their previously independent software, server, computer chip, and support service units into one vertical integration sales operation so customers now make just one call to meet any need. This masterstroke enables Sun to concentrate resources in a unique way for sustainable competitive advantage and also allows them to provide uniquely comprehensive service to their current customers. Sun believes this centralized system, along with improved customer interaction, will give them an intelligence edge in forecasting future trends and problems. Sun's customer service now includes pretesting customer software on every piece of hardware, remotely monitoring systems Sun has sold, and making on-site audits to improve operations for top customers.

Other companies, including IBM, Microsoft, and Oracle, are providing bundled software for e-commerce. Unlike Sun, none of those companies is also a dominant provider of the hardware that software must run on. To keep its sharpshooter computer servers firing, Sun is also investing an unmatched 10 percent of revenue in research and development, which should help them dominate this new segment even faster and more reliably while they service the dot-com industry.

Source: Adapted from Peter Burrows, "Sun's Bid to Rule the Web," *Business Week E.Biz,* July 24, 2000, pp. EB 31–42.

of the first movers. Older and larger firms attempt to invigorate their operations by entering new markets or forming joint ventures. Regulators, organized labor, and the government conspire to appropriate and tax the "profits" of new ventures. These so-called profits are in reality the early excess returns and may be needed for reinvestment to recoup the up-front investment, encourage future investment, and maintain the firm's technological or marketing advantages. Taxes and other appropriations leave the firm and, in aggregate, the industry underinvested and, therefore, smaller than they otherwise might have been. The result, of course, is diminished output, innovation, and employment. When this problem is recognized by policy makers, protection can be authorized, such as patent rights, tax abatements and credits, and accelerated depreciation schedules. An intelligence system may not be able to stop these trends, but a forewarned firm is in better position to protect its assets.

Transitional Industries

Transitional industries—those moving from emergence to stability—have certain recognizable features. At some point, there will be scarce resources, changes in customer tastes and values, and, finally, a shakeout. The shakeout period is crucial, for many firms go out of business at this time. The new venture can anticipate these developments, although their precise timing is always problematic.

Scarcity of Resources   As new firms enter the industry with an often dazzling array of products, strategies, and configurations, two powerful forces are at work. The first is that they bid up the prices of the resources they need to get started. Physical resources increase in price as they become more scarce. Scientific and managerial expertise costs more as people are lured away from current jobs with higher salaries and perquisites. Financial resources get more expensive as venture capitalists and investors demand higher yields from the later entrants. Overall industry costs rise as demand for industry inputs rises.

Customer Changes   The second force is the changing nature of the output market. Customers become more sophisticated and sure of what they want in terms of value, quality, and product characteristics. They become more powerful as they become more knowledgeable; they have more choices than they had earlier in the industry life cycle; and they are more likely to shop on price. The uncertainty of who the customer is and how large the market may be starts to fade as experience tells businesses who will buy and who will not. Competition for the existing customer base intensifies. Growth slows at the same time that shoppers become more price sensitive.

Survival Strategies in the Shakeout   What is the result of increasing production costs and decreasing selling prices? Smaller margins for everyone. Only the efficient survive. This is the transition phase, also known as the **shakeout**. Firms whose costs are too high will be forced out of business.[34] Firms that survive will be the ones that have resources with the four attributes of sustainable competitive advantage. When assets that are rare, valuable, hard to copy, and nonsubstitutable are deployed, the venture will be able to withstand price pressure and/or maintain lower costs than competitors.

The first priority in surviving the shakeout is to rationalize the resource base. This means pruning resources (of all six types) and the product/markets they serve if these resources are not earning rents and profits. During the emerging stage, firms often acquire excess resources, or slack. They do this for two reasons: (1) Because they are uncertain which resources will be the most important, they seek to gain control over as many as possible; and (2) growth is difficult to absorb, and as resources build, it is not easy to reinvest or deploy them quickly enough. During the shakeout period, as growth slows and margins are squeezed, slack must be wrung from the venture to restore it to agile, lean, and flexible conditions.

The next priority is to get the most out of reputational and organizational resources. These are often the last to develop for the new venture. Reputation is slow to develop because it takes time for the market and other stakeholders to gain experience with the firm. The organization, with its systems, processes, and routines, is also often a late-developing resource. The organization tends to evolve as the business grows, experimenting along the way. The interaction between the people, work flow, and policies that compose the organization tends to evolve as the business grows, experimenting along the way. The interaction between the people, work flow, and policies that compose the organization are complex. It takes time for all these components to come together. Even after they have coalesced, it takes practice and, therefore, time before that system can be perfected.

Reputation and organization are two of the most difficult resources to copy. As technology becomes more diffuse, as financing becomes more available to entrants, and as physical resources evolve toward commodity-type inputs, reputation and organization (and, by implication, human resources) are the best defense against increased competition and rivalry. Another potent strategy during the shakeout period is to buy cheap assets from the losers in the competitive game. As firms go out of business and their investors look to recoup whatever they can by selling the company or liquidating its assets, these assets often come to market at prices below their rent-earning capacity. The surviving firms, with superior human resources and organizational skills, can employ the liquidated physical resources, patent rights, licenses, and newly unemployed workers, managers, and staffers more effectively than their previous owners could. This firm-specific talent enables the survivor to collect a quasi-rent on the loser's former assets.

The strategy of expanding within the same business line by acquiring (by whatever method) other businesses is also known as **horizontal integration**. For example, horizontal integration and resource rationalization are the hallmarks of the shakeout in the biotechnology industry.

Shakeout Pitfalls   Firms must avoid pitfalls to survive this dangerous period. The most important of these is the "uniqueness paradox."[35] This is a blind spot that many companies have, especially those that are still relatively young. The uniqueness paradox occurs when people attribute unique characteristics to their own organization, characteristics that are, paradoxically, possessed by many other organizations. Although it may be good for internal cohesion for organizational members to differentiate themselves from their competitors by believing they are unique, it is bad for strategy. It is bad because it fools the firm into believing that some or all of its resources have the four attributes of SCA when, in fact, they do not. It makes the firm complacent and gives it a false sense of security. The firm is forced to react to outside pressures instead of generating its own proactive activities. This spells doom.

A second pitfall has already been mentioned, that is, keeping slack and excess capacity. The only thing worse than holding on to unused resources and facilities with too much capacity is acquiring new capacity that provides no rent-collecting possibilities, but firms do make the mistake of trying to "corner the market" on physical capacity even as growth slows.

A final pitfall is simply failing to recognize that the industry environment has changed. Sometimes the founders have difficulty adjusting to these new realities, and the entrepreneur is forced out and succeeded by a less creative but more managerially efficient executive. This is more probable when outside investors control the firm and fear that failure to act will cost them their investments.

Maturing Industries

It seems more appropriate to think of entrepreneurial strategies in the emerging and transitional environments because that is where the most visible and publicized entrepreneurial activity takes place. Entrepreneurs, though, are not limited by law, economics, or customers to these two phases of the industry life cycle. Entry can take a place in **mature industries** as well. Some flatly reject the idea that there is such a thing as a mature industry—there are only mature (and poorly run) firms. The argument is over the direction of causation. Does a maturing industry lower firm profitability, or does low firm profitability bring on the mature condition?[36]

Mature industries are characterized by slower growth, little pure innovation, more product and process improvements, more sophisticated customers, and increasing concentration of producers.[37] The last characteristic means that a few firms may produce 40 to 80 percent of the goods and services in the industry. This increased concentration also means that one or two industry leaders have emerged. An industry leader is the one the others look to for price changes and strategic movements. Sometimes mature industries appear to be friendly "clubs" with minimum competition and a general understanding of how to compete. The U.S. auto industry, the beef packers, the television networks, and the beer brewers spend as much time cooperating with each other to fend off attacks from outsiders (the Japanese automakers, the pork lobby, cable TV operators, temperance societies) than they do competing against each other.

However, entry is possible in mature industries, although the barriers are high. The computer hardware business is an example.[38] Start-up and entry in this industry is increasingly rare. The business is saturated. Ben Rosen, the venture capitalist who bankrolled Compaq Computer in 1982, says, "In terms of main-line, hard-core computer companies, it's very hard to define an area where you can get to a critical mass of $50 million to $100 million" in sales. Short of that size, the chances of making big returns and taking the company public are slim. Veterans of the industry are sadly concluding that the heyday is over. "It may not be possible to start a new computer manufacturing company," laments Richard Shaffer, publisher of *Technologic Computer Newsletter*. There are other problems as well:

- Capital costs have soared. "It costs $50 million just to find out if anybody cares."
- Limits on technological innovation are being reached. Firms promising breakthroughs are often disappointed.
- Replacements are being ordered by customers slowly. Much of the computer machinery just doesn't wear out.
- The industry's move to standardized parts and operating systems limits the innovation small companies can provide.[39]

Attacking the Leader   One possible strategy is to attack the industry leader (an imposing task, but not impossible).[40] Industry leaders can become vulnerable when the business cycle is on the upswing and things look good. Leaders may become complacent. Those with unhappy customers can also be attacked; they have grown arrogant and are no longer providing value. When leaders are under antitrust investigation, they are certainly less likely to retaliate, but never attack an industry leader with an imitative, me-too product or service. The challenger who does so has nothing to defend.

Three conditions must be present for the attacker. First, it must have some basis for sustainable competitive advantage. Some resources must possess the four-attribute qualities that would provide the entrant either a cost advantage or a sustainable difference. Second, the new entrant must neutralize the leader's advantage by at least matching the perceived quality of the leader's product. Last, there must be an impediment (more than one is even better) that prevents retaliation. These impediments are:

- Antitrust problems
- A cash crunch caused by overextension
- A blind spot such as the uniqueness paradox
- An overdiversified portfolio causing neglect of key areas
- A strategic bind (retaliation would jeopardize another business strategy)

If these three conditions are met, the entrant has a chance. One tactic is to **reconfigure** the ways of doing business. This means doing something startlingly different. For example, the makers of Grey Poupon mustard reconfigured the marketing of mustard by spending more on advertising than the mustard business had ever done in the past. French's, Heinz, and others were forced to give up share to this upstart. A second tactic is to **redefine the scope of service**. A new entrant can focus on a particular niche, serve that customer exceedingly well, and gain a foothold in a mature industry. For example, La Quinta motels focused on the frequent business traveler on a small budget. There was little retaliation, lest the entrenched competitors ruin their own pricing structure and demean the reputation of their core brands. Last, the challenger can attempt to spend its way to success. It can attempt to buy market share through exceptionally low prices and heavy promotion and advertising. This is risky business and out of the reach of all but the best-financed entrepreneurs.

Specializing   One additional entrepreneurial strategy can be used to enter a mature market. This strategy calls for the new venture to do something for a mature business better than it could do it itself. New firms and small firms can thrive in a mature market if they can take over some specialized activities for a big concern.[41] It is not unusual for a highly specialized small firm to have lower operating costs than large firms. The larger, more mature firms carry more overhead, have older technology, and do not focus on the cost drivers the way a smaller firm can. For example, Ameriscribe operates mailrooms for National Steel and does it better and cheaper than the firm can. The Wyatt Company, a consulting firm, did a survey and found that 86 percent of the nation's largest corporations had cut back on operations and contracted services to outsiders.

It should also be noted that there are costs to contracting out these services: legal contractual costs, monitoring costs, searching for contractors and processing bids, possible loss from opportunistic behavior, and recontracting costs. However, even after these transaction and agency costs are covered, it still may be cheaper to use an outside contractor. This is an example of the classic make-or-buy decision, and theoretical foundations of this problem are detailed in transaction cost theory and agency theory. Table 4-3 provides some additional examples of this phenomenon.

Declining Industries

Declining industries are characterized by the end of unit growth and by flat constant-dollar sales (i.e., adjusted for inflation). Finally, both of these indicators decrease.[42] Current examples of consumer industries in decline in the United States are tobacco and hard liquor. Industrial sectors in decline include manufacturers of carburetors for automobiles, certain defense-related manufacturers and aerospace contractors, and producers of bias-ply tires for original equipment manufacturers (OEM). The primary causes of industry decline are technological substitution, shifts in the tastes and preferences of consumers, and demographic factors.

Technological Substitution   When an older technology is replaced by a newer one, the older technology goes into decline. However, it does not immediately disappear. Even after the invention and adoption of the transistor, which replaced vacuum tubes in radios, televisions, and other devices in the late 1950s and 1960s, producers of vacuum tubes continued to exist. They supplied replacement parts for existing sets and produced for the hobby and collector markets. Similarly, producers of vinyl long-playing records still exist, although these have been rapidly and overwhelmingly overtaken by producers of compact discs and cassette tapes.

Changes in Tastes and Preferences   Changes in tastes and preferences shift demand to alternatives but do not cause immediate extinction of the declining industry. The declining consumer industries noted previously reflect changing tastes. For example, the underlying trend today is for healthier lifestyles. However, millions of Americans each year have a steak for dinner, accompanied by a whisky, and light up a cigar after dessert. The volumes of all three products continue to be high, but they are decreasing a little each year.

TABLE 4-3   Corporate Services Contracted Out to Smaller Firms

Company	Function and Service	Contractor
DuPont	Product engineering and design	Morris Knudsen
AT&T	Credit-card processing	Total Systems Services
Northern Telecom	Electronic component manufacturing	Comptronix
Eastman Kodak	Computer support services	Businessland
Mobil	Refinery maintenance	Serv-Tech
Whirlpool	Distribution center management	Kenco Group
National Steel	Mailroom operations and copying work	Ameriscribe
Security Pacific	Accounting and trust management	SunGard Data Systems
Texas Instruments	Packing and shipping materials	Harper Group

Source: Adapted from M. Selz, "Small Companies Thrive by Taking Over Some Specialized Tasks for Big Concerns," *The Wall Street Journal,* September 9, 1992, B1–2.

Changes in Demographics   Changes in demographics are reflected in overall product demand (see Chapter 3). As the baby-boom generation makes its way through the population cycle, its members first produced a boom in children's clothing and furnishings, followed by a decline in these industries. Then they bought automobiles and residential real estate, which boomed; now each of these industries is in decline. The boomers are aging, as are their parents, and health care is the fastest-growing segment of GNP. Guess what will occur when the boomers start to die off? Health care will decline, and the mortuary business will boom.

Achieving Success   Under certain conditions, new entrants can establish successful niches in declining industries. The key for the new entrant is to find ways to help the incumbents leave the industry and then purchase their assets at low prices. This is an imposing task, however, because a number of factors increase the height of the exit barriers for firms in declining industries:

- Low liquidation value of specialized assets
- Interrelationship of the business in decline with other businesses not in decline
- Potentially negative effects of exiting on financial markets
- Emotional and managerial effects of "calling it quits"

From the viewpoint of the entrepreneur, an opportunity exists if an industry is still attractive and the entrepreneur has or can acquire resources with the attributes of sustainable competitive advantage. Let's look at the example of Donald J. "Jerry" Ehrlich, chairman, president and CEO of Wabash National, a manufacturer of standardized and custom truck trailers.[43] Ehrlich manufactures a commodity product in a declining industry; total truck trailer production in the United States fell to 140,500 units in 1992 from 214,300 units in 1988. During the 1980s, many trailer manufacturers leveraged themselves with debt to the hilt, which meant they were in poor shape to modernize plants to meet the manufacturing challenges of the 1990s. Ehrlich saw this happen from close up when he was president of the Monon Corporation, a $250 million manufacturer of trailers. Monon declined when it became a leveraged buyout victim in the 1980s, and Ehrlich left to found Wabash National.

Ehrlich's initial resource endowment included two managers and 14 other employees from Monon who left with him, and his own 35 years of experience building trailers. His brother Rod joined him as chief of engineering. Ehrlich found cheap manufacturing space in an abandoned factory in Lafayette, Indiana, just 30 miles down the road from the Monon plant. Former customer Sears, Roebuck & Co., who had worked with Ehrlich for years, provided entry wedge momentum for the new company by ordering 10 trailers off the bat, with a promise to order 370 more if all went well. With this order in hand, Ehrlich employed underutilized resources and was able to buy manufacturing equipment at fire-sale prices from other bankrupt rust-belt companies. Ehrlich's strong reputation in the industry enabled him to raise $2 million in outside equity and generate an additional $3 million through industrial revenue bonds with government sponsorship.

How successful has Wabash become? In 1992, Wabash produced 100 trailers a day and had revenues of $300 million, representing sales of $180,000 per employee. In 1999, Wabash shipped a total of 69,772 units, corresponding to 191 units per calendar day.

Revenues grew to $1.454 billion in 1999, representing sales of over $259,000 per employee. The company believes it is now the world's largest manufacturer of truck trailers and bimodal rail/highway vehicles, and a wholly owned subsidiary is one of the leading retail distributors of new and used trailers and aftermarket parts. Wabash's 58-acre, 700,000-square-foot facility in Lafayette is the largest site of its kind in the world, and recent company acquisitions include Freuhauf Trailer Services, which was formerly one of its top competitors.

What factors will help Wabash continue to succeed in this declining industry? Jerry Ehrlich's strategic keys include the know-how to manufacture and market trailers, to build customer loyalty, to produce the product at the lowest cost in the industry, and to maintain a flexible and motivated workforce that can produce "15 different types of trailers for 15 different customers" on any given day.

Fragmented Industries

Figure 4-1 shows the life-cycle curve for an industry that has, over time, consolidated. Consolidation means that the number of firms decreases, the birth rate of new firms diminishes considerably, and larger firms have advantages of scale and scope. However, not all industries are dominated by large firms with megamarket shares. In other words, not all industries go through the life cycle of Figure 4-1. Industries that do not are called **fragmented industries**. Examples include professional services, retailing, distribution services, wood and metal fabrication, and personal care businesses, such as hairdressers and barbers.

The causes for fragmentation are diverse. Low-entry barriers can cause fragmentation because firms will always be faced with new challengers and, therefore, be unable to grow. An industry may not be able to generate economies of scale, because being larger brings no cost advantages. In these cases, firms do not get larger, and consolidation never takes place. Indeed, there may be diseconomies of scale; costs go up (on a per-unit basis) as the firms grow. High transportation and inventory costs may keep firms small and geographically limited.[44]

The effect of firm size on buyers and sellers also can keep an industry fragmented. If neither buyers nor sellers see advantages in dealing with larger firms, they will avoid such firms and negotiate with smaller, less powerful firms. Sometimes the market niches are too small to support larger firms because the needs of the market are so diverse. Any or all of these conditions can keep an industry from the path described in Figure 4-1 and, therefore, keep the firms in the industry small and relatively powerless.

Most of what we understand to be the small business sector of the economy is actually the set of fragmented industries and the ventures within them. Businesses in fragmented industries can be profitable, and they can grow to be relatively large. But by definition, if they are large enough to have a market share that can influence conditions, then the industry is no longer fragmented.

Overcoming Fragmentation   New ventures in fragmented industries sometimes have the potential to introduce strategic, technological, or managerial innovations that may help the industry overcome fragmentation. If the new venture enters with technologies that introduce economies of scale, the venture will grow larger. For example, the brewery industry used to be fragmented, with thousands of local brewers. The technological breakthrough that overcame this fragmentation was the refrigerated freight car, which enabled brewers to ship their beer long distances without danger of it spoiling.

Fragmentation may also be overcome by strategies that reconstruct the way firms operate. The "sneaker" used to be a fragmented product in the sporting goods industry. With few exceptions, it was sold as commodity footwear for kids (Keds, Converse). When it was reconstructed as an "athletic shoe," given technological developments, and promoted as a personal fashion statement, a highly profitable industry dominated by a few very large firms (Nike, Reebok, Adidas) emerged.

Another method of reconstructing an industry is to separate the assets responsible for fragmentation from other assets. This is known as "unbundling." Two classic examples are campgrounds and fast food.[45] These industries were characterized by thousands of small owners. Both require tight local control and supervision and must be located near their customers, but significant economies of scale in purchasing and marketing were achieved through franchising. Local control was maintained by the franchisee, and purchasing and marketing economies were obtained by the franchisor. The initial beneficiaries of these economies were McDonald's and KOA.

Investors, and especially venture capitalists, are increasingly targeting fragmented industries as neglected but high-potential opportunities. Why? Because a firm that overcomes fragmentation can become the industry leader, achieve enormous size and profitability, and provide rates of return in the thousands of percent range. The Chicago firm of Golder, Thoma & Cressy is often credited with originating this investment strategy. So far, it has applied its strategy to the nursing home, answering service, and bottled-water businesses. Other industries ripe for consolidation are small-niche food processors, small-town newspapers, security alarm companies, and (the ultimate local business) funeral homes.

The strategy is not easy to execute. First, the investor identifies and acquires a company in a fragmented industry, one with no market leader. Then a new management team is recruited to run the business. Together the investors and new managers identify and negotiate to buy a few additional companies in the target industry. The hardest part is next: consolidating all the companies under a common name and set of operating practices. If it works, the payoffs are huge.[46]

Coping with Fragmentation   Quite often the new entrant lacks the resources, means, or imagination to overcome fragmentation. Excellent money can still be made, however, from high-quality implementation, and the firm that learns to cope with fragmentation can thrive. A solid and profitable small business can be built on the following foundations:

- *Regimented professional management.* The introduction of managerial techniques and professionalism into small-business operations can keep the firm profitable even under strong price pressure.
- *Formula facilities or franchising.* High degrees of standardization and efficient, low-cost operations provide protection against eroding margins.
- *Serving specialized, focus niches.* A business that is highly specialized by product type, customer type, order type, or geographic area can achieve minor economies of scale and add high value for buyers.

Warning! A firm can be so specialized that it may not have enough customers to be feasible. Do not plan to open a pen repair shop, a shoelace boutique, or a restaurant based on the concept of toast.

E-NOTES 4-6

Industry Environment

Five different types of industry environments, each with its own unique lifecycle, include:

- emerging industries
- transitional industries
- maturing industries
- declining industries
- fragmented industries

EVALUATING STRATEGY AND ENTREPRENEURIAL OPPORTUNITIES

Recognizing, assessing, and exploiting opportunities are among the keys to entrepreneurial success. Opportunity assessment can be broken into five stages (Figure 4-2). Each stage focuses on analysis and the actions that must be taken. Analysis rests on the entrepreneur's understanding of the nature of the business that he or she wishes to create. Traditionally, entrepreneurs must ask the question, "What is my business?" They then attempt to answer the question in terms of a target customer and the target's buying needs, tastes, and preferences. In a world with volatile markets and changing tastes and preferences, keeping up is a dicey proposition. So, in opportunity assessment, entrepreneurs should initially assess the core stable set of *internal* capabilities rather than volatile external resources.

Stage 1: Identification

The first stage requires entrepreneurs to identify and classify the resources they currently have and can obtain control over in their initial efforts to create a new venture. Identification and classification should be structured using the six categories previously described: financial, physical, human, technological, reputational, and organizational assets. A resource is currently controlled if the entrepreneur and the top management team have immediate and unimpeded access to it, legally and physically. An asset is controllable to the extent that it may be obtained sometime in the future. For a rigorous analysis, a probability distribution can indicate the likelihood of obtaining the resource. If extremely high or low, this probability can be factored into the next part of the stage 1 assessment.

The second part of stage 1 entails determining the relative strengths and weaknesses of the resource bundle and configuration. The entrepreneur should then examine how to use these resources and explore what business opportunities exist to make

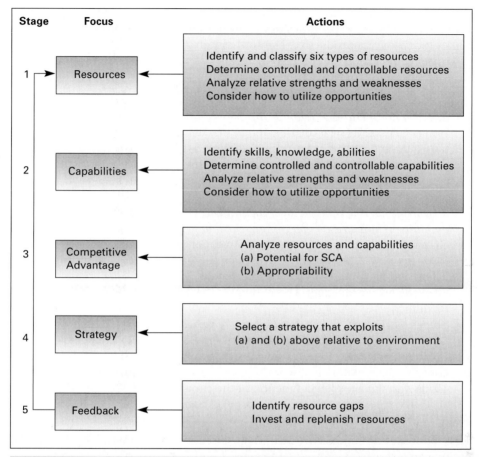

| Stage | Focus | Actions |

FIGURE 4-2   A Resource-Based Approach to Entrepreneurial Opportunity Assessment and Analysis

the most of them. What criteria should the entrepreneur use for this evaluation? The four attribute criteria: Is the resource under investigation:

- Rare?
- Valuable?
- Hard to copy?
- Nonsubstitutable?

The entrepreneur also needs to ask, to what degree? To the extent that the entrepreneur can answer "yes" to the first question and "quite a bit" to the second, he or she has the basis for competitive advantage.

Stage 2: Capabilities

The capabilities of a firm are the skills, knowledge, and abilities needed to manage and configure resources.[47] The second stage, then, is similar to the first, except the analysis focuses on capabilities instead of resources. Few resources, as pure inputs, can form the basis for a successful business. Usually these resources must be employed in some way — a way defined by the capabilities of the entrepreneur and his or her team.[48] Capability makes the resources productive. The firm requires capabilities to coordinate resources and foster cooperation for efficiency. The hardest part of this analysis is maintaining objectivity. Entrepreneurs are tempted to overestimate abilities and skills or dwell on past accomplishments they may not be able to generalize.

- *There is no one-to-one relationship between resources and capabilities.* Each firm can create its own relationship to manage its resources. The most important outcome of this relationship, though, is the smooth coordination and cooperation among the members of the teams who perform the routines. The routines themselves become intangible resources that may have the four attributes.
- *New firms have advantages over incumbents when developing routines and capabilities in industries undergoing great changes.* Older firms will have trouble changing routines to adapt to the environment; new firms can invent routines to fit the new realities. Of course, once the new venture has become established and its routines have been perfected, it is just as open to assault from an even newer challenger. This highlights the trade-off between efficiency and flexibility.
- *Some routines are widely distributed; others reside in the skills and abilities of one person.* For example, Walt Disney World is a complex amalgam of entertainment, art technology, traffic control, and highly motivated employees. In contrast, the junk bond underwriting at Drexel, Burnham, and Lambert in the 1980s was almost solely a function of the capabilities of Michael Milken.

Stage 3: Competitive Advantage

Stage 3 focuses on competitive advantage. Here we try to determine whether the competitive advantages(s) identified in stages 1 and 2 may be sustained and if the profits and rents can be protected. Sustainable competitive advantage depends on the firm's ability to move first and create isolating mechanisms. First-mover advantages and isolating mechanisms prevent other firms from copying and crowding the firm's profit. The entrepreneur should ask:

- Do isolating mechanisms exist for the firm?
- Which ones should be employed to protect our resource advantages?

Any rent that the firm can collect may be eroded. Physical resources can be depleted, be depreciated, be replicated, or become obsolete. The probability of appropriation is high, too. The environment will seek to get a share of the rents through taxation (government), increased wage demands (employees), rising input costs (suppliers), or litigation (competitors and lawyers). The new venture's founders and leaders must be sensitive and alert to these pressures.

Stage 4: Strategy

The next stage translates the assessment of competitive advantage into strategy. The firm requires two related strategies: one to protect and manage its resources, the other a product and market strategy. The first strategy has already been discussed in terms of isolating mechanisms and first-mover advantages. The second set of strategies entail dealing with the macroenvironment and the competitive environment described in Chapter 3.

Stage 5: Feedback

In stage 5, the entrepreneur should focus on feedback, that is, evaluating and reassessing the continuous process of new venture creation. Through the first four stages, resource gaps may have appeared and requirements for resources that are neither controlled nor controllable may become apparent. Recycling through the process after having identified the gaps is recommended. Gap-reducing and gap-eliminating strategies can be the focus of the next round. Also, resource bases are inevitably depleted and depreciated. The next cycle must account for these erosions and make plans for investments to maintain resources and investments and to replenish stocks and assets.

E-NOTES 4-7

Opportunity Assessment

The five stages of assessing entrepreneurial opportunities include:

- identifying resources
- analyzing capabilities
- evaluating competition advantage
- developing a strategy
- reviewing feedback

As we have seen throughout this chapter, no one strategy is best for all new ventures. Because choice is crucial and many paths can lead to success, we need a way to evaluate the strategy after it is chosen but before it is implemented. If we can do this, we can weigh various alternatives against one another and make a better choice without having to incur the consequences of a poor choice. The following four criteria may be used to evaluate proposals.[49] Each can be viewed as a test; if the strategy passes the tests, it is superior to strategies that fail the tests.

- *Goal consistency test.* Does the strategy help the firm to accomplish its goals? Are the strategy's outcomes predicted to be consistent with previous strategies and decisions? Will the strategy enable the firm to maintain its posture?
- *Frame test.* Is the firm working on the right issues? Does the strategy address resource issues and alignment with the environment? Does the strategy meet the requirements of the industry stage and help acquire and control resources possessing the four attributes of sustainable competitive advantage?
- *Competence test.* Does the firm have the ability to carry out the strategy? Can the strategy be broken down into problems that have solutions? Are these solutions that the firm can work out?
- *Workability test.* Will it work? Is it legal and ethical? Will it produce the desired end? Will the organization be willing to marshal its resources to carry out the strategy?

Summary

In this chapter, we reviewed a combination of theory and practice from both the strategic management and the entrepreneurship literature. Entry wedges and momentum factors are the initial entrepreneurial strategies. The major wedges are innovation, parallel types of competition, and franchising, and the various forms of sponsorship compose the momentum factors. Resource-based strategies are geared toward rent-seeking behavior. The most prevalent of four rent-seeking behaviors is the entrepreneurial strategy. The resource-based model also accounts for the rate and direction of a venture's growth strategies. Firms grow in the direction of underutilized resources and toward areas where they have distinctive competencies.

Quality as a strategy was discussed in the resource-based framework. The choice of a strategy of total quality management does not represent a sustainable competitive advantage for the firm. However, the implementation of such a program can provide advantages, because successful implementation requires superior market knowledge, complex service behavior from employees, and highly developed organizational systems. The best candidates for a successful TQM strategy are firms that already possess these resources.

We then looked at how industry conditions affect entry and strategy for a new venture. Five industry types were discussed: emerging industries, transitional industries, maturing industries, declining industries, and fragmented industries. Although new ventures can be successful in any of these environments, the emerging and fragmented environments provide the easiest entry and the most typical entrepreneurial case.

We concluded with a brief overview of the strategy evaluation process. Specifically, we identified four criteria for testing the appropriateness of a strategy before embarking on the market test itself. A strategy is appropriate if it is consistent with the goals of the organization, addresses the right issues, can be executed competently, and is workable both legally and ethically.

Key Terms

- Benchmarking
- Business-level strategy
- Competence test
- Continuous improvement
- Corporate strategy
- Customer contract
- Declining industry
- Emerging industry
- Enterprise-level strategy
- Entrepreneurial rent
- Entry wedge
- First-mover advantage
- Fragmented industry
- Frame test
- Franchisee
- Franchisor

- Functional strategy
- Geographic transfer
- Goal consistency test
- Horizontal integration
- Industry life cycle
- Isolating mechanisms
- Joint venturing
- Licensing
- Market relinquishment
- Mature industry
- Monopoly rent
- Outsourcing
- Property rights
- Quality circle
- Quasi-rent
- Reconfigure

- Redefine the scope of service
- Ricardian rent
- Second source
- Shakeout
- Spin-off
- Strategy
- Strategy formulation
- Strategy implementation
- Subfunctional strategy
- Supply shortage
- Switching costs
- Technological leadership
- Transitional industry
- Underutilized resource
- Workability test

Discussion Questions

1. Why do new ventures need strategies?
2. How do the major entry wedges help create momentum for the new venture?
3. How do the minor wedges supplement the major ones?
4. Evaluate the pros and cons of the minor wedges. Which would be the most or least effective in the long run?
5. Describe the four different kinds of rents. Give examples of how an entrepreneur might attempt to collect these.
6. How will firms employ their resources for growth? Explain the focus effects and synergy effects.
7. Discuss "quality" as a strategy. How can it be used to achieve sustainable competitive advantage?
8. What are the key elements affecting entrepreneurial strategy in these environments?
   a. Emerging industries
   b. Transitional industries
   c. Maturing industries
   d. Declining industries
   e. Fragmented industries
9. What are the five stages for assessing entrepreneurial opportunities?
10. What are the four tests of strategy? Why is it important to apply the tests before going into business?

Exercises

Develop a strategy for your new venture.
1. What entry wedges, major and minor, will you employ?
2. How will you attempt to collect and appropriate rents?
3. What industry environment are you entering? How will this influence your strategy?
4. Apply the four tests to your strategy. What questions do these raise? How would you answer these questions if posed by a banker or venture capitalist?

⟨ DISCUSSION CASE ⟩

A Strategy for Having Fun

Larry Schwarz makes unusual toys.

Put your hand inside the mouth of his Gus Gutz doll, and you can pull out 12 human organs. Reach into Harry Hairball, the stuffed cat, and you can remove a mouse, a goldfish, or a ball of yarn. There's even a letter carrier hiding down the throat of Freddy Fetch the dog. Schwarz says that his toys combine "the right amount of cuddly and gross."

Given the kind of innovative stuffed toys he has created, it may not be surprising that Larry Schwarz has reached inside himself to come up with an unusual way of marketing toys. A law school graduate who became a toy manufacturer because "I just thought it would be fun," Schwarz had already achieved the kind of market position most toy makers can only imagine. When his company, Rumpus Toys, was starting out, this entrepreneur maneuvered free national TV exposure by arranging a free guest appearance for his toys on the *Live! With Regis and Kathie Lee* daytime talk show. Just a few months later, Rumpus toys were on the shelves of Toys "R" Us, F.A.O. Schwarz (no relation), and other toy stores from coast to coast. In its first full year of business, Rumpus grossed over $12 million dollars.

But Schwarz, who prefers the title "Head Boy" to CEO, was not happy. He did not like traditional toy retailing. "It's a crappy business to be in," he says. Profit margins are slim, and manufacturers are hassled by returns from the stores that stock their products. Schwarz complained that it drove him wild to walk into a toy store and see his products lying around on the floor.

So Larry Schwarz yanked his toys off the shelves and floors of all those toy stores and decided he would sell his products strictly over the Internet. In fact, you could say that Rumpus is no longer in the business of selling toys. The Web has transformed them into an entertainment company that produces animated cartoons that happen to feature—and promote—more than 17 different Rumpus stuffed toys. Although Schwarz won't disclose the figure, he apparently had no trouble raising venture capital to make the transition to a dot-com company and was able to double the size of his staff to 40 employees.

Of course, the Rumpus Toys site is a little unusual, too. The bright and sassy Web page features photos and descriptions of their toys, and lists all the awards the toys have received. Reach inside, and you can pull out cartoons, games, and e-cards for each Rumpus character. During promotions, customers can earn free shipping or other shopping incentives by interacting with the site. Kids can sign up for an e-mail newsletter and even send a fill-in-the-blank message to their parents to personally beg for a particular Rumpus Toy product. The company is also developing a pilot for a Saturday morning TV show on the WB Kids network to complement their Web site efforts.

Head Boy Schwarz claims he made up his mind to transform his company after reading a horoscope prediction that said, "You will make a decision that will shock people." Although the financial figures have not been tabulated, Schwarz says, "I already think it was the right move."

(continued)

(*continued*)

CASE QUESTIONS

1. Given the target audience, do you think Rumpus Toys made a smart move by changing from traditional retail distribution to e-tailing? What are Rumpus Toys' specific advantages and disadvantages for both methods? Would you recommend a combined approach? Why or why not?

2. Larry Schwarz sent a box of his toys to a TV talk show to initially promote his product onto retail toy store shelves. What could he do now to publicize his Web site?

3. Several online toy sellers have failed recently. List some of the reasons why toy marketing might be particularly difficult on the Web. What products seem well-suited for e-tailing?

Source: Adapted from Paulette Thomas, "A Toy Maker Shelves His Cuddly Creations to Make Virtual Stars," *The Wall Street Journal,* November 1, 2000, p. B1; available at www.rumpus.com.

The Business Plan

5

Each plan, like a snowflake, must be different.
—Joseph Mancuso

Outline

Learning Objectives

After reading this chapter, you will understand:

- Why it is important to write a business plan
- The elements of a business plan
- How to write a business plan
- What kinds of questions people will ask about your business plan
- How to respond to critiques of your business plan

How do we want to use all the analysis and evaluation we did in Chapters 2, 3, and 4? We want to write a business plan. The development and writing of the business plan marks the transition from strategy formulation to the implementation stage of new venture creation. The entrepreneur or entrepreneurial team members have thus far collected information and analyzed it. They have examined their own preferences and goals to determine why they want to go into business. They have evaluated the venture's resource base and determined what is rare, valuable, difficult to duplicate, and nonsubstitutable. They have sifted through mountains of product and market data, analyzing environmental variables, market trends, and the competition. They have performed innumerable mental experiments to visualize what the business will look like, how the products or services will be produced or delivered, and how quality will be continuously monitored and improved.[1]

Now it is time for action. The document produced is known as the business plan. The **business plan** is the formal written expression of the entrepreneurial vision, describing the strategy and operations of the proposed venture. The business plan also goes by other names, depending on its intended audience. Presented to a banker, it may be called a "loan proposal." A venture capital group might call it the "venture plan" or "investment prospectus." Other audiences might be potential partners or top managers, suppliers and distributors, lawyers, accountants, and consultants.

Many firms start without business plans, meaning that their implementation stage begins with no plan. Most of these firms find eventually that they have to recreate their beginnings and write a plan at some point down the road. In today's complex economic environment, only the most reluctant entrepreneur with the simplest business concept avoids writing a business plan.[2]

This chapter is divided into four sections. The first section argues that every new venture should have a business plan and explores the benefits of developing one. The second section offers an extensive and detailed summary of the components of a business plan and explains how they combine to produce a comprehensive picture of the new firm. The third section explains what questions the entrepreneurs are likely to be asked by investors and others. The chapter concludes with suggestions for writing and presenting the plan. Business plans communicate more about the top management team than simply the scope of their entrepreneurial vision. Entrepreneurs are judged by the way they organize, write, and present the business plan. Therefore, it must be informative, concise, and complete.

WHY WRITE A BUSINESS PLAN?

Arguments can be made for and against writing a business plan. However, if the new venture is looking for financing from an outside source, it must have a plan. Writing a plan is not without its costs and sacrifices, but overall, the benefits far outweigh the costs.

The Costs of Planning

Entrepreneurs are often characterized as "doers," individuals who prefer action to planning and who let their deeds speak for themselves. One of the costs of writing a business plan is that the entrepreneurs must sit still long enough to do it. Hiring someone to write the plan is not an acceptable substitute; entrepreneurs should undertake the task personally. Although outsiders—consultants, accountants, and lawyers—should be tapped for their advice and expertise, the founder or the initial top management team should be responsible for the writing.[3] By personally writing the plan, the entrepreneurs ensure that they are familiar with all the details, for they will have to make decisions about the new venture and be responsible for those decisions. Moreover, investors expect the founders to be involved in and knowledgeable about the proposed enterprise.

Developing and writing the plan takes time, money, and energy. In launching the new venture, the entrepreneurial team may believe that actually working in the business is the best use of these resources. For short periods of time, that may be true. Over the long haul, though, the new venture team is the most valuable, rare, and unique resource the company has. The task of the entrepreneur is the task of the leader. The leader is the architect of organizational purpose.[4] The venture is created to achieve the vision of the entrepreneur. The best use of the entrepreneur's time and energy, therefore, is in creating, refining, and pursuing that vision.

Because every business plan must deal with economic uncertainty and the risks that the firm faces, one of the costs of writing a business plan is the psychological strain of admitting everything that can go wrong. Entrepreneurs are optimists, and they believe in the power of their own efforts.[5] They believe they will succeed. The serious business plan, however, exposes the possibilities that can lead to failure. To achieve full material disclosure for a potential investor, partner, or supplier,[6] the plan has to list the risks of the business, one by one. Recognizing these risks and facing an uncertain future can be psychologically uncomfortable for the entrepreneur. This is a cost, and it is one reason some business plans are never written.

A final reason for perhaps not writing a business plan is the fear, real or imagined, of prematurely closing off the new venture's strategic direction. There is some worthwhile debate about the breadth of market strategy employed by the firm. Should a new venture's strategy be very focused and oriented toward a narrow segment of the market? Or should the firm be more opportunistic and pursue a broad market strategy, basically striving to make initial sales wherever they can be found? If the purpose of a plan is to encourage focus, it could be argued that not planning is good because it enables the entrepreneurs to be more flexible. This is clearly the trade-off between planning and reacting.[7]

The Benefits of Business Planning

The business plan can personally benefit the entrepreneurial team. Founding a new business can be enormously fulfilling and exhilarating, but it is also an anxiety-ridden and tense experience. Usually a great deal of money is at stake, and the consequences of poor decisions can affect many people for a long time. In developing and writing a business plan, the entrepreneurial team reduces these anxieties and tensions by confronting them. By projecting the risks of the new venture into the future, the team comes to grips with potential negative outcomes and the possibility of failure. The knowledge that comes from this experience can reduce the fear of facing an unknown future.

Conflicts   Also on a personal level, the entrepreneur is potentially in conflict with the new business demands that he or she may find imposing. The entrepreneur may desire wealth and increased income, high esteem, a period of stability once the venture is off the ground, or more time for leisure and recreation. Each of these motivations, however, is impeded by the demands of the organization.

First, the new firm requires reinvestment; the more successful it is, the more money it will need for growth. This reality is in conflict with the entrepreneur's desire for short-term income. Second, the organization demands that the entrepreneur be a leader and a manager, but these responsibilities often require tough personnel decisions. The individuals who are hurt by these decisions may not hold the entrepreneur in high esteem. There is always the risk of not being liked and even of making enemies.

The entrepreneur may also anticipate a period of stability once the business is launched. The process of starting the new venture can be exhausting, and entrepreneurs may feel they deserve an interim period of consolidation and peace. But the organization may demand more risk-taking, additional crucial decisions may have to be made, and plans and strategies may have to be reformulated. Here again, the firm is in conflict with its creator. Last, once the business is off the ground, the founder may look forward to having more time for leisure or for family or community service. The venture, however, needs the entrepreneur's help with the daily tasks; he or she has to continue to make business decisions and lead the organization.

E-NOTES 5-1

Business Plan

A business plan:

- explains the entrepreneur's vision in writing
- demonstrates implementation (strategy and operations)
- may function as financing proposal or investment prospectus

---

The business plan helps the entrepreneur deal with these conflicts by recognizing the issues before they become serious problems. The entrepreneur decides which way the conflicts will be resolved. By anticipating these conflicting values and writing them into the plan, the entrepreneur can reduce the emotional strain that making these trade-offs entails. When the time comes for making a decision in a specific conflict, the entrepreneur can refer to the business plan as an objective standard for resolving it.

Planning and Performance   The firm also benefits from the planning process. Research shows there is a positive relationship between planning and performance in new and small firms.[8] *That is, firms that plan perform better and are more likely to succeed than firms that do not.*[9] There are four reasons why this is so.

1. *Comprehensiveness.* The business plan has to fully and completely treat all the major issues facing the new venture. It should leave nothing of importance out. This comprehensiveness enables the entrepreneur to see where trouble might come from and to develop contingent strategies to reduce the effects of these problems. It forces the entrepreneur to develop and demonstrate industry-related competence.[10]
2. *Communication.* The business plan is a document for communicating to various audiences the business's concept and potential. An effective plan succeeds in

communicating the excitement and vision of the founders and can help to attract resources to the new venture.

3. *Guidance.* The business plan sets goals and milestones for the new venture. It lays out the intentions of the entrepreneurial team and the values the founders wish to preserve in their organization. Therefore, the plan can be referred to repeatedly to guide decisions of the firm's managers and employees. "When in doubt, consult the plan" could be the motto of a new venture. In the exciting and turbulent months and years after starting, it is easy for the individuals in the organization to lose sight of the venture's original purposes and intended strengths. A readily available written plan fosters cohesiveness because everyone can see what the firm's desired objectives are.

4. *The planning process.* The process of putting together a business plan, consulting it frequently, and reviewing and revising it periodically can improve the venture's performance even though some aspects of the plan may become obsolete before the ink is dry. This improvement is brought about by collecting information, sharing analysis, developing norms for decision making within the organization, publicly enunciating the values of the organization's leaders, reviewing objectives, and linking these with action—all elements of highly effective organizations. In other words, the planning process itself helps make the company a better organization.

ELEMENTS OF THE BUSINESS PLAN

There are many variations on the theme of what goes into a successful business plan.[11] However, all these variations have the same essential elements:

PRELIMINARY SECTIONS
    Cover page
    Table of contents
    Executive summary

1. Type of Business
2. Company summary
3. Management
4. Product/service and competition
5. Funds requested, collateral, use of proceeds*
6. Financial history, financial projections*
7. Deal structure, exit*

MAJOR SECTIONS
  I. Background and Purpose

    A. History
    B. Current situation
    C. The resource-based concept

  II. Objectives

    A. Short term
    B. Long term

---

*Required primarily when the business plan is used as an investment proposal.

III. Market Analysis

    A. Overall market

    B. Specific market

    C. Competitive factors

    D. Microenvironmental influences

IV. Development and Production

    A. Production processes

    B. Resource requirements

    C. Quality assurance

V. Marketing

    A. Overall concept and orientation

    B. Marketing strategy and resources

    C. Sales forecasts

VI. Financial Plans

    A. Financial statements

    B. Financial resources

    C. Financial strategy

VII. Organization and Management

    A. Key personnel resources

    B. Human resource management strategy

VIII. Ownership

    A. Form of business

    B. Equity positions

    C. Deal structure*

IX. Critical Risks and Contingencies

X. Summary and Conclusions

XI. Scheduling and Milestones

    Appendixes

Preliminary Sections

The business plan has three preliminary sections, each of which is important. It has been reported that, on average, the reader will spend less than 10 minutes evaluating the plan for a new venture.[12] To make the reader want to go on to the main body of the document and evaluate the details, these beginning sections must be both attractive and informative.

Cover Page   Every business plan should have a cover page that includes the following information:

- The company name, address, telephone and fax numbers, and e-mail address, if it is available. The easier it is for the reader to contact the entrepreneur, the more likely the contact will occur.

---

*Required primarily when the business plan is used as an investment proposal.

- The name and position of the contact person, who should be one of the firm's top executives. The person designated as the contact person should be prepared to answer questions about the plan.
- The date the business was established (simply "established 1995," for example), and the date of this particular version of the business plan ("February 1997," for example).
- The name of the organization from which funding (or credit, or a supplier agreement, etc.) is being sought. The full name, correctly spelled, should be used.
- The copy number of the plan (for example, "copy 2 of 7 copies"). There are two reasons for this entry. The first is security. The entrepreneur must know how many of the plans are in circulation and who has them. Eventually, all of them should be returned. The business plan contains information that is sensitive and strategic. Unscrupulous competitors could put the firm at a disadvantage if the plan were to fall into their hands. The second reason for limiting circulation is exclusivity. It is not good practice to have dozens of copies of the plan circulating in the financial community. Financiers like to consider opportunities that are not being concurrently considered by others. If the plan is overcirculated, it could acquire the negative reputation of being "shopworn."
- The company's **logo**. Every firm should have a logo. A logo is a design, picture, or ideograph chosen to represent the company. The association of the company name with a pictorial design gives the reader (and eventually the customer) two ways of remembering your company and its products. A new venture can employ clip art or the latest computer technology to design its own logo, using a graphics or drawing program from a personal computer. A large firm with a substantial budget can have an advertising agency and a commercial artist design its logo.

Table of Contents   The page following the cover page is the table of contents. The table should follow the format of the elements of the business plan. Each major section should be numbered and divided into subsections, using two common numbering methods. The first is the Harvard outline method, which uses Roman numerals for the main headings, capital letters for the major sections, Arabic numbers for subsections, and the [number.letter] format for even smaller subsections. The second method is the decimal format. Each major heading is numbered, starting at [1.0], and subsections that follow are numbered as [1.10], [1.11] . . . [2.0], [2.10], [2.20]. The executive summary and the appendixes do not receive this form of numbering. The executive summary precedes the numbering and, therefore, has no number; the appendix numbers are in Arabic preceded by "A" to indicate that they are appendixes (A.1, A.2, and so on).

If the plan has a significant number of tables, figures, drawings, and exhibits, a separate table can be prepared that lists these with their titles and page numbers. Any consistent and coherent method for organizing these may be used. However, because the purpose of the table of contents and the table of figures is to make it easier for the reader to extract pertinent information from the business plan, complicated and arcane systems of cataloging should be avoided.

Executive Summary   The executive summary is the most important part of the business plan because it is the first section of substance that the reader sees. Most readers of business plans, especially investors, never read beyond the summary. They have too many plans to read and too little time to read them all. Thus, if the summary is not convincing, the reader goes on to the next plan. It is estimated that only 10 percent of all business plans are read thoroughly, meaning that 90 percent are rejected after the summary.[13]

Although the summary is the first part of the business plan that is read, it should be the last part written. It should be one to three pages in length, with absolutely no padding or puffery. A sample summary for a hypothetical company is presented in Street Story 5-1.

The company name and contact person should appear as they do on the cover page. Suggestions and recommendations for preparing the other sections of the executive summary follow.[14]

Type of Business   About 10 words are all that are necessary to describe the firm's industry or sector. Because particular investors will not invest in some industries, it is better to be clear up front and save time for everyone.

Company Summary   This summary should be a thumbnail sketch of your firm's history and background, and it should emphasize the positive. Be brief. More than half a page (150 words) is not a summary. State what your primary product or service is, but do not complicate matters by listing product extensions or auxiliary services. Stress the uniqueness of your product or service. If it is not unique, why will it succeed?

Management   Although who you are matters most, you do not have to provide much detail in the management description. List the top two or three people and emphasize their industry experience.

Product/Service and Competition   Mention the competition to illustrate the niche that your firm occupies. Again, this description should occupy no more than half a page (150 words).

Funds Requested   Briefly state exactly how much money you need to raise. What is to be the investment vehicle: debt, equity, some hybrid? If you are flexible, state your preference and your willingness to consider alternatives. The investor may make a counterproposal, and the deal can be restructured.

Collateral   If you have offered a debt instrument, you should indicate whether collateral is available and what form it will take. If there is none, you should say so. The more collateral you have, the lower the interest rate and the less equity you may have to give up.

Use of Proceeds   The financial section in the main body of the business plan should be specific about the use of proceeds. Here you should simply indicate how the money will be used. Avoid overly broad terms like "pay expenses" and "increase working capital." More specific statements such as "pay salaries" and "build inventory" are preferred.

Financial History   In presenting the firm's financial history, show only these major categories: revenues, net income, assets, liabilities, and net worth. Figures for the last 2 or 3 years should be shown. Make sure that the figures presented in the history are exactly the same as those in the main body of the plan. If the venture is completely new and has no financial history, omit this section.

Financial Projections   Financial projections should follow the same format as the financial history. Three years are usually sufficient. Again, the figures must match those in the main body of the plan.

Sample of an Executive Summary

Company: Del Cano, Inc.
1313 Mockingbird Lane
Springfield, MO 54545
Tel: (555-555-5555)
Web site: www.delcano.com
Contact: Andrew Rockafellow

Type of Business: Del Cano, Inc., develops, manufactures, and distributes a line of natural ingredient salad dressings and marinades. Unique international and ethnic offerings such as Asian Vinaigrette, Japanese Sesame, Moroccan, and Indonesian Peanut will be packaged in distinctive ceramic-capped bottles, offering time-strapped consumers an innovative meal solution. The product will be sold through distributors to specialty food retailers and to national food chains, once a critical sales mass is achieved.

Management: Del Cano is led by Andrew Rockafellow who has 5 years of experience in the consumer foods industry and has an MBA. The rest of the team has over 20 years of experience in sales, marketing, finance, and operations, including specific experience in retail and natural foods. All have MBA degrees.

Product and Competition: The salad dressing and marinade category is mature, with a variety of national and local competitors. National companies include Kraft (Seven Seas), Unilever's Lipton (Wishbone), and Clorox (Hidden Valley Ranch). Del Cano Salad Dressing and Marinade's advantages are its unique upscale position, supported by innovative packaging, usage ideas, and promotions. Our international theme, which will be updated regularly to reflect changing consumer tastes, offers a unique position in the marketplace today.

Funds Requested: $500,000 in cash funding, preferably equity

Use of Proceeds: Start-up and operating expenses, including $250,000 for sales and marketing, and $250,000 for the purchase of computers and office equipment plus slotting fees in retail stores.

Financial Projections:	*($000) First Year*	*Second Year*	*Third Year*
Revenue	$584	$1,061	$1,867
Net Income	(272)	(95)	167
Assets	203	76	355
Liabilities	(75)	(107)	5
Net Worth	278	(183)	350

Exit: At the end of 5 years, our projected value for the business is $3.1 million. Given the initial equity of $277,000, this represents an IRR of 62 percent. If market conditions preclude an IPO, sale of the business to a large food company will be pursued.

Exit   Investors expect to make money by selling their interest in the business to somebody else or back to the entrepreneur. This section of the executive summary indicates how and when the investor is most likely to accomplish this. A number of possible methods for investor exit will be discussed in Chapter 8.

Deal Structure   If complex combinations of investment instruments are being used to raise money, you should list them. For example, the deal structure might be:

Bank loan	$2,000,000
Subordinated debenture	1,000,000
Preferred stock	750,000
Common stock	250,000
Total	$4,000,000

Major Sections

The main body of the business plan contains the strategic and operating details of the new venture. Some redundancy among the sections is inevitable because the business is an integrated system and necessarily is self-referencing. This is not inherently bad. Some redundancy helps to focus the reader's attention. Where possible, a reference such as, "See Section III, Market Analysis" is preferable to repeating verbatim a long segment of the market analysis.

Background and Purpose

This section functions as an introduction to provide the reader with the context for understanding the business and its opportunity. Although history is not destiny in business, it is important for the reader to be able to gauge how far the firm has come and to comprehend where it is now in the new venture creation process. Suggestions and recommendations for preparing this material follow.

History   Briefly describe the history of your venture and its product or service. This section is especially important if the firm is offering a unique product or service. It tells the potential investor that you are a "first mover."

Current Situation   Briefly describe what your product is, to whom it will be marketed, and the technology necessary to make and deliver the product. This is known as the **product/market/technology configuration** (P/M/T). The P/M/T is the most concise statement of what your business is. You will have ample opportunity to expand on this statement later in the business plan. If the product or service is so technical that a nonexpert might not understand it, create an exhibit or appendix with a photograph or a drawing of the product, list its technical specifications, or present any available test results.

The Resource-Based Concept   Briefly describe the key resources that contribute to the firm's success. Explain how the resources are translated into a product or service that is distinctive and has a competitive advantage. This is the first appearance of your strategy statement.

Objectives

Objectives are desired outcomes. The new venture has three broad objectives: creation, survival, and profitability. These objectives are relevant for all new ventures, although for firms with an operating history, of course, only survival and profitability are pertinent.

Objectives can be thought of in terms of their time frame and how they are measured. **Short-term objectives** are outcomes that can be achieved within 1 year. **Long-term objectives** are generally goals that require more than 1 year to achieve, often having a 3- to 5-year time frame.

The measurement of how well an objective has been achieved can be either quantitative or qualitative. **Quantitative measures** are stated as numbers, for example, return on sales, return on equity, or employee turnover. Quantitative measures usually signal the degree of the firm's **efficiency**. They tell how well the firm has deployed a given set of resources in terms of their output. For example, a quantitative objective that indicates efficiency is operating or gross margin, which shows cost of goods sold and direct labor charges as a percentage of sales. A high gross margin indicates an efficient ratio of cost to revenue, and a low gross margin indicates inefficiency.[15] Quantitative objectives tend to be concerned with operating issues and the short term.

Qualitative measures, on the other hand, resist reduction to numbers. For example, the objectives "to be a good corporate citizen" or "to have a reputation for integrity" or "to develop innovative products" are hard to quantify. Qualitative objectives are more concerned with the effectiveness of the new venture. **Effectiveness** is the extent to which the firm is able to maintain and expand its position in the competitive environment and in the macroenvironment. Qualitative objectives, therefore, tend to be concerned with external and environmental issues and with the long term. Table 5-1 lists possible objectives that a firm might have. The entrepreneur should try to make the firm's objectives both realistic and challenging and should ensure that they are consistent with the rest of the narrative and with the plan's financial projections.

TABLE 5-1 Specific Objectives			
	Measurement of Objectives		*Time Frame for Objectives*
Objective	*Efficiency*	*Quantitative*	*Short Term*
Sales	↑	↑	↑
Profitability			
Market share			
Market position			
Productivity			
Product/service quality			
Innovation			
Employee morale			
Management training and development			
Social concern and responsibility	↓	↓	↓
	Effectiveness	Qualitative	Long Term

Market Analysis

The market analysis section should convince the reader or investor that the entrepreneur understands the competitive environment and the macroenvironment in detail. The purpose of this section is to demonstrate that (1) the market for the product or service is substantial and growing and (2) the entrepreneur can achieve a defendable competitive position. Suggestions and recommendations for the market analysis follow.

Overall Market   Describe the overall market for the firm's industry, its current conditions, and its projections for sales, profits, rates of growth, and other trends. Who are the leading competitors and why have they been successful? Where is the market located and what is its scope (international, national, regional, local)? Potential investors prefer industries with the potential for large sales volumes and high growth rates, so they should be given the big picture.

Specific Market   Narrow the focus to the specific target market, segment, or niche in which your firm will operate. Describe the current and projected conditions and the leading competitors. Describe the firm's customers—their needs, wants, incomes, and profits. How are purchasing decisions made, and by whom? If a market survey has been conducted, present the analysis in an appendix. What conclusions can be drawn from it? Present best-case, likely case, and worst-case sales projections for the total market segment. Who are the five largest buyers? What percentage of the firm's sales is projected to come from these customers? What are the trends for your customers' profits and incomes? How will the firm continue to assess its customer base and update information on its customers?

Competitive Factors   In this extremely important section, you should describe and explain how each of the factors covered in Chapter 3 affects the firm's sales and profitability. Analyze both the competitive nature of the firm's industry and the industry's attractiveness. Analyze the power of the buyers, the suppliers, substitute products and services, the height of entry barriers, and the nature of the current rivalry. Demonstrate how your resource base and strategy address these factors. For your most important competitors, evaluate their positions as well. Compare your strengths and weaknesses to those of the market leaders. Provide a summary statement of your firm's competitive position.

Macroenvironmental Influences   This is another vital section. Demonstrate your knowledge and competence by evaluating the impact of the macroenvironmental factors described in Chapter 3. Analyze the political, economic, technological, socio-demographic, and ecological factors that affect your firm. Develop scenarios for best, most likely, and worst cases. Draw a conclusion about the risks that each of these factors poses for your firm's survival and profitability.

Development and Production

This section emphasizes and describes the most important elements relating to the research, development, and production of your firm's basic product or service.

Production Processes   Outline the stages in the development and production of your product or service, briefly commenting on each stage. Detail how time and money are allocated at each stage in the production process or service delivery system. Discuss the difficulties and risks encountered in each stage. Create a flowchart to illustrate how the core function is accomplished. Evaluate each stage for its subcontracting potential. Where you face make-or-buy decisions, explain your choice. What resource-based competencies provide the firm with advantages during the production process?

Resource Requirements   Analyze each type of resource employed in the production process. These resources were described in Chapter 2 and include financial, physical, human, technological, reputational, and organizational resources. Where in the production process does the venture possess resources that are valuable, rare, hard-to-copy, and nonsubstitutable? Present the cost/volume economics of the production process or service delivery system. Describe trends in the cost of resource procurement.

Quality Assurance   Discuss the quality dimensions (product, user, process, value) described in Chapter 1. What is the firm's perspective on quality? Specify how quality will be defined and measured for the firm's production process. Will the new venture employ the techniques and systems of total quality management?[16]

Marketing

This section describes the actual marketing strategy of the firm or new venture. This strategy must be consistent with the objectives stated earlier. The marketing section explains how the firm will exploit its resource base to create a total marketing focus. It also describes how the new venture "connects" with its customers.

Overall Concept and Orientation   Return to the description of the venture's concept in the background section. Give it a marketing focus by transforming it into a statement of customer orientation. What benefits and positive outcomes will the customer derive from interaction with your firm? Evaluate the resources that the firm or new venture has or is capable of controlling in terms of their potential to create high levels of customer awareness and satisfaction. This introduction demonstrates your commitment to the marketing effort. Street Story 5-2 describes two entrepreneurs whose marketing concepts involve appealing to future entrepreneurs who dream of developing their own marketing plan.

Marketing Strategy   Briefly restate a description of your primary product or service's P/M/T along with that of the firm's major competitors. How does your marketing strategy support your product's strengths? How will it exploit your competitors' weaknesses? Next, identify your target market and show evidence of market research. Why are you competing in this particular segment? Why and how does your product appeal to this segment? How does your marketing strategy communicate and activate this appeal?

Describe the image of the firm you wish to portray. Show how this image is consistent with your product or service. Why is it appealing from the customer's viewpoint? How will you communicate this image? Describe the packaging, branding, and labeling plans for the product. What advertising, promotional activities, and campaigns will you initiate? Are you prepared to use a combination of techniques and media to get your message to customers? Prepare a budget and break down the costs of reaching customers by medium (usually in dollars per 1,000 people reached). If advertising materials (for example, copy, storyboards, photographs) are already available, present them in an appendix.

Discuss your pricing strategy. How do your prices compare with those of the competition? Is your pricing strategy consistent with the image you are trying to project? Does it create value for customers? What is your profit margin per unit under various

It's All How You Play the Game

Does creating a business plan seem like nothing more than an elaborate game to you?

That's apparently how it appeared to Jean Marc Fety and Jean Chistophe Marquis. Their *Start-Up 2000* computer simulation game allows players to pretend they are the CEO of a fledgling high-tech company. Players can base their imaginary company in one of three areas—interactive game consoles, mobile videophones or Internet TV—and then build and market more than 3,000 different products within that company. As the computer game's guide explains, the experience is "designed to help you complete the steps necessary to become the 'virtual Jeff Bezos of the twenty-first century.'"

Start-Up 2000 challenges players to make win-or-lose decisions about product development, production, and distribution. Players juggle employee supervision, implement marketing strategies, and combat competitors along the way. The goal is to help players complete the right steps to build a sustainable business and then take it to a successful IPO, but it isn't easy. One Amazon customer reported that "This game has a great engine, but it is impossible to win."

The game's instructions explain what the marketing, accounting, R & D, and other departments do in a real company, and then players interact with these departments in their simulated company. Virtual "employees" are the tools that makes every game session unique. They share information about competitors and the marketplace with their CEO during the game via "e-mail." Make-believeCEOs can play against the game itself or challenge up to eight additional players by connecting on the Internet or LAN.

The cofounders claim to have been inspired by the many hours they spent playing video games when they were university students in the 1980s. They left jobs at Andersen Consulting and Credit Suisse First Boston in 1995 to found Monte Cristo Multimedia to produce strategy and management simulation games. Today their company employs over 50 people and produces games with titles like "Wall Street," "Day Trader," "Airline Tycoon," and "Political Tycoon." In addition to dramatic real-life scenarios, all the games feature colorful graphics and an impressive attention to detail.

Start-Up 2000 may allow CEO wannabes to bask in the computer-screen glow of a successful business plan, but as the *Success* magazine review noted, "This is not a sim game for simpletons."

Source: Adapted from Paul Gallagher, "Business and Pleasure in 'Start-Up 2000,'" *Success* online, February 28, 2000; available at www.successmagazine.com, www.montecristogames.com, and www.amazon.com.

pricing schemes? Discuss your credit policy. Is it consistent with purchasing patterns within the industry? What is the firm's warranty policy? How will you continue to serve the customer after sales? Discuss your plans to create ongoing relationships with buyers and to encourage repeat business.

Explain how your product will be distributed. Describe the geographic scope of your distribution effort. What are the channels of distribution, and where is the power within these channels? Who will do your selling? What are the costs of reaching your market by using various channels?

Sales Forecasts In the section on market analysis, you provided figures to indicate how many buyers there are for the firm's products, where they are located, and how purchasing decisions are made. In this section on marketing, describe your efforts and strategy to reach these customers, sell them your product, and serve them after the sale. The natural conclusion to these two sections is the sales forecast. The sales forecast is a function of three elements of market analysis: (1) the size of the market in units and dollars, (2) the fraction of that market that your firm will be able to capture as a result of its marketing effort and strategy (market penetration rate), and (3) the pricing strategy.

Present your sales forecasts in an exhibit or chart. Prepare the forecast in terms of units of products (or number of services delivered) as well as in dollars. Multiply the product units by the predicted average price. State the justification for this price. Use a 5-year time frame. Present three sets of forecasts: a best-case, most likely case, and a worst-case scenario. What are the causes that separate the best, most likely, and worst cases? A graph might be used to illustrate sales trends and growth.

Financial Plans

The sales forecasts form the bridge between the marketing section and the rest of the firm's financial plans. The sales forecasts mark the end of the marketing portion of the business plan and the beginning of the financial analysis portion; they represent the "top line." The purpose of the financial analysis section is to illustrate the "bottom line." Bankers and potential investors evaluate this section to see whether enough profits will be generated to make the venture an attractive investment. It will also serve as the financial plan for the executives in the firm. This section is numbers oriented. Give the audience what it needs: rows and columns of figures carefully labeled and footnoted.

Financial Statements If the firm has an operating history, summarize its past and current performance. Summarize past performance by calculating ratios that highlight its profitability, liquidity, leverage, and activity. Compare these ratios with the averages for your industry that you have collected from trade data.

If the firm is a new venture, you must present the following:

- *Projected profit and loss statements (income statements) for 5 years.* Prepare these monthly for the first year, quarterly for the next 2 years, and annually thereafter.
- *Projected cash flow statements and analysis.* Prepare these monthly for the first year and until the firm has positive cash flow, quarterly for the next 2 years, and annually thereafter.
- *Projected balance sheets for the ends of the first 3 to 5 years.*

Reference and discuss each of these statements, but place the actual statements in a financial appendix. If the statements and projections indicate seasonality and cyclicality, comment on this. Draw conclusions for the reader by stating what each statement means and what message the reader should take away.

Provide a break-even analysis for the business. If it is a service business, show how many hours of the service must be sold. If it is a product business, indicate how many units of the product must be sold to break even. Present a table of break-even points in the appendix.

Financial Resources   Discuss the start-up costs for the business. Prepare a detailed list of all the physical assets the firm needs to purchase or lease and a statement of organizational costs such as legal, architectural, and engineering. State how much money the business will need. If debt is being sought, what will you use for collateral? How will you repay the loan? Make sure the financial statements reflect this repayment. How will you use the money? Create a use-of-proceeds exhibit. Investors generally believe that initial proceeds that are expensed, such as research and development and training costs, are riskier than money spent on capital equipment, land, and buildings.

If you have established credit that you will not initially need, provide the details and the references. If the firm has receivables, provide a list and an aging statement. What are the probabilities of collecting these receivables? If you have existing debt, describe it. List delinquent accounts and their amounts. Describe any accounts payable the firm has and state how long these debts have been outstanding.

Financial Strategy   The firm's financial strategy consists of two components. The first comprises the sources and uses of funds. State your preferences for sources of new capital. Is it from continuing operations, new debt, or new equity? What combination is appropriate, and what debt/equity ratio and degree of financial leverage is the firm targeting? On the use side, what are the firm's priorities for using the excess cash generated by operations and by additional financing? Is expansion and growth the priority or are dividends? Both the managers of the firm and the investors will be guided by these strategic decisions.

The second component of financial strategy comprises the internal control and monitoring systems. What safeguards are being proposed to ensure the security of the funds generated by operations and by any additional borrowings or equity offerings? Describe any systems or procedures that help monitor and control cash disbursement. Briefly describe the firm's internal audit procedures. Who are the firm's external auditors?

Organization and Management

From beginning to end, the business plan is a document with a purpose. In the preliminary sections, the plan introduces the firm in a general way. In the main body of the plan, the firm reviews its objectives, its market, and the strategy for reaching its objectives. The financial portion indicates the funds that will be required to launch the venture and the size of sales, profits, and growth that are predicted. The question that recurs to the reader throughout is: "Why should I believe any of this?" The answer comes in the section on organization and management. This section describes the firm's people — the entrepreneurs and top management team — as well as the firm's technical, reputational, and human resources. Before proceeding to the next section on ownership, which presents the deal and actually makes the request for money, the reader will want to be assured that the people are of the highest quality. The saying goes, "Give us a B plan with an A team over an A plan with a B team . . . every time."

Key Personnel Resources   Provide an organization chart with the names and titles of the key executives. Provide brief synopses of these individuals' previous experience, education, and related qualifications. The complete resumes of top managers and key executives may be placed in an appendix. State whether these people have worked together before and in what capacity.

What are these individuals' contributions to the company? Specify who will do what and why they were chosen for that role. What contractual relationships exist between the company and its principals, and between the principals? Are there employment contracts, severance packages, or noncompete agreements?

Describe the initial salaries, incentives, bonuses, pensions, and fringe benefits of the top people. Attempts should be made to keep initial salaries low to conserve cash and to keep deferred compensation (stock options and the like) high to produce long-term commitment. What key positions remain unfilled? Give the job descriptions of these positions and indicate the unique skills, abilities, and experience you will be needing. Describe your plans to continue to attract, develop, and retain the firm's key personnel. Without such plans, growth will be inhibited by people problems.

List the members of the firm's board of directors; include their ages, their relevant experience, their other corporate affiliations, and their connection with your firm. Also provide the names of the legal, accounting, banking, and other pertinent organizations (marketing or advertising agencies, consulting firms, and the like) that will guide the firm. How will these people assist the firm?

Human Resource Management Strategy   State the firm's basic philosophy concerning human resources and management. Does it favor close supervision or general supervision? Is unionization expected? What is the firm's approach to collective bargaining? Describe its strategy for employee compensation, profit sharing, and employee ownership. What is the rationale for such programs? How will the firm manage and control health-care and insurance costs? What are its strategies for employee and management development and training, for continuing education, and for hiring and promoting from within? What factors dictate criteria for promotion? How will performance be assessed?

How many employees does the firm currently have, or how many will be required to start the new venture? What are these employees' responsibilities, positions, and job descriptions? What percentages are skilled and unskilled? A pertinent analysis of the relevant labor markets by type of skill and geographic scope is required.

What equal opportunity employment regulations and other government requirements affect the firm and its work force? What strategies are in place to fulfill the firm's legal and regulatory obligations?

Ownership

In this section, the founders describe the legal form of the business, the contractual obligations of the owners to the firm and to each other, and, if the business plan is a proposal for financing, the nature of the deal. Note that only after the reader has become familiar with the experience, reputation, and character of the entrepreneurial team is it appropriate to ask for money.

Form of Business   Describe the legal form of the business—sole proprietorship, partnership, regular corporation, subchapter S corporation—and briefly explain why this is the best form for your firm (see Chapter 8). Discuss any special aspects of the ownership structure, for example, subsidiaries, holding companies, or cross-ownership agreements. If the firm is organized as a partnership, list the essentials of the partnership agreement, and include the actual agreement as an appendix.

Equity Positions   Prepare an exhibit to show the amounts that you and the other founders and executives of the company have invested in the business or will be investing in the near future. Also show the equity positions that these investments represent. Prepare another exhibit to show any rights to warrants and stock options, and indicate their nature (exercise price, expiration date). What proportion of equity would be controlled if these were exercised? If shares are held in beneficial trust, note this. Recent changes in the ownership of the firm should also be noted and explained. What percentage of stock is owned by the employees? (See Chapter 8.)

   If these investments are debt, specify for each the coupon, maturity, and any special covenants in the loan agreement. What is the priority (seniority) of repayment?

Deal Structure   Briefly describe the financing required to start up the business or to fund the development or expansion of current business activities (see Chapter 8). A 3- to 5-year time horizon for financial plans is appropriate. Is the preference for new debt or new equity? What are the potential sources for these funds? For what purposes will the money be used? For equity financing, how much of the company are you willing to offer for the stock? Present a structured deal,[17] including the following information:

1. The number of shares of stock available for the offering, and the percentage of total ownership that this represents
2. The price per share of each unit[18]
3. The revised number of shares and each founder's percentage ownership after the proposed financing is completed
4. The effect of dilution on new investors' shares[19]
5. The potential returns per share to the investor. These need to be consistent with the previously reported financial plans. Avoid projecting something here that has not been presented and validated earlier in the plan.

Critical Risks and Contingencies

   In this section, the new venture, following the rules of full disclosure, reveals all material and relevant information that a prudent investor needs before investing in the business. The nature of this information is inherently negative; the section lists every reason why someone would not want to consider an investment in the new venture. Having fully revealed this information, the entrepreneurs have performed their legal and moral obligation to be forthcoming and honest about the firm's prospects. Should the investors lose their investment, full disclosure may be a defense against claims of civil liability and criminal fraud. This section typically includes the following categories of information and the potential impact of each on the new venture:

1. Failure to produce the products and services promised
2. Failure to meet production deadlines or sales forecasts
3. Problems with suppliers and distributors

4. Unforeseen industry trends
5. Unforeseen events in the political, economic, social, technological, and ecological environments
6. Failure to survive retaliation by competitors with significantly more resources
7. The problems of unproven and inexperienced management
8. The problems of unproven and undeveloped technology
9. Difficulties in raising additional financing
10. Other issues specific to the firm in question

E-NOTES 5-2

Business Plan Body

The major section or body of a business plan details the new venture's:

- background and purpose
- objectives
- market analysis
- development and production
- marketing
- financial plans
- organization and management
- ownership
- risks and contingencies

Concluding Sections

There are still a few loose ends and details to report on in the concluding sections.

Summary and Conclusions

Briefly summarize the highlights and key features of your report. The most important elements to include are the firm's overall strategic direction, the reasons for believing the firm will be a success, a brief description of how the firm will be able to exploit its unique resources to advantage, the firm's sales and profit projections, its capital requirements, and the percentage ownership for the founders and for investors.

Because this is a summary, no new information should be reported here. You may even use the exact words you used in the earlier sections. Redundancy will reinforce your message and demonstrate that you are being consistent throughout the plan.

Scheduling and Milestones

The business plan outlines a number of actions that will be taken in the future. These actions are discussed in many different sections of the plan. To consolidate the timing of events, you should prepare a schedule, in chart form, of all of the important milestones that the firm expects to reach in the near and intermediate term. This helps the investor know when the firm will be needing additional capital infusions and allows the investor to track the firm's progress. Include the expected calendar dates for the following events that apply to the firm:

1. Seeking legal counsel and accounting services
2. Filing the documents necessary to set up the desired legal form of business, and completing licensing requirements
3. Completion of research and development efforts
4. Completion of a working prototype
5. Purchase or lease of production facilities, office and retail space
6. Selection of personnel: management, skilled, semiskilled
7. Ordering supplies, production materials, inventory
8. Beginning production
9. First order, sales, and payments
10. Other critical dates and events

Although it is usually desirable to speed up the timing of the new venture's launch, preparations will more likely take longer than expected. This is particularly true when the firm depends on some other organization or set of individuals for action before it can move on to the next scheduled task. Slack should be built into the schedule whenever possible.

Appendixes

Throughout our discussion of the elements of the business plan, we have suggested items, exhibits, and documentation that belong in an appendix. The business plan will usually have a number of appendixes. A partial list of possible appendix sections is shown below.[20]

1. A photograph or a drawing of your product (if appropriate) including title and labels if necessary. If the product or process is highly technical, and it is believed that investors will have the technical section reviewed by a consulting engineer, the entire technical section should be under separate cover.
2. A photograph or drawing of your intended location and physical layout (if appropriate), annotated if necessary
3. Sales and profitability forecasts in chart form
4. Market surveys and documentation of size and nature of market
5. Sample advertisements, brochures, and telemarketing protocols
6. Sample press releases
7. Price lists, catalogues, and mailing lists (just titles)
8. All detailed and footnoted financial statements, including income statements, cash flow statements, balance sheets, break-even calculations, and table of start-up costs
9. Fixed-asset acquisition schedule
10. Individual and corporate tax returns
11. Resumes of founders, board members, and key individuals
12. Letters of recommendation or character references from notable people
13. Any additional information deemed appropriate

CRITIQUING THE PLAN: QUESTIONS LIKELY TO BE ASKED

Although the entrepreneur has attempted in writing the business plan to answer all questions that might be raised, readers can still find problems. Professionals, like investors, will continue to ask questions and critique the proposal as they read it, and they need additional information when they meet the entrepreneur in person. It will be impossible to answer all the questions raised by the plan, or even anticipate what they may be. However, readers will have four major concerns, and the entrepreneur will have to address these in detail.[21]

Management

Repeatedly, entrepreneurs and the top management teams will be asked, "Who are you?" The reader must find a way to assess the entrepreneur's honesty. Although the business plan has been read and analyzed, no written document can answer doubts about the character and integrity of the entrepreneur. The entrepreneur's background will be researched and inconsistencies must be dealt with. (Everyone has inconsistencies in his or her background. No one is perfect. Even presidential candidates who have lived most of their lives in the public spotlight must refute these inconsistencies.)

If there is any doubt about the character of the entrepreneur, the financing will fall through. Entrepreneurs must be prepared to present their professional history, answer questions about their motivation, and discuss what they believe they can achieve.

Some entrepreneurs have been preparing for their new venture all their lives, and their previous careers are perfect matches for their intended new business. Student entrepreneurs sometimes have a chance to practice defending their management teams and other business plan issues before seasoned entrepreneurs, as Street Story 5-3 explains.

Resources

Investors are continually reviewing proposals for financing, and one way of differentiating between businesses with high potential and all others is careful scrutiny of the resource base of the firm. What rare, valuable, hard to copy, and nonsubstitutable resources does the firm have, can it control, or will it produce? Uniqueness is crucial. Also, the firm will need to demonstrate how it will keep the profits and rents generated by these resources. The entrepreneur should be prepared for dozens of "what if" questions that describe scenarios in which the resource-based strategy of the firm is attacked or undermined.

Projections and Returns

The firm's top management team will be asked to justify the assumptions underlying the sales forecasts, the cost estimates, the administrative costs, and the net profit figures. Because the entrepreneurial team will be required to defend these numbers, the data should have a concrete foundation in reality. At the same time, however, the projections need to be optimistic enough to indicate a solid return for the investors. This is a basic conflict in many new ventures, and inconsistencies will be examined thoroughly.

Your Plan Could Be a Winner

For some entrepreneurs, the first real-world screening of their completed business plan is not in a banker's office or room full of potential investors. More than 50 business plan competitions, hosted each year by American universities including Harvard, Massachusetts Institute of Technology, and Indiana University, give students an opportunity to present their ideas before a panel of judges that may include venture capitalists, business executives, accountants, marketing representatives, and other experts.

These competitions can be an important dress rehearsal. Potential entrepreneurs "stand a better chance of doing something special by going through a competition that teaches students how to present a plan and exposes them to the types of questions investors will be asking," according to Alex De Noble, professor of management and entrepreneurship at San Diego State and director of their annual competition. "Also, there is so much opportunity for networking."

Business professors credit these competitions as the incubators for many successful start-ups. They can be a virtual gold mine for students, too. Some competitions offer prize money; MIT awards $50,000 each year. Many fledgling entrepreneurs report that they have recruited mentors, advisors, board members, and even seed money after appearing at these events. All the competitors agree that they gain valuable PR. "It's a lot easier getting your foot in the door," notes Mike Cassidy, "if you can say you've won." Cassidy should know. He won the MIT competition while he was a student at Harvard Business School and later sold the Stylus Innovation software company he developed from that winning business plan for $13 million.

Although these competitions attract the cream of student business plans, they also echo with the same familiar criticisms. Michael Warshaw, a senior editor at *Inc.* magazine, reported on his experience as a division judge at the 15th annual Moot Corp. business plan competition at the University of Texas at Austin. Two of the five teams he and his fellow judges reviewed were eliminated for management issues (one for a failure to present enough details in the plan and the other for a language barrier that made the presentation difficult to understand); two other teams were eliminated for resource problems (a raw material that was falling in value and a product that was not unique). The judges even criticized the business plan of the team they selected as division winner for its indefensible numbers in financial projections and returns. That plan finished third in the overall competition. Warshaw reports that all the judges were "focused on the same basics: return on investment, product, management team, and whether the numbers make sense."

Warshaw reports that the teams who do not make it to the final round of the competition also chant a familiar refrain. Many of them refuse to acknowledge there could be a problem with their business plan. Instead, they claim they didn't win because "The judges just didn't get it."

Source: Adapted from Marc Ballon, "Upstarts: University Tournaments," *Inc.* online, December 1, 1998, and Michael Warshaw, "The Best Business Plan on the Planet," *Inc.* online, August 1, 1999. Information available at http://50k.mit.edu, www.moootcorp.org, www.bus.utexas.edu, and www.inc.com.

Exit

Investors need to know how and when they will recoup their money. Investors can exit by means of many alternative mechanisms, and, in any case, the exit will take place in the future after many other uncertain and risky activities. Thus, the exit is fraught with peril. However, this will not restrain investors from trying to pin down the exact details of the proposed exit. It is only natural for them to be concerned about their money, and the entrepreneur should expect the reader to pose many "what if" scenarios.

The overall evaluation of the plan may rest on the quality of the management team and the current status of the product or service. A useful tool to check the ranking an entrepreneur might receive is the Rich-Gumpert Evaluation System (Figure 5-1). The most desirable situation is the "4/4" firms.

FIGURE 5-1   Rich-Gumpert Evaluation System

Most Desirable ⟶

Product Service Level				
Level 4 Product/service fully developed. Many satisfied users. Market established.	4/1	4/2	4/3	4/4
Level 3 Product/service fully developed. Few (or no) users as yet. Market assumed.	3/1	3/2	3/3	3/4
Level 2 Product/service pilot operable. Not yet developed for production. Market assumed	2/1	2/2	2/3	2/4
Level 1 A product or service idea, but not yet operable. Market assumed.	1/1	1/2	1/3	1/4
	Level 1 A single, would-be entrepreneur.	Level 2 Two founders. Additional slots, personnel not identified.	Level 3 Partly staffed management team. Absent members identified, to join when firm is funded.	Level 4 Fully staffed, experienced management team.

More Desirable ⟶

Management Status

Source: From *Business Plans That Win $$$* by David Gumpert and Stanley Rich. Copyright © by David Gumpert and Stanley Rich. Published by permission of Sterling Lord Literistic, Inc.

E-NOTES 5-3

Key Business Plan Questions

- management: who are you?
- resources: are yours rare, valuable, hard-to-copy, and nonsubstitutable?
- projections: can they be justified?
- exit: how will investors recoup this money?

FORMAT AND PRESENTATION

The format of the business plan and its physical presentation make the first impression on the reader. Deliberate care and attention are needed in preparing the plan to make this impression a positive one.

Physical Appearance

Ideally the physical appearance of the plan is neither too fancy nor too plain. An extremely ornate binding and cover indicate a disregard for expense and a preoccupation with appearance over substance. Too plain an appearance may suggest a lack of respect for the reader and, ironically, not enough care for appearances. Rich and Gumpert recommend a plastic spiral binding and a pair of cover sheets of a single color.[22] They believe a stapled compilation of photocopied material will not be treated seriously.

The recommended length of the business plan is usually between 40 and 50 pages, plus appendixes. Because the appendixes and supporting documentation can be as long or longer than the plan itself, it is not unusual to bind these supplements separately.

The pages of the plan should be crisp and clean, with wide margins and easy-to-read type. Graphs and photographs should be of high quality, and all charts and exhibits should be labeled and referenced within the body of the plan.

Writing and Editing

It is extremely important that the plan be well written and edited. Irrelevant information and self-adulation should be excised, and length for its own sake should be avoided.[23] Bad writing will kill a plan, and yet it is not recommended that the writing be jobbed out. It is up to the entrepreneur and the new venture's executives and advisers to write the plan together. A basic guideline for writing a business plan or any kind of business assignment would include:

Prewriting

Begin by writing down your information and thoughts in an outline or organized way to find out what you know and need to know. At this stage, you should also think about the audience for your writing and arrange the material in a way that will suit the purpose of your piece and express your motivation.

Writing and Rewriting/Revising

Ideally every writer should be able to transform their outline into a fully articulated rough draft and then revise that initial piece for form, coherence, and style. Personal computers have made this process much easier. Clear and concise writing is always a goal, but don't get bogged down in the rewriting and revising part of the process. The best way to prepare for situations where you must write under a deadline is to practice writing every day.

Editing

Editing should be the last thing you do with any piece of writing. Make use of all the tools available today, including the computer's spell checker and thesaurus. The word-processing software on your computer may also include a grammar checker. If you have time, have a colleague or friend read and critique your writing piece before you review for a final time. Entrepreneurs should make sure that the plan says what they want it to say. Despite the availability of numerous published guides for writing business plans and general agreement on what the content should be, entrepreneurs continue to submit poorly written plans.[24] One researcher reviewed 20 business plans that were submitted to venture capitalists and found that:[25]

- Thirty percent failed to include a specific business strategy.
- Forty percent of the teams lacked marketing experience, and the marketing sections of the plan were most weakly developed.
- Fifty-five percent failed to discuss technical idea protection.
- Seventy-five percent failed to identify the details of the competition.
- Ten percent had no financial projections at all; another 15 percent omitted balance sheets; and 80 percent failed to provide adequate details of the financial projections.
- The more plan deficiencies, the lower the odds of gaining support from venture capitalists.

The complete business plan for Del Cano Inc., is presented as an appendix to this chapter.

Summary

Every new venture must have a business plan. The advantages of writing a business plan far outweigh the costs. The purpose of the plan is to enable the top executives of the established firm or new venture to think about their business in a comprehensive way, to communicate their objectives to individuals who may have a stake in the firm's future, to have a basis for making decisions, and to facilitate the planning process.

The essential elements of the plan are generally recognized. The preliminary sections set the stage for the reader. Make the first impression professional, concise, and informative because the reader may spend only a few minutes reviewing each plan. The major sections of the business plan describe the new venture's strategy, operations, marketing, management, financial plan, and ownership structure. These sections need to be as detailed as possible and internally consistent. The concluding sections provide details on timing, schedules and milestones, and a summary. The appendix contains reference material for documentation.

Each plan must be well written and organized, and it must anticipate the many questions that the reader will have about the business. No plan, however, can answer all questions that may arise. It is important, therefore, that entrepreneurs be familiar with all the details so they can respond to potential unanswered questions and critiques.

Key Terms

- Business plan
- Effectiveness
- Efficiency
- Logo

- Long-term objectives
- Objectives
- Product/market/technology configuration

- Qualitative measures
- Quantitative measures
- Short-term objectives

Discussion Questions

1. Discuss the costs and benefits of writing a business plan.
2. Who should write a business plan? Who should not bother? Who must write a business plan?
3. Why are the preliminary sections so important?
4. What information should be conveyed in the executive summary?
5. Distinguish between short-term and long-term objectives. Between quantitative and qualitative objectives. Between efficiency and effectiveness. Give examples.
6. How is the market analysis section linked to the marketing section?
7. How is the marketing section linked to the financial sections?
8. How are the financial sections linked to the management organization sections?
9. How are the management and organization sections linked to the deal structure and ownership sections?
10. What questions are likely to be asked by investors reading your business plan? Why are these concerns important to the investor?
11. Discuss the benefits of careful presentation and effective writing style.

Exercises

1. Draft an outline of your (or your team's) business plan.
   a. What information do you already possess? Write it in draft form.
   b. What information is still required? Prepare a plan to obtain this information.
2. Prepare as much of the executive summary of your business plan as you can. Be concise but informative. Follow the model given in the chapter.
3. Critique a business plan. Examples can be found in the case section of this book, the appendix to this chapter, or may be provided by your instructor.
   a. How well does the business plan address the key issues?
   b. What changes and improvements would you make to the plan?
   c. How well done is the presentation and writing? How has this influenced your impression?
   d. Would you be interested in investing in this business? Why or why not?

<DISCUSSION CASE>

Just Like a Real Business

A. Robert Moog says all he wanted was to "learn how to run a bigger business by first doing this *little* business." Fred Gratzon says his plan was "to do this business to support my family while I decided what to do with the rest of my life." Rick Shangraw says he was only going to work at his business until he could accept a college faculty job and make some *real* money. But today the stop-gap companies these entrepreneurs founded are established stars on *Inc.* magazine's list of the top 500 growth companies.

According to a survey done by the magazine, 10 percent of these company founders reported that mere survival was their initial business goal. A total of one-third of them said that they never hoped for fast growth, believing instead that their company would stay small or grow slowly. *Inc.* conducted a special survey of those 175 "Cinderella" fast growth companies and found that more than half of them thought they lacked the capital needed to place their start-up on the fast track. Almost as many (44 percent) wanted to limit growth as a means of keeping control. Some reported that they were fearful or cautious about fast growth (32 percent), or just didn't think that fast growth could happen in their situation (23 percent). Other founders said they underestimated the market demand (20 percent) or the economic conditions (20 percent), that they thought they lacked the business know-how to be truly successful (18 percent), or that they never intended to work hard enough to achieve fast growth (6 percent).

For A. Robert Moog, cofounder of University Games in Burlingame, California, fast growth was simply unintentional. After graduating from Stanford Graduate School of Business, Moog and a partner formed this company to produce a game called "Murder Mystery Party." Their plan was to sell the company after 3 years to provide seed money for a more ambitious venture, but their ambitions were met when the game became a national best-seller overnight. University Games now grosses $30 million a year, and ranks 494 on the *Inc.* 1996 list.

Fred Gratzon was broke and out of work when he started Telegroup, Inc., a discount long-distance phone service provider. Six years later, the Fairfield, Iowa, company has $210 million in annual revenues and ranks 151 on the *Inc.* list. The company's success has been a big surprise to Gratzon, who says that his whole idea for the new venture was accidental. He was inspired when he was trying to figure out a way to reduce his own phone bills, and he started investigating the package deals then being offered by AT&T.

Fifty-two percent of the Cinderella company founders responding to the *Inc.* survey said that their company has turned out "not even close" to what they expected. For many of them, success was a personal affirmation. Rick Shangraw had been fired from his consulting firm job when he pooled the resources of four credit cards to start Project Performance Corp., the environmental management firm that ranks 272 on the *Inc.* list. His

(continued)

(continued)

Sterling, Virginia, start-up went from a one-man show to a company with eight employees almost immediately. "Within 6 months it became clear that there was a market, that there were clients, and that I had the ability to build something."

Shangraw's experience echoes the stories of many of the entrepreneurs surveyed. Forty percent traced their motivation to start their business to a desire to be their own boss. Twenty-three percent said they wanted to prove that they could do it. Twelve percent reported they went into business so they could leave a job or recover from being fired. Only 17 percent claimed that their primary reason was to make a lot of money.

Not surprisingly, 41 percent of the top growers report that their initial financial projections were "understated." More than one-quarter said they didn't even have spreadsheets when they began. Thirteen percent said they were unprepared for fast growth when it occurred, and two-thirds said they were just starting to gear up when growth took off.

Most fast trackers said what they needed most when growth exploded was more employees (33 percent). Others said they needed more money (27 percent) or a better operating structure and internal procedures (21 percent). Even though their growth wasn't planned, only 10 percent said they need more experienced management. On the other hand, more than half of them reported that their personal lives have become "more complicated" since their company began to experience unanticipated fast growth.

Whether they planned for fast growth or not, many of these entrepreneurs have obviously enjoyed the surprise of success. Daniel W. Hunt started his Asphalt Specialties in Henderson, Colorado, with a five-man crew and a dream of putting away enough money to retire in comfort. Two years later, his company had 50 employees, annual sales of $8 million, and was 367 on the *Inc.* top growth list.

Hunt can recall the moment when he was out on a job, and he realized that he was surrounded by his machinery and his employees working on his project, and he suddenly thought, "This is just like a real company!"

CASE QUESTIONS

1. Why do some entrepreneurs want their companies to grow slowly or not at all?
2. Why do many new ventures grow despite the entrepreneurs' lack of planning?
3. Why are there so many false assumptions about growing the business?
4. What is the relationship between growth and resources?

Source: Adapted from Robert A. Mamis, "Growth Happens," *Inc.,* March 1997, pp. 68–74.

Appendix 5A

The Del Cano, Inc., Business Plan

I. BACKGROUND AND PURPOSE

History   The concept of using dressings, sauces, and marinades to flavor food has existed for many years. In this century, the proliferation of packaged consumer goods has provided consumers with an array of choices. Today, choices exist for a broad variety of tastes and preferences.

Our new venture seeks to identify and develop a market that we believe is underserved. The market is for dressings and marinades from international cuisines such as Japanese, Moroccan, and Thai. As people are exposed to these cuisines through ethnic restaurants, travel, and the media, they become interested in preparing these foods at home. This is the market in which will we operate.

Over the past several years, social and economic changes have brought about a tremendous shift in the way people prepare meals and eat both in and outside the home. Just 30 years ago, most meals, particularly dinners, were prepared in the home by using fresh ingredients and recipes that were passed from parents to children.

Several trends contributed to the decline of this tradition. First, many women work full-time outside the home. They simply don't have time to prepare complex meals in the evening. Second, as the children of these families reach adulthood, many have never developed basic cooking skills that for many years were learned as children at home. Third, the availability of alternatives, from restaurants, to prepared foods at the grocery store, to frozen meals, has created viable alternatives to the traditional meal.

These alternatives are attractive to many consumers much of the time. However, we believe a market exists (and our data support this belief) for a line of high-quality, natural dressings and marinades, representing cuisines from around the world that allow consumers to prepare delicious meals at home. The benefits of the product include:

- The simplicity it brings to meal preparation, from selecting the ingredients at the grocery store to setting them on the dinner table (we have created a meal solution, not just a product.)
- The variety it provides in terms of flavors and ingredients, from basic vinaigrette dressings to sophisticated marinades such as Moroccan and Japanese Sesame
- The pleasure it brings to people who are not accustomed to cooking at home, who can now prepare delicious meals for themselves, their family, and their friends
- The excitement and romance associated with trying something new and different, especially if it evokes memories of travel or a special dinner at a favorite restaurant
- The positive health effects from eating a freshly prepared meal with less fat and sodium than most prepared foods, especially when accompanied by vegetable or other low-fat side dishes

Current Situation

The Product   Del Cano Salad Dressing and Marinade is a ready-to-use bottled product that will initially be available in six to eight varieties. It can be used as a dressing for salads (such as lettuce, beans, or chicken) or as a marinade for meat and vegetables. Three attributes will provide consumer benefits that make this product truly unique:

- First, it is positioned not as a dressing that can also be used as a marinade, but as a meal starter with clear instructions on a variety of uses. Del Cano has done the preparation—now you simply finish the journey! The bottle will include an attractive card attached to the neck of the bottle with recipes and shopping lists for two or three dishes. This way, the entire meal can be visualized, understood, and planned in one step. We will make cooking easy for novices!
- Second, it will be presented in nontraditional, porcelain-capped bottles that are attractive on the shelf, functional as resealable containers, and fun to use as storage bottles when the product is gone. The package will make a statement about the buyer, reflecting sophisticated international tastes, a sense of adventure, and a willingness to try new things in the kitchen.
- Third, it will help people to connect with the very basic human need to create. Cooking has long been a pleasurable experience for many people, but there have been very few innovations that simplify fresh meal preparation. Most nonrestaurant-prepared foods are either frozen or prepared in-store. This product will promote cooking as an activity in itself, a pleasurable experience to be enjoyed with friends, where the results can be shared and enjoyed in your own home.

The Market   The primary target for this product will be young adults who are not accustomed to preparing meals at home and young families looking for an exciting alternative to traditional dishes. It will initially be available in specialty stores via food brokers and other distributors, with expansion into national grocery stores as soon as sales data enable us to obtain shelf space.

The central element in our marketing strategy is the positioning of Del Cano Salad Dressing and Marinade. In any specialty or national grocery chain, there is a section for prepared foods, which includes bottled marinades, and a section for condiments, which includes bottled salad dressings. Our product will be placed with the salad dressings for three specific reasons:

1. *Merchandising.* It is a high-traffic area, and it is easier to link use as a marinade to salad dressings than use as salad dressing to marinades. Our research indicates that salad ingredients are among the most frequently purchased items at the grocery store. Our goal is to take a segment of these buyers and get them to try our product.
2. *Convenience.* Infrequent and time-conscious cooks are more likely to explore the dressing than the marinade aisle. Because this is our target consumer, we want to be located where we will be seen.
3. *Uniqueness.* Our distinctive packaging will stand out in this aisle. The prepared-food aisle already has bottles of all shapes, cans, boxes, and a general sense of clutter. We want to rise above this and be seen as distinctive and sophisticated.

The Technology   We will outsource our manufacturing and packaging to a contractor. The role of our company will be to identify profitable product and market opportunities, develop business and operating plans that allow us to capitalize on these opportunities, and, through successful execution of these activities, build equity in the brand.

Resources

Financial   The founding partners will provide some of the equity, with the balance provided by venture capital investors.

Physical Rented facilities will include administrative offices and a test kitchen used for product development and quality assurance testing. We will outsource manufacturing.

Human Our team has experience in each of the primary functional areas required for this business, including marketing, sales, finance, operations, and information technology.

Technological The technology resources will be the recipes we create, which will be formulated in our own kitchens as we receive customer feedback through our Web site and other primary research. Recipes will be secret and protected by any employees with access to them, ensuring they remain within the firm.

Reputational Our reputational resources will be the brand identity we develop. This identity is composed of our distinctive logo, packaging, any trademarks we acquire, and the skill of our management team. Our message to consumers is that they can prepare delicious meals easily and enjoy healthful alternatives to frozen, prepared, and restaurant foods.

Organizational Del Cano creates value by developing a product, facilitating its manufacture, getting it into the hands of consumers through distributors and retailers, and even educating consumers in its use through packaging and marketing communications strategy.

II. OBJECTIVES

Short Term The near-term objective of Del Cano, Inc., is to gain acceptance in the natural and specialty food industry, with plans to enter the conventional grocery market in the long term. We will market our product to the natural foods market, working with food brokers and distributors. Initially, we will launch our product in the Midwest, targeting midsize to large-size cities including Cincinnati, Minneapolis, Columbus (Ohio), Indianapolis, and Chicago. We will educate the sales representatives of the superior quality and benefits of our products through trade shows, personal selling, and demonstrations.

Long Term Our long-term objectives are to gain commercial acceptance in the mass market. After 4 years in the natural foods market, reaching anticipated sales at $3.73 million, our products' proven sales record will increase the likelihood of gaining acceptance in national grocery chains. To enable this, we must gain distribution into national grocery chains, such as Kroger's, Dominick's, and Star Market.

III. MARKET ANALYSIS

Overall Market

Supermarket sales of pourable salad dressing totaled approximately $1.4 billion in 1996, up 6 percent over the year before, according to Information Resources, Inc., statistics. Despite the fact that many view it as a mature category, there is still growth potential in salad dressings, marketers say. In fact, the boom in sales of prepared salad mixes has been a major boom to salad dressing sales. Besides, trends toward healthier eating have endorsed the consumption of salads, which has had a direct impact on the dressing category.

The market leaders include:

- Kraft, with a 39.3 percent share of the total pourable salad dressings market, has a handful of brands including regular Kraft, Kraft Free, and Seven Seas
- Unilever's Thomas J. Lipton Co. (17.7 percent), with Wishbone,
- Clorox Co. (15.1 percent), with Hidden Valley Ranch

Last year saw a new entrant in the pourable salad dressings market: CPC has launched a line of Hellmann's and Best Foods pourable salad dressings in the United States, with the Hellmann's brand being used in the eastern United States and the Best Foods brand in the west. Although this new entry is likely to change the competitive pattern, especially in terms of market leadership, Del Cano's strategy is differentiated enough to appeal to consumers.

Private-label brands (about 5 percent in dollars and the same in units), many of them upscale lines or enhanced products, are also getting a lot of attention these days. In the 52 weeks ended January 29, 1996, dollar sales of private-label dressings shot up 16.6 percent, a rate three times better than the category itself, according to Information Resources, Inc., Chicago.

Specific Market

Major players in the pourable salad dressings category are finding it pays to segment the business into three distinct product niches: regular, light or reduced calorie, and fat free. Fat-free dressings are currently providing better than 60 percent of the category's sales. As in many other product categories, "fat free" is a major consumer hot button for salad dressings, marketers report. Kraft sells close to 50 percent of fat-free, reduced-fat pourable dressings. Del Cano will serve two of these categories: the regular and the fat free. We will not provide reduced-calorie dressings, because they generally contain chemical additives to achieve the texture of the regular dressings.

The growth of fat-free dressings can be attributed to consumers' healthier eating habits. More people are buying fat-free products, especially with the growth of bagged salads. Organic food sales have been growing 20 percent to 25 percent a year since 1990—versus 3 percent to 5 percent for the food industry overall. In contrast to the organic shopper of 20 years ago, today's typi-cal organic consumers are urban, affluent, educated, and very health conscious. They are looking for nutritious, wholesome, pure foods, spending 20 percent more than the average shopper. The existence of this segment highlights the premium people are willing to pay for quality, natural ingredient products. Consequently, we are planning a line extension into this area in the future.

In addition to the trend toward low-fat and fat-free products, there is also a trend toward more highly seasoned products and more exotic and ethnic offerings. Del Cano is responding to these trends by offering exotic flavors.

The new introductions to salad dressings are thus low- and no-fat, organic, all-natural, and gourmet-oriented. Many small companies try to establish themselves in these niches. Thus, prepackaged salads, the continuing influx of fat-free products, and the introduction of upscale, regional brands are helping to keep things flowing in the $1 billion-plus salad dressing category.

Competitive Factors

A comprehensive analytical tool for determining the attractiveness of the industry is Porter's model of competitive industry analysis.

The Bargaining Power of Buyers

Because there are numerous salad dressings available in the market, the buyer has power. If buyers have the choice, they naturally look for a reason to buy from a particular seller, and one good reason is a lower price. If the selling firm wants to draw the buyer's attention, it should then communicate to the buyer that its product is of high quality or has special features. Del Cano will differentiate its products, discouraging the buyer from basing its purchasing decisions exclusively on price.

Also, the buyer does not really face switching costs, which makes him all the more powerful. The buyer can make his own salad dressing if he wants to (and if he is able to do so, as well). In any case, such a probability is a threat for full integration.

The Bargaining Power of Suppliers

Suppliers in the salad dressing industry are not that powerful because there are many substitutes. The only way suppliers may gain bargaining leverage over their customers is by manufacturing their own products. In a word: integration.

The Threat of Relevant Substitutes

Four large competitors (Kraft, CPC, Unilever, and Clorox) share over three-quarters of the market among themselves. The rest is shared by a vast number of small- and medium-sized companies, not to mention the trend toward the development of private-label brands. The industry may also encounter an indirect substitute-product rivalry: The homemade salad dressing is an option and is most likely to jeopardize the sales in the pourable market.

The Threat of New Entrants into the Industry

The entry barriers are low as long as the entrant does not play on the same playground as the "Big Four," which means that a new entrant, if small, has to differentiate its products as well as its distribution channels so as not to encounter direct competition from established brands. Retaliation would indeed turn out to be decisive. New entrants do not usually have the financial assets to face large competitors.

However, the structural barriers are low because no tremendous financial resources are required to launch a new venture. This implies that the entrant focuses, at least in the short run, on particular nontraditional distribution channels, given the considerable access costs to national supermarkets. Del Cano will utilize a two-tiered approach for the industry, targeting the natural foods industry in the short run and conventional supermarkets in the long run.

The Rivalry Among Existing Firms

The presence of industry leaders helps maintain price discipline/reference and keeps the industry from engaging in destructive price wars. Within the "generic" dressing market, the intense competition can be noted through examining the advertising budgets of the major players. Kraft, for example, budgets approximately $40 million annually for their salad dressings. Thus, competitors are encouraged to differentiate. Although the salad dressing market is a fairly competitive and mature market, there is growth potential given the existence of several barely tapped niches with the organic/natural/fat-free/gourmet/ethnic trends.

Summary of the Competitive Forces

The salad dressing industry as a whole is marked by strong rivalry; low entry barriers; strong buyer, low supplier power; and high substitution. Although the general market is mature, the natural segment is growing rapidly. In addition, the margins are significantly higher for specialty and natural food products, such as Del Cano, than for the typical "commodity" salad dressing.

Macroenvironmental Influences

Political and Government Analysis

Reports in recent years about the possible cancer-causing effects of pesticides and chemical additives have raised consumer concern about conventionally cultivated food. Because of this—and the improved quality and lower prices of organic products as larger, more sophisticated producers have entered the field—industry analysts project wholesale organic product revenues to hit $4.4 billion this year, 25 percent higher than in 1996. The industry should also benefit from federal standards for organic products that are set to become law next year. Only 17 states now have rules pertaining to organic products, and their rigor and enforcement vary. The credibility conferred by a USDA-certified organic seal on everything from meat to processed foods will encourage many consumers to buy organic, which is a major asset in the organic salad dressing market.

Macroeconomic Analysis

The 1990s witnessed the emergence of the "environmental market." This is the market for equipment to clean and purify air and water and for agri-biological products to replace pesticides and herbicides. That green revolution has a strong effect on agricultural technology.

Technological Analysis

Research and development have been focusing recently on light, low-calorie, low-cholesterol products, easy-to-prepare, and individual-portion products. These are targeted at very specific consumer segments with a certain amount of purchasing power. They must be able to respond to the assumed or actual consumers' demands: flavor, service, safety, and health. To obtain those new product formulas, the food industry has been studying the use of alternative products among foodstuffs themselves, especially in terms of substitution: The fats are being replaced by substances having the same technical and organoleptic properties, but lower in calories because they have been lightened. Thus, the agri-food industry has been taking on a new dimension these last few years: Cracking agricultural products and assembling ingredients have become its new business. As a result, new technologies are being developed to allow product manufacturing under the most profitable conditions. They require significant investment in equipment rather than labor and are supposed to increase processing capacities.

Sociodemographic Analysis

Changing attitudes, demographics, and lifestyles are altering what Americans eat, how much they eat, and where they eat. A study conducted by McKinsey & Co. sees age, income, family composition, and ethnic-

ity as the drivers of total food spending, as well as the amount of money spent on food away from home and preference in eating places. McKinsey projects that by 2005, the population will have shifted significantly toward older groups, having an extremely positive impact on food spending. The percentage of people 45 or older will grow from 32 percent in 1995 to 38 percent in 2005. McKinsey analysts anticipate this group will continue its high relative spending on food.

Like other observers, McKinsey foresees a polarization of income in the United States in the future, but unlike some observers, the consultancy believes the middle class will shrink, increasing the ranks of the affluent. It is this segment of the population that we will target. McKinsey has identified six primary changing consumer attitudes and lifestyles.

- Consumers' greater need for convenience will lead to "just-in-time" meals.
- Consumers will be seeking more pleasure and fun from everyday life.
- More of life's meaning and enjoyment will be driven by family experiences.
- Continued concerns for health will be reinvented as total nutrition management.
- Consumers will demand more variety through customized eating experiences.
- Expectations for value will include no premiums for extras.

Ecological Analysis

Although all glass salad bottles are recyclable, ours are reusable: This will be encouraged on our packaging. We have chosen not to use plastic, even though it weighs less, due to its negative ecological reputation. The markets we will serve will definitely note the packaging materials utilized. Companies are expected to make allowances for ecological issues. As a result, the budgets of many larger firms have allocations for that area to comply with the macroenvironmental trend and avoid any possible conflicts.

IV. DEVELOPMENT AND PRODUCTION

Manufacturing

Del Cano products will be manufactured at a contract manufacturer's facility to be determined on the criteria discussed here. Del Cano views its recipes and marketing ability as critical to its success. Production capability, although important in terms of cost structure, will not lead to competitive advantage in the marketplace.

We have selected a contract manufacturer located north of Cincinnati, Ohio: LaSalle Manufacturing. LaSalle is an experienced manufacturer, meeting the needs of large companies such as Procter & Gamble in the food industry. Del Cano strives to provide only the best dressings and sauces using the best ingredients. LaSalle uses a similar pursuit-of-excellence mentality in its production processes.

Advantages of Contract Manufacturing

Contract manufacturing provides Del Cano with a flexible production capability while avoiding the excessive amounts of capital that would be required to build a plant of its own. This will be a clear advantage in the early stages of the company, because we expect some development time for our products to penetrate the marketplace. As our volume demand grows, LaSalle will be able to increase production, and Del Cano will be able to receive a lower rate per case on production costs. Our flexible contract provides the incentive to increase volume quickly to realize the lower rate schedule. The contract also highlights the increasing profit potential as the business develops.

We should note, however, that using a contract manufacturer does not eliminate the need to provide guidance in the production process and take ownership for the product quality. We have selected a facility that is reasonably close to our headquarters to ensure frequent visits to the plant to resolve problems and to create a close working relationship.

Selection Criteria

As mentioned earlier, LaSalle has prior experience in the food industry. One of the primary requirements was certification to meet governmental regulations. Production facilities must meet strict guidelines to safely produce goods for human consumption. LaSalle meets and exceeds all certification requirements and maintains this record. This allows Del Cano to focus on innovative products instead of production processes.

Measurement Control

LaSalle is accustomed to working closely with clients to ensure that products meet the highest quality standards. The production facility uses equipment with current measurement control systems to guarantee consistent quality of products. Precision is a critical element in both the producer and consumer areas. When consumers buy a bottle of Del Cano, they want to know that they are receiving a product that delivered the same unique flavor as a previous purchase. LaSalle's quality control will provide for consistent flavor for the consumer. Precision also is a critical factor in our ability to accurately forecast production costs by avoiding usage variances in ingredients.

Production

Steps in the production process are described here, and illustrated later in this section.

Receiving/Holding—Liquids An add-mix process will be used at LaSalle. This necessitates having holding tanks for bulk liquids to be delivered to LaSalle by tank car. Separate tanks will be used for liquids, such as various oils (olive, vegetable, canola, etc.) and vinegars (red wine, white wine, cider, etc.).

Receiving/Holding—Dry Materials   Dry ingredients such as herbs and spices will be received in bulk supersacks. These are large-capacity plastic bags in various sizes up to 2,000 pounds. Use of incremental sizes has two advantages for Del Cano. Variability will allow some flexibility to increase order sizes as production needs grow. Flexibility also avoids excessive investment in working capital because raw material inventory can be minimized.

Production Process   Production is begun by running liquid materials from holding tanks to a mixing tank. Measurement control will be accomplished either through flow meters or weight. Dry materials will be added by dumping premeasured quantities into the mixing tank from the supersacks as recipes warrant. Once all ingredients are added, an agitator (homogenizer) inside the mixing tank will be started to ensure that ingredients are thoroughly mixed before packaging. The agitator must continue to function throughout the packaging process to ensure consistent quality.

   Note: In some cases, an ingredient to increase viscosity (xanthan gum) may be added to ensure ingredients remain mixed while in packaging lines. Xanthan gum, though listed in ingredient statements, does not compromise taste and often breaks down after time.

Packing   Mixed product will run from the mix tanks directly to the filling lines where bottles will be filled. Bottles will then be mechanically capped and boxed for shipping.

Resource Requirements

Recipes and personnel constitute the primary assets of Del Cano. To that end, we will strive to develop the most unique yet genuine dressings and marinades of any offered in the marketplace. Company management takes pride in innovation and has a passion to pursue cooking-related opportunities that have the potential to have a larger exploitation in the high-end food market.

   As our business grows, we will continue to develop new recipes and will strive to hire people who also possess the drive to continue the Del Cano legacy of fine gastronomical flavors from around the globe.

Quality Assurance

Del Cano will strive to have the highest quality standards in the manufacture of its products. This desire has already been evidenced by the selection of a high-quality manufacturing site. We will also implement statistical sampling of our completed products for quality and taste characteristics. The sampling process will include the following areas:

Ingredient Content   This is to ensure that bottles contain the correct proportions of ingredients to deliver a consistent flavor to the customer.

Fill Weights   A scale system is included in the packing line to verify bottle content weight. Product fill levels must be measured to ensure that customers receive the amount as stated on the bottle, thus avoiding civil penalties. Control charts will be used to track performance and to identify problems as (if) they occur.

Leakage   Leakage is a primary concern for liquid products. This is predominantly a measure of customer satisfaction (distributors and grocery chains) versus consumer satisfaction. Chains have been known to charge back amounts or to deduct from invoices when they receive leaking products. To avoid this consequence, we will perform ship tests of Del Cano cases and resolve any issues during the beginning rollout stages of production.

Breakage   Breakage will be tested in the same manner as the leakage test.

   Product quality is only one aspect of the benefits a customer receives when they purchase Del Cano Salad Dressings and

Marinades. We will strive to acquire the highest quality ingredients, assuring customers a taste "voyage" unlike any other. The unique positioning of Del Cano as a salad dressing and as a marinade also gives our product a unique use and value quality discussed. Further, our price point, combined with our larger size, will also provide customers with a superior value impression.

V. MARKETING ORIENTATION

Marketing Segments

Today's dual income family has less time to plan and prepare healthful and nutritious meals. They are actively seeking fast and easy solutions to meet these needs. Supermarkets and restaurants are responding by offering home-meal replacements.

This trend is paralleled by a shift in consumer taste preferences. Twenty years ago, healthful and tasty cuisine from exotic parts of the world were generally unavailable unless one lived in a major metropolitan area. As ethnic groups continue to flourish in the United States, specialized food-oriented businesses have sprung up to meet their needs, but also to offer more entrenched Americans something new. Just as cultural traditions can define a nation or region of the world, cuisines have their own definitive spices, vegetables, and methods of cooking.

Finally, there is a dramatic shift in consumer demand for natural and organic foods. According to a recent survey conducted by the National Nutritional Foods Association, U.S. consumers can be segmented into the following six categories with regard to natural foods: unconcerned (18 percent), overwhelmed (30 percent), young recyclers (10 percent), affluent healers (12 percent), new green mainstream (23 percent), and true naturals (7 percent).

The unconcerned tend to be male and reject the idea that chemicals harm the environment. The overwhelmed tend to be women and in general are not optimistic; they feel they are struggling to just get by. The unconcerned and overwhelmed open no opportunities for our product. On the other hand, we will target the following four segments, with the greatest emphasis placed on the affluent healers and true naturals.

Young recyclers tend to be unmarried and are most concerned with packaging and recycling; they reject the notion of paying a premium for environmentally friendly products. Their eating habits are marked by a preference for eating more convenience foods than they should. The new green mainstream are interested in the environment but need a reason before they will act; they are not out to save the world. This group offers potential to be converted. The affluent healers tend to be highly educated, upscale, and are family and goal oriented. They are concerned about nutrition, exercise, and personal health and are willing to spend more for quality products that will benefit themselves or their family. Finally, the true naturals tend to shop at natural food stores and tend to be highly educated. They are totally committed to environmentally sound products, feel knowledgeable about environmental food issues, and like to learn more. They will go out of their way when they see quality and added value.

Other key trends indicate that people, due to their busy schedules, are purchasing or seeking "speed scratch" cooking solutions, more takeout, and more distinct ethnic food. Baby boomers, comprising 26.4 percent of the population, are value oriented and desire quality food, strong packaging, convenience, and good taste.

We will follow a two-tiered approach to reaching our target markets. First, we will enter the natural foods market via small and large specialty foods stores both directly as well as through natural foods distributors and brokers. Second, we will approach national distributors to help attain national presence in large chain supermarkets.

Marketing Strategy

Our primary strength lies in the value proposition our product offers. Currently, there are only two or three existing dressings and sauces that attempt to cross cultural segments. Product lines exist within certain cuisine, such as Asian and Mexican, or they tend to be Americanized in flavor and taste, such as "French" and "Italian" dressings. Our product, in contrast, offers ingredients providing a truer flavor that our food-conscious consumer desires. Tracking consumer trends will enable us to maintain up-to-date flavors, providing a competitive advantage. Recipes cannot be patented, as the slightest modification would allow the product to be virtually copied without legal ramifications. As such, we will leverage our own strengths, such as quality, product innovation, and marketing communications, to build brand equity that will solidify our competitive advantage.

Product

We will offer "food dressings" that can be used as both salad dressings and marinades. Our competitive advantage will be both quality and our ability to keep up with changing food trends.

Pricing

Our research indicates, not surprisingly, that the consumer wishes to pay the lowest price possible. After comparisons with other high-quality products, we have set a retail price of $3.99. In general, distributors demand a gross profit of 10 percent, and the retail grocer requires 20 percent. Working backwards, this leaves us with a wholesale price to distributors of $3.02. We will sell all products at the same wholesale price, encouraging retail prices to be identical across the product line. This will be encouraged for several reasons. Primarily, it will provide the consumer with the notion that all our products are identical in terms of quality, regardless of the ingredients. It will also simplify decision making during their shopping experience. Instead of purchasing by price, they will purchase based on their taste preferences. This will allow us to accurately assess which products are preferred due to taste and concept, as opposed to perceived price value.

Distribution

Initially, we will offer our product through specialty foods and natural foods distributors, such as Tree of Life and Blooming Prairie (natural foods distributors) and Kehe (a specialty food distributor located in Indianapolis, Indiana). We will utilize our contacts with the management and sales teams of these firms to help gain entrance into their product catalogs and order guides. To gain acceptance, we will meet with the distributor representatives and present our program. We anticipate a move into the national grocery chains during our fifth year. The first national chain we will target is Kroger. Their distribution is organized geographically, with 16 regional buying centers. We will present our product lines to each of the individual buying offices. Once three of the regions have accepted the product, it will be distributed through Kroger's central distribution center, Paytons. This will allow the product to be sold through all Kroger stores at a national level. We will use this same process to gain acceptance into other large chains, such as Star Market and Dominicks. At this time, we will also move into the large national distributors, such as Sysco.

Advertising and Promotion

The advertising and promotion budget is set at $200,000 for year 1; $200,000 for year 2; $400,000 for year 3; $600,000 for year 4; and $800,000 for year 5. These expenditures will be divided among both advertising (55 percent) and promotions (45 percent). This ratio will be maintained for the first 5 years.

Advertising

Print and radio advertising will be used to raise awareness of our product and encourage consumers to try it. Its position as a combination salad dressing and marinade will be explained. Our research indicates that people are comfortable with this positioning, but when you walk through the grocery aisles, only a couple of products in the salad dressing and marinade aisles mention both uses on the label. We want to leverage consumer acceptance of this positioning and build a brand image that reinforces quality natural ingredients, international flavor, and ease of use.

We will allot $30,000 for print ads, targeting consumers. They will be placed in local/regional natural food magazines such as *Conscious Choice* for the first 4 years. As sales expand, we will move to more national/mainstream magazines. We will spend $45,000 on radio advertising, airing commercials on hip radio stations with listeners between ages 25 and 40.

From the supply side, we will advertise our product in *Natural Foods Merchandiser.* We plan to join several trade group associations to build awareness in the industry. We will place the ads at the beginning of each quarter. First-year costs are estimated at $35,000.

Promotion

We will administer several promotional activities as part of our marketing concept. Despite the high design and printing costs, we will include hang tags as part of our packaging, because they will further differentiate our product as well as offer immediate recipes and alternative cooking solutions to the customer. These costs are estimated to be $5,000 for design and $20,000 for printing. In addition, we will ask the consumer to visit our Web page, where they can download and print these cooking solutions, devoted primarily to the fun exploration of Del Cano Salad Dressing and Marinade. We estimate the server costs and development costs to be $5,000 for the first year. This may seem low, but we will utilize our own pro-

gramming and design expertise to create our Web page. In addition, the Web page will allow us to quickly and easily update the recipe catalog. Finally, it will allow us greater input and feedback from the consumer. Consumers can easily e-mail us with their comments, suggestions, and perhaps even their own recipes.

Mail-in offers will increase purchasing continuity and broaden usage. Our initial program will offer a high-quality baking dish that can also be used for refrigerated storage and marinating. This product will be available at a discounted price when five UPC labels are submitted. This production is estimated at $50,000.

In addition, we will offer in-store sampling of the dressings to help promote the product. It has been shown that sampling can increase sales by up to 30 percent. This method will also help educate the consumer about the advantages and possibilities of our dressings as a cooking solution. Promotion of our product will be accomplished initially through in-store flyers and sampling. We will outsource this project. We will offer 50-cent coupons during the first month of the launch to increase impulse sales and product awareness. Costs for the coupons and in-store sampling are estimated at $17,000.

Product Packaging

Del Cano will be packaged in 16-ounce bottles that have resealable flip-top lids, similar to a *Grolsch* beer bottle, costing 30 cents each. There are several reasons for this packaging.

- It is distinctive on the store shelf and will create immediate interest due to its uniqueness. This is critical, given the large number of products and the uniformity of the packaging currently on the shelf.
- It is practical and reuseable. We will encourage buyers to reuse the bottles for other purposes, creating an environment friendly image. This packaging will

make the product more appealing to the new green mainstream.

- It reflects the image of the product itself: sophisticated, distinctive, and worldly.

Competitor Strengths

Our competitors in the major supermarket chains are formidable. They include the major dressing manufacturers, such as Kraft and Wishbone. The primary marinade producer is Lawry's. Although they may pose a threat in terms of shelf space and distribution, we will carve out a unique position as the only natural, ethnically diverse combination salad dressing/marinade. Therefore, these firms will compete at the margin of our target usage segment. These competitors can be viewed more as low-cost providers; we are positioning ourselves as a high-quality, superior value cooking solution provider. Their strengths also lie in their ability to manufacture with enormous economies of scale.

Because we are using a two-tiered market approach, the negative impact of the major dressing and marinade producers will be minimal. During the first 4 years, we will be selling through the natural food chains, thus competing within the second tier: the natural foods dressings, such as Annie's and Cardini's. By the time we gain acceptance into the national grocery chains, we will have developed brand recognition and a strong following. In addition to our market approach, it is our positioning, packaging, and superior flavors that further differentiate our products, cushioning Del Cano from competitive forces.

Our survey indicated that at a price of $3.99, nearly 50 percent of respondents perceived our product as unique and indicated high intention to purchase.

Sales Forecasts

In forecasting sales, we have used the market-potential/sales-requirement (MP/SR) method. This method allowed us to analyze anticipated sales from the top down; analyze needed sales levels from the bottom up; and compare the two to ensure that our needed sales levels were not greater than the market would support.

Our first step was to determine the market potential for our product. We will begin by producing and selling the six meal starters that were rated the highest by the respondents to our survey. Census data was collected for the metropolitan areas of the 20 cities selected for penetration during the first 2 years (see Exhibit IV). We defined Del Cano's target market as approximately 10 percent of the total population. We then defined the Del Cano trade area as 60 percent of our target market. Of this trade area, we assumed 3 percent market penetration and six annual purchases per customer. Years 3 to 5 show regional and then national expansion as the popularity of Del Cano's increases.

Second, we derived sales requirements. We did this by determining Del Cano's overall cost structure by adding estimated fixed-asset costs to estimated one-time start-up expenses and to estimated operating expenses—fixed and variable costs.

All pro forma financial statements are calculated based on the most likely sales scenario (see Exhibits I, II, and III).

VI. FINANCIAL PLANS

Financial Strategy

Source of Funds
Del Cano's preference for ongoing funding is to use proceeds generated from continuing operations. The firm is targeting a total initial debt of $30,000.

Uses of Funds
Our intended use of excess cash generated by operations and financing will be growth and expansion. Del Cano products have tremendous opportunity that can only be

EXHIBIT 1 Pro Forma Income Statement for Del Cano					
	Year 1	*Year 2*	*Year 3*	*Year 4*	*Year 5*
Sales	1,045,507	1,072,106	1,886,182	3,772,364	7,777,279
Less Expenses:					
COGS	466,417	631,334	1,110,720	2,221,440	4,579,823
Selling	250,000	250,000	500,000	750,000	1,000,000	Includes marketing to develop brand awareness
Administrative	41,820	42,884	75,447	150,895	311,091	Assumed 4% of sales
Salaries	125,000	125,000	125,000	125,000	125,000	5 partners@ $25,000
SNRI	300,000	300,000	100,000	–	–	Computers and office equipment, slotting fees
Depreciation	–	–	–	–	–	No PP&E to depreciate
Interest	3,000	2,812	2,605	2,377	2,126	$30,000 bank loan @ 10% over 10 years
Total Expenses	1,186,237	1,352,030	1,913,772	3,249,711	6,018,041
Net IBT	(140,730)	(279,923)	(27,590)	552,652	1,759,238
Income Tax Expense	(39,404)	(78,379)	(7,725)	146,343	492,587	Assumed 28% of IBT
Net Income	(101,325)	(201,545)	(19,865)	376,310	1,266,652

EXHIBIT II Pro Forma Cash Flow Statement for Del Cano

				YEAR 1 (First Half)				
Operations	*Year 1*	*January*	*February*	*March*	*April*	*May*	*June*
Net Income	(101,325)	(7,000)	(3,500)	(4,000)	(5,000)	(6,000)	(7,000)
Depreciation	–	–	–	–	–	–	–
(increase) Decrease in Accounts Receivable	(2000)	(138)	(69)	(79)	(99)	(118)	(138)
(increase) Decrease in Inventories	(15,000)	(1,036)	(518)	(592)	(740)	(888)	(1,036)
Increase (decrease) in Accounts Payable	1,000	69	35	39	49	59	69
Increase (decrease) in Salaries Payable	–	–	–	–	–	–	–
Increase (decrease) in Income Taxes Payable	(39,404)	(2,722)	(1,361)	(1,556)	(1,944)	(2,333)	(2,722)
Cash Flow from Operations	(156,730)	(10,828)	(5,414)	(6,187)	(7,734)	(9,281)	(10,828)
Investing							
Acquisition of Property, Plant, and Equipment	–	–	–	–	–	–	–
Cash Flow from Investing	–	–	–	–	–	–	–
Financing							
Issue of Long-Term Debt	30,000	2,500	2,500	2,500	2,500	2,500	2,500
APIC	550,000						
Cash Flow from Financing	580,000	48,333	48,333	48,333	48,333	48,333	48,333
Change in Cash	423,270	37,506	42,920	42,146	40,599	39,053	37,506
Cash, December 31, Last Year	–	–	–	–	–	–	–
Cash, December 31, Current Year	423,270	37,506	42,920	42,146	40,599	39,053	37,506

(continued)

EXHIBIT II *(cont.)*

	Year 1 (Second Half)					
Operations	*July*	*August*	*September*	*October*	*November*	*December*
Net Income	(8,000)	(7,000)	(5,000)	(4,690)	(4,000)	(40,135)
Depreciation	–	–	–	–	–	–
(increase) Decrease in Accounts Receivable	(158)	(138)	(99)	(93)	(79)	(792)
(increase) Decrease in Inventories	(1,184)	(1,036)	(740)	(694)	(592)	(5,942)
Increase (decrease) in Accounts Payable	79	69	49	46	39	396
Increase (decrease) in Salaries Payable	–	–	–	–	–	–
Increase (decrease) in Income Taxes Payable	(3,111)	(2,722)	(1,944)	(1,824)	(1,556)	(15,608)
Cash Flow from Operations	(12,374)	(10,828)	(7,734)	(7,254)	(6,187)	(62,081)
Investing						
Acquisition of Property, Plant, and Equipment	–	–	–	–	–	–
Cash Flow from Investing	–	–	–	–	–	–
Financing						
Issue of Long-Term Debt	2,500	2,500	2,500	2,500	2,500	2,500
APIC						
Cash Flow from Financing	48,333	48,333	48,333	48,333	48,333	48,333
Change in Cash	35,959	37,506	40,599	41,079	42,146	(13,748)
Cash, December 31, Last Year	–	–	–	–	–	–
Cash, December 31, Current Year	35,959	37,506	40,599	41,079	42,146	(13,748)

168

Operations	Year 2	Year 3	Year 4	Year 5
Net Income	(201,535)	(19,865)	376,310	1,266,652
Depreciation	—	—	—	—
(increase) Decrease in Accounts Receivable	(10,000)	(15,000)	(20,000)	(20,000)
(increase) Decrease in Inventories	(30,000)	(60,000)	(120,000)	(240,000)
Increase (decrease) in Accounts Payable	5,000	10,000	20,000	40,000
increase (decrease) in Salaries Payable	—	—	—	—
Increase (decrease) in Income Taxes Payable	(78,379)	70,653	75,689	416,897
Cash Flow from Operations	(314,923)	(14,212)	331,999	1,463,549
Investing				
Acquisition of Property, Plant, and Equipment	—	—	—	—
Cash Flow from Investing	—	—	—	—
Financing				
Issue of Long-Term Debt	—	—	—	—
APIC				
Cash Flow from Financing	—	—	—	—
Change in Cash	(314,923)	(14,212)	331,999	1,463,549
Cash, December 31, Last Year	423,270	108,347	94,135	426,134
Cash, December 31, Current Year	108,347	94,135	426,134	1,889,683

EXHIBIT III Pro Forma Balance Sheet for Del Cano on December 31

Assets	Year 1	Year 2	Year 3	Year 4	Year 5
Cash	423,270	108,347	94,135	426,134	1,889,683
Accounts Receivable	2,000	12,000	27,000	47,000	67,000
Inventories	15,000	45,000	105,000	225,000	465,000
Total Current Assets	440,270	165,347	226,135	698,134	2,421,683
Property, Plant and Equipment (net)	–	–	–	–	–
Total Assets	440,270	165,347	226,135	698,134	2,421,683
Liabilities and Owners' Equity					
Accounts Payable	1,000	6,000	16,000	36,000	76,000
Salaries Payable	–	–	–	–	–
Income Taxes Payable	(39,404)	(117,783)	(47,130)	28,560	445,457
Total Current Liabilities	(38,404)	(111,783)	(31,130)	64,560	521,457
Bonds Payable	30,000	30,000	30,000	30,000	30,000
Total Liabilities	(8,404)	(81,783)	(1,130)	94,560	551,457
APIC	550,000				
Retained Earnings	(101,325)	247,130	227,265	603,575	1,870,226
Total Owners' Equity	448,675	247,130	227,265	603,575	1,870,226
Total Liabilities and Owners' Equity	440,270	165,347	226,135	698,134	2,421,685

EXHIBIT IV Sales Forecast—Year 1

Population
U.S. Census 1995 Estimates

1 Akron, OH	678,834
2 Bloomington, IN	115,208
3 Cincinnati, OH	1,907,438
4 Chicago, IL	8,589,913
5 Cleveland, OH	2,224,974
6 Columbus, OH	1,437,512
7 Dayton, OH	956,412
8 Detroit, MI	5,279,500
9 Green Bay, WI	210,303
10 Indianapolis, IN	1,476,865

Year 1

	Total	January	February	March	April	May	June	1st 6 mos.	Notes
Market Potential	18,196,663	13,516,367	13,516,367	13,516,367	13,516,367	13,516,367	13,516,367	13,516,367	10 cities
Target Market	1,819,666	1,351,637	1,351,637	1,351,637	1,351,637	1,351,637	1,351,637	1,351,637	10% of market potential
Trade Area	1,091,800	810,982	810,982	810,982	810,982	810,982	810,982	810,982	
Number of Customers	43,672	32,439	32,439	32,439	32,439	32,439	32,439	32,439	4% penetration
Purchase Frequency	6.000	0.500	0.500	0.500	0.500	0.500	0.500	3.000	Average annual purchases
Total Volume	262,032	16,220	16,220	16,220	16,220	16,220	16,220	97,318	
Total Sales	**$1,045,507**	$64,716	$64,716	$64,716	$64,716	$64,716	$64,716	$388,298	
Trade Area % of Target Market	35,435	60%	60%	60%	60%	60%	60%		

(continued)

EXHIBIT IV *(cont.)*

	July	August	September	October	November	December	2nd 6 mos.	
Market Potential	22,876,959	22,876,959	22,876,959	22,876,959	22,876,959	22,876,959	22,876,959	10 cities
Target Market	2,287,696	2,287,696	2,287,696	2,287,696	2,287,696	2,287,696	2,287,696	10% of market potential
Trade Area	1,372,618	1,372,618	1,372,618	1,372,618	1,372,618	1,372,618	1,372,618	
Number of Customers	54,905	54,905	54,905	54,905	54,905	54,905	54,905	4% penetration
Purchase Frequency	0.500	0.500	0.500	0.500	0.500	0.500	3.000	Average annual purchases
Total Volume	27,452	27,452	27,452	27,452	27,452	27,452	164,714	
Total Sales	$109,535	$109,535	$109,535	$109,535	$109,535	$109,535	$657,209	
Trade Area % Coverage of 1–10 Target Market	60%	60%	60%	60%	60%	60%		

(continued)

172

EXHIBIT IV   Sales Forecast—Years 2–5 (*cont.*)

Population
U.S. Census 1995 Estimates   ***Population***

#	City	Population
1	Akron, OH	678,834
2	Bloomington, IN	115,208
3	Cincinnati, OH	1,907,438
4	Chicago, IL	8,589,913
5	Cleveland, OH	2,224,974
6	Columbus, OH	1,437,512
7	Dayton, OH	956,412
8	Detroit, MI	5,279,500
9	Green Bay	210,303
10	Indianapolis, IN	1,476,865
11	Kansas City, MO	1,663,453
12	Lexington, KY	435,736
13	Louisville, KY	987,102
14	Madison, WI	393,296
15	Milwaukee, WI	1,640,831
16	Minneapolis-St. Paul, MN	2,723,137
17	Omaha, NE	670,322
18	Pittsburgh, PA	2,394,702
19	St. Louis, MO	2,547,686
20	Toledo, OH	612,798

Year 2

	Total	***Notes***
Market Potential	36,946,022	20 Cities
Target Market	3,694,602	10% of market potential
Trade Area	1,477,841	
Number of Customers	59,114	4% penetration
Purchase Frequency	6.000	Average annual purchases
Total Volume	354,682	
Total Sales	**$1,072,106**	
20 Midwest Cities	40%	

Year 3

	Total	***Notes***
Market Potential	65,000,000	Midwest
Target Market	6,500,000	10%
Trade Area	2,600,000	
Number of Customers	104,000	4%
Purchase Frequency	6.000	
Total Volume	624,000	
Total Sales	**1,886,182**	
Midwest	40%	

(*continued*)

EXHIBIT IV *(cont.)*

Year 4

	Total	Notes
Market Potential	130,000,000	Midwest, West Coast
Target Market	13,000,000	10%
Trade Area	5,200,000	
Number of Customers	208,000	4%
Purchase Frequency	6.000	
Total Volume	1,248,000	
Total Sales	**$3,772,364**	
Midwest, West Coast	40%	

Year 5

	Total	Notes
Market Potential	268,014,000	U.S. domestic market
Target Market	26,801,400	10%
Trade Area	10,720,560	
Number of Customers	428,822	4%
Purchase Frequency	6.000	
Total Volume	2,572,934	
Total Sales	**$7,777,279**	
Nationwide	40%	

fully exploited through rapid growth maximizing penetration with major supermarket chains.

Internal Control and Monitoring Systems
Cash flow will initially be monitored by Rob Reader. A secondary, regular check will be performed by Andy Rockafellow. Financial records will also be reviewed by Bloomington, Indiana, accounting firm Hayden & Co., P.C.—a local accounting firm that specializes in handling business start-ups.

VII. ORGANIZATION AND MANAGEMENT

Key Personnel Resources

Karen Chatas, in addition to her marketing and design background, has developed a strong understanding of the natural food market as part of her work experience and cooking skills. She subsequently developed a number of contacts with distributors as well, which will be a definite asset to our company. Rob Reader, who has a finance background, will help the company assess and foresee its financial resources. Andrew Rockafellow is a finance major and acquired a solid experience of the consumer products market while working at Pillsbury and Procter & Gamble. Patrick Seiffert is a marketing major, with skills and experience in finance and sales. Bich-Quan Tran has a marketing and sales background with work experience in the consumer products market as well. She will also be able to provide an understanding of international prospects. The team's strength rests upon its balanced skills between finance and sales, which should enable the firm to grow safely.

Human Resource Management Strategy

Del Cano, Inc., will be run by the current team, each of us having developed skills in specific areas that will help the company reach a cruise speed. As a result, no tremendous financial resources should be involved in the human resources field because the company intends to remain closely supervised for the first couple of years. Also, this will enable us to be flexible about our wages according to the company's sales. Additional salespeople are nevertheless likely to be required from year 2 on, according to the company's net sales income. That number should then be doubled every other year, starting from the third year to meet the consumers' anticipated demand.

VIII. OWNERSHIP

Form of Business

The business is a limited liability partnership. As such, each partner is liable only for the amount of his/her personal investment in Del Cano, Inc. No other legal liability exists. The actual partnership agreement contains no special conditions or clauses.

Equity Positions

Owners' Equity Positions

Partner	Investment
Karen Chatas	$10,000
Rob Reader	$10,000
Andy Rockafellow	$10,000
Patrick Seiffert	$10,000
Bich-Quan Tran	$10,000
Total Owner's Equity	$50,000

Deal Structure

Del Cano, Inc., will require $500,000 to start up and grow at the rapid rate necessary for the organization to achieve its potential. The deal structure is to be negotiated with the investor.

IX. CRITICAL RISKS AND CONTINGENCIES

We feel that our company will be a success. As with any new venture, certain risks exist.

- No product currently exists; we are currently testing flavors and recipes.
- Although this is a start-up, we have strong experience in the foods and consumer products industries and can bring that knowledge to this company.
- Because we are in the food industry, we will not be able to obtain a patent for our product.
- We will outsource our salad dressing and marinade product to LaSalle Manufacturing. Although we feel we can maintain a strong relationship with this company, there is the potential that they may choose to manufacture our product for their own purposes. In addition, the company may cease production of our product for any variety of reasons. This could cause a shortage in supply. Inconsistent quality in the production of our dressing and marinade is possible, because we can not directly supervise its production. We feel this is highly unlikely due to LaSalle's reputation.
- The mainstream tier of competition (Kraft) has significantly more resources than Del Cano, but they focus on a larger mass market and cannot attack our strengths without incurring enormous costs.
- Although we have contacts within the midwestern natural and specialty food distributors, this is no guarantee that they will accept our product.
- Sales may grow rapidly, requiring additional capital to meet these needs. We feel that our producers will be able to

handle the increased demand, because they already produce for large companies such as Procter & Gamble.

- Sales may be less than expected. To counter this effect, we may have to temporarily reduce our profit margins, shifting the margin over to our distributors, encouraging them to push our product into the marketplace. We feel that our team has substantial selling expertise and thus will be able to obtain our desired growth rate through intense selling efforts.

- We are trying to initiate a shift in how salad dressings are viewed and used. This will depend greatly on how well this concept is accepted by the consumer. Our research and surveys have shown that the idea is acceptable, so we do not feel that this is a great threat.

- Significant delays in payment from our customers may cause a shortage of cash during the first year; this could be detrimental to the success of our company.

The company currently has no contingent liabilities as of October 1997. Each of these risks has been carefully assessed; we have incorporated preventative measures into the plan where possible. Although there are no guarantees, we have attempted to reduce risks wherever possible, and we anticipate the achievement of our goals.

X. SUMMARY AND CONCLUSIONS

We believe that our dressing and marinade concept will be accepted for the following reasons. First, market trends indicate a shift towards quick, easy, and tasty meal preparation. Our product is differentiated through its use and packaging, helping the end user to solve the problem of how to cook an exciting, fast, and nutritious meal. The sales, marketing, and financial experience of our team will provide the venture with the requisite skills to make this venture a success.

CHAPTER

6

The E-Entrepreneur

Everything has changed, nothing has changed.
—ANONYMOUS INTERNET PUNDIT

Outline

Learning Objectives

After reading this chapter, you will understand:

- Where the Internet is making the most impact
- Who is best positioned and enabled to take advantage
- Why value creation must be followed by value capture

- How the resources and capabilities of the venture influence success
- The nature of information economics on the Internet
- Which business models and strategies have been most successful

The opening quote indicates the ambivalence of this chapter. If everything has changed, then the older versions of marketing theory and practice are no longer quite so relevant for the creator of new ventures. Instead of analyzing the **four Ps of marketing**—price, place, product, and promotion—the new electronic or **e-entrepreneur** is mostly concerned with "click-through schemes and capturing eyeballs." If nothing has changed, however, then the fundamentals of marketing still apply to all businesses, including Internet ventures.

In previous editions of this book, Chapter 6 was called "Marketing the New Venture."* Much of our attention to e-entrepreneurship focuses on marketing, but many readers will be able to apply previous marketing courses, readings, and experience. Therefore, it seems appropriate to build on marketing foundations and offer a set of tools and frameworks for the Internet entrepreneur. This chapter will do just that—build on the foundations of new venture marketing but offer the e-entrepreneur as the practitioner du jour.

Of course, some things never change. You still cannot get rich from reading a book. Last year saw the publication of *The Complete Idiot's Guide to Making Millions on the Internet* (Que, $18.95). Just as the dot-coms' stock prices were crashing and their business models were crumbling, Nat Gertler (author of the *Guide*) claimed that the reader of his book may possess "the hands of a potential Internet billionaire, millionaire, or even simply a (future) happily employed Internet professional." Although early sales were brisk, the book will need a complete overhaul for its next edition. One reviewer notes that this time maybe they ought to call it *The Complete Idiot's Guide to Making Thousands on the Internet.*[1]

This chapter will not tell you how to make billions, millions, or even thousands on the Internet, but it will give you information that will enable you to identify where e-entrepreneurship is likely to be most successful and which people are most likely to be able to exploit this medium. The chapter will also show how the resource-based framework that we introduced in Chapter 2 can be used to develop strategies and plans to exploit Internet opportunities. In addition, we will review the basics of information economics. The key to information economics is that although information is costly to produce, it can be reproduced at almost no cost. High fixed costs, low marginal costs—that is the Internet's power and problem. We will also focus on business models for the e-entrepreneur—which ones seem to work, which ones seem like they will never work, and how we can evaluate the models that an e-entrepreneur develops for her own business.

If nothing has changed, you will be no worse off by adding e-entrepreneur skills to your tool kit. If everything has changed, then this is an opportunity for entrepreneurs around the world to take advantage of a marvelous technological innovation. They just need to know how.

---

*In the spirit of continuity, Chapter 6 from the second edition will be available either online at the Prentice Hall Web site for this book or in the *Instructor's Manual,* which can be copied and distributed to the class.

WHERE ARE THE E-ENTREPRENEURS?

There are two ways to think about the location of the e-entrepreneur. One is strictly on a geographic basis. The other is industry by industry. Let's take a look at the geography of the e-economy first.

Tables 6-1 and 6-2 show the basic computer infrastructure worldwide.[2] Table 6-1 illustrates that, at the current time, the United States still leads the world in the number of computers in use. Growth rates indicate that the Asia–Pacific region and the European Union countries may pass the United States by 2005.

Table 6-2 shows where the greatest growth per capita in computers has been and will be. These statistics show that the e-entrepreneur is operating internationally. It is also clear that the growth of the e-economy and Internet opportunities will be global and that e-entrepreneurs who possess some specialized advantage (such as language or contacts) in a particular high growth country will have distinct advantages.

These are not the only areas of the world where e-commerce and business will flourish. The non–U.S. e-entrepreneur will not only base business projections on the number of computers, but also on the number of digital handheld appliances like personal digital assistants (PDAs) and cell phones. Around the world, cell phones and similar handheld net-enabled devices are in huge demand. Table 6-3 shows where these subscribers are.[3]

TABLE 6-1   Computers in Use

Region	*1993*	*2000*	*2005 est.*
Asia–Pacific	25	116	257
European Union	44	135	250
United States	77	159	230
Latin America	3	18	44

TABLE 6-2   Growth Rate

Country	*Growth Rate (1993–2000)* *(%)*
China	1052
India	604
Russia	580
Brazil	565
Indonesia	552

Country	*Growth Rate Projected (2000–2005)* *(%)*
India	258
China	212
Poland	205
Ukraine	185
Turkey	171

TABLE 6-3   Cell Phone Users, 1990 and 1999 (in thousands)

Country	1990	1999
China	18	43,240
Egypt	4	465
Finland	226	3,445
France	283	21,434
Germany	273	23,470
India	0	1,195 (1998)
Ireland	25	1,400
Israel	15	2,800
Japan	868	56,849
Sweden	461	5,125
United Kingdom	1,144	23,944
United States	5,283	86,047

As Table 6-3 indicates, the delivery of information and services by cell phone and PDA is as significant as or more significant than delivery through the personal computer. Table 6-4 shows the growth rate of total Internet users and per capita Internet use. By 2005, even the late-developing African and Middle East markets will be substantial.[4] The main conclusion we can draw from this data is that the e-entrepreneur will be everywhere—everywhere there are personal computers, cell phones, or PDAs. Language capability and fluency in the local delivery language will be skills that the e-entrepreneur will need to possess or acquire.

We may also study specific industries to determine whether the Internet has caused major disruptions. The effect of the Internet revolution has not been felt the same way in every industry. Although the Internet was supposed to change everything, it changed some industries more than others. Basically, the Internet has the following potential:

TABLE 6-4   Total Internet Users and Per Capita Use (in thousands)

Internet Users by Region	1995	1998	2000	2005 e
Worldwide total Internet users	44,324	181,789	349,254	765,776
Worldwide total Internet users/1,000 people	7.8	30.7	57.5	118.0
North America total users	30,771	93,650	150,850	231,451
North America total users/1,000 people	104.9	311.2	492.6	720.6
West Europe/Scandinavia total users	8.713	42,006	87,743	213,670
West Europe/Scandinavia total users/1,000 people	22.1	105.8	220.5	529.9
Eastern Europe total users	375	3,800	10,806	45,472
Eastern Europe total users/1,000 people	1.3	13.0	37.2	157.7
Asia–Pacific total users	3,547	33,656	72,066	189,651
Asia–Pacific total users/1,000 people	1.1	9.9	20.7	50.9
South/Central American total users	410	5,647	10,629	56,051
South/Central American total users/1,000 people	0.9	11.4	38.4	101.2
Middle East/African total users	508	3,030	8.160	29,481
Middle East/African total users/1,000 people	0.6	3.0	7.9	26.1

- It lowers the cost of communication between people and companies, and within networks.
- It lowers the cost of transactions between people and companies and within networks.
- It lowers the cost of searching for information.
- It lowers the cost of monitoring transactions and search processes.

The areas where the Net may be revolutionary are the information-intensive industries where these costs are the greatest percentage of overall firm costs.[5] For example:

- *Financial services.* Most financial service transactions can be delivered electronically. Electronic fund transfers have been in use for many years. In many ways, financial services are ideal for the Internet because there is no physical product at all. However, banks have not yet figured out how to effectively deal with online bill paying.
- *Entertainment.* No physical product is delivered here, and much of entertainment can be digitized. This is ideal for the Internet because the consumption of entertainment services by someone does not affect the ability of someone else to consume the same services. However, no one quite knows the best business model.
- *Health care.* Although the delivery of health-care services usually requires a patient and health-care worker, much of the business end these days revolves around patient information and insurance transactions. The Internet can help with these, but who will reap the benefits? Service providers? Insurers? Patients?
- *Education.* Online learning and the delivery of courses over the Internet have become a fast growth business. Many students already do much of their institutional business online, from registering to checking grades to paying bills. The depersonalization of the educational experience is one potential criticism.
- *Government.* It is appealing for citizens to be in communication with the government. The government can deliver information about services, laws, taxes, and defense, and the citizen can give the government and its employees feedback and input. The infrastructure needed to do this would cost the government billions, and there may be other priorities for politicians.

The Internet impacts some industries only incrementally. These industries usually involve the creation, transformation, and transportation of some irreducible physical entity. These are industries where e-entrepreneurship may be difficult unless some e-entrepreneur finds a way to overcome the reality of the physical product.

- *Retailing.* Fancy Web sites and graphics received much of the attention in the original e-tailing revolution, but the reality of success was determined by back-of-the-house logistics and who could move the boxes around more efficiently. Never neglect the backend operations.
- *Manufacturing.* There is no substitute for high-quality manufactured goods. Intranet communications and supply chain management are important areas for electronic commerce, but the key is still the high-quality product, not the Web site.

- *Travel.* Transactions such as ordering tickets or making reservations are a good application; so are search processes that enable customers to check out hotels, resorts, and business sites. Eventually, someone has to get on an airplane or get in a car (or train, boat, or tram). That part of the travel industry suffers from real physical constraints.
- *Power.* Energy exchange and management are good applications. Enron.com (www.enron.com) became the largest marketer of natural gas and electricity by offering customers a portfolio of energy sources at a stable price, and reducing customer expenditures by analyzing their equipment and usage pattern. (Enron fell into bankruptcy after it lost investor confidence by misstating its earnings.) At the end of the day, however, the generation of power is a physical process and there is insufficient generating and transmission capacity at this time. These negative forces overwhelm the positives of exchange and management.

To summarize: The e-entrepreneur needs to scan and analyze both geographic regions and industries to spot opportunities. Some opportunities will depend on local knowledge of language, customs, and a network of contacts. Other opportunities may be constrained by industry and economic forces that remain unchangeable for the e-entrepreneur. However, entrepreneurs who are well prepared culturally have an advantage. Those that enter industries where the primary focus is information, not some physical product, may expect the best results.

E-NOTES 6-1

Internet Impact

The Internet is predicted to have the most impact on information-intensive industries, such as:

- financial services
- entertainment
- health care
- education
- government

The Internet is predicted to have less impact on industries that create, transform, or transport some physical entity, including:

- retailing
- manufacturing
- travel
- power

WHO ARE THE E-ENTREPRENEURS?

The e-entrepreneur comes in many modes. Young and ambitious, older and corporate-based, international and risk taking—these are just a few of the forms that the e-entrepreneur takes.

Many e-entrepreneurs are just like you. A recent survey of school placement offices shows that **e-commerce** start-ups are a serious consideration for business school graduates at some of the United States' most prestigious business schools. Although consulting and banking are still more popular (see Figure 6-1), start-ups have their attractions to many newly minted B-school graduates.[6]

The figure shows that as many as 15 percent of the graduating class from these schools may forego a corporate position to be part of a start-up in 2001 (Berkeley). Northwestern MBAs seem to be more conservative. Also note the drop-off in all three schools due to the "Internet bust" of 2000.

Quite a few ambitious undergraduates are pursuing their e-commerce dreams. They are going to school and starting Internet businesses. In a *New York Times* article, four such e-entrepreneurs were interviewed about their businesses.[7] When Jeffrey Gut, 21, started CollegiateMall.com, an Internet retailing company, he was a sophomore at Boston University. His motivation for the start-up was the frustration he had with the process of acquiring beanbag chairs and other trappings of college life. He returned to school in fall 2000 as a senior after taking a year off to get his company off the ground. He continues to serve as chief executive. He says that,

> When I started CollegiateMall, I was faking being a big company. The first 4 or 5 months, I had fake e-mail accounts, and I had six fake "employees" that would send e-mail to other people at companies. What's so neat about the Internet is that you can really front things—but not to deceive people. For example, when people wanted customer service, they'd e-mail "customer service" and "customer service" sends back an e-mail.

Mykolas Rambus, 21, is the chief executive of Lobby 7, a wireless services company. He graduated last spring from the Massachusetts Institute of Technology (MIT) with the other four founders of the company, which they ran from a dormitory room during their final semester. Lobby 7 is still based in Boston and has obtained venture capital from i-Group, an affiliate of Softbank. Rambus is now working to raise its next round of financing. Rambus says,

> I stopped really focusing on school in my sophomore year. I went to two or three lectures for certain classes. I just spent my time working with the resources of MIT—there's a vast array of networking opportunities, contacts you can make through professors, events to attend in the venture community . . . At MIT there are no rules, except that you can't have a corporate Web server running on one of their IP addresses.

Greg Y. Tseng, 20, was a senior at Harvard in the fall of 2000. He started Flying Chickens.com, a price-comparison Web site, after finding that he could save $40 by

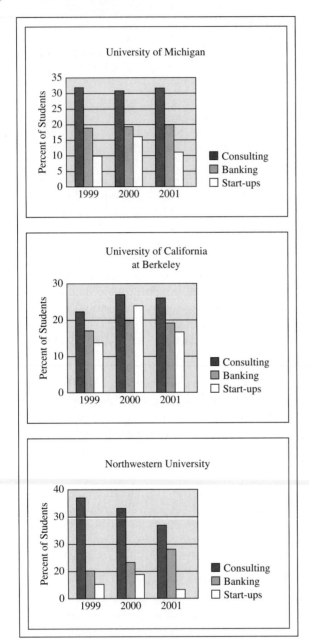

FIGURE 6-1 Start-up Plans for Business School Graduates

Source: School placement offices; 2001 figures are estimates.

buying a physics textbook online. The company's motto, "Fly the Coop," is a direct challenge to Harvard students to abandon the campus's main bookstore, the Harvard Coop. Tseng started his business during the summer after his sophomore year. Recently, the company merged with Limespot, a Web portal for college students that was also founded by college students. Tseng is now chief operating officer of Limespot. He says,

. . . I'm driven by achievement, and I'm also driven by impact. Right now I am only 20, and Limespot is not going to have the hugest impact in the world, but my professional ambition for life is to have a big impact. Microsoft has a big impact; Intel does, and presumably the next Intel would. But in a big machine where I'm steadily going up the ladder trying to express my views or make an impact and not being able to—I have no interest in that.

Alastair Rampell, 19, is a junior at Harvard and the chief executive of Rampell Software. The company provides a variety of software products and consulting services to consumers and corporate clients. Rampell has been a computer-programming whiz since elementary school. He wrote a program designed to ensure a lasting connection to America Online, which won him a significant following during notorious network overload problems in late 1996. He says,

One problem that you have with the Internet is this idea of perfect competition. I think it's going to have the effect of commoditizing a lot of goods. It's very hard to distinguish yourself based on price, because if you try to do that, then the people who are buying your products are not going to have any kind of loyalty to you whatsoever. If someone comes along with a lower price, because they have some kind of new efficiency or they're in a foreign country with cheaper labor costs, then you're finished. You've lost your customer base. It's hard.

These four young entrepreneurs and their statements indicate a high degree of risk taking and sophistication. They are dedicated to their businesses and to the life of e-entrepreneurship. It will be interesting to follow their careers over the next 50 years.

Clearly, not all e-entrepreneurs are from the United States. As in our geographic survey, e-entrepreneurship is a worldwide phenomenon. Consider the case of a Japanese e-entrepreneur, Sonny Koike.[8] Even after the Internet bubble had burst, Sonny's business continued to flourish. It is a consulting and incubator business known as "Netyear." Located on the edge of the Shibuya district of Tokyo, Netyear is one of the bright spots on an otherwise dimmed Tokyo Internet community. Kioke's other claim to e-entrepreneurship fame is that he started the Bit Valley Association. Modeled on Manhattan's New York Media Association, the Bit Valley Association brought together the brightest stars of the Japanese Internet business for deal making, seminars, financing, and partying. Unfortunately, the association "bit the dust" in February 2000 as the bubble burst, but according to Koike, the revolution is not over. He still believes in what he is doing. He believes the big business model in Japan is bankrupt, and that younger people will be gravitating to smaller, more entrepreneurial ventures. Again, we will wait and see.

Finally, let us cross the new venture border to include e-entrepreneurs within corporate America and across the world. The *e.biz* 25 is an annual listing of the top e-entrepreneurs published by *Business Week's e.biz* magazine. Table 6-5 lists these most powerful people by their achievements and contributions.[9] Each of these e-entrepreneurs has made a lasting mark on their industry, and aspiring e-entrepreneurs would be well served to know their names, study their businesses, and monitor future developments.

TABLE 6-5 The *e.biz* 25 for 2001

Name	Title	Company	Contribution	Challenge
Empire Builders	*Creating large markets and capturing large market shares*			
Monica Leuchtefeld	Vice President, E-Commerce	Office Depot, Inc.	Second largest e-tailer next to Amazon.com	Raise online customers to 50% from today's 40%
Stuart Wolf	Chairman and CEO	Homestore.com, Inc.	Showed that dot-coms can succeed by joining forces with the establishment	To keep growing despite the downturn, which could hurt housing sales
Meg Whitman	CEO	eBay, Inc.	Turned eBay into the largest site for e-commerce with 30 million registered users	Reach goal of $30 billion in transactions by 2005 in face of increased competition
Thomas Middelhoff	CEO	Bertelsmann	First European publisher to sell books, music and magazines on the Web	Use e-commerce to boost slow sales and profits
Steve Case	Chairman	AOL Time Warner	Brought the Net to 29 million people with AOL; now heads largest empire of new and old media	Generate synergies by using AOL's brand and TW's entertainment operations
Architects	*Building the infrastructure to capture billions of transactions and customers*			
Rick Belluzzo	President and COO	Microsoft	Reversed decline of Microsoft's Web business; MSN now #2	Build new Web business through subscriptions
Bill Coleman	CEO and Cofounder	BEA Systems, Inc.	Top provider of software for corporate e-commerce Web sites	Competition from IBM, Oracle, Sun Microsystems
Tony Ball	CEO	British Sky Broadcasting	Built the world's largest interactive TV system; over 5 million users	Persuading the couch potatoes to spend money online
Scott McNealy	Chairman and CEO	Sun Microsystems	"The network is the computer," and the Internet proved him right	Adjusting to the slowdown without losing major talent

Pekka Ala-Pietila	President	Nokia Corporation	Champion of the wireless Web; could sell 150 million Web-ready phones this year	Extending dominance will require software and competition from Microsoft
Michael Powell	Chairman	Federal Communications Commission	Pro-deregulation stance will aid mergers and consolidations	Going against big lobbies and vested interests
Visionaries			*Can see the future development clearly and persuade people to follow that path*	
Lawrence Lessig	Professor of Law	Stanford University	Promotes free expression online and argues that old industries are using Old Economy laws to stifle innovation	Persuading courts to adopt laws that balance existing rights while encouraging innovation
Hal Varian	Dean, School of Information	University of California, Berkeley	Net businesses adhere to the laws of economics	Convincing established firms that the changes are real
Innovators			*Creating new products and services, organizations and points of view*	
Courtney Love	Lead vocals, guitar	Hole	Suing her record label for more control over music on the Internet	If she loses, she could find it hard to get work again
Ray Ozzie	Founder	Groove Networks, Inc.	Substitute for Napster, Groove is peer2peer software that allows sharing	Make Groove a major player, sign up corporate partners
Paul Bourke	Chairman and CEO	Altra Energy Technologies, Inc.	Created first profitable independent online marketplace for energy	Must sign up new customers and maintain profitability
Takeshi Natsuno	Executive Director	NTT DoCoMo	Created the content for DoCoMo's i-mode service connecting to Net via cell phone	Transport i-mode to Europe and US, develop new services

(continued)

TABLE 6-5 *(cont.)*

Name	Title	Company	Contribution	Challenge
Websmart	*Ability to use the Web to create efficiencies and sustainable competitive advantages*			
Michael Dell	Chairman and CEO	Dell Computer Corp.	Wrote the book on e-business, keeps Dell profitable despite PC price war	Must find growth and products to sell online
Pradeep Sindhu	Founder and Chief Technical Officer	Juniper Networks, Inc.	Maker of network gear uses Web for everything, challenges Cisco dominance	Generating efficiencies and keeping costs down
Gary Reiner	CIO	General Electric Co.	Made GE e-business leader among large manufacturers, savings projected at $1.6 billion for 2001	Pushing cultural change for GE and raising percent of GE goods sold online
Jeffrey Skilling	President and CEO	Enron Corporation	Transformed Enron into North America's number 1 energy marketer	Proving bandwidth can be traded as a commodity
Steve Sanger	Chairman and CEO	General Mills, Inc.	Tops in cost-cutting using Web technology	Additional savings to offset slow growth core business
The Hot Seat	*Their business models and ideas are being tested; will they pass?*			
Jeff Bezos	CEO	Amazon.com	The gold standard for customer service	Profits, profits, profits
Marty Wygod	Chairman and CEO	WebMD Corporation	Put company on steady financial basis	Revolutionize health-care system
Masayoshi Son	President and CEO	Softbank Croporation	Aggressive investor in over 600 start-ups	Weather the storm, manage his portfolio

Source: Business Week e.biz, May 14, 2001, pps. 25–60.

WINNERS AND LOSERS

Beginning in March 2000, the stock market and the fate of many e-entrepreneurs began to plunge. What has been termed a "bubble" burst: Massive investment in e-commerce business had not produced a return for investors; suddenly, there were no more investors interested in these firms. Because the companies had not yet begun to earn profits, without additional investment they were eventually going to run out of cash. For many e-entrepreneurs, this is exactly what happened. For others, there is enough cash to last a few more months, or even a year or so. Without profits and/or additional cash infusions, though, the "burn rate" will catch up with all the sky-high promises of the first Internet bubble.

Digital Darwinism   Despite the positive demographics, the technological innovations and advances, the billions of dollars of investment, and the commitments of thousands of the best business minds, many new e-entrepreneurs fall victim to **digital Darwinism**.[10] That means they don't survive. They are "selected out" of the economy because they fail to either create value or capture value, or both. There are many examples of firms that failed on at least one of these criteria. Table 6-6 presents a sampling

TABLE 6-6 **Fallen Stars of E-Business**	
Adams Golf	Ashford.com
AskJeeves.com	Autoweb.com
Balanced Care	Buy.com
Caliber Learning Network	Coolsavings.com
Cypress Communications	Drkoop.com
DSL.net	Emultek
E-Stamp Corporation	Engage Technologies
FairMarket Inc.	Fastnet Corporation
Global Telesystems Group	Harvey Electronics
Horizon Medical Products	iBeam Broadcasting
Internet America	InterWorld Corporation
Ivillage	Juno Online Services
Knot Inc.	Launch Media
Log On America	Loudeye Technologies
Mail.com	Miller Exploration
NationsRent	Netpliance
NetZero	Nextera Enterprises
PeoplePC	Persistence Software
Quokka Sports	Razorfish Inc.
Salon.com	Shopnow.com
Talk City Inc.	Theglobe.com
24/7 Media Inc.	Valley Media
VarsityBooks.com	VitaminShoppe.com
Webvan Group	Women.com
Zany Brainy	Zapme Corporation

of e-commerce firms whose stock prices have fallen below $1 or were de-listed from the stock exchange.[11]

This is only the tip of the iceberg as digital Darwinism continues its inexorable process. *Fortune* magazine even publishes a dot-com deathwatch to enable its readers to anticipate the funerals.[12] What went wrong with so many of these companies, and how delusional were the e-entrepreneurs and investors who founded them? In some cases, the business models seems irresistible, yet the inability to capture value severely restrained the company's prospects. Consider the dual cases of Stamps.com and E-Stamps.[13]

Both companies were founded on the intriguing idea of using the Internet to purchase postage. The home office and small business market for postage is estimated at $22 billion. Businesses would be able to download "stamps"—no more trips to the post office; no more postage meters. Investors, however, were much more enthusiastic about this idea than customers. The United States Postal Service, which approved the plan, did not really make things easy. There was a 79-page technical manual about how to print the e-stamps; there was a $500 limit on purchases; and, although, the technology was proven, the market was not.

So, the firms struggled and lost millions of dollars. Their stocks plummeted 95 percent from their highs. Like many species that find themselves in a hostile environment, it was change or die. Both companies revised their plans and, using their secure printing technology, began offering shipping labels, concert and movie tickets, and other services. A check of their Web sites indicates that they have become more than e-stamp sellers: They have evolved into shipping and logistics solutions companies.

Success in the new economy requires more than innovation. There is in fact a glut of innovation.[14] There are so many new products and new product ideas out there that consumers are often overwhelmed by the choices. Unfortunately, customers are not always charged for the innovation. Either the innovators haven't the courage to require the customer to pay, or perhaps they haven't discovered how to collect for the innovation. Sometimes the attitude of the e-entrepreneur is based on the liberating but impoverishing credo—"information is free." Information is not free; it's just cheap to reproduce.

Investors have wised up, too. Venture capitalists have become wary of firms that create value but fail to capture it. It takes innovation and value creation as well as value capture to succeed.

Value Creation   The creation of value occurs when the company has the resources and capabilities to produce a product or service that is desired by market participants. For example, both Stamps.com and E-Stamps created value. They developed innovative technology. They put together a business plan that enabled home office users and small businesses to purchase their products. They saved the customer time and offered convenience. They let the customer avoid frequent trips to the post office. These are good things, valuable things, which were created by the companies in an effort to serve a customer and make some money.

Value Capture   Capturing that value means that the price charged covers the full cost of production and a return on investment. A firm must capture the value of its creation or else it is just an "intriguing idea" and not a sustainable business. Value capture has not been so easy for the e-entrepreneurs involved in the electronic stamp business. The post office, although approving the idea, made it difficult for the company to convince customers that this electronic postage would be accepted. The cost of providing the technology and service to customers was unexpectedly high, and although there surely were economies of scale, the critical mass of customers did not emerge. Therefore, these economies could not be exploited. Now Pitney-Bowes, the power of the metered-postage business, has entered the market, and the electronic stamp companies are in danger of running out of cash.

Does this mean that these firms are doomed? It might; but it might also mean that the firms will adapt to their environment and, building on their resources and capabilities, find a new ecological niche and a new strategy. What would this take? The reader is welcome to consider this on their own. In Street Story 6-1, a similar fate may be in store for many of Hollywood's e-entrepreneurs and dot-com firms.

Even the e-entrepreneur **incubator** must both create value and capture value, or perish. The incubator is supposed to create its own petri-dish environment that enables e-commerce start-ups to flourish. These incubators are a combination of venture capital investment, consultancy, human resource agents, and landlord. They create value for the start-up by doing a host of things for the start-up that the new venture cannot do as well for itself. Value capture, though, depends on the profitability of the companies in the incubator. That has not yet materialized. Therefore, incubators like Idealab!, CMGI, Divine Ventures, and Internet Capital Group all face serious problems in an indefinite future.[15]

Are all e-entrepreneurs and e-business ventures doomed? We don't think so. In fact, there are many successes, but we think that the creators of e-businesses would do well to follow some of the precepts of the resource-based view. They need to consider how the configuration of the venture's resources and capabilities will enable it to create and capture value. We also think that a deeper understanding of the rules of "information economics" would help the e-entrepreneur devise strategies that are winners. In the following sections, we will review how the resource-based view can be employed for e-commerce analysis and also explore the underlying economics of these businesses.

THE RESOURCE-BASED VIEW AND E-ENTREPRENEURSHIP

The resource-based view is our theory of what makes new ventures successful. It states that companies that possess resources and capabilities that are rare, valuable, hard-to-copy, and nonsubstitutable will be able to achieve a sustainable competitive advantage. The types of resources and capabilities are physical, reputational, organizational, financial, intellectual, and technological (**P-R-O-F-I-T**). Let's review these and see how they influence the success or failure of e-businesses.

Physical Resources   Physical resources, the things you can buy in a market, will seldom play a decisive role in the success of an e-business. This is the same conclusion we reached in Chapter 2, but there are a couple of physical capabilities that seem to matter—logistical capabilities and "bricks and mortar" presence.

Web-based businesses frequently need the capability to pick an order, box, ship, and deliver the product. There are **inbound logistics** of taking orders, and these are usually handled through the Web site. The **outbound logistics** require that the correct product be sent to the correct customer by the promised delivery date. This has proved more

Alas, HollyWeb Is Only a Bit Player

It should have been a star.

The Web site pop.com was one of the best and the brightest of the dot-coms created in the past few years to bring Hollywood-style entertainment to the Internet (where the sites have been dubbed "HollyWeb"). This site had $50 million in funding and included some of Hollywood's elite—Steven Spielberg, Ron Howard, and DreamWorks SKG—as its backers. It planned to produce and broadcast original Net-only programming, but pop.com never made it to the box office. Its Internet launch has been postponed indefinitely, and most of its 70 staffers have been given pink slips. "We were looking at throwing a lot of money away," says DreamWorks SKG principal Jeffrey Katzenberg about the decision.

The pop.com story is not unique. Many of the other HollyWeb Internet darlings, including Icebox.com, IFILM. com, Shockwave.com, and Digital Entertainment Network Inc., have either bitten the dust or retooled their plans significantly. "We know what doesn't work," says Frank Biondi, Jr., the former Viacom president who invested in several Holly-Web sites. "But what will work is far less clear to us."

The HollyWeb sites suffer from both value creation and value capture problems. Many original Internet programs were filled with sex, violence, and politically incorrect humor—in other words, content that pushed the limits of traditional TV and film venues and had a somewhat limited audience. Many sites wanted to broadcast short films or "Webisodes" produced by high-priced talent like Tim Burton or Steven Spielberg, or by wannabe-famous amateur filmmakers. The sites that were launched, however, suffered from low traffic and dismal advertising revenues. Part of the problem may have been technology; site managers did not understand that many consumers don't have the Internet connections necessary to view and download programs easily. Morgan Stanley Dean Witter estimates that only 35 percent of U.S. households will be hooked to cable modems and digital subscriber lines by the year 2004. "There just isn't a market out there, at least not now," notes Jeffrey Katzenberg. Or maybe there just isn't a paying market; the primary market for Web entertainment has been teenage boys and college kids, and many of them simply may not be willing to pay to be entertained on the Internet.

The sites that are surviving have made radical adaptations. Shockwave. com is replacing programs with online games. Former Disney Studio chairman Joe Roth purchased Mediatrip.com to promote films he hopes to make and to distribute those films and music online. IFILM has transformed itself from a consumer site to a unique business site. Subscribers now pay an annual fee as high as $35,000 for a unique way to network with other film industry professionals as a way of finding scripts or props or tracking film production.

"If we can give the industry the tools it needs to do business, we can become indispensable," explains IFILM chairman Skip Paul. They recently posted a 58-second film about an airplane landing on a freeway to attract industry afficionados to their site. The film was downloaded an astonishing 1 million times in its first 6 weeks—and the two computer graphic artists who made it were then signed to a contract by Creative Artists Agency Inc.

Source: Adapted from Ronald Grover and Stefani Eads, "HollyWeb Flops," *Business Week e.biz,* October 23, 2000, EB 124–134.

problematic for e-entrepreneurs. Many e-tailers (retailers on the Web) have failed to anticipate the problems of outbound logistics and failed to invest in the physical resources needed (warehouses and product-picking and moving equipment) to fulfill the orders that they have received. Others have decided to subcontract fulfillment of orders to independent businesses like Fingerhut Business Services, Inc. But these fulfillment companies have problems of their own, such as narrow margins and tough competition. Fulfillment itself is becoming a commodity business. An e-tailer has to make a choice:[16]

Choice 1. Build your own fulfillment capability. Pros: You have control. You know the system's capacities, timing, and quirks. It is dedicated to handling your own products exclusively. Cons: A state-of-the-art warehouse will cost around $20 million. There isn't this kind of cash available now that the investment bubble has burst.

Choice 2. Hire someone else. Pros: You don't have to invest millions, and you can save money through volume discounts that can be negotiated with companies like Federal Express. Cons: In busy times, the contractor may not be able to handle your order. The quality of the delivery service will vary from time to time. You can't control this.

The other issue of physical resources concerns whether or not an e-business should also have a "bricks and mortar" presence. Many companies started as physical businesses, a store or a manufacturing plant, and then added a Web-based capability. These companies have physical resources and an ability to relate to suppliers and customers directly at that location. Businesses that start the other way might be at a disadvantage. New ventures that are launched on the Web must consider whether or not the physical presence is critical to their success. There is simply not enough information and operating history available to be sure which is the right answer.

Reputational Resources A good reputation is critical to e-business success. First, it enables people to hear of your business through positive word-of-mouth (and word-of-e-mail) reports. Second, because of the remoteness of many forms of e-commerce, it requires trust to perform the transaction. As an example, consider eBay's rating system for buyers and sellers. At each transaction, the buyers and the sellers get to rate their satisfaction with the other party, and this rating is available to all other buyers and sellers. Trust and security are the keys, but how important is branding?

Branding is important, but it is not sufficient. You can have a great brand and still be a victim of all the other things that can go wrong in e-commerce. A cautionary tale is presented in Street Story 6-2.

Organizational Resources and Capabilities Once again, these are very important for the e-entrepreneur. Consider these statistics that illustrate the profile of an online shopper:[17]

- 45 percent demand timely responses to questions and inquiries
- 22 percent require informative content on the site
- 17 percent highly value communication with a real person
- 14 percent want the products displayed clearly and prominently
- 14 percent desire 24-hour availability

These customer demands and priorities put pressure on an organization to deliver. It takes coordination, commitment, and leadership to accomplish these tasks. Internal communication capabilities are essential to achieving high levels of customer

Web Business Wash-Out

The revolution in home appliances will have to wait.

For 8 brief months, the Brandwise.com Web site offered consumers a place where they could comparison shop for appliances like washing machines and refrigerators from the convenience of their home or office. The site posted Good Housekeeping Institute reports for every oven, dishwasher, and other appliance available, which customers could then examine at their leisure. The site also eliminated pushy salespeople, because consumers could use the site to purchase and arrange delivery of the item they wanted from a local retailer. The launch of Brandwise.com was widely applauded as a revolutionary step on the e-commerce ladder; both local and national media were so enthusiastic they actually encouraged consumers to shop at the site.

Brandwise.com may have been a good concept, but the reality is that it was a bad business. The site chomped through an estimated $10 million like a virtual garbage disposal before closing due to problems with both physical and reputational resources.

Like many sites, Brandwise.com stumbled over out-bound logistics in their rush to do business on the Web. As Dennis Moir, president of Western Appliances & TV in San Jose, explains, "Eighty percent of appliances purchased are replacements for things that broke. That person does not want to conduct research and get their appliance in 2 weeks. They want it yesterday." But retailers couldn't or wouldn't feed Brandwise.com accurate, up-do-date inventory information, which meant that delivery was anything but a sure thing. Brandwise.com got the customer complaint calls but, because they didn't control delivery, they couldn't make the appliances appear when needed.

Brandwise.com had indirect reputational problems, too. The idea for the site originally came from appliance megamanufacturer Whirlpool, although the business was a partnership between Whirlpool, the Boston Consulting Group, and Hearst Publications, parent of the Good Housekeeping Institute. But the name "Whirlpool" is what the public heard. Consumers were afraid the product reports were biased to favor Whirlpool products (although the Good Housekeeping Institute guaranteed testing was blind and unbiased), and retailers who didn't stock Whirlpool were afraid they would never get referrals. Brandwise.com did form alliances with national retailers like Sears and Montgomery Ward, but the real powerhouses like Kmart and Home Depot wouldn't sign on.

The Web site thought it could make money by charging retailers 5 percent of the sales price for every appliance sold through the Web. It also hoped to collect consumer data to sell to retailers and attract Web advertising, but Brandwise.com never got the number of visitors it needed to generate significant sales or data. Unexpectedly high costs for advertising outside of the Web doubled their customer acquisition charge, and they were forced to scale down their marketing campaign. In the end, traffic was too low to bother counting, and at least one of their retail partners never received a single referral during the entire 8 months.

(continued)

(continued)

Whirlpool now limits their Internet use for internal programs, like monitoring employee expense reports and retirement benefits. Ironically, their competitor, General Electric, has figured out a nonrevolutionary way to make the Internet work for them. GE uses the Web strictly to expedite delivery to retailers, allowing stores to handle all the traditional customer interactions. This appliance manufacturer is content to let consumers do their own comparative research.

Source: Adapted from Amy Kover, "Why Brandwise Was Brand Foolish," *Fortune,* November 13, 2000, 201–208.

satisfaction. Many e-tailers are first achieving this. The same survey reports that 83 percent of online shoppers were pleased with their last online experience and that 71 percent either strongly or somewhat agreed that online shopping is more convenient than buying products over the phone.

A critical organizational capability is the knack for using and organizing information to create and capture value. This exploits what the Web does best and most cheaply: collecting, arranging, manipulating, and sending massive amounts of data. "The vast majority of companies are not using the unique attributes of the Net," says Scott Kurnit, CEO of About.com. Value creation and capture on the Web requires "low-friction distribution, interconnectivity, and viral marketing," he concludes. These skills are organizational.[18]

Financial Resources   Financial resources, cash, credit, and access to capital markets did not prove to be the critical factors in determining e-commerce success or failure. Individuals and institutions invested billions of dollars, and the amount of the investment does not seem to be related to later survival. At times, it seemed that all that was needed in order to raise money to start an Internet company was an idea for one. Of course, there are some who would argue that even more money was needed.

For example, while an undergraduate at Yale, Michael Stern was able to obtain $1 million in commitments to invest in campus Internet ventures. He was a campus venture capitalist, but he has burned through most of that money and with no winners in his portfolio. "I wish we had had more money to put into companies. Ultimately, we would have done really well." Or, ultimately, he would have lost even more. "Maybe we were fools to give them the money in the first place. They were bright kids with ideas. We were all suffering from a mania," lamented Ben Karp of Dagim Consulting, who was the Yale students' original backer.[19]

Of course, as before, financial management skills and capabilities are different from the size of the financial endowment. With financial skill, the e-entrepreneur can marshal and maintain the endowments as long as possible. She can manage the "burn rate" better than those without obvious financial abilities. Great financial management might enable a company that is short on cash to survive long enough to turn a profit or find a partner. Poor financial management will destroy any company, no matter how large a cash pool it has.

Intellectual Resources and Intellectual Property The intangible property, knowledge, and skills of an e-venture are worth defending because these can form the source of sustainable competitive advantage. For example, eBay, the number one auction site, aggressively defends what it considers its intellectual property. There are a number of other, smaller auction sites that have challenged eBay, but some have done so by violating the agreement that eBay has with its buyers and sellers. One example is Auctiva, which links eBay's postings with their own. Because this violates eBay's rules, eBay has gone to court to stop the practice.[20]

Other e-commerce businesses also protect their intellectual property. For example, Amazon.com has patented its "one-click" buying process. Priceline.com has the rights to the "name your own price" business model. There is even a Web site that will help investors use statistical tools to value intellectual property.[21]

However, an interesting sidelight of the dot-com bubble and its deflation is how little the intellectual property of defunct dot-coms are worth. For example, eToys, which is in bankruptcy, has not been able to sell the proprietary management system that it developed to insure that over a million toys would be delivered in time for Christmas. It spent $80 million on a system that appears to be worthless. Firms that once had billion-dollar valuations and who spent millions on pricey Super Bowl advertising and marketing do not seem to be able to recoup much from their brands. When Petsmart.com bought Pets.com, it junked the sock puppet immediately. The brands, trademarks, and associations of failed dot-coms and failed business models bring little return to their former owners.[22]

Technological Resources and Capabilities Clearly, technological resources are valuable in the start-up and running of the e-commerce business. Many of these firms' basis for existing rests on their technological abilities. E-entrepreneurs who promise technological adeptness and cutting-edge technology products, and then cannot deliver, are simply doomed.

To review: The obsession that Internet companies had with their financing and the amounts that they raised was misplaced energy in the longer term. Financial endowments are not one of the critical resources, but financial management is. Organizational capabilities, intellectual property, and great technology are also sources of sustainable competitive advantage.

The business that is built on a great idea may find that the idea and its implementation create value for customers, but that is not the same as capturing that value and earning a profit. In order to capture the profit, the firm must be able to appropriate some of the surplus created in the value chain. This is why it is important to understand the rules of the information game.

INFORMATION RULES

Some of the most important insights about e-commerce come from a book by Carl Shapiro and Hal Varian called *Information Rules: A Strategic Guide to the Network Economy.*[23] Shapiro and Varian explain that the laws of economics still apply to the Internet revolution and that, like previous revolutions before it, these rules will provide us with strategic insights into the direction of industry evolution, and guidelines for success and wealth creation. Just like the railroad revolution of the mid- to late nineteenth century and the telephone revolution of the early twentieth century, the Internet and information age revolution of the late twentieth and early twenty-first century will follow certain predictable patterns. One significant difference, however, is the reality that this revolution is based on information: its collection, generation, copying, and distribution. There are certain qualities to information that are different from prior innovations, and these are important.

First, what is information? *Information* can be defined as anything that can be digitized. That means it is Web pages, textbooks, music, golf scores, movies, and stock quotes. These are all "information goods" in Shapiro and Varian's terms.

Second, information goods can be incredibly expensive to generate and collect. Consider digitizing all the world's phone books, or developing a database of all of the purchases made at Wal-Mart by all of its customers. The software needs to be developed and tested, enormous investment in hardware is required, and millions of human hours go into the constant analyzing, updating, and maintenance of the databases. Yet once built and employed, at any given moment it is virtually costless to make copies of the data analysis for people all over the Wal-Mart organization. A product (information) that is expensive to create is almost costless to duplicate. The implications of this will be discussed later.

Third, because information has different uses to different people, it will also have different values to different people. A golf score may have little value to the movie enthusiast, and stock quotes may have more value to the day trader than to the long-term investor. This provides the opportunity to discriminate in prices and segment the market.

Fourth, information is intellectual property and, therefore, can be protected and made a source of sustainable competitive advantage. E-entrepreneurs are urged to maximize the value of their intellectual property, not maximize the protection.

Last, information is an **experience good**. Although marketing people have long known how to market an experience good—free samples, early discounts, testimonials from trusted public figures—information is an experience good each time it is consumed. This requires that producers allow potential consumers to browse and peek at the information. Also, strategies for branding and reputation-building are needed. Reputation, as we have continually noted, is hard to develop and hard to copy and, therefore, can be a source of competitive advantage.

Now let us review the major tenets of the network economy and see how the e-entrepreneur can configure the new venture to make the most of the information rules.

Value Pricing

What is the value of information to the user? The answer is—it depends on the user. When a product is costly to produce but relatively inexpensive to duplicate, the price of information should depend on its value to the user, not the cost to produce the next unit (marginal cost). The imperative to the e-entrepreneur then is to segment the market according to the value of the information to the user and charge each segment what they are willing to pay to develop **value pricing**.

Consumers are not stupid, however, and they will be unwilling to pay more for a product than someone else (unless they are passengers on an airline). You must differentiate your product according to the personal needs of the purchaser so you can distinguish your high-value information-based product from your lower value products, and also differentiate your products from those offered by the competition. This requires you to know your customer well and track his or her moves, preferences, and feedback.

If you cannot differentiate your product, you must try to achieve a low-cost position and try to sell a lot of it. Reuse the information, repackage it, and resell it in many different ways. You can achieve economies of scale over large numbers of customers and reduce your average costs. This will be necessary for survival because the revenue streams obtainable for commodity information products will be quite limited.

Versioning

Versioning means producing a number of different options for your information-based product. Each option has to appeal to some customer who values it, so versioning goes hand in hand with value pricing. The prescription is to differentiate the product so that it adds value to a particular segment and then charge that segment whatever it will bear.

Information-based products can be versioned in many different ways:

- *Delay.* Some people want their information fresh, up-to-the-minute. Others can wait an hour, a day, or a month. Charge more for the timeliest data.
- *User interface.* Provide high-paying customers with superior user interface: better graphics, a more powerful search engine, increased sorting and filtering capabilities. Use design to make it look better, too.
- *Convenience.* You could restrict the time or location at which the information-based products are available. Convenience is related to delay.
- *Image resolution.* High-paying customers receive versions that are clear, with high-resolution images. Lower paying customers receive lower resolution or just text-based versions, no graphics.
- *Speed of operation.* Some sites may load quickly; some search algorithms may be more efficient than others. Customers are willing to pay for speed. This is true in hardware, too. Faster copiers and printers cost more than slower ones.
- *Capabilities.* Consider voice recognition software. How many words will it recognize? How many and which specialized vocabularies will be programmed into the software?
- *Features and functions.* The more features and functions, bells and whistles, the more you can charge. In fact, it often pays to develop the higher end version first and actually disable features and functions on the less-expensive models.
- *Annoyance.* "Nagware" are the pop-ups that appear with advertising or pitches of various kinds. Higher end versions do not have this nagging; lower end ones do.
- *Support.* Technical support is always available to the highest price payers. Lower levels of support depend on price segment. The lowest paying customer may receive no support, or just an online manual.

Because it often requires just a little imagination to produce many versions of the product, the e-entrepreneur needs to consider how many versions to actually produce. One of the ways to answer this is to see how many market segments there are that are large enough to support the production of an entirely separate version. Often this is hard to do because market research for a new information-based product is not going to be precise. One way around this problem is to employ "Goldilocks" pricing: Produce three versions. The first is the low-end standard version for the lowest paying customer. It has the least features and the least support. This will appeal to the lower value customers. Next, produce a professional version. This is for the business customer who uses it to create value at work or for the enthusiast who values more features and better design. Last, create a "gold" version that is the most expensive and is fully loaded with all features and speed. Many customers will buy the middle version due to a psychological trait called "extremeness aversion." They do not want to buy the cheapest (it harms their self-image), and they do not want to buy the most expensive (it harms their pocketbook). Just like Goldilocks, they choose the one in the middle. This strategy will enable the e-entrepreneur to get many people to trade up from the standard version and perhaps to sell some "gold" to customers who do not care about price or who have a high-status self-image.

Intellectual Property

Intellectual property is intangible property. The difference between tangible property and intangible property is that tangible property is "rivalrous in consumption." This means that if Tom eats a sandwich (the sandwich is tangible), Harry cannot eat the same sandwich. Intangible property has the interesting feature of being nonrivalrous. If Tom sees a movie or listens to a music CD, Harry can do so as well. There is almost zero additional cost to the producer and distributor when Harry sees the movie or listens to the music at the same time as Tom.[24]

The e-entrepreneur who publishes the content has two significant costs vastly reduced by the digitized intangible property. First, reproduction costs for the digital movie or music are drastically reduced. Second, digital technology allows distribution of the property to be accomplished quickly, easily, and cheaply.

The information rule for the e-entrepreneur is to maximize the value of the property, not the protection of the property. This means that the e-entrepreneur must design terms and conditions for the use and consumption of the intangible property that involve a basic trade-off: "The more liberal terms will tend to raise the value of the property to the consumers, but it may reduce the number of units sold."[25]

One implication of this rule is that it pays to advertise by giving away free samples. The samples cost the e-entrepreneur almost nothing, and the consumer gets to experience the good. Giving your product away, however, will make illicit copying and infringement easier, but the bootleggers have to identify themselves eventually. If they get big enough, they are easy to find.

Another implication is that strong copy protection imposes costs on consumers. Consumers take these costs into account before purchase or repurchase decisions. Additionally, if one e-entrepreneur has very strong protection, surely another e-entrepreneur will come along and compete based on loose protection. Although strong protection measures may have their place depending on the product, usually they will be defeated and invite competition.

Last, site licenses and group-pricing plans are valuable because they enable the producers to charge more for the property (without additional costs) while letting the consumers share the property without paying full individual prices. This is a win/win situation.

Lock-In

Lock-in is the same as imposing a switching cost on the customer (see Chapter 3). A switching cost imposed on the customer acts as both a barrier to entry for a potential competitor and a way of securing loyalty from the customer.

Customer lock-in is quite easily achieved in the information economy. The storage, manipulation, and communication of information require encoding, processing, and decoding. This comprises a "system," and the system usually consists of many computer programs and pieces of hardware. If a customer wants to change any one of these software programs or hardware items, a cost is involved. Usually, people do not switch unless the benefit of the switch exceeds the costs. There is also the cost of relearning a new system and process. "**Wetware**" (people's knowledge about how the system works) is a durable complementary asset, and changing it is costly. The e-entrepreneur can design several different kinds of switching costs into the digital business.[26] Table 6-7 illustrates some of the types of lock-in and the switching costs they impose.

The e-entrepreneur who can recognize lock-in and then manage it to ensure that the venture's customers remain loyal will begin to develop an "installed base" of customers. These customers can be counted on as a semipermanent revenue stream. The existence of an installed base raises the value of the venture significantly.

However, awareness of the e-entrepreneur's company is not the same as loyalty. Remember eToys? It had one of the highest brand awareness levels on the entire Internet. It was the killer toy seller that made shopping for toys a one-stop, low-cost option. During the Christmas season of 2000–2001, eToys gave signs that it might not be able to meet orders and that it might not be around much longer if it couldn't. This became a self-fulfilling prophecy as customers deserted the e-tailer. Even though eToys had advertised heavily in magazines and on television, awareness did not translate into loyalty, and the company failed.[27]

TABLE 6-7   Lock-In and Switching Costs

Types of Lock-In	Switching Costs for Consumers
Contracts and subscriptions	Damages for breaking the contract or ending the subscription before it expires
Durable purchases	Replacement of the equipment; switching cost declines as equipment ages
Brand-specific training	Customers have to learn a new system, process or technique; Loss of productivity during training period
Information and databases	Data conversion costs, potential for losing data; larger databases equal higher costs of conversion
Specialized suppliers	Search of finding new supplier; new supplier may not have precisely the same capabilities and quality of older supplier
Search costs	Aggregate of buyer and seller costs
Loyalty programs	Lost benefits from program; need to start over with another company's program

Networks and Positive Feedback

In the traditional economy that featured manufactured, tangible products, economies of scale dominated. Economies of networks are the driving force in the new economy. The basic idea of an **economy of network** is that the more people in the network, the more valuable being in the network is for each member. A network is a set of connections. When only one person owns a phone, it is almost valueless because there is no one to call. The same is true for a fax machine when there is no one on the other side to send or receive the fax. The same is true for an Internet connection. The more servers, companies, individuals, and organizations that are linked to the Internet, the more valuable being linked is to each one of these constituents.

Positive feedback is the effect of being in a large network. People value the network, they enjoy being in it, they want their friends to be involved, and they actively recruit others to participate. Consider two networks: one large and growing, and the other small and shrinking. One is becoming more valuable while the other is becoming less valuable to each member. Eventually, the small and shrinking network will be unable to sustain itself, and everyone will have migrated to the large and growing one. When there is positive feedback at work, the "strong grow stronger and the weak grow weaker."[28]

It is critical for an e-entrepreneur to be able to recognize when the business that has been founded is in a network. Without this accurate recognition, the e-entrepreneur could be developing and implementing a strategy that fails to take advantage of the effects of positive feedback. Worse, the e-entrepreneur can be steering the venture in the direction of not being in a network at all. How can this happen? An e-entrepreneur could mistake his or her nonnetwork status as a lack of competition and actually think that this is a good place to be. This is what happened, in some respects, to Apple Computer. While the rest of the industry was participating in the PC (IBM-based) revolution, Apple stuck to its proprietary hardware designs. Part of the reason for this was that it saw its lonely position as secure due to a lack of competition. In fact, its position was outside of the growing network of IBM-based producers and end users. As the world gained from the advantages of the transferability of software and skills developed on PCs, Apple saw its network shrink. It has stabilized at a relatively low figure, and now Apple forever has lost its initial foothold on personal computing.

Not all information-based industries will develop network economies. For example, there are no positive feedback effects for telephone handsets or PBXs as long as they meet the industry standards. When a product or service is purchased because someone else has purchased it, network effects will be present. When this happens, the market can tip and become a winner-take-all affair. This is what happened to the market for prerecorded and new videotapes. Two competing standards existed, Beta and VHS, but it was in everyone's interest to have one standard. When VHS began to get a small advantage due to price, everyone quickly moved to VHS, and Beta disappeared from the marketplace. The market tipped, and VHS won.

Street Story 6-3 illustrates how a network of real estate agents with home listings becomes more valuable as more brokers, buyers, and sellers use it. It also illustrates some of the reasons why cooperation and compatibility are important as well. The Web site for Homestore.com is www.homestore.com.

Make Money, Not Conflict

Got a job offer in Houston, Texas? Or a transfer to Helena, Montana? Dreaming about relocating to Honolulu, Hawaii?

Then, you're going to want to visit www.Realtor.com or one of the other Web sites under the Homestore.com umbrella. According to site-tracker Media Metrix Inc., it's the most visited real estate search site on the Internet. Maybe it's because it has the world's largest database of homes for sale. Maybe it's because the site allows shoppers to search for a new home by punching in a city, a zip code, the amount they want to spend, or even the number of bedrooms and bathrooms they want. Maybe it's because the site then shows shoppers color photos of the homes that match their requirements, tells them about the schools and the crime rate in that neighborhood, and then makes it easy for them to connect with a realtor, financing, insurance, movers, lawn care, furniture, and everything else they need to make a smooth transition. Other Homestore.com sites help consumers who want to build a home or rent an apartment.

Stuart Wolff, creator and chairman of Homestore.com, knew little about real estate when he created the Web site. He even admits to making a big mistake when he bought his first home. But Wolff, an electrical engineer who left IBM to design a computer system for his father's small chain of drugstores, understood something about doing business. "I grew up listening to stories about deals over the dinner table," he recalls. Intrigued by the Internet, Wolff worked for cable giant TCI for 4 years, investigating online business opportunities. In 1996 when he finally found a site with potential—a foundering Web page loosely operated by the National Association of Realtors—his employer was strapped for cash. So Wolff raised $7 million from other investors to take over the site.

Stuart Wolff's real skill was that he recognized that local realtors feared an Internet site would compete to take business away from them, or cut into their sales commissions. "From the beginning, I wanted to be a partner to the industry, not a threat," he explains. Instead, Wolff convinced real estate agents that his revamped site could work with them to enhance their marketing power. He set out to list more homes than anyone else on the assumption that more listings would attract more customers. Working with 740 regional listing services—and trading cash and stock for exclusive listing contracts with some realtors—Realtor.com has been able to list 90 percent of the homes for sale in the United States. Wolff made the site user friendly by loading it with educational tidbits about buying a home. Instead of taking a cut out of commissions, the site charges local realtors a small fee of about $40 a month to have their photo and phone number posted beside each of their home listings. One-third of the site's income comes from advertising from related businesses.

Building a cooperative network has made Wolff a rich man. In 2000, his 4.5 percent stake was estimated to be worth more than $80 million. That's a pretty good commission for a man who knew nothing about selling homes, but who knew a lot about working as a team, just a few years ago.

Source: Adapted from Christopher Palmeri, "The Architect of Homestore.com," *Business Week,* July 10, 2000, pp. 180–184; available at www.homestore.com.

Cooperation and Compatibility

The final information rule is about cooperation and compatibility. The key is to determine your allies and your enemies. Your allies will be part of your network (even if they are technically competitors, too). Your enemies will be forming competing networks (much more dangerous and threatening). Because this is a winner-take-all proposition, it is critical for the e-entrepreneur to correctly identify and attract allies, and to determine what the rules for cooperation and compatibility will be.

One of the basic rules will involve the development of standards. These are usually technical standards relating to how hardware and software interface. Technical standards will enable companies within the network to cooperate because their operating systems will be compatible. It will exclude from the network those firms that do not adopt standards or form networks with competing standards. Once the battle of the standards is fought, the industry will shift to more traditional forms of competition within the winning standard format.

The choice of standards should be made in a way to benefit customers and suppliers. This will make them allies, too, and help to win the battle against the competing standard. Doing this, though, will inevitably transfer some of the total industry profit potential to the customers (in the form of lower prices, higher quality, less lock-in) and the suppliers. The alternative to this is greed that may cause your customers and suppliers to bolt to the competing network, or sue you for antitrust violations or both (Microsoft's network victory has resulted in some of these consequences).

To summarize: The e-entrepreneur faces a set of choices that can be analyzed by using the traditional tools but using them in a very special way. These tools, the resource-based view of the firm and the "information rules" of economics, provide insight into the unique problems of buying and selling information-based products and employing the Internet effectively. Now that we have some basics in place, we will look at how different business models have evolved and how effective they are for producing sustainable competitive advantage.

E-NOTES 6-2

Rules for Information-Based Businesses

Information-based businesses are concerned with the following "rules" or tenets:

- value pricing
- versioning
- intellectual property
- lock-in
- networks and positive feedback
- cooperation and compatibility

BUSINESS MODELS AND STRATEGIES

Our last task is to investigate some of the different ways that companies have tried to exploit the new economy and the Internet to make money. We will look at the most popular business models and strategies that e-entrepreneurs have employed. A **business model** is a plan for earning a profit and the configuration of a business. The business models that we will be examining are business-to-consumer (B2C), business-to-business (B2B), business-to-business-to-consumer (B2B2C), the niche model, the clicks-and-bricks model, the process of roll-ups and conglomeration, the advertising model and, because of the problems that advertising models have, the pay-for-content model. We will conclude this section with some lessons learned from the Internet revolution.

B2C

In the **B2C business model**, the new venture is selling directly to the final customer and end user. It is sometimes called "e-tailing"—a derivation of retailing, meaning selling on the Internet. A host of products and services are now sold this way, from pet supplies to loan mortgages, from travel services to college courses.

Selling directly to the final consumer is the most ubiquitous form of online business. It is easy to set up a Web site for B2C commerce, but there are a number of large problems to solve in order to be successful.

- You have to have a way for customers to find you. There is much clutter on the Internet and much competition for the "eyeballs" of the customer and Web surfer. Be sure your site is designed so that customers can find it during searches. Use non-Web advertising and promotion methods to build awareness. Remember that awareness is not loyalty—the struggle for customer attention is never over. One way to build awareness, loyalty, and lock-in is to advertise using e-coupons.[29] These can be on your own Web site or positioned on other sites. Eighty percent of Americans clip coupons every year, and most everyone likes saving money. Here are the most popular categories of e-coupons:
  - Groceries   59 percent
  - Books   32 percent
  - Health   30 percent
  - Music   26 percent
  - Beauty   17 percent
  - Fast food   16 percent
  - Apparel   14 percent
  - Toys   14 percent
- Design a Web site for easy use. There is much you will want to try to do on your site to get the customer to buy, but overly ambitious sites that confuse the customer with many options and unnecessary details will lose sales. Keep it simple, fast, functional, secure, and private. The Web site should be a friendly place, as if it were a store or shop. One error that Web sites often make is that they do not allow customers to wander in and out of "departments" or product categories. This is done because e-tailers fear "abandoned shopping carts." An abandoned cart occurs when the customer chooses something to buy but

then does not click through to final purchase. E-tailers see this as bad, as if they lost business, but customers like the option of browsing and in real life frequently go in and out of stores without purchasing. Enabling the customer to browse and wander is a good idea.[30]

- Make sure it works. Check cross-browser functionality. Ensure that there are no broken links or missing images. Understand that if you sell on the Web, you are doing business globally. People all over the world can reach you, and they can reach you all the time. Be prepared.[31]

- Personalize the Web site. Make the Web site a customized shopping area for each consumer. Use the technology available to "remember" who is logging onto your site and what their previous browsing and purchasing experience has been. No one does this more effectively than Amazon.com. Visit their site and register and begin to see how they customize each view for the individual.

- Make sure you can get the product to the customer. This is called **fulfillment**. Taking orders is only a part of the problem. Fulfilling orders is also a big issue, and many e-entrepreneurs underestimate the problems of fulfillment. There are companies that specialize in this and will perform this for you for a fee. Ship the product on time or lose the customer forever.

You can even have a specialized company run your entire e-tailing operation for you. Consider a firm like Global Sports, Inc. Global Sports builds and runs e-tailing sites for other companies like Athlete's Foot, Sports Authority, and BlueLight.com. The established companies do the marketing and branding, but Global Sports does all the e-tailing operations, from site design to fulfillment.[32] It even buys the inventory from its clients to minimize client risk. The companies then split the revenue with Global Sports, with Global receiving 92.5 percent and the client 7.5 percent.

Will this business model work? Some are betting against it, and there is much "short interest" on Wall Street at this time. However, the company projects sales of $300 million by 2003. Who is right? Check the Web site at www.globalsports.com to see if the business is still operating at this time.

One particularly egregious failure in the B2C arena was the CueCat. With investors pouring over $100 million into this product, the story shows that a good idea is simply not enough to justify the expense. Street Story 6-4 fills in the details.

B2B

The Internet can also be used to sell in a **B2B business model**, meaning business-to-business. Here the final user is not an individual consumer, but another company. Some of this business is simply traditional wholesaling. Sometimes B2B represents selling technology and Internet networking services. There are many different ways an e-entrepreneur can create a venture that sells a product or service to another firm.

B2B is already a much larger transaction domain than B2C. Estimates for total B2B sales vary from $150 billion to $406 billion for 2000. The B2C market is estimated at only a tenth this size.[33] These numbers will grow steadily over time, even with the Internet bubble's deflation.

B2B consists of a number of separate models. The vast majority of B2B exchanges are simple purchase-order transactions that were formerly made by salespeople and that are now possible over the Web. A more controversial kind of business-to-business

Would Have, Could Have, Should Have

J. Jovan Philyaw is a super salesman.

A veteran presenter from the Home Shopping Network and QVC, Philyaw is credited with generating more than $4 billion in business-to-consumer sales during his 12-year career in direct marketing. "If you haven't see him, it's worth the price of admission," says Michael Dolan of Young & Rubicam Inc.

Philyaw's greatest sales accomplishment may be the selling of the CueCat, a handheld, cat-shaped scanner that allows consumers to access Web pages on their computer by electronically reading the bar code of any product. Need some soup recipes? Scan the UPC label on the side of your Campbell's soup can. Want to check the latest press release from Microsoft? Pass the CueCat over the bar code on the back of any Microsoft box, and your PC will head straight for their Web site. If your home newspaper is the *Dallas Morning News* or one of a handful of other Belo Corp. newspapers, you may be able to scan UPC codes that have been specially placed in ads to ease your Internet connections.

But CueCat did not score well with customers. Despite our addiction to trendy gadgets, both consumers and technology gurus seemed to hate the device. The amazing part of this story is the success that Philyaw and his Digital: Convergence Corporation had selling the CueCat to investors. Radio Shack Corp. invested $30 million. Young & Rubicam, Coca-Cola, and NBC all contributed to a pot of start-up capital that totaled more than $185 million. Almost all of that money is gone now, and 6 million Cue-Cats are sitting in a Digital: Convergence warehouse.

It's hard to say why CueCat didn't—or maybe hasn't—become a success. Companies liked it because they thought it simplified the Internet and made their sites easy to find; users thought it was just as easy to type in a Web address or a search. Computer columnist Walter Mossberg called the scanner "unnatural and ridiculous." If you visit the Digital: Convergence Web site (www.crq.com), you may still be able to get one for less than $5 and see for yourself.

Like its namesake, maybe the Cue-Cat has eight more chances to become a hot product. But for now, it's just an idea that should have worked, but didn't.

Source: Adapted from Elliot Spagot, "A Web Gadget Fizzles, Despite a Salesman's Dazzle," *The Wall Street Journal,* June 27, 2001, B1; additional information available at www.crq.com.

transaction is the buying and selling cooperatives that have been created by industry participants. These exchanges are industry specific (e.g. auto, grain, metal, chemicals) and allow the companies involved to save millions of dollars in back-office bookkeeping, sales, and administrative costs. Some are run by the buyers; some are managed by the sellers. They generate huge amounts of turnover and data. The data provide opportunities for price-fixing and collusion, and the Justice Department is investigating some of these exchanges.[34]

Most of the successful B2B Web sites are not dot-com upstarts but traditional suppliers who have moved their ordering process online to save money.[35] There are a few exceptions, such as Plumtree Software, which helps Procter & Gamble runs its B2B operations.[36] P&G hired Plumtree because it felt it needed the energy, innovation, and expertise that the start-up had. Plumtree benefited from the relationship because P&G is one of the best managed old economy companies in the world. As frequently happens, the collaboration between the big company and the small one led to great lessons for both. Table 6-8 summarizes these. The e-entrepreneur who contemplates starting a company that will depend on a partnership with a larger company should study these lessons closely.

To summarize: B2B is a much larger market than B2C, but traditional old economy suppliers who have shifted to the Internet to make purchasing more efficient frequently dominate it. Although there are opportunities for e-entrepreneurs in B2B, they will often require the collaboration of a larger firm or network of firms.

B2B2C

Business-to-business-to-consumer refers to Internet business models where the e-entrepreneur produces a product for another business that then markets it to the consumer. For example, the New York–based company Foodline.com offered restaurants in the New York area the opportunity to market their eateries to the public, enabling customers to make reservations online and collecting data about these customers. A similar company based in San Francisco called OpenTable.com does the same thing. These businesses sell their services to the owners of the restaurant, not directly to the public.[37]

Another example of the **B2B2C business model** is TrafficStation Inc. This Internet company provides traffic data for commuters and travelers. Although it does sell a few subscriptions directly to customers, the primary sources of revenue for its business model are other businesses: wireless service providers, wireless content providers, and carmakers. This enables them to offer different versions of their service and value price it to match their customers. Their own market research shows that only 20 percent of people would pay for traffic data if it were offered a la carte, but 61 percent would pay if other services were included. So TrafficStation has to piggyback its product and service onto the products and services of others. These partners will do most of the marketing directly to the customers. TrafficStation's expertise is in developing and

---

TABLE 6-8 Lessons for Start-Up Big Company Collaboration

Lessons for the Start-Up	*Lessons for the Big Company*
The big company's clout can help you in dealing with other customers.	The small company needs a very specific set of requirements. Supply the details.
Don't be arrogant. Serve the customers' needs, not your own egos.	Invest in the start-up and make sure that it has the resources it needs to do your job.
Pleasing the big customer is the make-or-break event in the life of the smaller firm.	Socialize with the employees of the smaller firm so that they know and respect you.
Find industry veterans to help guide the younger workers in the politics of big companies	Learn from the smaller company employees how to do things differently and develop cutting-edge skills.

managing the huge network of traffic information that comes out of the United States' metropolitan areas each day.[38]

Niches

Much has been made of the problems that dot-coms have faced and the nagging lack of business models that can sustain profitability. Despite this, there are e-entrepreneurs who are making a living on the Internet with their Web sites. These entrepreneurs occupy small niches with very motivated buyers, sellers, and participants.

A niche business on the Web can be defined as a firm that either targets a very specific market segment, provides that segment with a complete vertical supply chain, or specializes in a very specific kind of product or service and offers it to a number of different horizontal segments. The **vertical niche** market position demands that the e-entrepreneur be an expert in the customer segment that he or she is serving. This is because it seeks to be a full-service provider. The horizontal version of the niche position demands that the entrepreneurs possess the expertise in a small set of products. This is because the **horizontal niche** player seeks to sell these products, and only these products, to a wide variety of customers.

To summarize: The niche strategy possesses resources and capabilities to either serve a specific customer or offer a specific product, but usually not both.

For example, consider ElectricShaver.com, which specializes in replacement parts for—electric shavers. Gary Burns started this company in 1995. Burns is the technology-oriented son of the owner of Electric Shaver Service of Lincoln, Nebraska. Burns knew the Web and he knew shavers. He started his no-frills site by simply registering the right name early and off he went. He has many loyal customers, and the e-entrepreneur will gross nearly $1 million in 2001.[39] Or, consider nurse anesthetist Joseph A. Rybicki of New Jersey. He knows stethoscopes, so he is able to provide the intensely personal service of telling prospective parents which stethoscope can detect their baby's heartbeat. His domain name? Stethoscopes4u.com[40]

Of course, business models can be combined when necessary. For example, a company could have a B2B2C model and a niche position as well. That is the case for MightyWords.com. MightyWords was originally founded as a place for unpublished authors to electronically publish their works.[41] The business model called for people to pay to post their stories, poems, and plays. MightyWords.com would also be a destination site for readers wanting to pay to read these unknown authors' works. With the publication of novelist Stephen King's first electronic book and the future promise of digital books, this business model looked promising at first.

But, this model had problems. A consulting firm that was working with Mighty-Words.com on technology issues pointed out the difficulties of sustaining that business model: competing with Amazon.com and Barnes & Noble, who have vastly larger resources, and monitoring the quality of self-published, unreviewed work. Although it took awhile to convince MightyWords.com management to change their model, eventually they did. They decided to focus on one specific niche—managing the electronic online catalogue for other Web customers, like Barnes & Noble.

Now MightyWords manages the list, secures the transfer and sale of items, and works with authors. Revenue is shared between the destination site, MightyWords, and the authors. The MightyWords site has been relaunched with this new model, and although they were still doing some retail business, Chris MacAskill, the owner, plans to phase this out shortly.

Clicks and Bricks

The **clicks and bricks business model** represents a combination of a physical-presence business and an Internet business. Businesses in retailing, wholesaling, manufacturing, and various services (business, medical, consulting) can all take advantage of the clicks and bricks model. Having a physical presence and an Internet capability are complements that provide value to customers. Shoppers can browse the Internet and then come into a store for a touch-and-sample experience, or they can familiarize themselves with the product in person, but order in private. They should be able to return electronic purchases in the physical stores.

"Companies who can put together a winning multichannel value proposition are going to get a higher share of wallet than a pure online business," says David Court, a director at McKinsey & Co. in New York.[42] Court notes that multichannel shoppers spend more than just people who buy online. Therefore, giving your customer options and versions provides value and profits.

The kind of product you have to offer should also affect the decision to choose this business model. Table 6-9 shows the ratio of off-line versus online spending for a set of products and services. Clothing and apparel still require a strong physical presence in order to generate online sales, but auctions, books, and music do not and could be positioned just as e-tailing ventures.

When the e-entrepreneur has developed a strong brand, customers will come to the Web site to shop. Consider sporting goods discounter Campmor Inc. of Upper Saddle River, New Jersey. Campmor has only one store but has developed a large and loyal following over the years through its physical presence and mail-order catalogue sales. Now it is also selling over the Internet, and online sales have surged to triple-digit gains during the past 2 years. Online sales now represent 26 percent of all orders, reaching $18 million for 1999. This surpassed the big Internet-only launch of sporting goods

TABLE 6-9   Online Versus Off-line Sales Ratios

Product Category	Purchases Made Off-line for Every $1 Spent Online
Clothing/apparel	$2.92
Electronics	$2.89
Fitness/sports equipment	$2.50
Toys	$1.75
Computer hardware/peripherals	$1.50
Travel services	$1.01
Computer software	$0.99
Health/beauty and cosmetics	$0.93
Music/video	$0.83
Books	$0.68
Auctions	$0.05

e-tailer, Fogdog.com. Fogdog.com is now out of business, but Campmor is thriving. "There's a lot more to it than a big ad campaign and a snazzy Web site. It's getting the product out to the customer, and what you do when things get returned. Figuring all that stuff out takes a very long time, and we have been in business for a very long time," says Erich Eyler, Campmor's chief technology officer.[43]

Roll-Ups

The **roll-up business model** is a result of great competition within a fragmented market. The roll-up entrepreneur overcomes this fragmentation by buying up many of the smaller competitors. This enables the entrepreneur to reap the benefits of economies of scale and, when done on the Internet, economies of information.

Recently there has been great consolidation in the online wine-selling industry.[44] A company called eVineyard (evineyard.com) bought wine.com. Wine.com had previously merged with Wineshopper.com and VirtualVineyard.com. This industry is in the process of maturing, and companies are being rolled up into single units so that they can better compete. There is lots of competition, indicating more roll-ups will follow. Among the remaining competitors are Geerlings & Wade (www.geerwade.com) and winetasting.com (www.winetasting.com). Individual vineyards and producers are getting into the business, too.

A similar phenomenon occurred in the Web magazine business, or webzines.[45] They have had to join forces to survive. It was reported in the summer of 2000 that Automatic Media Inc. would be acquiring the content of *FEED* magazine and suck.com. They had already acquired alt.culture. *FEED* was originally founded by two freelance writers who saw the Web as a good outlet for their kind of literary journalism. They grew to eight full-time employees but could not turn the corner before their initial financing was depleted. Suck.com was founded by two Web producers in their 20s. They gained a reputation for attacking badly designed Web sites and then targeted popular culture in general. Even though they had been profitable, there were still benefits by selling out to Automatic Media. All of the sites owned by Automatic will retain their identity and brands, but all will share a common advertising sales force, technology developers, and administrative staffs. This should cut costs, increase efficiency, and make each webzine more sustainable.

Advertising Models

Once it was thought that the way to make money on the Web was to set up a site and sell advertising. The **advertising model** dollars would come because the site was targeted at exactly the market the advertisers needed. The ads would motivate people to **click through** to the sellers' sites, and the orders would flow like milk and honey in the promised land. Fantasy or reality? Fantasy.

Advertising turned out not to be the panacea for Web success. Although the novelty of Web advertising did enable some of the early models to be successful (30 percent click-through in 1994), the novelty quickly wore off (0.3 percent in 2001). Click-through rates are now lower than responses to direct mail solicitations. Advertisers began to cut their Web spending, and many advertising business model firms have gone bust.[46] Total Internet advertising revenue is estimated to be about $9 billion for

2001, and the rates per thousand views (also known as "CPM") is down to as little as $1 per CPM. Top traffic sites can still get $30 to $40 per CPM.[47]

Consider this: It is virtually impossible for a Web publisher to create its own content and survive on advertising dollars.[48] For example, suppose a credit card company wants to find customers online. It runs an advertising campaign to display its offer to 2 million viewers. Using industry averages of one click-through per 200 viewers and one sign-up for each 100 views, the campaign would yield 100 new customers. Because the new customer rate for direct mail or television would be $150 per, the credit card company would be willing to pay $15,000 to get 100 new customers via the Internet. For the 2 million views it received, that would be a CPM rate of $7.50.

However, the economics of running the Web site are brutal. Because the Web site probably does not have its own sales team, it pays 50 percent to the advertising network, such as DoubleClick. It is generating only $3.75 per CPM. If it is a successful Web site with 10 million viewers, that is $37,500 per month in revenue. Take out the costs for hardware, software, and bandwidth, and what is left might support a couple of employees. Most sites do not come close to 10 million viewers per month, and so most sites have no chance using just the advertising model. The e-entrepreneur will require multiple revenue streams for an online business.

However, there are some innovations that may start to reverse the trend. Instead of banner advertising, companies can use:[49]

- *E-mail.* Spending on e-mail marketing rose from $600 million in 2000 to an estimated $1.3 billion in 2001. You can pinpoint your market, and response rates are 5 to 15 times higher, but beware as e-mails clutter mailboxes and people delete without reading.
- *Skyscrapers.* These are the long, skinny ads that run along the sides of Web pages. According to one advertising network, response rates can be seven times higher than those for banner ads. Over time, these will diminish in effectiveness as people get tired of them, too.
- *Streaming video and audio.* Ads can be inserted into music and video clips by content networks like RealNetworks or NetRadio. This is much like the radio and TV market that advertisers are used to. According to RealNetworks, click-through rates are close to 3.5 percent, but high-speed connections are needed for this type of advertising.
- *Effectiveness tracking.* By placing "cookies" on the users' computers, companies can track the viewers' usage in the weeks after viewing an ad. This is a great way to see if the campaign is working, but it is expensive and time-consuming for the advertising company.
- *Minisites, pop-ups, and interstitials.* These ads come up on your screen uninvited and offer their products to viewers. One advantage is that it allows the viewer to stay at the site he or she is currently viewing without switching when they click through. Response rates are estimated at 5 percent, but these ads can be seen as intrusive and annoying.

To summarize: Advertising revenue can be a source of income for the e-entrepreneurial Web venture but probably not the only source if the business is to be successful.

Innovative advertising methods show promise, but it is usually going to be necessary for the e-entrepreneur to find someone who will pay for content or service or both.

Pay-for-Content Models

The **pay-for-content business model** means that users must pay to access a Web site; for example, *The Wall Street Journal* charges a subscription fee for its online edition. This model of the Internet is still in its infancy and will take time to develop. Although the marginal cost of reproducing information is very low, the average cost is still quite high. Companies can only survive if they cover their average costs. That includes all the expenses of producing the service.[50] Companies like *The Wall Street Journal* have chosen to share the costs of distributing their product between their print and Internet subscribers, even though the cost of posting news stories on the Internet is relatively low because they are already printing that material.

Many Web surfers have been spoiled with free Web sites that were subsidized by investors. Now that the investors are gone, Web sites will have to pay for themselves and make a return for the investor; this will require charging the customer for the product. As we saw mentioned earlier, it is possible to do this if the content of the site and the strategies for versioning, lock-in, value pricing, and network economies are correctly configured.

"Some people think that everything on the Internet should be free," says Ed Bernstein, CEO of PhotoPoint.com of San Francisco, "but those people are in for a surprise." PhotoPoint is a digital photography site with 1.6 million users. They have recently begun charging $19.95 to $29.95 per year for use of their posting and sharing services.[51]

However, it will be difficult to begin charging for services that used to be free. That is why some Web sites are easing their customers into the paying mode by offering a limited amount of service for free before starting to charge. This enables people to see if there is value and offers different customers different versions. For example, the San Francisco–based directory service 555-1212.com allows users to search for their first 30 phone numbers for free each month.[52] Salon.com, an online magazine, recently introduced a premium service (versioning) that includes "erotic" art, photography, and a daily column on the U.S. president called, "Bushed."[53] Other sites that require payment are Consumer Reports Online and some parts of Yahoo!

E-entrepreneurs will be challenged to find ways to have customers pay for content. According to Forrester Research, only 9 percent of consumers say that they are "likely" or "very likely" to pay for the content of books online. The percentages for music (7 percent), movies (7 percent), news (4 percent), and finance (4 percent) are even less encouraging. Even those who are willing to pay have an aversion to being "nickeled and dimed" to death. They would prefer one flat fee payment that covers most services.[54]

This is a difficult environment, but that is good for the e-entrepreneur with skills, capabilities, and creativity. If it were easy to make money on the Web, everyone would do it. If everyone could do it, the processes of competition would come into play, and only the profitable would be survivors. We will surely see the most creative and skilled entrepreneurs succeed in the long run.

E-NOTES 6-3

Business Models

Business models for e-entrepreneurs include:

- B2C model
- B2B model
- B2B2C model
- clicks and bricks model
- roll-up model
- advertising model
- pay-for-content model

WHAT HAVE WE LEARNED?

Fortune recently featured a cover story that discussed the lessons learned by e-entrepreneurs and their dot-com business ventures.[55] They say that we know that the dot-com era is over and that the intranet era is probably just getting started. In the process, here is what we have gleaned:

1. *The Internet doesn't change everything.* It is not a disruptive technology, but rather, helps complement existing businesses and forms of business.
2. *If it doesn't make sense, it doesn't make cents.* Businesses still need to make profits. The search for successful business models continues.
3. *Time favors existing businesses.* Many of the early upstarts taught incumbents important lessons of what not to do. Dot-com investors paid for everyone's education.
4. *Making money is harder than it looks.* Even B2B, which looked like it couldn't miss, now has the same gloomy status as B2C ventures. It's just not so easy.
5. *There is no such thing as "Internet time."* Things can change fast, and the Internet helped us understand that. Too often "Internet time" meant act before thinking or spend before analyzing, and it was a justification for a lack of discipline.
6. *"Branding" is not a strategy.* Historically, most companies grew organically, and they developed a brand by producing high-quality products or services over time. Instant branding—skipping the many years of fine service—doesn't work.
7. *Entrepreneurship cannot be systematized.* "The idea that you can institutionalize the creation of entrepreneurial ventures is bunk," according to venture capitalist Bill Unger. We agree. You must not follow the rules. You must break them.
8. *Investors are not your customers.* The ability to attract investors is different from the ability to serve customers and make a profit. If you can't do the latter, eventually the former says "no more money for you."

9. *The Internet still changes everything (despite what it says in 1).* It may not have changed the old industrial order, but it has changed the way that order does business.
10. *The Internet changes your job.* Information is everywhere, and if you can't do your job better because of it, watch out.
11. *The distinction between Internet and non-Internet companies is fading.* Clicks and bricks is a model that works. Everyone can improve purchasing with B2B networks.
12. *The real wealth creation is yet to come.* We were all too eager. These things take time. The dot-com revolution may be dead, but the Internet revolution is just beginning.

Summary

The relationship between marketing and electronic entrepreneurship might best be described as erratic. On one hand, the companies that have achieved a sustainable competitive advantage on the Internet have been the companies that have resources and capabilities that are rare, valuable, hard-to-copy, and nonsubstitutable. Like other businesses, companies doing business on the Web must rely upon the traditional precepts of marketing—price, place, product, and promotion—to attract and lock in their customers. Like other more traditional businesses, it has been the failure to create value or capture value that has eliminated many promising dot-coms.

On the other hand, doing business on the Web is unlike operating any other business. The Internet instantly transforms all Web-based businesses into global entities and potentially opens the door to any customer who has a computer, a cell phone, or a personal digital assistant. The Internet's main impact has been to lower the cost of communication. Therefore, although the Web spotlight initially celebrated e-tailers, it is in fact the information-intensive industries, such as financial services, entertainment, education, health care, and government, which appear to have the best chance to succeed on the Internet. Retailers, manufacturers, and businesses from the travel and energy industries will have a harder time making the Internet work for them. Our review of a variety of Internet business models, including B2C, B2B, B2B2C, clicks and bricks, roll-ups, advertising, and pay-for-content, bears this out.

It appears that doing business on the Internet doesn't make or break any business venture, and that Internet success reflects the same sound business and marketing choices that other business start-ups demand.

Key Terms

- Advertising model
- B2B business model
- B2B2C business model
- B2C business model
- Business model
- Clicks and bricks business model
- Click-through
- Digital Darwinism
- E-commerce
- Economy of network
- E-entrepreneur
- Experience good
- Four Ps of marketing
- Fulfillment
- Horizontal niche
- Inbound logistics
- Incubator
- Lock-in
- Outbound logistics
- Pay-for-content model
- Positive feedback
- P-R-O-F-I-T
- Roll-up business model
- Value capture
- Value creation
- Value pricing
- Versioning
- Vertical niche
- Wetware

Discussion Questions

1. Can you think of any businesses that are inappropriate or unsuited for the Internet? Why?
2. What are the Web sites that you visit most often? How many of them are information-intensive (financial services, entertainment, education, health care, and government) versus noninformation-intensive (retailing, manufacturing, travel, energy)? What are the best characteristics of each?
3. How could your college or university better utilize the Internet to benefit from versioning or value pricing?
4. What attracts you to a Web site? What features must a Web site have to get you to lock in as a repeat visitor?
5. What are some examples of Web businesses in a vertical niche, and some examples of businesses in a horizontal niche?
6. The Gap is a good example of a click and bricks Internet business. What do you think is the ratio of their online sales to their off-line sales? If you shop at the Gap, what is the ratio of your personal online purchases in the past year to your off-line purchases? What factors influence your decision to shop online or off-line at this vendor?
7. What kinds of businesses other than wineries and webzines might benefit from the roll-up business model now?
8. What kind of information or content on the Internet would you be willing to pay for right now?
9. Let's examine the well-known Web site Amazon.com (or another site of your choice). Amazon.com uses more than one business model; what are they? What other business models could this site consider using in the future?
10. If you were to describe one Internet business model as "most likely to succeed," which would it be, and why?

Exercises

1. Write a fictional résumé for a successful electronic entrepreneur. What kind of training and skills should he or she have? What kind of job experience should he or she have? Using the models described in this chapter, describe an e-business that this person's background has prepared them to pursue, and explain why.
2. Looking at Table 6-1 and Table 6-4, we see that the United States is predicted to remain world leader in the use of computers and the Internet in 2005. If you were starting a dot-com and wanted to target one of the regions listed in the tables as your audience, which region would it be, and why?
3. Using your last employer or a business you know, describe how one of the e-business models could be used to help that business grow.
4. Imagine that you have 1 million boxes of facial tissue sitting in a warehouse and that you must empty the warehouse in 30 days. Imagine that the cost of these tissues has already been absorbed by your company, so any income you produce is pure profit. Think of three innovative ways to use the Internet to empty this warehouse.

A Key in the Palm (Pilot) of Your Hand

It's not enough to know about construction if you want to work with Webcor Builders, Inc. You also have to know how to use the Internet.

Webcor, a $500-million-a-year general contracting company based in San Mateo, California, is one of the pioneers of the e-construction industry. "Using technology is the only way we can keep pace," explains company president Andrew J. Ball.

Construction projects generally represent a real communication challenge. Architects, engineers, contractors, suppliers, construction workers—not to mention owners—all need to keep in touch as decisions are made and unmade, problems are encountered, and blueprints and delivery schedules are changed. Other construction companies may use cell phones and fax machines, along with computers at their home office. Most companies generate mountains of paperwork—and hundreds of dollars in delivery service charges—to get the job done.

But Webcor, working with Blueline Online, sets up a multitiered, password-protected Web page for each of its 40 construction projects. It uses the site to post drawings and drawing changes, photos, delivery and completion status reports, and all the information the entire construction team needs. "People spend more time managing their work and less time on administrative paperwork," says Ball.

But it's actually access to technology that makes Webcor unique. Webcor presents a Web-linked PalmPilot to every customer once a contract is signed. There are PalmPilots in the back pocket of key supervisors on every job, and every field superintendent has a personal laptop and a digital camera. The office trailers at every site are also linked electronically to the Webcor home office so that "virtually" every employee on a job can be linked to the decision makers.

Technology has made a big dent in Webcor's bottom line. Reducing the number of copies, faxes, phone calls, and FedEx packages saved the company $10,000 a month in overhead on a recent project. Ball believes that Webcor's use of technology will eventually reduce building costs by 2 to 3 percent, which is significant in an industry where the profit margins are usually less than 10 percent. Reducing the time needed to approve changes and keeping better track of construction progress keeps customers happy, too. Thanks to a centralized Web page, Webcor was able to complete the Serrano Hotel in San Francisco in just 10 months instead of the 12 to 14 months originally scheduled, meaning that the hotel could open for business early. Web sites also create an electronic construction record, which comes in handy for building maintenance or to settle legal disputes.

Other big names in the industry, such as the Turner Corporation and the Bechtel Group, have started to use e-commerce sites like Citadon to bid for jobs, buy materials, and communicate with subcontractors. In 1995, it was Andy Ball who provided $50,000 in seed money and thousands of hours of his employees' time to mentor one of the companies that has today become Citadon. Despite Ball's advocacy efforts, Forrester Research says

(*continued*)

(continued)

that less than 1 percent of construction industry business is currently conducted online and that they expect the number to climb to just 4 percent by 2004.

Ball has encountered significant resistance to implementing technology, not only from his employees, but also from project partners like architects and suppliers. Webcor has responded by offering technology training. Ball predicts that in the near future the company will require employees and partners to be technology savvy in order to work on a job. "People will come to understand that this is how business will be done," he says. "Those who don't are just delaying the inevitable."

CASE QUESTIONS

1. List the ways that Webcor has used the Internet to create value. Have they also been able to capture value?

2. How can Webcor use technology to lock in their customers and suppliers?

3. What business models would you say Webcor uses?

4. What would you do to encourage Webcor's partners and employees to embrace the use of technology?

Source: Adapted from Margaret Young, "Wired at Webcor," *Business Week e.biz,* November 20, 2000, EB 59–62. Additional material for the case was found at www.webcor.com.

CHAPTER

Foundations of New Venture Finance

7

Anything for a friend, for a fee.
—FRED ALLEN, 1940S RADIO PERSONALITY

Learning Objectives

After reading this chapter, you will understand:

- How to determine the amount of *capital* a new venture will need
- The different types of *financing* available to the entrepreneur
- The different elements involved in *cash and working capital management*
- The pros and cons of different forms of financing—*debt versus equity*
- The major concerns of bankers and how *to approach them for a loan*
- The different methods for *valuing* a new venture

As the quote that opens this chapter indicates, it is now time to talk about money. New venture financing is about how much money the entrepreneur will need to start the business. However, it is more than that. It is also about creating value and wealth, allocating that value among the investors and founders, and determining financial risk for the business. This chapter and the next will explore and elaborate on these matters.

The quote has additional meaning for the financing of new businesses. It means that the parties to a transaction, especially an investment, should not take unfair advantage of each other; there should be consideration (a fee) for rights and privileges granted. Also, no matter how close a personal relationship the investors and founders have with each other, personal relationships should take a backseat to the overriding first priority—the successful launch of the new venture. The final inference to be drawn from the quote is that money is important, and this importance must never be minimized. People can and will talk about their devotion to the business, their concern for the products and customers, their involvement with the "cause." All of these may be true, and they are valid intrinsic motivations. Dismissing the importance of money and the creation and the subsequent protection of wealth, though, is naive and dangerous. People are concerned with financial issues, and some people care passionately about money. The entrepreneur may be one of these passionate people, and there are good reasons to believe that he or she is not alone.

Financing is one of the major hurdles that entrepreneurs must overcome. A Dun and Bradstreet survey reported that financial troubles (e.g., excessive debt and operating expenses, insufficient working capital) were responsible for 38.4 percent of business failures. Add in an additional 7.1 percent for inexperience (including financial inexperience), and it is clear why almost half of all ventures fail because of poor financial management.[1]

We begin the chapter by discussing the nature of financial resources. Next, we turn to the crucial issue of determining how much money the new venture will need for a launch. The initial financing requirement will depend greatly on the enterprise's cash and working capital management. We summarize the elements of cash and working capital management.

The chapter continues with a discussion of the sources and types of debt and equity financing. It concludes by presenting a number of models for valuing new firms. The valuation process is crucial to both investors and entrepreneurs as a vehicle for determining how the profits of the firm will be allocated. It sets the stage for financial negotiation and deal structures.

Just one word of caution before beginning our financial analysis. Modern financial theory was developed in an attempt to understand the performance of the stock market, specifically the New York Stock Exchange. Many of the concepts and tools taught as the foundations of financial theory are best employed when analyzing the types of events and companies represented on major stock, bond, commodities, currency, options, and futures exchanges. Because the underlying theory and techniques were not built with the entrepreneur in mind, applying them to new venture financing is questionable. The entrepreneur and the individuals and firms who invest in new ventures need to be aware that applying financial theory developed for stocks and bonds may provide incorrect signals for firm value and risk.[2]

DETERMINING FINANCIAL NEEDS

How much money does the entrepreneur need? One of the most important and difficult tasks for the start-up entrepreneur is determining how much money is needed to start the business. It is important because if the entrepreneur raises too little money by underestimating the business's needs, the firm will be **undercapitalized**. Undercapital-ized businesses may run out of cash, borrowing capacity, and the ability to raise addi-tional equity just when a new infusion of funds could get the firm over some difficulty. The result is that the firm will go out of business at that point. It is often said that for new firms "cash is king," because when the entrepreneur runs out of cash, the king is dead, and the business is often lost. Street Story 7-1 illustrates how difficult it can be for an undercapitalized entrepreneur to survive when cash is being "burned" at a fast rate.

Although it may not seem possible to many entrepreneurs, being **overcapitalized** is a sig-nificant danger as well. An overcapitalized firm has raised too much money and has exces-sive cash. Having too much cash sends the wrong signals to all the new venture's stakeholders. For example, it may signal to employees that the firm is doing better than it is, causing them to press for wage and benefit increases. Customers may take longer to pay if they think the new venture has plenty of cash on hand. Suppliers could demand payment quicker using the same logic. If the cash is spent on unnecessary perquisites or office upgrades, investors will be concerned that the firm does not respect money and lacks a frugal attitude. Also, excess cash earns no or very low returns. This diminishes the total return to investors.

There must be a balance between raising too little money and not being prepared for a down cycle and raising too much. If the entrepreneurs have raised too much, then they have sold (or encumbered) too much of their business. Entrepreneurs who can re-sist the temptation to continue selling equity beyond the amount truly needed will be able to sell additional equity sometime down the road when it is both really needed and much more valuable. This is called **phased financing**, and we will discuss it in more de-tail in the next chapter.

Working Capital and Cash Flow Management

The entrepreneur must focus on working capital and cash flow from the beginning of the financing process. Accounting profits do not pay the bills; only positive cash flow keeps the business solvent. It is estimated that over 60 percent of the average entre-preneur's total financing requirements are invested in working capital, 25 percent in ac-counts receivable alone.[3] Sufficient working capital is vital to the survival of the enterprise, and well-managed working capital and cash flow can significantly increase the profitability of the new venture.

Working Capital Concepts Working capital has two components. **Permanent work-ing capital** is the amount needed to produce goods and services at the lowest point of demand.[4] Although it may change form over the course of the cash flow cycle (for ex-ample, from inventory to receivables to cash), permanent working capital never leaves the business. As the firm grows and sales increase, the amount of permanent working capital increases as well. **Temporary working capital** is the amount needed to meet sea-sonal or cyclical demand. It is not a permanent part of the firm's financial structure. When these peak periods end, temporary working capital is returned to its source.

A firm that has too little permanent working capital runs the risk of losing business. If inventory levels are kept too low, stockouts occur and sales are lost. If the venture's accounts receivable policy is too restrictive, good customers who prefer to pay on credit may be turned away. If cash balances are too low, the venture runs the risk of not being able to procure supplies or pay its bills. This diminishes its ability to take advantage of short-term purchasing opportunities and damages its reputation.

Equity Angels

Whose face do you visualize when you think of an entrepreneur? Do you picture a man or a woman?

Apparently the majority of people—and equity investors—picture the face of a man. "There's a profile in the venture world of what a successful entrepreneur looks like," says Jennifer Gill Roberts, a partner in the Palo Alto office of Sevin Rosen Funds. "It's someone who's aggressive, very competitive, and hard driving. A lot of those are typical male characteristics. A woman may have all those qualities, but the way she demonstrates them may be very different."

Women may be different, but according to the Small Business Administration, they are much more entrepreneurial. For every start-up venture headed by a man, there are two ventures started by women. Women entrepreneurs, however, have problems attracting equity capital; women-led companies received less than 5 percent of the $36 million invested by venture capitalists in 1999.

Part of the problem may be the low numbers of women investors. Women hold only 20 percent of the management positions in U.S. venture capital firms. Those numbers are bound to grow as a new generation of venture capital firms led by women and focused on helping women entrepreneurs begin to flex their muscles. The Inroads Fund in Chicago now has more than $50 million in its portfolio; women-led and women-oriented funds in San Francisco, Washington, DC, Boston, and Cincinnati now have more than $70 million in equity under their management.

Women-focused venture capital firms have suffered from image problems. Sheryl Marshall from Boston's Axxon Capital Fund reports that when she started raising funds from institutional investors, many reacted by saying, "Ugh! A venture fund focused on women? How can that be successful?" Patty Abramson, cofounder of the Women's Growth Capital Fund in Washington, DC, feels she must defend these funds from the charge that they focus on gender alone. "We're not looking to invest in companies nobody else wants to fund. We're in the deals to make money."

New sources of equity funding for women entrepreneurs are also beginning to appear. After just a few breakfast meetings, the WomenAngels.net group in Washington, DC, had enrolled 90 members, each of whom agreed to contribute $25,000 a year for the next 3 years to a venture investment fund. Even more famous is Seattle's Seraph Capital Fund, whose 100 women members have been able to invest in 18 new ventures after women contributed amounts as high as $500,000 each. Although these women "angels" may have cash to invest, many of them don't have lots of financial expertise, so the Seraph Fund sponsors luncheons and seminars for its members to help them evaluate their investment decisions.

Another new source may come from a new venture incubator, the Women's Technology Cluster in San Francisco. Founder and former Cisco marketing chief Catherine Muther requires all the incubated ventures to pledge 2 percent

(continued)

(*continued*)

equity to a special fund. Right now, the fund is mostly warrants and promissory notes, but Muther hopes that one day the fund will fund the incubator and assist other female entrepreneurs.

Still, it's going to take some time for women to capture their fair share of the equity pie. "I don't think it's going to change dramatically until women have a greater presence in all areas, from angel financing and venture capital firms to government, law, and *Fortune* 500 companies," predicts Susan Preston, founder of the Seraph Fund.

Source: Adapted from D. M. Osborne, "A Network of Her Own," *Inc.* online, September 2, 2000; available at www.inc.com.

An enterprise with too much working capital for a given level of sales is inefficient. Stocks and inventory levels will be much higher than necessary to fulfill customer orders. Receivables will represent too large a percentage of sales, and the venture will find it is providing inexpensive financing for its customers. Cash levels will be more than needed for transactions and precautionary uses. Each dollar invested in working capital must return at least the internal rate of return of the rest of the venture's investment to be "pulling its weight" in the financial structure.

The Cash Flow Cycle   The **cash flow cycle** and its importance to the profitability of the firm is illustrated in Figure 7-1.

The top portion of the figure shows the **production cycle** from material ordering to finished goods inventory. It shows, too, the cash cycle from payment for raw materials through the collection of receivables. The bottom half of Figure 7-1 illustrates the corresponding sources and uses of cash and the formula for calculating the length of the cash cycle.

Segment 1 represents the time period of the accounts payable for raw material. It is a source of cash financing. Here it is the time that materials are received until approximately half of the raw materials are used. Segment 2 represents the time period in which raw materials remain in inventory. This segment corresponds to the time when they enter raw materials inventory until they enter work-in-process (WIP) inventory.

Segment 3 represents the time interval the WIP goods are counted in inventory. Segment 4 represents the time goods spend in finished goods inventory, and segment 5 represents the time that goods that have been sold are in receivables.

Figure 7-1 gives the formulas for calculating each of these ratios. The figures used to calculate these ratios will be found on the pro forma balance sheet and income statement for the new venture, or on the actual financial statements for the existing business. The total length of the short-term cash cycle is given by the sum of 2 through 5 minus 1.

Figure 7-2 demonstrates the significance of these ratios. The top illustrates a typical cash flow cycle for a sample firm, and the bottom half depicts a "controlled" cash flow cycle with much of the slack and waste removed.[5]

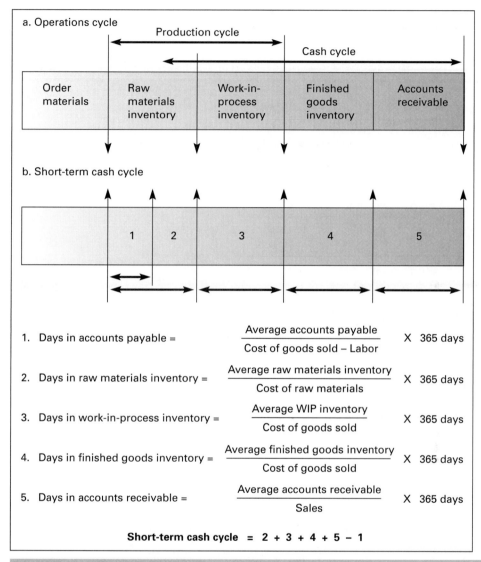

a. Operations cycle

b. Short-term cash cycle

1. Days in accounts payable = $\dfrac{\text{Average accounts payable}}{\text{Cost of goods sold} - \text{Labor}}$ X 365 days

2. Days in raw materials inventory = $\dfrac{\text{Average raw materials inventory}}{\text{Cost of raw materials}}$ X 365 days

3. Days in work-in-process inventory = $\dfrac{\text{Average WIP inventory}}{\text{Cost of goods sold}}$ X 365 days

4. Days in finished goods inventory = $\dfrac{\text{Average finished goods inventory}}{\text{Cost of goods sold}}$ X 365 days

5. Days in accounts receivable = $\dfrac{\text{Average accounts receivable}}{\text{Sales}}$ X 365 days

Short-term cash cycle = 2 + 3 + 4 + 5 − 1

FIGURE 7-1 The Cash Flow Cycle

The top half of Figure 7-2 indicates that the uncontrolled cash flow cycle is 120 days. This means that the firm, either through debt or equity, must finance every dollar of sales for 120 days. What does this mean in terms of firm profitability? If the firm had $5 million in sales, before controlling the cash flow cycle, the net working capital required for 120 days of sales value would be approximately $1,643,836 [($5,000,000/365) × 120]. The bottom half of the figure shows a hypothetical "controlled" cash flow cycle. After control measures are introduced and the cash flow cycle is tightened, the required working capital is reduced to $616,438 [($5,000,000/365) × 45]. Where has the difference of over $1 million gone? Typically, it goes to reduce debt or is invested in other assets that

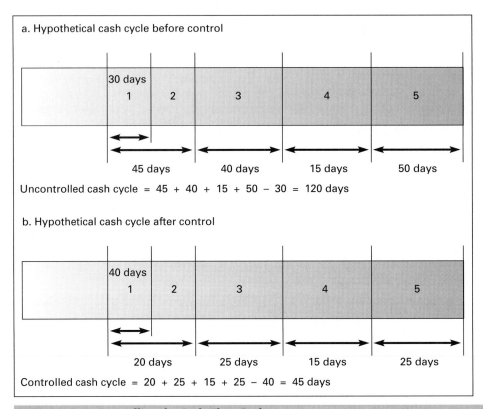

a. Hypothetical cash cycle before control

Uncontrolled cash cycle = 45 + 40 + 15 + 50 − 30 = 120 days

b. Hypothetical cash cycle after control

Controlled cash cycle = 20 + 25 + 15 + 25 − 40 = 45 days

FIGURE 7-2   Controlling the Cash Flow Cycle

can increase sales. For example, Figure 7-2 shows a marked reduction in the time it takes to process WIP inventory (segment 3; $40 − 25 = 15, 15/45 = 37.5\%$). The reduction in working capital requirements could be used to retire the debt incurred to purchase the machine that made manufacturing so much more efficient. This illustrates one of the dramatic effects of tightly managing the venture's cash; investments can be made to pay for themselves very rapidly.

Another way of seeing the dramatic benefits of cash management is to imagine that the owner of this hypothetical company needs to raise $1 million from venture capitalists in order to expand the business. Venture capital often requires rates of return of between 30 and 50 percent. If the entrepreneur can raise the $1 million through improved cash management techniques, the firm has saved between $300,000 and $500,000 per year in finance charges (dividends) paid to the venture capitalists. If the firm were netting 10 percent on sales of $5 million ($500,000), the cash control measures are the equivalent of increasing profitability between 60 percent and 100 percent.

Managing and Controlling the Cycle   Many excellent books detail the process of managing and controlling the cash flow cycle, so we will only summarize them briefly.[6] However, as the examples presented indicate, this is a subject that requires direct attention and tenacious control by top management.

Accounts payable. The longer the average accounts payable for the firm, the shorter the cash flow cycle. Therefore, the entrepreneur should develop relationships with vendors that enable them to extend payments when needed. Accounts payable are part of the permanent working capital of the venture and should be managed, not reduced.

Raw materials inventory. This is part of the permanent working capital of the firm, but look to keep it as low as possible. Just-in-time delivery systems, a good management information system, and accurate sales forecasting will help keep raw materials inventory down.

Work-in-process inventory. The Japanese *kanban* system of tagging and monitoring all work in process will help. Also, the introduction of efficient operations, worker training and incentives, and capital investment are all possible investments.

Finished goods inventory. Look to develop relationships with your buyers that enable you to deliver as soon as made. If your buyers can warehouse the goods, let them take delivery and thereby finance your finished goods inventory. Accurate sales forecasts and management information systems are vital.

Accounts receivable. The key variables are payment terms, credit limits, and collection programs. Your customers should be encouraged to pay their bills on time and given incentives to pay them early if the discount does not hurt margins.

E-NOTES 7-1

Financing a New Venture

Working capital, including:

- permanent working capital (to produce goods or services at lowest point of demand)
- temporary working capital (to meet seasonal or cyclical demand)

Cash flow cycle, including:

- operations cycle
- production cycle
- cash cycle
- short-term cash cycle

Managing capital and cash, including:

- accounts payable
- raw materials inventory
- work-in-process inventory
- finished goods inventory
- accounts receivable

Across the Venture's Life Cycle

Will the financial needs of the business change as the business faces different challenges? Of course. Over the course of the venture's life, financing needs will change. Entrepreneurs must be able to recognize where their firm is in its life cycle and specify precisely the uses of these funds. By demonstrating to investors how the financing will further the venture's objectives, the entrepreneur significantly increases the probability of closing the deal.

Early-Stage Financing   There are two categories of early-stage financing: seed capital and start-up financing. **Seed capital** is the relatively small amount of money needed to prove that the concept is viable and to finance feasibility studies. Seed capital is not usually used to start the business, just to investigate its possibilities. **Start-up capital** is funding that actually gets the company organized and operational. It puts in place the basics of product development and the initial marketing effort. Start-up capital is invested in the business before there are any significant commercial sales; it is the financing required to achieve these sales. Start-up capital is also known as **first-stage financing**.

Expansion or Development Financing   There are three sequential categories of financing within the expansion stage. **Second-stage financing** is the initial working capital that supports the first commercial sales. It goes to support receivables, inventory, cash on hand, supplies, and expenses. At this point, the firm may not have achieved a positive cash flow. **Third-stage financing** is used to ramp up volumes to the break-even and positive-cash-flow levels. It is expansion financing. Throughout the third stage, the business is still private, a majority of the equity still in the hands of the founding top management team. **Fourth-stage financing**, sometimes known as "mezzanine" financing (because it is between the cheap balcony seats and the more expensive but desirable orchestra seats) is the bridge between the venture as a private firm and the prospect of its going public. Relatively few ventures are successful enough to make it to this stage. For a firm to be considered for this, it must be attractive enough to lure professional investors and have the potential to be a public company (one traded on a stock exchange).

E-NOTES 7-2

Life Cycle Financing

Early-stage financing:

- seed capital: to prove concept is viable
- start-up capital: to make business operational

Expansion or development financing:

- second-stage financing: to support first commercial sales
- third-stage financing: to expand
- fourth-stage financing: to make the leap from private company to public company

SOURCES OF FINANCING

The initial financial objective of the entrepreneur is to obtain start-up capital at the least possible cost. Cost is measured in two ways. One is the return that will have to be paid to the investor for his or her commitment. The second is the transaction costs involved in securing, monitoring, and accounting for the investment. An investor may be satisfied with what appears to be a below-market return on investment, but if the cost of the transaction is significantly high, the entrepreneur may wish to consider an alternative source of financing.

The long-term sources of cash for the venture are debt and equity. In most cases, equity financing is more expensive than debt financing. This is because pure debt has a fixed return over a period of time; the potential gains to investors in equity financing are unlimited. Figure 7-3 illustrates how these two sources combine to build the liquidity level of the firm.

FIGURE 7-3   Permanent Sources of Venture Financing

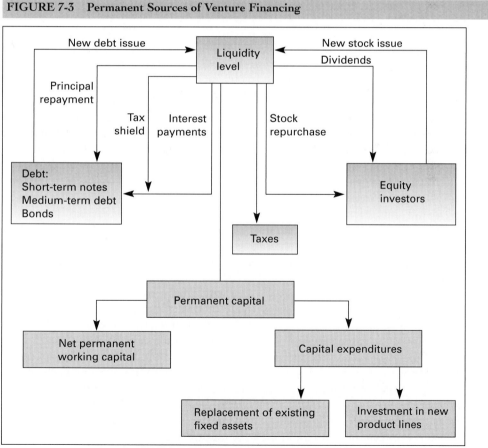

Source: Adapted from E. Walker and J. Petty, *Financial Management of the Small Firm,* 2nd edition (Upper Saddle River, NJ: Prentice Hall, 1986), 144.

The types and sources of financing available to the new venture depend on four factors:

1. The stage of business development
2. The type of business and its potential for growth and profitability
3. The type of asset being financed
4. The specific condition of the financial environment within the economy

The elements of the overall financial environment that should be considered are:

- Interest rates and their term structure[7]
- The level and trend in the stock market
- The health of various financial institutions, such as savings and loans, commercial banks, and international financial institutions
- Level of confidence in the economy
- Government monetary and fiscal policy

The entrepreneur and the top management team need to be sensitive both to threats to successfully financing the venture (such as low consumer and producer confidence) and to special opportunities, such as government finance programs and subsidies.

Equity-Based Financing

The liabilities and equity side of the balance sheet provides the general list of types of financing. On the balance sheet, they are listed in ascending order of risk, and therefore cost, to the investor. We begin from the bottom of the balance sheet with equity capital and move up to the less risky and cheaper types of financing.

Inside Equity   **Equity** finance represents an ownership stake in the new venture. All businesses require equity. Initial equity most frequently comes from the founder and the top management team and from their friends and relatives. Founders traditionally make a personal equity investment commensurate with their financial level. They do this for a number of reasons: It is often the easiest money to obtain, it shows commitment to future outside investors, and it provides the right incentives for the business owners.

Family and friends are the natural next place to look for money. Take the case of Matthew Oristano, the CEO and major shareholder of People's Choice TV of Shelton, Connecticut. This $25 million wireless-pay-tv company struggled for 8 years to secure the financing it needed to make a big impact in the industry. In the early days, family funds financed the future. Matthew offers this tip to other entrepreneurs employing family resources: "When you are dealing with family investors, it should be clearly defined which family members are actively involved in the business and which are involved only financially. To avoid confusion or misunderstandings, everything should be documented the same way any other financial relationship would be."[8]

At the beginning of the business, the risk is highest, and start-up equity carries with it the highest risk of total loss. Therefore, it also carries with it the highest returns if the business is successful later on. These initial investments are equity from the point of view of the firm, although the actual sums may have been borrowed. For example, an investor can borrow against the value of his home (and incur or increase the mortgage) to make an equity investment in the new venture. Equity from the owners, the top managers, friends, and relatives is called **inside equity** because it is generally believed that these investors will vote their stock in the best interests of the company "insiders."

Outside Equity   Outside equity comes from investors who have no personal relationship with the venture beyond their investment and their concern for its profitability and protection. Outside equity comes from three sources: private investors, venture capital, and public offerings.

Private investors.   Private investors, sometimes called "angels," are wealthy individuals interested in the high-risk/high-reward opportunities that new venture creation offers. A great deal of money is available from private investors, representing the largest single source of funds for new firms.[9] Wealthy investors exist in all communities and in all cities in the developed world. The best way to reach these people is through personal introduction by acquaintances or associates: lawyers, accountants, consultants, and others in the economic network of a community.

Wealthy investors will want to see the firm's business plan or offering memorandum. Obtaining expert legal counsel in this process is crucial. Many securities laws, both local (state) and federal, regulate the sale and distribution of stock.[10] Failure to comply with these laws and regulations may enable the investor to sue the entrepreneur for recovery of his or her investment if the company goes broke.

The main advantages of obtaining early financing from wealthy investors are its relative accessibility and the size of the investment pool. Also, these individuals may be in a position to lend their positive reputations to the venture to attract additional funds.

However, there are often disadvantages. Many wealthy people made their money in the professions or inherited it. They may lack the business expertise that would help the entrepreneur when advice is needed. Even when wealthy investors are businesspeople, they may have made their money in a different type of business or made it long ago when conditions were different.

A second disadvantage is the inability to invest more money sometime in the future (even rich people have limits). The most common range of investments from wealthy individuals is $10,000 to $500,000, with an average investment of about $50,000.[11] Although this may be enough in the early development stages of the firm, additional money will be needed later if the firm is successful. Additional sums may either be out of reach for the angel or represent too much risk in a single business for the wealthy investor.

A third problem concerns the relationship between the angel and the top management team. Private investors tend to be overprotective of their investment. They often call the entrepreneurs or complain when things are not going well. If the business is accessible and local, they may even personally visit, requiring extra time and creating headaches for the entrepreneur.[12]

Venture capital.   Venture capital is outside equity that comes from professionally managed pools of investor money. Instead of wealthy individuals making investments one at a time and on their own, they along with institutional investors pool their funds and hire professionals to make the investment and related decisions.

The venture capital industry has long been associated with new venture creation and has its own entrepreneurial history.[13] Also, like any industry, the factors that affect profitability within the industry are the power of the buyers (investors), the power of the suppliers (entrepreneurs who supply the deals), the threat of substitutes, the height of entry barriers, and rivalry between venture capital firms.[14] Also, macroenvironmental factors create both constraints and opportunities for these firms, just as they do for new ventures. These macro factors depend on the type of industry the venture capitalists specialize in. Because industry-specific knowledge is required for evaluating new-venture-financing proposals, venture capitalists tend to specialize in certain industries. For example, there are high-tech venture capitalists who prefer cutting-edge technological investments, distribution-type venture capitalists who invest in ventures that provide logistical benefits, and restaurant specialists who look to invest in the next Domino's or McDonald's restaurant chain. Venture capital firms have been raising and investing less money recently as a result of the decline in the economy and the end of the Silicon Valley boom of the late 1990s. Figure 7-4 illustrates recent trends for a number of industries popular with venture capitalists.[15]

Venture capital is risk capital. This means that the investors are aware of the high potential of receiving little or no return on their investment. To compensate the investors for this risk, venture capital looks for deals that can return at least 35 to 50 percent compounded over the life of the investment (typically a 5-year planning horizon). To achieve such lofty return on investment goals, the business opportunity must be extremely attractive, with the potential for very strong growth, and the venture capitalist must be able to own a substantial portion of the firm.[16] However, venture capitalists are often able to bring additional money to the table when needed. They can also provide advice based on experience and important industry contacts for the firm. We will return to the subject of venture capital in the next chapter, when we discuss how investors evaluate proposals, structure the deal, and negotiate.

Public offerings. The ultimate source of outside equity and wealth creation is the public offering. When you own 100 percent of a company that earns $500,000 per year, you make a very good living. When you own 50 percent of a company that makes $500,000 per year, is publicly traded, and is valued at 25 times earnings (25 × $500,000 = $12.5 million × .50 = $6.25 million), you are a multimillionaire. Often, in order to go from well-off to rich, the founders of the venture must take their firm public. This type of financing creates significant wealth because it capitalizes earnings at a multiple (the price-earnings ratio). "Going public" is done through an investment vehicle known as the **initial public offering (IPO)** and with the aid of an investment banker.

The IPO enables a firm to raise a much larger amount of equity capital than was previously possible. It also enables the entrepreneur and the top management team, as well as the earlier investors who still own shares of the firm, to sell some of their shares. This is an event that is often eagerly anticipated by founders and early investors, for it represents one of the most lucrative financial opportunities in a businessperson's career. It is estimated that the value of the firm increases by 30 percent at the completion of a public offering.[17] The appendix to Chapter 7 offers a detailed look at the process of going public.

For many entrepreneurs and top managers of entrepreneurial companies, the process and event of going public mark the culmination of years of hard work, public recognition of success, and long-delayed financial rewards. However, there are disadvantages and real costs to going public. Entrepreneurs should consider all of the costs and benefits of going public; the pros and cons are detailed in Street Story 7-2.

FIGURE 7-4 Venture Capital Investments from 2Q/2000 Through 1Q/2001

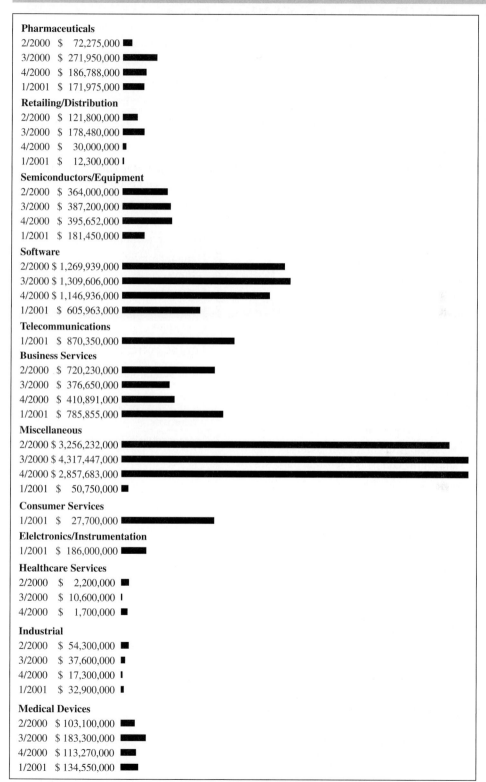

Pharmaceuticals
2/2000 $ 72,275,000
3/2000 $ 271,950,000
4/2000 $ 186,788,000
1/2001 $ 171,975,000

Retailing/Distribution
2/2000 $ 121,800,000
3/2000 $ 178,480,000
4/2000 $ 30,000,000
1/2001 $ 12,300,000

Semiconductors/Equipment
2/2000 $ 364,000,000
3/2000 $ 387,200,000
4/2000 $ 395,652,000
1/2001 $ 181,450,000

Software
2/2000 $ 1,269,939,000
3/2000 $ 1,309,606,000
4/2000 $ 1,146,936,000
1/2001 $ 605,963,000

Telecommunications
1/2001 $ 870,350,000

Business Services
2/2000 $ 720,230,000
3/2000 $ 376,650,000
4/2000 $ 410,891,000
1/2001 $ 785,855,000

Miscellaneous
2/2000 $ 3,256,232,000
3/2000 $ 4,317,447,000
4/2000 $ 2,857,683,000
1/2001 $ 50,750,000

Consumer Services
1/2001 $ 27,700,000

Elelctronics/Instrumentation
1/2001 $ 186,000,000

Healthcare Services
2/2000 $ 2,200,000
3/2000 $ 10,600,000
4/2000 $ 1,700,000

Industrial
2/2000 $ 54,300,000
3/2000 $ 37,600,000
4/2000 $ 17,300,000
1/2001 $ 32,900,000

Medical Devices
2/2000 $ 103,100,000
3/2000 $ 183,300,000
4/2000 $ 113,270,000
1/2001 $ 134,550,000

Source: "Venture Capital Survey, Fourth Quarter 2000"; available at wwdyn.mercurycenter.com/business/moneytree/report1.cfm. Reprinted by permission from *San Jose Mercury News,* San Jose, CA.

Going Public: Pros and Cons

Although going public may appear to be an entrepreneur's dream, it has its costs and benefits.

ADVANTAGES OF GOING PUBLIC

For the business:

1. Cash for the company to expand
2. Cash for the company for acquisitions or mergers
3. Greater accessibility to long-term debt for the company
4. Increased employee benefit plans and incentives with stock
5. Increased public awareness of the company

For entrepreneurs, top managers, and early investors:

1. Cash, enabling the entrepreneurs to diversify their personal portfolios
2. The establishment of an ascertainable value of the company for estate purposes
3. Equity available for executive incentives and compensation
4. Personal satisfaction for the top managers
5. Liquidity for the entrepreneurs
6. Entrepreneurs can maintain effective control of the company

Although there are clear advantages to going public, it can present some real obstacles. Several are detailed here.

DISADVANTAGES OF GOING PUBLIC

For the business:

1. Requirements to conform to standard accounting and tax practices
2. Lack of operating confidentiality
3. Lack of operating flexibility
4. Increased accountability
5. Demand for dividends from stockholders
6. Initial cost of offering and ongoing regulatory costs
7. Conflict between short-term and long-term goals

For the entrepreneurs:

1. More stakeholders to please and coordinate
2. Possible loss of control of the company in a takeover
3. Increased visibility for job performance
4. Increased accountability for earnings per share
5. Restrictions on insider trading, conflicts of interest
6. Focus on managing stock price
7. Internal bickering and politics

Sources: R. Saloman, "Second Thoughts on Going Public," *Harvard Business Review* 55 (September–October 1977): 126–131; S. Jones and B. Cohen, *The Emerging Business* (New York: Wiley, 1983).

Debt-Based Financing

Debt is borrowed capital. It represents an agreement for repayment under a schedule at an interest rate. Both the repayment schedule and the interest rate may be fixed or variable or have both fixed and variable components. In most cases, debt costs the company less than equity. Interest rates on debt are historically less than rates of return on equity. Why would entrepreneurs ever seek anything but debt? Because debt often requires collateral and its repayment always requires discipline. Discipline is required to meet the regular interest and principal payments; otherwise, the company will be in default, putting the company in jeopardy of forced bankruptcy. If the loan is collateralized (has a specific physical asset encumbered as assurance of repayment of principal), default may cause the loss of that asset. Therefore, the entrepreneur often seeks higher-cost equity because the owner of shares has no legal right to the dividends of the company, and the equity holder is the owner of last resort. If the company is forced into bankruptcy or liquidated, the equity shareholders receive only the residual value of the firm after all other claims are settled.

Some entrepreneurs finance their businesses with equity instead of debt for a second reason: They often cannot get a loan. Banks and other lending institutions are conservators of their depositors' money and their shareholders' investments. In certain economic climates, they are extremely reluctant to lend money to risky ventures. They are hardly ever in a position to lend money to start-ups. Thus, the entrepreneur is forced to raise equity capital in the initial stages, and forced to continue to raise equity even after passing the hurdles of the early stages. Because of the difficulty, new and small businesses have in procuring debt financing, various agencies and departments of the government offer special programs to help. One of the fastest growing and popular of these programs are the "micro lenders" that target women entrepreneurs and minority-owned firms.

E-NOTES 7-3

Sources of Start-Up Financing

Equity (ownership stake), including:

- inside equity: from founder, top management team, friends, family
- outside equity
- private investors
- venture capital
- public offerings

Debt-based financing (borrowed capital):

- asset-based debt
- cash flow financing

Micro Loan Programs   Women and minority-owned businesses have had difficulties getting debt financing, partly because they start the wrong types of business and partly because of discrimination. Too often these small start-ups are in-service industries, have no collateral, have high failure rates, and contain no entry barriers to protect against competition, yet the growth rates of start-ups by these individuals are high. For example, it is estimated that by the year 2000, 48 percent of all U.S. small businesses will be owned by women.

To address the gap between the need for debt financing and the availability of credit, the government has stepped in. In June 1992, the Small Business Administration announced a **micro loan** program to help women and minorities get loans of up to $25,000 at market interest rates. This program's initial loan budget was $24 million. "I hope this program will give an opportunity to the small cottage industry; people who haven't had a chance before. There used to be a day when your friendly local banker would give you a small loan on your signature. That no longer occurs. This [program] restores some of that," said Patricia Saiki, SBA administrator.[18]

The private sector is also trying to do more. Consider the case of the Earnings Resource Group, a $400,000 auditing firm owned and operated by Cynthia McGeever and Crisanne Buba. The firm is profitable, the owners are well educated, and both have been vice presidents at major banks. When their Wayne, Pennsylvania, company needed expansion capital, they found their prestigious client list and 30-percent operating margins insufficient. "Some bankers didn't even give us a follow-up phone call," recalled Buba.

But Earnings Resource Group did eventually land a loan ($600,000) from Compass Rose Corporation, a financial services company dedicated to women's business. It is a division of a large insurance company, Capital Holding Corporation. Although the parent company expects Compass Rose to earn a 16-percent return on investment, the subsidiary is still intent on changing traditional lending criteria. "We feel our lending formula captures life experience, not just balance sheet equations," says president Rebecca Maddox.

In addition to the loan program, Compass Rose offers a Harvard-like MBA program for women entrepreneurs. At $1,100 for a week-long training course, the education is not cheap, but it is valuable. Upon completion of the course, students have a business plan, one-on-one guidance, and guaranteed financing. Compass Rose hopes that the successful graduates will one day purchase insurance, Keogh plans, and other products from the company.

Says Cynthia McGeever, "If Compass Rose offers a product that I want, you can bet that I'll buy it from them because they've been there for us."[19] Anything for a friend, for a fee.

Positioning for a Loan   The time to establish a relationship with a banker, or lender, is *before* you need a loan. Because of their inherent conservatism, banks do not lend money in emergencies (unless they already have some money at risk) or on short notice. Call the president of the bank and introduce yourself. Ask to set up a meeting to tell the president about your business. Do not ask for a loan in this meeting. Ask the president who in the loan department might be a good match for your business-financing needs. When you call the person the president recommends, tell him or her that the president recommended that you speak directly with him or her. This is your referral.

The banker will be looking for the answer to four key questions when evaluating your business proposal. The answers to these questions should be clear and concisely communicated, both in writing and in discussion during the meetings the entrepreneur and the top management team will have with the lender.

1. *What will the money be used for?* Are there other sources of financing to help spread the risk?
2. *How much money is needed?* (Ask for too much, and you are paying for financing that you don't really need. Ask for too little, and you are unable to achieve your business purpose.)
3. *How will the money be paid back and when?* (Time is money, and the sooner the repayment, the higher the return and lower the risk for the bank.)
4. *When is the money needed?* Is it all going to be used now, or is it possible to draw down a balance over time?

Of primary importance to the lender is your ability to repay the loan. That is the first criterion. In considering the loan application, bankers will also be looking for five things (all beginning with the letter *C*).[20]

- *Character.* The banker's best estimate of whether you will be able (and willing) to repay your debt is your previous borrowing and business experience. If your reputation is worthy and your integrity is intact, you have passed the character test.
- *Capacity.* This is the numbers game. The banker wants to be sure that your business has the capacity (ability) to repay the loan, interest, and principal. Evidence of capacity is the cash flow of the business, the coverage ratio (earnings divided by debt service), and any personal guarantees that the banker may require.
- *Capital.* The lender is not interested in financing a business if the loan is the only source of long-term capital. This would mean 100-percent leverage. In case of default, the bank would be the owner of the business, and banks do not wish to be put in this situation. They are interested in situations in which there is sufficient equity to indicate that (1) the owners of the firm are putting up their own money in good faith because they believe in the deal and (2) the debt/equity ratio of the venture is in line with comparable types of businesses.
- *Conditions.* These are the particulars of the industry, the firm, the general economy, and the current risk position of the bank that add complexity to the lending decision. The entrepreneur's business may be in good shape and the entrepreneur of fine character, but if the economy is taking a turn for the worse and the venture's industry is leading the way (for example, construction), then the banker may think twice and still deny the application. The banker is always in a position of asking: "What can go wrong here and what happens to my depositors' money when it does?" The fallout of the savings and loan debacle of the 1980s has been to make already risk-averse professionals even more deliberative.
- *Collateral.* If a loan has collateral, then the creditor can sell a specific asset to ensure that the principal and accrued interest obligations are met.

Collateralized loans will generally have a slightly lower interest rate than unsecured loans. However, the quality of the collateral is important if the lower rate structure is to apply. Some assets may not be salable at anything approaching the value of the loan, and although these may be required as collateral, no lower rate will be extended. For businesses with short operating histories and service businesses with little tangible property, collateral often takes the form of personal guarantees and key-person life insurance.

Searching for a Lender   Entrepreneurs often find themselves in a seller's market when it comes to searching for a loan. Sometimes it may appear that the chances of receiving a business loan approach zero. However, the entrepreneur can do a few things to improve the chances. First and foremost, the entrepreneur needs to meet the requirements of the five Cs just described. Then the entrepreneur can begin to shop around as if the entrepreneur were hiring the bank to be its lender. Street Story 7-3 illustrates some of the problems and solutions that entrepreneurs have encountered.

As in any hiring situation, the entrepreneur should check the bank's references. Other people who do business with the bank will be able to tell the entrepreneur whether the bank is a friendly institution, one that is willing and able to work with the venture in good times and bad. Some banks have reputations for foreclosing early or calling in loans when the bank's balance sheet needs cleaning up. The bank's reputation is one of its most important assets, and a poor reputation should not be rewarded with the account.

Find a bank that has experience lending within your industry. Banks have different experiences, and their loan officers and lending committees have their own knowledge resources. If the lenders have experience, they will be more likely to understand the particulars of your loan application. Also, look for a bank that is the right size for your firm. A bank that is too small for your firm will not be able to finance follow-up loans. (Banks have regulations about how much they can loan to any single client.) A bank that is too big considers your account trivial, and you might feel lost among the megadeals being made. If your business is international, and you will be importing, exporting, or carrying on a banking relationship outside the home country, look for a bank that has both experience with these issues and correspondent relationships in your host countries.

Personal chemistry is important in choosing a banker. Do business with people you like and people who like you. Look for a bank that has someone who will be your "champion." A champion will try to present your firm and its prospects in a positive light within the bank itself, even when you are not personally there. Here are some other criteria you can consider when looking for a banker:[21]

Does it see you through adversity?   The Milwaukee architecture firm of Engberg Anderson geared up for a major construction project, and then ran into contract problems. The negotiations went on 4 months, and the company was hard pressed to meet their payroll, but their bank expanded their credit with good faith as their only collateral. "They understood the nature of the business," says founder Charles M. Engberg, "and saw us as a company they were willing to take a risk for."

Does it save you time?   The Mississippi Blending Co. may be located in Norwalk, Connecticut, but they bank in Keokuk, Iowa. Why? Because the bank there knows cornstarch, and Mississippi Blending blends food products made from cornstarch. When the

Hard Lessons in Financing

It was the best of times, and the worst of times: That's what a lot of entrepreneurs will tell you about their attempts to secure financing. Deals are always being made, but deals today often have lower valuations and tighter restrictions, and are based on investment and loan criteria that are stricter than they once were. Here are a few lessons that some entrepreneurs have learned the hard way in the financing fray.

1. *Make your financial projections realistic the first time around.*

   "The problem with many small companies' business plans is that they don't actually meet their projections," notes Fred Marcusa, a partner in Kaye, Scholer, Fierman, Hayes & Handler, which represents investors, lending institutions, and corporations in financing transactions. When a new venture goes back for additional financing 6 months or a year later, bankers are now evaluating less optimistic but more realistic numbers, and "that could further weaken an entrepreneur's chances of working out the right deal even in stronger markets."

2. *If you're unhappy with your financing source, move on quickly.*

   Lisa Argiris, a female and minority entrepreneur, had no problems securing a $50,000 line of credit from her local bank when she started a mail-order business selling musical instruments from her college dorm room. "It took me a long time to realize that my bank was really just interested in supporting me because of my public relations value to them—not because they really understood or believed in my business concept." Her company grew to $4 million in annual sales, but the bank was unwilling to extend Argiris new credit when she started a new company to rent instruments to local schools. Instead, Ar-

giris got a $1 million loan from Citibank. She now says, "Don't expect a bank to know what's best for your business."

3. *It's both* what *and* who *you know.*

   Mario Tolisano owns a construction company with annual revenues of $5 million. But even though he's been in business for 13 years, Tolisano can't find a bank to give him a line of credit large enough to cover payroll and operating expenses while Tolisano waits 30 to 60 days for his customers to pay him. Instead, Tolisano relies on personal savings and high interest rate contract-financing to cover his cash flow. He hopes things are going to change now that he's completed a 3-month course on financing alternatives, strategic planning, and accounting at the GE Capital Small Business College. "I'm hoping that the contacts I've made through the course will help me improve my financing prospects," Tolisano says.

4. *Be flexible, and be willing to make new friends.*

   Joe Elizondo, CEO of a fruit company that packages and distributes California dates, couldn't raise the $400,000 he needed in credit from a bank. "We didn't meet a bank's standards for financing, since the company's assets were encumbered by an SBA loan, its financial history had been troubled, there had been problems with the IRS under the old owners, and its new owners didn't have a lot of personal assets." Then Elizondo turned to Jesus Arguelles, a private investment banker, who put together a mostly-credit package worth as much as $800,000. One part of the package was "friendly-investor financing" where a private individual leased equipment Elizondo needed and leased it to the fruit company. "I could never have accomplished all this on my own," says Elizondo today.

Source: Adapted from Jill Andresky Fraser, "How to Finance Anything," *Inc.* online, March 1, 1999; available at www.inc.com.

company needed $2 million to cover a market bid, their bank got it for them in less than 24 hours without paperwork.

Does it treat you as an individual? The loan officer at a local bank practically overwhelmed Reynolds, a Lynnwood, Washington, retail-store-fixture manufacturer with detailed questions about his business. The company got the loan, and then the bank got the rest of the company's business. "I decided that if they were smart enough to ask these intricate questions, they must be worth banking with," explains Paul A. Abodeely, Reynolds CEO.

Does it teach and advise? The Tampa Bay Vending Company "couldn't believe it" when their banker volunteered to spend a day riding a company truck so he could learn about their business. However, the inside knowledge he gained that day transformed that banker into an expert consultant when Tampa Bay took over another company, started exporting their machines, and set up a retirement fund for their employees. As an added bonus, the banker even showed the owner's young son how to become a gumball machine entrepreneur.

Does it do something special for you? By 10 A.M. every morning, there's a report sitting on the desk of Jack Greenman, financial officer of the Sterling Healthcare Group, Inc., in Coral Gables, Florida, from his local bank. The report shows all the deposits and disbursements from the previous day, including the deposits from lockboxes in 19 states that the bank has swept into its central account. The service doesn't cost Sterling Healthcare a dime.

Does it accept responsibility for you? Garden-tool maker DeJay Corp. of Palm Beach, Florida, was upset when a bank posting error caused some of their checks to bounce. But they were smiling when the bank not only apologized, but also called every customer and vendor who might have received an unpaid check and explained that it was the bank's mistake.

Does it let you borrow against the future? The TPL technology-equipment manufacturer of Albuquerque won a big U.S. Army contract, and then were upset when they discovered their bank wouldn't increase their existing $250,000 line of credit. Another bank 100 miles away heard the TPL story through the grapevine and extended them the half-million dollars they needed, saying "You're the kind of company we need to encourage in New Mexico."

Does it find customers for you? A bank in Southern California played matchmaker for two of its customers, garment manufacturer Flap Happy and the local science museum. When the museum expanded its gift shop, Flap Happy hats were included in the retail mix.

These stories demonstrate that some commercial banks are willing to "go the extra distance" to attract small business customers, and that entrepreneurs need to shop around and communicate with their banking staff to find a lender who can be a true partner in their success.

Types of Debt Financing There are two basic types of debt financing: asset-based financing and cash flow financing. **Asset-based financing** is collateralized. The most common form of asset-based financing is trade credit. Trade credit is extended for the period between product or service delivery to the new venture and when payment is due. It is not uncommon to have a 25- to 30-day "grace period" before payment without penalty is expected. A discount is sometimes offered for early payment.

Asset-based debt.   A business usually borrows money to finance an asset. The asset may be short term—for example, seasonal accounts receivables—or long term—for example, equipment or property. When a specific asset is identifiable with the borrowing need, asset-based financing is appropriate. Table 7-1 illustrates some types of assets that are "bankable" and the typical maximum percentage of debt financing the firm can count on.

For example, a new venture with a positive cash flow conversion cycle (they spend before they receive) could borrow 70 percent of the money needed to finance accounts receivable, with the receivables themselves serving as collateral. Up to 60 percent debt financing is possible for inventory, with the inventory as collateral. Note that the more stable, long-term, and tangible resources have higher debt ceilings; the short-term, high-turnover assets have lower ceilings.

Smaller banks have traditionally turned away from asset-based financing because they lacked the ability to evaluate and dispose of collateral. However, increasingly these banks are moving toward developing special expertise in asset-based financing. In 1989, it was estimated that over $100 billion would be borrowed by small businesses with asset-based financing.[22]

Cash flow financing.   **Cash flow financing** refers to unsecured financing based on the underlying operations of the business and its ability to generate enough cash to cover the debt. Short-term (under one year) unsecured financing is usually for temporary working capital. A line of credit is an intermediate level of unsecured financing. Long-term unsecured financing takes the form of a note, bond, or debenture.

Because the debt is unsecured, banks may take other precautions to try to protect their asset (the loan). These protections, or **covenants**, are agreements between the lender and borrower concerning the manner in which the funds are disbursed, employed,

TABLE 7-1 Asset-Based Financing and Borrowing Limits	
Type	**Borrowing Limits**
Accounts receivable	For short-term receivables: 70%–80% For longer-term receivables: 60%–80%[a]
Inventory	Depending on risk of obsolescence: 40%–60%
Equipment	If equipment is of general use: 70%–80% If highly specialized: 40%–60%
Conditional sales contract	As a percentage of purchase price: 60%–70%
Plant improvement loan	Lower of cost or market appraisal: 60%–80%
Leasehold improvement	Depending on general reusability: 70%–80%
Real estate	Depending on appraisal value: 80%–90%
First mortgage on building	Depending on appraisal value: 80%–90%

[a]This is from a factor, a business that specializes in collecting accounts receivable and overdue debts for firms and lending them money against the total invoice amounts.

managed, and accounted. For example, an unsecured loan covenant might require the borrower to maintain a certain minimum balance in an account at the lending institution. In this way, the bank can restrict a portion of its funds from general use, raise the cost of the loan to the borrower, and potentially attach the balance in the account in case of default. Further details on this type of financing and its limits are discussed in the next chapter.

NEW VENTURE VALUATION

What is the new venture worth? How can it be valued? Determining its value is a problem that cannot be avoided, even though the methods for calculating value are uncertain and risky. When a new business is created by purchasing another business or its assets, a valuation is required to ensure a fair purchase price and to determine taxes.

A valuation is also needed when a new venture is created and the entrepreneurs are looking for equity investors. In this case, the valuation tells investors approximately what their investment might be worth in the future.[23] Investors need this information so that they can calculate their expected return on investment and bargain for the share (proportion of stock) in the venture that enables them to achieve this return.[24]

Because of lack of historical data, the valuation of new ventures and small businesses is difficult and uncertain. There is no efficient market to determine value, these ventures do not trade their equity on a stock exchange and thus have no market value in this sense, and they have no record of accomplishment to indicate potential future earnings. Unproven companies need to raise equity without being able to point to historical returns to investors.[25]

Despite these problems, valuations must be made. Three basic approaches to valuation include asset-based valuations, earnings-based valuations, and the use of discounted cash flow techniques.

Asset-Based Valuations

Asset-based valuations reveal the maximum exposure that investors face. The purpose of these valuations is to determine how much the venture would be worth if it were forced to cease operation and be sold for its tangible and intangible parts. Asset-based valuations can also be used to determine the cost of assets. There are four types of asset-based valuations: book value, liquidation value, and adjusted book and replacement value.

Book Value   The book value of an asset is the historical cost of the asset less accumulated depreciation. An asset that was originally purchased for $10,000 and has been depreciated on a straight-line basis for half its useful life will have a book value of $5,000. A fully depreciated asset will have a book value of zero, even though it may still have some economic value. Because accelerated depreciation schedules and techniques are employed primarily as tax shields, during the early life of an asset, the book value may understate the economic value of the asset. Frequently, the book value of an asset is completely an artifact of accounting practice and bears little relationship to its actual economic value.

Adjusted Book Value   Sometimes an asset's book value and its actual economic value are so at variance that it is necessary to adjust the book value to give a better picture of what the asset is worth. This adjusted book value can be higher or lower, depending on the circumstances. A frequent reason for an upward adjustment is to account for land values. Adjusted book valuations increase the value of real estate, which often rises over time, but because of accounting rules is always left on the books at historical cost. Many types of businesses are undervalued on the books because the land they own and control is worth many times the value of the business as an ongoing operation. Examples of this phenomenon include land-based businesses such as hotels, parking lots, and golf courses.

Land value can be adjusted downward if, for example, a parcel of property has major environmental problems and incurs cleanup costs. Also, sometimes neighborhoods and areas deteriorate for a variety of reasons, and property that was once valuable falls in value.

Inventory valuations are sometimes adjusted downward because the parts, supplies, or stock have become obsolete. A computer store retailer that maintained a stock of machines produced by out-of-business manufacturers might have to write down the value of the inventory. A clothing retailer who overordered and has a large stock of last year's fashions would be in a similar position. On the other hand, if held long enough, obsolete inventory and out-of-fashion stock can be a source of *increased* value. Eventually, this merchandise becomes rare. If a market in historical goods or collectibles develops, long-held "worthless" goods can become a source of revenue for the owner.

Replacement Value   Replacement value is the amount it would cost to duplicate the firm's current physical asset base at today's prices. When valuation is used for buying or selling a business, the replacement value of the assets can be a point of reference in the negotiation between buyer and seller. Because inflation is the historical trend in developed Western economies, the replacement cost of an asset is frequently higher than the original cost. However, because of technological and productive improvements, the replacement cost of computers and computing power is an example of an historical downward trend in replacement costs.

Liquidation Value   This is the value of the assets if they had to be sold under pressure. Sometimes firms face extreme cash shortages and must liquidate assets to raise cash to pay their creditors. At other times, courts order liquidation under bankruptcy proceedings. When buyers know that the venture is being forced to raise cash by liquidating, they can negotiate to pay below-market prices. Often liquidation is done at auction, and the prices paid might be only 10 to 20 percent of the market value of the assets. The liquidation value of the assets represents their absolute floor value. From the investor's point of view, the difference between the value of the investment and the liquidation value of the assets (after priority claims are met) represents the maximum risk or exposure for the investment.[26]

Earnings-Based Valuations

Earnings valuations entail multiplying the earnings of the venture by a price-earnings ratio or dividing the earnings by some capitalization factor (these are mathematically equivalent techniques). Two problems are inherent in this technique. The evaluator must determine which "earnings" should be used for the calculation and which "factor" is most appropriate for capitalization. The resolution of these issues is not trivial; differences in valuation provide arbitrage opportunities that can be practically riskless and very lucrative.[27]

Which Earnings?   Three possible earnings figures can be used in calculating an earnings valuation.[28]

Historical earnings.   **Historical earnings** are the record of past performance. Past performance is no guarantee of future achievement, but it is sometimes an indication. In cases of valuation for the purpose of buying or selling a business, sellers rely on past performance for their valuation; after all, it was their management that was responsible for that performance. However, because in most cases the sellers will no longer be part of management, the context within which the historical performance has occurred no longer exists. Therefore, historical earnings should not be used to value future performance.

Future earnings (historical resource base).   Calculations based on **future earnings** and the historical resource base represent a middle-of-the-road approach. They correctly identify the important earnings stream for the future out of which dividends will be paid. Also, the firm's future earning capacity will determine a market value. However, the use of the historical resource base assumes that the relationship between the firm's capabilities and its environment will remain unchanged. This calculation would represent the value to the current owner who anticipated no major changes in the assets of the firm, its strategy, or its competitive or macro situation. In a buy-sell situation, the buyer should not rely on this estimate, because the probability is high that the underlying resource base will indeed be modified under new ownership.

Future earnings (present and future resource base).   This is the most appropriate measure of earnings in both the buy-sell and new venture valuations. Future earnings are the basis for future returns. These future returns flow directly as a result of whatever new resources and capabilities are developed by the firm's founders and top managers. Therefore, valuation is always a forward-looking process, and its calculation requires estimates of future performance.

In addition to the problem of determining which earnings to include and under what circumstances to include them, valuation also must grapple with the problem of comparable earnings. Earnings can be stated and calculated in a number of ways: earnings before interest, depreciation, and taxes (EBIDT), earnings after taxes (EAT), and earnings before and after extraordinary items. Extraordinary items should be omitted from earnings calculations because they represent "nonnormal" operating situations and one-of-a-kind events. Because we are interested in valuation of an ongoing business, special situations should be factored out of the calculations.

Both EBIDT and EAT are legitimate earnings to use in the valuation process. The advantage of EBIDT is that it measures the earning power and value of the business fundamentals and underlying resources *before the effects of financing and legal (tax) organization*. From the viewpoint of a new venture in search of financing, as well as in a buy-sell situation, EBIDT is preferred, because future financial and legal structures may be altered according to the tax preferences of the owners. However, EAT is a reasonable and workable figure to examine. The important consideration is to be consistent in valuation methods. The entrepreneur should not employ EAT for one scenario and EBIDT for another.

Which Capitalization Factor?   Determining the capitalization factor is no less an exercise in estimation and judgment. The **capitalization factor** or **price-earnings (P-E) ratio** is the multiple that represents the consensus among investors concerning the growth and reliability of the firm's earnings over time. The P-E ratio is the price that an investor is willing to pay to buy a claim on $1 worth of current earnings. Higher P-E ratios mean that investors believe that earnings will be much higher in the future; lower P-E ratios indicate that investors do not believe earnings will increase very much.[29]

For example, large, stable, slow-growth businesses are often capitalized at five to 10 times earnings. Firms that are expected to grow as well as or slightly better than the economy as a whole might have price-earnings ratios in the teens to low twenties. Small firms with high-growth potential often come to market at IPO at multiples of 30, 40, and 50 times earnings. Their earnings are valued at higher ratios because certain investors look for the high-risk/high-reward stock that could be the next Intel, Microsoft, Cisco Systems, or Genentech.

No method of determining the correct price-earnings ratio for any specific new venture valuation is exact. The best process generates a range of potential values and evaluates outcomes within the range. In determining the P-E ratio, there are a number of reference points to check:

1. *Look for similar or comparable firms that have recently been valued and employ that capitalization rate as a base.* This is not easy, because there are few "pure plays" available for comparison.[30] Sometimes private valuations have been made by buyers or sellers, but these are not public information and may be difficult to access.

2. *Estimate the range for the stock market's overall P-E ratio for the period under evaluation.* If the market is expected to be a bull market, P-E ratios will be above the historical average. In this case, adjust the new venture ratio upward. In a bear market, ratios are down, and the new venture rate should reflect this.

3. *What are the industry's prospects?* Those under heavy regulation or competitive pressures will be valued lower than those that are considered "sunrise" industries—that is, industries just beginning their development under government protection and with little competition.

The earnings methods are commonly used because they are relatively efficient (you need only two reliable numbers) and easy to use for comparisons. They are volatile because any change in future earnings estimates produces a valuation change that is multiplied by what is sometimes a very large number. In addition, earnings from an accounting viewpoint are designed to minimize tax liability. They seldom represent the amount of cash actually available for returns to investors and owners. To examine these, we need a cash flow model of firm value.

E-NOTES 7-4

New Venture Valuations

Asset-based valuations:

- book value
- adjusted book value
- liquidation value
- replacement value

Earnings-based valuations:

- historical earnings
- future (historical resource base) earnings
- future (present and future resource base) earnings

Discounted Cash Flow Models

The value of a firm can also be estimated using discounted cash flow (DCF) models. DCF models were originally developed to estimate returns on specific projects over limited time horizons in the context of capital budgeting. They were then expanded for use in valuing publicly held firms traded on major stock exchanges. The application of DCF models to entrepreneurial opportunities is relatively new and must be applied with some caution.

Advantages of DCF Valuation   The DCF model of valuation can provide valuation estimates that are superior to asset-based and earnings-based methods if used appropriately. One advantage of the DCF model is that the valuation is based on the cash-generating capacity of the firm, not its accounting earnings. For new ventures, "cash is king"; when you are out of cash, you are out of business. An earnings model may depict the business as healthy, although it cannot pay its bills or open its doors to customers. A cash-based model is more sensitive to that issue.

Another advantage of the cash model is its inclusion of cash flows that can be appropriated by the founder/owner and the top management team. Cash payments to the entrepreneurs, such as contributions to Keogh plans and other retirement schemes, returns from debt repayments, interest payments, salaries, tax shields and advantages, dividends, and cash replacement perquisites (e.g., automobile insurance), can all be included in calculating the value of the firm to its owners. When a firm is "owned' by hundreds of thousands of small shareholders, these items are irrelevant. (Indeed, these decrease the value of the firm to the stockholders.) For a closely held firm, they are quite relevant.

Disadvantages of DCF Valuation   One of the most important disadvantages of the DCF model is that there are usually few other choices for the entrepreneurs to evaluate. Recall that DCF analysis was originally used for capital budgeting. In capital budgeting, the DCF model can provide a reliable ordering of alternatives. For the entrepreneur, there are few alternatives to the single new venture under consideration. Therefore, the benefit of reliable ordering is lost. If the other essential numeric inputs into the DCF calculation are also unreliable, the valuation will be a prime example of "garbage in, garbage out."

A second problem arises from estimating the numerical inputs into the DCF equation. Three major ones include the estimation of the period cash flows (usually annual), the estimation of the weighted cost of capital (discount rate), and the estimation of the terminal (or horizon) value of the firm. If these calculations are off, the valuation will be wide of the mark, too.

Discounted Cash Flow Example   To calculate the value of the firm with the DCF model, the following equation is used:

$$V = C_0 + C_1/(1 + k) + C_2/(1 + k)^2 + C_3/(1 + k)^3 + C_n/(1 + k)^n = \Sigma\, C_t/(1 + k)^t$$

where:

V is the value of the firm.
C is the cash flow in each period t.
k is the firm's cost of capital.

For example, suppose the entrepreneur had projected that a business could be started for $1 million and generate the cash flows listed in the following table. If an entrepreneur has a weighted cost of capital of 15 percent, and the firm's capitalization rate is .20 (its terminal value, or TV, then is $1,000,000/.20) = $5,000,000, then the value of the venture is $3,557,720.

Cash Flows in $000

Yr. 0	Yr. 1	Yr. 2	Yr. 3	Yr. 4	Yr. 5	TV 5
−1,000	200	400	800	1,000	1,000	5,000

Method: discount these flows by $(1 + k)^n$

The internal rate of return on this stream of cash flows is 68.15 percent. This is calculated by setting the initial investment ($1,000) equal to the 5-year stream plus the terminal value and solving for k. As long as the entrepreneur can finance this project at rates less than 68.15 percent, value is being created and appropriated by the firm. At rates above 68.15 percent, the value is appropriated solely by the investor.

Residual pricing model.   This brief example illustrates how an entrepreneur might use the DCF model to value the firm from his or her point of view, but it is also important to consider how an investor would value a new venture. One common method that investors employ is called the **residual pricing method**. It is called this because it is used to determine how much of the firm must be sold to the investor in order to raise start-up funds, with the "residual" left for the entrepreneurs.

From the investor's point of view, the pretax annual cash flows generated for years 1 through 5 are not important, because they generally will not be available to the investor. These will be paid out as perquisites to the entrepreneur and reinvested in the firm to keep it growing. The investor is interested in the after-tax profits at a point in time (let's say year 5). If the pretax cash flow were estimated at $1,000,000, let's say that the after-tax profits were $500,000. At a multiple (P-E ratio) of 10 times earnings, the firm is valued at $5,000,000 at the end of year 5.

Instead of using a weighted-cost-of-capital figure, say, 15 percent, the investor would use a "required-rate-of-return" figure. This is because the investor needs to see if the firm will be able to cover all the risk exposure, expenses, and the cost of no- and low-return investments the investor has made. The investor's required rate of return is invariably higher than the entrepreneur's weighted cost of capital (because the entrepreneur will also use low-cost debt when possible).

Let's say that the entrepreneur wants to approach the investor with a proposition: The entrepreneur wants to raise $500,000 from the investor for an equity share in the business. How much equity (i.e., what percentage ownership of the business) should the entrepreneur offer in exchange for a half-million-dollar stake?

To achieve a 40-percent return on investment, the investor would have to have $2,689,120 worth of stock at the end of year 5. This was calculated by taking the $500,000 initial figure and compounding it at 40 percent for 5 years $(1.4)^5$. The future-value factor of this term is 5.378. If the investor's stock must be worth $2,689,120 in 5 years and the total value of the stock will be $5,000,000 in 5 years $(10 \times \$500,000)$, then the investor must own 53.78 percent of the company ($2,689,120/$5,000,000).[31]

When the entrepreneur knows:

- The investor's required rate of return
- The amount of the investment
- The number of years the investment is to be held
- The after-tax profits for the horizon year
- The expected price-earnings multiple

The amount of equity ownership the investor will require can be calculated

As we will see in the next chapter, the investor may or may not actually require a 53.78-percent stake in the new firm. Elements such as potential dilution and management control need to be factored into a negotiation. No formula can fully express the complexity of a negotiation process or alleviate the desire of all parties to achieve the highest returns for the least amount of risk.

Summary

Entrepreneurial finance builds on traditional financial theory yet goes beyond it in certain ways that recognize that the entrepreneurial problem is unique and multifaceted. Financial resources are required, although seldom are they a source of competitive advantage. However, they are a formidable hurdle for the entrepreneur.

The entrepreneur must be able to accurately determine the venture's financial needs, not only at the beginning of the venture but throughout the venture's life cycle. Determining start-up costs, predicting cash flows, managing working capital, identifying sources of financing, and accessing this money are key activities. Equity must be raised both inside and outside the firm; debt, both asset-based and cash flow-based, will lower the overall cost of capital for the new venture.

In the process of raising the money, the entrepreneur will have to confront and solve the valuation question. Three types of valuations are possible: asset-based valuations, earnings-based valuations, and discounted cash flow models. All have their strengths and weaknesses. The use of a specific technique depends on the purpose of the valuation.

In the next chapter, we will examine more comprehensive and complex models of valuation and discuss the elements and structure of new venture financial deals.

Key Terms

- Asset-based financing
- Capitalization factor
- Cash flow cycle
- Cash flow financing
- Covenants
- Equity
- First-stage financing
- Fourth-stage financing
- Future earnings
- Historical earnings
- Initial public offering (IPO)

- Inside equity
- Management of financial resources
- Micro loan
- Outside equity
- Overcapitalized
- Permanent working capital
- Phased financing
- Price-earnings (P-E) ratio
- Private investors
- Production cycle

- Prospectus
- Residual pricing method
- Second-stage financing
- Seed capital
- Start-up capital
- Temporary working capital
- Third-stage financing
- Undercapitalized
- Venture capital

Discussion Questions

1. Why are financial resources not a source of competitive advantage even though they are a continuing hurdle for the new venture? (See Chapter 2 for review.)
2. Why is undercapitalization dangerous for a new venture? How can overcapitalization pose a problem?
3. What are the elements of the cash flow cycle?
4. How can managing and controlling the cash flow cycle save the entrepreneur money?
5. How do the financing needs of the enterprise change over its life cycle?
6. What variables affect the choice of financing sources for the entrepreneur?
7. What are the pros and cons of raising start-up capital from private investors?
8. What are the pros and cons of going public?
9. What steps should the entrepreneur take to position the new venture for a loan?
10. Discuss the models and methods of new venture valuation. What are the pros and cons of each method?

Exercises

1. Calculate the start-up capital needed to finance the new venture described in your business plan.
2. Analyze the cash flow cycle from your business plan pro forma statements.
3. Develop a plan to control your firm's cash flow cycle. Recalculate question 1. How much money did you save?
4. Calculate the prospective value of your new venture at the end of 5 years by adjusted book value or replacement value, by using the appropriate earnings method, and by using the discounted cash flow method.
5. Match your financing needs to the appropriate sources of capital.
6. Using the residual pricing method, how much equity would you have to sell in order to raise money from a venture capitalist?

DISCUSSION CASE

Socially Responsive Investment

Make no mistake; most venture capitalists aren't social do-gooders.

Most venture capitalists are strictly interested in making money. They want to invest their funds in high-tech or innovative ventures that need an influx of capital and maybe a little guidance to make company revenues soar. In the best-case scenario, venture capitalists want to empower companies that have the potential to go public and make everyone—including the venture capitalists—very rich.

However, a small group of venture capital funds are now focused on the "double bottom line." Their objective is not only to build the revenues of new ventures, but also to create new jobs in economically depressed communities. So far, the impact of these socially responsive firms has been quite small; it was estimated at the end of 1999 that these 70 funds had a total capital of $300 million, of which only about $100 million was invested in economically disadvantaged areas. But new legislation passed by the U.S. Congress in December 2000 should increase those numbers significantly.

According to the Small Business Administration, low-income communities in the United States are often unable to attract sufficient equity capital and technical assistance for new or expanding businesses, especially capital from the private sector. The U.S. government's response to this problem was to create the New Markets Venture Capital (NVMC) Program. This program will encourage the development of new, privately managed venture capital firms that are committed to creating jobs and promoting economic development in specific low-income geographic areas. Congress also appropriated $150 million in debenture guarantees for these new NMVC enterprises for 2001, along with $30 million for technical assistance programs. These allocations should come close to doubling the amount of money available to entrepreneurs in low-income communities.

Along with the money, there's lots of red tape. Potential NMVC firms had to pay a $2,000 fee and then spend an estimated 160 hours filling out an application form. The 15 to 20 that are approved will then have to raise $6.5 million from the private sector in less than 5 months in order to access the federal funds; they will then only receive those federal funds in a dollar-by-dollar match as they raise additional funds from the private sector over the next 2 years. The low-income geographic area where investments can be made are also limited. To qualify, an area must have a poverty rate of 20 percent or more and either be in a designated Urban or Rural Empowerment Zone, an Urban or Rural Enterprise Community, or be outside a metropolitan area.

The New Markets program has attracted considerable criticism. "There's a major distinction between putting money into depressed areas and actually doing good for low-income people," notes Julia Sass Rubin, who has studied venture capital's role in community development at Harvard. She cites San Jose, California, as an example. Ten years ago, San Jose had a high poverty level; thanks to venture capital investment, today it has a thriving economic base. "You could argue they got rid of poverty, but they didn't," claims Rubin. "They just got rid of the poor people."

(continued)

(continued)

Some existing "double bottom line" venture capital firms welcome the New Markets program because they think it may lead to better programs down the line, and because they feel it will legitimize economic investment in low-income areas. "It's not perfect—but it's better than no program at all," says Nick Smith, president of a Minnesota fund that had already invested $15 million in the creation of new jobs before your tax dollars created NMVC.

CASE QUESTIONS

1. As a taxpayer, how do you feel about this program? Do you think it's the role of the federal government to create jobs? What are the pros and cons?

2. If you were on the selection committee for NMVC firms, what kind of experience or credentials would you be looking for on an application?

3. Do you think a commitment to the "double bottom line" can be profitable? Is creating jobs a goal that is compatible with entrepreneurship?

4. Do you think this program will be successful over time? Visit the Small Business Administration Web site (www.sbaonline.sba.gov) to check the current status of the New Markets Venture Capital Program.

Source: Adapted from Julie Fields, "Venture Capital with a Conscience," *Business Week Online* February 7, 2001; additional information available at www.sbaonline.sba.gov.

Appendix 7A

The Initial Public Offering (IPO) Process

A public offering in the United States takes between 6 and 9 months to plan and execute. Administrative costs, printing, and legal fees may run from $500,000 to $1,000,000. The underwriters typically receive fees of 7.5 percent of the total proceeds as well as options to purchase additional stock at reduced prices.

The underwriter(s) are the investment bankers and brokerage houses that sell the stock to the public, generally through their retail distribution network. There are three types of selling efforts: best effort, best effort (all or none), and firm commitment. In the simple best-effort case, the underwriter agrees to sell as much as possible of the stock that is authorized, and the public issue goes into effect even if all the authorized stock is not sold. The best-effort scenario arises when the company is relatively small, the investment banker is regional, and the company's prospects are somewhat in doubt.

The best-effort (all or nothing) scenario requires the investment banker to sell all of the authorized issue or cancel the offering. This means that the company will not be public unless it can sell all its stock and raise all the money that it requires for financing its future. The advantage here is that the firm will not become public and undercapitalized. The disadvantage is that fees and costs associated with this strategy are not recovered if the offering is canceled.

The firm-commitment selling effort is the safest and most prestigious for the new venture's IPO. The underwriters guarantee that the entire issue will be sold by buying most of it themselves. Then they resell it to their customers. This selling effort is for companies that have the most solid backgrounds, products, and management. The underwriters share some of the risk of the offering by purchasing shares for their own accounts.

The process of going public begins long before the venture actually sells shares. The preliminary stages require the venture to meet the criteria of a public firm: a demonstrated record of growth in sales and earnings, a record of raising capital from other outside investors, a product that is visible in the market and of interest to investors, audited financial statements, clear title to the technology, an estimable board of directors, and a management team that is sufficiently seasoned to run the company and manage the IPO process simultaneously.[1]

If these criteria are met and the venture's managers have determined that the next step for the firm's financial strategy is a public offering, the process may formally begin. At this point, management will solicit proposals from underwriters for the IPO. Underwriters will respond with their philosophy, strategy, and tactics—as well as with the estimated costs of their services. Management must then select among the proposals and has the option of suggesting joint and cooperative efforts if that seems reasonable. Once the underwriter is hired, the offering begins.

1. Organization Conference This is the first meeting that brings together the three major parties to the IPO process: management, the underwriter, and the independent accounting firm that will prepare the financial statements. All parties bring their lawyers. They discuss the timing of the IPO, the nature of the offering in terms of amounts to be raised, the selling strategy, and the allocation of tasks. The lawyers inform all parties, but especially management, of the legal constraints of trading and disclosure that are now in effect.

2. Initial Registration Statement   There are three major parts to the paperwork that need to be done for the regulating authorities (the SEC). The first is the registration statement, a lengthy form that must be completed. Because of the detail and comprehensiveness of the registration statement, a significant number of appendixes are usually attached.

The second component is the prospectus. The **prospectus** is the document that is used to "sell" the new stock of the company. Although in some areas it must conform to certain regulatory standards, in other respects it is a great deal like the business plan. It describes the business, its product/market technology configuration, the competition and operations, and includes full audited financial statements. It is prepared under the rule of "full disclosure." This means that the company must reveal all information known to the company that might materially affect the decision of the investor to invest. From a practical standpoint, this means the company must reveal all risks, conflicts of interest (real and potential), and transactions that the top managers have had with the business that might be construed to be self-interest. This provides the firm some legal protection against claims of fraud.

The third component consists of supplemental data. This material is the equivalent of a huge appendix with such information as copies of leases the firm has entered into, the employment contracts of the top managers, sales and distribution contracts, and loan agreements. These can run to several hundred pages.

3. SEC Review and Comment   The package is then sent to the SEC for review and comment. In its review, the SEC staff looks for internal consistency of business plans and use of proceeds. It reviews the description of the issuer's unique risks that avoid the simple "boilerplate" disclaimers.[2] The SEC looks for areas in which the investor might be misled—for example, overoptimism concerning new-product development, overstatement of the actual size of the firm, overoptimism concerning contracts for work in hand and signed, and understatement of projected expenses for the use of proceeds. The SEC does not comment on whether the business will be a success; instead it looks for areas in which the investor should be protected against malfeasance and fraud.

4. Preparation of the Revised Statement   No IPO review is approved on the first submission. The SEC's review letter will request revisions and resubmission. Amendments are added to the application statement, deficiencies are corrected, and language is modified.

5. Preliminary Prospectus   Once the approval letter is issued, the preliminary prospectus can be prepared (it has been in process during this time) and then circulated. This prospectus is sometimes called a "red herring" because the border of the cover page is red and because of the speculative nature of IPOs in general. The number of shares and the price are not included in this document. The purpose of the preliminary prospectus is to gain visibility for the new issue within the investment community. It represents the beginning of the organization of the underwriting group or syndicate. The lead underwriter organizes a larger group of investment houses to help sell the issue and spread the risk.

6. Due Diligence   This is the process the underwriter must perform to ensure that the stock to be sold is a legitimate investment. If the underwriter were to sell stock without completing an investigation of the company, it, too, might be liable for fraud and damages (both from investors who lost money and from other brokers who lost money and reputation). Independent accountants review the company's financial picture, policies, and prospects and issue a letter to the underwriters explaining what they found. All the lawyers also write letters to each other describing the company's legal situation (current lawsuits as well as potential liability). All this investigative diligence is designed to weed out legal problems before they occur and to protect the underwriters, lawyers, and accountants from liability if they are "fooled" by the top managers.

7. Pricing the Issue   As the company gets closer to the time of actually declaring the date of the offering, negotiations begin to determine the price of the issue. Many factors are involved: the current state of the stock market, the earnings of the company, the total dollars the company is attempting to raise, the prices and performance record of other recent IPOs, and so on. There is a natural conflict of interest between the underwriters and the current owners of the company. The underwriters have the most to gain by slightly underpricing the issue: If the new issue comes to market at a discount, the underwriters' customers will be happy because the price will soon rise to its "market" level. Also, the underwriters will make additional profit, because they often take an option (called the "shoe") on as much as 10 percent of the issue. The current owners, on the other hand, want the issue to come to market at a premium. If the issue is slightly overpriced, they will receive more money for the shares they sell (personally), and the company will receive more money for whatever percentage of shares

are offered. As it gets closer to the time of the offering, the underwriter generally assumes control.[3]

8. Market Timing and Closing   The last step is the actual closing of the deal. The date of offering is set, and the underwriters and managers closely monitor the stock market in the weeks and days leading up to the offering. If the stock market starts to fall precipitously, the offering can be canceled up to the last minute. If the market is steady or rising, the night before the offering the final price is set, and a financial printer works all night to produce the prospectus for the IPO with the price on the front page.

NOTES TO APPENDIX

1. L. Orlanski, "Positioning for the Public Offering," *Bio/technology* 3 (1985): 882–885; and S. Jones and B. Cohen, *The Emerging Business* (New York: John Wiley, 1983).

2. L. Orlanski, "SEC Comments on the Offering Prospectus," *Review of Securities Regulation,* 17, no. 11 (1984): 887–896.

3. There is a good deal of evidence that new issues, on average, come to market underpriced. Quality new issues then rise quickly and the underwriters and those favored customers that were given the option of making early purchases then sell and make a quick profit. Within 6 to 18 months the shares are earning "normal" returns and no excess profits remain for investors. Low-quality new issues decline even quicker.

Securing Investors and Structuring the Deal

*Things may come to those who wait, but only the things left
by those who hustle.*

— ABE LINCOLN

Outline

Learning Objectives

After reading this chapter, you will understand:

■ What constitutes a *good investor,* and a *good investment*
■ The nature of the *investment process*
■ The *financial factors* that are involved in making a deal
■ How the entrepreneur can *create value* with a well-structured deal
■ The *legal forms of organizing* a business in the United States
■ The special conditions involving *taxes, private placements,* and *bankruptcy*

How does the entrepreneur obtain the money to launch the new venture? The chapter's opening quote implies that securing investors is an active process. If the era ever existed when investors beat a path to the door of the entrepreneur with a better mousetrap, it is gone. The entrepreneur cannot be passive and assume that financing will follow automatically from a well-designed business plan. There are many more entrepreneurs searching for financing than there are investors and money available to launch them all. The best deal will result from an aggressive, confident, and realistic approach.

What is a deal? It is usually much more complicated than a simple "Give me money, and sometime in the future, I will return it with gain." A **deal** is the structure and terms of a transaction between two or more parties.[1] For the entrepreneur, this definition has important implications. The first is that a deal has a structure. The structure indicates sets of preferences for risk and reward. These preferences depend on the personal characteristics of the bargainers, the current financial situation of the industries involved, as well as custom and tradition. The second implication is that terms must be negotiated— terms such as the rights and duties of the parties to the deal, the timing of the activities of the financiers and the entrepreneurs, and the constraints and covenants that establish the rules the entrepreneur and investors will follow. These are most often written so that the investors are assured, insured, and reassured that their money will be secure.

The final implication of the definition is that there may be more than two parties to the deal. It is unusual (and most of the time not preferred) for the entrepreneur to obtain all the financing from a single source. This may mean having debt from one source and equity from another. In reality, there are often layers of debt with different risk/ return characteristics, and there are distinct layers of equity as well. A deal is always a team effort, and many roles are available for the players.

The entrepreneur's key task is to create value. This is accomplished by making the whole greater than the sum of its parts. This process involves using the marketing concept of segmentation to raise financial backing. In essence, the entrepreneur is selling equity in the firm, ensuring cash flow, and guaranteeing return and repayment. Just as products and services have different characteristics that appeal to different people, financial instruments in a new venture financial deal also are differentiated, creating opportunities for market segmentation.

To be successful, the entrepreneur must demonstrate understanding and insight in three areas.[2] First, the entrepreneur and the top management team must understand their business. Without a clear understanding of the business and its environment, the entrepreneur and the investors will never be able to reach a consensus on the fundamentals, let alone the financing. Entrepreneurs must know the business well enough to understand the absolute amount of money they will need and when they will need it. They must understand the risks involved and the cause-and-effect factors because they will need to explain and defend their actions to potential investors. They need to understand the nature of the returns the business can offer—the sources of these returns, their magnitude, and their timing.

Next, entrepreneurs need to understand financiers and the context in which they make their decisions. Investors are interested not only in the amount of money they may make but also in the risk of the investment, the timing of the returns, the controls to protect their money, and the mechanisms needed to (1) reinvest, if necessary; (2) abandon, if prudent; and (3) harvest, when appropriate.

Perhaps most important, entrepreneurs need to understand themselves. What are their preferences for ownership, control, wealth, and risk? Without self-knowledge, entrepreneurs may make a deal that will not have long-term positive benefits for the founders and, indeed, can sow the seeds for a lifetime of discontent and bitterness.

This chapter explores the issues of structuring deals and financing new ventures. We review the process by which entrepreneurs approach investors and examine the criteria investors use to make investment decisions. Then we build two models to illustrate the issues of deal structure. A simple discounted cash flow example was illustrated in Chapter 7, and understanding this basic model is necessary to understanding the more elaborate models presented in this chapter. The chapter continues with a discussion of the negotiation process. Experience and common sense provide many of the guidelines for the "dos and don'ts" on deal negotiation. Last, we review legal and tax-related issues. Legal forms of organization, private placements, and the tax code all affect the final deal structure.

E-NOTES 8-1

A Deal

A deal is the structure and terms of a transaction between two or more parties.

APPROACHING INVESTORS

What do you need to know in order to meet with investors? Approaching investors requires knowledge of investing patterns and traditions. At its most basic, it is a selling job; the entrepreneur is selling a part ownership of the new venture (equity), a percentage of the anticipated cash flow (debt), or both. Every selling job requires knowledge of the customers, their purchasing habits, their sensitivity to price, and the substitutes and alternatives they face. In Chapter 3, we discussed selling products. A review of the concepts of "buyer power" applied to financiers provides some of the insight needed to plan an effective strategy to attract investors.

The Ideal Investor

Every entrepreneur has his or her vision of a dream investor. However, the ideal seldom exists in real life. What are the characteristics of the ideal investor? The ideal investor is one who:

- *Is actually considering making an investment.* An investor who is not liquid or has no desire to make an investment, no matter how rich, is unapproachable.
- *Has the right amount of money to invest.* An investor with too little money cannot buy into the deal. An investor with too much money may think your deal is trivial.
- *Is interested in the business.* Investors should have some, if not all, of the same enthusiasm and optimism about the business's prospects as the founders.

- *Has knowledge that can help the new venture.* Counseling from an investor who has experience, expertise, or network resources is ideal. The investor may be savvy about the business or industry or the geographic area where the business will operate. If the investor knows another individual who is interested in investing, this is important knowledge, too.
- *Is reputable and ethical.* The investor's reputation is part of the new venture's reputational capital. Ethical standards are important because investors could take advantage of inside information or manipulate their investment to the entrepreneur's disadvantage in a potential conflict of interest.
- *Has a good rapport with the top managers and founders.* The ability to communicate freely, to get along and see the situation from the founder's point of view, can go a long way to easing strain between management and investors.
- *Has experience in this type of investing.* Because of the wide swings in performance and emotions that are part of the entrepreneurial process, investors who know what to expect and can hang on for the duration are most desirable.[3]

Investors with all these characteristics are human resources that are rare, valuable, hard to duplicate, and nonsubstitutable. Therefore, they can provide sustainable advantage for the firm.

The ideal investor can exist within any of three primary investor groups.

1. Friendly investors such as family, friends, business associates, potential customers or suppliers, prospective employees, and managers
2. Informal investors such as wealthy individuals (e.g., doctors, lawyers, business-persons) and angels
3. Formal or professional investors in the venture capital industry

For example, professional investors were a source of outside funds and expertise for Software Artistry, Inc., a fledgling developer of artificial-intelligence software packages. The Indianapolis venture capital firm CID Equity Partners invested a total of $2.2 million in nine separate deals with Software Artistry over a period of 5 years. More importantly, CID encouraged the company to concentrate its efforts into developing Expert Advisor, a program that centralizes information from a business' internal experts at a central help desk. This unique and successful software has enabled businesses like Sony Electronics Inc., General Mills Inc., and the U.S. Senate to reduce the number of employees who handle customer inquiries, cut phone time, and slash the number of transferred calls within the organization. CID also recruited a new CEO for Software Artistry before the company went public in 1995. During the initial public offering, CID sold enough of its Software Artistry shares to recoup their cash investment but retained shares that still gave them a $40 million interest in the venture.[4]

After a long period of growth, the amount of money and the number of deals executed by venture capitalists have begun to decline. Venture capital investment and venture capital firms boomed in the mid-1990s. However, as returns to these investments declined in the new decade, a sharp drop in investment activity followed. This decline has continued through 2001 and is expected to endure through 2002.[5]

Ideal Investor

From the entrepreneur's viewpoint, a potential investor should have:

- liquid and sufficient capital
- knowledge of the business or knowledge that will help the new venture
- reputable and ethical standards
- good communication with management
- investment experience

The Ideal Entrepreneur and New Venture

Investors also have their "dream" investment. It has little risk, a big payoff, and takes place overnight. More realistic investment opportunities require careful study and evaluation. The five most important investment criteria are:[6]

1. *Market attractiveness.* There are four major elements of market attractiveness: size of market, growth rate of market, access to market, and need for the product. All enable a firm to build volume while sustaining selling margins.

2. *Product differentiation.* Product uniqueness and patentability are two dimensions of product differentiation. Both make the product hard to copy and are bases of sustainable competitive advantage. These result in higher profit margins. Value added through the employment of technical skills is also a component (part of the human and technical resource base of the venture).

3. *Management capabilities.* The skill levels of management and their implementation abilities are also key components. The development of organizational resources is the result of management capabilities. Also, the employment of inert resources, such as financial and physical assets, is enhanced by management and organization.[7]

4. *Environmental threats.* Research indicates that investors do not separate the industry environment from the macroenvironment, as we did in Chapter 3. The major threats indicated by investors are lack of protection from competitive entry, resistance to economic cycles (economics), protection from obsolescence (technology), and protection from downside risk.

5. *Cash-out potential.* This was the least important factor among all the evaluation criteria, not because money was not important, but because profitability and wealth are the result of all the other factors falling in place. The key items of this criterion were the potential for merger with another firm and other opportunities for exit. These factors are summarized in Figure 8-1.

An investor looks for the fatal flaw in an entrepreneur's plan, perhaps an inconsistency that negates all other positives. The investor attempts to view the new venture

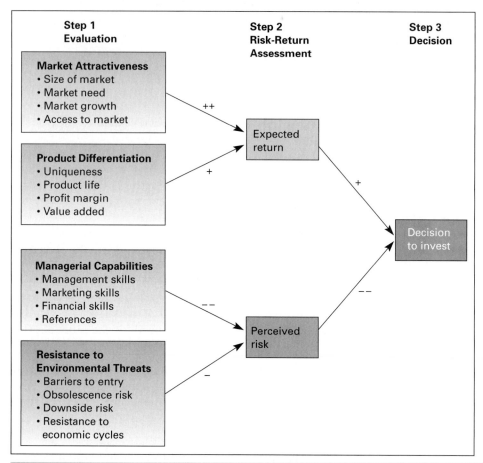

FIGURE 8-1   Venture Capital Investment Decision Process

Note: ++, +, −, −− symbols indicate the direction and magnitude of the parameters describing the relationships of the variables.

proposal as a business system, a set of interconnected parts. If the parts do not fit together, this is a red flag for investors—perhaps even a deal breaker, a "can't be negotiated demand," that catches the investor's eye and causes him or her to reject the proposal.[8]

Despite the crash of Internet entrepreneurs, not all e-commerce is off limits for investors. If the venture has the characteristics of the ideal entrepreneur, investors may still be interested. In Street Story 8-1, we see two Internet businesses that were still able to obtain financing, even after the bubble had burst.

Timmons sums up investor criteria in three broad strokes.[9] He says that the investment must be forgiving, rewarding, and enduring. A *forgiving* opportunity is one that has some allowance for variation. In other words, everything does not have to go perfectly for the venture to be a success. Because events seldom turn out perfectly, this is important. If the venture must be launched with the precision and perfection of a NASA

Playing the Dot-Com Financing Game

Could it possibly make sense to start a dot-com business now, while so many other dot-coms are failing? Analysts claim that success is indeed possible if you have the right idea, the right approach, and the right tool—especially if that tool is something you can . . . play around with.

Justballs.com is about—well, balls. The Web site features over 3,000 balls and related products from 40 different sports and 75 different manufacturers. They are the official supplier of balls for the Special Olympics and for a number of collegiate conferences, including the SEC, Big Ten, and the Big East. The site also sells clothing, trophies, and gift items, and many of their items can be personalized with a name or a corporate logo.

Justballs is happy to sell consumers a single softball or basketball, but their real target is the corporate or institutional client. "The values of competition, teamwork, perseverance, and winning are universal to corporate culture, and are brought to life in our line of high-quality sports-centric merchandise," says CEO Jim Klein. The company prides itself on developing personalized sports-related items for the corporate market. They provided engraved crystal basketballs for the VIP guests of the Gillette Company at an NCAA tournament and printed 15,000 cheer towels for Verizon for an A-10 Basketball tournament. They also created a foam football imprinted with a home-game schedule, which Temple University placed in the dorm room of every student.

Justballs is a good example of entrepreneurs knowing the business and understanding how finances work. Company management is not just a group of former jocks. CEO Klein was recruited to join the company after serving 3 years as the president of Universal Studios Consumer Products Group. Prior to that, he served in top management positions in companies that sold toys, gifts, and other merchandise. Jim Medalia, the president and founder of Justballs, has an extensive background in Web site design, desktop publishing, and graphic design; he includes companies like IBM and the BASF Corporation as his former clients.

The business experience of both men enabled them to make an attractive presentation to potential investors. Shortly after joining the company, Klein was able to raise a capital infusion of $13 million from venture capitalists. "I knew once I got in there I could turn people around," he says. Klein predicts the company will make a profit just 3 short years after it was created.

Other new dot-coms are finding innovative ways to secure investors. BabyPress Conference.com transmits videos of newborns in hospital maternity wards onto the Internet. Created by a former hospital association executive, the company makes most of its money by selling copies of videos and still photos, but the Web site has also found a new ideal investor. Toys "R" Us invested capital and linked the Baby PressConference site to its Babies "R" Us Web site, allowing new parents to steer anyone who watches their video to click through to a wish list of items for their newborn. Another potential investor is a company that hopes to market a service transmitting physician videoconferences. Teaming with BabyPressConference.com will allow this company to get their foot in the door of hundreds of hospitals.

The analysts may be right: Even in a declining market, the right dot-com not only makes sense, but could also make lots of cents.

Source: Adapted from Thomas E. Weber, "These Dot-Coms Say Investors Are Still There if You Have Good Ideas," *The Wall Street Journal,* January 29, 2001, B1; additional information available at www.justballs.com.

space shuttle, investors will steer clear. A *rewarding* opportunity is one that makes money. Returns do not have to be 100 percent compounded annually to be considered rewarding (although it helps). If early projections show returns in the 10 to 15 percent range, though, and the investors know that early projections are optimistic, then the project is not rewarding enough. Finally, the investment should be enduring. An enduring venture has a semblance of sustainable competitive advantage and is able to resist economic and competitive pressures. It must endure long enough to provide a clear exit for early investors as they pass the reward and risk to the next level of investors.

One of the characteristics of an ideal entrepreneur is track record. In Street Story 8-2, we see how an entrepreneur with a history of accomplishment does not have problems finding money—no matter how big the deal.

E-NOTES 8-3

Ideal Investment

For an investor, a potential new venture must be:

- *forgiving*—meaning that it must have enough market attractiveness and product differentiation to allow it to survive even if some things go wrong

- *rewarding*—meaning that it must have sufficient managerial capabilities and resistance to environmental threats to allow it to make an attractive profit

- *enduring*—meaning that it must have or generate enough sustainable competitive advantage so the investor can foresee the cash-out potential

---

Investor Processes

From the point of view of the investor, the investment process is a seven-phase cycle.[10] Each phase is designed to maximize the potential gain for the investor (or minimize the potential loss) at the least possible cost in terms of time spent evaluating proposals. Investors view the world as having many more proposals and entrepreneurs than they can afford to finance or even to review. This is especially true at the top of an investment cycle, like the one for Internet companies that lasted from the late 1990s through 2000. At the trough of a cycle (similar to the period from mid-2000 through 2001), there appears to be few entrepreneurs and too much money available.[11] Their emphasis is on getting the most likely proposals through their doors and eliminating others that waste time and human resources.

The Search   Investors scan and monitor their environment just as entrepreneurs do. When investors find an opportunity that appeals to them, they make the first contact through a reference or introduction from a mutual acquaintance or business associate. Cold calls are rare. The entrepreneur should attempt to emulate this behavior. There are, however, directories of venture capitalists for entrepreneurs who cannot arrange a personal introduction or reference.[12] The entrepreneur can save time and money by prescreening investors by size and investment preference. Once suitable investors have been identified, a letter of introduction (with a personal reference, if possible) followed by a phone call is customary.

Learning from Accomplishment

Sheldon G. Adelson must be a feisty guy. Less than 18 months after opening The Venetian hotel in Las Vegas, Adelson was fighting with everyone: suing the lead contractor for the hotel because they missed deadlines, squabbling with the culinary union because he didn't want them organizing his employees, bickering with the local government over the expansion of the Las Vegas Convention Center and the construction of a monorail on the strip. "I challenge the status quo," explains Adelson.

The only people he doesn't seem to be fighting is the Bank of Nova Scotia. They provided over 75 percent of the $1.2 billion he needed to build his glamorous hotel. The bank must love him, because the hotel is already generating more than $2,600 per square foot per day in profits, making it the fourth most profitable hotel in Las Vegas.

Adelson achieved that by challenging the status quo. The traditional Vegas hotel formula is to encourage customers to gamble by housing them in small hotel rooms and drawing them into the casino with cheap buffets. In contrast, The Venetian offers the largest standard hotel rooms in the country and equips them with minibars and fax machines. Guests at the hotel are invited to linger over meals at gourmet restaurants, which are staffed with handpicked nonunion help. Adelson is specifically courting business travelers, providing them with the creature comforts and business services they demand, and all the while betting that, although these hotel guests may do less gambling, when they do

roll the dice, they'll be staking a larger-than-average amount of money. The revenues indicate his hunch is right.

Adelson is familiar with business travelers because he is the creator of the world's largest trade show, Las Vegas' COMDEX computer exhibit. He was just a small-time venture capitalist and trade magazine investor when an article he read about desktop computers inspired him to create the show in 1979. Adelson has never used a computer, either then or now, but he understands how to make money by servicing a need. In addition to renting booth space, he pioneered other innovative ways to build trade show profits, including selling advertising for a special trade show newspaper, printing logos on tote bags distributed to attendees, and marketing space on banners that hung above the heads of the people shopping at the show. "I was criticized for squeezing every ounce of profit," he says. "I must admit I was good at that." Adelson sold his computer exhibit business to a Japanese company in 1995 for $862 million.

Now Adelson doesn't have to admit he's good at the Vegas hotel business, too, because as Bear, Stearns & Co. analyst Jason N. Ader notes, "Everyone is copying him." He plans to add another 1,000 hotel rooms to The Venetian and possibly build a new hotel and casino nearby in the future. He shouldn't have any trouble finding the financing. "This could be a rags-to-riches story," laughs this son of a Boston cab driver, "but my family was too poor to own rags."

Source: Adapted from Christopher Palmeri, "His Venice Isn't Sinking," *Business Week,* October 23, 2000, pp. 86–90.

Only a few investors should be contacted at a time. Whereas one-at-a-time contacts are too slow and deliberate, a shotgun approach should also be avoided. The investment community is small enough that soon everyone would know that everyone received your business proposal. It is estimated that 60 to 80 percent of the initial contacts made by phone result in rejection or at least a statement of noninterest.[13] For the 20 to 40 percent who are encouraged to follow up, the next step is to send the business plan or proposal to the investor for screening.

The Screen Once in the hands of the investor, the business plan is screened for further interest. In a large investment company, initial screening might be handled by junior staff people. (The criteria for investor screening were discussed in the previous section.) As the plan passes various tests, it may be moved along to more senior people for serious review. Timmons estimates that only one in five business plans or proposals are deemed interesting enough to invite the entrepreneurs in for a meeting and presentation. (A little arithmetic shows that if 20 percent of the proposals pass the search and 20 percent of those pass the screen, only 4 percent of total proposals have progressed this far.) A presentation by the entrepreneur to an investor committee follows. It enables personal factors and chemistry to enter the equation. The question-and-answer session that follows (or interrupts) the presentation will demonstrate the entrepreneur's mental agility. If the meeting goes well, the evaluation phase begins.

The Evaluation In this phase, the plan is dissected and evaluated from every conceivable angle as the investors perform what is known legally as "due diligence." Because professional investors are employing money that is not their own, they are legally obligated to protect their customers' finances by thoroughly investigating the potential of the proposed business. Legal opinions and certified accounting expertise are required. The process of due diligence has precisely the same intent as it does for the initial public offering described in Chapter 7. It is a time-consuming process lasting 6 to 8 weeks. It is also expensive, consuming hundreds of professional hours. The time and expense help explain why only 4 percent of proposals make it this far.

The Decision After the due diligence phase is completed, the investors are able to make a decision. If the decision is "no," the investors should be pressed for their reasons. The entrepreneur needs this feedback before beginning this long and frustrating process again. Common reasons for rejection include:

- *Technological myopia.* **Technological myopia** occurs when entrepreneurs are so caught up in the excitement of their technology, processes, or product that they have not analyzed the market or developed a marketing system.
- *Failure to make full disclosure.* The entrepreneurs may have failed to divulge pertinent facts that were later discovered. This stains the reputation of the team and makes them less trustworthy in the investors' eyes.
- *Unrealistic assumptions.* The entrepreneurs have exaggerated certain claims about the product or the market and used those exaggerated figures to produce highly optimistic and improbable forecasts and scenarios.
- *Management.* The investors do not believe in the capabilities of the top management team. Investors often say they prefer a B proposal with an A team to an A proposal with a B team.

If the proposal has been rejected and the entrepreneur has received feedback, he or she should respect the input and attempt to adjust to investor requirements. If the proposal is accepted, the negotiation phase begins, and the actual details of the deal will be hammered out.

The Negotiations   The objective of the negotiation phase is to come to an agreement concerning the rights, duties, contingencies, and constraints that will bind the parties to the deal. These results are later codified in a formal investment contract known as the "investment agreement." An outline of a typical investment agreement appears in Appendix 8A.

An entrepreneur who has created a venture that possesses many of the four attributes of sustainable competitive advantage has negotiating power. However, if the business is already using up cash faster than it can generate sales, the power may reside with the investors. The investors and the entrepreneurs must come to agreement on three crucial issues: the deal structure, protecting the investment, and exit.[14]

The Deal Structure   The two issues that need to be resolved here are (1) how is the venture to be valued? and (2) what investment instruments will be employed? We discussed valuation issues in Chapter 7. The entrepreneur will want to be able to justify the highest valuation possible, thereby requiring him or her to sell less equity and relinquish less ownership. For example, if the entrepreneur can reasonably negotiate a value of $2 million for the business, and a $1 million investment is required, the postinvestment value of the firm is $3 million. The $1 million investment represents 33.3 percent of the postinvestment ownership. If the original valuation had been only $1 million, the postinvestment equity ownership position of the investor would have been 50 percent.

The investment instruments are also an issue of negotiation. Investors prefer capital structures that maximize their return and minimize their risk. They try to negotiate deals in which their investment is preferred stock or some form of senior debt (with collateral, interest payments, and guaranteed return of principal) *unless* the business is a success, in which case they want their debt to be convertible into equity! Once converted, investors can share proportionately in the venture's profits. The entrepreneur, on the other hand, prefers a simple capital structure of common equity. It is simple and clean and does not require any cash payout unless and until the company can afford them.

Many other provisions and covenants are often included in the deal structure. Definitions, descriptions, and examples of these negotiable terms are provided in Appendix 8B.

The Harvest   For many investors, the primary source of returns occurs at the end of the investment's life—when the investor "cashes out" and **harvests** the profits. The details of the harvesting process can be negotiated and spelled out in the investment agreement. **Registration rights** enable the investor to register stock, at company expense, for sale to someone else. Because of restrictive regulation on the sale of private placement investments, investors are required to register their shares (an expensive and time-consuming process) before they may resell them. The two most common registration rights are piggyback rights and demand rights. **Piggyback rights** give the investor the right to sell shares on any registration statement that the company makes with the Securities and Exchange Commission for sale of shares to the public. **Demand rights** require the company to register the investor's shares for sale (at company expense) on demand whenever the investor wants. Demand rights are the more onerous to entrepreneurs because they can force the company to go public before it wants to do so. A demand registration exposes the venture to the high costs and external pressures of public ownership (see Chapter 7).

Other forms of investor exit may be negotiated. The entrepreneurs can negotiate a "put" contract, in which they agree to repurchase the investors' shares at a certain date for a certain price. If the put contract has a scale of dates and payment amounts, it can be considered a warrant held by the investors. Exit scenarios in case of merger or liquidation are possible, too. The entrepreneur must be careful not to be trapped in a situation where the investor can call for the liquidation of the business or an immediate cash payout when a merger/acquisition occurs.

Because the investment agreement cannot anticipate all contingencies, both sides will want to negotiate the process by which their rights under the contract can be modified. This may be done with a two-thirds vote of the board, for example.

Negotiations between investor and entrepreneur are paradoxical. While they are being carried out, the two parties are in conflict; one's gain is often the other's loss. The investor should be expected to do everything possible to secure his or her investment and increase the potential for return. The wise entrepreneur should also negotiate hard for economic rights and provisions favorable to keeping control of the company. Once the agreement has been reached, the two parties are partners, and their gains are often mutual and shared.[15] After the investment is made and the proceeds employed to grow the venture, the relationship between investor and entrepreneur is more like a marriage and less like a haggle over the price of beans. It would be extremely shortsighted for any party to the investment to pollute the atmosphere of the courtship and have that carry over into the marriage.

E-NOTES 8-4

A Seven-Step Process

- search
- screen
- evaluation
- decision
- negotiations
- deal structure
- harvest

STRUCTURING THE DEAL

At its most basic level, a **deal structure** organizes a set of cash inflows and outflows. It describes what monies are coming into the business as investment and what monies are going out of the business as payments in the form of dividends, interest, and return of principal. At another level, the deal structure indicates levels of risk and reward and addresses the questions of who gets what and when. By breaking the outflows down by type according to risk level, the entrepreneur is able to segment the investor market and sell the investor the level of reward and risk that best matches the investor's own profile.

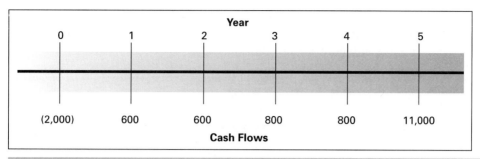

FIGURE 8-2 **Biotech Cash Flows Example ($000)**

Segmenting the Investor Market

A simplified deal structure is presented in Figure 8-2.[16] To understand the figure, imagine that the cash flows shown represent an investment and subsequent returns in a biotech company that does genetic engineering. The entrepreneurs have calculated that they need to raise $2 million to found the venture at year = 0. Figure 8-2 shows their final estimation of cash flows for the project for each year through year 5.

The internal rate of return on the cash flows in Figure 8-2 is 59.46 percent. This can be deemed sufficient to proceed with the analysis. The projection of 5 years is also sufficient and typical. However, the example shows only the aggregated bottom-line numbers on the deal. To segment the investor market, we need to break down these numbers into their original component parts. In this way, we can view the risk/reward attributes of each part of the cash flow.

Table 8-1 does this and indicates that for a $2 million investment, the project generates cash flows from three sources:

1. Tax incentives are positive in the first 3 years of the project but then become negative (tax payments) in years 4 and 5.
2. Free cash flow (CF) from operations is positive throughout the 5-year horizon, beginning at $200,000 in year 1 and rising to $1.2 million in year 5.
3. There is the projected terminal value of the business. In this example, it is predicted to be $10,000,000. This was derived (hypothetically) by taking the free cash flow for year 5 and subtracting the tax liability for year 5 ($1,200 − $200) and

TABLE 8-1 **Segmented Cash Flow Structure ($000)**

Source of Flow	Year 0	Year 1	Year 2	Year 3	Year 4	Year 5
Investment	($2,000)					
Tax incentive		$400	$400	$100	($200)	($200)
Free CF		200	200	700	1,000	1,200
Terminal value						10,000
Total CF	($2,000)	$600	$600	$800	$800	$11,000

Source: Adapted from J. Timmons, *New Venture Creation* (Homewood, IL: Richard D. Irwin, 1994), pp. 774–777.

applying a price-earnings multiple of 10 to the result $(10 \times \$1,000,000 = \$10,000,000)$. Note that the "Total CF" figure is the same as the one at the start of the example in Figure 8-2.

We can also calculate the net present value of each of the sources of cash flow by discounting the cash flows on any given line of Figure 8-2 by the internal rate of return on the whole project (about 59.5 percent). The net present value (NPV) of the investment component is $(-\$2,000,000)$, because it is in year 0. The other NPVs are calculated as follows ($000):

$$\text{NPV (tax)} = \frac{400}{(1+.595)^1} + \frac{400}{(1+.595)^2} + \frac{100}{(1+.595)^3} + \frac{-200}{(1+.595)^4} + \frac{-200}{(1+.595)^5}$$

$$\text{NPV (CF)} = \frac{200}{(1+.595)^1} + \frac{200}{(1+.595)^2} + \frac{700}{(1+.595)^3} + \frac{1,000}{(1+.595)^4} + \frac{1,200}{(1+.595)^5}$$

$$\text{NPV (TV)} = \frac{10,000}{(1+.595)^5}$$

The results are as follows:

NPV(Tax) = \$383,383, which is 19.1 percent of the returns
NPV(CF) = \$647,272, which is 32.4 percent of the returns
NPV(TV) = \$968,716, which is 48.5 percent of the returns
Total = \$2,000,000 (rounded off)

In this example, we see that most of the returns from this deal come from the terminal value of the company. This is the riskiest figure in the example, because it depends on a great many things turning out right 5 years from now. Deals like this are appropriate for venture capital firm investments.

Other Investor Segments But the entrepreneur would not want to go directly to a venture capitalist to finance this deal. There are two places the entrepreneur should go before approaching a venture capitalist. By finding a business angel (wealthy investor) and then a bank willing to lend money, the cash flows can be "sold" to investors who are less risk averse and accept lower returns than do venture capitalists. Table 8-2 suggests how these other flows might be partitioned.

The goal of our Figure 8-2 example is to raise \$2 million. The investment's tax benefits might appeal to a wealthy investor looking for a tax write-off. People in high

TABLE 8-2   Partitioned Cash Flow Structure by Investor ($000)

Source of Investment	Year 0	Year 1	Year 2	Year 3	Year 4	Year 5
Total CF	$600	$600	$800	$800	$11,000	
− Wealthy investor	400	400	100	(200)	(200)	
− Lending institution	100	100	100	100	1,100	
= Remaining	$100	$100	$600	$900	$10,100	

marginal tax brackets can often protect their incomes or cash flows by investing in businesses that may have high early losses. Let's assume that the entrepreneurs have been able to convince a wealthy individual with a required rate of return of 20 percent that the tax benefit cash flow projection is accurate and reliable.

How much would the wealthy investor be willing to pay for this cash stream? This can be determined by discounting the tax cash flow by the investor's required rate of return. In this case, we arrive at a present value of $492,155. This means that the individual should be indifferent to a choice between an investment of $492,155 and the cash flows from the tax benefits. After a modest amount of convincing, the entrepreneurs are able to receive a commitment from the investor for the money in exchange for the tax benefits (which could be larger if the firm loses more money in the early years).

With some money now in hand, the entrepreneurs are ready to approach a lending institution such as a commercial bank. Banks are not interested in tax benefits; few of them make enough money to pay very much in taxes anyway. They are interested in the ability of the firm to generate cash for interest payments and the repayment of principal. Although the free cash flows of the firm are relatively risky, some portion of them should be considered safe by conservative lending officers. For our example, assume that $100,000 (see Table 8-2) is considered fairly safe in any given year. If the entrepreneurs could find a bank inclined to accept an interest payment of $100,000 each year and a repayment of principal in year 5 with an interest rate of 10 percent, they could borrow $1 million.[17] Added to the $492,000 from the wealthy investor, the entrepreneurs need only $508,000 to complete the deal.

Selling Equity   There are not many alternatives for the remaining $508,000. So, the entrepreneurs are forced to sell equity in their business to a venture capital firm. Venture capitalists are interested in the riskiest portion of the deal, the terminal value. In exchange for this risk, they demand the highest returns (upwards of 50 percent). We can use the residual pricing method (Chapter 7) to determine just how much equity in the firm must be sold to the venture capitalists to raise $508,000 at a required rate of return. To calculate this, we discount the remaining cash flows not previously committed to the wealthy individual or bank (see Table 8-3) by the venture capitalist's 50 percent required rate of return. This gives a residual value of $1,796,707. The amount of the proposed venture capital investment is $508,000, which is 28.3 percent of $1,796,707. So the entrepreneurs offer the venture capitalists 28.3 percent of the common equity in their business for the $508,000. If the venture capitalists accept the offer, the entrepreneurs have completed their $2 million financing and have kept 71.7 percent of the firm for themselves. In fact, the entrepreneurs would be creating value for themselves at any point where they were able to raise money at less than the total internal rate of return (IRR) for the project (59.5 percent).

Risk Sharing

The previous example was intentionally simplified to show that investors have different risk/reward preferences and that entrepreneurs who can identify these needs have an advantage in securing financing for their ventures.[18] If the entrepreneurs in the example had gone directly to the venture capitalists (with their 50 percent required rate of return), they would have had to part with 79.9 percent of the equity to secure the entire $2 million.[19]

An additional assumption in the example was that the venture capitalists would take common stock and provide all of their investment up front, at the beginning of the initial period. These assumptions are relaxed in the example that follows.

Risk Sharing: Some Examples   Table 8-3 presents a simplified set of cash flows for a deal.[20] If we require this to be an all-equity deal with a required rate of return for the venture capitalist of 40 percent, then the NPV of the set of flows is $1,204. (The reader is encouraged to calculate this for themselves). The venture capitalist will demand 83 percent of the equity ($1,000/$1,204) for this investment, leaving 17 percent of the equity for the entrepreneurs. The net present value for the investors is $0, since 83 percent of this set of cash flows exactly equals the investment of $1,000, and the NPV for the entrepreneurs is $204.

However, the real world is not quite so neat. In a more likely scenario, both future cash flows and the appropriate discount rate are unknown. The parties to the deal will disagree about the amount and timing of the cash flows and the appropriate discount rate. The investors and entrepreneurs will disagree about interpretation of laws and regulations and the tax treatment of certain events. There will be conflicts of interest between the investors and founders; when one acts to protect his or her interest, it is at the expense of the other.

So let us relax just one assumption and say that instead of a certain $500-per-year cash flow, the amount is "expected" to be $500 per year, but the actual amount will be known only over time. How does this change the rewards and risks of the deal? The top portion of Table 8-4 shows the effects of this change on a common stock deal of proportional sharing.

If the probability is equal that the returns will be $450 or $550 (with the expected value still at $500), then the investor will receive $373 (.83 × $450) in the bad year and $456 (.83 × $550) in a good year. The expected annual return is the average of the two ($415), and the standard deviation (a measure of risk) of the PV to the investor is 83 percent of the total deal's NPV standard deviation of $102, or $85. The investor in this scenario receives 83 percent of the rewards and assumes 83 percent of the risk.

However, the venture capitalist will desire a different deal structure and, owing to the "golden rule" (whoever has the gold, makes the rule), will be able to bargain for it. The investor will negotiate for preferred stock with a fixed dividend and some liquidation preference. The sophisticated investor will probably want the preferred stock to be cumulative as well, meaning that any missed dividend payments accumulate and must be paid before any dividends on common stock are declared and paid. The bot-

TABLE 8-3   A Series of Cash Flows

	Period 0	*1*	*2*	*3*	*4*	*5*
Investment	($1,000)					
Cash flow		$500	$500	$500	$500	$500
Terminal value						1,000
Net cash flow	($1,000)	$500	$500	$500	$500	$1,500

Source: From "Aspects of Financial Contracting," *Journal of Applied Corporate Finance,* 1988, pp. 25–36. Reprinted by permission of Stern Stewart Co., New York, NY.

TABLE 8-4   Sharing the Risk

Common Stock (Proportional Sharing)	Venture Capitalist		Entrepreneur		Total	
Share of total stock		83%		17%		100%
Annual cash received: bad scenario	$373	83	$77	17	$450	100
Annual cash received: good scenario	456	83	94	17	550	100
Expected annual cash received	415	83	85	17	500	100
PV of cash received (incl. TV)	1,000	83	204	17	1,204	100
Net PV (incl. investment)	0		204		204	
Standard deviation of PV (and of NPV)	85	83	18	17	102	100

Preferred Stock	Venture Capitalist		Entrepreneur		Total	
Share of total stock		83%		17%		100%
Annual cash received: bad scenario	$415	93	$35	7	$450	100
Annual cash received: good scenario	415	73	135	27	550	100
Expected annual cash received	415	83	85	17	500	100
PV of cash received (incl. TV)	1,000	83	204	17	1,204	100
Net PV (incl. investment)	0		204		204	
Standard deviation of PV (and of NPV)	0	0	102	100	102	100

Source: From "Aspects of Financial Contracting," *Journal of Applied Corporate Finance,* 1988, pp. 25–36. Reprinted by permission of Stern Stewart Co., New York, NY.

tom half of Table 8-4 shows how preferred stock changes the risk/reward ratio in favor of the investors.

In this scenario, the investors receive their $415 expected cash flow dividend regardless of whether the actual cash flow is $450 or $550. In the bad year, the investors receive 93 percent of the cash flow; in the good year, 73 percent. All the risk of a bad year (and extra reward for the good year) is borne by the entrepreneurs. The standard deviation of the investors' returns is zero because there is no variation. The investors bear no risk (unless we include the risk of bankruptcy, which accounts for the 40 percent discount rate) because of the use of preferred stock instead of common stock.

So the investor will want preferred stock. There are two reasons for this preference in addition to minimizing risk. First, by enabling the entrepreneurs to achieve maximal gain under the "good year" scenario, the investors provide incentives for the entrepreneurs to work hard and smart to produce a good year. Second, if the entrepreneurs' forecasts are too rosy, and the entrepreneurs themselves do not think they can achieve these forecasts, they will have to admit to this before agreeing to this deal. Why? Because they know they will not be able to achieve the cash flows necessary for them to see any of the profits of the business. In essence, they will be working for the investors without hope of personal gain. This process is known as "smoking them out."

Staged Financing

Few deals require all the money up front. Most new venture development occurs in stages, and therefore most deals should allow for **staged** (or **phased**) **financing** as well. Let's say that the entrepreneurs need $20 million and are willing to sell 75 percent of the firm for this capital investment. Table 8-5 illustrates one possible way of staging or phasing, the financing. Often, first-stage financing is used for market studies, development of prototypes, and early organizational costs. The amounts are small relative to the entire financing plan and serve to prove the venture viable. In this scenario, $1 million goes to pay for these development and start-up costs and buys 50 percent of the venture. The implied valuation, therefore, is $2 million.

As the venture succeeds in its initial efforts, it becomes more valuable. Let's say that the second-stage money is needed to purchase plant and equipment for a small manufacturing facility that will enable the firm to test engineering concepts and design and to produce for a test market. Four million dollars are needed for this stage. The $4 million buys 33.3 percent of the firm. Because the investors already own 50 percent, this share is diluted, and they end up owning 66.7 percent at the end of this round. The company is more valuable at this point. Its implied valuation is now $12 million ($4 million $\times$ 3).

If the venture is on track and succeeding as planned, third-stage financing will be for a full production ramp-up. If this will require $15 million, the investor can be brought up to the originally determined 75 percent ownership by purchasing another 25 percent of the company. The postinvestment valuation of the firm is now $60 million. At each stage, the investor was willing to purchase less of the firm at a higher price.

Why was the investor willing to do this? Because the continued success of the entrepreneurs as they met their goals and milestones made the venture more valuable (and less risky).

The Option to Abandon

Not all staged-financing deals proceed as smoothly as the one depicted in Table 8-5. If things go wrong and the deal turns sour, the investors will not want to put additional money in, especially at the $4 million and $15 million dollar levels. That is, they want the **option to abandon**. The earlier example (Tables 8-3 and 8-4) shows what happens if staged financing is used and the entrepreneurs predict small variance in the expected cash flow of their venture. What happens if we increase the variance? If we increase the variance of outcomes to $50 cash flow in a bad year and $950 in a good year (the expected value is still $500), we increase the importance of being able to reevaluate the investment decision. In Table 8-4, with the spread only between $450 and $550, the investor was going to get paid in either case. With the wider spread, however, the investor will not get paid at all in the bad scenario.

TABLE 8-5   Phased Investment Scheme

Round of Financing	Amount Invested This Round	Percent Received This Round	VC's Share	Founder's Share	Implied Valuation (post money)
First round	$1,000,000	50.0%	50.0%	50.0%	$2,000,000
Second round	4,000,000	33.3	66.7	33.3	12,000,000
Third round	15,000,000	25.0	75.0	25.0	60,000,000

Formula for the second round: 50% + (33.3% $\times$ (1 − .50)) = 66.7%
Formula for the third round: 66.7% + (25% $\times$ (1 − 66.7)) = 75.0%

Source: From "Aspects of Financial Contracting," *Journal of Applied Corporate Finance,* 1988, pp. 25–36. Reprinted by permission of Stern Stewart Co., New York, NY.

Suppose the venture needs $500 in two stages. For this example, we need to compare two sets of rules for the investor. The first rule is that the venture capitalist has no choice but to invest in the second round, even if the cash flow is only $50. The second rule is that the investor may choose not to invest the $500 in the second round and thereby abandon the project. If the investor abandons the project, he or she forfeits any claims to an annual cash flow and receives a reduced share of the terminal value, $750. Table 8-6 illustrates the possibilities of these cash flow scenarios and rules.

The top portion of Table 8-6 illustrates a situation in which the investor is required to invest in both years. Because the discount rate is still 40 percent and the expected value of the annual cash flows have not changed from the original example (Table 8-4), the PV of the venture is still $1,204. But because $500 of the investment is delayed one period, the NPV for the entire project rises to $346 from $204.

The bottom portion of Table 8-6 is more complex and requires us to calculate the average of expected values of a good year and a bad year when the investor may

TABLE 8-6   The Option to Abandon the Project

	0	1	2	3	4	5	PV@ 40%
Rule I: VC Invest in Both Years							
Good scenario		$950	$950	$950	$950	$950	$1,933
Bad scenario		50	50	50	50	50	102
Expected annual cash		500	500	500	500	500	1,018
Terminal value						1,000	186
Expected cash inflow		500	500	500	500	1,500	1,204
Investment	($500)	(500)					(857)
Expected net cash	($500)	$0	$500	$500	$500	$1,500	$346

	0	1	2	3	4	5	PV@ 40%
Rule II: VC Has Option to Abandon in Year 1							
Good scenario							
Annual cash flow		$950	$950	$950	$950	$950	$1,933
Terminal value						1,000	186
Investment	($500)	(500)					(857)
Net cash flow	(500)	450	950	950	950	1,950	1,262
Bad scenario							
Annual cash flow		0	0	0	0	0	0
Terminal value						750	139
Investment	(500)						500
Net cash flow	(500)	0	0	0	0	750	(361)
Expected (or average) value of scenarios							
Expected net cash	($500)	$225	$475	$475	$475	$1,225	$451
Expected value of option to abandon (Rule I − Rule II): $105							

Source: From "Aspects of Financial Contracting," *Journal of Applied Corporate Finance,* 1988, pp. 25–36. Reprinted by permission of Stern Stewart Co., New York, NY.

abandon the project after the first period. The good scenario shows a periodic cash flow of $950 and an NPV of $1,262. The bad scenario shows an initial investment of $500, no cash flow, and a terminal value of $750. The NPV of this is (−$361). The average of a positive $1,262 and a negative $361 is $451. So, the value of the difference between the expected NPV of the first situation (top of table) and the expected NPV of the second situation (bottom of table) is $105 ($451 minus $346). Therefore, the investor can gain up to $105 in expected value by operating under the option to abandon. If the option is granted for "free," the investor gains the full $105. Clearly, the investor would be willing to pay up to $105 at the outset for the right to abandon. By changing the structure of the deal, the entrepreneur has created value and can sell that value in the form of an option to the investor.

Of course, this was a simplified example, and calculating options such as this is generally more complicated because there are more than just two possible cash flows ($50 and $950) and more than two possible investing stages ($500 in the first period and $500 in the second period). But the principle is illustrated—*the deal structure can create value.*

Other option types exist as well. For example, the option to revalue the project helps to determine at what price new capital will come into the deal if it is needed. A fixed-price option for future financing is also a possibility. If the value of the firm is above the exercise price, the investor will invest. If the value is below the exercise price, the investor will allow the option to expire or sell it to another investor who might find the option more rewarding because of a different risk/reward profile and preference.

Warrants

A **warrant** is the right to purchase equity and is usually attached to another financial instrument, such as a bond or debenture. Ordinarily, debt holders' returns are limited to interest and principal. The purpose of a warrant is to enable debt holders to add to their total return in case the venture turns out to be quite profitable. In this case, the warrant is sometimes called an "equity kicker" and, in fact, represents equity that, if the warrant is exercised, is off the balance sheet.

A callable warrant enables the entrepreneurs to pay the creditor off, thereby retiring the debt and recovering the equity according to a fixed schedule. The price of the warrant can be calculated for each period outstanding. Table 8-7 provides an example of the calculation of the price of a callable warrant.[21]

Let's assume that the investor has a subordinated debenture with a face value of $1 million, a coupon of 10 percent, and a warrant that guarantees the investor a total return of 15 percent. Calculating the call price (or value) of the warrant requires two preliminary steps. First, the analyst must determine the present value and cumulative present values of the interest payments. In Table 8-7, the third column shows the present value of the cash flow from the interest payments, discounted at 15 percent. Next, the analyst must calculate the future payment that makes the entire cumulative present value equal to zero at the guaranteed (in this case 15 percent) rate. The fourth column in the table shows the cumulative present value.

The actual calculation of the warrant's value, however, requires two additional steps. These are also described in Table 8-7. The first step calculates the total future payment, discounted (for *n* periods, in this case 5) at the required rate of return (15 percent in this case) that brings the cumulative present value (column 4; −$663) to zero. In this

TABLE 8-7 Calculating the Value of a Warrant

Period n	Cash Flow Interest Payments	Present Value @ 15%	Cumulative Present Value to Date	Value of the Warrant
0	−$1,000	−$1,000	−$1,000	
1	100	87	−913	
2	100	77	−836	
3	100	66	−770	
4	100	57	−713	
5	100	50	−663	$333

Assume: $1,000,000 subordinated debenture with a 10% coupon and warrants attached guarantee debt holder total return of 15%

1. Calculate the future payment in period *n* that will provide for a positive present value equal to the cumulative negative present value to date. This makes the entire present value equal to zero at the guaranteed 15% rate.

$$\text{For period 5: } \$663 = \frac{X}{(1.15)^5} = \$1,333$$

2. The warrant price is the difference between this value ($1,333) and the return of principal ($1,000) = $333.

3. This calculation can be made for any year, thus producing a schedule of warrant prices or values.

example, the amount is $1,333. The warrant price is the difference between this amount ($1,333) and the return of principal ($1,000), in this case $333.

Pitfalls and Problems to Avoid

There is only 100 percent of anything. This is true of the equity in a new venture and the cash flow from a start-up. Attempts to sell more than 100 percent of the equity and cash flow will come to grief (and prison). So each time the entrepreneur raises money, the future is somewhat constrained by the acts of the past. Each deal limits future options. In addition, each deal comes with covenants and legal restrictions that further bind the entrepreneur within a net of obligations. Unless the business is self-financing from the start, these constraints are inevitable, and the entrepreneur should focus on the controllable factors and not the uncontrollable ones.

First, the entrepreneur should avoid choosing investors and, especially, investment houses for their size or prestige alone. The choice should be made based on the needs of the business and not the egos of the founders. Conflicts of interest between the financiers, investment houses, and entrepreneurs are inevitable. The conflicts should be resolved in favor of what is best for the business. Bad advice abounds in these situations. Some of it results from ignorance, but much from self-interest. Although the entrepreneur is probably new to this game, the lawyers, brokers, and investors are not. Caution is advised.

The entrepreneur also needs to guard against his or her own greed. If he or she offers to give up too little—too little equity, too little control, too little authority—the investors will walk away. However, the entrepreneur must also guard against the appearance of giving up too much. This appears as either naivete or a lack of commitment to the new venture's future.

Last, the entrepreneur should prepare for the reality that future financing is always a possibility. The initial and early deals should not foreclose on this need. Incentives for the current investors to invest more should be built into each contract. Incentives for others to invest and not be crowded out or preempted by the initial investors should also remain. Everyone involved in the deal should have some latitude in their decisions and the ability to exit after a reasonable time period with their integrity intact (and maybe some money, too).

LEGAL AND TAX ISSUES

Obtaining experienced legal assistance and advice is critical to financing the new venture and resolving the legal and tax issues confronting it. Failing to obtain a good lawyer and accountant is worse than the trouble of choosing one.[22] Legal and tax assistance is needed for:

- The formation of business entities
- Setting up books and records for tax purposes
- Negotiating leases and financing
- Writing contracts with partners and employees
- Advising about insurance needs and requirements
- All litigation procedures
- Regulation and compliance
- Patents, trademarks, and copyright protections

Not all attorneys will be competent in all of the areas listed, but competent legal counsel knows its limitations, and experts can be brought in when required. As with many other aspects of business, there is no substitute for experience.

The best way to find competent legal service is word of mouth. The entrepreneur should then follow up by checking with legal referral services and interviewing lawyers personally to determine the rapport and the lawyer's understanding of the entrepreneur's business needs. Good legal counsel is not cheap; rates can run from $90 to $350 per hour. Some lawyers who specialize in getting new ventures up and running are willing to take equity in lieu of cash as payment for services.

There is an old saying that "a person who represents himself in a legal matter has a fool for a client." But if an entrepreneur insists on self-representation, he or she should be conversant with the content and the process of the law. A course in contracts and real estate law is recommended.

Sometimes, it is the investors who help provide legal counsel and advice. In addition, investors can help in many other ways. Street Story 8-3 shows how Charles River Ventures, a top-tier venture capital firm from Waltham, Massachusetts, provides extra tender loving care for its entrepreneurs.

Legal Forms of Organization in the United States

In the United States, there are five major types of legal organization: sole proprietorships, partnerships, corporations, S corporations, and limited liability companies (LLC).

More Valuable Than Money

Is there anything worth more to a start-up company than money?

The answer is apparently "yes" for a group of start-ups funded by Charles River Ventures, a venture capitalist company in Waltham, Massachusetts. In a program they call "CRVelocity," Charles River is offering business development services to 55 of their e-commerce and data communications ventures. These services include office space, legal counsel, consulting advice on topics ranging from marketing to debt financing to recruiting to real estate—even, in some cases, free lunches for employees.

Venture capitalist firms have always helped their start-ups by offering advice, recruiting their top personnel, and serving on their board of directors, but Charles River and a few other venture capital companies are offering much more now. "We're definitely seeing a growth in services—if not across the board, then very predominantly," says George Moriarty, editor of the *Venture Economics* trade publication. The support being offered is more "hands off" than the services provided by traditional business incubators and generally does not require the start-up to give up the same level of additional equity an incubator demands. Charles River Ventures says that it now requires a 15 percent equity stake for most of its initial investments; it was only requiring 10 percent before, but most incubators demand a 50 percent share.

Charles River has invested $10 million and hired as many as 30 staffers to run its CRVelocity program. "It's going to be a huge payoff for us," says Ted R. Dintersmith, a general partner at Charles River. "These companies are going to be a lot stronger." Participating companies won't have to waste time hunting for office space or for consultants, meaning they may be able to go public as much as 2 to 4 months more quickly. "Speed is critical," notes Izhar Armony, another Charles River partner.

Analysts note that venture capitalists are offering these services because their industry is becoming more competitive and because they recognize that investments in high-tech firms may require extra support, but not everyone approves. Some worry that fattening the staffs of Venture capital firms with support specialists will turn venture capitalists into bureaucracies unable to spot a good opportunity. They point out that many incubators are suffering because they tried to build their new ventures too fast. Some venture capital firms feel that it's inappropriate to play "Big Daddy" by providing these kinds of services for their start-up companies, and some start-ups agree.

Despite the critics, this new level of services has probably changed the venture capital business. "Venture capital is no longer about the money," says Donna Novitsky, partner in the California venture capital firm of Mohr, Davidow Ventures. "It's about the resources you bring to companies." Harvard Business School professor Paul Gompers agrees. "It's the evolution of venture capital from an art into a business."

Source: Adapted from Lynnley Browning, "Venture Capitalists, Venturing Beyond Capital," *The Sunday New York Times Business Section,* October 15, 2000, p. 1.

Each has its own characteristics in terms of legal identity and continuity, liability, taxation, and financing regulations.

Sole Proprietorships **Sole proprietorships** are the easiest to form and represent the majority of small businesses and self-employed persons. The company is simply an extension of the owner. For tax purposes, the sole proprietor completes an income statement (Schedule C). The sole proprietorship is taxed at the individual's rate, and earnings are subject to self-employment tax. A proprietorship ceases to exist when the owner dies, retires, or goes out of business; it cannot be transferred to another as a going concern. The owner is personally liable for all business activities (legal and financial).

Partnership A **partnership** is defined as a voluntary association of two or more persons to carry on as co-owners of a business for profit. All partnerships should be regulated with partnership agreements conforming to the Uniform Partnership Act. This agreement should cover such issues as:

- The contribution and participation requirements of each partner
- The allocation of profits and losses
- Responsibilities and duties
- Salaries and compensation contracts
- Consequences of withdrawal, retirements, or deaths
- The manner and means by which the partnership will be dissolved

Partnerships are not considered separate tax entities for tax purposes. The partners are taxed only at one level, that of the partner. Earnings flow proportionately to each individual, and the tax treatment is then similar to that of the sole proprietor. A partnership ceases to exist on the death, retirement, or insanity of any of the partners, unless a provision for continuation has been made in the partnership agreement.

There are two types of partnerships. A **general partnership** has only general partners and conforms to the description and limitations just listed. A **limited partnership** has both general and limited partners. The general partners assume responsibility for management and have unlimited liability for business activity. They must have at least a 1 percent interest in the profits and losses of the firm. The limited partners have no voice in management and are limited in liability up to their capital contribution and any specified additional debts. A limited partnership is limited to 35 owners.

One of the dangers of partnerships that is often unanticipated is that partners are agents for each other. The actions of one partner can cause unlimited personal liability for all the other partners. This is referred to as *joint and several liability.*

Corporation A corporation (also called a regular **C corporation** for the section of the law that describes it) is a separate legal person under the laws of the state within which it is incorporated. Its life continues even after the founders or managers die or retire. The central authority resides with the board of directors, and ownership resides with the stockholders. Shares may be bought and sold freely. No investor is liable beyond his or her proportionate capital contributions except for "insiders" in cases of securities fraud or violations of the tax code.

A corporation is taxed as a separate entity according to the corporate tax code and rates. Dividends declared by the corporation are "after-tax" from the firm's point of view, then taxed again at the shareholder level. This is known as the "double taxation" problem. To get around the double taxation problem, entrepreneurs often resort to tactics that are regulated by the Internal Revenue Service under the Federal Tax Code. These tactics usually revolve around issues of salary and interest expense.

For example, an entrepreneur could arrange to pay himself or herself a salary so high that it wipes out all profits of the corporation. Because the corporation has no profits, it pays no taxes, and the entrepreneur pays taxes just on the salary at individual tax rates. Under section 162 of the Federal Tax Code, the Internal Revenue Service can reclassify as dividends portions of salary that are unreasonably high. This creates a corporate tax liability in addition to the personal tax liability.

Interest expense is deductible from a corporation's pretax profits and, therefore, reduces its tax liability. This may tempt an entrepreneur to lend the new venture money for start-up and expansion capital instead of taking an equity position. This practice is considered legitimate, but only to a point. Under section 385 of the Federal Tax Code, a thinly capitalized company (one with a debt/equity ratio over 10:1) can have its debt reclassified as equity. Also, if the debt does not look like debt because, for example, it has conditional payment schedules instead of fixed coupon rates, it may be reclassified as equity. This means that what were tax-deductible interest payments are now double-taxed dividends.

The losses of regular corporations accumulate and can be used as tax shields in future years. The losses of proprietorships and partnerships are passed along to the principals in the year they are incurred. One exception to this involves "section 1244 stock." If this type of stock is selected in the firm's initial legal and tax organization, the owners of the firm would be able to deduct their losses from their regular income if the business goes bankrupt. If they had selected a regular corporation, their losses would be treated as capital losses at tax time.

S Corporation   An **S corporation** is a special vehicle for small and new businesses that enables them to avoid the double taxation of regular corporations. To qualify for S corporation status, the firm must:

- Have only one class of stock (although differences in voting rights are allowable)
- Be wholly owned by U.S. citizens and derive no more than 80 percent of its income from non–U.S. sources
- Have 35 or fewer stockholders, all of whom agree to the S corporation status
- Obtain no more than 25 percent of its revenue through passive (investment) sources

Although S corporations are incorporated under state law, for federal tax purposes they resemble partnerships. Usually, stockholders receive proportionally the profits or losses of the firm. This percentage is deemed to be a dividend. The monies paid to shareholders are considered self-employment income, but they are *not* subject to self-employment tax.

Limited Liability Company (LLC)   The **limited liability company** is a relatively new type of business organization that shares characteristics with both corporations and partnerships. Like a corporation, an LLC is legally a separate entity that provides liability protection for its owners. However, when it comes to taxes, LLCs are treated like a partnership, meaning that the LLC does not pay taxes itself and that all profits and losses *flow through* directly to LLC owners and are reported on their tax returns.

Although a corporation can be described by four basic characteristics (limited liability, continuity of life, centralized management, and free transferability of interests), an LLC maintains its tax status by selecting two and only two of these traits when it drafts its operating agreement. In other words, if an LLC decides that it will offer limited liability and be organized under a centralized board of directors, then it cannot legally continue as an entity after its owners die, or freely sell and trade its shares. An LLC receives some of the benefits of a partnership and some of the advantages of a corporation, but not all of them. For many firms, this means that either the partnership or the corporation remains the preferred choice.

LLC owners are called "members" and may be individuals, corporations, trusts, pension plans, other LLCs, or almost any other entity. The organization is required to file articles of organization with the secretary of state in the state where it operates and is also required to file some sort of annual report in most states, but an LLC still spends less time producing legal and tax reports than most corporations.[23]

Table 8-8 compares the different forms of legal organization on a number of important dimensions.

E-NOTES 8-5

Legal Organization

There are five major ways to organize businesses in the United States:

- sole proprietorships
- partnerships
- corporations
- S corporations
- limited liability companies (LLC)

Private Placements under U.S. Securities Laws

Whenever one party supplies money or some item of value expecting that it will be used to generate a profit or return for the investor from the efforts of others, a security is created.[24] All national governments regulate the issuance and redemption of securities, and all U.S. states do so as well. In the United States, the regulatory agency that oversees this function is the Securities and Exchange Commission (SEC). Because compliance with SEC regulations is always expensive and time-consuming, small firms and new firms have found it burdensome to comply. In response, regulations providing "safe harbors" for small and new businesses have been enacted. These safe harbors enable the smaller firm to issue securities (with constraints and limits) without conforming to the high level of effort necessary for large public offerings (see Chapter 7 on the IPO). These are called **private placements**. The specific regulations should be consulted directly for complete details. Experienced legal counsel should always be retained when interpreting

TABLE 8-8   Legal Forms of Organization Compared

Characteristic	Sole Proprietor	General Partnership	Limited Partnership	C Corporation	S Corporation	LLC
Limited liability for ALL owners	No	No	No	Yes	Yes	Yes
Owners can participate in management w/o losing liability protection	n/a	n/a	Partially	Yes	Yes	Yes
Easy to form w/o maintaining extensive record keeping	Yes	Yes	No	No	No	Yes
Number of owners	1	1 or more	1–35	2 or more	1–75	2 or more
Restrictions on ownership	No	No	Yes	No	Yes	No
Double tax	No	No	No	Yes	No	No
Able to deduct business loss on individual return	Yes	No	Yes	No	Yes	Yes

Source: Adapted from "Entity Comparison Chart," www.llcweb.com/entity20%comparison.htm. Used with permission of Steven E. Davidson, The Limited Liability Company Web site, www.llcweb.com.

these rules. Minor rule infractions and small deviations from the regulations can cause the firm selling unregistered securities to lose its safe harbor and leave it without any protections. These private financing regulations (found in regulations D and A of the SEC rules) include:

- **Rule 504.** Rule 504 is most useful when a venture is raising small amounts from many investors. A venture can raise up to $1 million during any 12-month period with up to $500,000 free from state registration as well. There is no limit on the number or nature of the investors, no advertising is permitted, and there are qualified limits on resale of these securities. Issuers cannot be investment companies.
- **Rule 505.** Rule 505 permits sale of up to $5 million to up to 35 investors and an unlimited number of "accredited" investors. No general solicitation or advertising is permitted, and there are limits on resale. Issuers cannot be investment companies. Disclosure is required to unsophisticated investors but not to "accredited" investors.
- **Rule 506.** Rule 506 permits the sale of an unlimited amount of investors and an unlimited number of qualified "accredited" investors. No solicitation or advertising is permitted. There is no limit on the nature of the issuer. Unsophisticated investors may be represented by purchasing representatives who can evaluate the prospectus.
- **Rule 147 (intrastate).** Rule 147 is for issues that meet the 80 percent rule for assets, income, and the use of proceeds. Investors must be residents of the same

state. There are no limits on the nature of the issuer, the number of purchasers, or the amount of the issue. There is a 9-month holding period before resale.

- **Regulation A.** Securities sold under this regulation must be less than $1.5 million in any 12-month period and sold only to "accredited" investors. Advertising is restricted, but there are no limits on the nature of the issuer or the number of investors. There are no limits on resale, but an offering circular must be filed and distributed. A "miniregistration" filing in the SEC regional office is required.
- **Rule 144.** If shares are sold and not covered by regulation A, then there are problems with resale (because the securities are not registered) unless they can be sold under Rule 144. Rule 144 requires a holding period and a filing registration before the shares can be resold.

These regulations refer to "accredited" investors. The term **accredited investor** has a very specific legal meaning.[25] Generally, accredited investors are investment companies, individuals with wealth and income above certain floors, and the officers of the issuer of the securities. The language of the regulation indicates the importance of having experienced legal counsel guide the process of issuing and selling private security offerings.

In addition, all the exemptions listed are subject to **integration principles**. This means that the securities should conform to a single plan of financing, for the same general corporate purpose, be paid for with the same consideration, and be the same class of securities. They should also be offered or sold at or about the same time; under Rule 147 or regulation D, any offering made 6 months prior or 6 months after will be integrated into the exempt offering. Violation of any of these principles violates the regulation, and the entire offering will be considered nonexempt and, therefore, in violation of the securities laws.

Last, in addition to compliance with all laws requiring securities registration, entrepreneurs must recognize the importance of providing potential investors with full and complete disclosure about the security, the use of funds, and any other consideration affecting the decision to invest. Both federal and state law make it unlawful to make any untrue statement of a material fact or to omit any material fact. A "material fact" is one that a reasonable investor would consider substantial in making an investment decision.

If an investor can show that the issuer misstated or omitted a material fact in connection with the sale of securities, the investor would be entitled to recover the amount paid from either the firm or possibly the individual directors and officers of the venture. Liability may also be imposed on the entrepreneur as the "controlling person" of the actual issuer. Actions such as these must begin within 1 year of the discovery of the misstatement and no later than 3 years after the sale of the security.

Cases such as these are complex and expensive. The court has the benefit of hindsight, which can lead to second-guessing the original issuer. The outcomes frequently depend on who can prove what was a "fact" at the time of the issue. A carefully prepared offering document can be invaluable in legal proceedings.[26]

U.S. Bankruptcy Laws

We have stressed the risky nature of entrepreneurial activity but have not directly confronted the ultimate negative consequences of risky behavior—bankruptcy. Bankruptcy is an option for dealing with financial troubles, primarily an impossible debt burden. The declaration of bankruptcy by a firm is an attempt to wipe the slate clean, equitably pay off creditors, and start again. Because of the potential rejuvenating effect of bankruptcy and the forgiveness of a portion of debts, a person or a corporation can declare bankruptcy only once every 6 years.

The prospect of bankruptcy is always with the entrepreneur and the firm's financiers. It partially accounts for the high required rates of return needed by equity investors. Because equity investors understand that in case of bankruptcy they are likely to receive no gains and even lose all their capital investment, they need high returns from the "winners." Our repeated discussions about the resources that provide sustainable competitive advantage for the venture have implicitly included the prospect of bankruptcy. Ventures created with resources that are rare, valuable, imperfectly imitable, and nonsubstitutable are more resistant to environmental threats, competitive attacks, and internal implementation errors than forms without these resources. Therefore, firms with a solid resource based strategy are more resistant to bankruptcy.

Warning Signs/Predictive Models   Bankruptcy seldom sneaks up on a firm. There are usually warning signs, and these signs can appear as early as a year to 18 months before the crisis actually occurs. Financial problems, specifically the inability to make interest and principal payments, are the usual precipitating event. However, any time the business has liabilities greater than its assets, it may file a bankruptcy petition. Because of the accounting rule that requires the acknowledgment of liabilities as soon as they are known, firms that may have cash to pay debts often find themselves with negative net worth. This can happen when a firm must recognize future liabilities for employee health costs or pensions, but the signals are evident earlier, and the longer-term cause is poor management. The early signs include unhappy customers, a faulty production or service delivery process, bad relations with investors or the bank, employee unrest and work stoppages, and, ultimately, poor financial management.

There are telltale signs of impending crisis. For example, when the firm changes management, its advisers, and especially its accountants and auditors, this is an indication that problems are mounting. These changes often result in late financial statements. Other indicators are:

- Qualified and uncertified accountants' opinions
- Refusal to provide access to key executives
- Sudden searching for an alliance partner
- New interest in a merger or acquisition without strategic reasons
- Writing off assets
- Restrictions in credit terms and availability

Because creditors can either save their investment or attempt to save the firm if they can become aware of the crisis early enough, research has been conducted to provide an early warning system for bankruptcy. The most famous of these predictive models uses information commonly available in financial documents.[27] There are two models, one for private companies, the other for public firms. The models are equations that calculate Z-scores from a discriminate analysis of the data. The models are shown in Table 8-9.

By plugging in the venture's actual financial ratios, multiplying these ratios by their weights (coefficients), and calculating the total, an analyst can determine whether the

TABLE 8-9 Predictive Model of Bankruptcy

Model 1: The Public Firm

Z-score = 0.012 (WC/TA) + 0.014 (RE/TA) + 0.033 (EBIT/TA) + 0.006 (MVE/TL) + 0.999 (sales/TA)

If the Z-score is less than 1.81, the firm is in danger of bankruptcy.

If the Z-score is greater than 2.99, the firm is considered safe.

Values between 1.81 and 2.99 are considered cautionary.

Model 2: The Private Firm

Z-score = 0.717 (WC/TA) + 0.847 (RE/TA) + 3.107 (EBIT/T) + 0.998 (sales/TA)

If the Z-score is less than 1.23, the firm is in danger of bankruptcy.

If the Z-score is greater than 2.90, the firm is considered safe.

Values between 1.23 and 2.90 are considered cautionary.

where:

$$WC = \text{Working capital}$$
$$RE = \text{Retained earnings}$$
$$EBIT = \text{Earnings before interest and taxes}$$
$$MVE = \text{Market value of the equity}$$
$$Sales = \text{Sales}$$
$$NW = \text{Net worth}$$
$$TA = \text{Total assets}$$
$$TL = \text{Total liabilities}$$

Source: E. Altman, R. Haldeman, and P. Narayanan, "ZETA-Analysis: A New Model to Identify Bankruptcy Risk," *Journal of Banking and Finance* (June 1977): 29–54.

firm is in danger of bankruptcy or is above the safe range. Ventures with Z-scores in the intermediate range need watching.

The Bankruptcy Reform Act of 1978   The Bankruptcy Reform Act of 1978 codifies three specific types of voluntary bankruptcy. These are known by their chapter designations: Chapter 7, Chapter 11, and Chapter 13. Each of these chapters details a separate manner by which the firm and its creditors can seek protection. A venture can be forced into bankruptcy (involuntary) by its creditors under the following conditions:

- When three or more creditors have aggregate claims that total $5,000 more than the value of their collateral
- When there is one or more of such creditors and the total number of creditors and claim holders is under 12
- When any one general partner in a limited partnership begins legal proceedings

The failure to pay on time is sufficient criteria for a filing of involuntary bankruptcy, even if the firm has the ability to pay. One way to avoid involuntary bankruptcy is to make sure that no three creditors are owed more than $5,000 in the aggregate and that the firm has more than 12 claim holders.

Chapter 7 bankruptcy.   A **Chapter 7 bankruptcy** provides for the voluntary or involuntary liquidation of the firm. The process provides for an accounting of all of the assets of the debtor, the identification of all creditors and claim holders, the appointment of a trustee to supervise the process, and a meeting of the creditors' committee to work out a plan of liquidation and distribution. The Bankruptcy Reform Act of 2000 added a means test to determine whether a person was eligible to file under Chapter 7.

Chapter 11 bankruptcy. A **Chapter 11 bankruptcy** is filed for the purpose of reorganizing the firm's debts so it can continue to operate. The goal is to keep the business running and eventually emerge from Chapter 11 as a healthier, albeit smaller, company. Creditors and claim holders may prefer this form of bankruptcy if they believe that there is a probability that they will receive more of their money than under Chapter 7.

Chapter 11 proceedings are often entered into voluntarily by the owners of the business because once the filing is made, all payments of debts and obligations are stopped until a settlement can be worked out. The process calls for the appointment of a trustee, the formation of a committee of general unsecured creditors, and meetings between the committee and the owners to work out a plan for reorganization. The debtor has 120 days to file the reorganization plan and 60 more days to obtain acceptance by the committee. The plan shows how the different classes of creditors will be treated and how the business will be operated until all the classes have had their reorganized claims satisfied. The court must approve the final plan. If the court approves the plan, the debtor is discharged of the old debts and obligated to the new debts as described in the plan.

However, many times firms do not emerge from Chapter 11. Then they are forced to liquidate anyway under Chapter 7. Evidence suggests that instead of forestalling liquidation and protecting the venture, Chapter 11 hastens the end. The chances of a small firm emerging from Chapter 11 are estimated at between 10 and 30 percent. The primary reasons for this are:

- The high costs of legal proceedings to discharge the debts
- The diversion of often shallow management to legal proceedings instead of business management
- Weakened bargaining power when creditors come face-to-face
- Market disruption because of negative publicity; customers and suppliers jump ship at the announcement of a bankruptcy filing

Sometimes it is recommended that the use of personal persuasion and negotiation be employed before the owner takes the precipitous and risky move of a Chapter 11 filing.

Chapter 13 bankruptcy. A **Chapter 13 bankruptcy** covers individuals, primarily sole proprietorships, with regular incomes of less than $100,000 and secured debts of less than $350,000. Its purpose is to discharge the debts of the person and protect the person from harassment by creditors. The plan can call for an extension of credit, paid in full over time, or a reduction in outstanding debt with a payment schedule over 3 years. The Bankruptcy Reform Act of 2000 requires debtors who file under Chapter 13 to repay either $15,000 or a quarter of their debts over 5 years.

Options and Bargaining Power Although debtors and owners in bankruptcy feel stigmatized and powerless, they often have a great deal of latitude and bargaining power. This is because the courts protect them from the full payment of debts. Creditors are usually loathe to see anything less than full payment. Therefore, in many cases, creditors will cooperate with the owners to avoid bankruptcy proceedings. The power of the owners derives from the conflicts of interest among the creditors. Because creditors are paid off according to the class to which they belong, they have different interests. Lower-priority creditors will be more hesitant to put the firm in bankruptcy because they will receive less. *Therefore, these lower-priority, or unsecured, creditors may even be a source of additional credit to prevent an involuntary bankruptcy filing!* It is often possible for the debtor to arrange postponement of payments, extended payment schedules, moratoriums on interest and principal payments, renegotiated leases, and the forgiveness of accrued interest under these circumstances. Of course, creditors do not have to be so understanding and can move legally against the firm. Good financial relationships and good personal relationships are extra insurance for the troubled business.

Some financing stories end in bankruptcy; others have happier endings. Street Story 8-4 could be a movie.

Summary

This chapter elaborated and expanded the ideas in Chapter 7. The entrepreneur must understand the criteria that investors use to evaluate the decision to invest in the new venture. Because different investors possess different criteria, the entrepreneur has opportunities to segment the financing market and sell investment vehicles that match the risk/reward preferences of the market.

Investors will use a seven-stage process in the investment cycle. They will search, screen, and evaluate proposals. After evaluation, they will make the decision, negotiate the details, structure the deal, and, last, harvest the investment. The elements of the deal structure (risks, rewards, and timing) help provide important positive incentives for both the investor and entrepreneur to make the new venture work. The types of investments offered, the manner in which they spread risk and reward, and the use of phased financing and options all combine to make the deal structure one of the more interesting, and potentially lucrative, aspects of entrepreneurship.

Last, the chapter covered some of the basic legal issues regarding new venture financing and start-up. The choice of organizational form affects business and personal liability, cash flow, and tax assessments. Careful consideration of securities laws can enable entrepreneurs and investors to avoid some of the more burdensome regulations. Bankruptcy, although always a negative from someone's point of view, can also be a bargaining tool for the new venture that needs a little more time and patience from its creditors. Expert legal advice is a must for all these issues.

Key Terms

- Accredited investor
- Antidilution provisions
- C corporation
- Chapter 7 bankruptcy
- Chapter 11 bankruptcy
- Chapter 13 bankruptcy
- Control issues
- Deal
- Deal structure
- Demand rights
- Disclosure
- Employment contracts
- General partnership
- Harvest
- Integration principles
- Limited liability company
- Limited partnership
- Option to abandon
- Partnership
- Performance and forfeiture provisions
- Piggyback rights
- Private placement
- Registration rights
- Regulation A
- Rule 144
- Rule 147
- Rule 504
- Rule 505
- Rule 506
- S corporation
- Shareholder agreements
- Sole proprietorship
- Staged (phased) financing
- Technological myopia
- Warrant

STREET STORY 8-4

Mom and Dad, Please Send Money

Imagine that you and your brother have started a business (if you don't have a brother, first imagine that you do). Imagine that your business revolves around an innovative way to bill clients for sales generated by advertising on the Internet, and that everyone thinks it has a lot of potential.

Then imagine that you and your brother are running out of money. You can't even meet your payroll; you have to borrow first $15,000, then $20,000, from your parents just to keep the doors open. But it's not enough. Imagine that you have to ask your parents to borrow against their home, their savings, their retirement account, and even their life insurance to help you raise the money you and your brother need to refine your technology and get some paying customers.

Imagine that you finally sign Barnes & Noble as your first customer. It's a promising start, but of course, one customer can't solve your cash problems. Meanwhile, your parents are having trouble making the payments for the money they lent you. Banks are calling them. Your mother says she can't sleep. Imagine that their lives and yours have become a nightmare.

This story is neither a dream nor a nightmare for Tom and Sam Gerace. This really happened to the Gerace brothers, and their parents really did risk every-thing they owned to give their sons' BeFree Inc. performance-marketing company a needed cash infusion.

Fortunately, no one has to imagine a happy ending. Just as the financial pressures on their parents were mounting, the Gerace brothers had an offer from a big Internet company to buy BeFree Inc. for more than $20 million. This would enable them to not only repay their parents, but also make both the brothers and their parents millionaires. Tom and Sam signed a 30-day "no shop" agreement with the Internet company, which meant they agreed not to talk to any other investors while they negotiated the deal.

But then a Boston venture capital firm convinced them they might be able to make a much better deal and still save their parents. The Gerace brothers agreed to meet with the venture capital organization at 1 minute past midnight on the night that their "no shop" agreement expired. Within 4 hours, they had worked out a deal where two venture capital firms each invested $5 million, which allowed the brothers to restore their parents' financial stability and give their company cash to work with, while the brothers still retained their ownership. Fifteen months later, BeFree Inc. went public. It had a market capitalization of $885 million 6 months after that.

Imagine that.

Source: Adapted from Hilary Stout, "These Parents Gambled Big Money Their Kids Really Were Geniuses," *The Wall Street Journal,* May 3, 2000, B1.

Discussion Questions

1. What are the components of a deal?
2. In the financing process, what three things must the entrepreneur understand in order to successfully complete the process?
3. What are the characteristics of the ideal investor?
4. What are the characteristics of the ideal entrepreneur and new venture?
5. Describe the investor process. What are the barriers and major pitfalls for the entrepreneur?
6. Why is the negotiation over the harvest so important?
7. How do risk preferences and risk sharing enter into the deal structure and the negotiation?
8. How do options and warrants add value to the deal?
9. Discuss the pros and cons of the various legal forms of organization.
10. How do U.S. securities laws aid in promoting entrepreneurship through private placements?

Exercises

1. Calculate the cash flows for your proposed venture if you have not already done so.
2. Partition these flows and segment your investor market.
3. Calculate the amounts you need to raise from each source.
4. Calculate the returns that each investor will make.
5. Develop a risk-sharing financing proposal. Include an option to reinvest.
6. Revise your financing plan to incorporate staged financing at the appropriate times.
7. Add a warrant for your debt investors to raise their return. Calculate the price of the warrant in a 5-year schedule.
8. Choose a legal form of organization for your proposed venture.

⬡ **DISCUSSION CASE** ⬡

Lying in the Jungle

There's an ancient Chinese axiom that states, "The fierce lion always dies in the jungle," meaning that an individual's most obvious trait is usually both their strength and their weakness.

For Bob Nelson, that trait is his high level of energy. A wisecracker with a laugh that sounds just like Woody Woodpecker's, Nelson has been a political campaign worker, a salesperson, and a consultant. Now he is an entrepreneur. While he was on the road a couple of years ago, traveling without his laptop computer, Nelson suddenly wished that he could check his e-mail by phone. Within a few months, Nelson and a speech-technology expert founded Cross Media Networks Corp. in the basement of Nelson's home.

CrossMedia's initial financing came from cash advances on Nelson's credit cards and investments ranging from $50,000 to $100,000 from a few wealthy individuals. That money enabled them to build a prototype machine where customers could dial a toll-free phone number and listen to a computer "voice" read their e-mail.

But CrossMedia needed more money—millions in additional investments—to develop their technology, and Nelson just couldn't seem to do that. His energetic pitch attracted investors who were willing to listen, but his sloppy attention to detail in his business plan made it almost impossible for him to close a deal. "The thing I worry about the most, and the thing I like the most, is you," one potential investor told him. Nelson also stubbornly insisted that he wanted Cross-Media to market both hardware and voice e-mail service, despite the fact that people inside and outside the company told him that he needed to concentrate on one or the other, and that he had the best shot of being successful by sticking to service.

As CrossMedia began to miss payroll deadlines, Nelson fell behind on other bills, and he became desperate. He spent money advanced to him by an investor even though he knew CrossMedia would be unable to meet all the conditions the investor wanted. He presented investors with a business plan built on selling software products, but included revenue projections from a service component that was otherwise missing from the plan. He frantically pursued multiple potential investors. Part of Nelson's panic stemmed from the fact that now other entrepreneurs had the same voice e-mail idea.

Finally, an investor that Nelson had been courting for months appeared to be seriously interested. A meeting between the investor and CrossMedia personnel went well until Nelson started talking about a new angle that he hadn't thought out or discussed with his colleagues. After the meeting, Nelson acknowledged his mistake by saying, "So, we'll get a call letting us down."

Ten days later, Nelson invited his management team into his office. As they were standing there he telephoned Cross-Media's bank. Everyone listened while a disembodied voice that sounded not very different from the technology they were trying to sell announced, "We just had a transfer of $500,000." Nelson's investor had made a down payment on a commitment for $5 million.

(continued)

(continued)

CASE QUESTIONS

1. Would you invest in CrossMedia Networks Corp.? Why or why not?
2. Would you be willing to accept a job working with Bob Nelson? What kind of role do you think Nelson should have in this company in the future?
3. Up until this point, CrossMedia has primarily solicited individual investors. Do you think they should pursue other sources of financing? What sources could they consider, and what would be the advantages—and disadvantages?
4. What kind of alliances with other businesses would you recommend that CrossMedia pursue?

Source: Adapted from Bryan Gruley, "Inside the Dream: A High-Tech Start-Up Begs for Cash, and Life," *The Wall Street Journal,* October 13, 1998, p.1.

Appendix 8A

Investment Agreement Outline

Following are the general contents of an investment agreement. The major sections are typical; details can be added or deleted depending on practice, tradition, and the negotiating skills of the participants.

I. *Description of the Investment*
This section identifies the parties, defines the basic terms, and includes descriptions of the amount of the investment, the securities issues, any guarantees, collateral, and subordinations. When the agreement includes warrants and options, the schedules and timing of exercise are included here. Registration rights, transferability provisions, and dilution effects are all essential parts of the investment and are described in this section.

II. *Conditions of Closing*
The closing of the deal is the actual transfer and execution of documents and funds. Typically, documents need to be submitted to close the deal. These are corporate documents and articles of incorporation, audited financial statements, contracts with related parties that could be construed to represent conflicts of interest, and important business documents, such as leases, supplier agreements, and employment contracts.

III. *Representations and Warranties by the Venture*
This section describes in full legal disclosure terms the material facts of the new venture's condition. Typical statements include the following:

- That the business is duly incorporated
- That the officers' decisions legally bind the company
- That the offering is exempt from SEC registration (if indeed it is)
- That all material facts have been disclosed

IV. *Representations and Warranties of the Investors*
These are the legally binding statements by the investors that they are indeed who they say they are and:

- That they are organized and in good standing
- That the investors' decisions legally bind their corporation (or organization)
- That they will perform all of their obligations if all conditions are met (usually this means that they come up with the money if conditions are met)

V. *Affirmative Covenants*
These are all the things that the entrepreneurs agree to do under the terms of the investment agreement and in the operation of their business. Typical covenants are:

- Pay taxes, file reports, obey regulations
- Pay principal and interest on debts
- Maintain corporate existence
- Keep books, have statements audited, allow investors access
- Maintain insurance
- Maintain minimum net worth, working capital, and asset levels
- Hold director's meetings

VI. *Negative Covenants*
These are all the things that the entrepreneurs agree not to do in the course of operating their business. Negative covenants may be abrogated with investor approval. Typical covenants are:

- Not to merge, consolidate, or acquire another business
- Not to change the corporate charter or bylaws
- Not to sell additional stock unless specified in the agreement

- Not to pay dividends unless specified
- Not to violate any of the affirmative covenants
- Not to liquidate the business or declare bankruptcy

VII. *Conditions of Default*
This section spells out the circumstances under which entrepreneurs are considered to have violated the agreement. These include:

- Failure to comply with affirmative or negative covenants
- Misrepresentations of fact
- Insolvency or reorganization
- Failure to pay interest and principal

VIII. *Remedies*
The specific remedies available to the investors if violation should occur, include:

- Forfeiture to the investor of voting control
- Forfeiture of stock held in escrow for this purpose
- The right of the investor to sell his stock back to the company at a predetermined price
- Demands for payment of principal and interest
- The payment of legal costs to ensure compliance

IX. *Other Conditions*
Anything not covered elsewhere.

Source: Adapted from J. Timmons, *New Venture Creation* (Homewood, IL: Richard D. Irwin, 1994), pp. 774–777.

Appendix 8B

Negotiable Terms to a Financial Agreement

COVENANTS AND PROVISIONS PROTECTING THE INVESTMENT

Investors have a legitimate interest in protecting their investment. They seek to do this in the following ways:

Antidilution provisions protect investors from having their investment's value diminish if the entrepreneur is forced to seek additional financing. It does not mean that the investors will never suffer a shrinkage of ownership percentage. As long as any new stock is sold at a price equal to or higher than the original investor's conversion price, the original investor will not suffer dilution. If the new stock is sold below the conversion price, the original investor loses economic value, and to prevent this, an antidilution provision, or "ratchet," is included.

There are two types of ratchets: full and weighted. A full ratchet is onerous for the entrepreneur because it requires the original investor to be able to convert all shares at the lower price. In our example, the investor purchased 33.3 percent of the company for $1 million. If shares were issued at $1 each, the investor would own 1 million shares. Let's say that a full ratchet is in effect and the company needs additional financing. Subsequently, it sells shares at 50 cents per share. The conversion rate for the original investor will drop to 50 cents. The 1 million shares becomes 2 million shares. If 250,000 50-cent shares have been sold, the total value of the shares outstanding is now $4.125 million (the entrepreneur's $2 million, the original investor's $2 million, and the new investor's $125,000). But the original investor's percentage of ownership has risen to 48 percent (2 million shares divided by 4.125 million shares). Over time and in case of financial crises, full ratchets severely reduce the share of ownership and value of the firm to the founders.

The weighted ratchet is more fair to the entrepreneurs. The conversion price is adjusted down by the weighted average price per share outstanding. The formula is:

$$X = (A \times B) + C/(A + D)$$

where

X = new conversion price
A = outstanding shares prior to the sale
B = current conversion price
C = amount received on sale of new stock
D = number of new shares sold

To illustrate from our example, if:

A = 3,000,000 shares
B = $1.00
C = $125,000
D = 250,000

then the new conversion price for the original investors is $0.9615, not the fully ratcheted $0.50:

$$\frac{(3,000,000 \times \$1.00) + \$125,000}{3,000,000 + 250,000} = 0.9615$$

This becomes a critical area of negotiation for the entrepreneur, especially when cheap shares of common stock are offered to officers, directors, employees, and consultants, as is common in start-up situations. A provision should be negotiated that these sales not trigger the antidilution provisions.

Performance and forfeiture provisions call for the entrepreneurs to forfeit a portion (or all) of their stock if the company does not achieve a specified level of performance. It protects the investor from paying too much for the company in the event the entrepreneur's original projections were too rosy. If the entrepreneur fails to meet the rosy projections, the entrepreneur pays the price of

reduced ownership in the company. Also, the forfeited stock can be resold to new executives brought in to improve the firm's performance. This provision serves to motivate the entrepreneur and protect the investor.

In a new start-up, a significant portion of the founder's equity may be at risk due to the performance/forfeiture provision. As the company achieves its early goals, the entrepreneur should negotiate less severe penalties and can legitimately negotiate an end to this clause because the firm's performance has shown that the initial valuation was reasonable. If the investors are reluctant to give in on this, the entrepreneur should insist on bonus clauses for beating the projections. In short, for each downside risk, the entrepreneur should negotiate for an upside reward.

Employment contracts serve to motivate and discipline the top management team. They often protect the investors from competing with the founders of the company if the founders are forced to leave. All terms of the founders' and top executives' employment contract (salary, bonuses, fringe benefits, stock options, stock buyback provisions, noncompetition clauses, conditions of termination, and severance compensation) are negotiable. The investors will want an employment contract that protects their investment in the venture. Especially if investors are buying a controlling interest in the company, the founder will want to negotiate a multiyear deal. The drawback to multiyear contracts is that if the entrepreneur wishes to leave early to do other things, investors can sue for breach of contract and/or prevent the entrepreneur from engaging in a competing business.

Control issues are negotiable and not solely dependent on the proportion of stock the investors have purchased. All minority stockholders have rights. A nationally recognized accounting firm will be hired to audit the financial statements, and important managerial positions may be filled with people recommended by the investors. All important business transactions (mergers, acquisitions, asset liquidations, and additional stock sales) will require consultation and consent. The entrepreneur who accepts a minority interest after the investment should negotiate for all the rights and options that the investor would.

Shareholder agreements are favored by investors to protect their stake in the company. Shareholder agreements can bind the company when offering new shares, forcing the firm to offer new shares to the original investors by giving them rights of first refusal. Sometimes agreements will call for the management to support the investor's choices when electing board members. Although these agreements are usually made at the insistence of the investor, entrepreneurs should ask for equal power as they negotiate for their stake in the new venture.

Disclosure is the process by which entrepreneurs provide investors with the full and complete details of the information and relationships under which the investor makes his or her decision. The investor requires audited financial statements, tax returns, and assurance that the company is in compliance with the laws and regulations.

Investors are especially concerned about contingent liabilities. Contingent liabilities occur when the company has future liability based on some prior event or action. For example, when producing a product, the firm has contingent liability if the product ultimately is dangerous, mislabeled, or causes harm, even if the company has no reason to believe in the present that this may happen. Because of the changing nature of U.S. environmental laws, contingent liability often resides in past decisions concerning waste management, the disposal of hazardous materials, or the use of building materials that prove to be dangerous or poisonous.

The entrepreneur should attempt to negotiate a cushion that will protect the founders and the new venture in case of an omission during the disclosure process. For example, if an omission is honestly made and results in company costs under a certain dollar amount, entrepreneurs will not be considered to be in breach of disclosure representations. This is also known as a "hold harmless" clause. The representations that the entrepreneurs make should also have a time limit attached, so that there is not liability for misrepresentation forever.

CHAPTER

9

Creating the Organization

Good fences make good neighbors.
—ROBERT FROST

Outline

Learning Objectives

After reading this chapter, you will understand:

- Some of the issues involved in creating and maintaining a *top management team (TMT)*
- The composition and responsibilities of a *board of directors*
- The concept of a *virtual organization*
- The principles of "built to last" ventures
- How different strategies create different *organizational structures*
- Some *ethical issues* facing entrepreneurs
- The balanced scorecard approach to venture performance
- Some successful strategies from the *entrepreneurial workplace*

W hen the entrepreneur creates the organization for the new venture, he or she is building fences. As the opening quote indicates, setting and determining boundaries—what is "in" versus what is "out"—has important effects on the venture's neighbors: its suppliers, customers, competitors, and stakeholders. "In" refers to the things the organization decides to do itself through its own people, administration, and hierarchy. "Out" refers to the things the organization lets other firms do by acquiring goods and services through the market at a price.

"Good fences" are boundaries that make sense for the venture's strategies, its transactions with its neighbors, and the resources that provide it with sustainable competitive advantage (SCA). When good fences are built, relationships with other organizations—with neighbors—will also be good—that is, profitable and sustainable for both vendors and customers. In setting boundaries, the entrepreneur makes choices about issues such as what to make versus what to buy, what to own versus what to let other firms control, how to grow, and what kinds of growth are sensible. These are all decisions relating to the creation of the organization and its boundaries.

Usually, before these boundaries are set and these difficult issues are addressed, the entrepreneur looks for help. Among the many tasks the entrepreneur has to perform is assembling the top management team. Members of the team help the entrepreneur determine organizational boundaries in two ways. First, by providing advice, they add input to the decision. Second, depending on their unique skills and experience either as individuals or collectively, they serve as human resources with the four attributes of SCA: rare, valuable, hard to copy, and nonsubstitutable. These people can help to determine the best places to draw the lines around the organization's activities.

We start by looking at the creation and development of the top management team from the viewpoint of the founding entrepreneur. We examine the characteristics of top managers and the process and dynamics of how teams are formed and maintained. Because research has shown that some teams produce at higher levels than others, we review the nature of high-performing teams.

Following this discussion, we present the basics and principles of what are called "visionary companies." These firms were started by ingenious entrepreneurs who figured out how to endow their companies with the kind of organizational culture and leadership that would stand the test of time. This section distills the major findings that were originally presented by Collins and Porras in their best-selling book, *Built to Last.*[1]

Next we examine the factors that affect the boundaries of entrepreneurial organizations. We describe an unusual but highly effective form of organization called the "virtual organization." From this follows a discussion of organizational design and structure. Given a set of boundaries and activities, each organization faces choices on how to delegate authority and responsibility and how to make use of the productive power of specialization. These are the key elements of organizational structure.

We next look at a system for managing organizational performance. This system, based on the work of Kaplan and Norton, is called the "balanced scorecard."[2] A balanced-scorecard approach to creating the organization assures that the firm is not missing any key components of performance and that the different elements of the organization are working in an integrated fashion.

The chapter concludes with a discussion of the major issues in creating and maintaining an entrepreneurial workplace. The ethical climate and culture should be consistent with high standards and the aggressive nature of the business. Entrepreneurs want the people who work for them to be as motivated, innovative, and productive as themselves. Examples of how entrepreneurs create an exciting environment for their workers are presented at the end of the chapter.

THE TOP MANAGEMENT TEAM

There is little doubt that the top management team (TMT) is a key component in the success or failure of the new venture.[3] The team is crucial to attracting investors, for investors look for experience and integrity in management.[4] The team is also a key element in new venture growth.[5] Without a team to plan, manage, and control the activities of the growing firm, the firm's growth will be limited to what the founder can personally supervise and manage.[6]

The general manager of any enterprise — here, the entrepreneur — has three leadership roles to play: organizational leader, architect of the organizational purpose, and personal leader. When the entrepreneur is putting the TMT together, all these roles are in action at once. Because the characteristics of the team will help determine the venture's performance,[7] creating and maintaining the TMT is one of the major responsibilities of the founding entrepreneur. As the **organizational leader**, the entrepreneur selects the members of the TMT and also works to blend their skills and expertise to ensure that the top management team will be highly productive. As the **architect of organizational purpose**, the entrepreneur serves as an analyst and strategist, helping the TMT determine what goals, objectives, and directions the business will pursue. Finally, as the **personal leader** the entrepreneur serves as a model for behavior in the organization.[8] This is the individual to whom people look for leadership about what is right and wrong for the organization. The entrepreneurial leader creates the climate and the culture of the workplace, and models the ethical standards of the venture for all to see. The roles of the entrepreneur are summarized in Figure 9-1.

Creating the Top Management Team

A **team** can be defined as "a small number of people with complementary skills who are committed to a common purpose, set of performance goals, and approach for which they hold themselves mutually accountable." How many is "a small number"? Some experts say it can be anywhere between 2 and 25.[9] However, teams with more than 12 to 15 members generally must form subgroups to facilitate communication and decision making. Subgroups begin to form hierarchies. The pace of group activity slows down, time is lost, and the logistics of meeting face-to-face becomes a problem.[10]

A useful distinction to make at this point is that between a team and a working group. A **working group** is a collection of individuals whose jobs are related to each other but who are not interdependent. The members are individually, as opposed to collectively, accountable. They do not really work together; they simply work for the same organization and are placed at about the same level in the hierarchy.

In contrast, a team is connected by the joint products of its work. Members of a team produce things together and are jointly accountable for their combined work. In the case of the TMT of a new venture, their joint output consists of the enterprise's managerial systems and processes. Team members value listening and constructive feedback, and

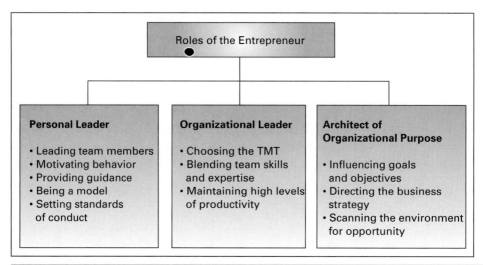

FIGURE 9-1   Roles of the Entrepreneur as General Manager

Source: Adapted from K. Andrews, *The Concept of Corporate Strategy* (Upper Saddle River, NJ: Prentice Hall, 1980).

they encourage each other in a supportive spirit. In a team, the whole is greater than the sum of the parts. Why? Because in addition to the individual's efforts, the venture receives the benefits of relationships. These relationships often transcend and overshadow individual contributions. When people are working on effective teams, they are sparked, motivated, and inspired by their interactions with the other team members.

The process of TMT formation should begin with an evaluation of the talents, experience, and personal characteristics that are required for the new venture's operating environment. This evaluation provides the entrepreneur with a map of the ideal team. This map guides the entrepreneur through the process of putting the TMT together and of answering the three fundamental TMT recruitment questions: From what sources will TMT members be recruited? What criteria for selection will be used? What inducements will be offered to potential members?[11]

Sources of TMT Members   TMT members are recruited either from people with whom the entrepreneur is already familiar or from "unfamiliars." **Familiars** may include family, friends, and current and former business associates. The advantages of choosing members of the TMT from among these groups are that the entrepreneur already has established trustworthy personal relationships with them, is acquainted with each person's capabilities, and may already have established working relationships with them. This prior knowledge and experience can help speed up team formation and decision making in the early stages of new venture creation. Recruiting familiars, however, can have disadvantages, and these come from the same sources as the positive factors. Familiars may come with the psychological baggage of former relationships when status and circumstances were different. Also, it is likely that familiars have much the same background, work experience, education, and world view. By duplicating the entrepreneur's own personal profile, they do not add complementary skills to the team.

Unfamiliars are people who are not known to the entrepreneur at the start of the new venture. They are individuals who have the potential for top management and may have had previous start-up experience. The entrepreneur can find these people through personal connections, business associates, or traditional personnel recruitment techniques: employment agencies, executive search agencies (headhunters), and classified advertising. Unfamiliars are a potential source of diversity for the TMT. They bring in new views, skills, and experiences that can complement the entrepreneur's. The most important potential negative factor is the lack of a prior working relationship with the founder.

Criteria for Selection   If the TMT is to be a highly effective group and an important contributor to enterprise performance, it should be composed of individuals with either of two primary characteristics. The TMT members should either personally possess resources that are rare, valuable, hard to duplicate, and not easily substituted, or they should be able to help the firm acquire and employ other strategic resources that do have these qualities.

Good personal chemistry and attraction to the entrepreneur can be a factor in selecting an individual for the TMT. It may be reassuring for the entrepreneur to work with people who have a mutual affinity. Such individuals put the entrepreneur at ease and help provide a comfortable working situation in which the entrepreneur can employ all of his or her talents and creativity.

More frequently, members of the top management teams are chosen for direct instrumental reasons. Entrepreneurs look for people who in some manner—perhaps through technical knowledge or functional expertise—complement existing human resources and add to the resource base. Other criteria include age, education, and tenure. For example, it has been found that when TMTs are composed of younger, better-educated, and more functionally diverse individuals, they are more likely to promote innovations and changes in the firm's strategy.[12] On the other hand, TMTs made up of older, longer-tenured people who are accorded high levels of discretion by the CEO tend to follow strategies that conform to the central tendency of the industry. They are able to achieve performance levels that are close to industry averages but not above average.[13] As the company grows, the needs of the venture change and so do the requirements for the TMT. As we see in Street Story 9-1, sometimes these changes affect the whole organization.

Money is frequently a reason for recruiting TMT members. The entrepreneur in search of financial partners usually allows the partners to be either members of the board of directors or working participants on the TMT. Connections (business, social, and technological) are also a good basis for choosing members of the TMT. These people help the new venture acquire or have access to new resources that would otherwise be beyond reach for the emerging business.[14]

Cultural Diversity   A final set of criteria address the potential need for demographic and **cultural diversity**. Because background and environment are major influences on individual perceptions and orientations, people from different demographic and cultural groups have different viewpoints. These differences, when expressed and processed by an effective group, can form the basis for a wider understanding of the firm's own environment. Each separate contribution adds to the firm's knowledge of its customers, employees, markets, and competitors, and to its awareness of factors in the

Letting Go

SIMOD Corp.'s purchasing agent wasn't sleeping on the job, playing hooky, or doing any of the bad things that sometimes cause people to lose their jobs. "It's much easier to fire someone who is not doing their job," observes Wells Richards, CEO of the telecommunications and data equipment distributing company. But Richards fired the purchasing agent just the same, even though she was . . . his sister. "It was probably the hardest thing I've ever done, but business is business," Richards says.

The personal relationship between Richards and his sister was a large part of the problem. "She was protective of me, and she was looking out for my back, but it upset everyone," explains Richards. Although he was glad to have someone he knew and trusted as a member of his initial top management team, his sister was also unable to adapt to the new systems and procedures SIMOD had to implement after 5 years of growth, when it became a company with revenues of $6.5 million. As the sister of the CEO, the purchasing agent felt free to make her own rules; as organizational leader, her brother the CEO had to fire her to demonstrate to the rest of his employees that he wouldn't tolerate anyone who wasn't a team player.

Richards' sister was not the only member of the company's first TMT that he had to let go. Although people who are willing to work for a struggling entrepreneur often demonstrate a high level of energy and commitment, they sometimes also have a highly developed ego. One of the first employees that Richards had hired for SIMOD was an excellent worker, but he had two problems: He didn't like working with women, and he had a fanatical devotion to the scheduling of his lunch hour. "When the company was small, none of that really mattered," explains Richards. But as other employees—including women—joined the company, problems developed. "He felt he didn't have to change, but as we grew, he had to get out of our way."

SIMOD's first bookkeeper was a young accounting student who worked part-time for the company. By the time the company had achieved the rank of #247 on the *Inc.* 500 list, they had outgrown her skills and the simple computer accounting program she knew how to operate. Richards tried to retain her as the assistant to the more experienced financial officer he hired, but she quit after a few months.

Richards remains troubled about his personnel actions. "In the end, I probably won't have any friends," he moans. But one of the company's top sales reps applauds his actions. "The general message is if you do your work like you're supposed to, you'll be here for a long time."

Source: Adapted from *Inc.* staff, "Hard Questions," *Inc.* online, October 15, 1998; available www.inc.com.

remote environment. It has even been suggested that TMTs should be composed to match the conditions of environmental complexity and change. Recent research has suggested that homogeneous TMTs tend to perform better in stable environments, and heterogeneous TMTs perform better in rapidly changing environments.[15] Therefore, because entrepreneurs most frequently operate in rapidly changing environments, a heterogeneous team should be most effective.

However, achieving the benefits of diversity is not easy. Some cultural groups, like the Japanese, fret about having to work with people of different cultures. They often attribute their success to cultural and racial uniformity. American managers, on the other hand, have more experience in diverse situations. Recent integration of European markets has made Europeans more sensitive to the power of diversity. European firms are now looking for people who are Euro-managers—people who can work well within any of the different cultures and ethnic communities in the European Union (EU).[16]

A recent study shows how diversity works.[17] Groups of students were formed to do case analyses in a principles of management course. About half the groups were composed of white males, and the other half were racially diverse. The groups had to do four case studies over the semester. The results showed that the homogeneous groups performed better at first, but that the diverse groups just about caught up by the end of the semester. The diverse groups took longer to learn how to work effectively with each other, but their rate of improvement was higher, and "by the end of the experiment, the diverse teams were clearly more creative than the homogeneous ones, examining perspectives and probing more alternatives in solving the final case study."[18] The study's senior author said that he believes that if the experiment had lasted longer, the diverse groups would have passed the others in overall performance.[19] In the real world of new venture creation, TMTs are expected to last significantly longer than one semester. Therefore, the long-term benefits of a diverse TMT can be achieved.

Inducements   The final issue concerning team composition is the range of inducements offered to people to join the team. These take the form of material and nonmaterial rewards. **Material rewards** include equity (stock in the company), salary, perquisites, and benefits. It is vital that most of the rewards of TMT membership be contingent on performance. This is true even in the early stages of new venture creation, when performance and profits may still be in the future. Moreover, the entrepreneur should consider the total rewards offered to the potential TMT member over the life of the opportunity. This will obviate giving too much too soon and will lead to the team member's commitment to the long term.[20]

Nonmaterial rewards can be equally important. A person may relish learning about the new venture creation process. People who someday will be entrepreneurs themselves may agree to participate in a start-up experience as preparation for their own endeavors. Being a TMT member is also a sign of upward mobility, distinction, prestige, and power—an additional inducement for many.

In the final analysis, the TMT will probably consist of some people whom the entrepreneur already knows and some unfamiliars. Some will be recruited for the team because they are strategic resources. For example, in the biotech industry where genome research is so highly specialized, companies are competing in the recruitment of biotech personnel for their TMTs. "All of the top-level scientists have probably been locked up [by companies]," reports Stanford University Nobel laureate Paul Berg.[21] The scientists themselves are the key resources in such companies. Firms cannot enter unless they have acquired this scientific expertise.

People can also be added to the TMT in a "just-in-time" fashion, that is, as they are needed.[22] This would argue for familiars in the early stages of a start-up, when there is the most uncertainty and the entrepreneur most needs trustworthy people for support. Later, team members can be recruited specifically for their money, connections, skills, and experience, as those resources are required.

Maintaining Top Management Teams

The recruitment of the top management team is only the beginning. Teams must learn to work together, and this takes time, especially if the group is composed of individuals from diverse backgrounds and cultures. A great deal of research has been conducted to determine the properties of highly effective work groups.[23] In this section, we will simply provide an overview of the properties as they relate to new venture TMTs.

Goals It is essential that the goals of the TMT be the goals of the new venture. Research has shown that agreement within a TMT on what the goals of the firm should be is positively related to firm performance.[24] However, over time the TMT will develop its own goals and objectives, subject to the overriding vision of the entrepreneur. These subgoals are essential if the team is to create its own identity and sense of mission. The accomplishment of these subgoals represents the joint work product of the team. Sometimes these goals are quite distinct; for example, the development and implementation of a management accounting system. Other goals might be fuzzy, as with becoming a leader in innovation. Fuzzy goals are acceptable, because they provide increased discretion and flexibility for the team.[25]

Norms and Values   Norms represent the team's shared standards for behavior, and values represent its desired outcomes. The most important of these norms and values are:

- *Cohesion:* the understanding that when the team gains, each individual member gains
- *Teamwork:* the acknowledgment that collective activities and accomplishments can surpass what any individual can achieve on his or her own
- *Fairness:* acceptance that rewards and recognition are based on the contributions of individuals to the team's efforts and its success. This implies an "equal inequality," because the rule is applied equally but the outcomes may be unequal.[26]
- *Integrity:* honesty and the highest standards of ethical behavior within the framework of the top manager's fiduciary relationship with the enterprise's owners and investors
- *Tolerance for risk:* the willingness to be innovative and to accept ambiguous situations
- *Tolerance for failure:* the willingness to accept that innovation and ambiguous situations sometimes lead to failures
- *Long-term commitment:* the obligation to promote the interests of the organization, its customers, employees, investors, and other stakeholders
- *Commitment to value creation:* the recognition that personal wealth will become a function of how valuable the new venture becomes as an ongoing, growing, and profitable entity

Roles   Within every group, certain people play certain roles. Sometimes people play multiple roles and can change roles as the situation warrants. **Contributors** are task-oriented and initiators. They are usually individuals with special knowledge or expertise in the area to which they are contributing. **Collaborators** are joiners. They align themselves with those making the contribution of the moment. The presence of allies adds to the likely acceptance of the contributor's initiative. **Communicators** aid in the process of defining that task, passing information from contributors to other members of the group, and restating positions held by potentially conflicting members. **Challengers** play the devil's advocate. They offer constructive criticism and attempt to portray the downside of the contributor's recommendations. Their role is to ensure that no course of action is taken or decision is made without considering what can go wrong or whether alternative courses might be more effective.[27] Over the course of a single meeting or day and certainly over the life of the group, any TMT member can play all of these roles successfully.

Communications   Highly developed interpersonal and communication skills are essential to the success of the TMT. Communications have three types of content: task, process, and self-serving. **Task-oriented communication** addresses directly the subject under discussion. Its purpose is to provide substantive information that helps the group make a decision. **Process-oriented communication** is concerned with how the group is operating and how people are behaving. It is reflective and attempts to make the group members aware of what is happening in the discussion. Both task and process communication are necessary for effective decision making. **Self-serving communication** contributes neither to task nor process but instead tries to put the speaker at the center of the discussion. The content of self-serving communications can vary, but frequently it can be identified as attempts to take credit, assess blame, or self-righteously accuse another of not adhering to the group's norms for behavior.

Effective communicators concentrate on task and process communication. Effective group members attempt to minimize self-serving communications.

Leadership The founding entrepreneur is both a member of the team and the team leader. In effective teams, however, leadership is often shared, depending on what the problem at hand is. If a particular individual possesses superior knowledge, experience, skill, or insight, that person takes the temporary leadership of the group.

E-NOTES 9-2

Maintaining the TMT

Important issues include:

- goals
- norms and values
- roles: who are the
    contributors?
    collaborators?
    communicators?
    challengers?
- communications

Benefits and Pitfalls of TMTs

The creation of a new venture top management team offers the benefits of team decision making.[28] These include breadth of knowledge, diversity, acceptance of decisions, and legitimacy.[29] The team approach to top management offers a balance of skills and attracts vital human resources to the emerging organization. It is also a test of the venture's viability—if no one will join the team, this raises questions about the venture's potential for market acceptance. A well-developed initial team will minimize the disruption caused by the loss of a single member and may save the time and energy needed for later recruitment. Such a team also demonstrates to external stakeholders that the founder has a willingness to be a people person and share authority and responsibility.[30]

However, the team approach to top management is not without potential problems and pitfalls. Timmons notes several possible problems in the process of forming a TMT for a new venture. For example, the TMT members may lack start-up experience, or they may be recruited too quickly, without careful attention to their commitment to the long term. Also, the team may be too democratic: In an effort to recruit, the entrepreneur may exaggerate the amount of decision-making discretion the team will have. Later discovery of such exaggeration is bound to be disappointing and demotivating, because in reality the new venture remains under the control of the founder and majority stock-holders. Last, the TMT may make decisions too rapidly under the mistaken impression that everything must be settled on day one.[31]

There are also the problems that can afflict any team, such as inefficiencies of time, groupthink, groupshift, and poor interpersonal skills.[32] Good group processes take time. People need a chance to discuss, communicate, revise their views, and develop new options. Sometimes time is of the essence, and the entrepreneur cannot wait for group discussion and consensus. Under these circumstances, the team must act quickly and forgo the "group process" it has carefully nurtured.

Groupthink prevents the team from critically evaluating and appraising ideas and views. It hinders the performance of groups by putting conformity ahead of group effectiveness as the priority. The principal symptoms are rejection of evidence that seems to contradict assumptions, direct pressure on doubters and nonconformists to drop their objections, self-editing by group members who are reluctant to present opposing points of view, and the illusion of unanimity. The best ways to avoid groupthink are to have the leader remain impartial until the end of the discussion and to develop norms that enable all members to express dissent without retribution.[33]

Groupshift is the phenomenon in which the collective decision of a team is either more risky or less risky than the disaggregated decisions of the team members. This means that sometimes people take larger or smaller chances in a group than they would on their own.[34] To make their point, people tend to exaggerate their initial positions in group discussions. As agreement is reached, the exaggerated positions become the ones adopted by the group. Moreover, when teams make decisions, the team is accountable. Sometimes this translates into "no one is accountable." This sense of diffused responsibility causes members to be less careful about what they approve.

Group effectiveness can also be ruined by the domination of a single member or a subgroup of members. If the discussions are so dominated, the advantages of diversity and breadth of knowledge are lost. Additionally, people are demotivated if they cannot contribute. Last, sometimes the person dominating the discussion may not be highly skilled or knowledgeable. When the mediocre control events, mediocre outcomes can be expected.

The Board of Directors

The top management team may be augmented by a board of directors. However, although the board and TMT members may overlap, the board is not the top management team and should not attempt to micromanage the venture.

There are two types of boards: an advisory board and a fiduciary board. The primary task of the **advisory board** is to provide advice and contacts. It is usually composed of experienced professionals who have critical skills important to the success of the business. For example, if the business is primarily a retail establishment, merchandising, purchasing, and marketing experience would be important resources. Also, people who have good contacts and are open-minded, innovative, and good team players are prime candidates for an advisory board.[35] A **fiduciary board** is the legally constituted group whose primary responsibility is to represent the new venture's stockholders. It is usually made up of insiders (the managing founder and senior TMT members) and outsiders (investors and their representatives, community members, and other businesspersons). In firms that are still very closely held—that is, those whose founder has not yet gone to the professional investment community for expansion funds—insiders tend to dominate. When venture capital has been used to support growth, venture capitalists often dominate the board.[36]

Members of the board, as trustees of the shareholders' interests, are the broad policy-setting body of the company. They also advise and mentor the founders and the TMT in the execution of their strategy. Specifically, the board exercises its power in seven areas, as follows.

Shareholder Interests   In representing shareholders, the board is accountable for the new venture's performance. It must approve the audited financial statements and all reports to the shareholders. The board must approve any changes in the venture's bylaws and then get shareholder approval for these changes. The board is also responsible for all proposals made to shareholders and approves the annual report prepared by top management.

Financial Management and Control   The board sets and declares all dividends. It sets all policies regarding the issue, transfer, and registration of company securities. It must also approve any financing programs; the TMT cannot seek financing that changes the status of current shareholders without board approval. The board must also approve the selection of the outside auditors top management has recommended. Then the shareholders, too, must approve the auditors.

Long-Range Plans   The board advises top management on its long-term strategy. The board does not make strategy, but it can help mold the venture's future from the recommendations of the top managers. The board establishes broad policies regarding the direction and means of growth. It must approve all acquisitions and mergers, subject to further approval by the shareholders.

Organizational Issues   The board elects its chairperson, the firm's president, and, usually with the president's recommendation, the other officers and top managers of the company. It writes and approves the chairperson's and president's job descriptions. It establishes their compensation levels, stock options, and bonuses, and it subsequently reviews their performance. From recommendations of the president, the board also approves the appointment, termination, promotion, and compensation of the other managers who report directly to the president.

Operational Controls   The board approves the annual operating and capital budgets. It reviews forecasts and makes inquiries about variances from forecasted amounts. It can request information and special reports from top management, which it may then use to carry out its other fiduciary duties. If performance falters, the board may recommend a reorganization, restructuring, or even voluntary bankruptcy to protect the shareholders.

Employee Relations   The board approves the firm's compensation policies, pensions, retirement plans, and employee benefit options. It also reviews the behavior of employees and top managers to ensure that they act in accordance with the highest ethical, professional, and legal standards.

Board Internal Operations   The board is responsible for its own internal operations. Based on the recommendation of the CEO and president, the board members approve their own compensation and expense accounts. They appoint subcommittees to study special issues, such as, for example, the protection of minority shareholder rights. They must attend board meetings at the request of the chairperson.

E-NOTES 9-3

Boards of Directors

Advisory board:

- provides advice and contacts
- composed of experienced professionals

Fiduciary board:

- legal group that represents stockholders
- composed of insiders (founder and key TMT members) and outsiders (investors, venture capitalists, community members, etc.)

Guidelines for Successful Boards

Information and research about top management teams and group processes can provide a set of guidelines for successfully selecting and employing advisory and fiduciary boards. These key factors should be part of the creation of the new venture's board of directors:

- Keep the board to a manageable size, 12 to 15 members at most.
- Board members should represent different capabilities and resource bases. For example, the board should have a balance of people with financial backgrounds, operational and industry experience, and local community knowledge.
- Because the board's primary responsibility is to the shareholders, both majority and minority shareholders should be directly represented.
- People with good communications skills and the ability to voice an independent opinion are needed. If everyone agrees about everything all the time, there is not enough diversity on the board.

Board Responsibilities

A board of directors exercises power in seven areas:

- shareholder interests
- financial management and control
- long-range plans
- organizational issues
- operational controls
- employee relations
- board internal operations

In Street Story 9-2, the experts offer some tips on putting together an effective board.

BUILDING AN ENDURING ORGANIZATION

The founder may not realize it when the venture is launched, but many of the earliest decisions made can influence the firm for its entire history. The culture of the organization is imprinted early, and the founder makes the largest impact on that culture. If the organization is going to survive a long time and become a "visionary-type" company, these initial conditions and decisions should be carefully considered.

These visionary companies are different from other ones. Collins and Porras reported in a large-scale study the dimensions upon which these differences were based. They reported their results in the now famous best-selling book, *Built to Last*.[37] Collins and Porras seek to identify the characteristics of these remarkable companies as well as the underlying causes of venture differences. For example, what factors explain how Motorola successfully moved from a humble battery repair business into car radios, televisions, semiconductors, integrated circuits, and cellular communications? Zenith started at the same time with similar resources but never became a major player in anything other than TVs. How did Hewlett-Packard remain healthy and vibrant after Bill Hewlett and Dave Packard stepped aside? Texas Instruments—once a high-flying darling of Wall Street—nearly self-destructed after Pat Haggarty stepped aside. What explains why the Walt Disney Company became an American icon, surviving and prospering through hostile takeover attempts, while Columbia Pictures lost ground, never became an icon, and eventually sold out to a Japanese company?

In their research, Collins and Porras found that visionary companies are firms that:

- Are premier institutions in their respective industries
- Are widely admired by knowledgeable businesspeople
- Made an indelible imprint on the world in which we live
- Had multiple generations of chief executives
- Have been through multiple product (or service) life cycles
- Were founded before 1950

Directors for a Board of Directors

Some entrepreneurs think their start-up venture doesn't need a board of directors, or that slots on a board are little more than titles to placate the egos of friends, family, or investors. "What entrepreneurs often don't realize is that a strong board can help a young or growing company build credibility in the outside world," says Bill Vogelgesang, a managing director in the investment banking firm of Brown, Gibbons, Lang & Co. He and other organizational experts have some advice for entrepreneurs who are assembling an advisory board for their new venture.

1. *The key issues in creating an effective board are control, credibility, and access.* Some entrepreneurs are reluctant to recruit talented or powerful board members because they're afraid the board may one day challenge their authority, or even usurp them. But a company with a good business plan and a strong management team has little to fear. "A well-connected board of experienced outsiders will give your company a lot of credibility in the business world as well as potential access to financing sources and other opportunities," says Ben Boissevain, managing director of the investment banking and advisory firm of E-Technologies Associates.

    Sally Smith, president of a company whose sales increased by 65 percent after recruiting a new board, says, "A board isn't there to replace management but to enhance it. I would expect our board members to look for ways to help us deal with our problems."

2. *Try to look at your prospective board the same way outside investors will.* Although the precise makeup of a good board may be open to debate, many experts believe that four out of every five seats should be filled by people from outside the company. The appointment of outsiders with strong credentials demonstrates the entrepreneur's commitment to making the best decisions for the company. A good board, adds Bill Vogelgesang, "reflects well upon a chief executive because it shows that he or she can take criticism and doesn't just want to impose one business vision on the company."

3. *Look for board members with lots of contacts and lots of experience.* "What you're looking for in an effective board is a group of mostly outsiders who have been through the entrepreneurial process many times. They understand the generic operating issues that a growth-oriented company typically faces," explains Michael E. Frank, general partner in the venture capital firm of Advanced Technology Ventures. "Good board members also have a very broad range of contacts that they can reach out to, which may include possible financiers, strategic partners, or even potential customers."

4. *Look for board members who have skills or experience you don't have.* "Very few entrepreneurs have all skills. It's rare for someone to understand operations, finance, sales and marketing, and human resources, and to be a great leader as well," observes Patrick J. Boroian, partner in the venture capitalist Sprout Group. "So what makes the most sense is finding board members who can complement your own skills set."

5. *Remember that your board is a public relations tool for the outside business community.* Bill Vogelgesang points out that many potential investors will contact board members to get information about a start-up company. If the board member makes a good impression, that's a plus. But Vogelgesang says, "If they wind up speaking to your brother-in-law or your best friend from kindergarten, that's not going to speak too well of you or your company."

Source: Adapted from Jill Andresky Fraser, "Building the Board," *Inc.* online, November 1, 1999; available www.inc.com.

This distinguished list includes such icons as Sony, Merck, American Express, 3M, Boeing, General Electric, Ford, and IBM.

Collins and Porras sought to understand why these companies were more enduring, more visionary, and better organized and managed than their counterparts. Their answer is easy to state but harder to do. Their conclusion is:

> *The continual stream of great products and services from highly successful companies stems from them being outstanding organizations . . . not the other way around.*

In other words, it is the organization—its processes, systems, routines, leadership, and culture—that makes the difference; no amount of great science or product development can overcome a poorly designed and administered organization. Management capability and skill are paramount.

Myths and Misinformation   That management capability is the most important ingredient in the visionary company mix is not an obvious conclusion, and there are many myths that Collins and Porras identify that entrepreneurs and managers believe. For example:

- *It takes a great idea to start a company.* No idea by itself is going to get the work done. I can tell you that a product that downloads the content of a newspaper and reads it to you while you drive to work is a definite winner, but until I start a company to produce, market, and distribute the product, it is just an idea. Management gets things done.
- *Visionary companies require great and charismatic visionary leaders.* There are not enough of these people to go around. Sometimes, their egos get in the way of successful management.
- *The most successful companies exist first and foremost to maximize profits.* If the firm exists only for money, then it will be satisfied when it becomes profitable. Visionary companies are never satisfied.
- *The only constant in a visionary company is change.* The core must be preserved, or the venture loses its identity and reason for existing.
- *Visionary companies are great places to work, for everyone.* Not everyone fits in. People who accept the challenge and vision are the ones who adapt to the culture. Those who don't must leave.
- *Highly successful companies make their best moves by brilliant and complex strategic planning.* If this was possible, everyone would do it.
- *Visionary companies share a common subset of "correct" core values.* There is no one set of "correct" values. What counts are commitment and action.
- *Blue-chip companies play it safe.* If they do, they die.
- *The most successful companies focus primarily on beating the competition.* Competition is important, but not as important as focusing on core values and exploiting unique resources and capabilities. Otherwise, you become a "me-too" organization.
- *Companies should hire outside CEOs to stimulate fundamental change.* Companies should do this only if the outsider also understands how to preserve the essentials of the business.

- *You can't have your cake and eat it, too, i.e., a company can't have homegrown managers and fundamental change.* You have to have both.
- *Companies become visionary primarily through "vision statements."* See the following sections.

The Venture's Vision How can you tell the difference between a vision and a vision statement? A vision is lived through the everyday experience of the people who work in and with the organization. A vision statement is the words written on a piece of paper. It makes sense that the beginning of the organization's development starts with the founder's or founding TMT's vision for the venture. The vision provides guidance about two essential elements—what core to preserve and what future for which to strive. The core represents the basic reason that the organization exists and the values and beliefs that it embodies. It is necessary to preserve the core, or the organization will lose its essential character and become a "nothing special–type" company. No company can survive for long by simply sticking to its founding principles: It must change and adapt. The vision must also include a commitment to change and progress. The vision must guide the venture's participants to keep the products and services fresh and worthwhile, but it must not deviate from the founding principles. The ideal vision is one that:

Preserves the core and stimulates progress

Therefore, the vision must have two components. The first is the **core ideology**. The core ideology defines the enduring character of an organization—a consistent identity that transcends product or market life cycles, technological breakthroughs, management fads, and individual leaders. The core ideology, in turn, is made up of two parts: the core values and the core purpose. **Core values** are a system of guiding principles and tenets—a small set of general guiding principles. These should not be confused with specific cultural or operating practices and should not be compromised for financial gain or short-term expediency. **Core purpose** is the organization's most fundamental reason for existence. It goes beyond "just making money": It should be a perpetual guiding star on the horizon and should not be confused with specific goals or business strategies. This is all better understood with an example. Let's look at the Disney Company. Numbers 1–4 are the core values; number 5 is the core purpose:

1. Fanatical attention to consistency/detail
2. Fanatical control and preservation of Disney's "magic" image
3. Continuous progress via creativity, dreams, and imagination
4. No cynicism allowed
5. "To bring happiness to millions" and to celebrate, nurture, and promulgate "wholesome American values"

Here is one more example from the Sony Corporation. Numbers 1–3 are the core values; number 4 is the core purpose:

1. Being a pioneer—not following others, but doing the impossible
2. Respecting and encouraging each individual's ability and creativity
3. Elevating the Japanese culture and national status
4. "To experience the sheer joy that comes from the advancement, application, and innovation of technology that benefits the general public."

The second part of the vision is the venture's **envisioned future**. An envisioned future can be defined by what an organization aspires "to become, to achieve, and to create." An organization must experience significant change and progress to attain that envisioned future. This includes a 10- to 30-year "big hairy audacious goal," or BHAG, and a vivid description of what it will be like when the organization achieves the BHAG.

A BHAG (pronounced "bee-hag") engages people—it reaches out and grabs them in the gut. It is tangible, energizing, highly focused. People "get it" right away; it takes little or no explanation. It is a huge and daunting challenge. A BHAG always:

- Is clear and compelling
- Serves as a unifying focal point of effort, and acts as a catalyst for team spirit
- Engages people
- Has a clear finish line
- Is tangible, energizing, and highly focused

Here is an example: In 1990, Sam Walton set the goal for Wal-Mart to achieve sales of $125 billion by 2000. At the time, the largest retailer in the world had sales of $30 billion. This sales target was incredibly audacious, but it was also easy to measure and focused the entire organization on a single future. How did they do? For fiscal year ending January 31, 2000, Wal-Mart reported net sales of $165,013,000,000. This was 32 percent better than their 10-year BHAG goal, and a 20 percent increase over the previous fiscal year. During this time, Sam Walton died, but the organization he created endured. Wal-Mart is built to last.

When writing your venture's BHAG, be so bold and exciting that it will stimulate progress even if the organization's leaders disappear before completion. Make it consistent with company's core ideology. Set it 10 to 30 years in the future. Remember, it is a goal, not a statement, and should be clear and compelling—no explanation needed. Finally, a BHAG needs to be outside the comfort zone. It may be ridiculed by outsiders and those who do not know your firm; to insiders, it is motivating, challenging, and inspirational.

The next step is to write a vivid description. This encompasses what your company will be like when it achieves its BHAG. It should be specific. For example, Henry Ford, founder of the Ford Motor Company, was quoted as saying, "I will build a motor car . . . so low in price that no man making a good salary will be unable to own one . . . the horse will have disappeared from our highways." It came to pass that the future envisioned actually occurred.

Time-Telling Versus Clock-Building   Which do you think is the more impressive and enduring capability—the ability to tell time or the ability to build a clock? Collins and Porras found that some founding CEOs were very good time-tellers, while others were more like clock-builders. (Of course, if the founder could neither tell time nor build clocks, their ventures failed early). Having a great idea or being a charismatic visionary leader is **time-telling**. Building a company that can prosper far beyond the presence of any single leader and through multiple product life cycles is **clock-building**.

A time-telling CEO has the ability to look around, scan the environment, gauge the resources needed to exploit an opportunity, and do it. The time-teller is a here-and-now person, living in the moment and taking advantage of current endowments. For example, Larry Ellison of Oracle might be considered such an entrepreneur. He is charismatic, hard-charging, and assertive, and he understood early the power of large database management. He is better known, however, for his many adventurous avocations than his executive skill. Many of his people have little loyalty to the organization, and Mr. Ellison's decision making is often under fire from the press.[38]

A clock-builder is a different breed of founder. The clock-builder focuses on the longer term. The metaphor of the clock refers to the organization. An organization is like a clock when it is possible for anyone to tell the time, and the capability to tell time resides within the organization. It doesn't depend on a single leader. Andy Grove of Intel is offered as a clock-builder. The founder of Intel is now retired, but his successor Craig Barrett oversees an organization that continues to lead the industry in the design, development, and marketing of computer chips, and computer networking and information products.

Recommendations for Entrepreneurs and Founders   Collins and Porras have some final recommendations based on their "preserve the core, stimulate progress" findings. Here is a summary of this advice:

1. Develop Cult-Like Cultures (preserve the core):
    Make your company a great place to work *only* for those who buy into the core ideology; reject those who don't fit with the ideology.
2. Homegrown Management (preserve the core):
    Promote from within, and make sure your senior managers are steeped in the core ideology of your company.
3. Big Hairy Audacious Goals (stimulate progress):
    Make a commitment to challenging and audacious goals and projects to stimulate progress.
4. Try a Lot of Stuff, and Keep What Works (stimulate progress):
    High levels of action and experimentation—often unplanned and undirected—produce new and unexpected paths of progress.
5. Good Enough Never Is (stimulate progress):
    Institute a continual process of relentless self-improvement with the aim of doing better and better, forever into the future.

E-NOTES 9-5

Built to Last

- preserve the core: core ideology and core values
- stimulate progress: BHAG and envisioned future
- leadership: time-telling or clock-building
- great organizations produce great products, not the other way around

THE ORGANIZATION'S BOUNDARIES

The previous discussion concerning the creation and maintenance of a top management team assumed that there was sufficient justification for building an organization. That is, the entrepreneur needed help and found that the best way to secure this help was to form a TMT and hire people to work in the company. But is it possible to be an entrepreneur without a TMT and, implicitly, without building an organization? The founder could conceivably rely solely on outside contracting and a network of independent suppliers and distributors to produce, deliver, and market the product or service. To understand the choice the entrepreneur faces when determining whether to use the market or build an organization, we need to understand the forces that determine the organization's boundaries.

The Virtual Organization

In Chapter 2, we defined entrepreneurship as "the creation of an innovative economic organization (or network) for the purpose of gain or growth under conditions of risk and uncertainty." At that time, we suggested that it was possible for an entrepreneur to develop a **virtual organization**. The virtual organization could be the model for the global business organization in the years ahead. It consists of a network of independent companies—suppliers, customers, and even rivals—linked by common goals and information technology to share skills, costs, and access to one another's markets. This new, evolving corporate model is fluid and flexible—a group of collaborators who quickly unite to exploit a specific opportunity.

For example, Kingston Technology Corporation of Fountain Valley, California, is a virtual corporation that has grown to over $500 million in sales. It is a world leader in computer upgrades, and it operates within a network of related firms that lead complementary corporate lives. This is not simply subcontracting. These companies share know-how, markets, and capital. Here's a typical example:

> On a recent Tuesday, a Los Angeles branch of ComputerLand received a call from Bank of America. It wanted 100 IBM PCs pronto. The problem: They needed lots of extra memory and other upgrades, the better to run Windows, Microsoft's ubiquitous operating system, and link into the bank's computer network. ComputerLand called Kingston, which snapped into action. Within hours, it had designed a sophisticated upgrade system—its particular specialty—and relayed "specs" to a key partner, Express Manufacturing. Express, which specializes in assembling electronic parts, cleared its manufacturing lines, filled Kingston's order, and sent the finished systems back that very afternoon. By evening, Kingston had tested all the components and returned them, via FedEx, to ComputerLand. By the weekend, Bank of America's computers were up and running. "You've heard of just-in-time inventory?" asks VP David Sun, referring to Japan's vaunted principle of cost-effective management. "This is just-in-time manufacturing."[39]

In the concept's purest form, each company that links with others to create a virtual corporation contributes only what it regards as its core competencies. Each firm is organized around the specific resources that are rare, valuable, hard to copy, and nonsubstitutable. All other resources are provided by other firms, which also possess the four attributes of sustainable competitive advantage. These advantages, however, remain protected within these other firms.

Technology plays a central role in the development of virtual corporations. Entrepreneurs in different companies can work together concurrently rather than sequentially on computer networks in real time.[40] To participate in a virtual corporation, an enterprise must focus on the things it does best and then forge alliances with other companies, each bringing its own special capability. Such an organization would be a world-class competitor, with the speed, power, and leading-edge technology to take advantage of market opportunities.[41] Street Story 9-3 shows how the Internet has given companies new design options.

E-NOTES 9-6

Virtual Organization

A virtual organization is an alliance of independent companies:

- linked by common goals and information technology
- that share skills, costs, and access to each other's markets

---

Traditional Organizational Structure

Virtual organizations can and do exist, but the question is, for how long? Kingston Technology may be long-lived because it has design capabilities that serve as its source of sustainable competitive advantage. In the case of Walden Paddlers, the alliances are built on trust, a much shakier foundation in a low-trust society such as the United States.[42] The more traditional view of organizational boundaries is based on the strategy-structure hypothesis.[43] The strategy-structure hypothesis states that "**structure follows strategy**." This means that the boundaries of the organization are adjusted periodically to meet the requirements of the firm's strategy.

Stage One: Simple Structure   A historical analysis of firm behavior provides the template for this hypothesis.[44] In the earliest stages of firm creation, an organization's boundaries began and ended with the entrepreneur and a few close associates. The strategy pursued by the top management team of such a new business was to increase sales volume. This simple structure is the first stage of the organizational structure life cycle.

Stage Two: Departmentalization   Historically, as the firm grew larger, entrepreneurs found themselves engaged in more and more administrative and fewer and fewer entrepreneurial tasks, such as allocating resources to various activities. This was detrimental to firm performance.

When the volume of the business grew so large that the entrepreneurs themselves could no longer make the top executive decisions that needed to be made, they hired managers: production managers, marketing managers, sales managers, engineering and design managers, and personnel managers. These managers supervised groups of similar activities that were combined together into departments. The firm now consisted of a main core, a center, that produced a product, and surrounding this core was a set of

Seeing Your Business Through Internet-Colored Glasses

They call them "plug-and-play" companies.

The expression, coined by Garth Saloner of the Stanford Graduate Business School, describes start-ups and other companies that use the Internet to outsource many of the functions that were previously done under one roof.

Nortel Networks, a company in Canada that builds high-performance Internet networks, is an example of how "virtual" integration can replace vertical integration. Over a 2-year period, the company sold 15 plants where it had previously manufactured products like printed circuit boards to other large producers in the field. Many of these firms were already doing business with Nortel, and they all signed long-term supply agreements with Nortel as part of the plant sales contract. Then Nortel established an Internet exchange called "e2open," which allows them to broadcast orders for new products to their network of suppliers so they can find the best, the cheapest, and the quickest source for materials.

The company has benefited from this changeover to a virtual organization in a number of ways. First, the e2open network allows them to be fast and flexible; orders that previously took the company up to 3 months to fill can now in some cases be completed in days. Nortel can also contract with a supplier that is close to their customer's location, which allows them to be more efficient in filling international orders. The company has now lowered costs because their suppliers can produce these core products cheaper than Nortel ever did because they have a high volume of sales. Outsourcing through the Internet network allows Nortel to take advantage of upgrades in production technology and, most importantly, allows the company to concentrate on the industrial and test engineering that it always did best.

Savvy entrepreneurs are also using the Internet to exploit profitable market segments. Brendan McLaughlin of Cambridge Technology Partners discovered that the production schedules of companies that make tapered roller bearings were being monitored via the Internet by a Scandinavian company that made replacement tapered roller bearings. This news plunged McLaughlin's client, who manufactured tapered roller bearings, into a panic because the bulk of his profits came from replacement parts. More virtual innovations undoubtedly lie ahead. Bill Sahlman, a professor at the Harvard Business School, says, "Our students go systematically, SIC code by SIC code, through industries, looking for ones to revolutionize."

Some established companies, such as Procter & Gamble and Staples, are spinning off new Internet ventures as a way of experimenting with virtual organization. Few companies, however, have been as brave or imaginative as General Electric. GE sponsored an Internet exercise so company managers could discover where their divisions were most vulnerable to competition from the Web. The name of the exercise was "destroyyourbusiness. com."

Source: Adapted from "The Shape of the New E-Company," *The Economist,* November 11, 2000, pp. 37–38.

functionally differentiated managers. **Departmentalization** is the second stage of organizational structure.

Stage Three: Divisional Structure   Volume can grow only so large in a single location. Constraints such as plant capacity, transportation costs, logistical problems, and the limits of the market itself meant that if a firm were to continue to grow, it had to expand to other locations. The next strategy that entrepreneurs undertook was geographic expansion. Initially, the firm continued to attempt to manage both the original location and the new geographic location from the origin. But as the number of expansion sites increased and the number of branches and outlets proliferated, this became impossible. Thus, the structure of the firm had to change to meet the demands of the new strategy. The new structure called for the grouping of units within a geographic region to form geographic divisions. This new structure was added to the functionally differentiated structure that was now clearly delineated as departments. Both reported to the firm's headquarters. This third stage of structural development is called the **divisional structure**.

Stage Four: Multidivisional Structure   Future growth in a single product, like the single location, was also a limiting strategy; there was satiated demand for the product and missed opportunities from related products and related markets. As the firm continued to pursue growth, it changed its strategy to one of related diversification and vertical integration. General Motors integrated with Fisher Body. Jersey Standard expanded its refining and marketing. DuPont developed new product groups based on its chemical research and development. Sears took on the insurance business and merged with Allstate Insurance. This diversification put new demands on the old divisional structure. Stress and strain were created. Inefficiencies occurred and finally a new structure was developed. This was the **multidivisional structure**, the fourth stage of development. Again, it grouped similar products and activities together so employees could achieve their highest productivity without the negative influences of other products or activities.

Stage Five: The Conglomerate   The fifth and final structure resulted from a change in strategy from related diversification to unrelated diversification. When firms began to enter businesses that were completely unlike any business in which they had previously engaged, the old structure again began to break down. The executives in the older divisions did not understand the new businesses, and they did not share the perspectives of the newer managers. There was no reason for these unrelated divisions to be grouped together, because they did not share markets, products, or technologies. In fact, it was better to keep them separate so that the performance of each could be measured independently. From this change in strategy came the **conglomerate**, also known as the **holding company**.

In summary, the "structure follows strategy" hypothesis says that an organization's boundaries are a result of the pursuit of different strategies. The boundaries are fixed for periods of time, but as the strategy changes and stress is put on the organization's structure, eventually a new structure arises. Each time a new structure comes into being, the enterprise's boundaries expand, and it takes on more activities within those boundaries.

Organizational Structure

Based on the "structure follows strategy" thesis, the organization of a business venture evolves according to the complexity of its product(s) and production.

Simple structure:

- structure designed to increase sales for new or small venture
- flat hierarchy of authority (two levels)
- employees not very specialized

Departmentalization:

- structure for a growing company
- management hierarchy differentiated by function

Divisional structure:

- structure for a company with more than one location
- management hierarchy differentiated by location and function

Multidivisional structure:

- structure for a company with more than one product
- management hierarchy differentiated by product, location, and function

Conglomerate:

- structure for a company with unrelated products
- management hierarchy differentiated by type of products, product, location, and function

---

ENTREPRENEURIAL PERFORMANCE: THE BALANCED SCORECARD

The great entrepreneurial organizations are going to perform at very high levels. The question is "levels of what?" Will it be levels of product innovation? Financial performance? Customer service? Internal efficiency? The answer is that great entrepreneurial organizations will operate at a high level on all of these dimensions. They will do so in a "balanced" way, not emphasizing one over the other because all of these dimensions need to work together to produce an organization that operates a successful system.

The balanced scorecard (BSC) is a systematic management process that generates objectives, activities, and measures for organizational performance.[45] The balanced scorecard is a set of measures that gives managers a fast but comprehensive view of their business. A good balanced scorecard has 15 to 20 different measures derived from the four basic dimensions of entrepreneurial performance:

- Financial dimension (How do we look to our investors?)
- Customer dimension (How do we look to our customers?)

- Internal operating dimension (What must we excel at?)
- Innovation and learning dimension (Can we continue to improve and create value?)

By developing a set of criteria on these four dimensions, entrepreneurs and the TMT can translate the venture's mission and strategy into a set of comprehensive operating and performance measures. All of the dimensions are linked, as illustrated in Figure 9-2.

Because the entrepreneurial venture's existence is characterized by change and growth, these measures can be fine-tuned to reflect changing circumstances. When the environment of the venture changes rapidly, old criteria can be discarded and new measures can be implemented.

This system is called "balanced" because it helps the entrepreneur balance:

- *The long term versus the short term.* Some of the criteria measures will capture a 3 to 6 month period's activity. Others will attempt to drive the organization to longer term goals, 3 to 5 years out.
- *Lagging indicators versus leading indicators.* Some criteria measure what has happened in the past, like financial performance or manufacturing productivity. These are the lagging indicators, and they tell the entrepreneur about the past. Other measures are leading indicators and relate to the future. Such measures and capital investment, training, new hires, and research intensity capture the venture's current activities in anticipation of a future payoff.
- *External performance expectations versus internal performance expectations.* Some of the measures deal with how the company is managing its relations with the external environment. Examples would be customer or vendor relations. Other measures deal with internal operations such as manufacturing efficiency and employee skill acquisition.
- *Financial versus nonfinancial performance.* The balance between these two is critical. Too much emphasis on financial results can choke growth as the entrepreneur seeks to maximize short-run opportunities. Too much emphasis on nonfinancial measures (such as "eyeballs" captured in Internet scenarios) risks running out of money and willing investors.

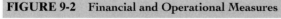

FIGURE 9-2 Financial and Operational Measures

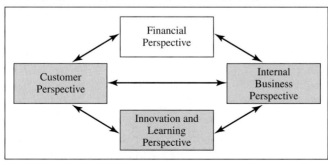

- *Driver measures of future performance versus financial measures of past performance.* The drivers are critically important because they indicate that a company is building the capabilities and acquiring the intangible assets it needs for future growth.

There are many good reasons to use the BSC approach. Frequently, entrepreneurs are really quite obsessed with financial performance, but this does not indicate how the company is developing for the future. Financial performance is a lagging indicator and measures the past; the entrepreneur should be focused on the future. It requires a balance of financial and other measures to give us the complete picture of how the firm is doing. In addition, the process of implementing the BSC in the venture makes people aware of the relationships among all four dimensions. All three of the nonfinancial measures must be linked to the financial ones. A good balanced scorecard is one where you can see the cause-and-effect relationships clearly in the measures chosen. However, the main lesson for entrepreneurs and the TMT is:

What you measure is what you get

Let us review the four dimensions of the balanced scorecard.

Customer Dimension   Customers' concerns generally fall into four areas: time, quality, performance and service, and cost. Examples of customer dimension goals might include:

Time—reduce delivery time
Quality—reduce defects or warranty claims
Performance and service—Increase value perception
Cost—reduce price or costs (e.g., delivery)

Examples of more specific measures of customers' goals are:

- Time: on-time delivery as defined by the customer
- Quality: percentage of sales from new and existing products
- Performance and service: market share, customer satisfaction rankings
- Cost: year-to-year cost reductions

It is up to the entrepreneur and the TMT to define the customer dimension goals and choose the measures for these. Each of the goals will be linked in some way to the financial measures and the other goals.

Internal Business Dimension   This dimension answers the question "what must we excel at?" and is directly related to the resources and capabilities possessed by the venture. The internal business dimension can be represented as a three-part value chain:

1. Innovation process—developing new technology and implementing it. An example of a specific measure is new product development and introduction versus the competition.

2. Operations process—developing manufacturing and delivery excellence. Examples of specific measures are reduced cycle time, reduced unit costs, and increased yield.

3. Post-sale service process—improving the service program. Examples of specific measures are reduced warranty costs and increased customer retention rates.

Innovation and Learning Dimension   This is also an internal dimension but focuses more specifically on the people in the organization. The goals for this dimension can be divided into three subcomponents:

1. *Employee capabilities.* An example of a goal in this area is the continued improvement in the technological capabilities of the employees and managers. A specific measure might be the time it takes to develop the next generation of technological product or service improvement. This goal makes it clear that there needs to be investment in employee training and development as well as the capital investment needed to sustain testing and quality.

2. *Information systems capabilities.* A goal in this area might be to develop an expert system of the manufacturing or throughput processes of the firm. A specific measure of this is how long it takes to develop and test the expert system.

3. *Motivation, empowerment, and alignment.* Examples of goals in this area include increasing employee focus on products and product information, or reducing time to market of a new item. A measure of the first might be the number of products that represent 80 percent of revenue; a measure of the latter might be a benchmark of time to market versus the competition.

Goals and measures are also directly linked to the other areas as well as financial performance. Balancing the needs of the organization requires attention to these people issues because people and their behaviors are instrumental in achieving the other objectives.

Financial Performance Dimension   The financial objective of every venture is to provide superior returns to investors. There are three primary ways to do this:

1. Through revenue growth and maximizing the mix of revenue streams. Some of the goals that can be set to achieve this include:
   - Designing and developing new products
   - Creating new applications for old products and services
   - Finding new customers and markets
   - Optimizing the product and service mix
   - Developing new relationships and strategic partners
   - Executing a new pricing strategy

2. Through cost reductions and productivity improvements such as:
   - Increasing productivity
   - Reducing unit costs
   - Improving distribution channel mix
   - Reducing operating expenses and overhead

3. Through superior asset utilization and investment strategies. These can be summarized as:
   - Improving the cash-to-cash cycle
   - Increased asset utilization rates

Typically, the specific measures of financial performance revolve around returns on invested capital, returns on equity, and returns on assets. Other important measures are gross and operating margins, market shares, and growth in sales.

As you construct your scorecard, remember that a good balanced scorecard has a limited number of measures that force managers to focus. They are not trying to achieve everything all at once. Four or five measures in each of the four dimensions are sufficient. A good scorecard brings together all of the dimensions in an integrated way and shows how activity on one dimension leads to activity and better performance on another. By showing cause and effect in this way, it guards against suboptimization and enables all the managers to see what the others are doing.

One company that has implemented the balanced scorecard is United Ad Label (now the Veriad Company). In Street Story 9-4, we see how the company used the four dimensions of the BSC to improve performance.

The benefits of using the balanced scorecard have been shown for many established companies over the years, and the same lessons apply for new ventures. Organization performance must be integrated and balanced. However, there are some other advantages to using the Balanced Scorecard approach since it is not only a measuring tool, but also a system of managing. Many companies have used the BSC to:

1. *Clarify* and gain consensus about strategy.
2. *Communicate* strategy throughout the organization.
3. *Align goals* (departmental and personal) to strategy.
4. *Link* strategic objectives to long-term targets and annual budgets.
5. *Identify* and align strategic initiatives.
6. *Perform reviews* (both periodic and systematic).
7. *Obtain feedback* to learn about and improve strategy.

E-NOTES 9-8

The Balanced Scorecard

- Has four dimensions: financial, customer, internal business, and innovation and learning.
- Balancing means considering long term versus short term, leading indicators versus lagging indicators, and financial versus nonfinancial measures.
- All four dimensions must work together with the other three leading to superior financial performance.
- Using the BSC is not only a way of measuring performance, but is also a system of management.

THE ENTREPRENEURIAL WORKPLACE

The new venture is not only a vehicle for the entrepreneur and the top management team to realize their dreams and ambitions; it is also the place where people work. The challenge of the entrepreneurial workplace is to enable employees to feel the same excitement, motivation, commitment, and satisfaction that the founders feel. Otherwise,

The Balanced Bus Approach

They started with a retreat.

Several years ago, each member of United Ad Label's TMT read *Balanced Scorecard: Translating Strategy into Action* and then spent 3 days as a group discussing how they could apply this approach to their own company. The 40-year-old manufacturer of industrial labels had recently been acquired by another company, and as human resources director Valerie Poole relates, "We needed a new compass to show everyone where we're heading and how we're going to get there."

During the retreat, the top management team analyzed the company as it currently was and then talked about new markets, competition, and what measures would be most meaningful to monitor and how to do that. But management still needed a way to communicate this new strategy to their 200 employees. They decided to use a visual analogy that everyone could understand. "We think of the scorecard as a bus, with the quadrants as the wheels," explains Valerie Poole. "'Everyone's on board the bus,' we tell employees. 'To take off, we need the proper amount of air pressure in the tires. We must pay equal attention to all four tires. We can't afford to have flat tires, and we shouldn't overinflate any one.' They could relate to that."

In the customer dimension or quadrant, United Ad Label, which is now known as Veriad (www.veriad.com), set a goal to have 70 percent of their customers reordering, and they started mailing coded report cards to customers to measure satisfaction. They also established focus groups from their customers to help develop new products and internally measured customer service activities like the on-time mailing of company brochures.

In their internal business quadrant, Veriad decided to concentrate on measuring operating income and cash flow. The statistics for things like production cycle time and customer returns are circulated to employees daily, and employees receive a bonus if the goals for operating income and cash flow are met.

In the innovation and learning dimension, Veriad implemented an employee assessment program that helps staff to evaluate their professional skills and also started to measure employee satisfaction, development, and retention. They also upgraded their phone system and are working on improving communication throughout the company.

In the financial performance quadrant, Veriad set mid- and long-term goals for sales, operating income and cash flow, return on capital, sales from new products and markets, and new business partnerships. Their overall goal is to be number 1 or 2 in market share in their industry.

Valerie Poole reports that Veriad is pleased with their balanced scorecard bus so far. In particular, the program has helped establish a strong sense of shared purpose throughout the company. "People see that every job counts. They know that if we keep our vision and values in line, the basic business strategies don't change much. They reflect our mission, and the way we uphold that mission—how we get things done—are the objectives and initiatives. When those change, we revisit the scorecard to see if we're still on track."

Source: Adapted from Karen Carney, "A More Balanced Scorecard," *Inc.* online, October 10, 1998; available at www.inc.com.

they will fail to carry out their tasks and responsibilities energetically and effectively. Part of the responsibility of the entrepreneur is to create an organization where the culture, the ethics, and the human resource management system are consistent with the goals and ambitions of the enterprise.

The Entrepreneurial Culture

The **culture** of the organization is reflected in its philosophies, rules, norms, and values. It defines "how we do things around here" for employees and consequently for customers. A strong entrepreneurial culture mirrors the entrepreneurial values of the founders. Entrepreneurs often start their business because they want to do things "their own way," and creating the entrepreneurial culture is their opportunity to see that everyone does it "their own way." Therefore, it is imperative that the entrepreneurs communicate what they believe is important for the organization to be doing. This communication can be face to face, or it can take place in meetings, employee newsletters, or in other written forms. Often the culture is communicated in rituals, rites, and the folklore of the company.[46] Entrepreneurial companies can do things their own way. For example:

> Amy Miller, president of Amy's Icecreams Inc., of Austin, Texas, is a self-described "hyperactive," so she wants her stores to be hyperactive, too. She encourages her employees to toss ice cream from scoop to bowl, and she allows and encourages employees to dance on the freezer tops. To recruit people as uninhibited as herself, she gives potential applicants a paper bag and asks them to do something creative with it.[47]

> At Tweezerman Corp. in Port Washington, New York, the slogan is "We aim to tweeze" and the goal is 24-hour service. Working for the tweezer and body-care products company can be frenetic and tense. Because the owner, Dal La Magna, does not employ secretaries, all the employees are constantly in a mad rush to answer phones, letters, and customer demands. The pace creates tensions and fights, so the company has "Fight Day" when all the stored-up steam can be let off once each month. Postponing the arguments gives most people a chance to cool off and get down to work. Also, the company has space set aside for employees to meditate when it gets to be too wacky.[48]

> Frank Meeks has 45 Dominos Pizza units in his Washington, DC, franchise area. Every week he and his managers do a no-nonsense 10-kilometer run before their meeting. "The company believes in integrating health and fitness," Meeks says. Recruits are told about the requirement before they are hired, and the only excuse not to run is a death bed plea. Meeks does not want any lazy people on the team. The competitive atmosphere created makes the meetings more like pep rallies than sales reports.[49]

The entrepreneurial culture is clearly different from the culture of traditional large organizations. It is future-oriented and emphasizes new ideas, creativity, risk-taking, and opportunity identification. People feel empowered to manage their own jobs and time. Everyone can make a contribution to the firm's success, and the common worker is a hero. Communication is frequently horizontal and bottom up—while the worker serves the customer, the manager serves the worker. Table 9-1 compares the organizational culture of the traditional firm with that of the entrepreneurial organization.

TABLE 9-1   **Organizational Culture: A Comparison**

Dimension	Traditional Organization	Entrepreneurial Organization
Strategy	Status quo, conservative	Evolving, futuristic
Productivity	Short-term focus, profitability	Short and long term, multiple criteria
Risk	Averse, punished	Emphasized and rewarded
Opportunity	Absent	Integral
Leadership	Top-down, autocratic	Culture of empowerment
Power	Hoarded	Given away
Failure	Costly	OK; teaches a lesson
Decision making	Centralized	Decentralized
Communication	By the book, chain of command	Flexible, facilitates innovation
Structure	Hierarchical	Organic
Creativity	Tolerated	Prized and worshiped
Efficiency	Valued, accountants are heroes	Valued if it helps realize overall goals

Source: Adapted from J. Cornwall and B. Perlman, *Organizational Entrepreneurship* (Homewood, IL: Irwin, 1990).

Entrepreneurial Ethics

An important part of the culture in the new venture is its ethical climate. The ethics of the organization are never clear enough. They are frequently ambiguous and shifting. Stereotypically, entrepreneurs are seen as having low ethical standards. The great robber barons of the American industrial revolution—the Rockefellers, Fords, Mellons, and Carnegies—were all seen in their time as ruthless and unethical.[50] In today's Chinese economic revolution, the use of public office for private gain, the lack of a "rule of law," and the endemic use of bribes contribute to the belief that the entrepreneur is an unethical, selfish economic animal. In fact, entrepreneurs and small business owners are neither more nor less ethical than managers and other people, but they have different tolerances for different types of unethical behavior. Table 9-2 reports the results of a large study of the ethical differences between managers of small and large businesses.

Entrepreneurs repeatedly face some ethical dilemmas. These all involve the meaning of honesty. At times the entrepreneur may feel that to be "completely honest" does a disservice to the new venture and his or her efforts to create it. Yet to be less than

TABLE 9-2   **Ethical Issues: Comparison Between Managers of Small and Large Firms**

Small Firm Manager More Tolerant of:	Large Firm Manager More Tolerant of:
1. Padded expense accounts	1. Faulty investment advice
2. Tax evasion	2. Favoritism in promotion
3. Collusion in bidding	3. Living with a dangerous design flaw
4. Insider trading	4. Misleading financial reporting
5. Discrimination against women	5. Misleading advertising
6. Copying computer software	

Source: J. Longnecker, J. McKinney, and C. Moore, "Do Smaller Firms Have Higher Ethics?" *Business and Society Review* (Fall 1989): 19–21.

completely honest puts the credibility and reputation of the entrepreneur and the new venture in question. These are the dilemmas of the promoter, the innovator, and the transacter.[51]

Promoter Dilemmas   When the entrepreneur is in the early stages of promoting the business to financial supporters, customers, potential partners, and employees, a certain euphoria is associated with the effort. The entrepreneur is in a very positive state of mind and trying to see the new venture in the best light possible. The entrepreneur gives positive impressions about the new venture even though the entrepreneur is quite aware of the dangers, risks, potential pitfalls, and barriers to success the firm faces. The entrepreneur weighs the pragmatic costs of revealing all this negative information against the benefits of being completely honest—the **promoter dilemma**. It is not clear at what point in the process and to what degree the promoter is obligated to communicate his or her most dire fears about the new venture.

Innovator Dilemmas   The creation of new businesses often means the creation of new technologies, products, and combinations. The **innovator**/entrepreneur frequently has the **dilemma** of expediting production and distribution or engaging in a long process of product testing for safety. Even if there is no reason to believe the product is unsafe, there is always the risk of the "Frankenstein" effect. If the unwitting entrepreneur creates a monster, a product that does harm or is perceived to do harm, the new venture will never recover. If the entrepreneur waits until the risk and uncertainty have been eliminated, someone else may be first to market.

Relational Dilemmas   Over the course of new venture creation, the entrepreneur becomes a member of a number of different networks, or groups of individuals and firms. Frequently, conflicts of interest exist. The ethical demands of membership in one group may conflict with those of another, creating a **relationship dilemma**. For example, the scientist/entrepreneur belongs to academic societies that insist that studies be reviewed by peers and published in professional journals to ensure that the science is valid. But by doing so the scientist may be revealing important proprietary information that is a source of SCA for the new enterprise.

A different type of relationship dilemma is a function of transactions that the entrepreneur engages in. An example often concerns investor relationships. One investor's commitment may depend heavily on the commitment of another investor, and vice versa. The entrepreneur may attempt to "ham and egg" it: Tell the first investor that the second investor has made a commitment, and tell the second investor that the first investor has done so as well. From the point of view of the new venture, complete honesty would mean that there would be no investor commitment. From the point of view of the relationship between the entrepreneur and the investors, there is less than complete honesty.

The entrepreneur faces additional tests of his or her ethical character. The "finders keepers" problem can occur when value is created by the collective efforts of many firms and individuals, but the entrepreneur has the ability to appropriate all of the gain for the new venture. Should the entrepreneur take all the gains, or should these gains be distributed among all the deserving parties? A second problem occurs when the goals of the firm and of the entrepreneur diverge. If the entrepreneur wants to live in a high style and spend more money than the business can afford, who is to say no? Often there is no one to control the entrepreneur in this situation. Last, the entrepreneur occasionally has to decide whether to engage in unsavory business practices, such as paying bribes, or forgo business opportunities. In some industries and cultures, such practices are commonplace. Refusing to pay the bribe simply means that someone else will and they will get the contract or sale. Should the entrepreneur go along or refuse to deal?

These are all difficult issues, and their resolution depends on the criterion used by the decision maker. A **utilitarian rule** would resolve the issue by asking, "Which choice produces the most good for the most people?" An **absolute rule** would decide the dilemma by consistently appealing to a moral or religious code—which almost invariably forbids lying, cheating, stealing, and taking advantage of less powerful people. A **relativist approach** to making these types of decisions looks at what everyone else is doing in the same situation and goes along with the crowd. To further complicate the ethics issues, it is not unusual to find a single individual using all three criteria at one time or another, depending on the situation.

E-NOTES 9-9

Entrepreneurial Ethics

Ethical issues facing an entrepreneur may include:

- promoter dilemmas
- innovator dilemmas
- relational dilemmas

MOST SUCCESSFUL HUMAN RESOURCE PRACTICES

There are few rules for successful human resource practices, because each company is different and human resource management is complex. Although standard practices and guidelines are easy to come by, these provide little insight into how to make the venture's human resource management a source of sustainable competitive advantage.[52]

Each business needs to identify its own managerial strengths and develop a system around them. That is what the companies described later have done, and it has earned them the reputation as some of the best entrepreneurial companies in the United States to work for.[53] These practices can be used by others as benchmarks, but the real challenge is to customize them to the special context of each enterprise.

Best Compensation Practices   The level of pay alone does not motivate workers, but it is an essential component. Pay fairness is equally important, as well as a transparent process that enables people to see how pay issues are determined. Rewards must be directly related to what the company wants its people to accomplish. It is fallacy to hope that people do A while their rewards come from B.

- A photo-image printer empowers employees to determine what skills are needed to do the job and then rewards them for proficiency and the ability to teach others. They grade themselves.
- A communications equipment maker sets compensation for each employee to the level of customer satisfaction. An annual customer survey and a measure of product service and reliability are used.
- A software services consultant offers customized pay packages with cafeteria-style benefits. A menu of annual salary, hourly salary, or a blend can foster mutual risk sharing between employer and employee.
- A midwest manufacturer instituted a **gain-sharing** program that rewards employees with a percentage of the savings or profits from their suggestions and innovations. Encourages ideas with a *Gainsharing News* newsletter.

Best Training Practices   Training is an investment in human resources, and exceptional training can be a source of SCA for the enterprise. Skill-intensive training improves the current level of employee productivity. Training can anticipate changes in the nature of work so that when job requirements change, there is no decline in productivity. Management training serves three purposes: It enables workers to better understand their managers' roles, it helps employees manage themselves, and it prepares people for promotion to management ranks.

- A computer systems installer enables employees to mentor each other. An expert employee spreads both skill and management knowledge to peers.
- An airplane furniture maker focuses training on "learning to learn" with Saturday sessions of exercises and role-playing where people can break down barriers to communication and improve teamwork.
- Coffee megastar Starbucks ties training to business strategy by formally building employees' identification with the company. In class, stresses everything from basic product knowledge to interpersonal relationships.

Best Job Autonomy   Employees who have authority and responsibility to do their jobs often display stronger motivation, better work quality, higher job satisfaction, and lower turnover. Job autonomy is one of the key components in making a company a great place to work. Not all employees can handle the freedom, but for those who can, it is the best way to manage people.

- An instrument manufacturer urges employees to "make it happen," to solve problems, to motivate themselves. Sets loose boundaries so everyone feels responsible for everything.
- A phone service reseller hires rigorously, trains intensively, and then turns people loose to perform. Little supervision is needed for most people. Reviews monthly or weekly progress reports.
- An automobile dealer empowers salespeople to cut deals on their own. Urges service department teams to boost customer satisfaction. Actively solicits and implements employee ideas.

Best Career Advancement   Employee advancement does not always mean a promotion up the ladder in the bureaucracy. Indeed, with increasing emphasis on flatter organizations, many businesses would be better off not having much bureaucracy at all. Then how are employees to advance and consider their jobs career opportunities?

- A temporary placement agency grows its own managers and hires from within. Hires for one or two levels up from the position available so that the employee can grow into the job as the company grows in its demand for managers.
- A linen distributor maps out career tracks up to 15 years in advance with the expectation that the new hire will retire with the company.
- A small agricultural business clearly communicates career growth opportunities to all employees. Promotes competent learners.
- A health policy consultant enables staff members to market their own ideas by developing personal interests that can create new businesses. Promotes lateral job moves if beneficial to all.

Best Quality of Life   Increasingly people are merging their work with their family life. Outside concerns about things such as child care, working spouses, and parental leave all influence job performance. People are concerned about the quality of their total life, not just the on-the-job part. The best companies to work for recognize this and make it possible for people to realistically combine their personal values and job requirements.

- A plumbing products manufacturer provides on-site school and child care before and after office hours. Offers financial support for adoptions. Offers benefits to part-time employees.
- A magazine publisher gives extended family leave at two-thirds pay plus 6 months' unpaid leave. Uses flexible scheduling, offers dependent-care assistance.
- A research lab established on-site adult day care and child care, employee fitness center, emergency counseling program.
- A commercial packaging maker made available on-site laundry facilities, English and high school equivalency classes, door-to-door transport, and a children's clothing swap center.

These small businesses and new firms have been creative and enterprising in developing human resource systems that integrate the needs of both the business and workers. When the venture's human resources are working to full capabilities, they are saving the company money, adding value for customers, adapting to the changing marketplace, taking responsibility, and managing themselves. The entrepreneur must consider the creation and development of the organization as an opportunity to achieve a sustainable competitive advantage.

Summary

This chapter has provided an overview of the theoretical and practical aspects of creating an organization. One of the top priorities for most entrepreneurs is the recruitment, selection, and organization of a top management team. The team serves as both the basis of sustainable competitive advantage by virtue of the uniqueness of its members and as the protector of the venture's resources.

The TMT and the founder are also responsible for ensuring that the organization has the potential to be highly successful in the long term. This requires preserving the core values of the business, while at the same time making sure that there are mechanisms in the organization that can stimulate progress and innovation.

Although some ventures can survive as virtual organizations, primarily using the market and alliances as support, most ventures create an organization that is hierarchical and divides authority and task responsibility among its members. As the firm's strategy changes and its industry develops, the entrepreneur must reappraise the earlier choices of which things to do internally and which to leave to the market.

The performance of the new venture should be measured on four different dimensions: financial, customer relations, internal business process, and growth and development. A balanced approach to performance helps the new venture develop the skills, capabilities, and resources necessary for survival and growth.

The entrepreneur and the TMT are responsible for the business's culture and ethical climate. Creating an exciting and motivating environment for employees is a challenge that must be met. The entrepreneur should employ innovative methods in compensation, training, promotion and advancement, job autonomy, and total quality of life. Attention paid to human resources can have long-term benefits for the firm and be a continuing source of advantage.

Key Terms

- Absolute rule
- Advisory board
- Architect of organizational purpose
- Balanced scorecard
- BHAG
- Built to last
- Challengers
- Clock-building
- Collaborators
- Communicators
- Conglomerate
- Contributors
- Core ideology
- Core purpose
- Core values
- Cultural diversity

- Culture
- Departmentalization
- Divisional structure
- Envisioned future
- Familiars
- Fiduciary board
- Gain-sharing
- Groupshift
- Groupthink
- Holding company
- Innovator dilemma
- Material rewards
- Multidivisional structure
- Nonmaterial rewards
- Organizational leader
- Personal leader
- Preserve the core

- Process-oriented communication
- Promoter dilemma
- Relationship dilemma
- Relativist approach
- Self-serving communication
- Simple structure
- Stimulate progress
- "Structure follows strategy"
- Task-oriented communication
- Team
- Time-telling
- Unfamiliars
- Utilitarian rule
- Virtual organization
- Working group

Discussion Questions

1. What are the three leadership roles of the entrepreneur? Give examples of each.
2. How is a team different from a working group? Give examples.
3. Where do the venture's TMT members come from? What are the pros and cons of recruiting familiars versus unfamiliars?
4. What are the arguments for and against a TMT that is culturally diverse?
5. What types of efforts must be made to maintain a TMT as a high-performing group?
6. What is the role of the board of directors? How can the board and the entrepreneur cooperate to make the venture a success?
7. What is a virtual organization? How can it exist and survive? When is a virtual organization an effective way of organizing the new venture?
8. Describe the changes in organizational structure that a firm might go through as it grows.

9. How do entrepreneurial organizations create and maintain culture?
10. What are some of the major ethical issues for the entrepreneur? Give examples. How should these be resolved?
11. How can the management of human resources reinforce the culture, the ethics, and the values of the entrepreneur? Give examples.

Exercises

1. Construct an "ideal" TMT for a new venture or for your business plan project.
2. Role-playing exercise: Recruit a potential TMT member away from a large corporation and convince this person to join your team.
3. Decide which activities your business plan project venture should do for itself and which it should rely on the market for.
4. Create an organization chart for your business plan project. What are the duties, responsibilities, and reporting relationships of the people represented in the chart?
5. What are the entrepreneurial values you wish to create and sustain in your business plan project organization? How will you do this?
6. Create a balanced scorecard for your new venture. What are your goals and what specific measures could you choose?

Building a Restaurant Organization

It isn't easy to get a job as a waiter at the Redeye Grill or Trattoria Dell'Arte in Manhattan. Proving that you're a whiz at remembering drink orders, have a Samson-like ability to lift heavy trays, or even that you have years of food service experience may not get you the job. Prospective waiters and managers at these restaurants are sometimes screened by a psychotherapist, and they have to demonstrate that they have *warmth*. "We pride ourselves on not just hiring smart people but people who still talk to their parents," says owner Shelly Fireman. "If their home was too dysfunctional, how can they present hospitality?"

Hospitality is very important to Fireman. You could say that he's obsessed with it. He passes out free hors d'oeuvres to guests waiting in the lounge at Shelly's, his Manhattan steak and seafood restaurant. The names of his most loyal customers are engraved on plaques that line the walls of the Brooklyn Diner, his ethnic Jewish restaurant. He even sends diners at the Redeye Grill out the door with fresh-baked cookies. "I try to build a place with personality, something that people will go home and remember," he says.

Fireman started life as a poor kid in New York. Today, he and his family still live above one of his restaurants, but now it's 41 stories above it in a penthouse apartment. He opened his first restaurant with $500 and a certificate from a 3-month food study course sponsored by the New York Public Library. Known as "The Hip Bagel," the restaurant was featured in a brief scene in a Woody Allen movie. Today, Fireman operates six New York restaurants that feed 5,200 people a day and produce annual revenues in excess of $55 million.

Fireman sees himself as a retailer, and not as a restaurateur. "He knows how to get to the bottom line," observes fellow restaurant owner Ken Aretsky. "He looks at food and liquor as someone else would look at pants and shirts." Fireman makes sure his merchandise tastes good, dreaming up new dishes and visiting each location to sample the menu. "This isn't it, darling," he tells a chef at the Brooklyn Diner after tasting the chopped liver. "I love you, but it isn't it." Ken Aretsky points out that some Fireman restaurants have gone through several name and menu changes before finding the winning formula. "Unlike a lot of us, he's not afraid to close a place and reopen it, to change it until he gets it right."

He gets it so right that Helen Hunt, Jerry Seinfeld, and Sarah Jessica Parker are among his regular patrons, and Fireman may be expanding some of his restaurants to national or international locations. But it's commitment to excellence and not pure culinary talent that seems to be responsible for Fireman's success. "I would have been successful at anything," he says. "I'm a hard-working, thinking being."

CASE QUESTIONS

1. In *Built to Last* terms, is Shelly Fireman a time-teller or a clock-builder? Why?

2. List what you think some of the Fireman restaurants' core values are. What would you say is their core purpose?

3. Suggest a BHAG for the Fireman restaurant organization.

4. What strategies could Shelly Fireman implement now to ensure that his restaurants will be "built to last"?

Source: Adapted from Joanne Kaufman, "A Restaurateur's Key Ingredient: Tenacity," *The Wall Street Journal,* August 7, 2001, p. A12.

CHAPTER

Corporate Venturing, Networking, and Franchising

Nothing is so firmly believed as what we least know.
—MICHEL DE MONTAIGNE

Outline

Learning Objectives

After reading this chapter, you will understand:

■ What intrapreneurship is, and why some corporations adopt it
■ The differences between intrapreneurship and entrepreneurship
■ The obstacles to intrapreneurship
■ The motivation for a business to form a joint venture
■ The kinds of business alliances and alliance behaviors
■ The pros and cons of franchising

O ur previous discussions of entrepreneurship have focused almost exclusively on the creation of independently owned and operated enterprises. Part of this focus was a function of our definition of entrepreneurship in Chapter 2: "the creation of an innovative economic organization (or network or organizations) for the purpose of gain or growth under conditions of risk and uncertainty." This limiting definition helped simplify much of the analysis, allowing us to examine the foundations of entrepreneurship that are common to all new ventures. In fact, the constraints of this definition do apply to a large proportion of entrepreneurial events. In this chapter, however, we will ease the constraints on this simplification and describe and analyze new venture creation in other contexts and environments.

First, we will relax the requirement that all entrepreneurship exists through the formation of independent firms. Large corporations create ventures, too. This phenomenon is called "intrapreneurship," with the prefix *intra* denoting "inside" the organization.[1] Intrapreneurship is different from entrepreneurship in a number of significant ways: the motivation for developing new ventures, the consequences and rewards to the individuals and teams involved, the process of new venture creation, and the barriers and opportunities along the way. Because intrapreneurship has become such an important aspect of the restructuring of U.S. businesses, guidelines for successful efforts in this area have been developed from a number of sources. These guidelines will be presented in this chapter.

The second part of this chapter deals with networking and alliances. Just as corporate venturing is one way for a large organization to expand its scope and still maintain control, networking and alliance formation enable the entrepreneur to control and leverage more resources. By joining with other organizations, both smaller and larger, our new venture can extend its reach and the scope of its activity.

The last part of the chapter examines franchising. Franchising has provided hundreds of thousands of people the opportunity to own and operate their own businesses. It is an important organizational form for both domestic and international business, and it has been the source of many entrepreneurial fortunes. Franchising is a hybrid form of organization in that it combines the entrepreneur's venture and resources in a unique way with other entrepreneurs' human and financial assets. The chapter concludes with a set of guidelines that can be used to evaluate a franchise opportunity.

INTRAPRENEURSHIP

In all sectors of today's global economy, large corporations are developing new products and services and creating innovative technologies and systems. When these creations are closely related to existing products or services, they take the form of line extensions, brand extensions, and related-product development. This is *not* what we mean when we identify intrapreneurship in the corporate setting. Brand proliferation and "line extensions can make a lot of money, but Honey Nut Cheerios and Diet Cherry Coke are probably not the path to world economic leadership."[2]

Similarly, if the technological innovations are natural extensions of contemporary scientific development, and if they are used to solve old problems in a more effective or efficient manner, this, too, is *not* what intrapreneurship is about. Although innovations and incremental changes are important to corporate success, they are not directly part of the intrapreneurship phenomenon.[3]

Intrapreneurship, rather, is the development, within a large corporation, of internal markets and relatively small autonomous or semiautonomous business units, producing products, services, or technologies that employ the firm's resources in a unique way.[4] It is something new for the corporation and represents, in its fullest manifestations, a complete break with the past. Intrapreneurship gives the managers of a corporation the freedom to take initiative and try new ideas. It is entrepreneurship within an existing business.

E-NOTES 10-1

Intrapreneurship

Intrapreneurship can be defined as:

- entrepreneurship within an existing business
- the development within a corporation of internal markets or autonomous or semi-autonomous business units that produce products, services, or technologies in a unique way
- an opportunity for corporate managers to take initiative and try new ideas
- an internal corporate venture (ICV)

The Need for Intrapreneurship

Why do existing businesses allow this internal entrepreneurship and encourage intrapreneurial efforts?[5] They do so because top executives in the corporate world generally recognize that the macroenvironment and the marketplace change much faster than a corporate bureaucracy can. Intrapreneurship provides large corporations the opportunity to adapt to the increasingly dynamic, hostile, and heterogeneous environment businesses face today.[6]

It also enables the corporation to diversify from its core business through internal processes. Many companies have an aversion to trying new technologies and products that were "not invented here." Diversification by acquisition and merger is often a risky business, with the corporation overpaying for an acquisition (known as Winner's Curse) or merging with a partner that does not share the goals and values of the company. Internal development is often preferred because it allows the corporation to manage the process and control its costs.

Intrapreneurship gives the corporation the ability and opportunity to conduct market experiments. These experiments can be compared to the evolutionary biological process of natural selection. Each intrapreneurial venture is a form of mutation of current corporate resources. These mutations provide diversity. If the corporate and economic environment is receptive to the mutation, it is "selected" and may grow into a large and profitable division or company. Other corporations may imitate the success, and a whole population of these types of businesses may emerge. Just as entrepreneurship can help to create entire new industries, so can intrapreneurship.

Intrapreneurship has additional value to established corporations. It can be used as a training ground for new managers. Corporations can develop future leaders by monitoring the progress of these intrapreneurs. Managers who can succeed in the new venture have much to offer the "mother" firm.

Also, intrapreneurial activities help to open new channels of distribution. This has been especially true with the emergence of the Internet. Established firms have used the Internet to sell directly to customers, to form cooperatives with other firms for selling and purchasing, and to develop consumer data and knowledge bases. Pepsico, for example, has used the Web to find a new generation of customers. Their Web site, pepsistuff.com, enables consumers to collect points for prizes on bottle caps. The results of this short campaign netted Pepsi 3 million logged and registered users, giving the company a database that would have cost millions and taken months to build. Sales volume rose 5 percent during the promotion, and the cost was about one-fifth of a mail-in project.[7]

Finally, established corporations use intrapreneuring activities to augment their bottom line. They do this primarily through direct investment in entrepreneurial companies. Table 10-1 lists the big corporate venture investors for 2000 by the volume of their IPO activity.

E-NOTES 10-2

Reasons for Intrapreneurship

Intrapreneurship provides a corporation with the ability to:

- adapt quickly to changes in the macroenvironment
- diversify from the core business
- conduct market experiments
- train new managers and leaders
- establish new channels of distribution
- invest and profit from new venture creation

A few U.S. companies are noted for their sustained ability to be intrapreneurial. Among these are Procter & Gamble, Johnson & Johnson, and the 3M Company of Minneapolis, Minnesota.[8] 3M has created over 100 new businesses or major product lines in its history. Four out of five of these have been successful. At 3M, any young engineer can pitch a new business or product idea to top management and be appointed head of the project if it is approved. The project or new venture is then set up as a separate business. The innovative product is assigned a project manager, who remains in charge of the venture until it is successful or abandoned. The project manager can mobilize all the skills and resources necessary for the product's development. The incentives for the new business team are aligned with the project's success—members of the team are rewarded and promoted as the business grows.

A newcomer and entrepreneurial venture itself, Virgin Group Ltd. of the United Kingdom has been one of the most intrapreneurial users of the Internet in the world. Street Story 10-1 gives us a rundown of Virgin founder and CEO Richard Branson's latest endeavors.

TABLE 10-1 Value Generated by Corporations Through IPOs in 2000		

Based on value of shares held by corporations minus original equity investment. Calculated using SEC filings and share price of company as of 12/31/00. Does not include stakes that corporations acquired through spinoffs or transfers of technology or assets.

Company	*Value Generated*	*Companies Taken Public*
Cisco Systems Inc.	$667 million	Corvis Corp., Equinox, NuanceComm., Oplink Comm.
Univision Comm. Inc.	$229 million	Entravision Comm.
Motorola Inc.	$221 million	Palm, Nextel Partners, Orchid Biosciences(1)
Nortel Networks Corp.	$183 million	Avici Systems, interWave Comm., Talarian Corp.
Dell Computer Corp.	$175 million	Corio, Divine Interventures, GoAmerica(2), Lante Corp., LivePerson, Neoforma.com, Storage Networks, WebMethods
Qualcomm Corp.	$139 million	Handspring
Global Crossing Ltd.	$124 million	Storage Networks
Compaq Computer Corp.	$108 million	Click Commerce, Matrix One(3), Storage Networks(4)
Novartis	$106 million	Tanox(5), Diversa Corp.
Genentech	$103 million	Inspire Pharmaceuticals, Intermune Pharmaceuticals
Emerson Electric Co.	$97 million	Click Commerce
PE Corp.	$89 million	Aclara Biosciences, Illumina
United Microelectronics Corp.	$89 million	Integrated Telecom Express
Sun Microsystems Inc.	$88 million	Caldera Systems(6), ONI Systems Corp., Resonate, ViryaNet Ltd.
ADC Telecommunications	$69 million	interWave Communications Inc., Vyyo, Mind C.T.I. Ltd.

(1) Invested in Orchid Biosciences, but amount not disclosed.
(2) Price at which Dell invested in GoAmerica not disclosed in S-1, so IPO price of $35 is being used to calculate investment.
(3) Amount invested in MatrixOne not disclosed, so IPO price of $25 is being used.
(4) Invested in Storage Networks, but amount not disclosed.
(5) Price at which Novartis invested in Tanox not disclosed, so IPO price of $28.50 is used.
(6) Invested in Caldera Systems, but holdings not disclosed.

Source: CorporateVenturing.com Used with permission from Asset Alternitives, Wellesley, MA; www.assetnews.com.

Comparison with Entrepreneurship

Compared to external markets and processes, the internal market for ideas, the resource evaluation process, and the individuals who champion intrapreneurship are different.[9] Both intrapreneurs and entrepreneurs seek autonomy and freedom and have fairly long-term perspectives. Intrapreneurs, however, must be much more sensitive to the corporate hierarchy and way of doing things. This means that intrapreneurs still respond

Like a Virgin

He already has an airline, a record label, a music store chain, and more than 165 other businesses. Now Richard C. N. Branson—who claims he doesn't use a computer himself—is operating the 12th most popular Web site in England and spending more than $225 million to develop an array of Internet businesses and services for his Virgin Group Ltd.

You can do more than get an airline ticket or a CD at virgin.com. You can buy a car, negotiate for a home mortgage, purchase securities, order a case of wine, contract for mobile phone service, bid on an online auction, arrange for gas and electricity service, or turn your computer into a digital radio tuner with access to 50 Net channels. Some services are currently available only in the United Kingdom, but Branson hopes to expand many of his Web ventures to the United States and international markets.

The Virgin Internet portal has transformed the company into a cyberconglomerate by linking all the diverse elements of its empire. "A lot of people never thought Virgin was very logical because we didn't specialize in any one area," says Branson. "But then the Internet comes along, and I'm able to pretend that it was all a carefully crafted plan." Web surfers visit the site for one reason, and end up staying for more. "I normally use Virgin's Web site for entertainment lists, but I was surprised by the amount of stuff they offer," notes Steven Scott, a London-based Web designer. Scott ended up purchasing CDs and pricing airline tickets after checking the movie listings.

The company's marketing for its new ventures has been aided by its easily recognizable red and white logo, its aggressive advertising, and the company's reputation for being "cool" and delivering exceptional service. Jaime Wood, head of European equity research at J.P. Morgan & Co., thinks it's a winning strategy: "The Web works best when a brand aggregates a variety of services into one place with a guaranteed level of service."

The Internet has also reduced Virgin's costs for everything from CDs to airline parts. Instead of inventorying items in a warehouse, Virgin now uses the Web to order items as needed, enabling them to reduce their costs by 15 percent.

Virgin.com's greatest success may lie ahead. Branson believes that cell phones, not personal computers, will be handling many Web transactions by 2005. The company is poised to take advantage of that trend because it already sells mobile phones and sponsors a wireless network. Cell phones will also give Virgin an innovative and inexpensive way to market directly to customers by using short text messages to promote its products.

Whether or not he's right, there's no denying that Virgin's intrapreneurial use of the Internet has not only diversified their core business, but also "virtually" changed that business. "Virgin.com isn't a company, it's a brand," observes Will Whitehorn, Virgin's director for e-commerce activities.

Source: Adapted from Kerry Capell, "Virgin Takes E-wing," *Business Week e.biz,* January 22, 2001, pp. EB 30–34.

to traditional corporate rewards and must be politically astute. Although intrapreneurs must deal with a bureaucracy and corporate culture, they also have a support system to help with their projects. Although intrapreneurs must gather approval, entrepreneurs must gather nerve.[10]

Both intrapreneurs and entrepreneurs disdain status symbols in the short term, preferring to get the venture off the ground. Entrepreneurs can maintain more independence in decision making, but they pay a higher price by putting financial resources at risk. Corporate intrapreneurs are just as likely as independents to have a technical background. Although independents have to rely on their own market research, intrapreneurs have to sell their ideas to their own organization before worrying about the outside market.[11]

Although entrepreneurs search markets to acquire resources for new ventures, intrapreneurs typically look inside the organization for resources that are not currently being used or employed efficiently. The intrapreneur can pry these resources for some current business operation; they probably closely resemble the corporation's core resources. In other words, the machines and physical plant the corporation is not using are probably not too different from the same resources actually being employed. The same can be said for human, technical, and organizational resources. The trick, then, for the intrapreneur is to employ these resources in a way that is sufficiently different from their traditional use.

There is also a basic difference between intrapreneurs and entrepreneurs regarding the separation of ownership and control.[12] Entrepreneurs own and control their businesses, so ownership and control are not separated and there are no inconsistencies. In a large corporation, however, the shareholders are the principals (owners) and the managers are the agents. However, when a manager wants to undertake an intrapreneurial venture, the manager needs to be able to act as a principal and have the same incentives as a principal. The owners of the corporation tend to discourage this because they are unwilling to trust managers and give them these types of incentives. Frequently, this means that intrapreneurs are forced to leave the company. Although this resolves the agency problem, it often leaves the corporation worse off, for managers leave with resources that are valuable, rare, hard to copy, and nonsubstitutable. Most often these resources are technical information, expertise, and the manager (the human resource). The corporation is left with less intrapreneurship than it needs to be successful.

The Process of Intrapreneurship

There are five recognizable stages in the process of intrapreneurship or corporate venturing.[13]

Problem Definition   Stage 1 begins with problem definition. Problems—or alternatively, opportunities—may come from sources within the company or industry. The key to recognizing intrapreneurial opportunities is to be sensitive to change and open to surprise. One source of ideas comes from unexpected occurrences[14]—either unexpected successes or unexpected failures. If customers are demanding a product or service into which the corporation did not put much effort or thought, this success can be a source of an entirely new business once enough resources are invested. Similarly, if a product is a failure, understanding why and determining what the customer really wants can also launch an intrapreneurial venture. For example, 3M developed an adhesive that no industrial user seemed to want and was ready to abandon the product. The engineer who led the project took the samples home and let his family use them. He discovered that his teenage daughters used the tape to hold their curls overnight. He recognized that there might be household and personal uses for the adhesive, later renamed Scotch tape.[15]

Incongruities—things that stick out as not being consistent—can also be the source of ideas.[16] That is, disparities between the assumption of an industry or business and economic realities give rise to ideas for intrapreneurial opportunity. Questioning the conventional wisdom ("everybody knows") or the perceived practice ("it's the way things are done") can point up these incongruities. When what "everybody knows" is no longer known and accepted by everyone, and when the way things are done doesn't work anymore, resources can potentially be redeployed to exploit an opportunity.

Coalition Building   Stage 2 requires coalition building. The intrapreneur must develop relationships within the corporate bureaucracy that help support the innovative project throughout its early development. This parallels the entrepreneur's search for legitimate partners and supporters. For an idea to attract support, it must in some way "fit" with the company and be congruent with company goals. This is a paradox of sorts, because if the innovation is too congruent, it is not innovative. To sell the idea, though, the intrapreneur does need to make this case. In addition to personal persuasion, the best vehicle for drumming up support and building a coalition is the business plan. We described the business plan for an entrepreneur in Chapter 5. The major differences between an intrapreneurial business plan and an entrepreneurial one are:

1. The intrapreneurial plan does not have an ownership section that details the conditions and requirements for selling shares. The corporation "owns" the venture.

2. The intrapreneurial plan does not seek outside financing. However, it does need to meet the requirements of the corporation's internal financing and capital-budgeting criteria.

3. The intrapreneurial plan needs a section to describe the relationship (strategic, operational, financial, and marketing) between the corporation and the internal corporate venture.

The business plan helps the intrapreneur find a sponsor or set of sponsors, who can then help get resources and pave the way for political acceptance. This is crucial, because corporate managers and the bureaucracy often see these **internal corporate ventures (ICVs)** as threats to the current power structure and resource allocation process. Also, the sponsor will help the intrapreneur remain objective about the prospects for success and failure. It is easy to lose objectivity when caught up in the excitement of creative innovation.

Resource Mobilization   Stage 3 calls for resource mobilization. The intrapreneur is looking for the same types of resources as the entrepreneur: physical, technological, financial, organizational, human, and reputational. To make the internal corporate venture a success: They must be rare, valuable, imperfectly imitable, and have no good substitutes. In the early stages of resource acquisition, the intrapreneur may be "borrowing" resources that are officially assigned to others in the corporation. As the project gains momentum and resource needs mount, official and formal recognition of the

ICV is needed. This will occur when the ICV passes the test of the corporation's internal capital market and receives its official budget.

Project Execution   Stage 4 is the actual execution of the ICV. It is parallel to an entrepreneur's official launch of a new venture, except that there are multiple levels of managers with different degrees of experience.[17] Otherwise, a similar set of conditions now surrounds the execution of the intrapreneurial strategy (see Chapter 4). The ICV must develop its entry strategy and determine its entry wedges. If it has first-mover advantage, it must employ isolating mechanisms to protect its advantage for as long as possible. It must assess the industry environment, both static and dynamic, and make appropriate operating and tactical decisions. It may be necessary to open the ICV to influences from external sources and to recruit personnel and technology from outside.[18] Finally, the venture must adopt a strategic posture and put criteria for evaluating performance and strategy in place.

Venture Completion   Stage 5 is the venture-completion phase. If the ICV has been less than a success, it can be dismantled and its resources reabsorbed by the corporation. If it has been successful, it can be continued and additional investment can be made. The more or less permanent position of the ICV in the organizational structure (see Chapter 9) should be established at this time. If the agency problem has proved too difficult to overcome for any reason (uncertainty, incentive alignment, opportunism), the ICV may become a spin-off—a completely independent company.[19] In such a case, the intrapreneurial managers can buy the assets from the corporation and then sell stock to the investment community or the public.

Even though they understand the process, recognize an ICV's potential benefits, and have extensive knowledge of the impediments to intrapreneurship, corporations nevertheless find the task daunting. They need to recognize, however, that intrapreneurs and a viable intrapreneuring process are two resources that are rare, valuable, imperfectly imitable, and nonsubstitutable. Thus, intrapreneurship is a source of sustainable competitive advantage.

Opportunities and Barriers to Intrapreneurship

Large companies have certain advantages in creating and exploiting intrapreneurial ideas. Some of these advantages relate directly to the intrapreneurs. Intrapreneurs are somewhat more secure operating from a position within a large organization. They already have a job and a steady income with benefits. They benefit from being part of a social network within the firm, a group of friends, colleagues, and knowledgeable individuals who can provide encouragement, resources, and technical aid.

Intrapreneurial Resources   The financial resources for the internal corporate venture come from the corporation. Although no corporation has unlimited financial resources, it must have resources well beyond the capabilities of private individuals and their friends and relatives. This source of financing lowers the personal financial risk for intrapreneurs. Of course, there is an element of career risk if an intrapreneur is unable to make the new venture a success. However, a supportive environment for intrapreneurship is more forgiving of failure than the external environment facing independent entrepreneurs.

Moreover, the corporation has all or most of the necessary resources that will make up the resource base of the new venture. It already has a set of organizational systems—marketing, engineering, personnel, legal, and accounting—that have many of the attributes that support its sustainable competitive advantage. Finally, most large corporations have a visibility and a reputation that can be extended to the new venture. These can provide early credibility and legitimacy for the intrapreneurial effort and act as strategic momentum factors.

Intrapreneurial Barriers   However, there are also barriers to corporate venturing and impediments to successful execution.[20] The major barrier is the corporate bureaucracy. Large corporations have many levels of management, and often all levels must approve the use of company resources for the intrapreneurial venture. Rules, procedures, and processes slow down decision making at the very time it should be expedited. A recent study shows that one of the ways that intrapreneurial efforts can be structured for success is through the image of a "loosely coupled system." The internal venture requires independence and limited contact with the corporate host.[21]

Sometimes the new venture threatens another product that the company produces, and incumbent product managers put up resistance. Frequently, there are opposing requests for resources in the corporation, and resources devoted to the new venture cannot be used to support established products and markets. Often people do not wish to change their orientations, goals, and behaviors to do the things necessary to implement change. The paradox here is that the very security the large corporation provides that enables a manager to take a risk also discourages people from taking any risks.

There are structural impediments as well. Internal capital markets lack venture capitalists. Venture capitalists can be very important contributors to the success of new ventures: They have technical expertise, contacts, and experience initiating new ventures that most corporate executives lack. Without venture capitalists, the investment process resembles a capital-budgeting exercise and may fail to capture all the subtleties of entrepreneurship. This can lead to the corporation's managing resources for efficiency and return on investment rather than for long-term advantages.[22]

In the same vein, intrapreneurs do not own the ICV. The incentives and risks are, therefore, different from those of independent entrepreneurship. Uniformly compensating everyone involved—a bureaucratic procedure—removes an important motivating force for the ICV. The result is that the corporation either abandons projects prematurely or escalates commitment to projects that have little chance of success.[23]

Some people doubt whether true entrepreneurship can ever exist inside a corporation.[24] Many companies that began as entrepreneurial ventures lose their fervor and excitement as they become investment-grade corporations. It is difficult to pay the rewards of intrapreneurship without incurring the resentment of other employees and managers. Shifting the major reward mechanism from status and rank to contribution to earnings is a challenge for the corporation.[25] Some companies may succeed for a while in motivating their brightest people to start ICVs, but because most of the rewards accrue to the corporation, these people are almost always destined to leave the confines of the larger corporation to start their own businesses.

Barriers to Intrapreneurship

- corporate bureaucracy
- internal product competition
- competing demands for resources
- resistance to change
- absence of "internal venture capitalists" for guidance
- employees' lack of ownership reduces commitment
- corporate environment not as free to creative people as entrepreneurial environment

---

Guidelines for Success

Intrapreneurship does not work without radical changes in the thinking of corporate managers and their stockholders.[26] Even when these changes have been implemented, successful intrapreneurship may develop only after the corporation has gained some experience and learned some lessons from the market.[27] Top corporate executives must nurture the atmosphere and supply the vision necessary to encourage their people to intrapreneurial activity.[28] Intrapreneurs practically need a bill of rights to set them free and enable them to simulate the external entrepreneurial environment within the organization. These "freedom factors," developed by Pinchot, are as follows:

1. *The right to appoint oneself as an intrapreneur.* Intrapreneurs cannot wait for the corporation to discover them and then promote them to an intrapreneurial position. People must have the right to take initiative themselves.

2. *The right to stay with the venture.* Corporations often force the originators of ideas and projects to hand off their creations as they require additional resources, expertise, and become better developed and bigger. Intrapreneurs need the right to continue with the project and see it through.

3. *The right to make decisions.* Intrapreneurs need the right to make the important decisions that affect the future of the venture. Pushing decision making up the hierarchy moves it from people who know and care to people who don't.

4. *The right to appropriate corporate slack.* In large bureaucracies, managers control resources so tightly it is often impossible to redeploy them to more productive uses. Intrapreneurs need discretion to use a percentage of their budgets, time, and physical resources to develop new ideas.

5. *The right to start small.* Large corporations have a home-run philosophy. They prefer to have a few well-planned large projects going. Intrapreneurs need permission to create many smaller, experimental ventures and let natural selection processes produce the winners.

6. *The right to fail.* Intrapreneurship cannot be successful without risk, trial and error, mistakes, and failures. False starts are part of the process. If intrapreneurs are punished for failure, they will leave the organization, and others will be reluctant ever to take chances again.

7. *The right to take enough time to succeed.* The corporation cannot set unrealistically short deadlines for intrapreneurial efforts to succeed. They must be patient with their investment.

8. *The right to cross borders.* Intrapreneurs often must cross organizational boundaries to put together the resources and people needed for the project. Corporate managers resist incursions on their turf. Intrapreneurs need passports and the freedom to travel.

9. *The right to recruit team members.* Intrapreneurs need the freedom to recruit for the cross-functional teams they must assemble for the project. The team must be autonomous, and members should have first allegiance to the team, not their former department.

10. *The right to choose.* Independent entrepreneurs can choose among many suppliers, financial sources, customer groups, and personnel. The intrapreneur must not face internal corporate monopolists who constrain the choices for procuring resources. The intrapreneur needs the freedom to choose from external sources when they are superior.[29]

NETWORKING AND ALLIANCES

According to Peter Drucker, large corporations that do not or cannot learn to innovate and intrapreneur will not survive. He says for some companies that means reinventing themselves. Increasingly, large companies are growing through alliances and joint ventures, yet very few of the big boys know how to manage an alliance. They're used to giving orders, not to working with a partner, and it's totally different. In an alliance or a joint venture, you have to begin by asking, "What do our partners want? What are our shared values and goals?" Those aren't easy questions for somebody who grew up at GE or Citibank and is now at the top or near the top of a huge worldwide enterprise.[30]

Today's entrepreneurs are deeply embedded in networks, partnerships, alliances, and collectives.[31] **Networking**, the process of enlarging the entrepreneur's circle of trust, is a negotiation process.[32] How entrepreneurs access networks and how those help them succeed are the subjects of this section.

Benefits and Motivations for Networking

Entrepreneurs usually have a wide range of friends, acquaintances, and business associates. They are able to make use of these **informal network** relationships to obtain resources and opportunities for their firms. These networks provide them with information about their environment, and they enable entrepreneurs to build reputation and credibility for themselves and their firms. Networks of people (and of other firms) are socially complex, casually ambiguous, and usually very idiosyncratic. They depend on that particular entrepreneur. The networks themselves can be sources of sustainable competitive advantage as well as a means of procuring other resources that can be a source of sustainable competitive advantage.

We have already touched on many of the opportunities that entrepreneurs have for various forms of networking. We talked about the pros and cons of taking in a partner in Chapter 8 when we discussed legal forms of organization. We illustrated the benefits of alliances called "virtual organizations" in Chapter 9. We talked briefly about joint ventures in Chapter 4 when we discussed momentum factors and entrepreneurial strategy. We saw how networks are important in finding sources of financing (Chapter 7). The modern "well-connected" entrepreneur has distinct advantages over the "rugged individual" of previous generations.

We can also distinguish four basic motivations for **formal network** participation or joint-venture formation.[33] (1) Joint ventures increase the internal capabilities of the venture and protect its resources, (2) joint ventures have competitive uses that strengthen the current strategic position, (3) joint ventures have longer-term strategic advantages that augment the venture's resource flexibility for the future, and (4) joint ventures further the social concerns and promote the values of entrepreneurs.[34]

E-NOTES 10-4

Joint Ventures

A joint venture is an organization:

- created by two or more independent organizations
- for a specific purpose
- over a set period of time

Internal Motivations   Internal uses of alliances are motivated by various cost and risk-sharing arrangements. These help reduce uncertainty for the venture. For example, sharing the outputs of minimum-efficient-scale plants avoids wasteful duplication of resources, utilizes by-products and processes, and maybe even allows the partners to share brands and distribution channels. Joint ventures can also be used to obtain intelligence and to open a window on new technologies and customers. These relationships can help a firm copy and imitate innovative managerial practices, superior management systems, and improved communications patterns.

For example, the Japanese industrial giant Matsushita came to Silicon Valley in the late 1990s to learn from the many start-ups there. They invested $50 million in an incubator and a venture capital fund and lured nine new high-tech American businesses to it. All of these companies are potential suppliers or partners for Matsushita's number one brand, Panasonic. They hope to learn from these companies as well as expand their innovation network.[35]

Sometimes businesses cooperate to save time. For example, Richard Kauflin, president of Supersign Inc., of Boulder, Colorado, which makes and installs signs, has an agreement with two other local companies. He can borrow supplies from them if he runs out, and he lends them his company's hydraulic-lift truck when they need it. In explaining the motivations for the cooperation, he says, "It's expedient. We'd have to wait a week to get some of these things delivered or go all the way to Denver to pick them up."

External Motivations   External motivations for alliance behavior lead to improved current strategic positions. A set of firms is more likely to be able to influence the structure of an industry's evolution than a single firm. Sometimes a joint venture can serve to preempt possible entrants and thereby give the partnership a first-mover advantage that is unlikely to be challenged. This first-mover advantage can be extended to gaining rapid access to the most desirable customers and obtaining their loyalty, expanding capacity to serve the entire market niche, and acquiring resources on advantageous terms before they become fully valued. Also, it is quite common to take on a foreign partner when entering that partner's domestic market.

Strategic Motivations   The third motivation concerns the future position and resources of the venture. Joint ventures can be undertaken for creative reasons, to exploit synergies, to develop new technologies, or to extend old technologies to new problems. Joint ventures can be a mechanism to give the firm a toehold in a market that is not completely ready for the product or service but needs long-term credibility. For example, many entrepreneurs are currently engaged in joint ventures in China and Russia. Most of these have no current payoff possibilities. But the entrepreneurs recognize that in the longer term, the relationships created and the knowledge developed will serve them well.

Social Motivations   A final motivation for entrepreneurs to engage in networking is to promote their own values and social agenda. One such network is the Social Venture Network (SVN). The primary goal of the members of the SVN is simple: They get to meet other entrepreneurs who are committed to social change through business. The network is a loose collection of entrepreneurs, social activists, corporate executives, and philanthropists. It has attracted some high-visibility entrepreneurs: Mitch Kapor of Lotus Development Corp.; Joe LaBonte, president of Reebok International Co.; Mel Ziegler, founder of Banana Republic and Republic of Tea; Anita Roddick, founder of The Body Shop International Inc., the British skin and hair-care firm; and, of course, Ben Cohen, cofounder of the ice cream maker, Ben & Jerry's Homemade Inc. You can visit the SVN online at www.svn.org.

The network brings individuals of common purpose together, but not just any individuals. "The idea is not just to get people interested in social action, but in social action by successfully growing companies," says Joshua Mailman, the cofounder of SVN. "We provide a peer network for people that's based on values, not just on business. We are the YPO [Young President's Organization] for the '90s."[36]

E-NOTES 10-5

Reasons for Joint Ventures

Businesses are motivated to participate in formal networks or joint-venture formation in order to:

- increase internal capabilities and protect resources (internal motivation)
- strengthen strategic position and competitiveness (external motivation)
- develop long-term strategic advantages that increase future flexibility (strategic motivation)
- further social concerns and values of entrepreneurs (social motivation)

Types of Networks

One type of network is known as the **personal network**. This is an informal network that consists of all the direct, face-to-face-contacts the entrepreneur has.[37] These include friends, family, close business associates, former teachers and professors, among others. The ongoing relationships in a personal network are based on three benefits: trust, predictability, and "voice."[38]

Trust enables the entrepreneur to forgo all of the activities and legal formalities that guard against opportunism. The entrepreneur can negotiate within a personal network without worrying about monitoring and controlling the other side. Trust can replace contracts and save the need to incur legal costs. Trust can enable the parties to enter into agreements without having to specify the details of who will do what, and when, and for how much. It means that the entrepreneur has the flexibility to call on resources and people very quickly.

Predictability reduces uncertainty. People within the personal network behave the same way time and time again. Their patterns of behavior are well known, as are their values and beliefs. Their consistent behavior enables the entrepreneur to have a mental map of the personal network—to know who will be where and when. Thus, he or she can navigate through the personal network rapidly when resources and information are needed for business purposes.

The third benefit of the personal network is **voice**—the permission to argue, negotiate, complain, and verbally dispute any problem within the network and still maintain good relations with the person on the receiving end. This permission, or norm, can be contrasted with the norm of **exit**. In some relationships characterized by less trust, once reciprocity is broken, displeasure is communicated, or a verbal argument takes place, the parties feel pressure not to do business anymore, and they "exit" from the network.[39]

Personal networks have **strong ties**.[40] Such ties are formed because the relationship may have a long history, there may be a family relationship, or people may share a common culture, common values, or common associations. Strong ties are especially important in the early stages of business formation, particularly in financing and securing the initial resources for new venture creations.[41]

The second type of network is the **extended network**.[42] Extended networks are formal, firm-to-firm relationships. The entrepreneur develops these by means of boundary-spanning activities with other owners and managers of enterprises, customers and vendors, and other constituents in the operating environment. These are the normal cross-organizational activities that are required for the operation as an "open system."[43] Extended networks become more important to the firm as it moves beyond the initial founding stage.

Extended networks contain more diversity than personal networks and, consequently, more information. The relationships are more instrumental and based less on trust. There is also more uncertainty and less predictability in these relationships. The customer of a customer may be included, as well as the supplier of a supplier. There may be many indirect associations in an extended network. As a result, these are **weak ties**.

But there is "strength in weak ties."[44] Weak ties enable the network to be much larger. As such, it will contain more diverse information, people, resources, and channels for the entrepreneur to use. Whereas strong ties produce trust but redundancy, weak ties provide unique information about opportunities, locations, potential markets for goods and services, potential investors, and the like. In addition, the extended network adds to the credibility and legitimacy of the firm and expands its reputational capital.

Outside directors who are involved in the enterprise and make a contribution provide a good example of the benefits of weak ties. These outside directors provide an invaluable check on the entrepreneur's decisions, and possible mistakes, by complementing the entrepreneur's information base and offering an objective outside viewpoint. Their fresh perspective can change the course of the venture's strategy. For example, Kurtz Bros. Inc, a landscape materials business in Cuyahoga Falls, Ohio, is a family business that decided to diversify a few years ago. It was ready to make a move into industrial materials, and initially its management forgot to consult the firm's three outside directors. When these directors heard of the plan, "They were pretty tough on us," concedes Lisa Kurtz, company president. "They told us we were fracturing our organization, and that we should stick to our knitting." The outsiders' views made a deep impression. The family owners quickly reconsidered their decision and liquidated the new unit.[45]

One technological example of the extended network is the proliferation of electronic bulletin boards that are designed and used by entrepreneurs to share and receive information. Take the case of Bill Vick, owner of a Dallas-based executive recruiting firm. When he needed some new ideas for getting clients and building his visibility and reputation, he put out a call for ideas on a bulletin board used by thousands of entrepreneurs. He received many suggestions, including one that proved to be a bonanza: Vick started mailing boxes of Vick's Cough Drops to sales executives with a postcard saying that his firm could "cure sick sales." A few days later at an industry conference, Vick was shaking hands and handing out more cough drops. "That one idea must have gotten me $25,000 worth of business," he says.[46]

Networking takes considerable time and money for the entrepreneur.[47] If the networking does not improve firm performance, it could prove detrimental to the enterprise and frustrating to the entrepreneur. Entrepreneurs should have both strong-tie personal relationships and weak-tie extended relationships. The ideal situation is for them to develop strong-tie extended relationships. By doing this, entrepreneurs can have the speed and flexibility of strong ties as well as the informational and resource advantages of the extended network.

Alliance Behaviors

Entrepreneurs engage in four basic types of alliances: (1) confederations, (2) conjugate alliances, (3) agglomerations, and (4) organic networks. These types are distinguished by two characteristics: (1) whether the relationship is direct or indirect (entrepreneur's business to alliance partner) and (2) whether the relationship is with competing or noncompeting firms.[48] The integration of these two dimensions produces the two-by-two matrix shown in Figure 10-1.

Confederate Alliances   Direct contact with competitors is called a **confederate alliance**, or simply a confederation. In concentrated industries, where a few firms have most of the market to themselves, confederate alliances are usually motivated by an attempt to avoid competition through techniques such as point pricing, uniform price lists, standard costing, and product standardization.[49] Because the alliance resembles a cartel, the firms may find themselves engaged in collusion that violates U.S. anti-trust law.

	Direct Contact	Indirect Contact
Competing Organizations	Confederate alliance	Agglomerate network
Noncompeting Organizations	Conjugate alliance	Organic network

FIGURE 10-1 **A Typology of Alliances**

Source: Adapted from G. Astley and C. Fombrun, "Collective Strategy: Social Ecology of Organizational Environments," *Academy of Management Review* 8 (1983): 576–587.

But smaller firms in fragmented industries—and this applies particularly to new ventures in emerging industries—have many opportunities for cooperation and alliances that are not illegally collusive. For example, firms can share transportation costs by ordering enough for a full-truckload shipment. Or they can engage in bilateral hiring practices. By hiring each other's workers on a regular basis, the firms can share expertise, information, and intelligence about the market, and they can upgrade each other's operational procedures by imitating the best of what the other has to offer.

Entrepreneurs must use good judgment in entering into confederate relationships. There is always the possibility of an unscrupulous competitor taking advantage of the trust inherent in such relationships. Another risk is that former rivals may be tempted to collude to raise profits by restraining production, raising prices, and holding back threatening new technologies. The lack of free-for-all competition can lead to complacency and the stifling of creativity and new ideas.[50]

Conjugate Alliances   Direct contact with noncompeting firms is called a **conjugate alliance.** Examples include long-term purchasing contracts with suppliers and customers and joint research and development projects. Companies that keep their separate identities and engage in conjugate relationships are mimicking the vertical-integration strategies of larger firms and attempting to obtain those benefits without incurring the inherent risks. An example would be a joint R&D effort that enables a manufacturer to test the operating characteristics of a supplier's materials (for a fee) and that reports back to the supplier how the material holds up under various real world operating conditions (an advantage for the supplier). Similar to the confederate form, the conjugate form is a task-oriented, tightly coupled, voluntary relationship within a weak-tie network.

By working together, conjugate networks can do things that no individual firm could accomplish. For example, in Indiana a network called the FlexCell Group combines makers of metalworking patterns and tools with mechanical engineers, producers of plastic injection molding, a prototype machine shop, and a contract machine shop. All the members are independent companies with sales of less than $10 million each. The result is a vertically integrated, "virtual" single-source supplier. Tom Brummett, the owner of the Columbus, Indiana, firm that supplies the network with marketing and management services, says that FlexCell "can offer its existing customer base more capabilities and quicker turnaround time, usually with more cost effectiveness. This is a way for small and medium-size companies to leverage their resources to compete in a global economy." Recently, FlexCell beat out two large multinational corporations from Europe and South America in its bid to produce engine components for a U.S. customer.[51]

Agglomerate Networks   An **agglomerate network**, or an agglomeration, is a set of indirect relationships between firms that are competitors. It serves as an information network that enables the firms to secure information about the capabilities and competencies that are regarded as necessary but not sufficient for success. Control of the network is maintained by dues and membership rules. An example of this type of network is a trade association. Such a network usually exists in highly fragmented and geographically dispersed environments that are populated by very small, homogeneous ventures, such as retailing and small farms. They are loosely coupled, voluntary, and have a low-task structure—no single member of the agglomeration can influence another member to do anything.

Organic Networks   An **organic network** is an indirect relationship (indirect in terms of the business, not the individual entrepreneur who represents the firm) between noncompeting organizations. These relationships are not task-oriented and may consist of strong-tie linkages such as friends and close business associates or weak-tie links such as might be found at the chamber of commerce or within a United Way campaign.

E-NOTES 10-6

Alliances

There are four types of alliances:

- confederations
- conjugate alliances
- agglomerations
- organic networks

Partner Selection Criteria

Choosing a partner for a joint venture, for an alliance, or even for one of the shorter-term relationships just discussed becomes a crucial issue for the entrepreneur.[52] A poor choice can doom not only the joint venture but also the entire enterprise the entrepreneur has worked to build. Two primary criteria must be met:

1. The potential partner must have a strong commitment to the joint venture.
2. The top managements of both firms must be compatible.

The first criterion must be met so that the firms have a mutual sense of responsibility and project ownership. If one side believes the venture is unimportant, it will devote less time and resources to the undertaking and be tempted to behave opportunistically. It may let the other side do all the work and take all the risks, while it enjoys the benefits of cooperation.

The second criterion must be met in order to join the two enterprises' cultures and to develop a strong sense of trust. The top managements of the two firms not only must be able to work together but also must be able to model cooperative behavior for their subordinates. When subordinates see that it is acceptable and even desirable for the two firms to work together and share resources and information, they will be much more likely to cooperate, too. The commitment and leadership of top management are essential.

After these two criteria are met, the other criteria for partner selection are typically contingent on the goals of the joint venture and its nature: product orientation, service delivery, technology sharing, or the like. Partners look attractive when they have complementary skills with little duplication and when the relationship creates a mutual dependency that makes cooperative behavior in everyone's self-interest. Good communications, similar cultures and values, compatible operating policies, and compatible goals—all make partners attractive for selection. A partner with a strong reputation is valuable because it enables the other firm to enhance its legitimacy.[53]

One additional issue for the entrepreneur is the size of the venture partner. Usually firms that meet the criteria listed are of approximately equal size. Many times, however, entrepreneurial firms are still quite small. There are some dangers when a small firm attempts to join forces with another enterprise that is considerably larger. Although sometimes this is justified—for example, when the smaller firm has a technology that is needed by the larger company—problems can be anticipated.

One problem is the distinct possibility that the larger firm will not be as dependent on the relationship for its survival or profitability as the smaller firm. Another is that the larger firm is more likely to have a bureaucratic culture in which decision making can be inflexible and slow. Smaller entrepreneurial firms are likely to feel paralyzed by the snail's pace at which the bureaucracy moves. The larger firm and its employees might feel that they should dominate the venture, because they are the older and historically the more successful of the two companies. This may make the personnel of the smaller firm feel resentful, because they, no doubt, believe that their contribution is just as significant as the larger firm's.[54]

However, not all strategic deals work out well, and frequently the goals and objectives of the large corporation do not meld well with those of the smaller entrepreneurial company. As we can see in Street Story 10-2, Disney and Toysmart's short-lived alliance ended in disaster for one of the partners.

Differences in decision making, flexibility, degree of dependence, and management style all decrease the trust and rapport of the two partners. This need not be fatal. A special operating environment, in which both sides have a free hand and consider themselves equal, can be created. This can reduce red tape and enable the larger firm's employees to feel as if they, too, are part of a smaller unit. Even when one partner is much larger than the other, the larger partner can find a smaller operating unit within its structure to be the counterpart of the small entrepreneurial venture.[55]

A Partnership That Lost the Magic

Toysmart.com looked like a winner.

The Web site started out with the goal of selling enriching and nonviolent toys over the Internet. BizRate, the consumer-rating site, gave it 4.5 stars out of 5. Boston consultant Patricia Seybold labeled it a top five retailing site. Media Metrix ranked it 24th among the most-visited sites on the Web at Christmas.

But it wasn't enough. The foundation for Toysmart was laid in 1997 when David Lord was hired as the chief financial officer for Holt Educational Outlet Inc., a Boston area toy store. One of Lord's first acts was to put the Holt toy business online. In 1998, Lord and Stan Fung, a partner in a venture capital firm, purchased the Holt business and rechristened the Web site as "Toysmart."

Toysmart started out with $500,000 from Fung's venture capital firm, but they decided they needed as much as $25 million to make their business grow. Lord says he had informal commitments for that much from other venture capitalists when he got a call suggesting a partnership with Disney. In addition to investing $25 million, Disney promised $20 million in advertising through Disney-owned companies.

Some small businesses "might think the big company is the salvation of their business plan," observes Chuck Davis, a former Disney executive who helped finalize the deal. "But it's a double-edged sword if the profits don't come in. Big companies are not used to supporting divisions without profits."

The partnership seemed troubled from the start. Delays that Disney caused as they finalized the paperwork hampered Toysmart's inventory build-up and media campaign as they entered the last 3 months of the year, a critical time in the toy business. Christmas sales totaled $6 million instead of the $25 million anticipated. Toysmart complained that they had little contact with key Disney personnel or board members and that the giant corporation kept changing their strategy for their Web-based partner. Disney objected to Toysmart's use of the phrase "good toys" because it implied that some of Disney's other partners made bad toys, and that Disney merchandise like the knife-flourishing characters from the animated movie *Mulan* might also be intrinsically bad. Even Disney advertising didn't help; one analyst claims that $2.6 million in "free" advertising on Disney's Go.com and Family.com Web sites in the fourth quarter produced a mere $66,000 in Toysmart sales.

After running through Disney's entire investment, Toysmart tried to redirect their site and find some new investors, but the Disney-controlled board closed Toysmart down after those efforts failed. A former Toysmart executive now complains that the company was treated "like a stepsister," but a Disney spokesperson responds by saying they could only "have patience where patience is deserved."

Source: Adapted from William M. Bulkeley, Joseph Pereira, and Bruce Orwall, "Toysmart and Disney Found a Tangled Web of Conflicting Goals," *The Wall Street Journal,* June 7, 2000, p. A1.

E-NOTES 10-7

Partner Selection

Both partners in a joint venture, alliance, or business relationship should have:

- strong commitment to joint venture
- compatible top management
- shared goals (product orientation, etc.)
- complementary skills
- good communications
- strong reputations

Processes of Reciprocity

How do entrepreneurs position themselves and their firms to enter into these alliances, networks, and cooperative partnerships? Why do people allow entrepreneurs to do this? From the business viewpoint, the primary reason is that the entrepreneurial firm has something to offer the partner—a skill, a process, a technology, a system for administration, access to a customer, or a desirable location.

But it is the entrepreneur who on a personal level initiates the contact and maintains the relationships so that they may be turned into contracts and formal arrangements. People allow entrepreneurs to approach them with these cooperative and collective strategies for four reasons:

1. *Friendship.* The entrepreneur has developed a nurturing and caring relationship with the people at the target organization.

2. *Liking.* There is pleasure and comfort in reciprocity and finding someone with an affinity and a liking for you.

3. *Gratitude.* The entrepreneur has put a member of the target's firm in his or her personal debt through a personal favor, and the discharge of that debt (reciprocity) is the mechanism for the cooperation.

4. *Obligation.* The target firm must repay some obligation it owes to the entrepreneur.[56]

In each of these cases, the entrepreneur has established a positive environment for cooperation by "being nice" and by doing it first. What kinds of things can entrepreneurs do to encourage cooperative behavior?

1. Share information with the target firm
2. Help the target firm solve a problem and be open to receiving help with a problem of its own
3. Give and receive favors, both business and personal
4. Create opportunities for others to receive recognition and achievement
5. Build and use networks and allow others access to these networks. The entrepreneur's strong ties can be another's weak ties
6. Ask others to make their networks available and piggyback on the reputation and credibility of the partner

E-NOTES 10-8

Forms of Reciprocal Agreements

alliance: an informal agreement between two or more businesses for a specific purpose

partnership: a formal bilateral agreement with pooled assets between two or more businesses for a specific purpose

network: a loose amalgamation for the sharing of information

collective: a group of businesses or individuals organized to work together as one unit

THE FRANCHISING ALTERNATIVE

Another way to expand the organization's boundaries and the reach of its activities is through franchising. **Franchising** is a marketing system by which the owner of a service, trademarked product, or business format grants exclusive rights to an individual for the local distribution and/or sale of the service or product, and in turn receives payment of a franchise fee, royalties, and the promise of conformance to quality standards.[57] The **franchisor** is the seller of the franchise, and the **franchisee** is the buyer.

To what extent is the franchise an entrepreneur? Any distinction between the two must focus on the concept of innovation. The franchisee creates an economic organization, perhaps a network of organizations. Gain and growth are clearly goals, and risk and uncertainty are ever-present. However, because the franchisee is contractually obligated to operate the business in a prescribed manner, he or she has little apparent room for innovation. Also, the franchisee does not usually have total control of the disposal of the business; franchisors usually reserve the right to choose or approve the next franchisee. However, franchisees frequently do make innovations that are either tolerated by the franchisor or adopted by the franchisor and incorporated into the system. For example, some of McDonald's best new product ideas originated with franchisees eager to improve their sales.

Franchising is one of the fastest-growing forms of business and now represents a major share of all business in areas such as fast-food restaurants, auto parts dealers, and quick-print copy shops. Also included in the vast array of franchise opportunities are automobile dealerships, major league sports teams, national and international real estate brokers, child-care centers, and accounting and tax services. A recent study by the International Franchise Association (IFA) was conducted by examining U.S. government data.[58] Some of the highlights of the report (which can be found at www.ifa.org) are:

- There were 1,398 franchising systems in the United States in 1998.
- The largest categories of existing systems are fast food (18 percent, 219 systems) and retailing (11 percent, 139 systems).
- The smallest categories of existing systems are travel (1 percent, 11 systems) and printing (1 percent, 18 systems).
- Lodging is the fastest growing category and now has 60 systems.
- Most franchise systems have between 11 and 50 units (25 percent).
- Sixty-two percent of all systems have been in business for 12 or more years.

- The majority of systems had initial franchise fees of $30,000 or less. Fast food averaged $20,095. Lodging and sports teams had the highest franchise fees.
- The average initial investment (excluding real estate) is under $250,000. It is over $1 million for lodging, but just $182,570 for fast food systems.
- For systems charging royalties based on sales volume, the greatest number of systems charged 4 to 5 percent.
- The median turnover rate (without transfers) for all systems was 5.54 percent.

The fantastic success of franchising is one of the fundamental changes in business in the post–World War II era, but why is franchising so successful for both franchisor and franchisee? How does it work?

E-NOTES 10-9

Franchising

A marketing system where the owner of a service, trademarked product, or business format:

- grants exclusive rights to an individual for local distribution or sale
- receives in return:
    franchise fee
    royalties
    promise of conformance to quality standards

Theoretical Foundations

Franchising is a method of implementing the growth strategy of the franchisor's venture. The successful franchisor possesses resources that are rare, valuable, imperfectly imitable, and nonsubstitutable. Usually these resources are a business concept, an operating system, a brand name, and an actual or potential national reputation. Franchising enables the franchisor to multiply the rents collected on the four-attribute resource through the franchise agreement. Each franchisee becomes an outlet for the value added by the special resource configuration. Franchising enables the franchisor's venture to grow using the franchisee's money, knowledge of the specific locale, and human resources. It also allows the franchisor to enjoy increasing economies of scale in purchasing, building development and improvements, and advertising and promotions. Finally, it enables the firm to enjoy two traditional strategic advantages at once: local control of costs through close supervision of the franchisee, and effective product and service differentiation nationally (or internationally) through the marketing efforts of the franchisor.[59]

Organizational Boundaries   Franchising is a way of setting the boundaries of the organization. Businesses that can expand by opening individual units always have the choice of establishing a chain through company-owned units or franchising. In fact, most franchising systems do contain a significant number of company-owned units in addition to the franchised ones. This enables the franchisor to conduct market experiments, gain knowledge of customer trends and changes, and maintain a solid understanding of procurement and operating costs. Frequently, the franchisor attempts to keep the best locations as part of the company-owned chain, even repurchasing these locations from franchisees who have made them a success.

Franchising is a hybrid form of organization and employs a hybrid mixture of capital and resources. The franchising agreement defines those boundaries by delimiting the organizational and financial constraints on the franchisor.[60] Therefore, it expands the organization's boundaries, which would otherwise be smaller because of limits on resources and money.

Additionally, franchising is a way of balancing the bureaucratic transaction costs of owning, monitoring, and controlling all the outlets or units of the venture (as a chain operation) with the market transaction costs of contracting with the franchisee.

The Agency Problem   The agency problem occurs when ownership and control are separated and the agent (or manager) substitutes his or her own goals and objectives for those of the owner. Because the franchisee is the owner/manager of the unit, the problems arising from the separation of ownership and control are greatly diminished. Because it would be difficult for the franchisor to monitor the quality and behavior of all the venture's outlets spread over the globe, the franchisor instead trusts that owners need much less monitoring than managers. Therefore, franchising is a partial solution to the agency problem.[61] A study using data from the U.S. Census on the food and motel industries found that franchising enables the franchisor to better control the most physically dispersed outlets and to protect the system's brand-name capital. The same study also indicated that franchising permits larger local outlets than using nonfranchised operations.[62]

However, franchising is only a partial solution because sometimes the owner of a franchise outlet also hires managers to run the business. Therefore, the agency problem still exists. Also, when franchisees serve a transient customer base, such as travelers on highways or in airports, they often let quality slip because they know there is little repeat business.[63] In summary, franchising enables the owner of a resource that is rare, valuable, imperfectly imitable (by the outsiders), and nonsubstitutable to make perfect copies of the resource without lessening its rarity. To do this, the franchisor must grant exclusive *local* operating rights to the franchisee so that, from the point of view of the final customer, the product or service is locally rare and somewhat hard to get.[64] The franchisor must build a national reputation. As we saw in Chapter 2, a reputation is one of the resources that can possess the four attributes of sustainable competitive advantage. So what franchisors give up in the complexity of local organization and the proprietary nature of technology or physical resources, they attempt to overcome with reputation, high visibility, and a system-wide culture of high performance.

Franchisor Considerations

The primary form of franchising is the **business format franchise**. The franchisor grants the right to the franchisee to operate the business in a prescribed way. The franchisor can sell these rights one unit at a time or for a geographic territory. The one-at-a-time approach enables the franchisor to maintain close control over locations and the speed of growth. The geographic area approach actually speeds growth, because it is usually in the interest of the franchisee to saturate the territory as quickly as possible. However, it enables some franchisees to become very large and powerful. This might be undesirable and risky from the franchisor's point of view because powerful franchisees can sometimes demand contractual concessions and resist royalty increases.

In the business concept format, the franchisor is selling the business or marketing system, not the hamburger or the quick-copy service. It is estimated that before the first franchisee is operating, the total costs for a franchisor of setting up these systems can run between $110,000 and $950,000. Table 10-2 shows the different cost drivers for the franchisor.

Franchising takes other forms in addition to the popular business format mode. A franchisor can grant an **exclusive right to trade**. For example, an airport or highway authority grants to specific companies the exclusive right to sell food and beverages in the airport or along the highway. A **distributorship** is also a form of franchise. An example would be a franchise to sell a particular make of automobile or computer. A **registered trademark franchise** enables the franchisee to use a name with the expectation that it is recognizable to the customer and that quality will be maintained. An example of this is the Best Western Hotel system. Each unit is independently owned and operated, but each uses the name Best Western and meets certain minimum standards.

The Franchiseable Business   Certain types of businesses are appropriate for franchising. The first and primary requirement is a successful series of **pilot stores**, locations, or operating units. The franchisor bears the cost of developing the formula during the pilot period. The franchisor must learn enough about how to make the business a success to be able to train others to be successful, too. This means learning the key elements of accurate site selection, efficient operations, internal and external financial keys and ratios, operating cost control, a consistent and workable pricing policy, and training procedures for both potential franchisees and their employees. In addition to systematically perfecting each of these areas, the potential franchisor must be sure that after all costs are met, enough is left over for the franchisee to earn a respectable return and pay the royalty to the franchisor.

TABLE 10-2   Estimated Costs of Franchising

Research and Development Costs
Associated with the creation of the initial product, market research for the product and the franchise system, and the franchising blueprint

Creation of the Franchise Package
Requires the hiring of a legal team to prepare the Uniform Franchise Offering Circular (UFOC) for the U.S. Federal Trade Commission. Franchisors are highly regulated by state authorities as well.

Marketing the Franchise
Will cost money for advertising the franchise's availability, recruiting and selecting franchises, further product and service development, and additional operational expenses

Working Capital
For ongoing operations such as training franchisees, continued promotions, further development and refinement, and possible financial capital to help franchises get started, plus some extra in reserve

---

Source: Adapted from R. Justis and R. Judd, *Franchising* (Cincinnati, OH: South-Western Publishing, 1989).

Businesses suitable for franchising often have a number of common elements. They have a product or service that is able to satisfy a continuing demand. Because it will take 2 to 3 years for both the franchisor and franchisee to see a return on their money, the franchise idea cannot be based on a fad or a quick "make-a-buck" opportunity.

The format of the franchiseable business needs to be simple and mechanical. A high degree of customized personal service or individual flair and skill may prove difficult for the franchisee to duplicate. Uniform standards of quality and appearance for the stores or outlets are important. This means that the franchisor must give serious thought to what quality means to the customer and be able to define and measure it accurately.

The franchisor looks for a simple and easy-to-remember name for the business. Strong advertising and promotional support are needed. The franchisee locations must be good enough to support the business but not so expensive that they absorb all the profits. This is why developing accurate site selection criteria is vital.

The administration of the franchise system should be kept simple. The franchisor needs a method to ensure that sales and profits of the franchisee are accurately reported and royalty payments are correct and timely. If possible, the franchisor should arrange for a bank or financial syndicate to provide financial assistance to prospective franchisees.

Even the best business format franchise system cannot long endure, though, if the original pilot operations do not have the resources to obtain sustainable competitive advantage.

Competitive Issues   The franchise system engages in two simultaneous sets of competitions: The franchisor competes to sell franchises, and the franchisee competes locally to sell the product or service. These are interrelated problems. If the franchisee is facing stiff competition and losses are accumulating, the franchisor will find it more difficult to sell franchises. Conversely, if the franchisor is having trouble selling franchises, this decreases the brand value, name recognition, advertising support, and purchasing economies of scale that the franchisee relies on for marketing and operations.

The dependency can run in the other direction, too. Franchisors depend on their franchisees for cooperation. A franchisee rebellion can be a serious problem for the franchisor. Although a franchisor can discipline individual franchisees who fail to live up to quality standards of contractual agreements, when the entire franchisee system rebels, the franchisor may have little choice but to negotiate or capitulate. Franchisee rebellions have occurred at some of the most famous and popular fast-food organizations, including Taco Bell, KFC, Holiday Inns, and Burger King. But for the most part, power is held by the franchisor, who screens and selects the franchisee, draws up the contracts, and collects the royalties.

Because of the preponderance of power on the franchisor side, the government regulates the franchise industry, primarily to protect franchisees. The franchising business is regulated both by the individual states and by the Federal Trade Commission (FTC). Much of the regulation has to do with ensuring that the franchisor provides the franchisee with the information necessary to make informed decisions. Franchisees contend that these rules are widely abused.

Under the current franchise rule, the franchisor must disclose all financial terms and obligations of the franchisee. Franchisors do not have to state how much money franchisees can expect to make, but if they voluntarily do so, they must document their claims. Civil penalties of $10,000 can be levied for each violation. However, individual franchises cannot sue the franchisor under the FTC rule; only the FTC can bring action in federal court.[65]

Despite regulation and potential problems with franchises, franchising remains popular because it enables businesses to expand quickly with other people's money and to have a self-motivated owner/manager control the operation. For franchisors to take advantage of these two benefits, they must be able to deliver a franchiseable product and business system. Street Story 10-3 illustrates a franchisor using the Internet as a tool for system operations.

Franchisee Considerations

Franchisees must be careful in evaluating franchise opportunities and choosing the franchising option best for them. Potential franchisees are urged to examine their personal preferences for risk, autonomy, and hard work. They should consider how their talents and experience will contribute to making the franchise a success. Because of the constrained nature of the franchise agreement, franchising is not for every entrepreneur "wannabe."

Franchisee Requirements   What are the most important things for franchisees to look for?

1. *Proven operating locations serve as a prototype for the franchisee.* This demonstrates do-ability to the customer. These stores have been tested and their operations refined. They are profitable, and the books should be open for qualified franchisees. The operation must be transparent enough so that the franchisee can believe that he or she can manage it.

2. *A credible top management team demonstrates to franchisees that they will not be alone and that there is sufficient expertise at the franchisor level to handle any emergency or contingency.*

3. *Skilled field support staff are the people who will train the franchisee and communicate the franchisor's message to the units in the field.* They help the franchisee attain his or her goals.

4. *A trade identity that is distinctive and protected will enable the franchisee to use the trademarks, signage, slogans, trade dress, and overall image.* The franchisee should be concerned that quality, perceived or real, is similar throughout the system.

5. *A proprietary operations manual comprehensively explains the proven methods of operation and management.* It should be easy to read and understand.

6. *Training programs, both on-site as well as at headquarters, should be regularly updated, and franchisee staff and management should be trained as well.*

7. *Disclosure and offering documents that meet all federal and state regulations are needed.* In addition, a franchise agreement that balances the needs of the franchisor and franchisee should be prepared. Table 10-3 summarizes the types of issues that need to be resolved in the contract.[66] Franchisees should retain competent counsel to advise them on all matters.

Computerized Child's Play

It used to be that when Michael Spehn, regional manager for Children's Orchard stores, wanted to distribute information to his 22 southern California franchisees, he had to make 22 phone calls. It used to be that when Walter F. Hamilton, Jr., CEO of this 100-store chain of children's boutiques that sell manufacturers' overstocks, new, and gently used merchandise, wanted to have an impromptu meeting with franchisees spread over 26 states, he had to arrange complicated and expensive conference calls.

But the creative use of technology by this retail franchisor has changed all that. Hamilton's goals when he purchased the chain in 1993 were to computerize and standardize the company. In the home office, he purchased new PCs, installed a network server, and hired a project manager to work on technology. In the field, he turned to the Internet.

Children's Orchard uses the Internet in a variety of ways. Visitors to their site (www.childrensorchard.com) can locate the store closest to them, or even explore the possibility of purchasing their own franchise. Hamilton estimates that half of his new store owners make their initial contact through the Web site. Those who already own stores can use the Web site to access a special intranet or private site. At this site, owners can read the company newsletter or messages from the CEO, request sales reports and other statistics, download documents and useful files for store management, check for late-breaking news and tips, and even have a live online chat with other Children's Orchard store owners.

Nancy Rigoglioso, a franchisee in San Diego, uses the site frequently. "In the past, I had to call Michael Spehn every week to ask about deals," she says. "Now I just log on." A recently posted deal led Rigoglioso to a children's dress factory, where she stocked up for a back-to-school promotion; in turn, she posted a tip for her fellow owners about a resource for clothes for preemie babies.

Children's Orchard has achieved Hamilton's standardization goal by enabling owners to order logo-imprinted bags, tags, and other supplies through the intranet site, and by posting an approved vendor list. The CEO also estimates that the intranet site has saved the company about $40,000 a year in communication costs and that it has played a big role in helping the $18 million company's income grow an average of 24 percent for 4 years in a row.

Many Children's Orchard franchisees are first-time business owners, and some have resisted computerization. Some of them don't have computers, or have old computers that connect at very low speeds, meaning that their connections to sites with pictures or graphics are very slow. However, other Children's Orchard owners have obviously embraced technology. Michael Spehn, who owns a store in addition to serving as regional manager, has set up his own supplemental company site for the stores in southern California. About half of his owners log in regularly. In the future, all new franchisees will be required to have Internet access. Says Spehn, "We're moving the process along by making it almost impossible to stay off the computer."

Source: Adapted from Emily Esterson, "Inner Beauties," *Inc.* online, November 15, 1998; available www.inc.com.

TABLE 10-3   Issues to Be Addressed in a Franchising Agreement

Issue	*Questions to Resolve*
1. Franchise fee	Amount? One time or per unit?
2. Royalties	Amount? As a percentage of net or gross? Sliding scale?
3. Quality control	Quality specifications? Inspections and monitoring? Rewards and sanctions?
4. Advertising	Fee? Local budget? National? Extensiveness and intensiveness? Messages and campaigns?
5. Offerings	Product line? Product mix? Required offerings? Alternatives? Franchisee-generated offerings?
6. Equipment	Required? Additional? Financing?
7. Location	Site selection requirements? Franchisor aid? Financing?
8. Operations	Signs? Hours? Maintenance? Decor? Personnel policies?
9. Reporting	Types of reports? Frequency? Auditing? Sanctions?
10. Dispute resolution	Methods? Equity?
11. Termination	Timing? Causes? Sanctions?

Source: Adapted from R. Justis and R. Judd, *Franchising* (Cincinnati, OH: South-Western Publishing, 1989).

8. *Advertising, marketing, public relations, and promotion plans should be prepared and available.* The franchisor should be ready to show how a national and regional product reputation will be developed for the benefit of the franchisee.

9. *A communications system establishes the ongoing dialogue that takes place between franchisor, franchisee, and the entire network of units.* This includes meetings, schedules of visiting, and attendance at association conferences, as well as random calls and inspections.

10. *Sufficient capital is needed to get the franchise system off the ground.* These are substantial costs to the franchisor. These were described in Table 10-2. The franchisee is responsible for due diligence before investing in any franchise operation. Many horror stories can be told of franchisees caught unaware and unprepared either by unscrupulous franchisors or simply by difficult economic times. Despite regulation, unprincipled dealers and susceptible buyers abound.

Take the case of all the would-be entrepreneurs who have been the alleged victims of such franchise opportunities as Juice Time, Cola Time, Lotto Time, Water Time, and Tater Time.[67] In each of these cases, a slick sales franchisor convinced hundreds of people to sink upwards of $40 million in these schemes. People were duped by the apparent connection of these business opportunities with such famous corporate giants as Coca-Cola and American Telephone and Telegraph. However, there were no opportunities here, only unfulfilled promises, nonexistent products and equipment, and training programs that never occurred. The results were millions of dollars lost and thousands of hours in court.

Even once-reputable franchisors fall on tough times, and the franchisees must bear the burden. In the mid-1980s, Nutri/System was a franchisor of diet centers with a bright future and optimistic prospects. But because of increased competition, negative publicity resulting from lawsuits from customers, and the heavy debt burden of a leveraged buyout, Nutri/System was in trouble. A severe financial crisis hit the firm in early 1993.[68] When the franchisor suffers, so does the reputation of its units, its advertising campaigns, and its field support and training. In the case of Nutri/System, the franchisees also depended on the franchisor to supply its exclusive line of diet foods for sale to customers. With no support, a failing reputation, and no product to sell, where were the franchisees to turn?

Franchisee Guidelines The potential franchisee should investigate a franchise opportunity by doing the following:[69]

1. *Perform a self-evaluation.* Is franchising really for you? If you are very entrepreneurial, franchising may not be for you, because it requires discipline to operate under someone else's concept. But if you are just getting started with the idea of owning your own business, franchising can give you some low-risk experience.

2. *Investigate the franchisor.* Visit other company stores and talk to other franchisees. Question earnings. Find out how the franchisor treats the franchisees, in good times and bad. Pay particular attention to the extent the franchisor respects the franchisee territory. You do not want to be in competition with your own franchisor.

3. *Study the industry and competition.* There are no sure things, and overall industry conditions and the nature of the competition will affect the individual franchisee. Also look at the degree of regulation in the industry. Many convenience store/gas station franchisees were stunned in the 1980s when they had to replace their underground gas storage tanks after the government-mandated tighter environmental controls. Few were prepared for the expense.

4. *Study the Uniform Franchise Offering Circular (UFOC).* The UFOC is the document required by the FTC of every franchisor. It contains some 20 items, including the history of the franchise, the background of the franchisors, a description of the franchise, the financial obligations of the parties, territories and sales restrictions, and matters related to copyrights, trademarks, logos, and patents.

5. *Investigate the franchisor's disclosures.* The franchisor is obligated to report any "fact, circumstance, or set of conditions which has a substantial likelihood of influencing a reasonable franchisee or a reasonable prospective franchisee in the making of a significant decision related to a named franchise business or which has any significant financial impact on a franchisee or prospective franchisee."[70]

6. *Know your legal rights and retain counsel.*

Summary

Typically, the entrepreneur has practically unlimited freedom to do business where and how he or she chooses. This chapter, however, has presented two types of business environments that are special cases of entrepreneurship because they limit this freedom of action. Both intrapreneurship and franchising raise organizational and contractual constraints to consider.

Intrapreneurship is entrepreneurship that takes place within a corporate setting. It is difficult to master and has many barriers to its success, most notably the corporate bureaucracy. For a corporation to be successful at intrapreneurship, it needs to give the intrapreneurs many of the same types of freedoms that entrepreneurs enjoy, thereby mimicking the external market system within the organization. But the intrapreneur must still conform to some, if not all, of the organization's values, goals, and processes. Political considerations within the organization are necessary hurdles for the intrapreneur to surmount.

Networking skills and alliance formation are vital to both new ventures and growing firms. Networking is actually a series of methods of securing resources without taking ownership. These include various forms of partnerships, alliances, and informal agreements. The ability to convince others of the desirability of an alliance and to negotiate favorable terms for the venture is a fundamental skill for today's entrepreneur.

Franchising presents the entrepreneur with the opportunity to expand the boundaries of the organization and, potentially, to retain control of the strategic resources that provide the basis of SCA. The franchisor contributes the key resource of the business system and the product or service's reputation. The franchisee contributes knowledge of the specific location, human resources, and a highly motivated owner/manager to maintain quality. The combination has led to tremendous growth in franchising systems.

However, the parties to the franchising agreement are also constrained. The franchisor must continue to support the franchisees through training, product development, advertising and promotion, and procurement assistance. The franchisee lives by the letter of the agreement and must operate the franchise as designed by the franchisor. Neither has the complete unlimited freedom of action of the entrepreneur, but the franchisee is particularly constrained and holds little power relative to the franchisor.

Key Terms

- Agglomerate network
- Business format franchise
- Confederate alliance
- Conjugate alliance
- Distributorship
- Exclusive right to trade
- Exit
- Extended network
- Formal network

- Franchisee
- Franchising
- Franchisor
- Informal network
- Internal corporate venture (ICV)
- Intrapreneurship
- Networking
- Organic network

- Personal network
- Pilot store
- Registered trademark franchise
- Strong ties
- Uniform Franchise Offering Circular (UFOC)
- Voice
- Weak ties

Discussion Questions

1. What benefits can corporations gain through successful intrapreneurship?
2. What are the important similarities and differences between entrepreneurship and intrapreneurship?
3. How is the intrapreneurial business plan different from the entrepreneurial business plan? Why is this so?
4. What impediments do large corporations impose on intrapreneurial efforts?
5. Why is networking important for the entrepreneur?
6. What is meant by the "strength of weak ties"?
7. Are franchisors entrepreneurs? Are franchisees entrepreneurs? Give reasons for your answers.
8. Why has franchising been so successful in the United States? Does it have the same potential worldwide?

9. Why is the pilot store so important for the potential franchisor?
10. What are the characteristics of a franchiseable business?
11. What is the nature of the dependency between franchisor and franchisee?
12. What should a franchisee look for in evaluating a franchise opportunity?

Exercises

1. Interview a local franchisee. Ask the franchisee about the relationship between the franchisee and franchisor. What are the problem areas and the positive points, and what does the future hold? Find out whether the franchisee is satisfied with the franchise and if he or she would do it again.
2. Request a package of material from a franchisor. Advertisements for these can usually be found in *Inc.* or *Entrepreneur* magazine, among other places. Evaluate the material you are sent. Does it answer the questions that a potential franchisee will have? Follow up by calling the franchisor. What additional information can you obtain this way?
3. Evaluate your own business plan for its franchiseability. Does it meet the criteria for franchising? If so, develop a franchise plan.

Networking Exercises

1. Identify a trade or professional organization that serves the type of business that you are writing your business plan for. Call or write this association and request materials. What does this organization do for its members? How can members get the most out of belonging to this group?
2. Attend a meeting of a professional organization or group. What types of activities go on? What kinds of behavior can you observe? Interview attendees. What reasons do they give for attending these meetings? What successes have they experienced?
3. Join a student club or group (if you do not already belong). Go to meetings and participate in a few activities. Make new friends. What kinds of things did you do to become friends with these people? What is the extent of the relationship? If you were going into business, how could these new friends help?

DISCUSSION CASE

Movies in Motion

Have you ever been stuck in an airport for hours, waiting for your flight? Have you ever booked a long flight, only to discover that you have already seen the movie they'll be showing?

If so, you're a potential customer for InMotion Pictures. The company rents digital videodisks (DVDs) and DVD players to travelers in U.S. airports. For $10 a day, you can rent a DVD, a battery-powered personal-size DVD player, and a headset. You can watch the movie in the airport, or even take it on your flight if you happen to be flying to an airport with another InMotion Picture rental kiosk. If you want, you can rent the player and an AC adaptor for the duration of your trip, get a free DVD rental for each day that you pay the $10 fee, and then return the equipment to the airport where you rented it. Disc players come with instructions and a 24-hour customer service hotline phone number.

You can also rent additional DVDs and headsets for a nominal charge. If you're traveling with a laptop that plays DVDs, you can rent a movie and use a prepaid mailing envelope to return it. You can even reserve movies by calling or using the company Web site (www. inmotionpictures.com).

The service has been a hit with business travelers and with parents who want to keep their children entertained with animated films or kids' movies. Established in 1998 by David Knight and brothers Barney and Mike Freedman, the company already has 22 kiosks in airports including Atlanta, Las Vegas, Denver, Orlando, San Diego, and San Francisco. Each location stocks approximately 170 titles, with choices including action, horror, comedies, and family films.

The company recently made two announcements: the opening of a "flagship" kiosk and training location for chain personnel at the Jacksonville International Airport, and the investment of an undisclosed amount by the movie rental megacompany Blockbuster. One additional announcement may affect InMotion Pictures' future: American Airlines reported that they will make DVD players available to some of their first-class passengers on international flights.

CASE QUESTIONS

1. Is InMotion Pictures a good candidate for franchising? Why or why not?
2. What are the potential pros and cons of the alliance with Blockbuster?
3. What do you think of this company's future prospects? Can you think of ways they could expand their business?
4. Do you think American Airlines' announcement is good news or bad news for InMotion Pictures?

Source: Adapted from Salina Khan, "Rental DVDs Entertain Fliers," *USA Today* online, November 17, 1999; available at www.usatoday.com; Eric Cravey, "InMotion Pictures Opens at JIA," *The Business Journal of Jacksonville* online, May 30, 2001; available at www.jacksonville.bcentral.com and www.inmotionpictures.com.

Case 1 Blitz

Tom Kinney and his three partners think they have a practical business idea and a do-able business plan, but no one wants to give them any money. Encouraging words have been easier to come by than financing, but they are not giving up: The search continues.

Tom and his partners—Eric Olson, Pat Dunne, and Kurt Moeller—all share a love for beach volleyball. Tom, in fact, was actively involved in the creation of the Professional Beach Volleyball League. It seemed like a natural for these four beach-loving friends to form Zuma SunCare, Inc., to market a new kind of suntan lotion to the consumer group they know so well: highly active men and women between the ages of 15 and 34. While other suntan lotion companies target children or athletes in their marketing plan, Zuma will be the first to gear their product specifically to the young adult market.

Zuma has developed a unique product to reach those consumers. Known as "Blitz," their suntan product is actually two different lotions packaged in a dual-chamber dispensing bottle. Blitz will allow sun worshippers to apply lotions with different SPFs to different parts of their body (a higher SPF for the face and sensitive areas, a lower SPF for areas where they want to tan quickly) without forcing consumers to purchase two separate products.

Zuma has a unique marketing plan for Blitz, too. Instead of selling the product in drugstores and supermarkets, Zuma wants to sell Blitz exclusively to gift stores and independent shops at resorts, hotels, cruise lines, and beaches. They feel that these outlets will be more receptive to a new brand, and that consumers will be more likely to appreciate the unique appeal of Blitz without the rows of competing products you find at a mass merchandiser.

Armed with multiple college degrees and lots of enthusiasm, Tom Kinney and his partners spent more than a year preparing their business plan. They produced research on the $620 million U.S. annual retail market for suntan and sunscreen products, which demonstrated that it was a growing market where other small companies with a special niche had succeeded. Their review of demographic statistics revealed that 64 percent of their target market of age 15–24 young adults currently use sun care products. A professional market survey by a reputable firm indicated that 60 percent of females and 29 percent of males in their target group expressed a strong interest in a dual-chamber bottle with multiple SPF suntan lotions. As long as the sun keeps shining, Blitz is sure to be a winner.

Now Zuma needs $485,000 to perfect the product, conduct additional market tests, refine packaging and advertising, and launch Blitz nationwide, but despite their well-documented research and carefully prepared financial projections, they can't seem to find an investor. They believe that the problem is that although all four partners have good credentials, none of them actually has any experience launching a new business, which makes potential investors leery.

Recently, Tom had an inquiry from a regional venture capital firm that might be willing to invest in Zuma. However, they would require Zuma to completely restructure their financial offer and to hire Steven Smith, an experienced entrepreneur they have worked with before, to be president and CEO of Zuma as a condition of their investment.

Tom just returned from lunch with Steven. This new venture veteran was impressed by Zuma's business plan, but he had two serious problems. First, he thought the name "Blitz" was a negative factor because it sounded too much like the word "blister." He suggested they needed a new name that would suggest the dual SPF concept. Steven also thought a marketing plan geared exclusively to small independent stores was inadequate, and that they should instead concentrate on nationwide mass marketers like Target and Wal-Mart.

Tom Kinney liked Steven, but his instincts told him that both the Blitz name and the exclusive marketing plan are 100 percent right for this product. He thought that 50-something Smith simply did not understand their target market. Tom was uncertain whether he or his original partners would be willing to change their plans after they'd put so much time and energy into developing the concept, even if it meant losing their investment.

BACKGROUND AND PURPOSE

The market now has a preponderance of health and beauty aid products targeted at consumers with youthful, active lifestyles. The founders of Zuma SunCare realized, however, that one product, perhaps more readily identified with "fun" and "youth" than any other, had not found a home with these consumers: suntan lotion. Thus, Blitz SunTan Lotion, the sun protection product of the young and active, came into being.

Current Situation

Blitz SunTan Lotion is a line of tanning and sun protection products, with varying degrees of SPF levels for varying degrees of tan promotion and sun protection. Blitz will be marketed to the 15- to 35-year-old age group, those with active, youthful lifestyles. The technology needed to make the product is the specialty of the manufacturers and packagers to whom we will subcontract orders for the product. The product will be delivered to market through direct sales of our own, the sales efforts of brokers in the

industry, and through established channels of experienced health care and beauty aid distributors.

Our Resources

This section describes the key resources that the founders bring to Zuma SunCare, as well as other important factors that contribute to Zuma SunCare's success.

Human Resources

The founders of Zuma SunCare are unique in the levels of vision, drive, creativity, and intelligence. The insight that enabled the founders to recognize an unexploited market niche, and the creativity behind the inception of the dual-chamber dispensing bottle, were not one-time-only phenomena. The founders possess unique skills that will enable them to continually perceive opportunities where others do not, and thus ensure that Zuma SunCare will remain at the forefront of suntan lotion marketing innovation.

President and CEO Tom Kinney brings with him an enormous amount of relationship capital. Having grown up playing volleyball on the beaches of southern California, Mr. Kinney is intimately familiar with the driving forces behind the burgeoning sport of professional beach volleyball. The marketing appeal of professional beach volleyball to young and active consumers is strong, and Mr. Kinney's contacts in the sport promise unique access to an excellent source of promotional capital.

Reputational Resources

Because Blitz SunTan Lotion will be the first brand-name sun care product exclusively aimed at the young and active, it will garner enormous first-mover brand loyalty. With continued high-profile marketing to the young and active, Blitz's name will be inextricably linked to the concepts of "fun" and "youth." Blitz will be able to retain a firm hold on market share in its niche, even in the face of competition from "me too" imitators.

Organizational Resources

Zuma SunCare's organizational structure will be lean, tight, and flat. Consequently, Zuma SunCare's decision making will be fast and responsive to perceived market opportunities. In combination with the strong human resources of the firm, Zuma SunCare's organizational resources promise to help make it a success.

OBJECTIVES

Short Term

The short-term, 1-year goals of Zuma SunCare are as follows:

From October 1996 through January 1997, Zuma's goals are to perfect the formula, packaging, and advertising of Blitz SunTan Lotion by conducting concepts tests in a college/beach community such as Gainesville, Florida. Through a series of participative panels, screenings, and tests, Zuma will be able to determine the ideal Blitz formulation (scent, consistency, color, etc.), which packaging provides the greatest appeal, and which advertising schemes generate the greatest response.

Beginning in February 1997, Zuma SunCare will begin promoting and selling the perfected Blitz product in a limited test market representing a microcosm of Blitz's eventual national market. Again, Gainesville, Florida, might represent a community selected for the test. The market test will enable Zuma to gain valuable experience establishing distribution channels and implementing its marketing and advertising strategy, but will not require large financial losses.

The concept and market tests will assist Zuma SunCare in realizing its short-term goals: creating the optimal product, crafting highly effective marketing and advertising strategies, honing the implementation of those strategies, and perfecting the establishment of sales and distribution channels.

Long Term

The long-term, 2- to 5-year goals of Zuma SunCare are as follows:

Using the knowledge and skills gained from its concept and marketing tests the previous year, Zuma will ramp up its advertising and sales strategies for a national launch of Blitz SunTan Lotion in 1998. Zuma will attempt to maximize market share as early as possible with intense media and trade promotions. This strategy will be important to defend competitive threats. The company will minimize direct competition from mass-market brands (Coppertone, etc.) by targeting regional convenience stores, surf shops, and beach and ski resorts. The national brands have less impact on these channels because their sales are concentrated on national supermarket and drugstore chains. By the end of this first year of national operations, Zuma SunCare projects that Blitz will achieve approximately 1 percent share of the total sun care market, and earn $779,007.

By the end of its fourth year of national operations, Zuma projects a 2.5 percent market share for Blitz, earnings of $2.8 million, and the ability to tender a successful initial public equity offering if desired.

An additional goal of Zuma during years 2 through 5 is to exploit the high brand-name recognition that Blitz SunTan Lotion will have established with consumers. Zuma wishes to cash in on the intangible value of the Blitz name by branding out into other product lines bearing the Blitz name, such as apparel and gift items.

MARKET ANALYSIS

Overall Market

Zuma SunCare will compete in the $620 million U.S. retail market for suntan and suncreen products. This market has averaged a 5 percent annual growth (Exhibit 1), representing a trend that is expected to continue with the growing concern for the harmful effects of the sun's rays. The entire skin-care industry is one of the fastest growing segments of the personal products category. The distribution channels that have shown the most growth have been mass merchandisers and alternative markets such as direct sale (The Body Shop) and informercial/cable TV. Specific high-growth niches are expected to be ethnic and men's markets, as well as all-natural products. The European market will also be important because sales there are about twice as those in the United States.

There has been a strong proliferation of health and beauty products developed over the past 10 years, particularly among sunscreens and sunblocks. Seventy percent of the suncreen market has gone to products with an SPF of 15 or higher, as consumers become more concerned about the harmful effects of the sun's ultraviolet rays. Also, recent segmentation efforts have prompted manufacturers to develop brands that fit consumers' lifestyles, not just an SPF factor. The high growth of products specifically for children is a result of studies that indicate regular use of sunscreen before the age of 18 reduces the likelihood of melanoma skin cancer by 78 percent. Likewise, sunless tanning products have boomed, currently comprising 15 percent of the sun care market. A deluge of new sunless tanning products is expected to be introduced in both mass market and prestige channels.

Leading Competitors The market is divided between a half-dozen major manufacturers and a multitude of small, independent, and private-label brands (Exhibit 1). Currently, the strongest player in this market is Schering-Plough with its brands Coppertone, Coppertone Kids, Coppertone Sport, Water Babies, and Shade. These lines comprise 33 percent of the market and have achieved this by having a long brand history, heavy marketing expenditures (over $30 million annually), and the resources of a large pharmaceutical and packaged goods corporation. Their closest competitors, Banana Boat and Hawaiian Tropic, have less than half Coppertone's market share, yet have aggressively expanded their lines and sharply increased media spending. Other firms sell prestige market sunscreens in department stores, aimed at high-end users, with cosmetic-oriented brands toward women. The major brands sell products across the United States as well as overseas; the smaller companies concentrate sales in regions with heaviest use, such as the southeast and west coast.

Despite the strength of the major brand names, numerous start-ups have successfully entered the market with niche positioning. About 30 percent of the market is divided among numerous smaller companies that stress ties to a particular region or a reputation gained by word of mouth at beaches and resorts. This segment, rather than the mass-merchandised segment dominated by the major brands, is the one in which Zuma will directly compete in the early years.

Specific Market

Target Market The Blitz brand will be specifically marketed to the segment of young men and women between the ages of

15 and 34 who live highly active lifestyles. Particular emphasis will be placed on college students between ages 18 and 24. Both the 15 to 19 and the 20 to 24 age groups are expected to grow significantly faster than the general population (Exhibit 2), and they have traditionally been among the highest users of sun care products. About 38 percent of this segment uses sun care products on a regular basis, which creates a base of 28.9 million users. Given this, it is estimated that the "young adult" portion of the retail market is $318 million retail.

Based on preliminary market surveys, this market purchases according to price, product efficacy, and brands that appeal to this lifestyle. Sixty-four percent of respondents use sun care products "to achieve a good tan without burning"; 27 percent want complete protection from UV rays. This agrees with secondary research that indicates a growing trend for many young adults to limit exposure to the sun altogether.

A significant number of respondents tend to use more than one product at a time, using higher SPF products on their face, neck, and shoulders. Eighty percent of females and 29 percent of males expressed a strong interest in a dual-chamber bottle with multiple SPFs. They saw value in being able to carry multiple suncreen types in one company package. It is very inconvenient to carry two or three separate bottles. One-hundred percent of females and 43 percent of males would also like smaller packaging when going to the beach or sporting events. The lower response rate from males is consistent with the fact that men in general use less suncreen, are less involved in sun care purchases, and often borrow lotion from others.

Most purchasing is "on the go" at supermarkets or convenience stores, as active people enjoy outdoor activities. Because 70 percent of all sun care sales are the result of impulse buying, countertop displays of Blitz will be incorporated in the retailing plan. Zuma SunCare's marketing efforts will concentrate initially on the 15-million college students enrolled in the United States, particularly during summer and spring break vacations (see marketing strategy).

Direct Competitors Direct competition consists of other manufacturers that sell to our market segment and carry the beach promotional theme. This includes two national brands, Banana Boat (Playtex) and Hawaiian Tropic, as well as several lesser known regional brands (BioTropic, Sunbrella, Malibu Tropic, etc.).

Competitive Factors

Below the top four or five manufacturers, the sun care market is highly fragmented in terms of both product offerings and target markets. Generally, a new firm has three options in which to carve a niche:

Create a superior formulation. This is difficult to achieve. R&D costs are high, development takes a long time, and manufacturers must meet guidelines for FDA over-the-counter drugs.

Have a "me-too" product at a lower price point. Although it is possible to earn some market share, profits are limited. Retailers and distributors will be less likely to carry the product for similar reasons. They will not see much differentiation between a new brand and the ones they already carry.

A hook. With a new packaging or marketing angle, a generic formulation can gain shelf space, as evidenced by successful start-up brands from BioTropic and Sunbrella. Distributors, retailers, and consumers are intrigued by a unique *looking* product because many assume the lotion inside is about the same. This requires minimal capital with little or no R&D costs because all manufacturing and packaging can by outsourced. This is the approach Zuma SunCare will follow.

With the success of Zuma's positioning strategy for Blitz, major competitors may target the 18–35 market in retaliation. However, Schering-Plough will not enter the fray with the total commitment and zeal of Zuma for fear of jeopardizing its appeal to the overall market, securing Blitz's position. Start-up imitators will also not be able to supplant Blitz from its position.

Industry Analysis

Buyer Power   Several factors indicate consumer buyer power: low switching costs, several competitive products, and a trend toward higher retail prices. As prices rise, and as consumers begin to use sunscreen as an everyday product, buyers will become more price sensitive. On the other hand, buyer power is limited because they do not threaten to integrate and they do not always possess full market information. In many cases, consumers will buy whatever product is readily available, particularly at resorts and surf shops.

The heaviest buyer power lies with the distributors and retailers. Just like consumers, they have many sun care products from which to choose. Selling the distributors on the unique positioning of the product will be critical to ensure penetration at the retail level. However, retailer interest in sun care products is expected to grow for several reasons:

- Sun care products offer retailers high margins, between 30 percent and 50 percent off list price.
- More retailers are stocking the products during nonsummer months, hoping that consumers will purchase before traveling to vacation spots.
- Many retailers are advertising earlier in the season to impress consumers that the products are already available in stores.

Supplier Power   Due to the great number of suppliers for blow-molded plastic bottles, injection molded caps, and labels of comparable quality, they do not possess as much power as individual suppliers. Although fewer in number, there are several contract fillers of sun care formulas as well.

Substitute Products   Direct substitutes include products with sunscreen additives, such as moisturizing lotion, insect repellent, and antiaging cream. These categories have shown recent growth, although most of these substitutes are aimed at older consumers outside our target segment.

Rivalry Among Firms   Although rivalry is substantial, it mainly exists between brands that share common distribution channels. Based on that, the whole market can be subdivided into three segments:

- High-end cosmetics sold in department and drugstores (Clinique, Estee Lauder, Neutragena)
- Mass-market national brands sold in national chain drug and supermarket stores (Coppertone, Hawaiian Tropic, Banana Boat)
- Small independent brand, sold primarily through independent surf shops, beach and ski resorts, and local convenience stores (Body Drench, BioTropic, etc.)

Zuma SunCare will focus on the third segment, earning shelf space at the independent shops and resorts where the strength of the national brands is diminished. The resorts, hotels, and cruise lines are more receptive to carrying new brands because of closer sales relationships and slightly higher retailer margins. These are ideal outlets for Blitz because the consumers are captive, without the opportunity to purchase at a mass merchandiser.

Macroenvironmental Influences

Demographics   As mentioned earlier, the target age groups of 15–19 and 20–24 are both expected to rise over the next 10 years. Much of this is attributed to the "baby boomlet," or the children of baby boomers who will demand the bulk of the household spending for the rest of the decade (Exhibit 2).

The sun care market is affected more by annual weather than by the business cycle. Although sun exposure is relatively constant, consumers have tended to purchase more in years of warmer temperatures.

Social Trends and Values Perhaps the strongest factor for this industry's macro-environment is a general trend toward healthier lifestyles, particularly as consumers value health over vanity. Concern about melanoma, skin cancer, and the harmful effects of the sun's UV rays has risen dramatically. About a million cases of non-melanoma skin cancer are diagnosed each year, equal to all other kinds of cancer combined. Because one in six people can expect to develop skin cancer, the American Academy of Dermatology (AAD) recommends that people use sunscreen with an SPF of 15 or higher on a daily basis. SPFs of 15 and above continue to drive the category, currently accounting for more than 50 percent of sales. Also, the UV Index, which describes the level of UV hitting the ground, will become part of daily weather forecasts, advising people to wear a sunscreen with an SPF of 15. After this index was introduced 3 years ago in Canada, sunscreen sales increased, and American manufacturers are expecting a similar trend here. The pale look is becoming "in," but that has not stopped people from enjoying outdoor activities. Due to marketing efforts by the largest manufacturers, people are beginning to think about sunscreen 365 days a year. The popularity of sunless tanning products has already made sun care a year-round category.

Government Regulation In recent years, FDA rulings have actually stimulated the sun care market by allowing manufacturers to use SPF numbering and cancer-prevention claims as marketing tools. In the near future, the FDA monograph on sunscreens is expected to be modified, which will regulate labeling and product claims. Some of the expected changes include:

- No SPFs greater than 30, because the FDA does not believe that they provide significant added benefit
- Suncreens to carry a static and water-resistant SPF
- Must show a sun alert warning stating the damage of the sun's rays on the skin
- A tanning products warning for products without a sunscreen, stating that fact
- Products claiming to inhibit exposure from UV rays and declaring an SPF to be regulated as a drug

Zuma SunCare plans to follow each of these when necessary, even welcoming the change. We predict that stricter labeling rules will weed out competitors that sell low-quality products that claim sun protection but do not have UV-inhibiting active ingredients. The new regulation will be more of a challenge to makers of cosmetic products with "added sunscreens," which have been stealing a piece of the overall market.

DEVELOPMENT AND PRODUCTION

Production Processes

Zuma SunCare, Inc., plans to contract the manufacture of its lotions, bottle caps, and labels. This is the most cost-effective way of entering the market. It avoids up-front capital costs in research and development and manufacturing. It allows Zuma to take advantage of contract manufacturers' expertise and economies of scale in manufacturing these products. Our long-term plan (more than 5 years into operations) is to bring these steps in-house, beginning with development of new lotion formulas.

Zuma will contract for the manufacture of two-chambered bottles with two openings. The bottles can contain sunscreens of two SPF factors, or a sunscreen and an after-sun product. The sunscreen manufacturer will receive the two-chambered bottles, plus the caps and labels. The manufacturer will fill the bottle, cap the bottle, and add the label. The manufacturer will ship the filled bottles to Zuma's warehouse. Then Zuma will send the sunscreen to distributors, brokers, and retailers (Exhibit 3).

We have talked with a contract manufacturer to determine costs. The costs will range from $1.35 for a bottle with sunscreens of SPF4 and 8 to $2.63 for a bottle with sunscreen of SPF 30 and aloe (Exhibit 4).

Resource Requirements

Zuma SunCare, Inc., believes that subcontracting production to those companies with the resources to produce sunscreen and the experience in manufacturing sunscreen will be helpful in several ways.

- It will lower capital required. Zuma will not need to spend money to buy or lease land, buildings, and manufacturing equipment.
- It will allow Zuma to focus on its competency, marketing. Companies are increasingly specializing in areas where they excel and subcontracting other parts of their operations. Companies are only concerned with working on areas where they can add value. Zuma is not a manufacturer; it is a marketer. Companies with whom Zuma subcontracts will have expertise in making bottles, caps, labels, and sunscreen.

As Zuma's sales grow and its finances become more stable, Zuma will examine the benefits of bringing product development and production in-house. Doing so would require many new facilities and personnel:

- A laboratory to research and develop new formulas and sunscreens
- A factory to produce the sunscreen
- Trained scientists to invest and thoroughly test new sunscreens
- Experienced manufacturing managers to start, refine, and monitor the production processes

- Employees to work in the manufacturing plant

Product Differentiation

The biggest factors differentiating Zuma's product will be its bottle and label. The two-chambered bottle is something no other sunscreen manufacturer offers. It will enhance profit margins and be more convenient for consumers. As discussed in the "Target Market" section, survey results indicate that many consumers carry more than one bottle of sunscreen, for such reasons as wanting varying degrees of sun protection on different body areas, or wanting an after-sun product.

The label will be designed by Zuma's marketing department. We will aim for a unique, flashy label that will grab consumers' attention. It will be designed to appeal to the 15–34 age bracket, not the wide range of consumers most sunscreens target.

Quality

Zuma will ensure quality by carefully selecting contractors. We will choose only firms that have consistently delivered excellent products to small companies in the past. Zuma will diligently monitor the products suppliers deliver and randomly test them to confirm that the products meet the standards specified.

MARKETING

Overall Concept and Orientation

Blitz will combine tanning safety with a fun-youthful, high-energy, and stylish image. The "MTV Generation" of 15- to 24-year-olds use sun care products on special occasions, either at the local beach or on a spring break vacation. For them, getting a safe tan is important, yet they do not want to feel they need a medicinal product to do so. Brand image particularly influences their purchase intentions, even more so than product efficacy claims. Blitz will appeal to these attitudes with high-impact, fresh graphics, radical promotional images, and sponsorship of popular events such as volleyball tournaments, swimwear contests, and outdoor concerts.

Marketing Strategy

Based on preliminary market research, we view the young adults to be an untapped segment in the sun care industry. Based on the competitive map in Figure 1, most products appeal to a slightly older crowd of 30- to 44-year-olds, predominated by female users. Zuma SunCare will aim for the hole in this map of 18- to 24-year-olds with a stronger appeal toward male users. The secondary target group will be males and females flanking this age group, down to 15-year-olds and up through 34-year-olds.

Communication of the Image

The critical elements and costs required to execute the marketing plan are outlined in Table 1, followed by detailed descriptions of each. (Other annual costs are included in Exhibits 5, 6, and 10.)

Packaging Beyond the image of the Blitz brand, Zuma SunCare will appeal to another consumer need—convenience. This will be accomplished with a unique dual-chamber bottle that allows users to carry a high and low SPF in one package. Our consumer research has indicated a strong tendency to use multiple SPFs, such as SPF 8 or 15 on the body and SPF 30 on the face. A combined sunscreen and after-sun aloe vera gel will also be available (see Exhibit 4 for product line). All of the sunscreens will be PABA free, waterproof, and moisturizing.

Advertising Zuma SunCare will communicate Blitz's cool image with a three-pronged advertising strategy:

- *Print advertising.* Bold images and attention-getting slogans (i.e., "Hey, don't get fried, Get Blitzed!") will be used in ads placed in college newspapers, youth-oriented magazines (*Wired*, *Spin*, etc.), and alternative urban newspapers.
- *Radio spots.* Initially, radio spots will be run on low-cost college radio stations and stations in "spring break" locales.
- *Billboards.* Initial use of billboards will be bus billboards.

Promotions and Sponsorship Once Blitz establishes sufficient brand recognition, Zuma SunCare will sponsor local volleyball tournaments and other beach-oriented events. Free samples will also be important to induce early trial and raise brand awareness. These promotions will occur at college campuses, spring break parties, and sponsored events. Other sales promotions directed at retailers will include point-of-purchase countertop displays and discounted initial orders to earn shelf space.

Zuma SunCare will aggressively market the Blitz brand at industry trade shows. The purpose is not only to expand brand exposure but to line up key distributors, brokers, and retailers.

Pricing Strategy

An 8-ounce, dual chamber bottle of Blitz SPF 15/30 will retail for $8.95. This price point is high enough to reflect the quality ingredients and provide a significant profit, yet slightly lower than competitive brands in order to meet the target market's need for value. Lower SPF products will have a slightly lower price due to the lower cost of the active sunscreen ingredient, which is typically the highest cost item per ounce. Single application packets will cost $1.25 for 0.75 ounces.

Distribution

In order to maximize penetration in retail channels, Zuma SunCare will need to established strong relationships with distribution partners. This will be done in three ways:

- *Health and beauty aid distributors/ wholesalers.* Their margin ranges from

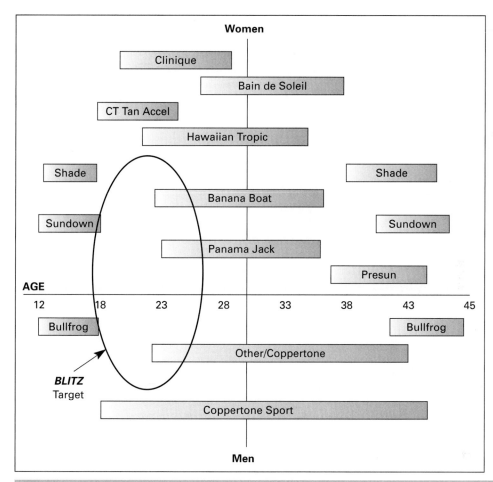

Women

Clinique

Bain de Soleil

CT Tan Accel

Hawaiian Tropic

Shade   Shade

Banana Boat

Sundown   Sundown

Panama Jack

Presun

AGE

12   18   23   28   33   38   43   45

Bullfrog   Bullfrog

Other/Coppertone

BLITZ
Target

Coppertone Sport

Men

FIGURE 1   Demographic Map of Competing Brands

5 to 15 percent depending on the level of extra services they provide to retailers. Retailers earn between 40 percent and 50 percent of the retail price.

- *Sales brokers.* Sales brokers will act as Zuma SunCare's agents, selling to smaller surf shops and resort stores. They will make additional sales to distributors as well. Commissions range from 5 percent to 7 percent.

- *Direct sales.* Direct sales calls made by Zuma's owners. These efforts will concentrate on resorts and surf shops in vacation spots throughout Florida and Mexico. Additionally, the owners will begin to establish contractual agreements with beach resorts, ski resorts, cruise lines, and collegiate football stadiums to become preferred suppliers of sun care products with direct sale, discounted price. These arrangements may allow dual branding of the product with each venue, such as "Club Med Sunscreen, *from the makers of Blitz.*" The single-application packets show particular promise for concession sales at warm weather football stadiums.

TABLE 1 Summary of Marketing Costs

	Year 0 (market test)	Year 1	Year 2	Year 3	Year 4	Year 5
Package design	15,000					
Logo and art work	10,000					
Advertising development	75,000					
Other R&D	20,000					
Media Spending						
Television	0	0	524,333	545,307	562,432	584,929
Radio	5,000	100,833	104,867	109,061	112,486	116,986
Print	7,000	25,208	26,217	27,265	28,122	29,246
Billboard	8,000	25,208	26,217	27,265	28,122	29,246
Trade shows	0	50,000	52,000	56,243	63,266	74,012
Promotion						
Sponsorships	0	75,000	78,000	84,365	94,899	111,018
In-store promos	0	35,500	36,920	39,933	44,919	52,549
Free samples	5,000	5,000	5,200	5,624	6,327	7,401

Based on these estimates, average revenue is calculated as a 55 percent margin of total retail dollar sales.

Marketing Time Line

Concept Testing During the first year, Zuma SunCare will conduct concept tests in a representative market in order to finalize the details of product form, pricing, advertising, and distribution. Two to three variations of the product will be shown to consumers, each with a different mix of product ingredients (moisturizers, fragrances, etc.) and label graphics. We will also test different advertising mock-ups to determine which elicits the best consumer response. Estimated cost of this testing period is $172,000. During this time, the founders will establish relationships with distributors of health and beauty items, as well as brokers specializing in sales to independent retailers.

Market Testing Once the product concept is finalized, production will ramp up for sales to a specific region selected as a representative sample of our total market (i.e.,

Gainesville, Florida). We will launch an intense promotional campaign of local radio advertising, print media in youth-oriented magazines, and moving billboard (bus) advertising. Direct sales efforts will be made to retailers within this test market, particularly hotels, resorts, surf shops, party stores, and convenience stores. The purpose of the market testing is to forecast future sales, fine-tune promotional strategy, and strengthen our distribution network.

Full-Scale Production If the market test indicates that Blitz will reach a target 2 percent share of the Gainesville young adult market, Zuma SunCare will initiate full-scale marketing and production. Zuma will attempt to maximize market share as early as possible with intense media and trade promotions. Once a foothold is achieved, this strong marketing effort will continue in order to defend against competitive threats.

Although the long-term goal is to achieve national distribution, Blitz will initially be launched in the coastal resort communities in California and Florida. Subsequent regions (every 6 to 8 months) will be added, including Cancun, Mexico, Texas, South Carolina, and the southeastern seaboard. In addition to these regional targets, marketing promotions will continue at major universities throughout the country, anticipating student travel to our target regions.

Sales Forecasts

Based on the market-potential/sales-requirement (MP/SR) method, estimated sales for the first full year of production (after the concept and market tests) are $3.76 million. Beginning with the market potential technique, sales were forecasted with the following assumptions:

- The target market of 15- to 34-year-olds has a population of 77.2 million; of those people, 28.9 million are regular users of sun care products (Exhibit 2).
- Average retail dollars spent per person is $11 annually, which was calculated by dividing total retail market over total sun care users. This amount averages those that buy more and those that buy less.
- Total dollar market of the segment is, therefore, $318 million.
- Successful independent sun care start-ups have been able to achieve 1 to 2 percent of the *total* $620 million retail market.
- With concentrated marketing efforts to the youth segment, Zuma SunCare could expect to earn 1.1 percent of the overall segment or 2.15 percent of the young adult segment.
- 2.15 percent × $318 = $6.84 million retail; 1.1 percent × $620 = $6.20 million.
- With an average gross margin of 55 percent of retail, this translates into company revenues of $3.76 million.

With the sales requirement technique, the break-even point for the first year of full production is 330,547 bottles of lotion. This requires a 0.45 percent share of the overall retail market, which is feasible with Zuma SunCare's strong marketing push.

Detailed sales forecasts appear in Exhibits 8–10. Monthly sales for the first year are adjusted to account for seasonality, with more shipments expected in the early spring and summer months.

FINANCIAL PLANS

Financial Statements

Projected profit and loss statements for Zuma SunCare appear in Exhibits 8–10. The statements report monthly data for the first year of full operations (1997); quarterly data for the first 3 years; and annual data for the first 5 years. Sales for the first year average 67,943 bottles per month over the period. Because sale of suntan lotion is subject to seasonal trends, the number of bottles sold in each month is multiplied by a seasonality factor (see Exhibit 7). Over the first year of production, sales are projected to grow by 5 percent each month, and net income is projected to be $779,007. Sales grow in the following 4 years by 30 percent, 35 percent, 30 percent and 20 percent, respectively, and net income grows to $2,799,612.

Quarterly balance sheets for the first 3 years of full operations, and annual balance sheets for the first 5 years, appear in Exhibits 13–14. The growth in sales of Blitz leads to a growth in Zuma SunCare's assets from $1,095,538 at the end of year 1, to 7,989,813 at the end of year 5. Accounts payable are assumed to be paid on a net 90-day basis. All sales are made through accounts receivable, and allowance for doubtful accounts is 5 percent. Accounts receivable will also be paid on a net 90-day basis, insuring that Zuma will have adequate working capital.

Statement of cash flows for Zuma appear in Exhibits 11–12 on a quarterly basis for the first 3 years, and on an annual basis for the first 5 years. Due to the contracting out of manufacturing and bottling, Zuma makes no cash investment in property, plant, and equipment. Accumulated depreciation pertains to office equipment and computers purchased in 1996. Zuma will receive its third and final cash infusion from investors just prior to the beginning of operations in 1997. Consequently, the statement of cash flows shows no cash from financing activities, and a beginning cash balance of $200,000. The founders of Zuma project a growth in cash flow from operations from $770,926 in 1997 to $2,723,325 in 2001.

Financial Resources

Zuma's start-up costs appear in Exhibits 5–6. The concept test will require approximately $172,700, of which $30,000 will come from the owner's initial investment, leaving a need for $142,700 in outside funding. Because Blitz's image is the key to its success, much of these funds, $50,000, will be needed for advertising development. The rest of the funds will go towards the basics of conducting the test, the majority being earmarked for salary and living expenses. Zuma is contracting out all manufacturing and bottling, so other than the cost of desks and computers, no funds will be needed for physical equipment.

The market test will require an additional $172,700, which will be comprised of another $30,000 investment from the founders and $142,700 in outside funding. The primary use of these funds will be for salary and living expenses, and the remainder used to conduct the test. Just prior to the beginning of full operations in 1997, a final infusion of $200,000 in outside resources will be required to fund initial production and marketing costs. Following this last infusion, the business will be funded internally from operations. The total outside funds required will be $485,400.

The incurred debt will require interest payment of 15 percent paid at the end of each fiscal year, beginning in 1997. At the end of Zuma's third full year of operations, investors will have the option of converting the debt to an equity ownership position equaling 20 percent of the company's outstanding shares. Should investors choose not to convert, Zuma will have the right to call the loan and repay the debt in full. The entries in the income statement, statement of cash flows, and balance sheet reflect the scenario of Zuma repaying the loan in full at the end of the third year.

Financial Strategy After the final installment of funds from its investors, Zuma will be able to fund all necessary expenditures out of cash flow from operations. At the end of its fifth year of full operations, Zuma will tender an initial public offering. At that time, we will examine ways to use that money to help Zuma grow, such as purchasing a competitor and achieving economies of scale, or vertically integrating by beginning our own manufacturing and bottling operations.

MANAGEMENT AND ORGANIZATION

Key Personnel Resources

Zuma SunCare's four founders will take crucial roles within the company. They have varied backgrounds and skills, which will allow Zuma to function well as a firm.

Tom Kinney, the company's president and CEO, has extensive knowledge and contacts in the professional beach volleyball tour. He grew up playing volleyball on the beaches of southern California. Mr. Kinney understands and can anticipate consumers' needs in the area of sun and beach products.

Eric Olson, the company's vice president of finance, was previously an officer in the United States Marine Corps. While in the service, he developed numerous leadership and communications skills, a keen ability to plan and coordinate the actions of others, and an acute sense of attention to detail. This experience enables him to view the business from a strategic angle with long-term growth as an objective. Other experience includes a position with the internal audit department of a *Fortune* 500 firm. Specific projects included capital projects audits, benchmarking studies, and due diligence analysis. Furthermore, Mr. Olson has extensive experience creating and refining complex financial models that allow accurate sensitivity and scenario analysis in dynamic circumstances.

Pat Dunne, the company's vice president of marketing, has 5 years' experience in product design and marketing communications. He has extensive project management experience at a multimillion-dollar entrepreneurial firm that specialized in custom trade show programs and displays. Mr. Dunne's responsibilities included helping clients position their products in the marketplace, plan and design their displays, and effectively market those products.

Kurt Moeller, the company's vice president of production, has experience working in just-in-time manufacturing environments. He has identified and maximized opportunities in new areas for previous employers. Mr. Moeller can quickly learn about new topics and pinpoint the most important questions.

The founders will receive salaries of $40,000 per year, payable in equal, biweekly checks.

Zuma's founders will have significant ownership stakes in the company. Their shares in the company will provide incentive for them to continue working toward Zuma's success. However, the founders will have to forfeit all of their shares if they leave the company before it has completed 3 years of operations. Founders will have to relinquish 8,000 shares if they leave the company during its fourth year of operations. They will have to forfeit 4,000 shares if they leave the company during its fifth year of operations.

Founders will sign noncompete contracts with Zuma. They will be prohibited from working for another sun care products company during the first 5 years Zuma conducts operations and for 12 months after they leave Zuma.

Human Resource Management Strategy

Zuma will have few employees. The founders will have the vast majority of responsibility for such tasks as marketing, distributor and manufacturer relations, and financial controls and performance measures. Zuma's main need will be for employees to take orders, serve customers, and help coordinate logistics between Zuma, its suppliers, and its distributors.

Zuma will not incur future liabilities on behalf of its employees. The company will not sponsor a defined-benefit or a defined-contribution pension plan. Zuma will try to pool with other small businesses and receive discounted health insurance rates.

Zuma does not anticipate that any employees will be covered by a collective bargaining agreement.

OWNERSHIP

Form of Business

Zuma will be formed as a limited liability corporation (LLC). Nearly every state in the United States permits LLCs. These allow corporate profits to be passed to owners as dividends, without being taxed twice. LLCs limit investors' liability to only the money they have put into the company. They do not have restrictions on investors in the company, such as a maximum of

35 investors and no foreign owners, that "S" corporations have.

Equity Positions

Zuma will begin with 100,000 shares. Each founder will own 20,000 shares. The remaining 20,000 shares will be reserved for investors who can convert their debt into equity.

Founders will have the first right to purchase shares sold by other founders. Founders will also be able to vote the shares of any founder who has relinquished his shares, which have been returned to the corporate treasury.

Deal Structure

Each founder will make an initial investment of $15,000 in cash, plus $5,000 in physical capital. That investment will purchase 20,000 shares apiece.

Zuma plans to raise the rest of the money Zuma needs by issuing debt that can be converted into equity. We recognize that start-up ventures are risky, and investors need appropriate assurances and rewards to compensate for those risks. By holding debt, investors will have first claim on the firm's cash flow, but the debt's convertibility will allow investors to enjoy great rewards if Zuma succeeds.

Zuma will ask investors for money at three points. Zuma wants to minimize losses that founders and other investors might suffer if Zuma is unsuccessful. Zuma will conduct two separate tests to be as certain as possible that Blitz SunTan Lotion will be a success. We will ask for funding to conduct a concept test, and we will ask for additional funding if a concept test is successful and if a market test is successful.

Zuma's founders will invest $30,000 in cash before the first test, the concept test. Zuma will ask outside investors for $142,700 before the concept test. This test is designed to determine formulation, packaging, and advertising likely to appeal to Zuma's largest market. It will begin in October 1996 (see Exhibit 5 for more details).

Zuma's founders will invest $30,000 in cash before beginning the second test, the market test. Zuma will ask outside investors for an additional $142,700. This test will occur only if the concept test is successful. The market test will begin in February 1997 in a limited market representing a microcosm of Zuma's eventual national market. This test is expected to help Zuma develop distribution channels and refine and implement its marketing strategy (see Exhibit 6 for more details.)

If both tests are successful, Zuma will ask outside investors for $200,000. That money will be used to fund the beginning of operations. Those will begin in October 1997.

Investors will receive quarterly interest payments, starting in the first quarter Zuma begins nationwide operations. These payments will be at an annual interest rate of 15 percent per year. During the first 30 days of fiscal year 2000 (Zuma's fourth full year of operations), investors will have the option of converting their debt into equity. Their ownership stake will be worth 20 percent of the company. If the outside investors choose not to convert their debt into equity, Zuma will have the option of converting the debt to equity and buying out investors by paying them the value of their equity.

Zuma hopes to obtain all venture capital funding from the same source and to line up commitments for that funding before beginning the concept test. That will allow Zuma's founders to focus their efforts on successfully developing and marketing Blitz SunTan Lotion, instead of needing to devote their time and efforts to raising more capital.

Zuma realizes that the investment in the concept test is the riskiest. However, because Zuma is receiving all its funding from the same source, Zuma will pay investors the same interest rate and allow them to convert their principal to equity.

Summary of Funds Needed

Date	Amount	Use	Interest rate
Sept. 1996	$142,000	Concept test	15%
Feb. 1997	$142,700	Market test	15%
Sept. 1997	$200,000	Nationwide launch	15%

Value of the Company ($000s)

	1997	1998	1999	2000	2001
Revenues	3,759	5,082	7,136	9,648	11,577
Net income	779	791	1,400	2,235	2,800
P/E ratio	22	22	22	22	22
Total value of equity	17,138	17,402	30,800	49,170	61,600
Value of equity offered				6,160	

Zuma has valued itself at a P/E ratio of 22. This is the value the stock market has typically assigned comparable consumer products companies: Schering-Plough, Johnson & Johnson, and Procter & Gamble. These companies are more stable and have a long track record of consistent growth. However, Zuma's small size and entrepreneurial culture will give it the ability to grow more quickly than those large companies, which already sell many products over large geographical areas.

Potential Returns to Investors ($000s)

If Conversion Occurs:	Year 0	Year 1	Year 2	Year 3	Year 4	Year 5
Investment	(485.4)					
Interest		72.8	72.8	72.8		
Equity received				6,160		
Percent of equity owned				20%		
Value of company				30,800	49,170	61,600
Terminal value						12,320

If Conversion Does Not Occur:	Year 0	Year 1	Year 2	Year 3	Year 4	Year 5
Investment	(485.4)					
Interest		72.8	72.8	72.8	72.8	72.8
Principal						485.4

Corporate Governance

Zuma will have a nine-person board of directors. Each founder will sit on the board. Entrepreneurs with experience in consumer product development and marketing will be asked to sit on the board; Zuma hopes to find two such entrepreneurs. The remaining three directors will be chosen by investors. Investors from each of the three issues of convertible debt will choose one director.

Each share of stock will be worth one vote. Convertible debt offering will allow outside investors one vote for every two shares of stock they would hold if they converted their debt into equity.

Zuma plans to obtain legal, accounting, and promotional services from companies with experience helping entrepreneurial firms grow quickly.

CRITICAL RISKS AND CONTINGENCIES

Any new business venture poses significant risks to investors. There can be no guarantee that investors will receive the principal they have invested. Here are some of the larger risks that will face Zuma SunCare, Inc.

Failure to Produce the Product As Required This could result from the inability of Zuma to reach of viable agreement with manufacturers of bottles, caps, labels, or sunscreen. This could also arise from the inability of the manufacturer to deliver a suitable product or to refund Zuma's payments once an agreement is reached.

Failure to Meet Production Deadlines If products are not produced or shipped quickly enough, Zuma could miss the peak selling season for sunscreen. This could also hurt Zuma's efforts to coordinate its marketing for Blitz SunTan Lotion with the product's introduction; customers could seek the brand but be unable to buy it. This would give competitors a greater chance to imitate Zuma's plans and build the awareness of their brands.

Inability to Convince Distributors and Retailers to Carry the Product Manufacturers introduce many new products, only a small fraction of which succeed. Zuma will have to persuade distributors to haul an unproven product from a new company. Zuma will also have to convince retailers to use their finite shelf space to stock Blitz SunTan Lotion.

As mentioned earlier, Zuma will do several things to persuade distributors to carry its products. We will give distributors, brokers, and retailers a full refund for any products unsold after 4 months. Zuma will offer its middlemen a similar margin as other leading regional sunscreens. However, Zuma will still be able to retail for about 20 percent less than those brands. Zuma will stress the benefits of having a sun care product targeted to a specific age group that frequently spends time in the sun.

Failure of the Market to Embrace the Product Simply put, Blitz SunTan Lotion may not appeal to the consuming public. Or it may appeal to the public, but it may not be appealing enough to convince consumers to buy the product. This would result in lower revenues, because of lower prices per unit and/or lower unit sales. The subsequent revenue decrease could result in Zuma being unprofitable and unable to repay its investors.

Difficulty Raising Additional Financing Zuma has to raise funds three times. By doing this, Zuma hopes to prevent investors from unnecessarily risking capital. However, this could cause Zuma to not have enough funding to launch its products nationwide, even if both preliminary tests are successful. That would leave Zuma unable to fully recover its investors' initial investments.

A Large Sun Care Product Manufacturer Invading Zuma's Niche One of the large sunscreen manufacturers may see what Zuma is doing and try to copy it. Zuma will trademark its name, logos, and advertising tag lines, but Zuma's product and two-chambered bottle will not enjoy patent protection. A larger competitor would have the ability to do more product promotions and advertising. It could sustain deeper short-term losses than could Zuma and try to underprice Zuma.

Zuma will combat this in several ways. In the contract with our bottle manufacturer, we will prohibit that company from selling two-chambered bottles for use by other sun care product manufacturers. We will also suggest that Zuma's retail price be about 20 percent below the retail price of our nearest competitors, other regional sunscreen makers. Those companies will have larger overhead and advertising budgets, which should deter self-destructive price competition.

Management Is Unproven This is the first entrepreneurial venture Zuma's managers will have launched. There will be setbacks and challenges that may surprise Zuma's founders. Zuma's founders may be at a disadvantage with potential suppliers and customers because of their inexperience.

This quartet has also not worked together extensively as a team. The founders could discover that they do not function as a cohesive group when working together on a daily basis.

SUMMARY AND CONCLUSIONS

Zuma SunCare, Inc., is a focused firm that can provide added value to sunscreen users and a significant return to investors. Zuma's unique two-chambered bottle concept enables consumers to conveniently carry and use varying levels of sunscreen protection. Furthermore, Zuma plans to combine sunscreen protection along with an after-sun moisturizing product, providing further value and convenience. Zuma will aim its marketing at a niche targeted only lightly by major sunscreen manufacturers: the 15–34 age group. Sunscreens sold by most competitors appear to have little appeal to people in this age group, who frequently enjoy the sun.

Zuma will minimize capital costs by subcontracting research, development, and production of its Blitz SunTan Lotion. This will enable Zuma to concentrate on its area

of expertise: marketing. The firm's president and CEO understands sunscreen consumers, in part because he grew up playing volleyball on the beaches of southern California. Another founder has extensive experience designing and creating companies' marketing and displays at trade shows.

Although marketing costs in this industry are high, Zuma will still be able to have substantial margins. Because Zuma is not capital-intensive, owners will be able to make a large return on their investment. By the end of year 5, Zuma projects sales of $11.6 million (2.5 percent of the marketplace) and after-tax profits of about $2.80 million. Zuma plans to allow outside investors to buy a 20 percent ownership stake. Zuma will divide the remaining shares equally among the four founders.

SCHEDULING AND MILESTONES

Before September 1996	Make founders' investments into company Incorporate company Obtain accountant, legal counsel
During or before September 1996	Acquire initial financing
October 1996	Begin concept test
During or before January 1997	Obtain second round of financing
January 1997	Reach agreements with subcontractors to begin producing Zuma SunTan Lotion
February 1997	Begin market test
During or before September 1997	Obtain third round of financing
October 1997	Begin nationwide launch of product

| During or before
December 1997 | Reach agreements
with manufacturing
subcontractors
Reach agreements
with brokers, distribu-
tors, retailers | December 1997

During or before
January 1997 | Begin repaying
investors' debts

Make first sales
Receive initial cash
from sales |

EXHIBIT 1   The SunCare Market

	1991	*1992*	*1993*	*1994*	*1995*
(in millions)					
Retail market share	$500	$520	$593	$600	$630

Retail Market Share—Suntan Products

	1994
Schering-Plough	33%
Banana Boat	11%
Hawaiian Tropic	10%
Bain de Soleil	9%
Vaseline IC	6%
Others	31%
Total	100%

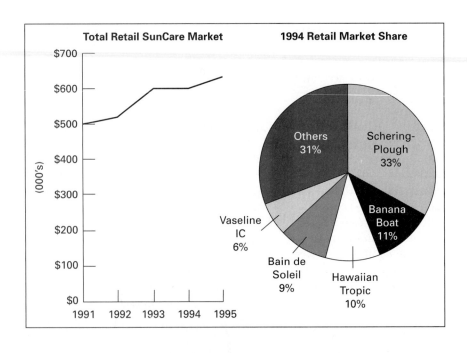

EXHIBIT 2   Population Trends

Age Group	1994	1999	2005	Regular Users
15–19	17.6	19.6	21.0	34.8%
20–24	18.4	17.7	19.8	38.3%
25–29	19.1	18.3	18.1	38.0%
30–34	22.1	19.8	18.4	38.3%
Total 15–34	77.2	75.4	77.3	
Total U.S. population	260.2	272.5	286.3	33.0%

Age Group	(in millions)
15–19	6.1
20–24	7.0
25–29	7.3
30–34	8.5
Total User Base	**28.9**
Average annual retail $ spent	$ 11.00
Estimated young adult segment ($ retail)	**$318**

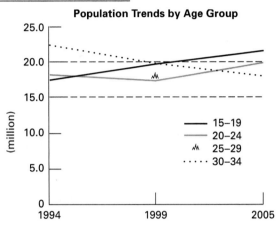

Source: Department of Commerce, Population Series, p. 25.

EXHIBIT 3   Production Process

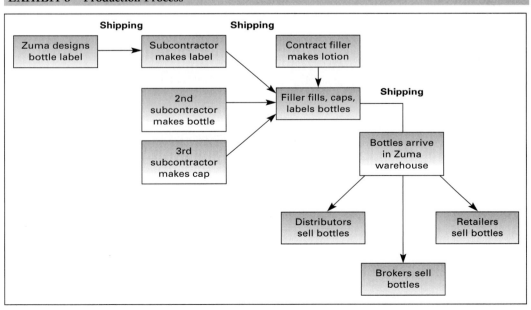

EXHIBIT 4 **Initial Sales and Costs Forecasts**

Sales and Costs Estimate by Category
Based on Estimated Average Monthly Sales in the First Year

Cost per Ounce	SPF4	SPF8	SPF15	SPF30	Aloe Vera Gel
Active ingredient	$0.05	$0.08	$0.16	$0.25	$0.25
Inactive ingredients	$0.05	$0.05	$0.05	$0.05	$0.00
Bottle	$0.20	$0.20	$0.20	$0.20	$0.20
Caps	$0.15	$0.15	$0.15	$0.15	$0.15
Label	$0.08	$0.08	$0.08	$0.08	$0.08
Cost per 8-ounce bottle	$1.23	$1.47	$2.11	$2.83	$2.43

Per Unit Cost for Bottle Sold

Costs per Bottle	SPF4 & SPF8	SPF4 & SPF15	SPF8 & SPF15	SPF8 & SPF30	SPF15 & SPF30	SPF4 & Aloe	SPF8 & Aloe	SPF15 & Aloe	SPF30 & Aloe
Active ingredients	$0.52	$0.84	$0.96	$1.32	$1.64	$1.20	$1.32	$1.64	$2.00
Inactive ingredients	$0.40	$0.40	$0.40	$0.40	$0.40	$0.20	$0.20	$0.20	$0.20
Bottle	$0.20	$0.20	$0.20	$0.20	$0.20	$0.20	$0.20	$0.20	$0.20
Caps	$0.15	$0.15	$0.15	$0.15	$0.15	$0.15	$0.15	$0.15	$0.15
Label	$0.08	$0.08	$0.08	$0.08	$0.08	$0.08	$0.08	$0.08	$0.08
Total unit costs	$1.35	$1.67	$1.79	$2.15	$2.47	$1.83	$1.95	$2.27	$2.63
Estimated unit sales amount	2000	2500	6900	6700	6700	4000	12500	13500	9500
Estimated retail price	$7.25	$7.49	$7.95	$8.49	$8.95	$7.49	$7.95	$8.49	$9.49
Estimated unit sales price	$3.99	$4.12	$4.37	$4.67	$4.92	$4.12	$4.37	$4.67	$5.22
Margin per bottle	$2.64	$2.45	$2.58	$2.52	$2.45	$2.29	$2.42	$2.40	$2.59

Total number of sales	64300
Weighted average retail price	$8.38
Weighted average sales price	$4.61
Weighted average cost	$2.14
Weighted average profit per bottle	$2.47

EXHIBIT 5   Concept Test Funding Requirements

Additional Funds Needed
Year 0 Concept Test
in Months 1–5

Use of funds:	
Production and start-up expenses	$10,000
Research and development	$15,000
Package design	$10,000
Bottle mold	$10,000
Market research expenses	$5,000
Travel expenses	$5,000
Advertising development	$50,000
Logo and artwork development	$10,000
Legal fees	$2,000
Salary and wages	$40,000
Total	$157,000
Plus contingency	$15,700
Total funds needed	$172,700
Founder's initial investment	$30,000
Total outside funding required	$142,700

EXHIBIT 6   Market Test Funding Required

Year 0
Additional Funds Required
Market Test in Months 6–12

Use of funds:	
Product production	$10,000
Package design	$5,000
Research and development	$5,000
Travel expenses	$10,000
Advertising development	$25,000
Media expense	$20,000
Legal fees	$2,000
Salary and wages	$80,000
Total	$157,000
Plus contingency	$15,700
Total funds needed	$172,700
Founder's additional investment	$30,000
Total outside funding required	$142,700

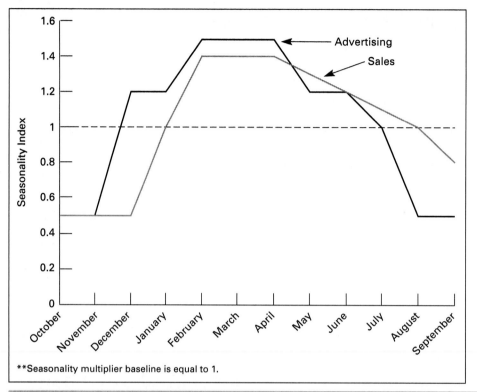

EXHIBIT 7   Seasonality Market Trends*

*Seasonality multiplier baseline is equal to 1.

EXHIBIT 8 Monthly Sales for Year 1997

	October	November	December	January	February	March	April	May	June	July	August	September
Number of bottles sold	32,150	33,758	33,758	67,515	94,521	94,521	94,521	87,770	81,018	74,267	67,515	54,012
Number of cases sold	1,340	1,407	1,407	2,813	3,938	3,938	3,938	3,657	3,376	3,094	2,813	2,251
Revenues												
Sales	$148,234	$155,646	$155,646	$311,292	$435,808	$435,808	$435,808	$404,679	$373,550	$342,421	$311,292	$249,033
Cost of goods sold	$68,753	$72,190	$72,190	$144,380	$202,132	$202,132	$202,132	$187,694	$173,256	$158,818	$144,380	$115,504
Gross Profit	$79,482	$83,456	$83,456	$166,911	$233,676	$233,676	$233,676	$216,985	$200,294	$183,602	$166,911	$133,529
Operating Expenses												
Interest expense	$7,665	$7,700	$7,700	$8,421	$8,999	$8,999	$8,999	$8,855	$8,710	$8,566	$8,421	$8,133
Rent	$833	$833	$833	$833	$833	$833	$833	$833	$833	$833	$833	$833
Utilities	$417	$417	$417	$417	$417	$417	$417	$417	$417	$417	$417	$417
Salary	$13,333	$13,333	$13,333	$13,333	$13,333	$13,333	$13,333	$13,333	$13,333	$13,333	$13,333	$13,333
Wages	$1,600	$1,600	$1,600	$1,600	$1,600	$1,600	$1,600	$1,600	$1,600	$1,600	$1,600	$1,600
Broker expense	$2,965	$3,113	$3,113	$6,226	$8,716	$8,716	$8,716	$8,094	$7,471	$6,848	$6,226	$4,981
Travel and entertainment	$3,333	$3,333	$3,333	$3,333	$3,333	$3,333	$3,333	$3,333	$3,333	$3,333	$3,333	$3,333
Shipping costs	$5,000	$5,000	$5,000	$5,000	$5,000	$5,000	$5,000	$5,000	$5,000	$5,000	$5,000	$5,000
Depreciation	$333	$333	$333	$333	$333	$333	$333	$333	$333	$333	$333	$333
Advertising												
Television advertising	$0	$0	$0	$0	$0	$0	$0	$0	$0	$0	$0	$0
Radio advertising	$4,167	$4,167	$10,000	$10,000	$12,500	$12,500	$12,500	$10,000	$10,000	$8,333	$3,333	$3,333
Print advertising	$1,042	$1,042	$2,500	$2,500	$3,125	$3,125	$3,125	$2,500	$2,500	$2,083	$833	$833
Billboard advertising	$1,042	$1,042	$2,500	$2,500	$3,125	$3,125	$3,125	$2,500	$2,500	$2,083	$833	$833
Promotions												
Sponsorships	$3,125	$3,125	$7,500	$7,500	$9,375	$9,375	$9,375	$7,500	$7,500	$6,250	$2,500	$2,500
In-store promos	$1,479	$1,479	$3,550	$3,550	$4,438	$4,438	$4,438	$3,550	$3,550	$2,958	$1,183	$1,183
Free samples	$208	$208	$500	$500	$625	$625	$625	$500	$500	$417	$167	$167
Trade shows	$2,083	$2,083	$5,000	$5,000	$6,250	$6,250	$6,250	$5,000	$5,000	$4,167	$1,667	$1,667
Office supplies	$292	$292	$292	$292	$292	$292	$292	$292	$292	$292	$292	$292
Insurance	$500	$500	$500	$500	$500	$500	$500	$500	$500	$500	$500	$500
Miscellaneous expenses	$1,250	$1,250	$1,250	$1,250	$1,250	$1,250	$1,250	$1,250	$1,250	$1,250	$1,250	$1,250
Total Operating Expenses	$50,667	$50,850	$69,254	$73,089	$84,044	$84,044	$84,044	$75,390	$74,623	$68,598	$52,056	$50,522
Income before tax	$28,814	$32,606	$14,202	$93,822	$149,632	$149,632	$149,632	$141,595	$125,671	$115,005	$114,856	$83,007
Taxes	$10,085	$11,412	$4,971	$32,838	$52,371	$52,371	$52,371	$49,558	$43,985	$40,252	$40,200	$29,053
Net Income	$18,729	$21,194	$9,231	$60,985	$97,261	$97,261	$97,261	$92,037	$81,686	$74,753	$74,656	$53,955
Break-even volume (bottles)	20,495	20,569	28,013	29,564	33,996	33,996	33,996	30,495	30,185	27,747	21,056	20,436
Excess volume sold (bottles)	11,655	13,189	5,744	37,951	60,525	60,525	60,525	57,275	50,833	46,519	46,459	33,576

EXHIBIT 9 Quarterly Sales for 3 Years

1,059,921

	1997				1998				1999			
	Q1	Q2	Q3	Q4	Q1	Q2	Q3	Q4	Q1	Q2	Q3	Q4
Number of bottles sold	99,665	256,557	263,309	195,794	129,565	333,524	342,301	254,532	174,912	450,258	462,106	343,618
Number of cases sold	4,153	10,690	10,971	8,158	5,399	13,897	14,263	10,605	7,288	18,761	19,254	14,317
Revenues												
Sales	$459,526	$1,182,908	$1,214,037	$902,746	$621,279	$1,599,292	$1,641,378	$1,220,512	$872,275	$2,245,405	$2,304,495	$1,713,599
Cost of goods sold	$213,133	$548,645	$563,083	$418,703	$288,155	$741,768	$761,288	$566,086	$404,570	$1,041,442	$1,068,849	$794,785
Gross Profit	$246,393	$634,263	$650,954	$484,043	$333,123	$857,524	$880,090	$654,426	$467,705	$1,203,963	$1,235,646	$918,814
Operating Expenses												
Interest expense	$23,064	$23,820	$25,120	$26,419	$29,578	$43,186	$43,772	$37,915	$33,070	$52,176	$52,998	$44,776
Rent	$2,500	$2,500	$2,500	$2,500	$2,600	$2,600	$2,600	$2,600	$2,704	$2,704	$2,704	$2,704
Utilities	$1,250	$1,250	$1,250	$1,250	$1,300	$1,300	$1,300	$1,300	$1,352	$1,352	$1,352	$1,352
Salary	$40,000	$40,000	$40,000	$40,000	$41,600	$41,600	$41,600	$41,600	$43,264	$43,264	$43,264	$43,264
Wages	$4,800	$4,800	$4,800	$4,800	$14,976	$14,976	$14,976	$14,976	$26,997	$26,997	$26,997	$26,997
Broker expense	$9,191	$23,658	$24,281	$18,055	$12,426	$31,986	$32,828	$24,410	$17,446	$44,908	$46,090	$34,272
Travel and entertainment	$10,000	$10,000	$10,000	$10,000	$10,400	$10,400	$10,400	$10,400	$10,816	$10,816	$10,816	$10,816
Shipping costs	$15,000	$15,000	$15,000	$15,000	$20,800	$20,800	$20,800	$20,800	$21,632	$21,632	$21,632	$21,632
Depreciation	$1,000	$1,000	$1,000	$1,000	$1,000	$1,000	$1,000	$1,000	$1,000	$1,000	$1,000	$1,000
Advertising												
Television advertising	$0	$0	$0	$0	$95,333	$182,000	$169,000	$78,000	$99,147	$189,280	$175,760	$81,120
Radio advertising	$18,333	$35,000	$32,500	$15,000	$19,067	$36,400	$33,800	$15,600	$19,829	$37,856	$35,152	$16,224
Print advertising	$4,583	$8,750	$8,125	$3,750	$4,767	$9,100	$8,450	$3,900	$4,957	$9,464	$8,788	$4,056
Billboard advertising	$4,583	$8,750	$8,125	$3,750	$4,767	$9,100	$8,450	$3,900	$4,957	$9,464	$8,788	$4,056
Promotions												
Sponsorships	$13,750	$26,250	$24,375	$11,250	$14,300	$27,300	$25,350	$11,700	$14,872	$28,392	$26,364	$12,168
In-store promos	$6,508	$12,425	$11,538	$5,325	$6,769	$12,922	$11,999	$5,538	$7,039	$13,439	$12,479	$5,760
Free samples	$917	$1,750	$1,625	$750	$953	$1,820	$1,690	$780	$991	$1,893	$1,758	$811
Trade shows	$9,167	$17,500	$16,250	$7,500	$9,533	$18,200	$16,900	$7,800	$9,915	$18,928	$17,576	$8,112
Office supplies	$875	$875	$875	$875	$910	$910	$910	$910	$946	$946	$946	$946
Insurance	$1,500	$1,500	$1,500	$1,500	$1,560	$1,560	$1,560	$1,560	$1,622	$1,622	$1,622	$1,622
Miscellaneous expenses	$3,750	$3,750	$3,750	$3,750	$3,900	$3,900	$3,900	$3,900	$4,056	$4,056	$4,056	$4,056
Total Operating Expenses	$170,771	$241,177	$234,057	$171,175	$296,538	$471,060	$451,284	$288,590	$326,613	$520,189	$500,142	$325,745
Income before tax	$75,622	$393,085	$416,897	$312,868	$36,585	$386,464	$428,806	$365,836	$141,092	$683,774	$735,504	$593,069
Taxes	$26,468	$137,580	$145,914	$109,504	$12,805	$135,262	$150,082	$128,043	$49,382	$239,321	$257,426	$207,574
Net Income	$49,154	$255,506	$270,983	$203,364	$23,781	$251,201	$278,724	$237,794	$91,710	$444,453	$478,078	$385,495
Break-even volume (bottles)	69,076	97,555	94,675	69,240	119,948	190,542	182,543	116,733	132,114	210,415	202,306	131,762
Excess volume sold (bottles)	30,589	159,002	168,633	126,554	9,616	142,982	159,758	137,798	42,798	239,843	259,801	211,855

EXHIBIT 10 Annual Sales for 5 Years

	1997	1998	1999	2000	2001
Number of bottles sold	815,324	1,059,921	1,430,894	1,860,162	2,232,194
Number of cases sold	33,972	44,163	59,621	77,507	93,008
Revenues					
Sales	$3,759,216	$5,082,460	$7,135,774	$9,647,567	$11,577,080
Cost of goods sold	$1,743,563	$2,357,298	$3,309,646	$4,474,641	$5,369,570
Gross Profit	$2,015,653	$2,725,163	$3,826,128	$5,172,925	$6,207,510
Operating Expenses					
Interest expense	$98,424	$154,450	$183,021	$134,239	$161,087
Rent	$10,000	$10,400	$10,816	$11,249	$11,699
Utilities	$5,000	$5,200	$5,408	$5,624	$5,849
Salary	$160,000	$166,400	$173,056	$179,978	$187,177
Wages	$20,000	$62,400	$112,486	$126,532	$148,024
Broker expense	$75,184	$101,649	$142,715	$192,951	$231,542
Travel and entertainment	$40,000	$41,600	$43,264	$44,995	$46,794
Shipping costs	$60,000	$83,200	$86,528	$67,492	$70,192
Depreciation	$4,000	$4,000	$4,000	$4,000	$4,000
Advertising					
Television advertising	$0	$524,333	$545,307	$562,432	$584,929
Radio advertising	$100,833	$104,867	$109,061	$112,486	$116,986
Print advertising	$25,208	$26,217	$27,265	$28,122	$29,246
Billboard advertising	$25,208	$26,217	$27,265	$28,122	$29,246
Promotions					
Sponsorships	$75,000	$78,000	$84,365	$94,899	$111,018
In-store promos	$35,500	$36,920	$39,933	$44,919	$52,549
Free samples	$5,000	$5,200	$5,624	$6,327	$7,401
Trade shows	$50,000	$52,000	$56,243	$63,266	$74,012
Office supplies	$3,500	$3,640	$3,786	$3,937	$4,095
Insurance	$6,000	$6,240	$6,490	$6,749	$7,019
Miscellaneous Expenses	$15,000	$15,600	$16,224	$16,873	$17,548
Total Operating Expenses	$817,181	$1,507,471	$1,672,690	$1,735,191	$1,900,414
Income before tax	$1,198,472	$1,217,691	$2,153,438	$3,437,734	$4,307,096
Taxes	$419,465	$426,192	$753,703	$1,203,207	$1,507,484
Net Income	$779,007	$791,499	$1,399,735	$2,234,527	$2,799,612
Break-even volume (bottles)	330,547	609,767	676,597		
Excess volume sold (bottles)	484,777	450,155	754,297		

EXHIBIT 11 Quarterly Cash Flows for 3 Years

	1997				1998				1999			
	Q1	Q2	Q3	Q4	Q1	Q2	Q3	Q4	Q1	Q2	Q3	Q4
Operating Activities												
Net income	$49,154	$255,506	$270,983	$203,364	$23,781	$251,201	$278,724	$237,794	$91,710	$444,453	$478,078	$385,495
(Increase) decrease in accounts receivable	($37,769)	($59,456)	($2,559)	$25,586	($51,064)	($80,385)	($3,459)	$34,592	($71,694)	($112,860)	($4,857)	$48,567
(Increase) decrease in inventories	($17,518)	($27,576)	($1,187)	$11,867	($23,684)	($37,283)	($1,604)	$16,044	($33,252)	($52,346)	($2,253)	$22,526
Increase (decrease) in accounts payable	$4,379	$6,894	$297	($2,967)	$5,921	$9,321	$401	($4,011)	$8,313	$13,086	$563	($5,631)
Increase (decrease) in notes payable	$44,758	$70,458	$3,032	($30,320)	$60,513	$95,259	$4,099	($40,992)	$84,960	$133,743	$5,755	($57,553)
(Increase) decrease in prepaid rent	($7,500)	$2,500	$2,500	$2,500	($7,800)	$2,600	$2,600	$2,600	($8,112)	$2,704	$2,704	$2,704
Increase (decrease) in interest payable	$23,064	$23,820	$25,120	($72,005)	$29,578	$43,186	$43,772	($116,535)	$33,070	$52,176	$52,998	($138,244)
Increase (decrease) in accumulated depreciation	$1,000	$1,000	$1,000	$1,000	$1,000	$1,000	$1,000	$1,000	$1,000	$1,000	$1,000	$1,000
Net Cash from Operations	$59,569	$273,145	$299,186	$139,026	$42,244	$284,899	$325,532	$130,491	$113,994	$481,957	$533,989	$258,862
Investment Activities												
(Purchase) sale of equipment	$0	$0	$0	$0	$0	$0	$0	$0	$0	$0	$0	$0
Net Cash from Investing												
Financing Activities												
Issuance of equity	$0	$0	$0	$0	$0	$0	$0	$0	$0	$0	$0	$0
Issuance of long-term debt	$0	$0	$0	$0	$0	$0	$0	$0	$0	$0	$0	($485,400)
Payment of dividends	$0	$0	$0	$0	$0	$0	$0	$0	$0	$0	$0	$0
Net Cash Flows from Financing												($485,400)
Beginning Cash Balance	$200,000	$259,569	$532,714	$831,900	$970,926	$1,013,169	$1,298,068	$1,623,601	$1,754,091	$1,868,086	$2,350,042	$2,884,032
Ending Cash Balance	$259,569	$532,714	$831,900	$970,926	$1,013,169	$1,298,068	$1,623,601	$1,754,091	$1,868,086	$2,350,042	$2,884,032	$2,657,494

EXHIBIT 12 Annual Cash Flows for 5 Years	1997	1998	1999	2000	2001
Operating Activities					
Net income	$779,007	$791,499	$1,399,735	$2,234,527	$2,799,612
(Increase) decrease in accounts receivable	($74,198)	($100,316)	($140,844)	($57,394)	($39,648)
(Increase) decrease in inventories	($34,414)	($46,528)	($65,325)	($26,620)	($18,389)
Increase (decrease) in accounts payable	$8,603	$11,632	$16,331	$6,655	$4,597
Increase (decrease) in notes payable	$87,928	$118,878	$166,905	$32,666	($26,848)
(Increase) decrease in prepaid rent	$0	$0	($0)	($0)	$0
Increase (decrease) in interest payable	$0	$0	$0	$0	$0
Increase (decrease) in accumulated depreciation	$4,000	$4,000	$4,000	$4,000	$4,000
Net Cash from Operations	$770,926	$779,166	$1,380,803	$2,193,834	$2,723,325
Investment Activities					
(Purchase) sale of equipment	$0	$0	$0	$0	$0
Net Cash from Investing	$0	$0	$0	$0	$0
Financing Activities					
Issuance of equity	$0	$0	$0	$0	$0
Issuance of long-term debt	$0	$0	($485,400)	$0	$0
Payment of dividends	$0	$0	$0	$0	$0
Net Cash Flows from Financing	$0	$0	($485,400)	$0	$0
Beginning Cash Balance	$200,000	$970,926	$1,754,091	$2,657,494	$4,851,328
Ending Cash Balance	$970,926	$1,750,091	$2,649,494	$4,851,328	$7,574,653

EXHIBIT 13 Quarterly Balance Sheets for 3 Years

	1997				1998				1999			
	Q1	*Q2*	*Q3*	*Q4*	*Q1*	*Q2*	*Q3*	*Q4*	*Q1*	*Q2*	*Q3*	*Q4*
Assets												
Cash and marketable securities	$259,569	$532,714	$831,900	$970,926	$1,013,169	$1,298,068	$1,623,601	$1,754,091	$1,868,086	$2,350,042	$2,884,032	$2,657,494
Accounts receivable	$37,769	$97,225	$99,784	$74,198	$51,064	$131,449	$134,908	$100,316	$71,694	$184,554	$189,411	$140,844
Inventories	$17,518	$45,094	$46,281	$34,414	$23,684	$60,967	$62,572	$46,528	$33,252	$85,598	$87,851	$65,325
Other assets	$15,000	$10,000	$5,000	$0	$23,681	$18,481	$13,281	$8,081	$32,639	$27,231	$21,823	$16,415
Equipment	$20,000	$20,000	$20,000	$20,000	$20,000	$20,000	$20,000	$20,000	$20,000	$20,000	$20,000	$20,000
Less depreciation	$1,000	$2,000	$3,000	$4,000	$5,000	$6,000	$7,000	$8,000	$9,000	$10,000	$11,000	$12,000
Net equipment	$19,000	$18,000	$17,000	$16,000	$15,000	$14,000	$13,000	$12,000	$11,000	$10,000	$9,000	$8,000
Total Assets	$348,855	$703,033	$999,965	$1,095,538	$1,126,598	$1,522,965	$1,847,361	$1,921,016	$2,016,671	$2,657,425	$3,192,116	$2,888,077
Liabilities												
Accounts payable	$4,379	$11,274	$11,570	$8,603	$5,921	$15,242	$15,643	$11,632	$8,313	$21,399	$21,963	$16,331
Notes payable	$44,758	$115,215	$118,247	$87,928	$60,513	$155,771	$159,871	$118,878	$84,960	$218,703	$224,458	$166,905
Prepaid rent	$7,500	$5,000	$2,500	$0	$7,800	$5,200	$2,600	$0	$8,112	$5,408	$2,704	$0
Interest payable	$23,064	$46,885	$72,005	$0	$29,578	$72,763	$116,535	$0	$33,070	$85,246	$138,244	$0
Other liabilities	$0	$0	$0	$0	$0	$0	$0	$0	$0	$0	$0	$0
Long-term debt	$485,400	$485,400	$485,400	$485,400	$485,400	$485,400	$485,400	$485,400	$485,400	$485,400	$485,400	$485,400
Total Liabilities	$565,102	$663,774	$689,722	$581,931	$589,211	$734,377	$780,048	$615,910	$619,855	$816,156	$872,769	$183,236
Owner's Equity												
Common stock	$80,000	$80,000	$80,000	$80,000	$80,000	$80,000	$80,000	$80,000	$80,000	$80,000	$80,000	$80,000
Equity in excess of par	$0	$0	$0	$0	$0	$0	$0	$0	$0	$0	$0	$0
Retained earnings	($296,246)	($40,740)	$230,243	$433,607	$457,387	$708,589	$987,313	$1,225,106	$1,316,816	$1,761,269	$2,239,346	$2,624,841
Total Owner's Equity	($216,246)	$39,260	$310,243	$513,607	$537,387	$788,589	$1,067,313	$1,305,106	$1,396,816	$1,841,269	$2,319,346	$2,704,841
Total Liabilities and Owner's Equity	$348,855	$703,033	$999,965	$1,095,538	$1,126,599	$1,522,965	$1,847,361	$1,921,016	$2,016,671	$2,657,425	$3,192,115	$2,888,077

EXHIBIT 14 Annual Balance Sheets for 5 Years					
	1997	*1998*	*1999*	*2000*	*2001*
Assets					
Cash and marketable securities	$970,926	$1,754,091	$2,657,494	$4,851,328	$7,574,653
Accounts receivable	$74,198	$100,316	$140,844	$198,238	$237,885
Inventories	$34,414	$46,528	$65,325	$91,945	$110,334
Other assets	$0	$8,081	$16,415	$35,665	$66,941
Equipment	$20,000	$20,000	$20,000	$20,000	$20,000
Less depreciation	$4,000	$8,000	$12,000	$16,000	$20,000
Net equipment	$16,000	$12,000	$8,000	$4,000	$0
Total Assets	$1,095,538	$1,921,016	$2,888,077	$5,181,175	$7,989,813
Liabilities					
Accounts payable	$8,603	$11,632	$16,331	$22,986	$27,583
Notes payable	$87,928	$118,878	$166,905	$134,239	$161,087
Prepaid rent	$0	$0	$0	$0	$0
Interest payable	$0	$0	$0	$0	$0
Other liabilities	$0	$0	$0	$84,581	$62,162
Long-term debt	$485,400	$485,400	$0	$0	$0
Total Liabilities	$581,931	$615,910	$183,236	$241,806	$250,832
Owner's Equity					
Common stock	$80,000	$80,000	$80,000	$80,000	$80,000
Equity in excess of par	$0	$0	$0	$0	$0
Retained earnings	$433,607	$1,225,106	$2,624,841	$4,859,368	$7,658,981
Total Owner's Equity	$513,607	$1,305,106	$2,704,841	$4,939,368	$7,738,981
Total Liabilities and Owner's Equity	$1,095,538	$1,921,016	$2,888,077	$5,181,175	$7,989,813

The original research for this case was prepared by Tom Kinney, Eric Olson, Pat Dunne, and Kurt Moeller under the supervision of Marc Dollinger in the fall of 1996. The data in the case are real. Some of the names and places have been disguised.

Case 2   Tellme Networks: Dial Tone 2.0?

It was close to midnight on a brisk night in November 2000, and Mike McCue, co-founder and CEO of Tellme Networks, was on yet another recruiting mission.[1] His targets: top computer-engineering students at Stanford University. His secret weapon: free pizza. McCue planned to personally deliver pizzas to the Stanford computer lab in hopes of convincing a handful of top students to quit school and join Tellme, the leading provider of Web content that could be accessed using simple voice commands over a regular telephone. The now 32-year-old McCue himself had skipped college and joined IBM as a graphics specialist.[2] As CEO of Tellme, McCue spent about 60 to 80 percent of his time recruiting employees. "It's not hard to get money these days," he claimed. "It's getting the right people that's difficult."[3]

Indeed, it had not been hard for Tellme to win over financial backers. In fact, its success at raising money—an astounding $238 million as of the end of 2000[4]—made the voice portal war Tellme's to lose. Its list of backers was a virtual Who's Who of the venture capital world. Tellme had raised $125 million in October 2000 despite immense volatility in the stock markets and the general downturn of technology stocks. The substantial investments—not to mention an alliance with telecommunications giant AT&T—gave Tellme a significant leg up on the competition. Still, the company faced increasing pressure to deliver on its ever-evolving business plan.

"Our long-term goal is to create Dial Tone 2.0," McCue said, envisioning a future when users would not even need to dial Tellme. Instead of getting a dial tone when they pick up the phone, users would be connected directly to their personal Tellme virtual assistant, ready at their disposal.[5] Would Tellme succeed in becoming the Yahoo! of the voice portal market? How would the company capture and sustain profits in this rapidly evolving market?

COMPANY BACKGROUND: "NETSCAPEES"

McCue got involved with computers at a fairly young age. He wrote several video games in high school, and after graduating he joined IBM as a graphics specialist.[6] In 1989, he left IBM and founded Paper Software, which went on to develop 3-D Internet software that enabled Netscape Navigator to display complex graphics. In February 1996, McCue sold his company to Netscape Communications for an estimated $20 million and joined the firm as vice president of technology. After America Online acquired Netscape in 1998, McCue, like dozens of Netscape's other top engineers and middle managers, left the company to start his own venture.

In January 1999, McCue and 22-year-old computer whiz Angus Davis, a fellow "Netscapee," founded Tellme Networks in Mountain View, California. McCue also

MBA candidates Yi-Hsin Change, Quyen Chu, Kedric George, Dhruv Mohindra, and Zinnie Yoon prepared this case under the supervision of Professor Christopher L. Tucci for the purpose of class discussion rather than to illustrate either effective or ineffective handling of an administrative situation. Distributed by the Berkley Center for Entrepreneurial Studies at the Stern School of Business, New York University. To order copies, phone: 212-998-0070, fax: 212-995-4211, or e-mail: bces@stern.nyu.edu.

quickly brought on one-time arch nemesis Hadi Partovi, formerly the group program manager for Microsoft's Internet Explorer, as part of Tellme's founding management team, which consisted of several other Netscapees. (See Exhibit 1 for details on Tellme's management team.) In July, former Netscape CEO Jim Barksdale and former Microsoft senior vice president Brad Silverberg, along with Tellme's roughly 20 employees, contributed $6 million as seed money for Tellme.[7]

Thanks to the pedigree of its founders and management team, Tellme raised an additional $47 million in December 1999 from leading venture capital firms Benchmark Capital and Kleiner Perkins Caufield & Byers. (See Exhibit 2 for details on Tellme's advisers.) In May 2000, AT&T invested $60 million in Tellme as part of a strategic relationship in which Tellme would use AT&T networking services and collaborate with AT&T to develop business and consumer applications. In October, Tellme raised an additional $125 million in financing from a group of well-known technology institutional investors. (See Exhibit 3 for a company timeline.) With its more than 250 employees, the company expected that the latest round of financing would carry the company through to profitability.[8]

"TELLME MORE"

Tellme offers Web content via a toll-free number (1-800-555-TELL). Users can call Tellme and access news, weather forecasts, sports scores, stock quotes, traffic reports, horoscopes, and movie and restaurant listings using simple voice commands, such as "Tellme news" or "Tellme more." Users can also set "Tellme Favorites," including specific cities for weather forecasts and different types of news through Tellme's Web site. In addition, Tellme can connect users to major airlines and a local taxi service anywhere in the country.

"Simple, everyday tasks for simple, everyday people on simple, everyday devices—telephones," explains, McCue, who wanted to create something as attractive to consumers as the Web without a technology barrier.[9] "Everyone from my grandmother to my baby brother can understand this," he says. "Nothing to buy, download, install, or set up—just pick up the phone and dial." There are only a couple of hundred million Web-enabled devices in the world today, but there are 1.5 billion telephones.[10] With Tellme, anyone with access to a phone can access Web-based content without any additional hardware.

Industry experts are calling this interplay of Web-based content and the telephone a "voice portal," much like a Yahoo! except via phone. Tellme began a nationwide 3-month trial of its free voice portal service in April 2000 and officially launched its service in July after completing 1.6 million calls during the test period. Through the trial, the company increased its voice-recognition accuracy to an average of 95 percent.

DEVELOPMENT OF TELLME

Although its service relies heavily on advanced voice-recognition software, Tellme actually outsources the technology and licenses it from companies such as Nuance and Lernout & Hauspie. Tellme combines the voice-recognition technolgoy with proprietary user interface tools and a new programming standard called VoiceXML (VXML) to encode Web content in such a way that a voice browser can automatically recognize and retrieve information.[11] McCue equates Tellme to "radio on demand," a combination of a speech-recognition portal and search engine designed to save time and money.

Tellme sells advertising and charges an undisclosed fee to list companies on its 1-800 directory. The company also makes money as an application service provider

(ASP) by hosting applications for existing Internet sites. "The real money is in the ASPs," says Yankee Group analyst Megan Gurley. "The e-commerce and advertising revenue will be chump change."[12] Eventually, Tellme plans to offer commerce as well, which would allow users to order items and services from e-tailers such as Amazon.com using just a telephone. The idea is that Tellme would take a cut of every order placed using its service. "It's about hearing a song on the radio, and being able to call Tellme and buy it," McCue says.[13]

After its most recent round of financing, Tellme recently began emphasizing professional services for building phone sites and providing other voice-enabling services to businesses. Tellme offers businesses a technology called Tellme Studio (studio.tellme. com) that is free and offers extensive tools necessary to get a simple phone site up and running using a Web browser and an ordinary phone. Since Tellme Studio uses familiar Internet standards such as HTML, HTTP, Javascript and SSL, companies can use their existing Web sites and Web technologies to build their phone sites. Once the phone sites are built, Tellme offers additional services, for a fee, to further improve these sites.

"This is all about recreating the Web phenomenon on the telephone network," says McCue. "By bringing the Internet's open standards to the phone, we expect to see the creation of thousands of compelling phone sites linked together to form a 'phone Web' that can be used by nearly anyone, anywhere."[14]

OVERVIEW OF THE VOICE PORTAL MARKET

Voice portals allow callers to use toll-free numbers to access the Internet from a telephone without an Internet connection. (See Exhibit 4 for an illustration of how a voice portal works.) Forrester Research estimates that voice-driven e-commerce could reach and exceed $450 billion in revenue by 2003, which is three times the projected revenue for online retailing.[15] Market research firm Kelsey Group projects that more than 18 million U.S. consumers will use a voice portal service by 2005.[16]

While mobile professionals are the likely target market for voice portals, other potential customers include commuters needing traffic updates, consumers wanting local information via audible yellow pages, disabled individuals who cannot utilize a keyboard but can access information audibly, and the estimated 55 percent of U.S. homes still without Internet access.[17]

Existing Web portals expect voice portals to be popular with regular Web users, who would hopefully log on more often if they could do so using their cell phones. They also anticipate tapping a vast and entirely new audience of users who do not own PCs, which amounts to about half of all U.S. households.

COMPETITION

Tellme faces roughly 30 to 35 start-up competitors in the voice portal market. Many players in this market are focusing on distinct services, such as providing driving directions or reading the user's e-mail out loud, or on specific markets, such as those outside of the United States, as a means of differentiation. (See Exhibit 5 for details on Tellme's main competitors and Exhibit 6 for a list of infrastructure companies supporting the voice portal market.)

While competition among voice portal start-ups is already intense, established technology and Internet companies have also started to get in the mix. America Online recently took a small stake in Speechworks International, a Boston-based voice-recognition software maker, and acquired voice portal Quack.com.[18]

Tellme's key competitive advantage against its competitors may not be its technology or toll-free service offerings, but rather its seasoned management team, its blue-chip investors—including Kleiner Perkins and Benchmark Capital—its strategic alliance with AT&T, and its $238 million war chest. That is significantly more money than all of its rivals combined.[19]

TELLME ALLIANCES

As a voice portal, Tellme needs content providers such as CNN Radio and *The Wall Street Journal* to feed news reports. However, Tellme's most important alliance has been its deal with telecom giant AT&T. Both AT&T and Tellme are gambling that consumers will want Web access when there is no good Web connection available.

For Tellme, AT&T's $60 million investment gave the start-up much-needed validation and credibility in the eyes of consumers—not to mention the much-needed cash. The alliance also solidified Tellme's leadership position in the voice portal market, and gave Tellme access to a wide range of advanced networking capabilities, a scalable infrastructure, networking management, professional services, and Internet hosting. In short, AT&T brought McCue & Co. one step closer to replacing the dial tone.

For AT&T, the deal gave the telecom giant a foothold in the voice portal market, putting it first in line to reap any benefits if voice portals really take off. In essence, AT&T was able to outsource its research and development (R&D) in this area to Tellme. In addition, AT&T stood to benefit with increased phone traffic as more and more consumers started using voice portals.

THE FUTURE OF TELLME

The day after McCue's latest pizza delivery/recruiting mission at Stanford, Tellme held a staff meeting that was part company meeting and part evangelical revival.[20] McCue sent out a rallying cry: "The next few months are the most important we've had—perhaps we'll every have—at Tellme. We need to stand and deliver now!"

After the meeting, McCue wondered how Tellme would maintain its lead in the voice portal market in the face of increasing competition to eventually become Dial Tone 2.0. The company's latest round of investors had very high expectations and wanted Tellme to push ahead in offering more business-to-business services. McCue asked himself: Should Tellme continue to build out its consumer-based Web site, or should it concentrate on increasing revenues from business customers? Could it do both? Or would Tellme be spread so thin that it would never become the Yahoo! of the voice portal market?

Notes

1. Based on actual account. McNichol, Tom. "Capturing Eardrums," *Wired,* May 2000. (www.wired.com/wired/archive/8.05/tellme_pr.html)
2. *Ibid.*
3. *Ibid.*
4. Silverman, Steve. "Tellme Announces New Funding and Focus," *Redherring.com,* October 4, 2000. (www.redherring.com/vc/2000/1004/vc-tellme100400.html)
5. Nee, Eric. "Who Wants to Talk to the Web?" *Fortune,* November 13, 2000, p. 317.
6. McNichol, "Capturing Eardrums."
7. Kalish, David E. "Former Netscape and Microsoft Execs in Unusual Internet Collaboration," The Associated Press, July 18, 1999.
8. Silverman, "Tellme Announces New Funding and Focus."
9. Madeo, Mark. "Tell Me Something New," *Business 2.0,* March 1, 2000. (www.business2.com/content/magazine/fiter/2000/03/01/11086)
10. Swartz, Jon. "Tellme Networks Wants to Reinvent the Telephone," *Forbes,* March 21, 2000. (www.forbes.com/2000/03/21/feat2.html)

11. Nee, "Who Wants to Talk to the Web?"
12. Patsuris, Penelope. "The Latest Web Gadget May Be the Phone," *Forbes,* July 28, 2000. (www.forbes.com/2000/07/28/feat.html)
13. Kapustka, Paul. "Big Fish: Calling Mike McCue, CEO," *Redherring.com,* July 26, 2000. (www.redherring.com/companies/2000/0726/com-bigfish072600.html)
14. "Tellme Introduces the World's First Open Platform for the Telephone Network." *Wireless Developer Network—Daily News,* June 14, 2000. (www.wirelessdevnet.com/news/2000/166/news7.html)
15. "The Value of Voice Portal Solutions." (www.intel.com/eBusiness/products/momentum/voice.html)
16. *Ibid.*
17. *Ibid.*
18. Cleary, Sharon. "Speak and You Shall Receive." *The Wall Street Journal,* September 18, 2000, p. R25.
19. Reinhardt, Andy. "The Good Ole Telephone Becomes a Hot New Web Tool," *Business Week,* April 24, 2000. (www.tellme.com/newsclips/bizweek4.html)
20. McNichol, "Capturing Eardrums."
21. Tellme Web site (www.tellme.com/about/management/).
22. *Ibid.*
23. Silverman, "Tellme Announces New Funding and Focus."

EXHIBIT 1 Tellme Management Team[21]

Mike McCue CEO, Chairman and Co-Founder	Formerly vice president of technology at Netscape, McCue played a leading role in establishing product, technology, and business strategy for the company's client, portal, and server businesses. Prior to Netscape, McCue was founder and CEO of Paper Software, which won nearly 80% market share in 3-D Internet software from competitors SGI and Microsoft. Netscape acquired Paper Software in February 1996. McCue left Netscape to co-found Tellme Networks in January 1999. At Tellme, he is responsible for the overall leadership and direction of the company.
Angus Davis Director of Production and Co-Founder	Formerly Communicator product manager at Netscape, Davis was responsible for Netscape's next generation browser technology. He co-authored "Netservices," a plan to transform Netscape from a software company to a services company, and worked on early strategy planning for Netcenter, the portal Web site. Having joined Netscape in 1996 when he was only 18, Davis was for some time the company's youngest employee. At Tellme, Davis helps develop corporate business strategies and strategic partnerships, and guide the future direction of the company.
Hadi Partovi VP, Production, Board Member	Formerly the group program manager for Microsoft's Internet Explorer, Partovi had broad responsibility for product strategy, design, and project management on the Internet Explorer team, where he helped direct four major releases of the browser software. Partovi left Microsoft to join his former arch-enemies from Netscape as part of Tellme Network's founding management team. At Tellme, he is responsible for delivering the consumer service that will bring the power of the Web to the telephone network. Partovi graduated from Harvard University with M.S. and B.A. degrees in Computer Science.
John Giannandrea Vice President, Platform Development, CTO, and Board Member	Formerly chief technologist and principal engineer in the browser group at Netscape/AOL, Giannandrea led the development of many important Web browser technologies and contributed to many of today's Web standards and protocols. At Netscape, Giannandrea was involved with every release of the Navigator product, from the first beta of 1.0 through 4.5. Prior to Netscape, he worked on the Telescript and MagicCap technologies at General Magic. As vice president of platform development and chief technology officer at Tellme, Giannandrea is responsible for all technical aspects of Tellme's service offerings.
Charles Moldow SVP, Business Development and Sales	Prior to joining Tellme, Moldow was general manager of MatchLogic, Excite@Home's digital marketing technologies and solutions company. Prior to the merger with Excite in January 1999, he was vice president of @Media Sales and Marketing. Previously, Moldow was vice president of business development for @Home Network, where he managed all facets of the company's development and deal efforts. Before joining @Home Network, Moldow worked at TCI, founded two companies in the marketing/publishing industries, and spent 4 years at Merrill Lynch in the mergers and acquisitions practice.
Andrew Volkmann VP, Finance and Administration	Volkmann comes to Tellme from Netscape, where he spent 3½ years in various financial roles. As the senior director of finance, he was responsible for the financial planning and analysis for Netscape's Netcenter division. Prior to the Netcenter position, Volkmann served as the director of finance for Netscape's enterprise software research, development, and marketing groups. Prior to Netscape, he served as a product line finance manager at National Semiconductor and as worldwide planning manager at Hitachi. At Tellme, Volkmann is responsible for all general and administrative functions.

EXHIBIT 2   Tellme Advisers[22]

Jim Barksdale Board Adviser	Barksdale is managing partner at The Barksdale Group, a full-service investment advisory firm he founded in April 1999. Before that, Barksdale was president and CEO of Netscape Communications.
Peter Currie Board Member	Currie is a partner at The Barksdale Group. Before that, he served as executive vice president and chief administrative officer of Netscape Communications. From April 1989 to April 1995, Currie held various management positions at McCaw Cellular Communications.
John Doerr Board Adviser	Doerr is currently a partner at venture capital firm Kleiner Perkins Caufield & Byers, where he has sponsored a series of investment (Compaq, Cypress, Intuit, Macromedia, Lotus, Netscape, Sun Microsystems, Symantec) that led to the creation of over 30,000 jobs.
Kevin Harvey Board Member	Prior to founding Benchmark Capital in 1995, Harvey started two successful software companies: Styleware, which pioneered integrated software for the Apple II personal computer and was ultimately purchased by Claris Corp., and Approach Software, the first easy-to-use client/server database for Windows. Approach was acquired by Lotus Development in 1993.
Mike Homer Board Adviser	Homer is currently a senior vice president at America Online. Prior to Netscape's acquisition by AOL, Homer held various executive positions at Netscape Communications, including executive vice president and general manager of Netscape Netcenter.
Chip Pitts Board Adviser	Pitts formerly worked at Nokia, where he negotiated key transactions and disputes, and also helped develop and implement Nokia's Internet strategy. Prior to Nokia, Pitts was a partner at Baker & McKenzie, the world's largest law firm, where he assisted many businesses in protecting and exploiting their intellectual property globally.
Brad Silverberg Board Member	Silverberg is currently a founding member of the venture holding firm Ignition, investing in wireless and other technology start-ups. He was formerly a senior vice president at Microsoft, where he served as a member of Microsoft's nine-person Executive Committee, its top decision-making body. Silverberg ran the Windows business from 1990 to 1995, and then directed Microsoft's Internet turnaround.
Jaleh Bisharat Board Adviser	Bisharat was most recently vice president of marketing for Amazon.com. At Amazon.com, she oversaw customer acquisition and retention, brand marketing, public relations, market intelligence, and the customer experience group.
Scott Bedbury Board Adviser	Bedbury has established himself as one of the world's most successful brand architects, helping Nike make "Just Do It" part of the global lexicon and fueling Starbucks' drive to reinvent a 900-year-old commodity. Bedbury directed Nike's worldwide advertising efforts from 1987 to 1994 and later served as Starbuck's chief marketing officer.

EXHIBIT 3	Tellme Company Timeline
January 1999	Tellme Networks, Inc., founded by Mike McCue, former vice president of technology at Netscape, and Angus Davis, former Communicator product manager at Netscape. McCue brings on Hadi Partovi, former group program manager for Microsoft's Internet Explorer, as part of Tellme's founding management team.
July 1999	James Barksdale, former CEO of Netscape, and Brad Silverberg, former senior vice president and member of Microsoft's executive committee, along with Tellme's employees, invest $6 million in Tellme. Silverberg and Peter Currie, former executive vice president and CFO of Netscape and a partner at The Barksdale Group, join the company's board of directors.
December 1999	Tellme raises $47 million from leading venture capital firms Benchmark Capital and Kleiner Perkins Caufield & Byers. Seed-round investors The Barksdale Group and Brad Silverberg also participate in this round of financing. Kevin Harvey, a founding partner at Benchmark, joins the company's board of directors.
April 2000	Tellme begins nationwide trial of its free voice portal service. Users can call a toll-free number and access news, weather forecasts, sports scores, stock quotes, traffic reports, horoscopes, and movie and restaurant listings using voice commands.
May 2000	AT&T invests $60 million in Tellme as part of a strategic relationship in which Tellme will use AT&T networking services and collaborate with AT&T to develop business and consumer applications based on Tellme's Internet platform and delivered over AT&T's network.
July 2000	Tellme officially launches 1-800-555-TELL, ending a 3-month trial in which the company completed 1.6 million calls and brought its voice-recognition accuracy to an average of 95 percent.
October 2000	Tellme raises an additional $125 million in financing from institutional investors Attractor, Amerindo Investment Advisors, Bowman Capital, Essex Investment Management, Ignition, Van Wagoner, and others including original investors Benchmark Capital, Kleiner Perkins, and TheBarksdale Group.[23]

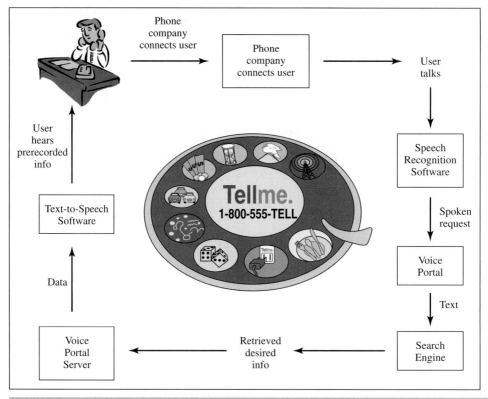

EXHIBIT 4   How a Voice Portal Works

EXHIBIT 5	Tellme's Main Competitors		
Voice Portal	Features	Powered By	Notable Characteristics/Recent Developments
Be Vocal	• Nationwide Business Finder • Driving Directions/Traffic Updates • Flight Information • News, Weather, Sports, Stock Quotes	Nuance Communications	• Application service provider (ASP) featuring commercial hosting (selling private label voice portals) and development hosting (developers can prototype, test, and run their own voice portal via 1-800 BEVOCAL) • Recently raised $45 million in 2nd round financing from Mayflower Partners, Technology Crossover Ventures, and Trans Cosmos USA
Quack.com	• Traffic Updates • Weather, Sports, Stock Quotes • Movie Information • Restaurant Information	Speechworks	• Acquired by America Online, Fall 2000 • The firm plans to use targeted advertising as a source of revenue • Offers Web Hosting—Provide the platform that allows companies to set up unique phone sites
PhoneRun.com	PhoneRun specializes in "phonecasting," where users access different phone channels that broadcast: • Traffic • Horoscopes • Lottery Results • Restaurant Guides • News, Weather, Sports, Stock Quotes Plus: • Books on Tape • CEO Speeches • Live Sporting Events	Lucent Mobile Communications System (MCS)	• Unique, broader content • On June 20, 2000, WorldCom announced it will let customers browse the Internet and get Web content using technology from PhoneRun.com • Content partnership with CNN

(continue)

EXHIBIT 5 *(cont.)*

Voice Portal	Features	Powered By	Notable Characteristics/Recent Developments
TelSurf	• E-mail (will read messages to you) • Instant Messaging • Traffic • "Hometown Radio" – Over 1,000 Internet radio stations • News, Stock Quotes	N/A	• Pricing; plans to use targeted advertising, but will also offer its service ad-free for 6 cents per minute • ASP strategy • Website provides personalized Web portal services
Audiopoint	• Traffic • News, Weather, Sports, Stock Quotes • Entertainment • Horoscopes	Speechworks	• Plans to use heavy advertising (one 5–10 second ad every 45 seconds) • Provides information only from its content partners (PC Quote/Hyperfeed (stock quotes), Screaming Media (sports), SmartRoute (traffic) and AccuWeather (weather)
iNetNow	• Full service "Internet concierge" manned by live human "surfers."	Traditional phone technology connects user to a live human being.	• 24/7 Live Access to a professional internet surfer • Subscription revenue model. Plans range up to $21.95 per month for unlimited calls
HeyAnita	• E-mail (will read messages to you) • News, Weather, Sports, Stock Quotes • Flight Information • Movie Information • Horoscopes • Package Tracker	N/A	• Offers Web hosting, providing the platform that allows companies to set up unique phone sites • Commercial Hosting (selling private label voice portals)

EXHIBIT 6   Infrastructure Companies Supporting the Voice Portal Market

Firm	Product/Focus
Nuance Communications	Creates speech-recognition software. Used by Tellme and BeVocal.
Lernaut & Hauspie	Creates speech-recognition and translation software. Used by Tellme.
Speechworks International	Creates speech-recognition and translation software. Used by Quack.com. Also, Yahoo! plans to use Speechworks software to convert text messages (e-mail) into voice. AOL holds minority stake in the company.
Phone.com	Merged with Software.com and renamed Openwave Systems, Inc., in November 2000. Openwave serves over 150 communications service providers with an aggregate of over 500 million subscribers. The new firm's portfolio of products includes wireless Internet infrastructure and browsers, unified messaging, mobile e-mail, directory services, voice processing, synchronization, and instant messaging.
Lucent (MCS)	Creates a voice platform believed to be more scalable than competitors. Used by Phonerun.

Case 3   Stamps.com: Bringing Electronic Postage Online

INTRODUCTION

If the post office had only opened before John McDermott's 8:00 A.M. finance class, Stamps.com might have never been born. Out of stamps and unable to mail the resumes he had been up all night preparing, McDermott instead decided that the inconvenient hours of the post office just weren't making the grade. And so an idea was born.

Wondering why he couldn't just print stamps using his own computer, McDermott mentioned his idea to fellow UCLA MBA students Ari Engelberg and Jeff Green. After doing some research, the trio discovered that the United States Postal Service (USPS) had released a specification under the new Information Based Indicia Program (IBIP) for a product that allowed consumers to print postage from their PCs.

While the original USPS specification called for a hardware device that would store postage "value," the three were convinced that a more convenient, simple, and cost-effective solution could be delivered— without the hardware—by harnessing the power of the Internet.

With financing secured, a technology team in place, and an intensive period of development complete, the group received approval to test market its service from the USPS in August 1999. And with minimal advertising and marketing, the company had nearly 100,000 preregistered users only 1 month later.

Since that time, it has been a battle of the postage providers. With Stamps.com

firmly behind the concept of delivering postage with just a computer, a printer, and an Internet connection, the company now stands head-to-head against both traditional postage providers, such as Pitney Bowes, as well as its most substantial competitor in the online postage arena, E-Stamp Corporation.

Who will win—paper stamps, Stamps.com's software solution, E-Stamp's hardware solution, or a yet unnamed competitor in the electronic postage space? The battle lines have been drawn, and McDermott and his team prepare to fight as the wars unfold.

WHAT IS ONLINE POSTAGE?

USPS Information Based Indicia Program

The Information Based Indicia Program (IBIP) is the USPS office responsible for delivering a higher level of convenience and security to customers through the development of a secure form of digital postage and introduction of higher security systems for the purchase and printing of PC postage products.

While the IBIP office establishes performance and evaluation criteria, the products themselves are developed solely by private industry and are submitted to the USPS for qualification as "PC Postage" products. The USPS does not specify design requirements, but all products are evaluated and must meet published performance criteria to ensure optimal security, financial and system integrity, and operational interface

MBA candidates Ping Chen, Beth Flom, Rachel Glube, Margot Krikorian, and Karen Rothenberg prepared this case under the supervision of Professor Christopher L. Tucci for the purpose of class discussion rather than to illustrate either effective or ineffective handling of an administrative situation. Distributed by the Berkley Center for Entrepreneurial Studies at the Stern School of Business, New York University. To order copies, phone: 212-998-0070, fax: 212-995-4211, or e-mail: bces@stern.nyu.edu. No part of this publication may be used or reproduced without written permission of the Berkley Center. Copyright © 1999 by the Stern School of Business and Christopher L. Tucci. All rights reserved.

before being approved for commercial distribution. There is no limit on how many companies can submit products to the IBIP for evaluation.

Technology

Information Based Indicia (IBI) represent the next generation of postage—digital postage generated from personal computers. The IBI "stamp" is a two-dimensional barcode that is printed on an envelope in the upper-right-hand corner, or on a label for an envelope or package. It conveys evidence that postage has been paid and contains mail processing data requirements, including licensing zip code, destination delivery point, date of mailing, postage, digital signature, rate category, and the indicia version number. In addition, the IBI contains security-related data elements (See Appendix E for visual representation of IBI).

The distinction between the IBI and PC Postage is made as follows: The IBI is the marking printed on the envelope, while PC Postage is a trademark owned by the USPS for use on products developed by private industry to print IBI. All fees associated with the use of PC Postage products and services are established by the product providers.

Beta testing for PC Postage products commenced in March 1998. By year end, the USPS had authorized four companies— E-Stamp Corporation, Stamps.com, Neopost Inc. and Pitney Bowes for field-testing. After 3 90-day testing phases, Stamps.com was the first software-based service approved for commercial distribution in August 1999 and was commercially distributed in November 1999.

WHO IS STAMPS.COM?

Management

The founding UCLA MBA students, John McDermott, Ari Engelberg, and Jeff Green, have fervently worked to recruit a management team capable of taking the company through all phases of growth. In August 1998, John Payne was appointed CEO of Stamps.com. Bringing extensive expertise as former president and CEO of two software companies, Payne provided the perfect blend of management and technology.

Under Payne, the company has rapidly assembled a "dream team" adding former postmaster general Marvin Runyon and USPS executive Loren Smith to its board of directors. In October 1999, Payne was additionally made chairman of the board, and Smith was appointed president and chief operating officer.

Target Market

Stamps.com targets the 45-million strong small office/home office (SOHO) market, which has not previously had a specific postage solution tailored to its needs. With no sign-up costs, no long-term contracts, and no equipment to purchase, Stamps.com is the only electronic-postage provider to give its SOHO customers the flexibility to get everything online. Customers simply download free software, register online, pay a monthly fee, and begin printing postage.

By targeting SOHO users with a software-based Internet postage solution, Stamps.com hopes to capture a substantial portion of mind share from users seeking a cost-efficient alternative to traditional postage methods.

INDUSTRY OVERVIEW

USPS Statistics

The 1998 USPS *Annual Report* indicates that of the 7 million customers who visited a U.S. post office each day last year, approximately 70 percent purchased stamps. In 1998, the USPS processed over 197 billion pieces of mail, despite the growth in the use of e-mail. The total U.S. postage market was approximately $58 billion, of which approximately $38.9 billion was represented by first-class, priority, and express mail. Keenan

Vision, an independent research firm, estimates that revenue from first-class, priority, and express mail should grow to $46.2 billion by 2002.[1]

Traditional Mail Versus E-mail

In 1995, e-mail usage was approximately 100 billion messages. However, only 3 years later, e-mail messages have skyrocketed to an excess of 500 billion. At the same time, while first-class mail usage grew 7 percent in 1988, that number has decreased to a less than 2 percent growth rate in 1998, causing little concern for Stamps.com's future growth.[2]

Internet Usage

According to the International Data Corporation (IDC), Internet connectivity and commerce is expected to continue unabated for the foreseeable future. The number of Internet users worldwide will grow from an estimated 100 million in 1998 to 319 million by 2002.[3] Additionally, 73 percent of adult Internet users rate the Internet as either "somewhat" or "very indispensable" (eStats).[4]

SOHO Statistics

The SOHO market represents a large and growing customer segment. There were 44.7 million small businesses and home offices in the United States in 1998, a number that is expected to grow to 57.7 million by 2002. Yet Morgan Stanley Dean Witter reports that there were only 1.7 million postage meters in the United States, leaving a vastly untouched market.[5]

In 1999, there were 22.7 million SOHOs online. Of these businesses, 63 percent were already ordering products online and were spending an average of $171 monthly on postage. As Internet dependence increases among small businesses and as additional small business migrate online, the segment should continue to be significant within the

e-commerce market. In fact, it is also estimated that small businesses accounted for $4.4 billion of e-commerce in 1998 and should account for approximately $100.4 billion of e-commerce activity in 2002.[6]

DRAWING THE BATTLE LINES

Product

Stamps.com's product is free downloaded software that allows customers to print postage at any time of the day or night with just a computer, printer, and Internet connection. This product enables customers to print first-class, priority, and express mail and send everything including packages, postcards, and letters.

The software prints postage from laser or inkjet printers on all standard mail pieces and on labels for leading parcel carriers such as the U.S. Postal Service and the United Parcel Service. Other value-added product features include an address verification system, integration with popular small business software, 24-hour customer service, automatic postage calculation, and customizable addressing.

Pricing

The Stamps.com software is free. It can be downloaded from the Stamps.com Web site or obtained on a CD-Rom, distributed by multiple vendors, including Intuit and Office Depot. Once customers open an account with Stamps.com and purchase a minimum of $10 of postage, they can start printing. Any postage purchased is refundable.

Stamps.com customers can choose from two pricing plans depending on their postage needs. The business service plan starts at $3.99 and has a maximum price of $19.99 per month for unlimited postage. The personal service plan starts at $1.99 per month for 12 months and lets customers use up to $25 in postage per month.

Partnerships

Stamps.com has partnerships with a variety of major companies including America Online, IBM, Microsoft, Office Depot, Lotus, ZDNet, Avery Dennison, Quicken.com, Westvaco, and other leading office supply and technology companies, which provide access into the SOHO and consumer markets.

AOL In October 1999, Stamps.com and AOL formed a broad distribution and marketing alliance that positioned Stamps.com as the exclusive provider of Internet postage on AOL, Netscape, and CompuServe branded CD-ROMs, giving millions of small business customers access to Stamps.com software. Under the 3-year agreement, Stamps.com will have access to the more than 20 million combined members of AOL and CompuServe, and to millions of additional Netscape Netcenter and Digital City visitors. AOL's $56 million investment made under this agreement strengthens an existing alliance between the two companies that helped increase the number of pre-registrants to over 100,000 consumers and businesses.

"Stamps.com is a leader in Internet postage, an industry of growing interest to many different segments of the online community," said Bob Pittman, president and chief operating office of America Online. "Whether it's individuals, small businesses, or corporate enterprise, working together AOL and Stamps.com will be able to make this service both easy to use and easily available."

Microsoft In August 1999, Microsoft formed an alliance with Stamps.com to provide its millions of Microsoft office users with Stamps.com service through the popular Microsoft Office Update Web site. Customers will be able to download the Stamp.com free software directly from the Microsoft Office Update download catalog

and begin printing postage from their desktops within moments from signing up for the service.

Stamps.com also integrates seamlessly with existing address books, word processors, and other applications, including Microsoft Word and Outlook, so that customers can verify mailing addresses instantly and print postage directly from the software applications they currently use.

"Microsoft is excited to have Stamps.com provide our small office and home office customers online access to postage from within their Office applications," said Taylor Collyer, business development manager, Microsoft Corp. "With office 2000, Microsoft has shown how the Internet can bring seamless integration of value-added services to the world's premier productivity suite. The Stamps.com Internet postage service is a great example of how Office 2000, a PC, and the Internet combine to make people more productive," added Collyer.

iShip In October 1999, Stamps.com acquired privately held iShip.com, a leading provider of Internet-based shipping technology. This acquisition positioned Stamps.com as the only online postage service that offers small business, consumer, and corporate enterprise customers a single source for all their mailing and shipping needs.

The agreement joined iShip.com's unique Web-based multicarrier shipping technology with Stamps.com's core Internet postage service. This gives customers one-stop access to mailing, shipping, and tracking services, as well as label printing for such leading parcel carriers as the U.S. Postal Service and United Parcel Service (UPS). Together they will enable carriers to reach new customers.

The iShip.com service includes online rate and service comparisons—including the U.S. Postal Service, UPS, FedEx and Airborne Express—and the ability to purchase and print labels online. iShip.com was founded in 1997 by the same management team that developed UPS Online Professional, the world's most powerful shipping and tracking software.

"This merger will build a single marketplace on the Web for shipping and mailing services and information, in a way that benefits both customers and carriers," said Stephen Teglovic, president and CEO of iShip.com. "As a combined company, we will be able to double our market opportunity and provide the most comprehensive service on the Internet to manage all mailing and shipping needs. The complementary technology that Stamps.com and iShip.com bring together, matched with strong management teams on both sides, will make this a great partnership for the mailing and shipping industries."

EncrypTix In November 1999, Stamps.com announced the formation of EncrypTix, a subsidiary that provides highly-secure, authenticated online printing of tickets, vouchers, and certificates for events, travel, and financial service industries. EncrypTix will utilize Stamps.com's technology to enable companies to complete transactions over the Internet to customers who can print the documents using their laser or inkjet printers. The alliance leverages Stamps.com's technology to open the door into different markets and a new way of doing business on the Internet. The formation of EncrypTix expands Stamps.com from a consumer electronic postage provider to a business-to-business technology provider.

"We have created EncrypTix to establish and develop new, alternative uses of Stamps.com's technology for Internet-based transactions," said John Payne. "By creating EncrypTix and enlisting Jim Rowan's very capable leadership as the CEO and president of EncrypTix, Stamps.com can continue to focus on growing the user base for its Internet postage service and developing a complete, one-stop mailing, shipping, and tracking solution on the Internet."

EncrypTix will be a wholly owned subsidiary of Stamps.com. Upon completion of technology licensing and intercompany operating agreements, EncrypTix will seek capital from key strategic investors in addition to Stamps.com. EncrypTix is also planning to develop strategic customer and partnership relationships with other providers in the events, travel, and financial services industries.

WAGING THE WAR

As electronic postage proliferates, Stamps.com faces multiple challenges. In essence the company must fight a war on three fronts: (1) electronic postage versus traditional postage, (2) software solutions versus hardware solutions, and (3) online brands versus off-line brands.

Changing Traditional Behaviors

Not all small business owners are savvy, innovative, computer-literate professionals. And not every small business owner actually purchases his or her own stamps. While "techie" professionals in urban areas are traditional "early adopters" of electronic postage, other stamp buyers have been slow to catch on to Internet postage.

It takes time to change consumer behavior. Taking a trip to the post office is a habitual activity for many individuals. Others may wonder, how can you drop a letter in the mailbox when your computer and printer are back at the office? In fact, sticking on or peeling off a stamp can be more convenient than logging on. Change doesn't come easy.

Additionally, it is doubtful that all consumers will switch to digital postage. Yet industry players question whether it is even necessary. While traditional postage may slow Stamps.com's ability to establish critical mass as quickly, it should not present a long-term challenge. Traditional and digital postage can coexist in the marketplace. With nearly 60 million businesses in the SOHO market alone, the market is large enough for both players.

The Fight for a Dominant Standard

In 1996, all participants in the IBIP (potential Stamps.com competitors) were basing their product on a hardware device that connected a user's computer and printer. The United Postal Service required this external equipment in their original specifications for IBIP—its function was to store the postage purchased by the user.

However, the Stamps.com product design was based on software. Its customers would download free software over the Web, register as users, and then print postage as needed. Its service was meant to easily accommodate professionals carrying their laptops, and SOHO users who wanted to print their business logo as well. Despite the difference in standards established by USPS, Stamps.com was approved to distribute digital postage on August 9, 1999.

On that very same day, another Web-based start-up, E-stamp Corporation, was approved for distribution of electronic postage. But consumers couldn't use the E-stamp product right away. To become a customer, one must sign up at the E-stamp Web site, pay $50, and then wait for their "Starter Kit"—including hardware apparatus and an Address Match CD-ROM—to arrive via USPS Priority Mail (3 to 5 days). Both the device and CD-ROM are necessary components of the E-stamp product.

Early critics have found numerous flaws with E-stamp Corporation's product. First, the hardware requirement takes away from the convenience and immediacy of purchasing online. Additionally, some users experienced functionality problems (i.e., printer would not print postage, yet customer's account would be debited). And many are concerned about the potential for related computer problems resulting from the use of an external device.

Competition Intensifies

As these new e-commerce businesses vie for consumer brand awareness, fight the battles between platforms, and invest extensively to educate the market about electronic postage, other established players in the mailing industry are preparing their attack. These off-line brands are threatening to steal a big piece of the pie!

Neopost Neopost has operations in 70 countries and is the number one supplier of mailroom equipment in Europe, second worldwide. The company's U.S. division received approval from the USPS in 1998. Its product, *Simply Postage,* requires a special "stamp dispenser," special Neopost labels, and a Neopost scale for weighing packages.

Pitney Bowes Known for its postage meter, used by medium- and large-sized companies, Pitney Bowes is now courting SOHO users with its recently approved Clickstamp.com. Originally, the product was hardware based—used in combination with Pitney Bowes' computerized meter remote setting system and Postage by Phone. More recently, Pitney Bowes has introduced a software-based product, offering many of the same features as Stamps.com. "I'd guess they could grab 35 percent of the market before long," said B. Alexander Henderson, an analyst at Prudential Securities Research.[7]

WINNING THE STANDARDS WAR

Competitive Advantages

One of Stamps.com's distinct competitive advantages lies in its postage server. It automatically interacts with common word processing applications, contact and address management software of popular e-mail interfaces (i.e., Microsoft Outlook), and accounting applications. Also, a built-in calculator automatically applies the exact amount of postage each time. Other unique advantages include an Address Matching System that catches address mistakes and automatically provides missing information (i.e. zip +4 code) and reports that track personal purchase history, and the specifics (i.e., date, weight, postage amount) for each piece of postage ever printed. No CD-ROMs or hardware peripherals are needed.

Brand Equity

As the first software provider to market, Stamps.com has a certain first-mover advantage. "At this piont, I think Stamps.com is ahead of the game," said Bonnie J. Brooks of Creative Strategies, a consulting company in Campbell, California. Being first has a significant online advantage, because "the first to market usually does well."[8]

It is that first-mover advantage that will help to create top-of-mind awareness for Stamps.com over its competitors. With its first-mover advantage, strong partnerships, and beneficial pricing plan, the Stamps.com brand is already on its way to becoming synonymous with Internet postage. Additionally, the company's successful IP has also afforded Stamps.com additional marketing and advertising dollars to beef up its brand image.

Various alliances have further enhanced its popularity, as well. By aligning itself with Microsoft, AOL, IBM, and others, Stamps.com was successful in registering over 100,000 members before its official launch. These alliances have resulted in a new way of doing business for many small home office businesses as the technology simplifies the postage process.

RECOGNIZING STAMPS.COM'S WEAKNESSES

John Payne realized that although his company offered many benefits to the marketplace, there were some weaknesses that still needed to be addressed.

Critical Mass

Of his many concerns, achieving critical mass in the marketplace is close to the top of Payne's list. He predicts that the company that achieves this will become the standard. There is also the limit to the company's expansion internationally since this would be a different postal market. Currently, Stamps.com is only marketed to domestic small businesses and its customers total 100,000, giving it a long way to go to achieve such market mass.

Appropriability

Stamps.com's intellectual portfolio is protected by three U.S. patents related to secure software rental systems. Additionally, the company has four filed U.S. patent applications. Experts—and the company's recent alliance with EncrypTix—suggest that Stamps.com will be able to apply all competencies and endowments toward other authenticated documents such as concert and airline ticket, both within the United States and internationally. Payne, however wondered, "How much does this really protect Stamps.com from competitors developing similar software platforms?"

Low Barriers to Entry

Like many Internet companies, Stamps.com may well face a highly competitive environment. There are low barriers to entry for Internet companies since there are minimal costs and difficulties to setting up a Web site. While the USPS must approve all PC Postage product distributors, approvals have been rapid and multiple, potentially creating a situation where any number of competitors can establish a working site on any given day.

Additionally, concern has been raised about the entrance of the powerful and well-known Pitney Bowes into the market. Leveraging its $4.2 billion revenues,[9] Pitney

Bowes has far deeper pockets than its start-up rivals. And with high brand recognition, a quality software product and an established installed base of traditional postage users, Pitney Bowes might pose the largest threat to Stamps.com yet.

Regulatory Threats

Currently, both Stamps.com and E-stamp face lawsuit claims submitted by Pitney Bowes that the companies have infringed on Pitney Bowes' technological patents for developing the Internet postage technology. Stamps.com is refuting this accusation, and believes that its competitor served this suit merely to hinder its competition. Supporting this stance, a federal investigation into Pitney Bowes' accusations was launched in June 1999. Investigators are also questioning the legality of the suit.

THE NEXT FRONT

With traditional postage posing only a limited threat to electronic postage, and the software-based model winning the standards war, Payne has only one more battle to win. In the war against additional software-based competitors, he must fend off traditional off-line competitors looking to stake a claim—particularly Pitney Bowes.

And Pitney Bowes has been doing its homework. The corporation is spending substantial marketing dollars to reinvent itself from the "postage meter" company to a provider of quality business solutions. The community-based Web site offers "Small Business Solutions," showcases the Pitney line of mailing products, and promotes the company's line of financial solutions, as well as its electronic postage product. Will this comprehensive Web site result in more loyalty and customer lock-in to the Clickstamp product? And how does Stamps.com effectively fight Pitney Bowes' marketing muscle,

distribution network, established brand, and installed base?

With the window of opportunity rapidly closing, Payne realizes he has an important decision to make. Should he continue fighting the wars or succumb to the competitive environment posed by rivals such as Pitnew Bowes? Should Stamps.com leave the consumer electronic postage arena and leverage its authentication technology in the business-to-business world through initiatives such as EncrypTix? Can it survive doing so?

Bibliography

Adelson, Andrea. "Getting In on the Ground Floor in the Cyberpostage Market," *The New York Times,* February 18, 1999.

Afuah, Allan N., and Tucci, Christopher L. *Internet Business Strategies,* Chapter 5, McGraw Hill Higher Education, 2000.

Alexander, Ryan B., and Chouch, Mia K. "Stamps.com Inc.: A Wit Capital Research Report," July 21, 1999.

Associated Press. "Justice Department Investigates Internet Postage Suits," *The New York Times,* June 22, 1999.

BusinessWire. "Bob Newhart Stab in Stamps.com's New Innovative Advertising Campaign," October 18, 1999.

Business Wire. "Stamps.com Establishes Subsidiary EncrypTix. Inc; EncrypTix to Explore Secure Printing Applications for the Events, Travel, and Financial Services Industries," November 16, 1999.

Campanelli, Melissa. "E-Stamp, Stamps.com Duel over SOHO," *DM News,* November 1, 1999.

CNET. "Postal Service Gives Stamp of Approval to Stamps.com, E-Stamp," August 9, 1999, www.CNET.news.com.

Deutsch, Claudia. "Now Putting a Big Stamp on the Era of the Internet; Pitney Bowes Is Updating the business," *The New York Times,* November 8, 1999.

Manes, Stephen. "Going Postal—Digitally," *Forbes Magazine,* September 6, 1999.

Web Sites for Additional Research

www.neopost.com

www.pitneybowes.com

www.stamps.com

www.usps.gov

www.hoovers.com

Notes

1. Alexander, Ryan B., and Chough, Mia K. "Stamps.com Inc.: A Wit Capital Research Report," July 21, 1999.
2. Manes, Stephen. "Going Postal—Digitally," *Forbes Magazine,* September 6, 1999.
3. Wit Capital Report.
4. Campanelli, Melissa. "E-Stamp, Stamps.com Duel over SOHO," *DM News,* November 1, 1999.
5. Wit Capital Report.
6. Wit Capital Report.
7. Deutsch, Claudia. "Now Putting a Big Stamp on the Era of the Internet; Pitney Bowes Is Updating the Business," *The New York Times,* November 8, 1999.
8. Adelson, Andrea. "Getting In on the Ground Floor in the Cyberpostage Market," *The New York Times,* February 18, 1999.
9. www.pitneybowes.com

APPENDIX A Statements of Operations (9/30/99)

	3 Months Ended		9 Months Ended September 30, 1999	January 9, 1998 (inception) to September 30, 1998	January 9, 1998 (inception) to September 30, 1999
	September 30, 1999	September 30, 1998			
Revenues					
Costs and expenses:					
Research and development	2,370,848	292,382	5,049,459	548,200	6,581,270
Sales and marketing	7,640,454	—	10,856,087	—	11,488,436
General and administrative	4,412,467	513,959	8,275,706	1,125,584	10,291,636
Total costs and expenses	14,423,769	806,341	24,181,252	1,673,784	28,361,342
Loss from operations	(14,423,769)	(806,341)	(24,181,252)	(1,673,784)	(28,361,342)
Other income (expense):					
Interest expense	(40,269)	(4,349)	(121,968)	(4,814)	(149,592)
Interest income	766,044	1,732	1,200,123	2,682	1,211,957
Net loss	$(13,697,994)	$ (808,958)	$(23,103,097)	$(1,675,916)	$(27,298,977)
Basic and diluted net loss per share	$ (0.40)	$ (0.17)	$ (1.59)	$ (0.35)	$ (2.44)
Pro forma basic and diluted net loss per share	$ (0.40)	$ (0.07)	$ (0.74)	$ (0.17)	$ (1.10)
Weighted average shares outstanding used in basic and diluted per-share calculation	34,101,500	4,897,500	14,495,600	4,738,400	11,186,100
Weighted average shares outstanding used in pro forma basic and diluted per-share calculation	34,101,500	10,984,700	31,259,500	9,612,800	24,794,800

APPENDIX B   Comparison of Stamps.com Versus E-stamp.com (as of 10/99)

	Stamps.com	*E-stamp.com*
Date of foundation, location	Founded in 1996, Santa Monica, California	Founded in 1994, San Mateo, California
Date of receiving national approval from U.S. postal office	August 9, 1999	August 9, 1999
IPO date, capital raised from IPO	June 25, 1999, IPO capital $60 million	October 8, 1999, IPO capital $110 million
Product differentiation	*Software based:* Need to be online to print postage	*Hardware based:* Link print and PC with an electronic vault, load postage to the vault from Internet, then print postage off-line
Pricing scheme	No charge for software; *Business Plan:* 10% service fee on the postage used; minimum $3.99/mo., maximum $19.99. *Personal Plan:* Use up to $25 in postage per month. $1.99 per month OR $19.99 for 12 months.	Give away $10–$25 postage to new customers; $50 start-up charge; 10% convenient fee on the postage used, minimum $4.99, maximum $24.99. No monthly fee.
Size of user base	100,000	10,000

APPENDIX C Stamps.com Major Alliances (as of 10/99)

America Online — In December 1998, AOL and Stamps.com announced comprehensive distribution and marketing agreement. Stamps.com free Internet postage download to be available across AOL Network, CompuServe, AOL.COM, AOL and Digital City, and to be bundled with new member CD-ROMs.

Office Depot — In February 1999, Stamps.com entered into a partnership with Office Depot that would provide Stamps.com with a download link to sign up for the Stamps.com service available from the Office Depot Online Superstore. That agreement would also incorporate a "point of purchase" advertisement campaign.

Dymo/CoStar — In March 1999, Stamps.com entered into a distribution relationship with Dymo, a label maker, that is part of Esselte, an international office and business supply company. Stamp.com's agreement with Dymo/CoStar provides that the Stamps.com software will be bundled on all software installation CD-ROMs included in CoStar LabelWriter printer boxes. In addition, the Stamps.com software will be downloadable from the CoStar Web site.

Seiko Instruments — In March 1999, Stamps.com entered into a distribution agreement with Seiko Instruments USA, a supplier and marketer of printer mechanisms, PC peripheral color printers, and specialty black and white printers. That agreement provides that the Stamps.com software will be bundled on software installation CD-ROMs included in Seiko Smart Label Printer boxes. In addition, the Stamps.com software will be downloadable from the Seiko Web site.

Westvaco — In April 1999, Stamps.com entered into a distribution and codevelopment agreement with Westvaco, a manufacturer and supplier of paper materials, envelopes, and other packaging products. As part of that agreement, Westvaco would promote the Stamps.com service on boxes of Westvaco's Columbian brand laser and inkjet envelopes. In addition, the Stamps.com service would be promoted on the Columbian brand Web site.

Intuit — In May 1999, Stamps.com entered into a promotional agreement with Intuit. That agreement provides Stamps.com with an electronic link to the Stamps.com Web site available from various channels within the Intuit network of Web sites.

MySoftware — In July 1999, Stamps.com entered into a strategic partnership with MySoftware, a provider of productivity software and Internet services for small and mid-sized businesses. Under that agreement, MySoftware will integrate the Stamps.com service with the MySoftware suite of Internet direct marketing software products, including the MyDeluxeMailList application.

Microsoft — In August 1999, Stamps.com announced partnership with Microsoft. Following installation and registration of Stamps.com free software, Microsoft users will be able to download and print postage directly from their desktops. This partnership provides Stamps.com with an extremely ubiquitous platform into which the company can penetrate.

3M — In September 1999, Stamps.com announced a partnership with 3M to market the Stamps.com service with 3M's stationery products after January 2000.

IBM — In October 1999, Stamps.com announced a strategic alliance with IBM to distribute Stamps.com's service to the over 1 million members of the IBM Owner Privileges Program, which is designed for owners of IBM's Aptiva PC and ThinkPad i Series.

iShip.com — On October 25, 1999, Stamps.com announced the acquisition of iShip.com, a provider of Web-based shipping technology that allows customers to compare and select rates and services from multiple carriers, including UPS, FedEx, Airborne Express, and U.S. Postal Service. The combined entity should provide consumers, small businesses, and corporate enterprise customers with one-stop access to mailing, shipping, and tracking services, as well as label printing for parcel carriers, such as the U.S. Postal Service and the United Parcel Service (UPS).

EncrypTix — On November 16, 1999, Stamps.com announced the formation of a new wholly owned subsidiary, EncrypTix, Inc., to provide distributors of tickets, vouchers, and other forms of bearer value with a secure, authenticated online printing solution. EncrypTix will adopt Stamps.com's proprietary, Internet-based technology to complete online transactions through a customer's laser or inkjet printer.

APPENDIX D	Major Events
1996	StampMaster, Inc., was founded and joined the Information Based Indicia Program (IBIP), a program initiated by the USPS to introduce a new form of postage to the public—postage that can be delivered via the Internet to a user's computer.
8/98	U.S. Postal Service has approved StampMaster, Inc., beta and market testing of its new service for delivery of postage over the Internet.
12/98	StampMaster, Inc., announced that the company has changed its name to Stamps.com.
12/98	AOL and Stamps.com announced comprehensive distribution and marketing agreement.
2/99	Stamps.com completed $30 million private financing with major investors such as Vulcan Ventures, Inc., Chase Capital Partners.
6/99	Pitney Bowes filed a patent infringement lawsuit against Stamps.com in the United States District Court for the District of Delaware. Pitney Bowes' suit against Stamps.com alleges that Stamps.com infringes upon patents related to postage application systems and electronic indicia.
6/25/99	Stamps.com commenced its initial public offering, the initial offering of 5,000,000 shares was priced at $11 per share.
8/9/99	Stamps.com receives approval for electronic postage from U.S. postal service.
8/9/99	Microsoft partners with Stamps.com to bring Internet postage to Microsoft Office users.
8/21/99	America Online, Inc., and Stamps.com form major alliance to bring Internet postage to millions PC. The new alliance expands existing agreement; AOL also makes multimillion-dollar investment in Stamps.com.
10/18/99	Bob Newhart started multimillion-dollar campaign with television and print buys.
10/22/99	Stamps.com launched Internet postage service to customers nationwide.
10/25/99	Stamps.com announced the acquisition of iShip.com.
11/16/99	Stamps.com announced the formation of the wholly owned subsidiary EncrypTix, Inc.

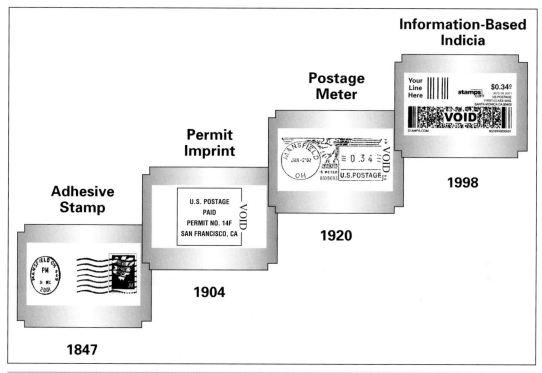

APPENDIX E   IBI Visual Representation

Case 4 Rubio's: Home of the Fish Taco (A)

Rubio's Restaurants Inc., formerly known as Rubio's Deli-Mex, is a family-owned and operated Mexican restaurant located in southern California. Rubio's specializes in authentic, fresh-tasting Mexican food using authentic Mexican recipes. Rubio's is best known, however, for its fish tacos, which were relatively unknown in San Diego prior to Rubio's entry in 1983. Although Rubio's is known as the "Home of the Fish Taco," the menu also offers a variety of other, more traditional Mexican favorites such as burritos and carnitas. Designed as a fast-food restaurant, the food may be ordered for consumption on the premises or for carryout. Rubio's offers an alternative to the full-service Mexican restaurant without sacrificing quality. The success of this concept has been phenomenal. After opening in 1983 with one location near Mission Bay, Rubio's has, in just 9 years, grown to include 12 restaurants extending from San Diego to Orange County.

HISTORY

The concept for Rubio's restaurants was first developed in the late 1970s during one of Ralph Rubio's camping adventures in San Felipe on the Baja peninsula, Mexico. According to the legend, it was on one of these excursions that Ralph observed numerous American tourists lined up to purchase fish tacos from the San Felipe beach vendors. Over the years, taco stands proliferated in San Felipe. Figuring that fish tacos would be as popular in San Diego as they were in the Baja, Ralph solicited one of the veteran beach vendors, "Carlos," to move to San Diego and open a restaurant that featured these tacos. Although Carlos declined, he provided Ralph with his "secret family recipe" for fish tacos. Ralph carried this recipe with him for 5 years after his 1978

graduation from San Diego State University. Armed with his liberal arts degree, 8 years' experience in the restaurant industry, and $30,000 from his father, Ralph opened the first Rubio's on January 25, 1983. It was located on East Mission Bay Drive in the Pacific Beach area of San Diego, California, on the site of a previously failed hamburger restaurant. Despite Ralph's lack of a menu just 2 days before the restaurant's scheduled opening, the first week's sales averaged $250 a day and the restaurant was packed. Within 3 years, sales at the restaurant grew to $2,000 a day. Based on the success of the first restaurant, in March 1986 a second location was opened on College Avenue near San Diego State University. Shortly thereafter, in August 1987, Rubio's opened its third location near Pacific Beach. Rubio's expansion has continued at a rapid rate. Rubio's now has 12 locations from as far south as Chula Vista to as far north as Irvine.

THE FAST-FOOD INDUSTRY

The United States food service industry estimates its 1991 sales at $248.1 billion. The second-largest category of restaurants in the food service industry are the limited-menu outlets, which consist largely of fast-food restaurants such as Rubio's. Sales in this category of food providers are estimated for 1991 at $74.1 billion. According to the National Restaurant Association (NRA), fast-food restaurants have enjoyed rapid growth. In fact, from 1970 to 1990, sales in these limited-menu restaurants have increased at an estimated 12.9 percent compound rate, compared with 7.9 percent for the remainder of the U.S. food service industry.

The success of the fast-food industry, a relatively mature, highly competitive business, is believed to be the result of changing demographics and lifestyles. Over the past several decades, more Americans have been turning to restaurants for their meals. Dual-income families made the option of dining out a necessity because of the families' lack of spare time. At the same time, additional income made dining out more affordable. The fast-food industry has also managed to sell its customers on the value and convenience their products and services offer. This perception has been enhanced by the addition of drive-through windows, which enable customers to order and be served in their cars. Restaurants have further catered to customers' idea of convenience by adding delivery to the current list of services offered. Despite these positive indicators, Rubio's, as a competitor in the fast-food industry, faces several challenges in the imminent future. The relatively weaker economy of 1991 and 1992 has led to higher unemployment and an increase in meals prepared and consumed in the home. The fast-food industry is also threatened by several other factors, including environmental pressures, increased nutritional awareness, the AIDS scare, and governmental legislation. As a player in the fast-food industry, Rubio's must monitor the arena in which it participates and respond to the following opportunities and challenges.

Changing Demographics

Aging Population   The United States is simultaneously experiencing a rise in life expectancy and a decline in the number of people age 15 to 34. The net effect of these trends is an aging U.S. population. This change in demographics is likely to have a significant impact on the fast-food industry. First, as the population of consumers grows older, it is likely their tastes will shift toward midscale restaurants and away from the fast-food industry. In fact, according to a 1988 study conducted by the NRA, customers age

18 to 24 spend 79 percent of their time attributed to eating out at fast-food restaurants; individuals age 45 to 54 spend only 60 percent of their time eating out at fast-food restaurants. The difference between these age groups is allegedly the result of older patrons' higher disposable income and their desire for additional amenities.

The Baby Boomers   The second impact from the changing demographics results from the recent rise in birth rates. Although double-income families have less time for food preparation, baby boomers are now having families of their own. As a result, there are more households with small children who are less likely to dine out. Instead, these families are utilizing such conveniences as microwaves and take-out and delivery services.

The Decline in Teenagers   Finally, the decline in the birth rate in the early 1970s has resulted in a decrease in the number of youths between the ages of 16 to 20. The fast-food segment of the restaurant industry has traditionally relied on this category of individuals as its main source of labor. As a result, fast-food restaurants have had a harder time attracting and retaining employees. This has, to a degree, been alleviated by the vast amount of unemployment resulting from the current recession. However, the overall change in demographics is forcing the fast-food industry to adjust accordingly.

Nutritional Concerns

In addition to the changes associated with an aging population, the fast-food industry must also respond to changes in customers' needs and concerns. Baby boomers are becoming preoccupied with healthier eating, and fast-food restaurants are responding accordingly. Individuals are now concerned not only with value and convenience, but also with the fat and cholesterol content of the items offered by fast-food restaurants. As a result, restaurants are changing their menus and product offerings to emphasize, or deemphasize, the benefits of their products.

In an effort to lure customers, McDonald's launched the new McLean Deluxe, a burger that boasts only 9 percent fat because of the use of seaweed substitutes. Although purportedly healthier, the new item costs the consumer a $0.20 premium over the usual quarter-pounder, which has twice the fat. McDonald's also followed the lead of other fast-food restaurants by switching to 100 percent vegetable oil from a blend containing beef tallow for cooking fries and hash browns. Encouraged by consumer acceptance of these products, McDonald's replaced its ice cream with lowfat yogurt, introduced lowfat milk shakes, and even added cereal and bran muffins to its menu. In June 1991, McDonald's introduced, as limited time promotional items, a 90-calorie Diet Coke float and a 275-calorie grilled chicken sandwich. Other fast-food restaurants, such as Burger King and KFC, have also changed their product offerings to cater to consumers' health concerns. These changes reflect the need of fast-food restaurants to change in response to the needs and concerns of a changing population.

Governmental Legislation

Teen Labor Laws　The fast-food industry must also deal with changes in the legislation that affects it. One such area of legislation is teen labor laws. Current legislation prohibits 14- and 15-year-old persons from working on school nights after 7:00 P.M., a time when restaurants usually need a full staff to deal with the dinner crowd. Representatives in the industry have been advocating changes in these restrictions to permit teenagers (1) to work a maximum of 4 hours on days preceding school days, 1 hour more than currently allowed, and (2) to work until 9:00 P.M. on school nights, 2 hours past the current restriction. Industry advocates are also seeking an extension of the cooking and baking activities these workers are legally permitted to perform. These proposed changes would help ease the pressures on restaurant managers who are attempting to deal with the limited workforce. However, the industry's lobbyists met much resistance. In fact, several legislators were seeking to enact certain bills that would increase the pressures on the fast-food industry's hiring practices. One proposed bill would substantially increase penalties for serious infractions of federal teen labor laws to include prison terms for employers whose willful violations resulted in the serious injury of a teenage employee. Another provision of the bill sought a requirement that all applicants under the age of 18 secure a state-issued work permit if they do not possess a high school diploma. Industry representatives believe that regulations such as these would decrease the number of teenagers hired, thereby hurting the exact individuals whom the laws were designed to protect.

Federal Minimum Wage Hike　Legislation in other areas may also affect the fast-food industry. On April 1, 1991, the federal minimum wage rose from $3.80 to $4.25, with a subminimum exception for persons who have never before held a job. Payroll expenses generally account for 26 percent of all sales dollars. According to a survey conducted by Oregon State University, fast-food outlets were relatively unscathed because the majority of their employees already earn between $5.50 and $6.00 an hour. Although full-service restaurants were hit the hardest by this legislation, labor is the second-biggest cost for all restaurant operators.

Mandated Health Plans　The food service industry also faces an increase in labor costs from legislation related to mandated health plans. Legislators are pushing for a bill that would require employers to provide all their employees with health insurance or face a special payroll tax of 7 to 8 percent.

The special payroll tax would then be used to fund a federally administered insurance program for low-income Americans. If enacted, the industry fears that many small restaurant operations will be forced out of business by the expensive plan. As an alternative, industry advocates are seeking tax breaks and other incentives designed to encourage restaurant owners to voluntarily provide health insurance to employees.

Discrimination in the Workplace The fast-food industry is also monitoring proposed legislation intended to curtail job discrimination by allowing workers the right to have juries decide lawsuits against employers suspected of discrimination in the workplace. The act would permit the victims of discrimination to seek both compensatory and punitive damages, an option previously restricted to persons charging racial discrimination. Industry advocates contend that this legislation would shift the burden of the culpability test to require a business to prove its innocence rather than requiring the plaintiff to prove its guilt. As such, restaurants would be forced to resort to hiring persons because of their demographic traits rather than their abilities. Although the original form of the act would not have passed, proponents have negotiated a compromise with the White House guaranteeing its passage.

AIDS, E. Coli, and Customer Health The fast-food industry cannot escape the effects of the AIDS controversy. According to the executive vice president of the NRA, Bill Fisher, a number of restaurants are identified as employing individuals either suffering from AIDS or infected with HIV. Once identified, the restaurants suffer a rapid decline in business and are often forced to close. As of July 1990, food service lobbyists were attempting to revive the Chapman Amendment (as it was known in the House), a measure that would exempt food service operators from providing employees with AIDS the same rights and privileges as their

healthy peers. Employers would then be able to reassign infected employees to positions of comparable salary that did not involve any food handling. Contrary to the food industry's desires, the Senate enacted the Hatch Amendment, which is similar to the Chapman Amendment with one added qualification. It provides that the secretary of the U.S. Health and Human Services Department specify annually the diseases that can be transmitted through food. The Hatch Amendment further provides that only persons with a designated illness may be reassigned. According to Dr. Louis Sullivan, former secretary of the U.S. Health and Human Services Department, AIDS cannot be spread through food or beverages. The net effect of enacting this law is that food handlers with AIDS may retain their posts, and restaurants are virtually defenseless against consumers' fears.

The winter of 1993 saw an outbreak of illness caused by *E. coli* bacteria infection. A total of 475 cases of illness and three deaths were reported in the west, predominantly in the state of Washington. The cause has been attributed to tainted hamburger meat served at fast-food establishments operated by Foodmaker, Inc. (Jack in the Box). Review of meat vendor qualifications and cooking procedures was immediately undertaken, but a precipitous decline in sales could not be avoided. Whether a full recovery by Foodmaker is possible and what sort of regulations may emerge at the state or federal level are as yet unknown.

Environmental Pressures

The fast-food industry has also been facing increasing pressure from environmental groups to become more concerned over the ecological effect of its products and packaging. According to these environmental groups, chlorofluorocarbons (CFCs) used in the production of the plastic packaging used by the fast-food industry are responsible for damage to the ozone layer, which protects life on earth from the harmful effects of the sun's ultraviolet rays. Environmentalists also contend that the plastic packaging made of polystyrene foam takes up valuable space in landfills, takes decades to decompose, and has no viable recycling market. Despite some studies that indicated that the packaging is environmentally sound, McDonald's, the world's largest restaurant chain, began replacing plastic packaging in favor of paper. Although the paper is not recyclable and requires tremendous chemical and industrial processes to create it, it is biodegradable if composted and requires less space than foam packaging when discarded. McDonald's explained some of the factors leading to its switch, citing its lack of success at recapturing the packaging that leaves its restaurants and the lack of an infrastructure in the plastics-recycling industry. However, it appears that the company's 1990 annual report explains the real impetus for McDonald's change: "Although scientific studies indicate that foam packaging is sound, customers just don't feel good about it." Several other fast-food companies have also initiated environmental policies that involve recyclable polystyrene and compostable paper and plastic. McDonald's plan, however, is the most sweeping in the industry. The company will also replace its large white take-out bags with brown recyclable ones, convert to smaller napkins, install stainless steel condiment dispensers to eliminate the need for packets, compost eggshells and coffee grounds, and test starch-based spoons, knives, and forks as substitutes for current plastic versions. The company is further challenging its vendors to recycle and will require periodic progress reports that evidence the suppliers' use of recycled material in containers.

Suppliers

Food and beverage suppliers to the fast-food industry exert power on the participants by raising prices or reducing the quality of their products and/or services. One way a restaurant may deal with its suppliers is through backward integration. McDonald's entertained such a move and entered the business of raising cattle. Naturally, the environmentalists who condemn the use of plastics also condemn the raising of cattle—their grazing habits cause erosion and their waste pollutes the ground and air.

Rivalry Among Competitors

As a member of the fast-food industry, Rubio's competes with numerous types of restaurants, ranging from individual independent operations to franchises and chains. Rivalry among competitors results from a number of factors, including fixed costs. Fixed costs in the restaurant industry, which include labor costs, utility bills, and the interest expense on buildings, land, and equipment, are quite high. Restaurants have developed a variety of alternatives to compete by reducing their fixed costs.

Contract Services   PepsiCo Inc.'s Taco Bell has adopted one way to reduce high fixed costs. Since the mid-1980s, Taco Bell has been shifting as much of the food preparation to outside providers as possible. By contracting with these outside suppliers, Taco Bell has been able to reduce not only labor costs but kitchen space as well. This reduction in fixed costs has allowed Taco Bell to slash its menu prices, thereby attracting 60 percent more customers and reaching sales of $2.6 billion, a 63 percent increase.

Robotics   The desire of fast-food restaurants to reduce the labor costs has resulted in several more imaginative alternatives. Taco Bell is investigating whether robotics in the kitchen will increase savings by reducing space and labor requirements. Within 2 years, they are expected to adopt automatic taco makers and soft-drink dispensers. Carl's Jr. restaurant is utilizing an automated ordering system, dubbed "Touch 2000," which allows customers to enter their own selections on a touch-sensitive counter-top menu. The menu is connected to an IBM computer that checks the order and prompts the customer for more specific information if it is not satisfied. When satisfied, the computer relays the order automatically to the kitchen and the cashier. Burger King is currently evaluating the system as well. Although robotics reduce labor costs, increase productivity, and virtually eliminate boring jobs, not all fast-food restaurants are converting to their use. Today's economy has made human labor more available, reduced restaurant profits, and forced cutbacks in spending on research and development.

Reduced-Sized Restaurants Restaurants are also developing downsized units in an effort to reduce costs and gain access to towns that were previously dismissed because of their inability to generate sufficient sales to sustain a full-size outlet. McDonald's new prototype, called the "Series 2000," is 50 percent smaller and costs 30 percent less to build. These new units seat 50 patrons and employ only 20 persons per shift. McDonald's traditional units seat twice as many customers and require, at a minimum, 40 employees per shift. These downsized units will not only allow the chain to enter small towns but will also allow the company to secure locations in congested markets that were previously inaccessible because of the limited size of available sites.

Value Menus Fast-food restaurants have also explored a variety of strategies to attract customers during hard economic times. In an attempt to compete for the consumer's dollar, Red Lobster, a dinner house, launched a value menu that boasts numerous entrées for less than $10. In addition, the chain upgraded its china, uniforms, and napkins to enhance its image of providing the customer with value. Although fast-food restaurants must proceed cautiously to ensure that the customer's need for quick service is satisfied, many fast-food restaurants

are also opting for expanded menus to attract customers. McDonald's has also unveiled new menu selections designed to boost sales. Of particular concern to Rubio's is the addition of two Mexican items, the breakfast burrito and the chicken fajita. McDonald's is also testing turkey and pizza as other menu options. McDonald's U.S. president Ed Rensi does not anticipate that the addition of these new products will dilute the company's concept of serving hot fast food in a pleasant environment at a low cost. In fact, new technology should enable McDonald's to broaden its menu while maintaining good service times. Other fast-food restaurants have responded to this threat by promoting time-intensive products on a limited basis only.

Taco Bell, the nation's leading Mexican fast-food restaurant, is credited with having started these discount wars with the addition of its 59- and 39-cent value menu items. As operating profits for the third quarter of 1991 decreased, analysts wondered whether Taco Bell's value menu had discounted the chain out of a profit margin. However, according to Taco Bell president John Martin, the chain will not need to raise prices for at least 5 years because of its systemic restructuring and cost-saving technological changes in operational methods.

Marketing Strategies Restaurants have also explored other marketing strategies in an attempt to attract customers. Burger King developed a Kids Club to capitalize on the power of children to influence the purchases of their parents. Burger King entices its 2.7 million members with six newsletters "written" by well-known cartoon characters. The members also receive iron-on T-shirt logos and activity booklets. Burger King analysts credit the club for a recognizable increase in the chain's business. Burger King is also investigating other marketing alternatives to increase consumer spending. To further reach its teenage market, Burger King is buying time on Channel One, a satellite service that beams 12 minutes of programming and commercials each day into school classrooms. It is believed that a 30-second commercial on Channel One reaches 40 percent more teens than a commercial on MTV. Finally, Burger King is spending a portion of its advertising budget on local tie-ins to help build traffic at its franchises.

Delivery Service   Fast-food restaurants such as Burger King are also attempting to prod the dinner crowd, who would ordinarily select a midrange restaurant, by offering limited table service during the dinner hour. Customers place their orders at a walk-up counter, serve themselves a drink, and select a seat. When ready, their order is served to them at their table. Although Burger King does not intend to raise its prices as a result of this new service, the effects remain to be seen.

Acknowledging that the 1990s will be a decade dedicated to convenience, pizza restaurants may not be alone in their home delivery service. Although KFC franchisees are reluctant and anticipate operational difficulties, KFC is planning to add delivery service to all 500 of its domestic units. Because no other chicken segment player offers home delivery, it is an opportunity to preempt its competitors and gain a competitive edge.

Payment Convenience   Fast-food restaurants are also experimenting with the use of bank cards and ATM cards as alternative methods for payment. MasterCard, which wants people to use its card for everyday transactions, estimates that 70 percent of the people who eat at fast-food restaurants have a bank card. Arby's tested the system and discovered that bank card transactions exceed cash purchases by 30 to 60 percent. As a result, Arby's will install the system in all company-owned stores. McDonald's is also experimenting with a McCharge card for use in its outlets.

Expanding Distribution Channels   In addition to expanding product lines, restaurants are also looking for new points of distribution. Aided by new technology, fast-food restaurants have moved into many nontraditional outlets. PepsiCo, which owns Taco Bell, Pizza Hut, and KFC, will expand into any outlet where it may tempt hungry consumers. As a result, PepsiCo's food service brands may now be seen in supermarkets, convenience stores, movie theaters, student unions, amusement parks, fairs, hospitals, airports, and sports arenas. Taco Bell is also entertaining the possibility of selling packaged meals on supermarket shelves, a potentially lucrative market given that a quarter of the people age 35 to 44 are single.

THE RUBIO'S CONCEPT

Product Line

Rubio's main draw is its $1.49 fish tacos. A fish taco consists of a soft corn tortilla, pieces of deep-fried fish fillet, salsa, white sauce, cabbage, and a lime. The white sauce is made up of a mixture of mayonnaise and yogurt. Although the basic ingredients in the fish taco are known, because of local taco wars Rubio's batter for the fish remains a company secret. As a result, the batter is now packaged at a location other than the individual restaurants. Rubio's also offers a fish taco especial, which costs a little more but is prepared with such extras as guacamole, jack and cheddar cheese, cilantro, and onion. For those patrons who do not savor the idea of a fish taco, Rubio's menu offers such other traditional Mexican favorites as burritos, tostadas, nachos, and nonfish tacos. Consistent with the company's desire to satisfy the needs of its customers, menu items have been added or modified in response to customer input. All these items, including the fish tacos, are prepared to order using authentic Mexican recipes and fresh ingredients. A copy of Rubio's current menu is attached as Exhibit 1.

In addition to providing authentic, fresh-tasting Mexican food, Rubio's differentiates itself by offering a cold food menu, enabling customers to purchase select ingredients to prepare their own meals at home. In essence, customers may purchase the makings for almost every item on the menu.

Facilities

Rubio's original restaurant locations were selected based on Ralph Rubio's knowledge of the areas and the characteristics of their population. Although Rubio's target market varies to some extent by store location, on the whole its market consists of young and middle-aged upscale professionals and students. Members of these groups typically value their health and enjoy such social activities as the beach, athletic competition, musical entertainment, and dining out. As a result, the facilities are typically located in fast-growing retail areas with high traffic and visibility. Rubio's also considers the land use mix within a 3- to 5-mile radius. As a result, the restaurants are located in areas with high percentages of residential and office or industrial uses. Unlike the typical inaccessible mall location, these locations provide a greater number of customers with the characteristics of Rubio's target market and more flexible operating hours.

Under the Rubio family's direction, the exterior style and interior design of each of Rubio's restaurants is consistent throughout their 12 locations. The typical unit features a walk-up order counter with a large red-and-white-lettered menu behind it. Paper menus, which detail the company's phone-in order policy, are also provided. The units' decor is contemporary, with light wood, green wallpaper, color framed prints, and Mexican tile tables. A mural of the company mascot, Pesky Pescado, usually appears on one wall. (Pesky is an animated fish, standing upright on his tail, with a taco shell wrapped around his body.) The typical unit also features decorations that emphasize a beach theme, including surfboards, palms, green-and-white walls, ceiling fans, and beach scenes. This upscale atmosphere is further enhanced by a sound system that plays authentic mariachi music.

Although the units vary slightly by location, most have 2,200 square feet, with a cooking area, a dining area for approximately 50 people, and an outdoor patio. Each restaurant features an area where customers may purchase deli items and/or a variety of promotional items, such as T-shirts, bumper stickers, and decals. All units, other than the original one near Mission Bay and the SDSU location, have beer and wine licenses, a feature intended to strengthen Rubio's image as a fast-food alternative to fine Mexican restaurants. Consistent with the company's emphasis on service and convenience to the customer, one restaurant site also features a drive-through facility.

Each Rubio's location also has a designated receptacle for recycling bottles and cans used in the restaurant. Given that there is no consensus on whether plastic or paper is better for the environment, Rubio's will continue to use clamshell containers, which have better thermal retention. Rubio's has, however, switched to tray service to reduce the amount of paper used in each facility. Therefore, each facility also has an area designated for tray storage. As the recycling infrastructure grows, Rubio's continues to monitor plastic recycling. Once the decision to recycle is made, each facility will also have to designate space for plastics recycling.

In addition to these 12 restaurant locations, in April 1990 Rubio's joined the concession lineup at Jack Murphy Stadium. By May, Rubio's had expanded to the plaza level in an effort to meet the enormous demand at the stadium for its product. More recently, Rubio's joined the concessions at the Irvine Meadows Amphitheater.

Unit Operations

The typical unit has 15 to 25 employees, depending on the amount of customer traffic. Each unit has one general manager, two assistant managers, a cashier, an expediter, a prep clerk, four line clerks, a shift leader, and a customer service employee. To ensure uniformity throughout its facilities, the company has developed job descriptions for each of these positions. A sample of these descriptions is contained in Exhibit 2.

Despite the increase in the federal minimum wage rate, Rubio's employees have not been affected. On average, the employees make an hourly wage that already exceeds the new federal minimum. Unit structure and wage scales are presented in Exhibit 3.

In addition to a higher minimum wage, full-time employees are also offered various benefits, such as health insurance. Although Rubio's offers its full-time employees health insurance, only 30 percent currently take advantage of this benefit. Rubio's believes that this may result from cultural differences. As a result, Rubio's is currently engaged in direct marketing of its health insurance plan to its employees in an effort to increase participation rates to 70 percent. Rubio's is making this effort despite the anticipated increase in costs to the company.

Marketing Strategy

Despite the fact that San Diego shares a border with Mexico, Ralph Rubio recognized that no other restaurant in the area was serving authentic Mexican food. By offering fresh-tasting, authentic Mexican food in a contemporary, clean atmosphere, Rubio's is targeting a key segment of the market: young, upscale professionals and students, age 18 to 49, with a taste for better food. Rubio's success is, therefore, the result of carving out a special niche in an otherwise crowded fast-food market.

During the first couple of years of operation, Rubio's rarely advertised. Instead, early efforts were concentrated on ensuring that the total concept, from the menu to the decor, was designed to satisfy the customer's needs and desires. Yet despite this lack of

advertising, Rubio's was attracting new and repeat customers. Rubio's now promotes its business in at least three media—print, radio, and television—that appeal to consumers within its targeted market. Rubio's is currently investigating the idea of poster panels and billboards as an additional medium to access its target market. Current advertising objectives and strategies are:

ADVERTISING OBJECTIVES:
- Increase "trial" visits to Rubio's within target audience, adults 18 to 49
- Encourage repeat visits to Rubio's
- Increase overall awareness of Rubio's
- Generate awareness of Rubio's new location(s)

ADVERTISING STRATEGIES:
- Implement a consistent, chainwide media plan in San Diego that will effectively reach target market
- Execute local store marketing efforts in San Diego for grand openings and locations with special needs
- Implement a localized media and promotions plan in Orange County with emphasis on the Irvine location
- Administer sales promotion during heavy advertising periods

As in the past, Rubio's utilizes local cable television channels and radio stations to promote its products. Although the commercials have been relatively simple, they are designed to increase consumer awareness of Rubio's products. By tying the commercials to specific promotions, the effect is to increase regular foot traffic in Rubio's facilities as well as to attract first-time customers unfamiliar with fish tacos. Current advertising also seeks to generate awareness not only for Rubio's products but for its new locations as well.

Rubio's also uses direct mail to attract customers. With direct mail, Rubio's has been able to identify potential customers within a

5-mile radius of a new or existing restaurant. Rubio's believes that if it is able to persuade potential customers to try its product once, they will become repeat customers.

In addition to direct promotions, Rubio's participates in numerous indirect promotions. Rubio's has sponsored local athletic events such as the San Diego International Triathlon. Rubio's has also sent a 15-foot inflatable version of Pesky Pescado to local parades, sporting events, and restaurant openings. Pesky, Jr., an inflatable human-sized costume, also makes local appearances. These marketing efforts represent 2½ percent of sales, or $256,000. As Rubio's expands throughout southern California, it will continue to educate its potential customers through the use of these media and promotions.

Management

Despite its growth from one small restaurant in 1983 to over 12 locations throughout southern California, Rubio's remains a closely held corporation with ownership split among the family members. Ralph and Ray Rubio (Ralph's father) are the founders and majority stockholders. Ralph Rubio is acting president of the company. Ralph's brothers and sister fill the other key positions in the company: Robert is vice president of operations, Richard is vice president of expansion, and Gloria is vice president of training. The youngest Rubio, Roman, assists Gloria at corporate headquarters with training. Although Rubio's has brought in outside people to fill management positions, the family intends to maintain ownership and control for as long as possible.

As a relatively young, family-owned organization, Rubio's is characterized by centralized management and control. The company offers extensive training programs for its managers and employees to ensure efficiency and standardization in the production of its products. This policy is evidenced by its thorough and detailed operations manual. As the business expands, managers are provided with a sufficient degree of flexibility to handle day-to-day operations tailored to the needs of each individual store. Ultimate authority, however, remains with the Rubio family.

Finances

As a privately held company, the majority of Rubio's growth has been achieved with funds generated from within. Recent expansion has also been assisted by bank financing. The company's growth has been relatively slow and cautious. Sales, however, have not been slow. The combined sales from the 12 restaurant locations average over 10,000 fish tacos per day.

Including sales of other menu items, the average Rubio's store had sales of $700,000 during 1991. This figure represents a decline from 1990, when the average store had sales of $745,000. Each store unit is, however, designed to handle $1 million in annual sales, leaving plenty of opportunity for an increase in sales. Rubio's goal for the next several years is to increase the average store's sales to over $800,000.

Even with the current decrease in sales, the stores are quite profitable. To break even, the typical store must achieve monthly sales of approximately $30,000 to $35,000. The main cost difference among Rubio's facilities results from different lease costs. Labor and material costs remain the same across facilities. Food ingredients represent about 16 percent of the sales price of menu items. The ingredients breakdown for the fish taco and the fish taco especial are presented in Exhibit 4.

A LOOK TO THE FUTURE

Ralph's belief that the fish taco would be as popular in San Diego as it was in the Baja was correct—and judging from the amount of sales and the number of imitators, it is here to stay. Although Rubio's already has 12 restaurant locations, its goal is 50 company-owned restaurants in southern California averaging sales of $40 to $50 million annually. Fast-food industry figures also show that the Mexican food segment is still experiencing lucrative growth nationwide. Rubio's plans, therefore, to continue its expansion into new geographic markets. Although Rubio's has already expanded into Orange County, it will continue its investigation of northern California.

Yet as Rubio's approaches its tenth anniversary, the company faces many decisions and challenges that will affect its future. First, the company must determine issues related to future expansion:

1. Is there a market on the east coast for fish tacos?
2. Is international expansion a viable alternative?

Assuming that such expansion is feasible, the company must then determine how to establish operations in distant locations:

3. Should the company consider franchising, licensing agreements, partnerships, or even joint ventures?
4. Should the company attempt to remain a closely held, family organization?

Alternatively, Rubio's may focus its attention on expanding its distribution channels:

5. Should Rubio's manufacture its fast-food products for distribution in nontraditional outlets?
6. Should Rubio's offer a packaged version of its product in supermarkets and grocery stores?

Moreover, given the importance of limiting or reducing costs, Rubio's must also consider the feasibility of assorted cost-saving investments:

7. Should Rubio's centralize the preparation of some or all of its food products once the company reaches a specified number of outlets?
8. Should Rubio's integrate into its own sources of supply?

Menu...

Welcome to Rubio's... Home of the Fish Taco! Founded in January of 1983, we have since served over <u>6 million</u> of our delicious San Felipe style fish tacos to happy customers all over San Diego. Our philosophy is to provide delicious Mexican food served in a clean attractive atmosphere, while maintaining that original Baja flavor. Please enjoy your visit and come back soon!   ¡Hasta Luego! *Pesky*

Los Otros

QUESADILLA   we spread guacamole on your flour tortilla, sprinkle with cheddar cheese and top it with salsa, we fold it, then heat until it's hot and melted...................**$2.09**

TAQUITOS   three tacos deep-fried and topped with guacamole, salsa and cheese **$1.79**

NACHOS REGULAR   our own homemade chips topped with a melted jalapeno cheese sauce...**88¢**

NACHOS GRANDE   the mas mucho o' nachos. over a bed of chips, you'll find cheese sauce, beans, salsa, guacamole, sour cream, and a black olive at the very top.......**$2.95**

CHIPS   a bag of our fresh tortilla chips, we cut them and fry them right here, every day.....**60¢**

BEANS   a plate of our spicy delicious baked pintos, sprinkled with cheese..............**75¢**

PALETAS   frozen fruit sticks...............**75¢**

CHURROS   ....**75¢**

Combinations

all served with homemade chips and beans

#1   any two tacos
beef carnitas or fish...........................**$2.29**

#2   chicken burrito, beef taco.........**$3.89**

#3   carnitas, burrito, fish taco.........**$3.00**

#4   beef burrito, carnitas, taco.........**$3.70**

#5   fish burritos, fish taco...............**$3.27**

NEW **#6**   carne asade, burrito, fish taco.....**$3.89**

PESKY COMBO   two fish tacos especiales with beans and chips.......................**$2.09**

Tacos

FISH TACO ESPECIAL   for the supreme of fish tacos we provide one of our regular fish tacos dressed with guacamole, cheddar cheese and cilantro/onion. go ahead try one.....................................**$1.79**

SHREDDED BEEF   in a soft-shell corn tortilla with guacamole, salsa, cilantro/onion and shredded with lettuce.......................**$1.59**

CARNITAS   shredded pork, served on a soft-shell corn tortilla with salsa, cilantro/onion and lettuce.............................**$1.94**

FISH   tacos san tempe-style, a strip of fish battered and deep-fried then placed in a soft-shell corn tortilla with salsa, our special white sauce and cabbage, add a squeeze of lime and you have an authentic fish taco........**$1.00**

NEW **CARNE ASADA***   marinated chunks of steak, seasoned, skillet-seared and placed in a soft-shell corn tortilla with guacamole, salsa, cilantro/onion and cabbage, es deliciosa...**$1.34**

Burritos

BEEF   a soft flour filled tortilla with guacamole, beans, spicy shredded beef, salsa, cilantro/onion and a little lettuce. Moo-y delicious.....**$2.49**

CARNITAS   shredded pork on a flour tortilla with beans, salsa, cilantro/onion, and lettuce. one of our specialties........................**$2.44**

CHICKEN   chicken simmered in a spicy tomato sauce with onions and peppers, then served on a flour tortilla sprinkled with cheddar cheese, cilantro/onion, and lettuce **$2.49**

FISH   a local favorite. fish filets in a flour tortilla and guacamole, beans, salsa, white sauce, cilantro/onion and cabbage. so mucho tasty.......................................**$2.54**

BEANS AND CHEESE   beans on a bed of cheese with salsa and cilantro/onion......**$1.09**

MACHACA   our shredded beef and egg with salsa and cilantro/onion, a great way to start the day.......................................**$1.98**

CHORIZO   mexican pork sausage scrambled in egg with cilantro/onion and salsa, good and spicy......................................**$1.98**

NEW **CARNE ASADA***   from the streets of Mexico City, a recipe that includes tasty chunks of steak marinated and skillet-seared served on a flour tortilla with beans, slasa, cilantro/onion and guacamole...**$2.55**

Tostadas

BEEF   a deep-fried tostada shell covered with beans, salsa, lettuce, chopped tomato, onion, cheese, sour cream, and garnished with a black olive................................**$2.18**

CHICKEN   our shredded chicken on a bed of beans, salsa, lettuce, chopped tomato, onion, cheese, sour cream and an olive......**$1.05**

BEAN   beans cover the tostada shell and are then topped with salsa, lettuce, chopped tomato and onion, cheese and an olive........**$1.49**

SALAD MEXICANA   our spicy shredded chicken on a bed of fresh lettuce and tortilla chips covered with chopped tomatoes, jack cheese and sour cream. add our special salsa dressing and you have a light tasty meal that is "mucho" healthy!...............**$2.95**

Drinks

pepsi. diet pepsi. rootbeer. orange slice. slice. iced tea. coffee. lowfat milk. big kahuna fruit juice.

cerveza available at most locations

EXTRA ITEMS   guacamole, cheese or sour cream on any item................................**..25¢**

■ all orders packaged to go
■ phone in orders welcome

Cold Food Menu

Corn Tortillas.................. .80 Doz
Flour Tortillas...............1.20 Doz
Beans................ 1.00 Pt 1.80 Qt
Taquitos.................. 1.00 set (3)
Guacamole.................. 3.75 lb
Cilantro & Onion........... 1.00 lb
Shredded Beef.............. 3.75 lb
Carnitas..................... 3.75 lb
Chicken...................... 3.75 lb
Shredded Cheese (Jack Ched)...... 3.00 lb
Shredded Mexican Cheese........... 3.00 lb
Chips........................... 1.75 lb
Quesadillas............................. 2.09 each
Salsas................ 1.60 Pt 3.00 Qt

Note: We do not sell our cold food products in increments less than a pound, pint or dozen.

CALL – IN ORDER POLICY

■ Please call in your orders before 1:30 am. No call-in orders will be accepted between 11:30 am and 1:30 pm.
   Note: No call-in or pick-up orders between 11:30 am and 1:30 pm at our Kearney Mesa and University City stores

■ Be aware of our two locations in Pacific Beach to avoid misplaced orders

■ Customer phone numbers will be required on all orders over $10.00

■ When picking up your order, please stand and pay in the cashier line.

■ Please allow 24 hours notice for any large deli orders over $25.00

Thank you, Rubio's

Locations

MISSION BAY 4504 Mission Bay Dr 272-2801	*CHULA VISTA* 789 N. El Camino Ave 427-3811
S.D.S.U. 5187 Colten Ave 206-3844	*ENCINITAS* 481 Hemingway St. 632-7395
PACIFIC BEACH 925 Grand Ave 270-4800	*EL CAJON* 298 Magnum Ave 440-3325
POINT LOMA McCloud & Vista Blvd 223-2631	*KEARNEY MESA* 1420 Cameron Mesa Blvd 268-5770
SAN MARCOS Vine & Mesa Way 745-2962	*UNIVERSITY CITY* 8935 Towne Center Rd 453-1606

Our Fish Tacos are now featured at
JACK MURPHY STADIUM!

Now in Tustin & Irvine

*Available all stores June 15
Prices may vary according to location and are subject to change without notice*

Rubio's
Home of the Fish Taco©

EXHIBIT 1   Rubio's Menu

EXHIBIT 2	Rubio's Job Descriptions
Prep	Responsible for prepping all the food product, cleanliness and organization of walk-in, and care of equipment.
Line 3	Under the direction of Line 1; Line 3 heats the tortilla, fries fish, taquitos, and churros, and cooks machaca and chorizo.
Line 2	Under the direction of Line 1; Line 2 works the condiment table, wraps the food, keeps the condiment table stocked, and his area clean.
Line 2B	Works alongside Line 2; responsibilities are mainly the wrapping of food to help expedite the food more quickly. This position is implemented during peak hours.
Line 1	The "Quarterback"—sets the pace in the kitchen, reads the ticket, works the steam table and gives direction to Line 2 and Line 3. Line 1 is directly responsible for how smooth the shift goes. He/she is the leader.
Expediter	Responsible for bagging orders correctly and putting out orders. Responsible for restaurant cleanliness. Restocks throughout the day. Always says "thank you" to customers. Must wear the tag provided by the company.
Cashier	Greets the customer, takes the order, and cashiers throughout the day. Responsible for the cash drawer. Keeps area clean and, along with the expediter, helps clean the dining area. If time, helps put out orders. Must wear the name tag provided by the company.
Shift Leader	Responsible for upholding the company's standards and procedures to the highest possible level in every aspect of the restaurant operations. Responsible for the maintenance of the restaurant's operations while under the direction of the management crew. Shift leaders will adhere to the management demeanor and dress policies.
Customer Service Employee	Hired by the special service organizations for the disabled to meet the needs of our customers during the busy lunch. Responsible for bussing, wiping tables, restocking, sweeping, getting napkins and utensils for customers already seated, and any other duties specified by the particular store.

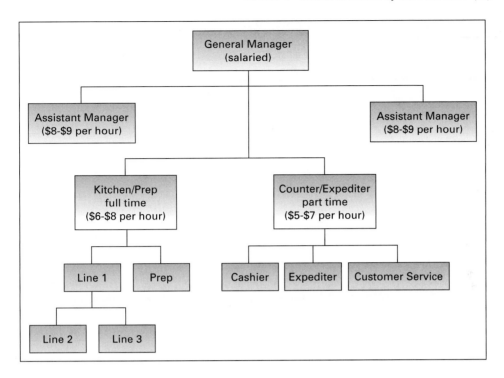

EXHIBIT 3   Typical Rubio's Store Structure

EXHIBIT 4 Menu Recipe File

		Fish Taco	
Ingredients	*Portion*	*CPU*	*Cost*
Fish (pollack)	1.25 oz	0.1031250	0.1289063
White sauce	0.50 oz	0.0215625	0.0107812
Cabbage	0.75 oz	0.0133547	0.0100160
Limes	1.00 slice	0.0069179	0.0069179
Corn tortilla	1.00 each	0.0291667	0.0291667
Fish batter	0.75 oz	0.0218750	0.0164063
Salsa	0.75 oz	0.0227422	0.0170566
		Cost	$0.2192510
		Menu price	$1.44
		Item cost (%)	15.226%
		Gross profit	$1.2207490

		Fish Taco Especial	
Ingredients	*Portion*	*CPU*	*Cost*
Corn tortilla	1.00 each	0.0291667	0.0291667
Fish (pollack)	1.25 oz	0.1031250	0.1289063
Fish batter	0.75 oz	0.0218750	0.0164063
Salsa	0.75 oz	0.0227422	0.0170566
White sauce	0.50 oz	0.0215625	0.0107812
Cabbage	0.75 oz	0.0133547	0.0100160
Guacamole	0.50 oz	0.0641875	0.0320937
Cheese	0.50 oz	0.0812500	0.0406250
Cilantro/onion	0.25 oz	0.0248750	0.0062187
Limes	1.00 slice	0.0069179	0.0069179
		Cost	$0.2981885
		Menu cost	$1.79
		Item cost (%)	16.659%
		Gross profit	$1.4918115

This case was prepared in 1992 by Professor Kenneth E. Marino of San Diego State University with the assistance of graduate student Linda Kelleher Carter. It is intended as a basis for class discussion rather than to illustrate effective or ineffective handling of an administrative situation.

Case 5 Rubio's: Home of the Fish Taco (B)

Rubio's Restaurants Inc. is a publicly held corporation that owns and operates 128 high-quality, quick-service Mexican restaurants in California, Arizona, Colorado, Nevada, and Utah. Known for its Baja-style Mexican food and signature fish tacos, Rubio's has undergone phenomenal growth in the past 10 years, from 12 stores in 1992 to a planned 138 stores by 2002 and franchising another 14 stores. Rubio's focuses on offering a high-quality product at the price and speed of a fast-food restaurant, and its success has been phenomenal, as is evident in its growth both in number of stores and sales. Since opening in San Diego County in 1983 as a family-owned restaurant, Rubio's has helped define the quick-service Mexican food segment of the restaurant industry. Management intends to continue doing so at a national level well into the future.

THE RESTAURANT INDUSTRY

The restaurant industry, which is defined by the National Restaurant Association (NRA) as encompassing all meals and snacks prepared away from home, including all takeout meals and beverages is expected to achieve sales of $399 billion in 2001. This represents an increase of 5.2 percent over 2000 sales and will mark the tenth consecutive year of real sales growth for the industry. Sales at quick-service (fast-food) restaurants alone are forecast to reach $112 billion in sales, or 28 percent of total restaurant industry sales.

With sales projected to equal 4 percent of the U.S. gross domestic product (GDP), the restaurant industry is a cornerstone of the nation's economy, employing 11.3 million people (making it the largest employer in the country outside the government). In close to 30 years, the number of locations that offer food-service has nearly doubled, from 491,000 in 1972 to 844,000 in 2000. This phenomenal growth has been parallel to the growth of the restaurant industry's share of the food dollar, which has risen from 25 percent in 1955 to 45.8 percent in 2000. (The average annual spending on food away from home was $2,030 per household, or $812 per person.) In addition, it is projected that by 2010, 53 percent of the food dollar will be spent on food away from home. This industry growth has been driven by the growth in the number of higher income households and the rising need for convenience and value. On the other hand, the large growth in sales has helped foster a fiercely competitive environment, consisting of 844,000 dining locations. As a result, restaurant owners are focusing on the physical settings of their facilities (i.e., design, decor, and atmosphere) as a basis for differentiation, rather than on food and service (as has been the focus in the past).

In addition to a highly competitive environment, restaurant owners have several other challenges to address. Labor, purchasing, and operational costs have continued to rise, and energy costs, especially in California, have soared. Workplace safety has become increasingly important, as labor laws have become more stringent, and worker's compensation insurance has become more costly. Use of technology has become widespread in ordering supplies, processing

This case was prepared in 2001 by Jennifer Quinnet (MBA) under the direction of Professor Kenneth Marino, Department of Management, San Diego State University.

transactions, and providing information (via Web sites) to suppliers and customers. As a participant in the fast-food segment, Rubio's must monitor its competition and face these challenges in order to remain successful in this competitive environment.

Regional Trends

Western Region Although total employment, disposable personal income, and population growth was higher than the national average in 2000, the region's economy is predicted to slow simultaneously with the nation's economy. However, at the state level, California is expected to continue leading the nation in total sales volume and total employment in the restaurant industry. Unfortunately, California is quickly becoming saturated by full-service and quick-service restaurants, and other states may provide more opportunities to new businesses.

Mountain Region The mountain region achieved the strongest national growth in total employment and total population in 2000, as well as a higher than average growth in disposable personal income. At the state level, Nevada and Colorado are expected to lead not only the region but also the nation in eating-place sales growth in the future.

Central Region In the midwest and central regions, the economy, total employment, disposable personal income, and population growth increased at a rate well below the national average. Furthermore, the region is expected to continue with these trends, posting the lowest restaurant industry sales growth in the nation.

Eastern Region Economic growth in the mid-Atlantic and New England regions of the eastern part of the nation slowed in 2000, while the South Atlantic region posted economic growth well above the national average. In fact, at a regional level, the South Atlantic is expected to lead the nation in restaurant sales in the future. New England's eating-place sales are expected to increase at the national rate, with New Hampshire and Rhode Island leading the way for the region.

Major Market Trends

Education Food and drink sales by contract food-service providers at educational institutions are expected to increase in the future as a consequence of, and in correspondence with, the continued increase in academic enrollment. The higher education sector of the educational market is expected to increase at the fastest rate.

Recreation Food and drink sales at recreation and sports centers are projected to increase at a higher rate than sales in the educational sector due to increased event attendance and the growth in the number of higher income households. For example, attendance at spectator sports such as ice hockey and baseball is increasing, and attendance at theme parks is up as a result of new and improved attractions and repeat visitors.

Transportation The transportation market is expected to experience the highest increase in food and drink sales. Railroad depots are projected to post the largest sales increase due to increased passenger traffic, especially for short trips. Airports provide another venue where substantial numbers of travelers seek preflight and between-flight meals.

Lodging Places Although food and drink sales at lodging places are expected to grow, the increase is expected to be less than in other markets due to the slower growth in personal and business travel. This will be most evident in the hotel-restaurant segment.

Business Places Sales by contract food-service providers are predicted to increase slightly at commercial and office buildings. The rate is equivalent to expected employment growth in areas such as finance, insurance, real estate, and government.

Economic Trends

Sales at quick-service restaurants are expected to reach $112 billion in 2001, which is a 4.4 percent increase over the segment's 2000 sales of $107 billion. When adjusted for inflation, (real) sales are actually increasing at a rate of 1.8 percent in 2001, slightly less than the 2.1 percent growth in 2000. This decrease in the growth rate of real sales is a result of a slower growth in the national economy, as well as slower unit growth within the quick-service segment. Slower unit growth is believed to be the result of a move toward franchise-owned versus company-owned stores, and a trend toward cobranding or multiconcept branding at a single establishment (e.g., Carl's Jr. with The Green Burrito, and KFC with Taco Bell).

Unemployment Although the restaurant industry as a whole continues to benefit from the nation's steady economic growth, individual restaurant owners are finding it difficult to attract and retain employees during this prosperous time when the employment rate has reached a 30-year low. Furthermore, high turnover rates plague the restaurant industry. In fact, in 1998, fast-food restaurants reported a median annual turnover rate of 117 percent. Additionally, the median tenure for workers in food-service occupations is 1.3 years, well below the median of 3.6 years for all wage and salary workers in the nation. Because of low unemployment and high turnover rates, restaurant operators believe that recruiting and retaining employees will continue to be one of the top challenges their businesses face. As a result, many employers are devoting more time and money to employee development by expanding overall training programs and implementing cross-training programs. In addition to training, it is equally important for employers to communicate the career paths available to employees in the restaurant industry. If workers can begin to see their jobs as part of a longer career path in the restaurant industry, they may be more inclined to remain in a particular job and loyal to a single organization.

Labor Force

Labor Statistics According to the Bureau of Labor Statistics (as reported in a March 2000 article in *Restaurants USA Magazine*), 4 percent of all employed men, 6 percent of all employed women, and 20 percent of all employed teenagers worked in food-preparation and food-service jobs in 1998. Furthermore, the number of total workers in the restaurant industry is projected to reach 12.5 million by the year 2008 (an increase of nearly 15 percent from 1998). According to the Restaurant Industry Employee Profile (a National Restaurant Association), the typical employee in a food-service occupation is:

- Female (58 percent)
- Under age 30 (59 percent)
- High school graduate or less (71 percent)
- Single (71 percent)
- Living in a household that includes:
  relatives (82 percent)
  two or more wage earners (80 percent)
  average U.S. household income
- Part-time employee working an average of 25.5 hours per week
- An individual with relatively short job tenure

Women in the Workforce The number of women in the workforce has steadily been increasing over the last 2 decades and is expected to continue to outpace growth in male employment. With regards to employment, the restaurant industry is more likely than other businesses to hire women. As an illustration of this trend, in 1998, women made up 46 percent of the total employed labor force, and they constituted 58 percent of those employed in food-service occupations. Furthermore, women predominated

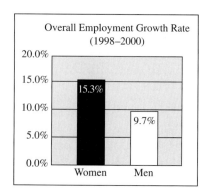

men in a majority of positions: supervisors, wait-staff, kitchen workers, and (front) counter staff. However, women are less likely than men to be employed full-time, as is evident in 1998, when 66 percent of all part-time employees were female.

Minorities in the Workforce   As minority populations continue to grow in the United States, so does the number of minorities working in the restaurant industry. In 1998, Hispanics accounted for 17 percent of all persons employed in food-service occupations, and African-Americans accounted for 12 percent. As a basis of comparison, Hispanics comprise 10 percent of the national population of employed persons, and African-Americans represent 11 percent. In terms of staffing positions, both minority groups are more likely than average to be employed as cooks and miscellaneous food works, and Hispanics are also more likely than average to be wait-staff assistants.

Job Growth   Although the employment rate in the food-service industry has been increasing annually for nearly a decade, it has been lagging in comparison to the nation's overall growth rate for the past 3 years. However, the industry continues to be a major job-creator, creating more than 1.5 million jobs during the 1990s, making it the third largest private-sector job-creator

in the U.S. economy (following businesses services and health services).

Consumer Needs and Lifestyles

Consumers' need for convenience continues to increase as employment increases, leaving little spare time to prepare meals at home. In 1999, a typical person (age 8 and older) consumed an average of 4.2 meals prepared away from home per week. Therefore, quick-service restaurants are increasing their efforts to provide fast and easy service to customers in order to keep up with their busy lifestyles. According to the 2000 Consumer Survey conducted by the NRA, 47 percent of adults between the ages of 18 and 24 reported that takeout food is essential to the way they live. Furthermore, 77 percent of adults, ages 18 to 24, indicated that consuming takeout or delivery meals allowed them more time to spend on other activities.

Along with increased convenience, restaurant owners are continually trying to meet the changing tastes and preferences of their customers. In fact, 76 percent of quick-service operators reported that they introduced new food items in 2000, and 66 percent stated that they intend to do the same in 2001. In addition, because customers are seeking more value for their dollar, many restaurants offer a variety of promotions throughout the year, such as weekly or monthly specials, as well as bundled-meal discounts. Promotional offerings are determined largely by the type of customer quick-service restaurants are trying to attract. Quick-service operators indicated the following customer groups to be the most important (in order of significance): (1) businesspeople; (2) teenagers; (3) senior citizens; and, (4) tourists and parties that include children.

Ethnic Cuisines   During the 1990s, the market for ethnic cuisines grew with consumers' desire to experience menus based on different cultures. In fact, the growth was so widespread that Italian, Chinese, and Mexican restaurants, which are the most popular, have become mainstream rather than exotic and new. Many ethnic foods have become more readily available and are offered at "nonethnic" restaurants. Therefore, ethnic restaurants can no longer rely solely on their menus to attract their target consumers, who are typically younger and living in major metropolitan areas. Service, value, and atmosphere are as significant factors as in any restaurant.

Seafood   Seafood consumption has been on the rise, as consumers are looking for healthier and more innovative alternatives in restaurant menus. Customers have indicated the primary reason for eating seafood is the taste, followed by health, diet, and caloric reasons. Most people perceive seafood to be healthful, more so than beef and pork products. However, consumers are more likely to order seafood at a fine-dining or casual restaurant than at a fast-food establishment due to concerns regarding freshness, limited preparation options, and a preference for hamburgers or chicken when eating fast food. In fact, the most common reasons for not eating seafood include lack of convenience or availability, dislike of the taste, high prices, and food-safety concerns.

Restaurant Setting   The physical setting in which customers dine is becoming a more integral part of the restaurant experience, as well as a basis on which to compete. Design, decor, and atmosphere have become the focus of many restaurant owners and managers. In the NRA's Restaurant Settings 2000 Survey, approximately 66 percent of the respondents reported using the services of an interior designer, and 75 percent worked with an architect in the design of their restaurants. Restaurant owners are

particularly interested in keeping their settings modern yet timeless.

Of course, customer satisfaction with food and service has been and continues to be of utmost importance to restaurant owners, which is why most of their time is still devoted to these areas; if food and service are unsatisfactory to the customer, physical setting is likely to be insignificant in the overall dining experience. Once food and service needs are met, restaurant owners can focus on the physical environments of their restaurants, focusing on the type of experience the customer is seeking. However, in general, the physical setting is often less important at mid-scale restaurants where patrons spend less time and are usually interested in just getting something to eat quickly, in contrast to upscale restaurants where consumers are looking for a complete dining experience, where physical setting becomes integral.

External Pressures

Energy Costs   As energy prices continue to soar, restaurant owners look for new ways to maximize their energy usage and subsidize the rising costs in other ways, one of which is by raising menu prices. California businesses are not only facing doubled energy costs, but also rolling blackouts, which shut down a business's energy for a minimum of 1 hour, causing a loss in business and often product when the refrigeration system shuts down. As energy prices and blackouts continue, many businesses will be forced to shut down their facilities and move to places where traffic and costs allow them to operate.

Workplace Safety   Improvements over the last decade in workplace safety, along with more stringent requirements regarding worker's compensation insurance, have successfully reduced occupational injuries and illnesses in the restaurant industry. Lower rates of injury and illness have helped restaurant owners maximize labor productivity while, at the same time, managing heath-care expenses.

Technology Technology has become prominent in every facet of business. In the restaurant industry, technology is used for a variety of tasks, both at the corporate and store levels. Examples may include (1) ordering and purchasing supplies from vendors, (2) maintaining computerized accounting systems, (3) taking customer orders electronically, and (4) designing and hosting a Web site. The Internet has become a competitive business tool in every industry, and approximately half of the respondents to the NRA's 2000 Tableservice Operator Survey reported that they have a Web site. Restaurant Web sites are typically informational in purpose, providing consumers with information such as locations, menu items, and promotions. Other more technologically advanced restaurants offer online reservations and online ordering capabilities. Regardless of its use, technology is taking over business and being used to increase efficiency while decreasing long-term costs.

Competition Competition in the quick-service segment of the restaurant industry is stronger than ever, not only from other quick-service restaurants, but also from other food-service providers and segments of the restaurant industry that offer takeout menus. Some of the key competitive factors in the restaurant industry are food quality, price and value, service quality, restaurant location, and the dining atmosphere.

THE RUBIO'S CONCEPT

Product Line

Rubio's menu features burritos, soft-shell tacos, quesadillas made with marinated chargrilled chicken breast and lean steak, and seafood such as chargrilled mahi mahi, sautéed shrimp, and their signature Baja-style fish taco. All items are made-to-order, and side items such as chips, rice, and beans are made fresh daily. Rubio's restaurants offer a self-serve salsa bar where customers can choose from three freshly made salsas. Prices for menu items range from $1.89 for the signature fish taco to $6.29 for a Lobster Combo. Most of the individual establishments also offer a selection of imported Mexican and domestic beers, along with a variety of soft drinks.

Most restaurants also offer a Health-Mex menu and Kid Pesky meals for children. The HealthMex items are designed for the nutritionally conscious consumer and have less than 20 percent of their calories from fat. The Kid Pesky meals offer a choice of a fish taco, chicken taquitos, quesadillas, or a bean burrito served with a side dish, drink, churro, and toy surprise.

To add variety, Rubio's occasionally offers limited-time promotional menu items, such as the tequila shrimp burrito. However, most of these items are not permanently added to the menu due to the seasonality and limited availability of the product.

Facilities

Rubio's targets high-profile, major metropolitan areas that offer appealing demographic characteristics such as high-traffic patterns; high density of white collar families; medium to high family incomes; high education levels; a large concentration of daytime employment; residential, retail, and entertainment developments; and limited competition. The senior management team is actively involved in selecting new markets, and each new site must be approved by the Rubio's Real Estate Acquisition Committee.

Once the site is approved, Rubio's leases rather than purchases the appropriate facility space in order to minimize the cash investment associated with each unit.

Historically, the typical restaurant size has been 1,800 to 3,600 square feet but is expected to range from 2,000 to 2,400 square feet for future sites. On average, the total cash investment required to open an individual restaurant is $380,000 to $450,000, not including preopening expenses of $19,000 to $25,000.

Once the space is leased, construction begins to design the interior and exterior according to Rubio's usual specifications. Some of the design elements include colorful Mexican tiles, saltwater aquariums with tropical fish, beach photos, surfboards, and authentic palm-thatched patio umbrellas. The intent of the decor is to create a relaxed and casual environment in which customers can enjoy an authentic Baja Mexican meal.

Unit Operations

The typical restaurant employs one general manager, one to two assistant managers, and 18 to 22 hourly employees, 60 percent of which work full-time. All employees working over 30 hours per week are eligible for health-care benefits, and employees over 18 years of age that work more than 20 hours per week are eligible to participate in Rubio's 401(k) plan. In addition, managers are offered performance-based cash incentives that are tied directly to sales and profitability, and they have the option to buy shares of common stock when hired or promoted.

Besides unit management and employees, Rubio's also employs district managers, each of whom reports to a regional manager and is responsible for all phases of restaurant operations as well as opening new units.

Marketing Strategy

As Rubio's has grown to 128 stores in five states over 18 years, it has built upon its original "fish taco" concept to expand its menu and position itself between the quick-service and casual-dining segments of the restaurant industry. The key elements of Rubio's market positioning are:

- Distinctive, fresh, high-quality food
- Casual, fun dining experience
- Excellent dining value

To achieve its positioning goals during its first 18 years of operation, Rubio's advertising had been handled in-house. However, as of January 2001, Team One Advertising was hired to help build the Rubio's brand, develop promotional advertising, increase awareness, and generate trial in new markets. In addition, Rubio's plans to hire local public relations firms to help establish brand awareness in the new markets.

Broadcast advertising, both television and radio; coupons; and in-store point-of-purchase displays have been used as marketing tools to increase brand awareness, attract new customers, and build customer loyalty. The promotional theme is designed to portray Rubio's as a high-quality, quick-service Mexican food restaurant, as well as to publicize special offers.

All of the marketing strategies employed are designed to help accomplish and reinforce the business objective of becoming the "leading high-quality, quick-service Mexican restaurant brand nationwide" (Rubio's 10-K, 2000).

Competition

The restaurant industry is fiercely competitive and segmented, based on the type of service, food, and price being offered. In the quick-service, high-quality Mexican food segment, Rubio's direct competitors include Baja Fresh, La Salsa, and Chipotle (see Exhibit 7). Rubio's indirect competitors include full-service Mexican restaurants such as Chevy's and El Torito, as well as fast-food restaurants, especially those concentrating on Mexican food offerings such as Taco Bell and Del Taco. Although Rubio's is able to compete favorably in the restaurant market, many of its competitors are better established nationwide with greater financial, marketing, and management resources.

Franchise Opportunities

To enhance the company's expansion strategy, Rubio's implemented a franchising program in 2000 (see Exhibit 8). Management and financial resources will be provided by Rubio's to build the infrastructure of the newly franchised units, and franchisees will in turn pay area development fees, new store opening fees, and royalties to Rubio's. As of February 2001, Rubio's had two signed franchisee agreement, one to open eight units and the other to open six.

Financials

For 2000, Rubio's had 90 units open the entire year, which generated an average sales per unit of $896,000, an average operating income per unit of $130,000 (14.5 percent of sales), and an average cash flow per unit of $166,000 (18.6 percent of sales). Comparable restaurant sales (for units open and operating over 12 months) increased 0.6 percent in 2000, much lower than the 6.0 percent increase from the previous year; overall sales increased 40.9 percent over 1999 sales, an increase that is partially a result of the opening of 36 new restaurants in 2000. Of the 90 units open the entire year, 22 are located outside of California. Those 22 units generated an average sales per unit of $733,000, an average operating income per unit of $36,000 (4.9 percent of sales), and an average cash flow per unit of $75,000 (10.3 percent of sales).

Abbreviated Annual Financials

Income Statement All dollar amounts in millions except per share amounts.	Dec-00	Dec-99	Dec-98
Revenue	$95.7	$67.9	$44.5
Cost of goods sold	$32.6	$23.0	$15.0
Gross profit	$63.1	$44.9	$29.5
Gross profit margin	65.9%	66.1%	66.3%
SG&A expense	$61.9	$42.0	$28.8
Operating income	$1.2	$2.9	$0.7
Operating margin	1.3%	4.3%	1.6%
Total net income	$(0.2)	$1.7	$0.9
Net profit margin	—	2.5%	2.0%
Diluted EPS ($)	$(0.03)	$0.20	$0.14

Balance sheet All amounts in milllons.	Dec-00	Dec-99	Dec-98
Cash	$1.3	$3.5	$0.8
Net receivables	$1.4	$0.8	$0.3
Inventories	$2.0	$0.6	$0.4
Total current assets	$12.1	$12.9	$4.5
Total assets	$52.3	$50.0	$25.8
Short-term debt	$0.0	$0.0	$0.7
Total current liabilities	$7.7	$5.8	$5.9
Long-term debt	$0.0	$0.0	$1.1
Total liabilities	$9.3	$6.9	$7.8
Total Equity	$43.0	$43.1	$17.9
Shares Outstanding (mil.)	8.9	$8.9	1.0

Source: Information from www.hoovers.com.

In May 1999, Rubio's made an initial public offering in order to raise capital for the operation and expansion of the business, yet does not anticipate paying any cash dividends in the foreseeable future. Unfortunately, although restaurant revenues have continued to increase, Rubio's stock price has been spiraling downward (see below).

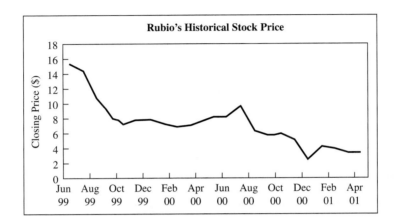

Rubio's attributes the depressed stock price to higher labor, energy, and food costs, which have led to a number of underperforming restaurants

A LOOK TO THE FUTURE

Although Rubio's has been reasonably successful thus far in the highly competitive restaurant industry, the company has some challenges to face in the near future. The company already plans to raise menu prices and focus their marketing efforts to improve sales in order to offset some of the cost pressures. Although the long-term plan is to grow to nearly 2,000 restaurants nationwide, Rubio's is slowing store growth in the immediate future in order to preserve capital and focus on operational excellence.

Although Rubio's management is taking steps to overcome the challenges they face, there are a number of issues to be considered regarding current strategy and future growth:

1. Is Rubio's expansion plan feasible?
2. Is the Rubio's concept transferable to other regions of the country? If yes, where should expansion efforts be focused?
3. What other markets and distribution channels could Rubio's penetrate? (for example, university campuses, frozen foods in grocery stores, etc.)
4. Is franchising a good option?
5. What are other possible solutions to offset the drop in stock price?

EXHIBIT 1   Rubio's Baja Grill

EXHIBIT 2   Rubio's Baja Grill Total Assets Versus Total Liabilities for 1998–2000

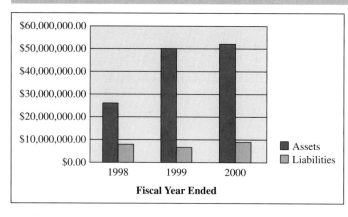

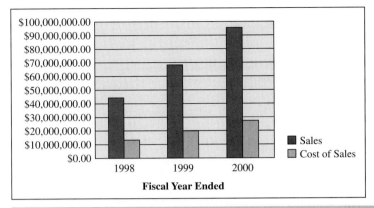

EXHIBIT 3   **Rubio's Baja Grill Sales Versus Cost of Sales for 1998–2000**

EXHIBIT 4   **Rubio's Baja Grill Net Income for 1998–2000**

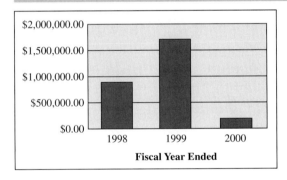

EXHIBIT 5   Risk Factors

1. If we are not able to successfully pursue our expansion strategy, our business and results of operations may be adversely impacted.
2. Our operating results may fluctuate significantly due to seasonality and other factors, which could have a negative effect on the price of our common stock.
3. We may not be able to obtain and maintain state and local permits necessary to operate our units.
4. We have recently initiated a franchise strategy. We may be unsuccessful in fully executing this program.
5. Unanticipated costs or delays in the development or construction of our restaurants could prevent our timely and cost-effective opening of new restaurants.
6. We may be unable to fund our substantial working capital requirements and may need additional funding sooner than we anticipate.
7. The ability to attract and retain highly qualified personnel to operate and manage our restaurants is extremely important, and our failure to do so could adversely affect us.
8. Our resources may be strained in implementing our business strategy.
9. If we are not able to anticipate and react to increases in our food and labor costs, our profitability could be adversely affected.
10. The restaurant industry is intensely competitive, and we may not have the resources to compete adequately.
11. Our failure or inability to enforce our trademarks and trade names could adversely affect our efforts to establish brand equity.
12. As a restaurant service provider, we could be subject to adverse publicity or claims from our guests.
13. Our restaurants are concentrated in the southwest region of the United States, and, therefore, our business is subject to fluctuations if adverse business conditions occur in that region.
14. The large number of shares eligble for public sale could cause our stock price to decline.
15. Our common stock may not develop an active, liquid trading market.
16. The market price of our stock may be adversely affected by market volatility.

EXHIBIT 6   Rubio's Baja Grill Nutritional Information—HealthMex Menu Only

At Rubio's, we've always had one goal in mind: serving the freshest and best-tasting food around. We're dedicated to the idea that food doesn't have to be boring to be good for you. So, whether you order from the HealthMex menu or our regular menu, your food is always made fresh to order, using only the highest quality ingredients. We use only boneless, skinless chicken breast and lean, trimmed steak. We use only 100% cholesterol free canola oil. And we never add lard or MSG. Never.

HealthMex

All items on our HealthMex menu have less than 22% of calories from fat.

Menu Item	Calories Fat Cholesterol Sodium Carbohydrate Protein
HealthMex Taco w/Chicken	180 3g 20mg 340mg 24g 14g
HealthMex Taco w/Mahi Mahi	190 2g 35mg 260mg 25g 18g
HealthMex Burrito w/Chicken	380 9g 30mg 960mg 48g 28g
HealthMex Burrito w/Mahi Mahi	380 8g 60mg 740mg 48g 32g
HealthMex Combo	690 13g 72mg 1735mg 93g 51g

(continued)

EXHIBIT 6 *(cont.)*		

Menu Item	Calories Fat Cholesterol Sodium Carbohydrate Protein	
HealthMex Taco Combo w/Chicken		
	480	
	8g	
	47mg	
	1195mg	
	68g	
	33g	
HealthMex Combo w/Chicken and Mahi Mahi		
	490	
	7g	
	62mg	
	1115mg	
	69g	
	37g	
HealthMex Taco Combo w/Mahi Mahi		
	500	
	7g	
	77mg	
	1035mg	
	70g	
	41g	
Rice and Bean Burrito		
	340	
	7g	
	5mg	
	990mg	
	58g	
	11g	

Source: Information found at www.rubios.com/nutritional.htm.

EXHIBIT 7 Competitive Analysis

	Rubio's Baja Grill	Chipotle	La Salsa Fresh Mexican Grill	Baja Fresh Mexican-Grill
Locations	Arizona California Colorado Nevada Utah	Arizona California Colorado Illinois Kansas Maryland Minnesota Missouri Ohio Texas Washington DC	Arizona California Colorado Connecticut Indiana Nevada Ohio Puerto Rico Texas Utah	Arizona California Colorado Illinois Maryland Nevada Ohio Oregon Texas Virginia
Menu Offerings	Tacos Burritos Combination Platters Side Dishes HealthMex Menu Baja Bowls Kid Pesky Meals Party Packs Catering	Tacos Burritos Fajita Burritos Side Dishes	Tacos Burritos Combination Platters Side Dishes Party Packs (Grande Trays) Catering	Tacos Burritos Combination Platters Salads Side Dishes Party Packs
Fish Tacos	Original Fish Taco Grilled Mahi Mahi Taco Shrimp Taco	N/A	Baja Style Fish Taco Sonora Style Fish Taco Baja Style Shrimp Taco	Baja Fish Taco Baja Style Shrimp Taco
Price Range	$1.89–$6.29	$4.55–$5.25	$2.35–$7.45	$1.85–$6.95
Web Site	www.rubios.com	www.chipotle.com	www.lasalsa.com	www.bajafresh.com
Franchising Opportunities	Yes	No	Yes	Yes
Publicly or Privately Held	Publicly Held	Privately Held	Publicly Held	Privately Held
Ticker Symbol	RUBO	N/A	SBRG	N/A
Planned Expansions	24 units	Unknown	3 units	10 units
Areas of Expansion	None	N/A	None	Washington, DC

EXHIBIT 8 Franchise Opportunities with Rubio's Baja Grill

WELCOME TO RUBIO'S FRANCHISE PAGE AND THANK YOU FOR YOUR INTEREST!

This is the beginning of an exciting period for Rubio's, because we are franchising for the first time in our 17 year history!

We are seeking experienced, well-capitalized partners that have the financial and operational where-withal to develop multiple locations within a given market area.

We have a minimum financial requirement of a net worth of $500,000, with liquid assets of $250,000. Based on the number of restaurants to be built as part of the area development agreement, we will require that you have the financial capability to meet the development objectives. If you meet our minimum financial requirements and would like some additional information, please contact us at:

E-mail:
Franchisedepartment@rubios.com

Facsimile:
(760) 929-8203

Corporate Address:
Rubio's Restaurants, Inc.
1902 Wright Place, Suite 300
Carlsbad, CA 92008
Attn: Franchise Department

Thank you again for your interest.

Rubio's Baja Grill Restaurant franchises are available only in certain states. We do not offer any franchises in jurisdictions where we are not yet registered (or otherwise qualified) to make offers or sales. The information on this Web site is not an offer to sell or solicitation of an offer to buy a Rubio's Baja Grill Restaurant franchise. An offer for a Rubio's Baja Grill Restaurant franchise is made by prospectus only.

Source: Information found at www.rubios.com.

Steak, Fish and Chicken "Tres Tacos"

"BAJA" FISH TACO

FRESH snapper, lightly breaded, topped with cabbage, Pico de Gallo salsa, our own tangy dressing and a squeeze of lime.

ORIGINAL " BAJA STYLE " TACOS

Mini soft corn tortillas with chopped onion and cilantro, hot or mild salsa, and your choice of:

    CHARBROILED MARINATED CHICKEN

    CHARBROILED STEAK

    CHARBROILED "WILD" GULF SHRIMP

EXHIBIT 9   Baja Fresh Web Site

When you keep
life fresh, things stay
interesting.

La Salsa
FRESH MEXICAN GRILL®

CLICK HERE

EXHIBIT 10   La Salsa Web Site

EXHIBIT 11   Chipotle Web Site

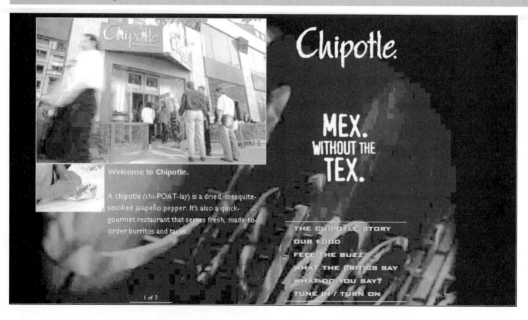

TABLE 1   Rubio's Baja Grill Balance Sheet (1998–2000)

Balance Sheet Statement Fiscal Year End	December 2000	December 1999	December 1998
Assets			
Cash and equivalent	$ 1,300,000.00	$ 3,500,000.00	$ 800,000.00
Receivables	$ 1,400,000.00	$ 800,000.00	$ 300,000.00
Inventories	$ 2,000,000.00	$ 600,000.00	$ 400,000.00
Other cur assets	$ 7,400,000.00	$ 8,000,000.00	$ 3,000,000.00
Total cur assets	$12,100,000.00	$12,900,000.00	$ 4,500,000.00
Gr fixed assets	$50,200,000.00	$36,300,000.00	$22,600,000.00
Accum depr and depl	$12,300,000.00	$ 8,400,000.00	$ 5,500,000.00
Net fixed assets	$37,900,000.00	$27,900,000.00	$17,100,000.00
Oth Noncur asset	$ 2,200,000.00	$ 9,200,000.00	$ 4,100,000.00
Tot Noncur asset	$40,100,000.00	$37,100,000.00	$21,200,000.00
Total Assets	$52,300,000.00	$50,000,000.00	$25,800,000.00
Liabilities			
Accounts payable	$ 4,300,000.00	$ 3,200,000.00	$ 2,900,000.00
Short-term debt	$ —	$ —	$ 700,000.00
Other cur liab	$ 3,400,000.00	$ 2,600,000.00	$ 2,300,000.00
Total cur liab	$ 7,700,000.00	$ 5,800,000.00	$ 5,900,000.00
Long-term debt	$ —	$ —	$ 1,100,000.00
Oth noncur liab	$ 1,600,000.00	$ 1,100,000.00	$ 800,000.00
Tot noncur liab	$ 1,600,000.00	$ 1,100,000.00	$ 1,900,000.00
Total Liabilities	$ 9,300,000.00	$ 6,900,000.00	$ 7,800,000.00
Stockholder's Equity			
Preferred equity	$ —	$ —	$17,700,000.00
Common equity	$43,000,000.00	$43,100,000.00	$ 200,000.00
Retained earnings	$ 1,400,000.00	$ —	$ 100,000.00
Total Equity	$43,000,000.00	$43,100,000.00	$17,900,000.00
Tot Liab and Stk Eq	$52,300,000.00	$50,000,000.00	$25,700,000.00

TABLE 2 Rubio's Baja Grill Income Statement (1998–2000)

Income Statement Fiscal Year End	December 2000	December 1999	December 1998
Revenues/sales[a]	$95,700,000.00	$67,900,000.00	$44,500,000.00
Cost of sales[b]	$28,300,000.00	$20,000,000.00	$13,100,000.00
Gr Oper Profit	$67,400,000.00	$47,900,000.00	$31,400,000.00
S, G & A expenses	$61,900,000.00	$42,000,000.00	$28,800,000.00
Op Prof Bef Depr	$ 5,500,000.00	$ 5,900,000.00	$ 2,600,000.00
Deprec and amort	$ 4,300,000.00	$ 3,000,000.00	$ 1,900,000.00
Oper inc aft depr	$ 1,200,000.00	$ 2,900,000.00	$ 700,000.00
Other icome, net	$ 800,000.00	$ 700,000.00	$ 500,000.00
Inc avail for int	$ 300,000.00	$ 2,900,000.00	$ 900,000.00
Interest expense	$ 100,000.00	$ 200,000.00	$ 300,000.00
Pretax income	$ 400,000.00	$ 2,800,000.00	$ 800,000.00
Income taxes	$ 200,000.00	$ 1,100,000.00	$ 100,000.00
Net inc cont ops	$ 200,000.00	$ 1,700,000.00	$ 900,000.00
Net inc tot ops	$ 200,000.00	$ 1,700,000.00	$ 900,000.00
Special inc/chrg[c]	$(2,300,000.00)	$ 700,000.00	$ 300,000.00
Normalized income	$ 2,100,000.00	$ 2,400,000.00	$ 1,200,000.00
Total Net Income	$ 200,000.00	$ 1,700,000.00	$ 900,000.00

[a]REVENUE. Restaurant sales increased $23.2 million, or 51.8%, to $67.9 million for the 52 weeks ended December 26, 1999, from $44.7 million for the 52 weeks ended December 27, 1998. This increase was principally due to the $8.9 million in sales generated by a full year of operations from the units opened in 1998, which have been opened for less than 15 months, combined with the $11.9 million from the 31 units opened during 1999. In addition, comparable unit sales increased $2.4 million, or 6.0%. Units enter the comparable store base after 15 full months of operation. The comparable unit sales increase was primarily driven by (1) the success of the 0.99 Fish Taco, Tequila Shrimp Burrito, Lobster Burrito, and the Crab and Shrimp Enchilada promotions, (2) slightly weaker sales in the early part of 1998 due to poor weather, and (3) a price increase of approximately 1.5% at the beginning of 1999.

[b]COST OF SALES. Cost of sales as a percentage of sales increased to 29.6% in the 53 weeks ended December 31, 2000, from 29.4% in the 52 weeks ended December 26, 1999, primarily due to inefficiencies in our new markets and higher costs incurred relating to certain menu changes made in July 2000.

[c]LOSS ON ASSET IMPAIRMENT. In 2000, we recorded a $2.2 million charge related to the impairment of a select number of underperforming restaurants as required under Statement of Financial Accounting Standards No.121, "Accounting for the Impairment of Long-Lived Assets and for Long-Lived Assets to Be Disposed Of." We currently do not plan to close any restaurants. There was no impairment expense recorded in 1999.

TABLE 3   Rubio's Baja Grill Statement of Cash Flows (1998–2000)

Statement of Cash Flows Fiscal Year End	December 2000	December 1999	December 1998
Net income	$ 200,000.00	$ 1,700,000.00	$ 900,000.00
Deprec and amort	$ 4,300,000.00	$ 3,000,000.00	$ 1,900,000.00
Deferred inc tax	$ 500,000.00	$ 100,000.00	$ —
Oper gains (loss)	$ 2,300,000.00	$ 100,000.00	$ —
Chg receivables	$ 600,000.00	$ 500,000.00	$ 200,000.00
Chg inventories	$ (1,400,000.00)	$ 300,000.00	$ 100,000.00
Chg oth cur asset	$ —	$ 400,000.00	$ 700,000.00
Chg payables	$ 1,100,000.00	$ 300,000.00	$ 1,200,000.00
Chg oth cur liab	$ 1,300,000.00	$ 600,000.00	$ 1,200,000.00
Net cash cont ops	$ 6,200,000.00	$ 4,600,000.00	$ 4,200,000.00
Net cash fr ops	$ 6,200,000.00	$ 4,600,000.00	$ 4,200,000.00
Sale ST invest	$ 35,300,000.00	$ 102,600,000.00	$ 32,900,000.00
Purch P, P and equip	$(16,600,000.00)	$ (13,800,000.00)	$ (6,900,000.00)
Purch ST invest	$(27,200,000.00)	$(112,400,000.00)	$(29,600,000.00)
Net cash fr inv	$ (8,400,000.00)	$ (23,600,000.00)	$ (3,600,000.00)
Issuance of debt	$ —	$ 1,000,000.00	$ 2,200,000.00
Issuance cap stk	$ —	$ 23,600,000.00	$ 500,000.00
Repay LT debt	$ —	$ (2,900,000.00)	$ (2,900,000.00)
Repur capital stk	$ —	$ —	$ 400,000.00
Net cash fr fin	$ —	$ 21,700,000.00	$ 700,000.00
Net chg cash and eq	$ (2,100,000.00)	$ 2,700,000.00	$ 100,000.00
Cash begin period	$ 3,500,000.00	$ 800,000.00	$ 900,000.00

TABLE 4   Rubio's Baja Grill Quarterly Stock Price for 1999–2000

	High	Low
Second quarter 1999	$16.50	$13.25
Third quarter 1999	$15.50	$ 6.50
Fourth quarter 1999	$10.00	$ 6.00
First quarter 2000	$ 9.00	$ 6.28
Second quarter 2000	$ 8.69	$ 6.13
Third quarter 2000	$10.25	$ 5.81
Fourth quarter 2000	$ 6.63	$ 2.56

Case 6   Suzy's Zoo

INTRODUCTION

Suzy's Zoo, a closely held greeting card company located in San Diego, California, is in its 25th year of operations. Owner and president Suzy Spafford is the creative and driving force behind the menagerie of characters that make up Suzy's Zoo. The company has managed to secure a profitable and safe niche with a devoted following among its customers. The "Zoo" consists of approximately 35 cartoon characters that come and go; however, a few characters have proven to be especially long-lasting. For example, the most popular character is Suzy Ducken, a fluffy, yellow bird with Mary Jane shoes and white ankle socks. Also popular is the laid-back Jack Quacker, who sports rubber sandals. Other popular zoo characters are Ollie Marmot, Corky Turtle, and D. J. Ducken. Each character has a distinctive personality, and characters are eventually retired when they lose their appeal in the marketplace.

The company and its products are conservative, appealing to middle-American, homespun tastes. As Spafford would say, "Suzy's Zoo cards are G-rated."

Although the beginning was entirely in greeting cards, the company has expanded into a variety of products, including balloons, rubber stamps, and party supplies. Through licensing agreements, the characters appear on needlework, sleepwear, baby gifts, and mobiles. Other licensed goods that have been in the product line but are currently awaiting new licensees are stuffed animals, coffee mugs, and figurines. By finding a market niche, and with a philosophy of slow growth, Suzy's Zoo has always operated profitably. It has also expanded into international markets; currently, Suzy's Zoo products are sold in 46 countries worldwide.

HISTORY

Suzy's Zoo founder and president Suzy Spafford started the business in the mid-1960s when she was working toward her bachelor of fine arts degree at San Diego State University. To earn extra money for school, she worked summers and weekends at local artmarts creating colorful pastel and water-color drawings, particularly cartoon characters custom-designed to buyers' tastes. She sold her drawings for $3 apiece, generating $3,000 to $4,000 per summer. During her senior year in college (1967), Bill Murr, a Berkeley, California, medical instrument manufacturer, saw Spafford's work at an artmart in San Diego. He proposed they team up and start a small greeting card business. Murr provided $600 in funding, and Spafford created eight card designs and agreed on a 90 percent (Murr) to 10 percent (Spafford) split. Suzy's Zoo was officially launched.

Spafford worked out of her home, creating designs that were shipped to Murr in Berkeley, who supervised the printing, then boxed and distributed them to local stationery stores. The cards immediately sold well in the Bay Area and on a smaller scale in Washington and Oregon. Within 2 years, the cards were selling throughout California. Sales increased steadily through the first several years. In the early 1970s, Murr decided he no longer wanted to handle the day-to-day operations. Spafford bought Murr's inventory and reversed the financial

This case was prepared in 1992 by Professor Kenneth E. Marino of San Diego State University with the assistance of graduate student Terry Wittbrot. It is intended as a basis for class discussion rather than to illustrate effective or ineffective handling of an administrative situation.

arrangement, with Murr retaining 10 percent ownership and no involvement in the actual running of the company. Suzy's Zoo was incorporated in 1976.

Suzy feels the key to her early success was in keeping the company small enough to produce on demand. No warehousing costs and low overhead allowed Suzy's Zoo to completely turn its inventory three to four times per year, a routine the company still tries to practice.

By the mid-1970s, Suzy's Zoo cards were being distributed nationally, and her characters were appearing on novelty items such as calendars. During the next several years, new products were added to the Suzy's Zoo line: invitations in 1977, gift wrap and party goods in 1985, Mylar balloons in 1987. In the late 1980s, Suzy's Zoo expanded into the international arena through European and Far Eastern licensing arrangements.

Until recently, Suzy's Zoo depended solely on Spafford for character and product design. Spafford felt that keeping Suzy's Zoo a one-artist company was central to its success. A conscious policy decision was made to maintain a pattern of slow growth.

THE GREETING CARD INDUSTRY

Greeting cards are a $5.6 billion-per-year industry dominated by three companies. As Exhibit 1 shows, Hallmark cards is the leader, enjoying approximately a 46 percent share of the market; American Greetings Corp. has a 30 percent share; and Gibson Greetings has about an 8 percent share. The remaining 16 percent of the market is divided among close to 1,000 other companies.

The effect is that two levels of competition operate. The three big card companies are competing against each other on one level, and all the rest of the card companies are competing with each other on another level; but the small companies are not really competing against the big companies.

Ninety percent of all card purchasers are women. Unit sales growth in greeting cards has been 1 to 3 percent per year. However, this is a maturing market that recently has been threatening to stop growing for the first time since 1945.

The late 1980s saw vicious price wars in the greeting card industry. Retailers perceived greeting card companies as all alike; every big card manufacturer's profitability suffered in a discounting frenzy. Greeting card companies are, therefore, having to develop new strategies to maintain their share, or get a large piece, of a pie that is not growing.

The greeting card market is made even more competitive because barriers to entry are very low. This means that it does not take too much to get into the greeting card business. Anyone with an idea, some talent, and a little start-up money can give it a try. This makes for high turnover, as companies enter the market, fail, exit the market, and are replaced by other newcomers. It should be noted that this information pertains to entry into that 16 percent share of the market where the smaller card companies compete; barriers to entry into the arena where the three large card companies compete are very high.

In an effort to maintain their market share or boost sales in this static environment, the three big competitors have come up with a variety of strategies. Hallmark is trying to persuade today's too-busy-to-write Americans to let it express their sentiments for them. Midway between Father's Day (in June) and Halloween (October 31) is the worst time of year for American publishers of greeting cards. Retailers sell fewer cards at this time than at any other time of the year. Trying to boost sales during this dry spell gave birth to the "nonoccasion" card. Hallmark has produced a series of 500 nonoccasion cards for adults and in 1989 added a new line of adult-to-child cards, "To Kids with Love," to help children ages 7 to

14 and their parents cope with growing up. Nonoccasion cards now account for more than 10 percent of the 7.3 billion greeting cards sold in America each year.

American Greetings has on staff a psychiatrist and various other experts to help come up with new products. The psychiatrist is good at identifying stressful situations in which people have a "psychological need for a card." To further enhance its competitive position and increase declining earnings, American Greetings instituted a cost-cutting program and improved its customer service. Unprofitable subsidiaries and excess costs were trimmed. Just-in-time (JIT) processes in manufacturing and card development allowed American Greetings to reduce inventories and decrease the time it takes to bring cards to market. As part of its emphasis on customer service, in 1991 American Greetings established its Retail Creative Services Department. This unit emphasized working with customers to create seasonal displays designed to boost store traffic. In early 1992, American Greetings formed its Information Services Department to develop software to analyze retailers' sales patterns and track inventories for many different products. Apparently these innovations are paying off; sales of American Greetings cards and related products such as wrapping paper grew 10 percent in 1991, while Hallmark reported only a 1 percent increase in revenues for the same goods.

Both Hallmark and American Greetings have gone high-tech with computerized greeting card services that allow customers to choose graphics, write messages, and print their personalized messages on blank cards in minutes. It is presumed that this service would appeal to nontraditional card buyers such as men and younger people. Projections indicate that this could become a substantial portion of both companies' business in the future.

For smaller greeting card companies, other strategies have been useful. Finding a niche in the market is one way to compete. The goal is to develop a unique concept or style that will appeal to a wide segment of the buying public without disappearing into the shadows of the giants. For example, use of a distinctive sense of humor, stylized artwork, or messages that appeal to specific groups such as college students could establish a marketing niche.

Many small cardmakers have found that it is very important to listen to their retailers and sales representatives. To compete in an industry dominated by the big companies, the smaller companies have to be better, turn over more quickly, and be more profitable for the retailer.

SUZY'S ZOO TODAY

Operations

The company is a nonunion operation with approximately 50 employees (see organization chart, Exhibit 2).

Spafford makes all the major decisions regarding the company except for personnel and financial matters. Minority owner and vice president Ray Lidstrom takes the lead in those areas.

Suzy's Zoo currently operates out of a two-story, 52,000-square-foot warehouse/office suite in the Mira Mesa area of San Diego. The company moved into this facility in February 1990. Operations include product design, marketing, warehousing, and shipping. No manufacturing is done on-site; rather, manufacturing is accomplished through subcontractors.

The facility is set up to ensure the efficient flow of products through the warehouse (see operations diagram, Exhibit 3).

Shipments of manufactured goods arrive at the receiving dock from various locations via common carrier on palletized boxes and in cartons. The boxes are placed into a racked bulk-storage area adjacent to the receiving dock. Handtrucks and forklifts are used to move stock.

As product is needed, cartons are broken down, and the shelves are stocked in the "picking" area. The picking area consists of merchandise organized by product number on a shelving system, where pickers fill orders by progressing up and down the aisles pulling items called for in the order. Product is stocked from the backside of the shelves (the alleys) so that workers stocking product do not interfere with workers filling orders. As orders are retrieved, they are placed in cardboard cartons, sealed (shrinkwrapped), labeled, and shipped by common carrier to customers' locations. Machinery used in these operations consists of a counter/collator and a shrink-wrap oven.

An office staff of approximately 12 is maintained for accounting, purchasing, credit, marketing, and customer service functions.

Although the vast majority of sales are wholesale, a small showroom/retail outlet is operated at the front of the building for walk-in traffic. The receptionist performs her office duties from the sales counter and rings up the sales.

Product Line

Spafford is still very involved in product development, and many of her ideas come, as they always have, from her customers. Greeting cards account for about half of Suzy's Zoo sales. The Suzy's Zoo line has expanded to include coloring books, calendars, gift wrap, and paper party supplies. Most non-paper goods are sold under licensing agreements. Currently, the company is considering the incorporation of coffee mugs into the product line, because mugs are commonly marketed through retail greeting card outlets. The alternative to this is to license the use of the characters to mug manufacturers.

In the case of Suzy's Zoo, licensees are renting the artwork for a stated period of time so that they can apply Suzy's Zoo character images to their own products, such as mugs and T-shirts. A typical Suzy's Zoo license has a term of 3 years with an option to renew for an additional 2 years. The licensing fee is calculated as a percentage of sales and ranges from 3 to 6 percent. International licensees pay higher fees (10 to 12 percent), but this is split between Suzy's Zoo and its international broker. A list of Suzy's Zoo international brokers, the products they license, and their territories can be seen in Exhibit 4. This approach to international expansion allows Suzy's Zoo to penetrate new markets that it cannot enter in other ways, without assuming much of the risk. No one knows if a product will sell, and with licensing, the licensee assumes the costs of manufacturing and getting the product to the marketplace. The major disadvantage of licensing, from Spafford's point of view, is the loss of creative control; she admits to the need for many compromises in this area. In addition to licensing images for nonpaper products, Suzy's Zoo images are also licensed to other manufacturers of greeting cards, such as Current, a large mail-order house based in Colorado.

Marketing Strategies and Distribution

The most important source of marketing to an organization like Suzy's Zoo is its network of independent sales representatives. These individuals are in continued contact with retailer store owners, who can provide the most accurate information on consumer preferences. A decision was made to go with the mom-and-pop shops as the stores of trade and to stay away from the large department store business. These smaller stores have been Suzy's Zoo's "bread and butter"; they place their orders and pay their bills. According to Spafford, "It's clean business and we make a better profit that way." Some of the larger independent card companies are now encroaching on Suzy's Zoo shelf space in these stores. Some smaller independent card companies have merged to compete against the big companies; Suzy's Zoo is not considering such a move. The company has maintained a simplified merchandising policy for sales—no fancy displays, no giveaways, "just simple, plain, honest business," Spafford says. In today's environment, continuing to operate under this policy is becoming more of a challenge. Retailers expect deals, discounts, merchandising, and guarantees from the manufacturer to take back unsold stock. If Suzy's Zoo does not begin to offer some sort of consideration to the marketplace, maintaining shelf space may become more difficult.

Within the United States, manufacturers' representatives sell Suzy's Zoo merchandise to retailers. These representatives operate on a nonexclusive basis, getting standard commissions of 20 percent on the sales they make. Suzy's Zoo does not employ an in-house sales force. Suzy's Zoo products are sold internationally through international licenses, international distributors, and direct sales.

Marketing strategies have had to change over the years to keep up with the growth. The cards have been a boutique item, but other products such as tablecloths, invitations, cups, and plates are mass-marketed in high-volume stores. Revenues from cards have plateaued, and the overall increases in revenues can be attributed to other products. If people do not want to buy cards with cute images anymore, then Suzy's Zoo will put the artwork on other products that people will buy—that is why you see it on items like children's sleepwear and baby products.

As consumer consciousness has been raised, recycled paper products have become more important. Some consumers will not buy paper goods without the recycling code. Another change in recent years is that all Suzy's Zoo products are bar-coded, which has allowed Suzy's Zoo merchandise to be sold in some of the larger retail outlets.

Suzy's Zoo participates in approximately six trade shows per year. The two big national shows are the National Stationery Gift Show in New York and the Los Angeles Gift Show. Participation in trade shows is another way to expose the product line to different types of retailers that sales representatives do not currently call on. Suzy's Zoo also participates in regional trade shows through participation by its sales rep organizations.

Sales

In 1976, the year Suzy's Zoo was incorporated, total sales were $600,000. In 1992, total sales will exceed $6 million. In recent years, total sales have increased 4 to 5 percent annually. Approximately 85 percent of Suzy's Zoo annual revenues come from sales to U.S. retailers, 10 percent come from licensing agreements, and almost 5 percent come from export sales shipped directly from the Suzy's Zoo warehouse. Table 1 shows sales data for the past 4 years.

THE FUTURE

The company philosophy remains as always to "give them what they want at a reasonable price," says Spafford. This philosophy has given Suzy's Zoo a great reputation in the card industry. Suzy envisions constant growth. Her goal is to keep turning out cards and products people can relate to. One of the biggest impediments to Suzy's Zoo's growth is that there is only one Suzy Spafford. Spafford hopes to one day stop drawing every greeting card herself and has begun work on a character "bible" containing drawings and specifications detailing how each character should look and things they might say. This will enable the continuity of the line's look. Spafford is currently training three artists and likens herself in this respect to Walt Disney in the 1930s. She has hired very talented people but has to teach them how to draw the characters the way she would draw them. Spafford feels the business needs more talented people to push the company to the next level.

	Total Sales ($000)	Sales to U.S. ($000)	Percent of Total	License Income ($000)	Percent of Total	Export Sales ($000)	Percent of Total
TABLE 1 Sales Figures for Suzy's Zoo							
Year							
1989	$5,350	$4,775	89.2	$475	8.9	$100	1.9
1990	5,650	4,977	88.1	500	8.8	173	3.1
1991	5,900	5,090	86.3	550	9.3	260	4.4
1992	5,950	5,083	85.4	600	10.1	267	4.5

Suzy's Zoo fiscal year ends June 30.

Suzy's Zoo will never become a giant in the greeting card industry. "We can't compete with Hallmark or American Greeting Cards, nor do we want to." Greeting cards, however, will continue to make up a significant percentage of the product line.

Currently, Spafford is looking forward to turning some of the characters from Suzy's Zoo into storybook characters. Spafford plans to develop her characters within a storybook world where they will have names, personalities, and even their own dwelling places—there are endless possibilities for stories. Spafford will be more involved in story-line development and illustration, with other artists doing the drawing for greeting card products. Spafford envisions a series of children's classics similar to "Winnie-the-Pooh." A decision has already been made to publish the first book independently and distribute it through the company's existing distribution base. Then the goal is to find a large publishing house to work with on future projects through some type of joint venture arrangement. In the meantime, Suzy's Zoo is currently consulting with a major licensee in the stuffed-animal market. It is hoped this effort will coordinate with the introduction of the first children's book to enhance character recognition.

After books, Spafford wants to try animation. The plans in this area are still vague, but Spafford hopes to create video either for television broadcast, such as a Saturday morning children's cartoon, or for direct sales to video stores. Her ambition is to attract the attention of the Disney company for a possible joint project. If animation becomes a reality, then, of course, this would necessitate the addition of other artists to create this specialized form of drawing. She is also unsure whether the company will create a book and video division or whether the characters will be licensed to an outside video production company.

In addition to these product development ideas, nurturing and growing the greeting card business and responding to changes in retail requirements are also priorities. Internal issues of succession, organization design, and management development have been highlighted by the continued growth of the business.

In any event, it is hoped that books and video will have a circular effect on Suzy's Zoo business as the increased recognition that will come from these higher-profile exposures will boost sale for all products sporting the Suzy Zoo character images.

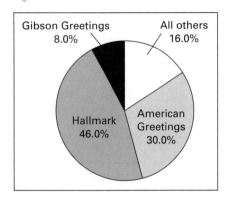

EXHIBIT 1   Greeting Cards Industry: Market Share Comparison

EXHIBIT 2   Suzy's Zoo: Organizational Chart

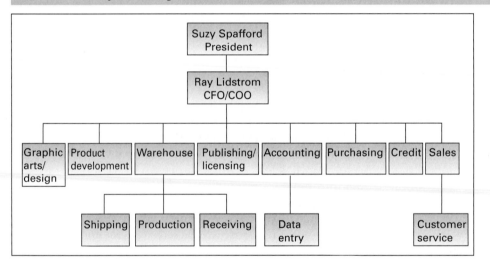

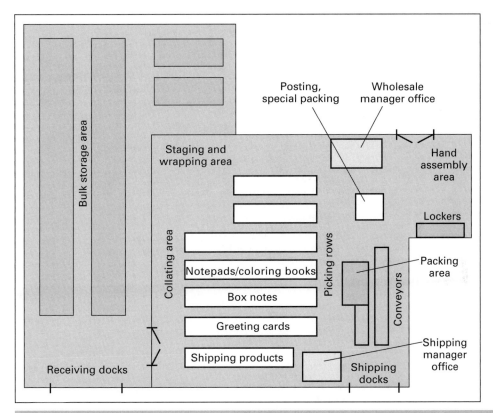

EXHIBIT 3   Suzy's Zoo: Warehouse and Order Assembly Plant Layout

EXHIBIT 4	Suzy's Zoo International Brokers	
Name of Company	*Product*	*Territory*
Introduct Holland, BV	Self-adhesive stickers	Finland, Sweden, Norway, Denmark, United Kingdom, N. Ireland, Eire, Belgium, Netherlands, Luxembourg, France, Italy, Spain, Portugal, Greece
Korsh Verlag GmbH & Co.	Kitchen calendars	Germany, Austria, Switzerland
Karto Oy	Greeting cards, postcards, invitations, gift wrap	Finland
Karl Walter GmbH & Co. KG	Photo albums	Europe
AB Pictura Sweden	Gift wrap, carrying bags, gift boxes, greeting cards, postcards	Europe
Reithmuller GmbH	Balloons, lanterns, blow-outs, garlands	Europe
Murfett Regency Pty Ltd.	Greeting cards, paper products	Australia, New Zealand, South Pacific
Stanley Newcomb	Greeting cards, paper products	Australia, New Zealand, South Pacific
Trumura Pyxis Intl., Co., Ltd.	Children's products	Japan
Copyrights Europe	Various	All European countries
Alkor GmbH	PVC foil	Europe
George Bruckner GmbH	Cone-shaped paper bags, school friend albums	Germany, Austria, Switzerland

Case 7 TiVo: Television the Way You Want It

Our company is revolutionizing the way people watch television and our personal television service is truly shaping the future of home entertainment.[1]

—MIKE RAMSEY, PRESIDENT AND CEO, TiVo

As Michael Ramsay looked on at the festivities at the TiVo IPO celebration, he wondered what that writer at *The Wall Street Journal* was thinking about his company now. Just months after the company's loyal employees were mourning the potential damage created by a negative article in the *Journal* about their new personal video recorder and service, his company was now a $1.1 billion contender.

Since its inception, TiVo has made great strides in the home entertainment industry. In just a matter of months, TiVo has built a powerful network of alliances encompassing the whole value chain. Companies ranging from Philips, Sony, NBC, and America Online all want to be part of the personalized television phenomenon that TiVo has helped to create. The investor enthusiasm for this new class of television technology has been remarkable. However, after their third quarter report, the first report since the IPO on September 31, 1999, TiVo has only 4,300 subscribers to its service.[2]

The race is on to beat the competition. Not far behind TiVo is Replay Networks Inc., whose own personalized video recorder offers strikingly similar features and functionality. Then there is Microsoft, the most formidable player of all. Their new version of WebTV promises not only to captivate the public, but also to knock the teeth out of a few competitors along the way. Knowing that there will be many difficult challenges ahead for TiVo, Ramsay wonders how long the 'honeymoon' will continue.

A REVOLUTION IN THE TELEVISION INDUSTRY

The rapidly evolving market for home entertainment goods and services is intensely competitive, composed of both established competitors and young upstarts. The market is subject to rapid technological change, and the delivery of video and television programming is particularly competitive as new products and services continue to be introduced and marketed. Critical success in this market depends on how well a company can establish name recognition, performance, pricing, ease of use, and functionality. (See Exhibit 1 for a list of competitors.)

These new product introductions compete with products and technologies that have established markets and proven consumer support such as VCRs, DVD players, cable and satellite television systems, and the Internet. A new product also faces competition from Internet service providers and other Internet companies such as WebTV,

MBA candidates Carl Lei, Joanne Lupatkin, Dan Miller, Joe Pezzimenti, and Dana Sze prepared this case under the supervision of Professor Christopher L. Tucci for the purpose of class discussion rather than to illustrate either effective or ineffective handling of an administrative situation. Distributed by the Berkley Center for Entrepreneurial Studies at the Stern School of Business, New York University. To order copies, phone: 212-998-0070, fax: 212-995-4211, or e-mail: bces@stern.nyu.edu. No part of this publication may be used or reproduced without written permission of the Berkley Center. Copyright © 1999 by the Stern School of Business and Christopher L. Tucci. All rights reserved.

America Online, and X-TV. These competitors are seeking to meld Internet browsing and traditional broadcast, cable, or satellite television programming into a single medium. For example, WebTV and Echo-Star Communications have released the DishPlayer, which is a product that combines Internet access with a program guide and the ability to pause live television. (See Exhibit 2 for 1998 TV-related statistics.)

As the reach and popularity of television has grown, so too has the amount of programming available to viewers. The explosive growth in available channels resulting from cable and home satellite television systems has led to an overwhelmingly diverse selection of programming and content. Channels have been created to deliver programming to target groups such as women or children, or to deliver specialized content, such as news, cartoons, classic movies, golf, comedy, or educational programming. Subscription-based premium channels such as HBO and Showtime also offer specialized programming, including major motion pictures, made-for-television movies, and sporting events. Clearly, there is more television programming to choose from now than ever before.

Personal Television Products

Accordingly, a new class of electronics known as personal television products or personal video recorders has sprung up to address this deluge of programming. Personal video recorders allow consumers to control their television viewing. These devices sit between the television and cable box, satellite receiver, or antenna, and can be programmed to act as a personal assistant, changing channels, recording programs of interest, and letting users watch what they want, when they want. They also support TV buffering or caching, namely automatic recording of live programming. According to market researcher International Data Corp., sales of personal video recorders are predicted to reach 200,000 units by the end of 1999 and 1.6 million in 2000. By 2003, sales are expected to top 9.6 million units a year.

TiVo INC.

Company Background and Culture

Michael Ramsay and James Barton had been friends since their days at Silicon Graphics Inc. in the early 1990s. (See Exhibit 3 for profiles of cofounders). The two of them had dreams of starting a business and initially came up with the concept of building home-based servers to retrieve Internet files. The idea was pitched to financiers in Silicon Valley to no avail. The product lacked definition and was likely to confuse potential customers.

Going back to the drawing board, Ramsay and Barton refined their concept to better analyze consumer needs. They discovered there was a market for personalized television and that the existing products out there were rudimentary. Ramsay and Barton re-pitched their refined concept to financier Randy Komisar a second time. Impressed by the founders' tenacity and the product's market potential, Komisar signed the deal. In August 1977, TiVo was created to service the gap in the market for personal television. Headquartered in Sunnyvale, California, TiVo has been obtaining subscribers and selling personal video recorders since March 31, 1999.

TiVo employees (there are about 150) describe the company as "hip" and "amazing" with a strong family-like culture. TiVo would rather hire someone that is less experienced, easy to work with, and highly motivated than someone who is very experienced and conceited. People wear shorts and T-shirts (with the TiVo logo, of course) to work. Many people on the marketing staff were former engineers and vice versa. Employees take on multiple responsibilities; "If people want to do something, they do it." In order to foster entrepreneurism, employees are not clustered into particular departments. Any new ideas are welcomed; the only philosophy that the company has is that any new software created should be able to run on the previous TiVo box. In addition, the office space is designed to facilitate interaction with top management. For example, all employees work in cubicles, including the CEO and founder. This is to ensure an open and collaborative atmosphere. No formal titles or hierarchical ranking structures exist. For example, TiVo's WebMaster has business cards that have "Admiral" or "Head Wrangler" as his title.

The Product

*I watch live TV almost never. I press the
pause button and wait 15 minutes, then
I don't see any commercials for the
rest of the evening.*

—RICHARD BULLWINKLE,
WEBMASTER, TiVo[3]

The Concept   The TiVo service allows consumers to watch what they want when they want, giving customers greater control, choice, and convenience over their television viewing. (See Exhibit 4 for selected product details from the user guide.) The TiVo service also creates a new platform that enables broadcasters, advertisers, and network operators to deliver television programming, advertising, and in-home commerce.

The Technology   TiVo comprises three key components: the personal video recorder, the TiVo remote control, and the TiVo Broadcast Center.

The personal video recorder enables the basic functionality of the TiVo service. As a recording and storage device, the box automatically records live television and archives viewer preferences. It uses an advanced disk scheduling technique, which manages the recording and deleting of pro-

grams on the system. Two models of the personal recorder are currently marketed, one supporting 14 hours and the other supporting 30 hours. On a nightly basis, the personal video recorder will automatically dial into the TiVo Broadcast Center via telephone to download the TiVo features, services, and software upgrades. The personal video recorder works with analog broadcast, cable, and digital satellite systems.

The TiVo remote control operates both the personal video recorder and the television set. The remote allows the viewer to navigate programming options, select shows to be recorded, enable advance-viewing features, and indicate personal preferences with the Thumbs Up/Thumbs Down buttons.

The TiVo Broadcast Center is a series of computer servers that manage all of TiVo's programming and service data. The Broadcast Center distributes proprietary services and specialized content such as the on-air program guides, Network showcases, TiVolution Magazine, and other content provided by TiVo's partners. Currently, the transmission of data occurs over phone lines. In the future, satellite and cable bandwidth will be utilized.

The Service   The TiVo service is a subscription-based service enabled by a personal video recorder using the TiVo technology. The features that distinguish TiVo from traditional television viewing include (see Exhibits 5 and 6 for service and feature details):

1. *The ability to locate and record multiple shows quickly and easily:* Viewers can timeshift their television shows and create a customized lineup of several shows for viewing at anytime.
2. *The ability to control live television:* Viewers can pause, rewind, instant replay, and playback in slow motion any live television broadcast.
3. *Availability of viewing preferences and programming suggestions:* Viewers can

utilize the Thumbs Up/Thumbs Down rating mechanism to direct the TiVo service to deliver program recommendations based on the user preferences.

4. *Specialized content:* Includes broadcaster-created Network Showcases that feature selected programming, upcoming movies, special events and miniseries, as well as editorial content from TiVolution Magazine.

5. *Menu-driven navigation and viewer interface:* By using the TiVo Central menu screen, viewers can browse through an on-air program schedule guide and easily access all features of the TiVo service. TiVo is currently developing new features on its open technology platform. The company anticipates future services to include:

- Active promotions: iPreview will enable customers to schedule and record programming featured during previews.
- Active ads: Advertisers will have the ability to target consumers with personalize advertisements based on the viewer's stored preferences.
- In-home commerce: iBuy will allow viewers to get more information about the featured product and possibly purchase the items through the TiVo remote control.

Business Model

Strategy   TiVo strives to be a service company, not a "hardware manufacturer." Their primary strategy has been (1) to develop partnerships and (2) to engage in licensing agreements. TiVo anticipates gaining future revenue from service fees, as well as from advertising and selling of consumer data to services such as A. C. Nielsen.

Licensing   TiVo invented both the technology and the box, and companies like Philips who were interested in the technology approached them early on. TiVo agreed to license the technology to Philips (and later

Sony) for free. In return for manufacturing the hardware, Philips and Sony agree to integrate the TiVo service into their product offerings. Their future strategy includes licensing their technology to television, DVD, DSS, and cable box manufacturers to include the TiVo technology and service with the product. TiVo's goal is to continue to provide their technology at a price of at or near zero and to receive all of their revenues through subscriptions and partnership revenues (advertising and market research). To further entice manufacturers to build the unit and promote the service, TiVo is subsidizing the cost of the boxes and sharing future subscription revenue.

Partners   In addition to alliances with manufacturers, TiVo also has a number of partnerships with other industry segments. For example, A. C. Nielsen purchases data on TiVo users. Because of the contact between the viewer and the TiVo servers, the data obtained through TiVo could be more accurate and less costly to collect than current A. C. Nielsen data gathered on "people-meter" systems. Also, because of the push technology that TiVo provides, content providers will be eager to try to partner with them in order to put their program on their lists. General advertisers may also be interested in partnering with TiVo because of the potential ability for targeted, personal advertising. TiVo can deliver advertising to a particular viewer depending on past viewing activity in that household and demographic factors.

Finally, one of TiVo's more interesting partners is the NBC network. At first, the television networks were not pleased with this new technology that would allow viewers to essentially skip all commercials. However, because the networks were convinced that this was the future of television, they felt that they had no choice but to embrace the new technology and get involved as quickly as possible. NBC's investment in

TiVo has not only secured them a place on the TiVo board but is also giving them a first-hand view and a significant role in driving how the technology will progress in this industry. NBC has already started working with TiVo and others to pilot a new service called Ipreview. For network and cable programmers, it offers the ability to reach their target audiences in a more effective manner. These interactive promotions provide added convenience for consumers and a new way for networks to promote their upcoming content.

> *TiVo's Ipreview creates a powerful direct connection with our viewer by transforming NBC promotions from passive to interactive. Ipreview makes our promos even more compelling, offering a call to action.*
> —JOHN MILLER, PRESIDENT, NBC ADVERTISING AND PROMOTION

NBC and Showtime Television have participated in the development of the new service and will be among the first networks to deliver promotional programming to TiVo subscribers. In early 2000, TiVo viewers will see a small icon appear in the corner of the promotional programming on their television screens, indicating an Ipreview. The interactive Ipreview icon that appears on screen will be unobtrusive and should not distract from normal viewing. The Ipreview symbol in live television programming will remain interactive in recorded shows. TiVo will charge the networks a fee for promoting shows, and will earn money for every "successful call-to-action," operating much like the "per-click" fee system used by Internet marketers and affiliates.

Pricing and Distribution Priced at $499 per unit, the TiVo system can be ordered online, via fax, or from a local store. The TiVo subscription service is priced at $9.99 per month. Users also have the option of buying "lifetime" service for $199.

The Phillips Personal TV Receiver with the TiVo Service is available in 520 retail stores nationwide, including Best Buy, Circuit City, CompUSA, and Sears. TiVo and Philips also chose to sell their product online at 800.com, Amazon.com, CircuitCity.com, and ROXY.com because of their quality product presentation and superior service. These are among the highest volume retailers online and include the premier consumer electronics products on the Internet.

During the third quarter, Sony Corporation of America made a significant equity investment and signed a letter of intent for the manufacturing of personal video recorders and integration of original content and services. Also announced was an alliance with America Online for AOL TV. TiVo and AOL will bring consumers a new interactive experience by combining TiVo's personal TV services with AOL TV's enhanced interactive television capabilities. In addition, AOL made an equity investment in TiVo. Moreover, TiVo received equity investments from CBS, Comcast Corporation, Cox Communications, Discovery Communications, Inc., The Walt Disney Company, Liberty Media, Advance/Newhouse, and TV Guide Interactive.

THE COMPETITION

Although TiVo has claimed the lead in the market for personalized television products, the competition is rapidly catching up. Replay TV and WebTV are major threats to TiVo's existing and future business.

Replay Network's ReplayTV

Led by a new CEO, Kim LeMasters of CBS fame, ReplayTV is a direct equivalent to TiVo. With the ReplayTV platform and service, users can create personalized

"Replay Channels" that feature their favorite shows, themes, or actors for selective viewing. ReplayTV also lets consumers pause/rewind live broadcasts, record and playback simultaneously, and archive shows. The box, which supports 10 hours of programming, retails at $699. ReplayTV can currently be purchased on Amazon.com; there are no physical retail partners.

ReplayTV received the "Best of Show" honors at the 1999 International Consumer Electronics Show in Las Vegas, Nevada. In August 1999, a group of leading companies, including Time Warner, The Walt Disney Company, NBC, and Matsushita Kotobuki (Panasonic) invested $57 million in the company. Additionally, Marc Andreesen of Netscape contributed funding to the company claiming that "ReplayTV will do for TV what the browser did for the Internet. It's the browser for TV. While WebTV tries to integrate the Internet with television, Replay is an effort to enhance the TV experience first and foremost."

However, Replay has been very slow to get off the ground. Why? "They lost out because they designed the product for the high-end user," said Bullwinkle. "They never understood the mainstream consumer. Replay came out with an elaborate marketing campaign but couldn't deliver results. Replay has zero retailers."[4]

Microsoft's WebTV

WebTV was supposed to be the ultimate TV appliance for Web-savvy consumers, but so far, it has not yet lived up to expectations. Early iterations of the service were described as "clunky," and analysts wondered if consumers were really ready (or would ever be ready) to think of their televisions as Internet devices.

In June 1999, WebTV Networks announced new versions of its Classic and Plus hardware. The products deliver on WebTV's promise of getting users hooked onto the Net using the TV as a portal; however, said one computer magazine, PC enthusiasts probably will want to stick with their desktop modems.[5]

The high-end system, WebTV Plus, has caught a lot more attention. The WebTV Plus by Philips is a set-top box with a V.90 56-kilobit-per-second modem, and increased on-board memory takes the place of the WebTV hard drive, which is used to store interactive channel guides and software upgrades. Features that remain from the older design include a smart-card slot, a printer port, a microphone port, and the IR Blaster, which allows users to control their cable set-tops with the WebTV remote and makes multiple remotes a thing of the past. The hardware makes it easy to surf the Web and watch TV using a picture-in-picture configuration. And there's still plenty of interactive programming that has Web hooks or WebTV-specific hyperlinks.[6]

They will throw in a ton of money on the marketing campaign and offer to sell the product at a fraction of the cost to get market share. The quality of the product will not be better than TiVo's.

— RICHARD BULLWINKLE,
WEBMASTER, TIVO[7]

Microsoft's product is different than TiVo's in many ways, but nonetheless is expected to be the biggest competitor to TiVo. They are expected to transform WebTV to more closely resemble a personal TV product by next year. By letting the smaller players come to market first, Microsoft can steal the best features from TiVo and Replay TV. TiVo believes it has an advantage over Microsoft because it was first to market. They are also working hard to develop their own strong brand equity and consumer awareness. TiVo's strong alliances with Philips

(#1 brand in Europe) and now Sony (#1 brand in the United States) is a huge leap forward. However, both electronics giants are also manufacturing units for Microsoft.

STANDARDS IN THE INDUSTRY

Currently, there are no standards around the "digital VCR" software and technology. However, there are standards being developed for the larger interactive television market. The Advanced Television Enhancement Forum (ATVEF) is a cross-industry alliance of companies representing the broadcast and cable networks, television transports, consumer electronics, and PC industries. The ATVEF is committed to "accelerating the creation and distribution of enhanced television programs so that consumers can receive enhanced television programs in the least expensive and most convenient way possible."[8] The founding companies (listed in Exhibit 7) are developing a specification and directing ongoing marketing activities to accelerate the development of HTML-based television products and services. Companies including Microsoft, B3TV, Liberate Technologies, Mixed Signals Technologies, and PowerTV are in compliance with the ATVEF standards. Currently, TiVo has not chosen to follow these standards for Interactive TV.

AN UNCERTAIN FUTURE

The line between television, Internet, and e-commerce is blurring, and TiVo has recognized this as both an opportunity and a threat. TiVo is devoting research and development efforts in hopes to unlock this potential market. As Ramsay jots down some notes for the next management team meeting, the underlying issues surrounding the direction of the company troubled him. Specifically:

- How can TiVo fend off Microsoft's threat to dominate this space with the relaunch of WebTV?
- Will TiVo be able to sustain profits from their innovation?
- Is TiVo's strategy of market penetration through alliance building the most appropriate model? Or, is TiVo partnering too much?
- What will become the dominant design in the future? Will the industry experience a shakeout? Who will be the winners and losers?

ENDNOTES

1. Please visit www.tivo.com and click through for a tour of the products history and recent developments.
2. Robertson Stephens, Digital Media Infrastructure Research analyst report, October 26, 1999.
3. Phone interview with Richard Bullwinkle, October 14, 1999.
4. Phone interview with Richard Bullwinkle, October 14, 1999.
5. *Inter@ctive Week,* June 16, 1999, "Digital Devices: I Want My WebTV," www.zdnet.com/intweek/stories/news/0,4164,407184,00.html.
6. *Ibid.*
7. Phone interview with Richard Bullwinkle, October 14, 1999.
8. www.atvef.com/

EXHIBIT 1 Interactive TV (ITV) — The Players

Who	Product	Current Stage	Future Plans	Business Model
America Online www.aol.com **Vienna, Virginia**	AOLTV	Brainstorming	Partnered with Liberate on software, Philips on hardware, DirecTV on broadcast, TiVo on recording device	Not announced
B3TV www.b3tv.com **San Francisco**	E-commerce/transaction functions for ITV broadcasts based on ATVEF standards	Aired a B3TV-enhanced Domino's Pizza commercial for WebTV and EchoStar DISH Network subscribers in mid-August	Interest marketers in ATVEF-compliant enhancements	Charges marketer for enhancements, plus gets a piece of transaction fees
Liberate Technologies www.liberate.com **San Carlos, California**	Software that goes inside set-top boxes to add Net capability to broadcasts in compliance with ATVEF standards	This Oracle spin-off has fewer than 50,000 subscribers through NTT Japan and NTL Europe	Deals with AOLTV, Cable & Wireless, US West, Comcast, MediaOne and Cox to deploy platform	Sells client/server software to both network operator and set-top box manufacturers
Microsoft www.microsoft.com **Seattle**	WebTV	Owns WebTV; led ATVEF standards; invested in Wink and in worldwide cable broadcasters	Further involvement in ITV landscape through WebTV deals and cable investments; Windows is currently being used on a General Instrument set-top box	Charges ISP fees through WebTV, sells WebTV software to set-top box manufacturers
Mixed Signals Technologies www.mixedsignals.com **Culver City, California**	Tools for adding interactivity to broadcast content based on ATVEF standards	Built interactivity for *Wheel of Fortune*, *Jeopardy*, the Weather Channel and MSNBC	Signed deals with Oxygen, ATT&T, EchoStar, Fox and American Movie Classics to create interactive content	Sell ITV tools and/or services to content provider
OpenTV www.opentv.com **Mountain View, California**	Software that goes inside digital set-top boxes to enable interactivity in digital MPEG broadcasts; not based on ATVEF standards	Deployed in 3.5 million European homes	U.S. deployment through EchoStar's 3 million satellite subscribers beginning in December	Sells system to broadcasters

472

PowerTV **www.powertv.com** **Cupertino, California**	An operating system for interactive TV inside set-top boxes based on ATVEF standards		This Scientific Atlanta spin-off deployed in 420,000 European homes	Sells client/server software to both network operators and cable set-top box manufacturers
ReplayTV **www.replaytv.com** **Mountain View, California**	A digital VCR with added capabilities including a commercial-skip button	Sells box	Continues to seek partnerships with hardware companies to make Replay boxes	Sells box to consumer; no monthly service charges
Sony/Columbia TriStar **www.sonypictures.com** **Culver City, California**	Interactive versions of *Wheel of Fortune* and *Jeopardy* through Columbia TriStar	Debuted *Wheel* and *Jeopardy* on Oct. 4th; invested in Mixed Signals and Liberate	Will trial and ITV service through CableVision in New York; will manufacture TiVo box	Not announced
TiVo **www.tivo.com** **Sunnyvale, California**	A digital VCR with added capabilities including intelligent-agent technology	Sells box and monthly service	Filed IPO in July; partnered with Sony to make TiVo box and programs; partnered with AOLTV	Sells box; charges monthly service fee of $9.95
Wink **www.wink.com** **Emeryville, California**	Software that goes inside set-topboxes; adds interactivity through a proprietary network	Has 150,000 subscribers	DirecTV will offer Wink-enabled broadcasts soon; other deals are in the works	Licensing to broadcasters and set-topbox firms; will promote interactive Wink ads and take a fee

Source: The Industry Standard, Interactive TVs New Approach, Leslie Anderson. October 11, 1999, www.thestandard.com/article/display/0,1902,6661,00.html.

EXHIBIT 2   1998 TV-Related Statistics Reports

- 98.0 million, or more than 98% of all U.S. households, owned at least one television.[a]
- U.S. households owned, on average, 2.4 televisions.[a]
- U.S. households spent an average of 7 hours and 15 minutes per day viewing television.[a]
- 66.1 million U.S. households spent $30.9 billion to receive subscription-based cable television services.[b]
- 10.6 million U.S. households spent $5.3 billion to receive subscription-based satellite television services.[c]
- $47.4 billion was spent on television advertising. This represents over 23% of total advertising spending.[d]
- Over 60% of U.S. cable subscribers had access to more than 53 channels, compared to less than 10% in 1985.[e]

[a]Nielsen Media Research.
[b]Paul Kagan Associates.
[c]Satellite Industry Association.
[d]McCann-Erickson, Inc., a market research firm.
[e]1998 Television & Cable Fact Book.

EXHIBIT 3   TiVo's Cofounders

Michael Ramsay

- Served as TiVo's chairman of the board of directors, chief executive officer, and president since its inception in August 1997.
- From April 1996 to July 1997, Mr. Ramsay was the senior vice president of the Silicon Desktop Group for SGI, a manufacturer of advanced graphics computers.
- From August 1994 to April 1996, Mr. Ramsay was president of Silicon Studio, Inc., a wholly owned subsidiary of SGI focused on enabling applications development for emerging interactive media markets.
- From July 1991 to August 1994, Mr. Ramsay served as the senior vice president and general manager of SGI's Visual Systems Group.
- Mr. Ramsay also held the positions of vice president and general manager for the Entry Systems Division of SGI.
- Prior to 1986, Mr. Ramsay held research and development and engineering management positions at Hewlett-Packard and Convergent Technologies.
- Mr. Ramsay holds a B.S. degree in electrical engineering from the University of Edinburgh, Scotland.

James Barton

- Served as TiVo's vice president of research and development, chief technical officer, and director since its inception.
- From June 1996 to August 1997, Mr. Barton was president and chief executive officer of Network Age Software, Inc., a company that he founded to develop software products targeted at managed electronic distribution.
- From November 1994 to May 1996, Mr. Barton served as chief technical officer of Interactive Digital Solutions Company; a joint venture of SGI and AT&T Network Systems created to develop interactive television systems.
- From June 1993 to November 1994, Mr. Barton served as vice president and general manager of the Media Systems Division of SGI.
- From January 1990 to May 1991, Mr. Barton served as vice president and general manager of the Systems Software Division of SGI. Prior to joining SGI, Mr. Barton held technical and management positions with Hewlett-Packard and Bell Laboratories.
- Mr. Barton holds a B.S. degree in electrical engineering and an M.S. degree in computer science from the University of Colorado at Boulder.

Source: SEC S1 filing.

EXHIBIT 4   The TiVo Personal Television Service

The TiVo Personal Television Service provides all of the personal TV functions to your PTV receiver. Your receiver will have severely limited functionality without the TiVo Service. The PTV receiver uses the phone line to connect to the TiVo Service. This daily, toll-free call provides:

- Updated **Network Showcases** (daily)
- **TiVolution Magazine** (daily)
- Program Guide Data (daily). Every day the TiVo Service sends you the latest program guide data to make sure you always have up to 2 weeks' worth of listings. The TiVo Service also checks for changes in the network programming that has already been downloaded, and makes corrections. This program guide data allows you to schedule recordings, set up Season Passes (i.e., automatically record a specific show anytime it appears on TV), and use the What's on Live TV Guide. It also enables the **TiVo's Suggestions** (a listing of programs that you had given one or more THUMBS UP to in the past).
- Software updates from TiVo, as they become available. As TiVo adds new features and make enhancements, we will send these updates to your PTV receiver. You'll see a message on your screen when this has occurred.

The toll-free call takes place when you're not using your phone line, and you can continue to use your TV and PTV receiver during the call. If you need to use the telephone, simply pick up your phone. The TiVo Service call will automatically disconnect and try again later.

Source: Personal TV Owner's Guide, Philips.

EXHIBIT 5   Key Features of TiVo Personal Television Service

- **Ability to Play with Live TV:** You can pause or rewind up to 30 minutes of live programming. When you change channels, the current recording clears, and new recording begins on the new channel.
- **Ability to Find Your Favorite Programs and Set Up Recordings:** The TiVo service allows the viewer to record programs in one of five ways: (1) By Name, (2) By Channel, (3) By Time, (4) Manually, (5) or via TiVo's Suggestions. TiVo's Suggestions is a list of programs that were created based on what programs you have given a THUMBS UP to.
- **TiVolution Magazine:** The TiVolution Magazine is an interactive content area that provides you with the opportunity to select themed packages of programming from a wide variety of networks. This guide to the "Best of What's On" is written and produced by the TiVo editorial staff. The key difference with this feature is that it allows the viewer to choose programming via themes (like the perils of dating, twenty-somethings, twisted TV, etc.).
- **Network Showcases:** The Network Showcases are listings of the best programs offered by television's biggest networks (like Flix, HBO, NBC, Showtime, CNBC, The Movie Channel, etc.)
- **Thumbs Up and Thumbs Down:** This feature allows TiVo to know what channels/programs you like (THUMBS UP) and dislike (THUMBS DOWN). Based on what program you like, TiVo looks through the program listings for new shows that you might like, but might not have known about. These programs are listed on **TiVo's Suggestions.** The programs are listed by how closely they match your TV preferences. Over time, as your personal TV preferences become more detailed, the list of TiVo's Suggestions will become more and more accurate.

Source: Personal TV Owner's Guide, Philips.

EXHIBIT 6   ATVEF Founders

The ATVEF founders comprise the leaders in four key industry segments:

1. Broadcast and cable networks
2. Cable and satellite service providers
3. Consumer electronics
4. Personal computers and software industry

Founders
1. CableLabs
2. CNN Interactive
3. DIRECTV
4. Discovery Communications, Inc.
5. Intel Corporation
6. Liberate Technologies, Inc. (formerly NCI)
7. Microsoft and WebTV Networks
8. NBC Multimedia
9. NDTC Technology, Inc.
10. Public Broadcasting Service (PBS)
11. Sony Corporation
12. Tribune
13. The Walt Disney Company
14. Warner Bros.

Case 8 LiveREADS: Valuing an E-Book Start-Up

READING AND A NEW FRONTIER

At 2:34 A.M. on Friday, November 17, 2000, Neal Bascomb finally turned off his computer. Five errors—he had found and corrected five errors in the final version of *Orpheus Emerged,* a newly discovered novella by Beat legend Jack Kerouac. Bascomb's new e-book publisher LiveREADS would introduce the novella in a revolutionary new e-format 3 days later on Monday, November 20. *Orpheus Emerged* would be the first e-book published to include an interactive, multimedia design. Too restless to let things go, CEO and cofounder Bascomb had insisted on reading both the Adobe GlassBooks and Microsoft Reader editions himself to be sure that there were no errors. Now, over 600 pages later, he was ready for bed. Later that day, he would deliver both versions to bn.com, the exclusive e-tailer for this inaugural LiveREAD.

As he attempted to fall asleep, Bascomb ticked through the implications of Monday's launch in his mind. After raising about $700,000 in a series of angel rounds, cash was starting to run low. He and cofounder Scott Waxman had used the bulk of the money to enter into contracts with 20 *New York Times* best-selling writers, paying them for options to original works the company had to exercise within 4 to 6 months (see Exhibit 1 for description of authors). They desperately needed to make the leap to the next level and raise $5 million in order to begin publishing the next series of LiveREADs before the options expired. Venture capitalists had been lukewarm on a content play, but might be swayed if *Orpheus Emerged* made a big enough splash. And then there was the question of a strategic investor. The venture arm of a major media company had recently approached the founders to merge LiveREADS with an e-book publisher it had been incubating in an all-stock deal. Should the founders take the deal or hold out for a venture capitalist that would let them retain control and a larger piece of the pie? How would the founders even know what to accept from a VC or from this entertainment behemoth? How much was their company worth to these two different investors, and what other factors should they take into consideration?

ONCE UPON A TIME, THERE WAS LIVEREADS . . .

Nearly a year before, cofounder Neal Bascomb had been an agent at one of New York's more exclusive literary agencies, Carlisle & Co. He had helped Michael Carlisle, a respected veteran in publishing, break free from the giant William Morris Agency to go out on his own. Previously an editor at St. Martin's press, Bascomb was one of the first employees at Carlisle in the summer of 1998 and quickly set to work building a long and profitable client list.

MBA candidates Diane Bartoli, Chris Lemmond, Ashok Sinha, Daniel Urbas, and Stephen Wells prepared this case under the supervision of Professor Christopher L. Tucci for the purpose of class discussion rather than to illustrate either effective or ineffective handling of an administrative situation. Distributed by the Berkley Center for Entrepreneurial Studies at the Stern School of Business, New York University. To order copies, phone: 212-998-0070, fax: 212-995-4211, or e-mail: bces@stern.nyu.edu.

Competitors joked that if he didn't pace himself he would be the Prefontaine of the agenting world, making reference to the champion runner who started with a flash and ended as fast. But pacing wasn't in Bascomb's vocabulary, and by the end of year 1 he laid claim to nearly $1 million in book contract sales with major publishers, one of the most successful first years for an agent witnessed by the industry.

After that banner first year, Bascomb started to dream about running his own publishing house. First he went to his boss, Michael Carlisle, and talked about how the agency could be a bit more entrepreneurial in how it made money. Perhaps they should do more in exploiting the digital rights for their clients' works. But it seemed this was outside the scope of what Carlisle felt they were capable. Nearly a year and a half after starting at Carlisle, Bascomb decided to venture out on his own.

Bascomb began writing the business plan for what would eventually become Live-READS. He called on every entrepreneur and visionary he knew in the business and interviewed them about future trends and the viability of an e-publishing model. Among the first of these interviewees was Scott Waxman, a young industry player who had started his own very successful agency a few years before. Although only 32, Waxman had a full head of salt-and-pepper hair and the self-assuredness of a veteran. In fact, when he learned that Bascomb left Carlisle & Co., he immediately attempted to convince him to join The Waxman Agency as a partner. But when Bascomb introduced the idea of an e-publisher, Waxman realized the true potential of a different kind of partnership. Shortly after reading Bascomb's business plan, he called to say he wanted to help launch the business. Knowing that Waxman had a host of expertise as well as publishing and e-world contacts to bring to the table (Waxman's brother was a founder of Flooz.com), Bascomb was eager to accept the offer.

After officially incorporating in February 2000, the two founders immediately set about trying to find funding for their new venture. They talked to venture capitalists, angel investors, investment arms of media companies—anyone who would take a meeting with them. Rather than money, what they mostly got was advice. But they also found a lead angel investor in former Sony Corp. chairman Michael "Mickey" Schulhof, who helped finalize their e-publishing model as a business-to-consumer play that would build on the brands of established best-selling writers. In addition, LiveREADS would use the full extent of the digital medium by enhancing e-books with video, audio, animations, live links, and additional information all keyed to the text (see Exhibit 2 for information on characteristics of the LiveREAD product). Schulhof based his investment on a series of milestones the founders had to reach. These milestones were mostly in the form of author contracts, initially targeting a total of 15 contracts.

LET'S MAKE A DEAL

Since they had limited funds, Bascomb and Waxman constructed a contract similar to a movie option contract that would allow Live-READS to gain access to some of the most successful writers in America for a relatively small cash outlay. In a traditional book contract, a publisher pays an author advance against royalties in three stages: on signing, on delivery of the manuscript, and on publication. LiveREADS adapted that model by paying each author $10,000 in cash on execution of a contract that locked the writer into an option for 4 to 6 months. The remainder of the advance would then be made in the same stages as in a traditional contract, minus the option price of $10,000. All the works commissioned had never been published. In addition, LiveREADS specifically commissioned medium-length works to avoid the "book length" options most writers were bound to with their traditional publishers. LiveREADS was not responsible for the remainder of the advance unless it chose to exercise the option. Payments for the remainder of the advance were tied to exercise of the option, delivery of the manuscript, and the publication of the work, thereby limiting LiveREADS' overall exposure. LiveREADS did not retain the print rights; however, it did retain rights for electronic text, multimedia, dramatization, worldwide translation, audio (which can be worth as much as half the value of the total advance) and perhaps most importantly, an option on the author's next mid-length original work in the electronic medium, which held the author bound to LiveREADS for 18 months to 2 years.

With this blueprint in mind, Bascomb hired a publisher to help sign the authors. Paul Bresnick had most recently been an executive editor at William Morrow, a large traditional publisher. But his 30-year career spanned from *Spy* magazine to *Penthouse,* to Doubleday Publishing. Over the course of his career, Bresnick had published renowned authors James Baldwin, T. C. Boyle, Betty Friedan, Joyce Carol Oates, Lawrence Block, and perhaps most notably, Bill Cosby. Cosby's *Fatherhood* was one of the biggest bestsellers of the 1980s and one that announced the dawn of the celebrity book. Now Bresnick was on board at LiveREADS to use his deep connections in the old world to see the dawn of yet another revolution in publishing—the emergence of the e-book. Bresnick's traditional experience was a neat counterbalance to the e-knowledge CTO Tim Cooper brought to the table. Cooper was the founder and president of a technology and programming consultancy that, among other things, developed digital products for the publishing industry.

By the beginning of September, the team at LiveREADS had met with virtually every major literary agency in the business and concluded deals with more than 20 major *New York Times* best-selling writers. Each deal required a long and complicated contract negotiation because LiveREADS was breaking new ground in the assignment of digital rights in respect to the combination of electronic text with multimedia (audio, video, animation) as well as e-commerce and advertising/sponsorship sales. This investment of time was vital to the success of the company—Bascomb and Waxman considered their contracts with these major agencies as valuable assets and key barriers to entry protecting LiveREADS from other fledgling e-publishers looking to compete in the space.

Having signed the targeted number of authors, and with the remainder of the angel financing in the bank, the company was ready for the next step in the business plan: raising the series A round of financing. In preliminary meetings with venture capitalists, the founders soon learned that despite their impressive roster of writers, VC investment would not happen without more proof of concept. To prove themselves and their business model, and gain credibility with potential investors, they needed to publish their first LiveREAD.

MAKING THE LEAP

With time working against them, Bascomb and Waxman rallied the team. They had to publish their first LiveREAD within 1 month. Bresnick called literary agent, Sterling Lord, and told him the company would be exercising the option for a never-before-published novella by Jack Kerouac, *Orpheus Emerged.* Over the next month, LiveREADS would not only design and produce the interactive e-book, but also put together a series of marketing and distribution deals necessary to reach its target market. But before they could get started, they first needed to determine the price for their first LiveREAD.

There were a few factors to be considered in setting the price. There was a relatively short history of established e-book prices that ranged from $1 (Stephen King's *The Plant*) to as much as 10 percent below the traditional book price (about $18). In addition, mass market paperback books (the most inexpensive books on the market) ranged from $5.50 to $9.00. Bascomb and Waxman wanted to price *Orpheus Emerged* inexpensively enough to encourage customer adoption. At $3.95 the founders felt it was cheap enough to encourage readers to take the leap. Plus, at $3.95 Bascomb estimated that they would need to sell only 20,000 copies to break even, a mere fraction of Kerouac's sales.

LiveREADS chose bn.com, the online arm of the Barnes & Noble superstore, as the exclusive distributor on the guarantee of a significant marketing campaign (including advertising and keyword searches on Yahoo!, AOL, MSN) and affiliate network push (over 400,000 sites would be offered the opportunity to carry the title). Furthermore, bn.com would build a boutique within its site that promoted LiveREADS and its first publication. With that distribution deal in place, LiveREADS began building its own marketing network based on revenue sharing deals. Apple, Blah-blah Network, Flooz, Adobe, Salon.com, and tens of other sites would promote the lost Kerouac classic. On the day of the launch, direct online marketers EMAIL SHOWS and Zooba would e-mail over 300,000 people. Tens of thousands of flyers would be distributed on over 50 college campuses across the country. And a national publicity campaign, including stories in the *LA Times* and on National Public Radio's *Fresh Air,* would begin on November 20. As the head of bn.com's e-book division said: LiveREADS was the the first company to actually be "publishing" an e-book instead of simply making a digital version of a preexisting work available.

THE BURGEONING E-BOOK MARKET

The e-book market gained a legitimate toehold in 2000 by attracting the attention of the most powerful players in new media, including Rupert Murdoch's News Corporation, Microsoft, Adobe, Amazon, Barnes & Noble, and the world's largest publishers, including Bertelsmann and Time Warner.

Still in its infancy, the e-book and digital publishing industry was marked by a virtual cacophony of players staking claims and forming alliances, all with public pronouncements of tempered, cautious optimism about the future of the market. Lower forecasts of the market potential reflected sheer derision of the format, while higher estimates reflected the belief that e-books would inevitably dominate book publishing.

Some analysts estimated the market would grow to $218 million by 2002.[1] An industry-financed study performed by Andersen Consulting estimated that e-books would represent $2.3 billion, or 10 percent of the book market by 2005[2] Forrester, on the other hand, forecast e-book market share of only 2 percent by 2005.[3]

As of November 2000, bn.com carried 2,700 e-book titles in three competing formats,[4] and Amazon carried 1,000 e-book titles available in the Microsoft Reader format.[5] Tom Turvey, e-books manager at bn.com remarked:

"Digital content is something that began slowly a few years ago and now is something that really has picked up steam. Even a year ago, this may have been a smaller part of our business, but with the strong partners, and now the strong original content from within the author community, it really has gained a lot of traction even in the last 6 to 8 months."[6]

How fast the industry would grow would depend on the settlement of issues that had similarities to those facing the music industry. Importantly, authors and publishers wanted to ensure that published works were protected from piracy, and that technologies and standards protected their intellectual property rights. Additionally, booksellers were cautious about the potential of cannibalization of their current "hard" book business, and printers and distributors feared that they would be disintermediated out of the book publishing supply chain.

COMPETING AND DISTRIBUTORS FORMATS, PUBLISHERS

One of the most crucial issues for the growth of the e-book industry was the extent of consumer adoption of the digital format. Consumers had three ways to view digital content at the end of 2000. Consumers could download books directly to their personal computers to be read off the computer screen, or they could download e-books to a specialized e-book reader. Or, for a smaller portion of book titles, consumers could download to a personal digital assistant (PDA) using Microsoft's Reader or Reciprocal software.

Faced with these options, a number of manufacturers were striving to become the dominant standard. However, the existence of competing, incompatible formats exacerbated the problem for the industry. The main players included two of the largest software providers, Microsoft and Adobe, and Gemstar International's e-book reader format. Additionally, Reciprocal, a small software provider, was introducing a format to download e-books to both personal computers as well as PDAs using the Palm Operating system. Except for Adobe's Glassbook Reader, all competing formats adopted the "Open E-Book" (OEB) standard, which used common HTML and XML Web programming. The first LiveREAD, *Orpheus Emerged,* was made available in both Adobe Glassbook and Microsoft Reader formats. It is important to note that only Glassbook allowed for the full effects of the connectivity and innovative design LiveREADS developed, despite the fact that it was impossible to print the novella from this edition. Although only plain text, the Microsoft Reader edition was printable. The following table outlines the various attributes of the competing formats.

	Microsoft	*Gemstar International*	*Adobe*	*Reciprocal*
Products	Microsoft Reader	Rocketbook and Softbook	Glassbook	Reciprocal
Availability	MSN.com, online bookstores, Windows CE 3	Retailers	bn.com	TBD
Price	Free	$299–$699	Free	TBD
Standard	Open	Open	Closed (PDF)	Open
Additional comments	Over 1 million downloads in 3 months after 8/2000 launch	Murdoch backed company, encryption supported by publishers	Preferred by LiveREADS	New—launched in November 2000, allows for download to Palm o/s

While concerned about cannibalization of their current hard books, the major publishers embarked on various initiatives that encompassed selling e-books on their own content Web sites, to distributing to traditional book e-tailers, to developing entirely new content. For current, fast-moving titles, the e-book model would be "time-phased," where e-books would be released prior to print publication at print or print discount prices. Industry incumbents Random House and Warner Books had already announced new e-publishing divisions. In addition, new pure-play companies were coming on the scene. The most notable of these was Mighty Words (see Exhibit 3 for a description of publishers' efforts). Internet book retailers and other content sites had announced their own plans to distribute e-books (see Exhibit 4 for a description of these companies' efforts).

SELLING OUT? ACQUISITION BECOMES AN OPTION

In early November, LiveREADS management was approached with an all-stock buyout offer. A newly formed investment and incubation group majority owned and backed by a global entertainment giant had spent the previous few months creating an e-book company and hoped to merge with LiveREADS to create a digital publishing and distribution company and Web site. Bascomb and his partners would receive shares in the resulting new company in exchange for their entire equity stake in LiveREADS.

The incubator had been formed as a subsidiary of the parent's music, motion picture, television, and related entertainment division. Its mandate was to create, incubate, operate, invest in, and acquire digital media companies. Given his business's dependence on consumer acceptance of new forms of entertainment technology, Bascomb saw this mission as a natural complement to LiveREADS.

The incubator focused on core digital media technology areas including broadband services, wireless, personal broadcasting, e-mail/direct marketing, digital asset management, e-commerce facilitation, and professional Internet services. In addition to equity financing, it provided portfolio companies with critical support in areas including strategic planning; infrastructure needs ranging from office space, phones, administrative assistance, computers, network, and Internet connectivity to full human resources support, accounting, access to credit and financial administration; Web development and design; recruitment; product management; marketing; and a rich network of distribution partners in both online and off-line channels.

Bascomb was impressed with the company's portfolio and expected that if LiveREADS was acquired, many synergies could be realized for the new digital publishing company. These included a private, high-speed broadband network, a full-service digital rights management (DRM) solution, and a leading global infrastructure technology platform for the aggregation, distribution, and seamless integration of digital content to Web sites, portals, and wireless networks. The incubator had also helped manage well-known media and technology start-ups that had ultimately gone public or had been acquired by industry heavyweights.

The potential acquirer was focused almost exclusively on enabling technologies that would help consumers optimize their online entertainment experiences. The merger would provide LiveREADS with access to the parent's rich library of entertainment content, which could be integrated into future products. But Bascomb worried about the management and direction of the acquiring firm—it had received a substantial sum from its parent company, and although it had only been operational for a few months, there was little evidence that any real progress had been made.

Bascomb wondered how to value the new stock offer. His partners, investors, and he would receive stock in the merged publishing entity. But what would that be worth? How could he justify accepting an all-stock offer when he and his colleagues had worked for so long with little income and when his investors had already given him much cash? Should they accept stock in the new merged entity, and if so, how much?

GETTING MONEY "THE VC WAY"

Like every other start-up, LiveREADS embarked on the campaign of raising money. LiveREADS had started by raising $700,000 from angel investors. In the four angel rounds, equity was distributed to the investors in installments amounting to 10 percent each. This meant that the LiveREADS

founders ended up keeping 60 percent of the company (see Exhibit 5 for details of previous financing rounds). Now LiveREADS was considering the first round of venture capital fund-raising, hoping to raise $5 million.

When asked about how the VCs place a money valuation on LiveREADS, Bascomb replied, "VCs look at your stage of business development, the type of company—in our case it is a content-driven company, and the valuation from the last angel round."[7] VCs would then look at projected net income after a certain period (for instance, 5 years) to determine how much of the company they would need to own to realize an appropriate return on their initial investment. The following table shows a typical calculation, with the appropriate P/E multiple crucial in determining the value of the company after an appropriate investment horizon, and the amount of equity VCs will require.

Time to exit	5 years	(investment horizon generally between 2 and 7 years)
Year 5 net income	$1.7 mill	(LiveREADS projections)
Year 5 valuation	$1.7 \times X$	(X is an appropriate P/E multiple)
VC investment	$5 mill	
Est. VC annual return	40%	(required return varies between 40–70%, depending on the risk of the company. LiveREADS was shipping product, so estimated return is lower)
Cumulative 5-year return	5.4 times	(5 years of 40% growth per annum)
Future value of VC inv	$26.9 mill	($5 mill investment multiplied by required 5-year return)
VC equity share	26.9/Year 5 valuation	Amount of the company the VC would require to obtain the required return.

In terms of the stage of development, LiveREADS had accomplished few significant milestones, and the initial launch would also demonstrate a viable business model, if successful. Nevertheless, much needed to be done (see Exhibit 6 for future milestones).

The fact that LiveREADS was a content-driven company could also prove to be an issue. While plenty of funds were available for investment, and the VCs had

substantial amounts of funds, there was a perception that funds were not being invested in companies. In particular, content companies appeared out of favor with the VC community.

However translating these generalities into a specific valuation to take to the VCs would be difficult—Bascomb needed to know what specific factors the VCs would take into consideration when valuing the company in order to come up with a value. Bascomb knew that the core assets of the company, specifically the contracts with the authors, would play a large part. However, achieving their required return on investment, ownership and control issues, and other factors would also be under consideration in dealing with the VCs.

From a control perspective, Bascomb knew that if he went the VC route, the LiveREADS founders would end up giving away another 30 to 40 percent of the remaining equity to VCs while if he chose to accept the buyout offer, LiveREADS founders' equity would likely be diluted to 5 percent of the new company.

most likely outcome. While recognizing that start-ups don't often proceed according to plan, Bascomb also felt the natural urge to ensure that any exit allowed them to reap some of the reward from the sweat equity invested in the company, and should be liquid to a certain degree. Control issues were also important in the overall decision, as was the value that each of the different investors would bring to the company in addition to their capital contribution.

These and other issues were under consideration as CEO Neal tried to decide which route to pursue, and how he should value the company to present his "price" to each of the potential investors.

CONCLUSION

In deciding which avenue to pursue, Bascomb also had to take a number of other factors into consideration. LiveREADS was burning approximately $30,000 per month, which gave the company a fume date of mid-February 2001, although the company could theoretically proceed at a reduced pace without the additional capital. However, while cash outflows could be slowed, the company was anxious to exercise its author options before they expired, and deliver the product to market. Aside from generating revenues, it would also provide credibility and assist in signing additional authors and raising capital.

Strategically, Bascomb had to determine how each financing route fitted with potential exit strategies. The feeling of the founders and angel investors was that if all went according to plan, the best time to exit would be within 2 years, with a trade sale the

ENDNOTES

1. *The Sunday Patriot-News* (Harrisburg), 11/05/2000.
2. "E-Books Still Long Way off from Joining Best-Seller List," John Dorschner, 10/16/00 *Chicago Tribune.*
3. "New Flare-Up in Battle Over E-Books," Mary Jo Foley, 11/06/00, *ZDNet News.*
4. "A New Chapter in the History of the Book," Paul Kendall, 11/07/00 *Daily Mail.*
5. "Hot Copy Publishers Ponder Paperless Books," Paul D. Colford, 11/07/00, *New York Daily News.*
6. "Barnesandnoble.com Set to Sell Bevy of E-Books," Kevin Featherly, *Newsbytes News Network,* 10/30/00.
7. Team interview with Neal Bascomb, November 13, 2000.
8. Ibid, *New York Daily News,* 11/7/00.
9. Ibid, *New York Daily News,* 11/7/00.
10. "Mighty Words Titles to Be Offered at BN. Com." Paul Hilts, 11/06/00, *Publishers Weekly.*

EXHIBIT 1 Author Characteristics

20 brand-name best-selling authors

6 *New York Times* #1 bestsellers

The #1 travel writer in America

The #1 personal finance writer in America

The #1 adventure writer in America

The #1 popular science writer in America

The #1 sports writer in America

National Book Award winner

Over 75 million copies sold by authors

EXHIBIT 2 Characteristics of LiveREADS' Product

- Original—A new experience that surpasses other mediums
- Size—Digestible size of between 50–100 pages long
- Compelling—It has to be worth the time it takes to read; hold reader's attention
- Unique—No other comparable online options available
- Frequently refreshed—Sense of urgency and timeliness
- Topical—Meets the reader's expectations
- Professional—Clean and easy to read and maneuver; accurate
- Entertaining—Delivers written word in a fun, immersive way
- Thorough—Leaves the reader satisfied

EXHIBIT 3 Publishers' E-Book Initiatives

Random House (Bertelsmann)
Mary Bahr, editorial director of @Random, scheduled to launch in January 2001, said the new division would offer titles for consumers who "don't necessarily read book reviews or frequent bookstores."[8]

Warner Books (Time Warner)
Warner announced the March 2001 launch of iPublish.com, which would utilize digital content to test market new talent and develop printed books. Greg Voynow, general manager, announced that iPublish might offer a subscription series of romantic short stories for "an insatiable fan to read at her desktop or print it out, on her lunch hour or at work, or before she puts her kids to bed."[9]

Mighty Words
A first mover in digital publishing, Mighty Words' parent, Fatbrain, received $35 million in funding from Microsoft cofounder Paul Allen. With an existing large-scale operation, the bulk of its operations related to "vanity press" type publishing. Like LiveREADS, the bulk of its works were short original works. In November, bn.com agreed to carry Mighty Words content. According to Chris MacAskill, Mighty Words' CEO, "business, technology and mind/body titles make up about 80 percent of our titles, with fiction and other nonfiction titles comprising only about 20 percent. Our bread is buttered by professional titles today, because at this stage it's still an early-adopter market. On bn.com today, there are 120 titles, 85 percent original and exclusive."[10]

EXHIBIT 4   Retailers' E-Book Initiatives

Amazon
Amazon created a special e-book section for its Web site and supported the Microsoft Reader format only. Amazon would not push e-books for the holiday 2000 season, as it had not yet worked out secure encryption technologies to enable e-book gift-giving. Amazon typically retained 55 percent of revenues from its e-book offerings.

bn.com
The Barnes & Noble Web site, 40-percent owned by Bertelsmann, offered e-books available in the Microsoft Reader, Gemstar e-book, and Adobe Glassbook formats. Like Amazon, it retained 55 percent of e-book revenues

Contentville
Contentville offered a limited range of titles that utilized the Microsoft, Gemstar, and Adobe Glassbook formats.

Lycos
In November, Lycos announced that it was entering into a 5-year, nonexclusive commitment to carry Random House's "Modern Library" collection of downloadable new and old classics, available at Lycos Shops.

EXHIBIT 5   Previous Financing Rounds

Date	Pre-Money Valuation	Amount Raised	Post-Money Valuation
15 May 2000	$900,000	$100,000	$1,000,000
1 July 2000	$1,350,000	$150,000	$1,500,000
1 September 2000	$1,800,000	$200,000	$2,000,000

EXHIBIT 6   Milestones

Based on the company's projections, the following milestones are instrumental to LiveREADS' plans:

2nd/3rd Quarter, 2000
- Develop online demo and begin site development
- Hire a chief technology officer, vice president of content development
- Sign 25 *NYT* best-selling writers
- Begin investigating content delivery platforms
- Secure $700,000 in angel financing and set advisory board

4th Quarter, 2000
- Sign 10 *NYT* best-selling authors
- Secure $5 million in financing
- Coordinate content partnerships with portals and major media sites
- Build out Website and technology infrastructure
- Hire chief operating officer, vice president of marketing, vice president of business development, and creative director

1st Quarter, 2001
- Create 6 LiveREADS for launch
- Develop strategic e-commerce partnerships for LiveREADS
- Launch version 1.0 of Web site
- Further integrate production/packaging abilities in-house
- Obtain 50 content affiliates

2nd Quarter, 2001
- Launch 8 LiveREADS
- Develop key strategic partnerships
- Sign 20 additional *NYT* best-selling writers

Case 9 Windsor Industries, Inc.

Windsor Industries, of Akron, Ohio, was founded in 1980 by E. L. Gibitz, then 66, to sell an industrial-grade tool board to automobile manufacturers. By 1993, annual sales averaged $405,000 and had seemed to hit their peak. Gibitz felt that there was significant potential for tool board not only in the automotive market but also in the marine service area and, especially, the consumer "do-it-yourself" market. Windsor was originally licensed by a similar company in Great Britain with sales in excess of $5 million a year. Although Great Britain has only 1/16 the GNP of the United States, Windsor's sales had never approached that level. Gibitz often wondered what needed to be done to reach a comparable sales level on this side of the Atlantic.

Although 13 years had passed since its founding, the organization still consisted of just three people. Gibitz did everything from making sales calls to packing the product for shipment to placing orders for materials. All manufacturing was outsourced, with material coming from both local and international (Korea and Taiwan) suppliers. Windsor simply designed the tool boards, sold the product, and shipped to the customer. In addition to Gibitz, Windsor employed a sales representative and a receptionist, both of whom participated in the packing function when a large order was to be shipped. Most current customers were automotive manufacturers who bought directly or required their dealers to buy the tool board along with required "essential tools." (Automobile manufacturers require dealers to buy these "essential tools" for each model year of car. Each dealer must retain these tools for 5 years.) Windsor's recent venture into the marine market was met with positive customer response, but it remained a small portion of sales.

PROBLEM IDENTIFICATION

Although there seems to be a strong market for tool board, Windsor Industries has one major problem. At 79, Gibitz does not have the energy level he had when he began the enterprise. Although he enjoys the activity, it is certain that he is not able to maximize the company's potential. It is likely that he would sell the business, given an acceptable offer.

A team of potential buyers emerged. The group was composed of three recently graduated MBA students, one of whom was Gibitz's grandson. But before he could sell the business, and the team could buy it, Gibitz needed to develop a business plan. The business plan proposed the purchase of the company by the team and outlined a strategy for increasing sales to about $3 million in 5 years. But the plan doesn't address two crucial questions: (1) What is the viability of selling the business? (2) What is the value of the business?

Excerpts of the business plan follow.

THE PRODUCTS

Windsor has two primary products in its tool-board line. The basic tool board, called "Loc-Board," is similar to Peg-Board in function but is constructed of reinforced steel and uses a patented screw-in hook that holds up to 160 pounds. With over 100 different hook styles available, the board can hold any tool. The shape of the tool is silk-screened either

---

This case was written in 1991 under the supervision of Professor James R. Lang by Jon Littlefield, The R. B. Pamplin College of Business, Virginia Polytechnic Institute and State University.

directly on the board or on an adhesive vinyl overlay that allows easy updating for each new model year. In addition to the hook attachments, the product offers extensive bin storage as well as a tool storage cart developed so that the mechanics' tools are close to the workstation at all times, further increasing the mechanics' efficiency.

A second product, called "Forever Peghook," uses the same screw-in philosophy to attach to standard Peg-Board. This is the main product that would be targeted toward the consumer market. Consumers might also be interested in a standard Peg-Board vinyl overlay with shapes of common household tools such as various screwdrivers, hammers, and pliers. This product could also be targeted toward service bays that already use some sort of existing Peg-Board.

The Loc-Board system has two advantages. First, studies have shown that up to 70 percent of an automotive dealer's "essential tools" are either misplaced or missing altogether when audits are conducted. This requires mechanics to spend an average of 6 to 8 hours per month searching for tools. Second, when this search comes up empty, the mechanic may attempt to do the job without the correct tool, possibly leading to unsafe repairs. As a result, this tool board increases both the efficiency of the mechanic and the safety of the repair.

CURRENT MARKETS

Most of Windsor's sales to date have been to automotive manufacturers. Japanese manufacturers Nissan and Subaru have purchased tool-board sets for all their dealers. Other customers are such diverse corporations as Ford (Tractor) and Harley-Davidson. Additional possibilities exist in the marine service market; a recent direct-mail campaign to Mercury Marine dealers has elicited positive response, and a follow-up piece is in the making.

Growth potential exists in two main areas. The first is the industrial and commercial area, primarily foreign automotive manufacturers. Further penetration of the domestic automotive-manufacturing market, the marine-manufacturing market, and other specialty markets (fast oil-change centers, for example) would produce large custom orders.

The second potential growth area is the retail market for individual tool boards. Although this is currently being handled by mail order, there is an opportunity to set up distribution channels through national discounters such as Wal-Mart, Kmart, and Sears Roebuck & Co. Additionally, such national and regional hardware discounters as Hechinger and Lowe's are likely prospects. Finally, distribution through auto parts retailers will help reach the retail market.

In addition to steel tool board, Windsor also markets a vinyl overlay designed to cover the traditional Peg-Board that already exists in many applications. Suzuki U.S.A., for example, has recently furnished its 300-dealer network with these overlays combined with the screw-in Forever Peghook designed to secure the hooks to the Peg-Board. The industrial, commercial, and retail potential of this Peg-Board add-on are significant.

PROFIT POTENTIAL AND RESOURCE REQUIREMENTS

As is typical in small businesses, neither revenues nor profits are consistent. Average annual revenues for the past 4 years (FY 1989 to FY 1992) have been $405,477, with a standard deviation of $78,194. Gross profit as a percentage of sales has averaged 57.0 percent; net income has averaged $36,229, or 10.3 percent of sales.

Significant improvements can be made in these results. First, the revenues can be substantially higher with additional sales effort, as Table 1 shows. Projections indicate that increased selling effort can produce sales growth of over 650 percent for the first 5 years of operation. We propose three people in direct sales, each focusing on the automotive market. Second, as is common with entrepreneurial ventures, income may have been understated to avoid federal income taxes. As a result, projected figures will be substantially higher.

Both cost of goods sold and operating expenses will increase to a lesser extent than revenues, as economies of scale in selling and purchasing begin to take place. This yields a pretax net income that grows faster than sales.

After purchasing the company from Gibitz, the new owners' strategy will emphasize sales growth. Automobile manufacturers will play a large part in this expansion effort, as they have traditionally been the largest customers for the product. This will be the focus for the first year and a half. Additionally, a niche exists in the retail market with distribution through large discount retailers (Hechinger, Lowe's) and direct-mail order for a tool board and hook set.

These sales growth targets can be achieved for two reasons. The first is increased sales effort. The second is an increasing trend toward safety in automobiles, as evidenced by such recent additions as the air bag and antilock brakes. A mechanic who cannot find the correct tool with which to make a repair will use a different tool, per-

haps resulting in a dangerous repair. The Loc-Board system ensures that the mechanic can find the correct tool.

Capital Requirements

Requirements for capital fall into two categories, the capital to purchase Windsor Industries and the influx of cash necessary to expand the business beyond its current three-person operation. Purchase of the business would include the company and product names, patents, tooling, and other assets. It might also include an annual lease agreement for the existing headquarters facilities at an additional charge.

Growth requirements are difficult to estimate. The first few years of operation will be focused on marketing and sales, resulting in significant advertising and travel expenditures. With the substantial growth rate that has been projected, the buyers estimate that an additional $200,000 will be required.

THE INDUSTRY

The nearest competitor to the Loc-Board system, although far behind in durability and strength, is standard Peg-Board. The five largest Peg-Board–producing companies produce 50 million square feet of standard Peg-Board annually. At current retail prices of approximately $0.30 per square foot, this is a $15 million market. In addition to these five large companies, hundreds of small local and regional producers exist, multiplying this figure many times. It is also

TABLE 1 Selected Financial Data (projected)						
	Year 0	*Year 1*	*Year 2*	*Year 3*	*Year 4*	*Year 5*
Sales	$368,919	$725,000	$1,250,000	$1,600,000	$2,100,000	$2,800,000
Cost of goods sold	154,946	304,500	525,000	672,000	882,000	1,176,000
Operating expenses	113,603	305,537	351,794	425,966	604,639	700,842
Pretax net income	$100,370	$ 59,963	$ 318,206	$ 447,034	$ 558,361	$ 868,518

estimated that 500 million hooks are sold annually—an additional $31.25 million.

Market Size and Trends

The two main markets, automotive and residential, are large. The total number of distinct dealer franchises in the United States was 41,368 in 1992. With a historical average of 10 tool boards per dealer and an average selling price of $75 per board (including overlays, hooks, etc.), the total automotive market for the product would be $31,026,000. Growth is likely to be zero in the number of automotive dealerships—the number tends to remain relatively constant—so this is an accurate figure for the total market size for later years as well.

Market size for the residential market is not as easy to estimate. A recent survey of households by Rubbermaid, Inc., estimated that about half of the 80 million single-family homes in the United States had some type of Peg-Board. If the market for the Windsor Loc-Hook Starter Set alone (retail price is $14.95) is considered, the total residential market is $598 million.

Customers buy the product for four reasons. First, the Loc-Board system mitigates risk. Mechanics are more likely to use the correct tool for the repair. Second, the product decreases time wasted searching for tools, and thus increases productivity. Third, the screening of the tool on the board improves the likelihood that the tool will be replaced correctly, reducing the dealer's tool replacement expense. Finally, the system organizes the whole work area, increasing the public's perception of the dealership's service quality.

Competition and Competitive Edges

Windsor faces no direct competition. Some indirect competition comes from traditional Peg-Board and from other tool storage systems. Additionally, Kent-Moore and Owatana Tool Company both market a board similar to Windsor's, but they supply the boards only as part of a total package. Both of these companies (which supply to the large domestic automotive manufacturers) buy the accompanying hooks from Windsor.

Competitive advantage comes primarily from the substantial benefits that customers receive. This "value added" consists of increased safety and less downtime for mechanics. Tools are not lost nearly as much. As mechanics currently spend 7 to 8 hours per month looking for tools, this represents significant time savings. Additionally, repairs done without the correct tools can be a safety hazard.

Other competitive advantages come from the following:

1. *Legal aspects.* Patents held for the company's hooks represent a competitive advantage, although it may not be economically feasible to defend these.
2. *Informational aspects.* Current customer lists and historical business information are competitive strengths. The founder's experience with parts outsourcing and low-cost foreign suppliers is also a competitive plus.
3. *Quality characteristics.* The product is highly differentiated. Its level of quality has been consistently high—it is a simple product, but is stronger and more durable than standard Peg-Board.
4. *Market characteristics.* The market is obscure, making competitive entry less likely. Once customer contacts are cemented and the company grows, competitive position will become more defensible. Thus, losing patent protection in a few years becomes less of a factor. Windsor Industries has already established itself as the primary player in this market. Price sensitivity is low, and quality of the product is high compared with standard Peg-Board, the closest form of competition.

Estimated Market Share and Sales

At the current price of $750 for one tool-board set (of ten tool boards), the estimated sales level will be 967 sets for year 1. This assumes that if each of the three salespeople obtains only two additional large contracts in the automotive area, with the average contract yielding $100,000 to $150,000 in sales, this sales level can be achieved. Subsequent years' sales will increase further based on resales of overlays and other follow-up sales, and expansion into the retail and direct-marketing (catalog) areas.

ECONOMICS OF THE BUSINESS

Operating margins for the automotive segment of the business dominate the analysis because this is the largest segment of current sales. The new owners will focus primarily on the automotive market during the first year and a half of operation. Table 2 summarizes the pricing margins based on a set of 10 tool boards for which the average dealer pays $750. The average purchase cost for a tool-board set is $320, which leaves a $430 gross margin. Profit after taxes is almost $80 per set—over 10 percent of the sales price.

With the infusion of cash from an increase in debt in year 1, sales are expected to grow to $2.8 million in year 5, producing gross profit of $1.624 million and net income of $625,000. Additionally, there is ample reason to believe that sales will continue to increase well past the $3 million level.

Durability of the profit stream will come primarily from the momentum that will have been built up by past sales contacts, the reputation of the company and product, and a substantial increase in the selling effort. As has been previously discussed, the threat of new entrants into the specialized segment of the Peg-Board industry that has been created by Loc-Board is minimal because of the relative obscurity of the product offering and perceived barriers to entry. Additionally, Windsor enjoys a significant cost advantage in production of hooks for standard Peg-Board and for the specialized Loc-Board. Last, the depth of Windsor's hook offering will further prevent other companies from attempting to grab market share.

Fixed and Variable Costs

Because past sales trends have fluctuated greatly, the risk of internal manufacturing is currently not outweighed by the economic benefits. Thus, the company currently owns few fixed assets, no real estate, and little inventory. Assets to be purchased will be the company name, customer lists, the patents, and the current tooling for hooks. Although economies of scale could be attained with in-house production, a significant loss in flexibility would likely result.

Fixed costs beginning in year 1 include selling, advertising, rent, utilities, salaries, and interest expense. These increase after year 1, but they are generally tied to sales. As a result, if sales are greater than or less than expected, these fixed costs will change. These costs are summarized in Table 3.

TABLE 2 Product Costs and Profitability

	Cost per Unit (set of 10)	*Percent of Sales*
Purchase costs	$320.00	42
Gross margin	430.00	58
Fixed costs	316.00	42
Profit before taxes	114.00	15
Profit after taxes	$ 79.80	10.6

TABLE 3   Fixed-Cost Breakdown

	Year 0	Year 1	Year 2	Year 3	Year 4	Year 5
Sales	$368,919	$725,000	$1,250,000	$1,600,000	$2,100,000	$2,800,000
Selling expense	9,111	97,000	97,000	126,000	140,000	158,500
Advertising expense	21,689	40,000	50,000	50,000	50,000	50,000
Telephone and utilities	2,724	5,500	5,500	5,500	5,500	5,500
Rent expense	10,000	12,000	15,000	18,000	21,000	24,000
Salaries	41,599	100,000	100,000	120,000	150,000	180,000
Postage	9,620	18,905	32,595	41,722	54,760	73,013
Interest expense	0	55,000	55,000	55,000	55,000	55,000
Total fixed costs	$ 94,743	$328,405	$355,095	$416,222	$476,260	$546,013
As percentage of sales	25.70%	45.30%	28.40%	26.00%	22.70%	19.50%

MARKETING PLAN

Current customers are top prospects for updates in overlays and hooks, and perhaps additional boards as well. Additionally, other import manufacturers are good prospects. Windsor has yet to sell to a Big Three domestic manufacturer. Tapping this market will be a top goal of the sales team during the first year and a half.

The second group of targeted customers are homeowners. Rubbermaid's study estimates that 40 million single-family households in the United States have Peg-Board. This creates a huge market not only for sales of the Forever Peghook but also for sales of stronger, higher-durability replacement boards.

Marketing strategy will focus on automobile (and other) manufacturers for the first year and a half, as this will be the key to reaching positive cash flow. After this time, the marketing effort will be expanded to include coverage of large discount chains targeted at the homeowner or home improvement market and increased direct mail effort with advertising in national magazines.

Pricing

Current prices are based on the superiority of the Loc-Board system to other avail-

able alternatives—namely Peg-Board—and thus leave a comfortable profit margin. The response in volume to changes in price seems to be relatively inelastic, so there is no reason to change the current pricing policy. The new owners may determine in the future that they must drop prices at least temporarily to secure orders from large customers. If this is the case, once the new customer sees the value of the tool storage system, it is likely that they will be willing to pay a higher price. At any rate, with the high profit per board, there is substantial leeway available to secure this type of order.

Sales Tactics

Certainly, the sales and marketing function will take priority among all activities during the first few years of the new venture. The new owners expect to travel a great deal, and this is reflected in the comparatively high budgeted expenses for sales activity. Because major customers are located in Detroit and on the west coast, the directors will likely spend at least 30 to 40 weeks per year on the road selling.

The automotive business will be the first to receive focus. This has been the Loc-Board system's traditional strong area, so it must be saturated by the sales effort. Other large manufacturers will get attention during this first phase of the sales process. Included will be marine manufacturers and other manufacturers with well-developed dealer networks. After the first year and a half, the retail market will be added to the marketing focus, with emphasis on large discount chains and chains specifically targeted to homeowners and do-it-yourselfers.

Service and Warranty Policies

Service and warranties are an important part of the marketing process. The boards are warranted for durability and strength, and the boards are in fact stronger than most customers expect them to be. Additionally, because the hooks are welded, they, too, are much more durable than standard peg hooks. Installation of the boards is simple. Both the shape of the tool and the hook number are silk-screened on the board (or overlay). The installer merely has to match the hook number to the location on the board to install the hook.

Advertising and Promotion

Advertising expense doubles in the first year of the new venture. A focus on creating awareness by significant advertising expenditures in automotive magazines and other trade publications will expand demand in the automotive and retail markets. Also, new product releases will be sent to major product-related publications in an effort to gain publicity at minimal cost.

Distribution

Three channels exist for distribution of the Loc-Board system. First, direct sales will be used to tap the auto-manufacturing market. This will involve a total selling cost of approximately $90,000 in year 1. Subsequent years will focus increasingly on direct sales to major retailers and catalog marketers.

Shipping costs are the main distribution cost. These costs depend on shipment size; smaller orders go through UPS, larger orders through independent freight carriers.

Per-unit shipping costs decrease as order size increases. Freight costs have averaged $17,340 over the past 5 years, roughly 4 percent of revenue.

MANUFACTURING AND OPERATIONS PLAN

A manufacturing plan for the Loc-Board system logically focuses on purchasing because 100 percent of the manufacturing is outsourced to different companies. The actual tool board is made in Ohio; the hooks that secure the tools on the face of the tool board have been made in Seoul, South Korea, for the last 5 years. Tooling is being fabricated for a new, lower-cost production facility located in Taipei, Taiwan. Additionally, there are domestic suppliers for the hooks and the vinyl overlays. A freelance graphic artist designs the screens used to silk-screen the tool shapes on the vinyl overlays and boards. No formal order-processing system is being used currently because the nature of the business does not require time- or quantity-based ordering. At present, the different components are ordered when a sale is made to an automobile manufacturer or dealer. When the company grows to the level of multicontractual sales, a formal order-processing system may need to be implemented.

Geographical Location/Facilities and Improvements

Windsor Industries is based in Akron, Ohio. This is where the administrative office and the packaging center are located. All inbound shipments from suppliers are received and repackaged according to order specification. The repackaged items are then shipped to the customer (the dealer or manufacturer). This home base in Ohio will be sufficient to grow the company to the projected level in 5 years. At that time, further analysis will be conducted to determine whether inhouse manufacturing facilities would be less expensive per unit than total outsourcing. Yearly analyses will be conducted to see whether a larger storage facility may be required to handle increased sales levels.

STRATEGY AND PLANS

The strategy that will expand this company from $400,000 in sales to about $3 million in sales in 5 years will consist of intense selling and marketing efforts to large automobile manufacturers, automobile dealers, and large retail hardware outlets, along with penetration of the do-it-yourself market through direct-mail catalogs. A second strategy is to research all available suppliers of each component that is outsourced. This will reduce the power of the current suppliers, enable Windsor Industries to keep costs as low as possible, and prevent overloading a single supplier with a large order.

The only quality control check Windsor will have on suppliers is the acceptance or rejection of a shipped component lot. This is another reason to research alternative suppliers; if a supplier continually sends poor lots, an alternative supplier can be used. Even if this new supplier has a higher cost, the lost sales resulting from time-consuming and unnecessary reshipping can be minimized. However, supplier relations have been favorable since the business incorporated in 1980. Quality control to the customer is measured in friendly customer service, timely product shipments, and, of course, quality products. Products shipped should be of the highest quality because of the initial quality control check of supplier shipments.

LEGAL ISSUES

The only legal issue pertains to the patent on the screw-in hooks. This patent was granted in 1984 and remains protected until 2001. However, as the company operates in a small market niche with relatively no large-scale exposure, it is doubtful anyone would test the strength of the patent. The patent number is still displayed in current catalogs. More legal issues will arise when the growth of the company leads to large contracts. At this time, consultants and/or lawyers can be hired on an as-needed basis to ensure fair and binding contracts.

ORGANIZATION AND KEY MANAGEMENT PERSONNEL

Windsor Industries is owned and operated by E. L. Gibitz, who would like to sell the business and retire. The incoming entrepreneurial team consists of Jon Littlefield (Gibitz's grandson), Greg Brink, and Tim Middleton. Full ownership (capital stock on the balance sheet) will be transferred to the entrepreneurial team with the following equity split: Littlefield–55 percent; Brink–22.5 percent; Middleton–22.5 percent.

The duties of each team member will overlap considerably. The main focus and effort will be on sales and marketing to each market. For the first 18 months, expansion in the automotive industry will be the goal. After that, each team member will focus on penetrating new markets. Brink will have responsibility for the automotive and industrial business. Because Brink has selling experience as well as a strong interest and background in automobile technology, he is the most qualified to expand in this market.

Middleton will concentrate on developing the direct catalog sales market. Currently, this is an ongoing project of Windsor Industries, but it is restricted to advertising in other magazines and limited distribution of company catalogs. Middleton's expertise and experience in conducting reliable market research will be utilized to determine the size of this market, the location of potential customers, and the most cost-effective way to reach them. Customers will be reached by direct mailing of catalogs and increased print advertising in magazines that they frequently read. The goal is to present the product to customers well and often so that they can see and comprehend the value added.

Littlefield will be in charge of a new market area, large retail outlets such as Wal-Mart, Lowe's, and Hechinger. In the first year to 2 years, he will conduct interviews by phone and in person with purchasing managers in these large stores. If the results of the interviews are positive—and they are projected to be—a test market of stores will be supplied with the products. These stores will be located in towns and cities that are relatively close to Akron but are diverse enough to represent different market areas. The success of these test market stores will determine the rate of expansion in the retail sector.

CRITICAL RISKS, PROBLEMS, AND ASSUMPTIONS

Some risks will exist while trying to grow the venture:

1. Manufacturers (or other customers) may decide to produce their own version of our tool-board set. A manufacturer's decision to produce a similar product in-house and distribute it to all dealers could take away a substantial amount of the venture's potential market. By use of suppliers in foreign countries (Taiwan, for example), the management team hopes to keep costs and prices low enough to convince manufacturers that in-house production is not worthwhile.
2. Customer orders have traditionally been sporadic. This is mainly the result of a lack of selling "intensity" by current management. Sales are expected to become more stable and predictable when a dedicated sales force is in place.
3. Sales projections represented in the business plan may be somewhat inaccurate because of the nature of the business. The venture will grow at a rate that depends on the type of customer the entrepre-

neurial team can attract (manufacturer, independent dealer, or retailer). The entrepreneurial team feels confident that a substantial growth rate can be achieved with an intense selling effort by all members of the venture team.

4. As the venture becomes more lucrative, the market niche will become more attractive to potential competitors. The management team does not feel the market will become large enough to attract major attention for 3 to 4 years. By this time, the team hopes to have an extensive customer base and contracts with customers aimed at maintaining business.
5. As sales grow and product demand increases, there is a risk that suppliers to the company may be overwhelmed. The management team plans to prevent any supply problems by close study of supplier capacity and possible alternate supplies. The team will decide in future years if products should be produced in-house.

The company (venture) in question has been a going concern for many years. Although the risks listed are real, they have not presented themselves in any tangible way to the current management of the company. The entrepreneurial team feels confident that these risks are minimal.

THE FINANCIAL PLAN

Pro Forma Income Statement

The income statement contains the company's current-year statement and projections for the first 5 years of operations under the management of the venture team. For the projected years, several items are held as a constant percentage of sales. These include cost of goods sold, freight, and postage. Other items are held constant or only slightly increased (rent expense, depreciation, etc.). Major expenses to consider are significant increases in selling expense, salaries, and advertising expense. These line items must be emphasized to increase sales. Because of the company purchase recorded in year 1, there is a net income drop from $87,924 to −$13,487 in year 1. Net income and cash flows remain positive in subsequent years.

To test the volatility of earnings with a lower sales projection, the venture team has determined that a 20 percent reduction in sales results in a 35 percent lower net income figure in year 5. The resulting net income figure is still over $400,000, as shown in Table 4.

Pro Forma Cash Flow Analysis

The company is expected to produce sufficient cash flows in subsequent years to fund operations (funding from cash flows and $200,000 from initial debt financing). If cash flows from operations do not prove sufficient to cover the costs of outsourcing, the company has the ability to establish lines of credit to finance current assets. The company has been successful doing so in the past.

The venture team does not expect any problems with receivables, and the founder's experience would support this. Most of Windsor's customers do not have financial difficulties and are able to pay for products easily. Receivables and inventory are expected to grow in proportion to sales in years 1 through 5. The team does not foresee any major capital equipment purchases because of the outsourcing practices of the company. As sales and cash flows increase, management may decide to purchase a manufacturing facility in the United States to gain some additional control over costs and scheduling.

TABLE 4 Sensitivity Analysis of Net Income (20% sales projection decrease)						
Pro Forma Income Statement	**Year 0**	**Year 1***	**Year 2**	**Year 3**	**Year 4**	**Year 5**
Sales	$368,919	$580,000	$1,000,000	$1,280,000	$1,680,000	$2,240,000
Cost of goods sold	154,946	243,600	420,000	537,600	705,600	940,800
Gross profit	213,973	336,400	580,000	742,400	974,400	1,299,200
Expenses						
Selling expense	9,111	97,000	97,000	126,000	140,000	158,500
Advertising expense	21,689	40,000	50,000	50,000	50,000	50,000
Telephone and utilities	2,724	5,500	5,500	5,500	5,500	5,500
Freight	13,750	21,617	37,271	47,707	62,615	83,487
Rent expense	10,000	12,000	15,000	18,000	21,000	24,000
Salaries	41,599	100,000	100,000	120,000	150,000	180,000
Depreciation	5,110	5,110	5,110	5,110	5,110	5,110
Early payment of loan	0	0	0	0	100,000	100,000
Postage	9,620	18,905	32,595	41,722	54,760	73,013
Total expenses	113,603	300,132	342,476	414,039	588,985	679,610
EBIT	100,370	36,268	237,524	328,361	385,415	619,590
Interest expense	0	55,000	55,000	55,000	55,000	55,000
EBT	100,370	−18,732	182,524	273,361	330,415	564,590
Taxes (credit)	12,446	−5,245	51,107	76,541	92,516	158,085
Net income	$ 87,924	$−13,487	$ 131,417	$ 196,820	$ 237,899	$ 406,505

*Year 1 and subsequent years are projections.

Case 10 Sony PlayStation 2: Trojan Horse in the Living Room?

. . . The Trojans came out of Troy to receive the huge horse as an offering of peace, and decided to celebrate, far into the night. In the small hours of the morning, while everyone was drunk or asleep, the Greeks inside the horse climbed down from it. Silently, they killed the Trojan sentries at the city gates. The gates were then opened to the bulk of the Greek army. In their drunkenness, the Trojans had not seen the Greek fleet return to their shores . . .[1]

It was approaching midnight on October 25, 2000, and anxious consumers jostled for position outside a Wal-Mart in Harvey, New York. With voices raised and minor scuffling, the scene resembled a live enactment of *Street Fighter EX3,* a new video game title developed by Capcom for the Sony PlayStation 2. But just before the first karate chop could be thrown, the doors of the retailer opened, and the crowd flooded inside.

The crowd had been waiting to buy the much-anticipated Sony PlayStation 2, or "PS2" to avid fans, which would officially go on sale in North America on October 26. In September, Sony had announced that due to parts shortages, it would be able to ship just half of the 1 million units it had expected to ship to North American retailers by the launch date. After that, the company would be able to ship only 100,000 units a week

through the end of December. This represented a critical shortfall for Sony, especially during the key holiday 2000 season.

This made Ken Kutaragi, the brash and outspoken CEO of Sony Computer Entertainment, quite anxious. In 1999, the Computer Entertainment Division was responsible for 40 percent of Sony Corporation's profits, and the PS2 was expected to provide a critical boost to the company's fortunes in 2000. Sony had missed earnings targets in the first two quarters of 2000, and a number of key executives left the firm or were fired.[2] With just a small supply of PS2s, Kutaragi worried that arch rivals Sega and Nintendo would fill the holiday void with their own advanced game systems.

Kutaragi also wondered if gamers and reviewers would like the new machine, priced at $299, and the new titles, priced at $49 each. Would they *not* buy the PS2 and hold out for the new Sega DreamCube or Microsoft XBox gaming console, due to launch in 2001? Or, would they buy the PS2 and subsequently reject it when the alternatives hit the marketplace? The PS2 featured the most advanced gaming features to date: a 128-bit central processing unit with floating point performance of 6.2 Gflops rendering 66 million polygons per second. In other words, it offered super high performance with the most impressive graphics to date in a home gaming system. The system was

MBA candidates Pamela Bierman, Sheryl Cohen, Kenneth Globerman, Jodi Hirsch, and Christopher Lemmond prepared this case under the supervision of Professor Christopher L. Tucci for the purpose of class discussion rather than to illustrate either effective or ineffective handling of an administrative situation. Distributed by the Berkley Center for Entrepreneurial Studies, at the Stern School of Business, New York University. To order copies, phone: 212-998-0070, fax: 212-995-4211, or e-mail bces@stern.nyu.edu. No part of this publication may be used or reproduced without written permission of the Berkley Center. Copyright © 2000 by the Stern School of Business and Christopher L. Tucci. All rights reserved.

backward compatible with old PlayStation game titles, and the company offered 26 new PS2 titles for the October 26 launch (See Exhibit 1 for pictures of PS2, GameCube and Dreamcast).

Beyond the holiday season, Kutaragi's bigger worry was a more strategic one. While game systems and titles were a lucrative business, he believed the future of home entertainment offered the potential for vastly greater riches. Kutaragi saw his PS2 as a Trojan Horse into people's homes. He envisioned the PS2 and the future PS3 exploiting the potential of broadband Internet and interactive television applications. The PS series could become the central home information and networking appliance connecting the PC, the TV, the stereo, and the Internet.

In addition to cutting edge gaming features, the PS2 featured the ability to play Compact Disc recordings and DVD movies, both with Dolby Digital sound. Additionally, it contained a 295 mHz processor, 32 SDRam, a bay for a 3.5-inch hard disk drive, and an expansion unit for interfacing with a network for future functionality upgrades. It has no modem per say, but a port for a network card (not included with the console) to plug into a high-speed broadband connection. The console is equipped with two USB and one IEE1394, or Fire-Wire, port for eventual (400 megabit-per-second) data transfers from peripherals ranging from hard drives to digital video cameras. Together with USB and i.Link interfaces, the PS2 was able to expand into a home network.[3]

PS2 also had an impressive co-processor to handle heavy duty graphic-rendering and other functions. The PS2's screen resolution was also impressive with up to 1280 × 1024 screen pixels, or double that of the Dreamcast's 640 × 480.[4] (Exhibit 2 compares game consoles on various attributes.) Kutaragi wondered if his self-described Trojan Horse strategy would work. All the major telecom-

munications providers, as well as the leading software, computer manufacturer, and content providers, were scrambling to get a "magic box" into people's homes that could capture the promise of eventual media, data, and content convergence. He was worried about Microsoft, which was maneuvering to place its operating system on current home set-top boxes, and was developing its XBox, which would contain many, if not more features than the PS2. Microsoft announced that it would support the fourth quarter, 2001, launch of the XBox with $500 million in advertising and promotion.[5]

Kutaragi was also concerned about AOL's new interactive TV initiative, and wondered if the company would be successful in leveraging its 25 million subscribers to the TV set. Who were the appropriate partners for Sony to guarantee the scale necessary for the Trojan Horse strategy to work? And could Kutaragi succeed in leveraging his all-in-one PlayStation vision by overcoming his own company's music, movie, and electronics unit initiatives, many being pursued independently of each other?[6]

SONY COMPANY OVERVIEW

Sony is a recognized name in the areas of audio-visual electronics, information technology, music, motion picture, and television both in the United States and worldwide. (See Exhibit 3 for an outline of Sony's Divisions.) In addition to its success with the original PlayStation game console, and potentially with the new PS2, Sony has demonstrated an impressive history of successful product innovations. Not only was Sony the co-developer of the CD and DVD, it has invented a wide variety of audio-visual products including the Walkman personal stereo, flat screen FD Trinitron WEGA televisions, Memory Stick, Handycam Camcorders, and Mavica Digital Cameras. (See Exhibit 4 for illustrations of Sony innovations.)

RECENT SONY INITIATIVES

Launch of PlayStation 1

The original Sony PlayStation was launched in December of 1994 and spurred the market's demand for more compelling on-screen action. Sony decided to take advantage of this market opportunity with a 32-bit CD-based format as opposed to 16-bit cartridges. It rapidly gained market share, displacing Super Nintendo Entertainment System as the market leader. It also maintained a dominant position in the video game industry when Nintendo introduced its 64 system. By the spring of 1998, nearly 33 million PlayStation consoles and 236 million software units had been shipped worldwide.

Entrée into PC Business: PC Interface

In September 2000, Sony launched personal information terminals in Japan, named "CLIE." They interface with PCs and enable the management of data such as schedules, address lists, display images, and also allow the utilization of networks to send e-mail messages and browse Web pages by connecting to wireless phones. In December 2000, Sony intended to launch a personal IT television in Japan named "airboard," which allows users to enjoy both TV broadcasts and the Internet on a single terminal, and enables users to enjoy it anywhere inside the home by using the latest wireless technologies.[7]

Sony also collaborated with Intel in 2000 in an effort to give consumers the ability to share electronic content between PCs and various consumer electronic devices such as digital cameras, digital camcorders, and portable music players. In addition, the two companies will work to enable PCs with the Digital Video Interface, which provides high bandwidth, plug-and-play digital connections for high-quality displays. Both firms hope that the effort will establish an industry-wide adoption of DVI to assure compatibility among the next-generation flat-panel PCs.[8]

HDTV

Sony introduced the industry's first direct-view flat screen HDTV set in September of 1998. The set is a 34-inch wide-screen TV, featuring Sony's proprietary FD Trinitron flat screen picture tube. The Sony HDTV set is designed to display free, over-the-air digital broadcasts when connected to an optional, external antenna. Jim Palumbo, vice president of Sony's Display Marketing Division said, ". . . Sony's HD component input may serve the cable industry and consumers by allowing cable subscribers access to broadcast HD programming if local cable operators elect to provide set-top boxes with HD component outputs." Sony's focus, according to Nishida, is to maximize consumer convenience. The proprietary technology of Digital Reality Creation (DRC) converts standard definition video signals to four times their original image resolution, from sources including broadcast TV, cable, videotape, digital satellite systems, DVD, and WebTV Internet terminals.[9]

Palm-Powered Personal Entertainment Organizers

Sony positions its personal entertainment organizer as one of the strategic products of the coming broadband network era and strives for the creation and growth of the new market segment. In November of 1999, Sony and Palm Inc. agreed to collaborate in the development of next generation Palm OS software with AV functionality. Sony also plans to expand Memory Stick Expansion Modules that will add various new applications to the personal entertainment organizers as well as other devices for 2001.

GAMING INDUSTRY TRENDS

The video game industry is a $15 billion global business, and includes consoles and game titles. Video game usage at home has exploded since 1994 with the introduction of "next generation" systems such as the Sega Saturn (1994), Sony PlayStation (1995), and Nintendo 64 (1996). Sony leads the market with Nintendo and Sega distant followers. Between 1997 and 1998, consoles experienced 20 percent growth as retail sales of games grew from over $5 billion to just over $6.3 billion. Competition within the industry is generally difficult to predict due to changing technologies and consumer tastes for new games. In 1998, the penetration of video game consoles in U.S. homes started to decline, down 2 percent to 35 percent. This decline can partially be attributed to the increasing use of the PC as a game machine.[10]

Games are considered the "razorblades" of the marketplace as most profits are generated through successful games rather than the consoles themselves. The games segment reached $8.4 billion in revenue in the United States last year, including PC game software, according to industry tracker NPD. (See Exhibit 5 for game sales rankings.)

Despite its widespread availability and the feature of a built-in modem, the Sega Dreamcast has not enjoyed nearly the buzz created by PS2. A strong factor is that top game software developer Electronic Arts chose to not make games for Sega so that it could focus on development for PS2.[11] Nintendo is betting that gamers frustrated by PS2 shortages will buy its current game console, N64, even though it is not as powerful. To stir interest in N64, Nintendo released a sequel to its popular *Zelda* adventure. Microsoft may find itself behind in the market with fewer games and with no prior system from which games could be played.[12]

Sega Dreamcast

Sega Enterprises, Ltd., based in Tokyo, develops, markets, and distributes Sega video-game systems.[13] The 128k Dreamcast system retails for $149, and comes equipped with an upgradeable 56K modem and a Web browser designed by longtime strategic partner Planetweb. Sega plans to add new fea-

tures to the Dreamcast browser at least once every 3 months. It recently introduced a $21.95-a-month online gaming service, complete with Internet access and e-mail, offering a $150 rebate for an 18-month subscription to SegaNet.[14]

By plugging the system into a phone jack and dialing through AT&T WorldNet (with whom Sega has an alliance) or another ISP, gamers can be transported to the Sega Dreamcast Network. The network will function like any other Internet portal, offering e-mail service and Web browsing. The service also allows players to participate in Web-based chat sessions about Dreamcast products.[15] The network will keep players apprised of upgrades and gaming cheat codes, as well as provide downloadable game demos. Editorial content, including news and reviews of Dreamcast products, will be supplied by IGN.com.[16] While Dreamcast will not support broadband Internet services such as cable modem access, Sega has not ruled out future upgrades for the console.[17]

Microsoft Xbox

Microsoft is actively promoting its Xbox, its attempt to transfer its success in the PC industry to the console market. This console will have the power of a high-end gaming system as well as the flexibility of a personal computer. "We are developing a game console that will bring a new dimension to the gaming experience," Microsoft said in a statement.[18] The console will have "movie quality" 3-dimensional graphics and a connection to high-speed Internet services that will allow users to take part in multiplayer games as well as connect to the Web and exchange e-mail.[19]

Nintendo GameCube

Nintendo is a worldwide leader in the creation of interactive games and succeeded with its Super Mario line of games, making Mario a household name. The company introduced the first portable hand-held game with interchangeable game packs.[20] Game cartridges for the N64 will not play on the GameCube, which will be a dedicated game machine much like Nintendo's current N64, but with much better image quality. The GameCube will feature a central processor from IBM and a graphics processor from ATI Technologies. The games will be offered on 3-inch disks designed by Matsushita Electric Industrial Co., the Japanese manufacturer of Panasonic products. The format, incompatible with standard CD and DVD drives, was chosen in part to discourage piracy. In addition to the regular gamepad, there will be a wireless version available that works from as far away as 30 feet. Modems for regular phone lines and faster connections for Internet play will also be available.[21]

Online Trends

As PS2 game consoles with hard drives and broadband pipes grow, the means by which consumers acquire and play games will be transformed as downloading entire games or parts of games will be common. Analysts estimate that by 2004, 14 percent of online game sales will come from downloads. This will lead to the evolution of new content and business models as gamers pay by monthly subscription or per play for downloads of game demos, updates, and new episodes of continuing stories. Sony is looking to capitalize on broadband by skipping over a dial-up modem and instead including a broadband adapter.

Microsoft's XBox will be a late entrant into the market.[22] Microsoft believes the hard disk and online capabilities of XBox will create opportunities to give games life beyond the retail purchase and open doors for new opportunities in game design. The hard drive is not just a massive memory card on which to store saved games, although it can be utilized for that purpose. The hard drive actually adds additional benefit to the game developers who are seeking new ways to extend the life of their games, whether it is through new downloadable content or on-line multiplayer play.[23]

Licensing

The gaming industry is also leveraging the star power of Hollywood and athletic celebrities to draw people to its games. Such agreements represent enormous branding implications for the celebrities and well as the cable channels bringing them into homes through a new venue. New technological advances to consoles have further enhanced licensing agreements. Madden NFL is one such game that has enjoyed phenomenal success with "real life" stars.

As the game industry booms, franchising is a natural progression, according to Ed Roth of the market research firm NPD Group. "Video games are so engrained in our culture, it makes sense to port successful game concepts to films and other mediums."[24] (Examples of agreements are shown in Exhibit 6.)

TROJAN HORSE: CAPTURING CONVERGENCE

Buzzwords like "convergence," "smart appliances," "set-top boxes," and "interactive TV" continue to take center stage in the media entertainment world. Industry has long waited for real technology to catch up to the vision that consumers will enjoy the combined power of traditional entertainment with the connectivity and information-rich content of the Internet. Given its near ubiquity (see Exhibit 7), many believe that the television should be the default platform of choice. Tasks once confined to the PC, like Web surfing and e-mail, could now be performed from a couch.

Early attempts at this vision were met with poor results. Convergence advocates going back to the days of the Philips CD-I,

Time Warner Full Service Network (the infamous Orlando project), and 3DO multiplayer machines of the early 1990s have argued that the combination of TV and computing will lead to an entirely new, tightly integrated, and highly successful entertainment platform. In fact, none have succeeded, primarily because they could never get their costs down with so many functions.[25] ICTV, for example, was founded in 1990 to develop a proprietary video-on-demand system. "The technology worked, but the business model didn't," says CEO Wes Hoffman. "In 1995, we basically had to restart the company because the Internet had taken hold and moved everything away from proprietary platforms to open standards."[26]

More recent efforts have kept convergence hopes alive. WebTV was launched in 1995 and was sold to Microsoft for $425 million. By 1999, it garnered a subscriber base of approximately 800,000 viewers. According to Steve Perlman, one of the founders of WebTV (who has since left the company), "All televisions will probably be Internet-capable devices within 5 years. The cost is coming down so rapidly that there's no reason for that not to be true."[27] With respect to how consumers' orientation to TV viewing will change, Perlman comments, "Suppose I'm watching a football game—I really want to see the stats that I'm *interested* in seeing. I want to look up related stuff at the same time, and I don't want to be limited to the little stats meter on the side of the screen."[28] Although WebTV and recent entrants such as Phillips-AOLTV can provide these capabilities, their success hinges on the availability of programming content. "If Hollywood and the cable companies don't produce content for the interactive TV," says Sean Kaldor, analyst at IDC, "then there's nothing these companies can do."[29]

Another recent attempt to harness the power of convergence comes in the form of "enhanced TV." Sony itself (and others, notably Phillips and Panasonic) has manufactured a set-top box that uses technology developed by TiVo to create "smart television." By combining television broadcasting (cable, satellite, pay-per-view, or antenna) and digital recording into one box, TiVo technology enables the viewer to control the broadcast experience. Consumers can pause, rewind, and replay LIVE television at the touch of a button. Moreover, TiVo smart technology offers added benefits such as TiVo Suggestions and Wishlist, which can record consumers' favorite programs (without the need to set timers) and make programming suggestions based on viewing patterns.

While the long-term prognosis for media convergence remains strong, its implications for the gaming industry remain unclear. Gaming console manufacturers (Sony, Nmtendo, and Sega) have sold more than 125 million units worldwide, achieving remarkable penetration into consumer households. In addition, given that 91 percent of people who buy a home PC use it to send e-mail, 56 percent to access the Internet, and 58% to play video games,[30] gaming consoles are in a strategic position to offer these services, potentially displacing the traditional computer. As interactive TV and technologies such as TiVo and Replay catch on, PC-like activity will begin to move from the home-office to the living room—exactly where today's gaming consoles exist. Hence the movement toward the manufacturing of next generation consoles, which many claim are essentially PCs in disguise.

While Sony's PS2 is marketed as the future of entertainment in the home, Dean Takahashi of Red Herring takes a different view. "Convergence will arrive, but PS2's success will not hinge on its 'Trojan horse' strategy in 2001," he says. "With high-speed Internet access lagging behind (projected to exist in only 30 percent of U.S. homes by 2008, according to Paul Kagan Associates), and the price-point of stand alone DVD players coming down (below that of PS2),

PlayStation2 will succeed due to Sony's marketing strength, the power of its brand image, and the quality and variety of its games."[31] Moreover, Microsoft's XBox division believes that gaming itself should be the sole purpose of its upcoming XBox machine. "'Convergence is bull#&!," says Seamus Blackley, Director of Advanced Technology for the Xbox.[32] Nintendo backed up this view, as it will not design its next generation console, the GameCube, with the ability to play DVD movies.

Nevertheless, most agree that broadband will arrive, convergence will hit critical mass, and the nature of home computing will forever change. The question no one can answer accurately is, "When and how?"

KUTARAGI'S NEXT STEPS

Ken Kutaragi was brash and confident, but the success of his Trojan Horse strategy would depend on whether he could preempt competitors and build scale with the all-in-one PS2. He knew that forming the right alliance partners would be the key to his and Sony's success. He opened his Roledex and began dialing his phone.

ENDNOTES

1. Summarized from darter.ocps.k12.fl.us/ classroom/who/darterl/trhorse.htm.
2. Li, Kenneth. "Power Player," The Standard, 8/15/00, www.thestandard.com/article/ display/0,1151,17526,00.html.
3. www.playstation2.com/hardware/future/ future/jhtml, 10/26/00.
4. Fields, Jason. "Review: PlayStation 2 Vs. Dreamcast," AP Online, 11/02/00, www.djinteractive.com.
5. "Daily Media Update—Electronic Arts to Develop Games for Microsoft XBox," Dow Jones Business News, 12/13/00, www. djinteractive.com.
6. Li, "Power Player."
7. www.world.sony.com/IR/Financial/index. html.
8. Sony Press Release, "Intel and Sony Team on Connecting PCs and Consumer Electronic Devices in the Home," February 2000.
9. Sony New Release, "Sony Launches Industry's First Direct-View HDTV Set as Portal to Digital Future," September 1998.
10. "Games People Play: The Sony PlayStation Story," NYU Stern Case 982-081, NPD.com Special Report, November 6, 1998.
11. Fields, "Review."
12. "Nintendo Unveils GameCube, New Game Boy," *USA Today,* www.usatoday.com/life/ cyber/tech/review/games/cgg217.htm.
13. "Games People Play: The Sony PlayStation Story," NYU Stern Case 982-081: Sega Company News.
14. Berman, A. S. "Online Pay Still a Dream for Dreamcast," usatoday.com, 11/23/99, www.usatoday.com/life/cyber/tech/review/ crg225.htm.
15. *Ibid.*
16. "SegaNet: Trawling for Online Players," *USA Today,* 9/05/00.
17. Berman, A. S. "Online Play."
18. "Microsoft Talks Xbox, J. Allard, General Manager of XBox, Talks Launch Strategy, Exclusive Games, Broadband, Square, and More." GameSpot VG, 11/22/00, www. zdnet.com/gamespot/stories/news/ 0,10870,2631156,00.html.
19. "Microsoft 'X-Box' Draws Mixed Reaction," *USA Today,* 03/10/00, www.usatoday. com/life/cyber/tech/review/games/cggll49. htm.
20. "Games People Play: The Sony PlayStation Story," NYU Stern Case 982-081: Nintendo Company News.
21. "Nintendo Unveils GameCube, New Game Boy," *USA Today.*
22. "SegaNet: Trawling for Online Players," *USA Today,* 9/05/00.
23. Ajami, Amer, and Kennedy, Sam. "Microsoft Announces X-Box Bill Gates and a Bevy of Third-Party Developers Talk About Microsoft's Entry into the Console Marketplace," GameSpot VG, 03/09/00, www. zdnet.com/gamespot/stories/news/ 0,10870,2541759,00.html.
24. Saltzman, Marc. "Video Games Spur Books, Movies," *USA Today,* 02/03/99,

www.usatoday.com/life/cyber/tech/review/games/cg020.htm.

25. Takahashi, Dean, "Antitrend—Converged Appliances May Beckon and Promise, but They Still Aren't Ready for Prime Time," *Red Herring,* December, 2000, pgs. 167–170.

26. Zerega, Blaise. "Sell a Vision—With Recent Advances, Interactive TV May Finally Be Able to Deliver on Earlier Promises," *Red Herring,* October, 1999, pgs. 144–146.

27. Malony, Janice. "Programming in Perlman," *Red Herring,* October, 1999, pgs. 148–151.

28. Ibid, Malony.

29. Zerega, Blaise. "Sell a Vision."

30. *Source:* Forrester Research. Quoted ftom Craven, Delia, "Playing the PC Game," *Red Herring,* October 1999, pgs. 136–140.

31. Interview conducted with Dean Takahashi, reporter for *Red Herring* magazine, 11/21/00.

32. Takahashi, "Antitrend."

EXHIBIT 1 Comparison of Game Consoles

	Price	Number of Games Available	U.S. Introduction	Central Processing Unit	Video Chip	Total Memory	Expansion/Network Options	DVD
Sony PS2	$299	26 (52 by year-end and plays all 800 PS1 games)	October 2000	295 MHz Sony Proprietary	147 MHz Sony Graphics synthesizer	38 MB	Two USB ports, Firewire port expansion slot, modem enabled	Yes
Nintendo GameCube	N/A	N/A	Autumn 2001	405 MHz PowerPC	203 MHz ATI chip	40 MB	Two serial ports, parallel port, modem enabled	No
Sega Dreamcast	$149	170 (200 by year end)	Current system	200 MHz Hitachi SH-4	NEC Power VR	26 MB	Serial port, modem enabled	No
Microsoft XBox	About $300	About 30 expected	Autumn 2001	733 MHz Intel Pentium III	300 MHz X-Chip by nVidia	64 MB	USB port, Ethernet port, HDTV support	Yes

Source: The New York Times, 10/26/00.

EXHIBIT 2   Sony Divisions

Sony Electronics, Inc.
Sony Electronics manufactures, markets, and sells consumer and professional audio and video equipment, telecommumcation products, computer products, recording media and energy products, semiconductors, and other electronic components. Its Consumer Electronics Group is responsible for manufacturing and marketing the audio-visual product innovations listed above, in addition to products such as home entertainment systems, VAIO PCs and peripherals, cordless telephones, and car stereo products. Sony Electronics also includes a broadcast and professional company and a media and components group.

Source: www.sony.com/SCA/outline/electronics.html.

Sony Computer Entertainment America Inc.
Sony Computer Entertainment America Inc. is a wholly owned subsidiary of Tokyo-based Sony Computer Entertainment. It handles the marketing and distribution of the PlayStation game console in North America, as well as the development and production of software for the PlayStation, the PC, and online markets. Game titles include: NFL GameDay series, Cool Boarders Series, and Everquest.

Source: www.sony.com/SCA/outline/computer.html.

Sony Broadband Entertainment (3 subsidiaries)
Sony Music Entertainment produces, manufactures, distributes, and markets music, video, DVD, and SACD. Its U.S. division includes labels such as American Recordings, Columbia, Epic, and Legacy records, and artists such as Aerosmith, Lauryn Hill, Michael Jackson, Billy Joel, Jennifer Lopez, Ricky Martin, Will Smith, and Bruce Springsteen. Products include CD, CD-ROM, DVD, DVD-ROM, Minidisc, audiocassettes, and videocassettes.

Sony Pictures Entertainment's global operations encompass motion picture production and distribution, television programming and syndication, home video acquisition, operation of studio facilities, development of new entertainment technologies and distribution of filmed entertainment in 67 countries. Also a part of this division is Sony Online Entertainment, which includes TheStation@ Sony.com (a popular online game site), Sony Music Online, SPE Online, and InfoBeat. In addition, SPE owns the Game Show Network, a 24-hour programming service with an extensive library of game shows, as well as new interactlve game shows.

550 Digital Media Ventures was formed to create, incubate, operate, invest in, and acquire digital media companies.

Sources: www.sony.com/SCA/outline/music.html; www.sony.com/SCA/outline/pictures.html; www.sony.com/SCA/outline/corporation.html.

Sony Plaza Public Arcade & Sony Wonder Technology Lab
Sony Wonder Technology Lab, located in New York City, is a free interactive entertainment and educational museum.

Source: www.sony.com/SCA/outline/plaza.html.

Metreon
Metreon is a 350,000 square foot Sony urban entertainment center in San Francisco, which hosts a combination of theatres, IMAX, attractions, restaurants, and shopping.

Source: www.sony.com/SCA/outline/metreon.html.

EXHIBIT 3   Sales Charts

The new console sales charts reveal that Sega's Dreamcast is picking up steam as Shenmue becomes the top-selling console title for the week ending November 11, 2000. Nintendo still holds three of the top four slots while just one PlayStation 2 game makes the cut.

Top-Selling Console Games—All Brands
1. Shenmue—Sega/Dreamcast
2. Pokemon Silver—Nintendo/Game Boy Color
3. Pokemon Gold—Nintendo/Game Boy Color
4. Legend of Zelda: Majora's Mask—Nintendo/Nintendo 64
5. NBA 2K1—Sega/Dreamcast
6. Tony Hawk's Pro Skater 2—Activision/Dreamcast
7. Tony Hawk's Pro Skater 2—Activision/PlayStation
8. The World Is Not Enough—Electronic Arts/Nintendo
9. Madden NFL 2001—Electronic Arts/PlayStation 2
10. Madden NFL 2001—Electronic Arts/PlayStation

Top-Selling Sega Dreamcast Games
1. Shenmue—Sega
2. NBA 2Kl—Sega
3. Tony Hawk's Pro Skater 2—Activition
4. NFL 2Kl—Sega
5. Crazy Taxi—Sega
6. Ready 2 Rumble Round 2—Midway
7. Jet Grind Radio—Sega
8. Tony Hawk's Pro Skater—Crave
9. Quake 3 Arena—Sega
10. Sonic Adventure—Sega

Top-Selling PlayStation 2 Games
1. Madden NFL 2001—Electronic Arts
2. Tekken Tag Tournament—Namco
3. Nascar 2001—Electronic Arts
4. SSX—Electronic Arts
5. NHL 2001—Electronic Arts
6. Summoner—THQ
7. Ready 2 Rumble Round 2—Midway
8. Dead or Alive 2: Hardcore—Tecmo
9. TimeSplitters—Eidos
10. Dynasty Warriors 2—Koei

Top-Selling Nintendo 64 Games
1. Legend of Zelda: Majora's Mask—Nintendo
2. The World Is not Enough—Electronic Arts
3. Hey You Pikachu!—Nintendo
4. Mario Tennis—Nintendo
5. Disney's Tarzan—Activision
6. Madden NFL 2001—Electronic Arts
7. Tony Hawk's Pro Skater—Activision
8. Star Wars: Episode I Racer—Nintendo
9. Star Wars: Rogue Squadron—Nintendo
10. NFL Blitz 2001—Midway

Top-Selling PlayStation Games
1. Tony Hawk's Pro Skater 2—Activision
2. Madden NFL 2001—Electronic Arts
3. Tony Hawk's Pro Skater—Activision
4. NBA Live 2001—Electronic Arts
5. Medal of Honor: Underground—Electronic Arts
6. Spyro: Year of the Dragon—Sony
7. Gran Turismo 2—Sony
8. Dave Mirra Freestyle BMX—Acclaim
9. Driver—Infogrames Entertainment
10. Tekken 3—Namco

Source: www.zdnet.com/gamespot/filters/top/10/0,11997,6014070,00.html.

EXHIBIT 4   **Examples of Gaming Licensing Agreements**

Creator	Licensor	Type	Features
Acclaim	HBO	Boxing	35 renowned boxers. Commentary by Jim Lampley, Larry Merchant, etc.
Codemaster	MTV	"Music Generation"	
Electronic Arts	Warner Brothers	Harry Potter	Games
Electronic Arts Sports	Tiger Woods	Golf	TPC at Summerlin, among others.
ASC Games	Jeff Gordon	Nascar Racing	Reproduces every small detail of racing.
Electronic Arts	James Bond	Secret Agent	Likeness of Pierce Brosnan as James Bond, and Denise Richards as Christmas Jones.

Sources: Gamespot VG 11/20/00, 11/21/00, *USA Today* 2/03/99, 8/20/99,10/24/00.

EXHIBIT 5   **Digital Appliance Penetration in American Households (%)**

Appliances	1992	2000	2008
Color TV	98	99	99
VCR	76	87	91
DVD player	0	15	41
CD player	42	55	59
PC	27	61	77
Digital set-top box	0	11	44
High-speed internet	0	4	30
Digital video recorder	0	1	37

Source: Paul Kagan Associates/4th Wave.

Notes

Chapter 1

1. C. Handy, *The Age of Unreason* (Cambridge, MA: Harvard Business School, 1990).
2. Ibid.
3. Ibid.
4. Ibid.
5. Ibid.
6. Ibid.
7. "Know Your Future," *The Economist,* December 23, 2000. From the special "Survey the Young," 6–9.
8. J. Boyette and H. Conn, *Workplace 2000* (New York, Dutton, 1991).
9. Boyette and Conn, 1991, 44.
10. M. Low and J. MacMillan, "Entrepreneurship: Past Research and Future Challengers," *Journal of Management* 14 (1988): 139–161.
11. The term "network" was added here to anticipate the possibility that the entrepreneur could create a "virtual" organization. This is an organization that employs other organizations, almost exclusively, to carry out the functions that are ordinarily thought of as within the enterprise.
12. H. Stevenson, M. Roberts, and H. Grousbeck, *New Business Ventures and the Entrepreneur* (Homewood, IL: Irwin, 1989).
13. M. Morris and F. Jones, "Entrepreneurship in Established Organizations: The Case of the Public Sector," *Entrepreneurship: Theory and Practice,* 24, 1 (1999): 71–91.
14. W. Baumol, *Business Behavior: Value and Growth* (New York: Harcourt Brace, 1967).
15. J. Carland, F. Hoy, W. Boulton, and J. Carland, "Differentiating Entrepreneurs from Small Business Owners: A Conceptualization," *Academy of Management Review* 9 (1984): 354–359.
16. E. Penrose, *The Theory of the Growth of the Firm* (New York: John Wiley, 1959), especially pp. 56–57. This book was the precursor of the development of the resource-based theory that is the foundation for this text.
17. G. O'Driscoll, K. Holmes, and M. Kirkpatrick, "Who's Free, Who's Not," *Wall Street Journal,* November 1, 2000, A26.
18. M. Jordan, "How One Woman Stormed Vietnam to Realize a Dream," *Wall Street Journal,* May 5, 1994, 1.
19. J. Vitullo-Martin, "Moscow Entrepreneurs Seize Golden Opportunity," *Wall Street Journal,* January 20, 1997, A11.
20. A. Grimes, "A Liberal Entrepreneur Finds Room to Grow; Then Politics Intrude," *Wall Street Journal,* October 5, 2000, A1.
21. T. Richman, "Creators of the New Economy," *Inc.'s The State of Small Business* (1997): 44–48.
22. Ibid.
23. Ibid.
24. In fact, one professor of entrepreneurship referred to the teaching and taking of entrepreneurship courses as oxymoronic—the juxtaposition of two incompatible ideas.
25. Although a case can be made that the origins of the theory can be claimed by E. Penrose in her 1959 book, *The Theory of the Growth of the Firm* (New York: Wiley), it really is not until the mid-1980s that the resource-based theory of sustained competitive advantage began to be explored and developed in management terms. Two particularly salient articles are: J. Barney, "Firm Resources and Sustained Competitive Advantage," *Journal of Management* 17 (1991): 99–120, and K. Conner, "A Historical Comparison of

Resource-based Theory and Five Schools of Thought within Industrial Organization Economics: Do We Have a New Theory of the Firm?" *Journal of Management* 17 (1991): 121–154. Barney and Conner make the initial claim that this theory may supersede others as a theory of the firm.

26. These terms will be defined and their meanings elaborated in the next chapter.

27. Conner, 1991.

28. Rather than repeat the four desirable attributes of resources over and over throughout the book, we will adopt the convention of calling them "the four attributes" of the resource-based model.

29. J. Bain, "Economics of Scale, Concentration, and the Conditions of Entry in Twenty Manufacturing Industries," *American Economic Review* 44 (1954): 15–39; M. Porter, *Competitive Strategy* (New York: Free Press, 1980).

30. W. Gartner, "A Conceptual Framework for Describing the Phenomenon of New Venture Creation," *Academy of Management Review* 10 (1985): 696–706.

31. This brief discussion owes its genesis to Chris Argyris' discussion of the ethics of a consultant in *Intervention Theory and Method: A Behavioral Science View* (Reading, MA: Addison Wesley, 1973).

32. S. Caminiti, "A Payoff from a Good Reputation," *Fortune,* February 10, 1992, pp. 74–77. This is a quote from Laurel Cutler.

33. D. Garvin, *Managing Quality* (New York: Free Press, 1988). See Chapters 3 and 4 for a detailed discussion. This is one of the seminal books that launched the "quality" revolution in the United States.

34. Garvin, 1988, p. 41.

35. Garvin, 1988, p. 43.

Chapter 2

1. J. Barney, "Strategic Factor Markets: Expectations, Luck and Business Strategy," *Management Science* 32 (1986): 1231–1241.

2. Here is a personal example. Two business professors teaching in Hong Kong, one an expert in management, the other in marketing, have endlessly discussed how to make money in China. After all, the rumor is that everyone is getting rich in China and these two professors are smart, talented, and even speak Chinese. But in spite of the myriad of opportunities, they are unable to create a new venture. Why? Because they have no resources and all they know how to do is teach class and write academic papers.

3. Recently a new debate has been opened about whether or not the resource-based view of the firm is a complete theory. See the following for the details:

R. Priem and J. Butler, "Is the Resource-Based 'View' a Useful Perspective for Strategic Management Research?" *Academy of Management Review,* 26 (2001), 1, 22–40; J. Barney, "Is the Resource-Based 'View' a Useful Perspective for Strategic Management Research? Yes." *Academy of Management Review,* 26 (2001), 1, 41–56; R. Priem

and J. Butler, "Tautolgy in the Resource-Based View and the Implications of Externally Determined Resource Value: Further Comments," *Academy of Management Review,* 26 (2001), 1, 57–66.

In fact, this book generally adopts Barney's approach to the problems and issues of entrepreneurship, and although I agree that Priem and Butler's work add to the dialogue, in the end I believe that Barney's arguments carry the day.

4. S. Winter, "Knowledge and Competence in Strategic Assets," in D. Teece, ed., *The Competitive Challenge* (Cambridge, MA: Ballinger, 1987), pp. 159–184.

5. History is often not studied when it comes to the social sciences such as psychology and sociology and even to some extent economics. One of the finest works in management and organization theory is a set of histories by A. Chandler, *Strategy and Structure* (Cambridge, MA: MIT Press, 1962); and entrepreneurial histories abounded as an early form of study. See II. Livesay, "Entrepreneurial History," in C. Kent, D. Sexton, and K. Vesper, eds., *Encyclopedia of Entrepreneurship* (Upper Saddle River, NJ:

Prentice-Hall, 1982). To understand how history and science are related, see any works by Stephen Jay Gould.

6. Barney, 1986.

7. Barney, 1986. Barney also makes a case that "luck" has a much larger role in entrepreneurship and business success in general. This can also explain why there is an incongruence between "rich" and "smart."

8. J. Timmons, *New Venture Creation* (Homewood, IL: Irwin, 1990). Timmons uses these three general criteria for assessing the worthiness of an entrepreneurial effort. We will discuss in more detail the evaluation of business opportunities and business plans in this and later chapters.

9. J. Schumpeter, *Capitalism, Socialism and Democracy,* 3rd ed. (New York: Harper & Row, 1950). Schumpeter first coined this phrase "destructive capitalism" in his description of entrepreneurship as the force that initiates change in capitalistic systems.

10. H. Stevenson, M. Roberts, and I. Grosbeck, *New Business Ventures and the Entrepreneur* (Homewood, IL: Irwin, 1989). Especially Chapter 1.

11. J. Barney, "Firm Resources and Sustained Competitive Advantage," *Journal of Management* 17 (1991): 99–120.

12. See, for example, A. Thompson and A. Strickland, *Strategic Management: Concepts and Cases* (Homewood, IL: Irwin, 1992).

13. Barney, 1991.

14. Barney, 1991.

15. For more on culture and its effects see: C. Enz, *Power and Shared Values in the Corporate Culture* (Ann Arbor, MI: UNI Research Press, 1986); and G. Hofstede, *Culture's Consequences: International Differences in Work-Related Values* (Beverly Hills: Sage Publications, 1984).

16. Barney, 1991.

17. M. Dollinger, P. Golden, and T. Saxton, "The Effects of Reputation on the Decision to Joint Venture," *Strategic Management Journal* (1997) 18, 2, 127–140. See also C. Fombrun and M. Shanley, "What's in a Name? Reputation Building and Corporate Strategy," *Academy of Management Journal* 33 (1990): 233–258.

18. Prahalad and Hamel refer to organizational resources, particularly those that confer strategic advantage on the firm as "core competencies." See C. Prahalad and G. Hamel, "The Core Competencies of the Organization," *Harvard Business Review* (1990), May–June, 79–91.

19. G. Huber, "The Nature and Design of Post-Industrial Organizations," *Management Science* 30 (1984): 929–959. This article takes a futuristic approach to organizational design and is still ahead of its time.

20. Huber, 1984.

21. C. Brush, P. Green, M. Hart, and L. Edelman, "Resource Configurations over the Life Cycle of New Ventures," *Frontiers of Entrepreneurship Research,* 1997 edition, babson.edu/entrep/fer/papers97/brush/bru1.htm.

22. R. Grant, *Contemporary Strategy Analysis* (Cambridge, MA: Blackwell, 1992).

23. J. Freear and W. Wetzel, "The Informal Venture Capital Market in the 1990s," in D. Sexton and J. Kasarda, eds., *The State of the Art of Entrepreneurship* (Boston: PWS-Kent, 1992), pp. 462–486.

24. Grant, 1992.

25. We qualify this a bit when we say, "on a strictly financial basis." Clearly, money raised from organized crime activities is neither morally nor contractually equivalent to a loan from the local commercial bank.

26. G. Markham and R. Baron, "Social Skills and Entrepreneurs' Financial Success: Evidence That the Ability to Get Along with Others Really Matters," *Frontiers of Entrepreneurship Research,* 1998 edition, babson.edu/entrep/fer/papers98/IV/IV_B/IV_B.html.

27. O. Richard, "Racial Diversity, Business Strategy and Firm Performance: A Resource-Based View," *Academy of Management Journal,* 43 (2000), 2, 164–177.

28. Sometimes relational capital is referred to as "networking." For more information, see S. Birley, "The Role of Networks in the Entrepreneurial Process," *Journal of Business Venturing* 2 (1985): 155–165; M. Dollinger and P. Golden, "Interorganizational and Collective Strategies in Small Firms: Environmental Effects and Performance," *Journal of Management* 18 (1992): 696–717.

For alliance information see J. Baum, T. Calabrese, and B. Silverman, "Don't Go It Alone: Alliance Network Composition and Start-Ups' Performance in Canadian Biotechnology," *Strategic Management Journal,* 21, March 2000, 267–294.

For the use of outside consultants, see J. Chrisman and W. McMullan, "A Preliminary Assessment of Outsider Assistance as a Knowledge Resource: The Longer Term Impact of New Venture Counseling," *Entrepreneurship: Theory and Practice* 24 (2000), 3, 37–53.

29. Barney, 1991.
30. J. Carland, F. Hoy, W. Boulton, and J. Carland, "Differentiating Entrepreneurs from Small Business Owners: A Conceptualization," *Academy of Management Review* 9 (1984): 354–359.
31. D. McClelland, *The Achieving Society* (Princeton: D. Van Nostrand, 1961).
32. See R. Brockhaus, "The Psychology of the Entrepreneur," in C. Kent, D. Sexton, and K. Vesper, eds. *Encyclopedia of Entrepreneurship* (Upper Saddle River, NJ: Prentice Hall, 1982), pp. 39–71.
33. J. Rotter, "Generalized Expectancies for Internal Versus External Control of Reinforcement," *Psychological Monographs* 80 (1966): Paper 609.
34. Brockhaus, 1982.
35. R. Brockhaus, "Risk-Taking Propensity of Entrepreneur," *Academy of Management Journal* 23 (1980): 509–520.
36. W. Gartner, "Who Is the Entrepreneur? Is the Wrong Question," *American Journal of Small Business* 12 (1988): 11–32.
37. A. Cole, "Definition of Entrepreneurship," in J. Komives, ed., *Karl A. Bostrum Seminar in the Study of Enterprise* (Milwaukee: Center for Venture Management, 1969), pp. 10–22.
38. A. Shapero and L. Sokol, "The Social Dimensions of Entrepreneurship," in C. Kent, D. Sexton, and K. Vesper, eds., *Encyclopedia of Entrepreneurship* (Upper Saddle River, NJ: Prentice Hall, 1982), pp. 72–90.
39. R. Amit, "'Push' and 'Pull' Entrepreneurs," *Frontiers of Entrepreneurship Research, 1994 edition,* www.babson.edu/entrep/fer/papers94/amit.htm.

40. Professor Pyong Gap Min, quoted in D. Lorch, "Ethnic Niches Creating Jobs That Fuel Immigrant Growth," *New York Times,* January 12, 1992.
41. Based on a story by Timothy Noah that appeared in *The Wall Street Journal,* August 2, 1992.
42. Noah, 1992.
43. Noah, 1992.
44. S. Birley, "The Role of Networks in the Entrepreneurial Process," *Journal of Business Venturing* 1 (1985): 107–118. We will return to this topic in a later chapter.
45. For a discussion of this and other background characteristics, see Chapter 3 of R. Hisrich and M. Peers, *Entrepreneurship* (Homewood, IL: Irwin, 1991).
46. This is not an uncommon situation, but it is a difficult one. Consider the employee (for example, an accountant, salesperson, or consultant) who services a customer who then encourages the employee to go into business for himself. Implicit here is the notion that the customer will switch to the new entrepreneur. This is a common situation. But is it ethical? Does the employee have a responsibility to an employer not to steal the customer? Should the employee report the offer and try to do a better job servicing the customer within the current employment relationship? There is an economic side as well. A firm with a single customer is vulnerable. The customer may feel the entrepreneur is in some way obligated to give the customer the best deal because of the history between them. The new firm's employees will, of course, know the circumstances of their firm's founding and may replicate it when their time comes.
47. Much of the discussion on spin-offs is adapted from D. Garvin, "Spin-Offs and the New Firm Formation," *California Management Review* 25 (1983): 3–20.
48. U. Gupta, "Blending Zen and the Art of Philanthropic Pastry Chefs," *The Wall Street Journal,* January 2, 1992.
49. Shapero and Sokol, 1982.
50. H. Stevenson, M. Roberts, and H. Grousbeck, *New Business Ventures and the Entrepreneur* (Homewood, IL: Irwin, 1989).

Chapter 3

1. The model has antecedents in the work of many industrial organization economists, but it was Michael Porter's book *Competitive Strategy* (New York: Free Press, 1980) that made the analysis compulsory for noneconomics majors in all business schools.

2. L. Fahey and V. K. Narayanan, *Macroenvironmental Analysis for Strategic Management* (St. Paul, MN: West Publishing, 1986).

3. Focus groups are small panels of experts or interested individuals who have special knowledge of the problem at hand.

4. J. Pearce and R. Robinson, *Strategic Management* 4th ed. (Homewood, IL: Irwin, 1991).

5. Fahey and Narayanan, 1986.

6. In a totalitarian state, the property of others can be confiscated by the state by force. We recognize this as immoral, although there may not be much, short of risking life and limb, that an individual can do about it. In a democracy, one group of people can vote itself the rights to the money and economic productivity of another group. Few of us consider this immoral, yet it has the same effect.

7. "Japanese Business Methods," *The Economist,* April 4, 1992, 19–22.

8. This section is largely derived from Fahey and Narayanan, *Macroenvironmental Analysis,* 1986.

9. There is an extensive literature on technological change, technological diffusion and the adoption of innovations, and the role of technology in society. However, these topics are beyond the scope of this book.

10. B. Wattenberg, "America by the Numbers," *The Wall Street Journal,* January 3, 2001, A11.

11. C. Kluckhorn, "Values and Value-Orientation," in T. Parsons and E. Shils, eds., *Toward a General Theory of Action* (Cambridge, MA: Harvard University Press, 1962), 338–433.

12. Distributive justice refers to the desirable distribution of the wealth of society among its members.

13. The World Commission on Environment, 1987.

14. Comments by Frank Popoff, CEO and chairman of Dow Chemical Company, at the Graduate Business Conference, April 3, 1992, Indiana University, Bloomington, Indiana.

15. P. Drucker, *Innovation and Entrepreneurship* (New York: Harper & Row, 1985).

16. Drucker, 1985.

17. Drucker, 1985, 108.

18. The story is an old one and often makes the rounds in graduate economics classes. However, I was reminded of it by reading S. Oster, *Modern Competitive Analysis* (Oxford University Press: New York, 1990).

19. A frequently heard question when challenging a new venture opportunity is: "If this is such a good idea, why has not someone already done it?" As we can see, this is actually an economic question in sheep's clothing. The correct answer to this line of questioning is: "Because no one else has been smart enough, until now."

20. B. Wernerfelt and C. Montgomery, "What Is an Attractive Industry?" *Management Science* 32 (1986): 1223–1230.

21. These three strategies are known as "generic" strategies because other strategies are derivatives of these three. Porter originally argued that a firm must choose to pursue one of the three strategies because the firm could not adhere to more than one strategy within a single market. He called this being "stuck in the middle." Empirical research has demonstrated that sometimes firms can achieve differentiation and the low-cost position simultaneously. C. Hill, "Differentiation Versus Low Cost or Differentiation and Low Cost: A Contingency Framework," *Academy of Management Review* 13 (1988): 401–412; A. Murray, "A Contingency View of Porter's 'Generic Strategies,'" *Academy of Management Review* 13 (1988): 390–400; P. Wright, "A Refinement of Porter's Strategies," *Strategic Management Journal* 9 (1980): 93–101.

22. This is the model developed and popularized by Michael Porter in his two books, *Competitive Strategy* (New York: Free Press, 1980) and *Competitive Advantage* (New York: Free Press, 1985). Although this chapter borrows heavily from these two books

and relates the Porter analysis to the problems of new venture creation, there is really no substitute for reading the originals.

23. Often the argument is offered that quality improvements pay for themselves, either by increasing customer loyalty or increasing customer base. All this may be true if the increased loyalty decreases the price elasticity of demand and the cost increases can be passed on to the new customers.

24. There are some interesting counter-examples, however. When competition heats up in the automobile industry, factory rebates (price concessions from manufacturers) plus the normal bargaining process within the dealerships can produce final sales prices lower than the average variable cost for the combination of manufacturer and dealer. In an overheated housing market, buyers often bid up the price of the house against each other instead of bargaining for lower prices. This can be true even if the supply of houses is greater than the demand. It is the inflationary expectations that drive this process. People feel that the prices will be even higher if they do not buy quickly. Of course, this is a self-fulfilling prophesy for the group of buyers, even if it benefits a particular buyer.

25. This is especially true when a third party is paying for the airline ticket (for example, your employer), but the flyer receives private credit for the miles.

26. Example from Porter, 1980.

27. The presence of entry barriers is prima facie evidence that perfect competition does not exist. But does actual entry have to occur to keep incumbents from earning above-normal returns? It can be argued that the threat of entry is itself sufficient, as long as that entry is relatively costless and irreversible. This is known as the "contestability theory." This theory makes a distinction between competitive markets, where actual entry enforces price discipline, and contestable markets, where the threat of entry enforces discipline even though the industry looks like an oligopoly. See W. Baumol, J. Panzer, and R. Willig, *Contestable Markets and the Theory of Industry Structure* (New York: Harcourt, Brace, Jovanovich, 1982).

28. The general model to determine if entry will be profitable can be written as an equation where the sum of all future discounted cash flows from the new venture is set against the sum of the direct investment attributable to the new venture, plus the sum of the expenses related to overcoming the structural barriers, plus the sum of the expenses related to retaliation costs (such as price concessions, marketing and legal expenses). All too often entrepreneurs make their calculations and include only the direct investment costs (property, plant equipment, and initial organization costs). An opportunity that looks profitable based on direct costs might not be profitable when the barrier and retaliation costs are factored in.

29. Exit barriers are those structural impediments that prevent inefficient firms from leaving an industry even when the firms are unprofitable and have little prospect of achieving profitability. Examples of exit barriers are psychological commitment by the firm's owners, specialized assets, fixed costs of exit (e.g., labor agreements), and government policy (e.g., Chrysler and Lockheed in the United States).

30. Porter, 1980, 18–20.

31. The Federal Trade Commission maintains a classification scheme for all businesses known as the Standard Industrial Classification code, or SIC code for short. All products and services are assigned codes that range from two to seven digits. Two- and three-digit SIC codes are too broad and general to identify competitors, and five-through seven-digit codes may be too narrow. The four-digit SIC code is the generally accepted level for current and potential competitor analysis.

32. See Chapter 2 for complete definitions and descriptions of the resources and their attributes.

33. Included in the general term *strategy* here would be such elements as the firm's goals and future goals, its assumptions about itself and its industry, and its own assessment of its strengths and weaknesses.

Chapter 4

1. Quoted in A. Deutschman, "America's Fastest-Growing Companies," *Fortune,* October 5, 1992, 58–82.
2. There are a number of fine textbooks on the subject of strategic management. The following list is not meant to be complete or exclusive: G. Dess and A. Miller, *Strategic Management* (New York: McGraw-Hill, 1993); H. Mintzberg and J. Quinn, *The Strategy Process* (Upper Saddle River, NJ: Prentice Hall, 1991); Pearce and R. Robinson, *Strategic Management: Formulation, Implementation and Control* (Homewood, IL: Irwin, 1992); A. Thompson and A. Strickland, *Strategic Management: Text and Cases* (Homewood, IL: Irwin, 1992).
3. D. Hambrick, "Some Tests of the Effectiveness of Functional Attributes of Miles and Snow's Strategic Types," *Academy of Management Journal* 26 (1983): 5–26.
4. The original concept and description of entry wedges was developed by Karl Vesper in *New Venture Strategies* (Upper Saddle River, NJ: Prentice Hall, 1980). Revised 1990.
5. Vesper, 1980.
6. P. Drucker, *Innovation and Entrepreneurship* (New York: Harper and Row, 1985).
7. Drucker, 1985.
8. R. Berner, "Kissing Off the Cosmetics Counter," *Business Week,* October 30, 2000, 108–112.
9. S. Winter, "Knowledge and Competence as Strategic Assets," in D. Teece, ed., *The Competitive Challenge* (Cambridge, MA: Ballinger, 1988), pp. 159–184.
10. Winter, 1988. Winter provides an example that some readers may relate to. A brain-damaged man may retain the ability to play golf and hit a one-iron a good distance and in the desired direction. This type of competency cannot be easily transferred by any known method of communication. However, if the damage is to the part of the brain that process declarative information, the man might not recall where the ball landed or be able to keep track of his score.
11. J. Emshwiller, "Federal Research Labs Can Help Small Firms Compete," *The Wall Street Journal,* December 9, 1992, B2.
12. M. Wright, R. Hoskisson, and L. Busenitz, "Entrepreneurial Growth Through Privatizations: The Upside of Management Buyouts." *Academy of Management Review* (2000): 25, 3, 591–601.
13. S. Walsh and B. Kirchoff, "Can Entrepreneurial Core Competencies and Capabilities Overcome Poor Strategy?" *Frontiers of Entrepreneurial Research* (1998); online at babson.edu/entrep/fer/.
14. J. Mahoney and J. Pandian, "The Resource-Based View Within the Conversation of Strategic Management," *Strategic Management Journal* 13 (1992): 363–380.
15. These rewards can rightly be characterized and defined as entrepreneurial rents, the difference between a venture's *ex ante* cost (or value) of the resources combined to form the venture. See R. Rumelt, "Theory, Strategy and Entrepreneurship," in D. Teece, ed., *The Competitive Challenge* (Cambridge, MA: Ballinger, 1988), pp. 137–158.
16. J. Doh, "Entrepreneurial Privatization Strategies: Order of Entry and Local Partner Collaboration as Sources of Competitive Advantage," *Academy of Management Review* (2000): 25, 3, 551–571.
17. M. Lieberman and D. Montgomery, "First-Mover Advantages," *Strategic Management Journal* 9 (1988): 41–58.
18. Winter, 1987.
19. Winter, 1987.
20. Lieberman and Montgomery, 1988; R. Rumelt, "Theory, Strategy and Entrepreneurship," in D. Teece, ed., *Competitive Strategic Management,* (Upper Saddle River, NJ: Prentice Hall, 1988), pp. 556–570.
21. This section follows Mahoney and Pandian, 1992.
22. Quoted in Mahoney and Pandian, 1992, from W. Starbuck, "Organizational Growth and Development," in *Handbook of Organization,* J. March, ed. (Chicago: Rand McNally, 1985), 451–533.

23. E. Penrose. *The Theory of the Growth of the Firm* (New York: John Wiley, 1959).

24. "Special Report: Quality," *Business Week,* November 30, 1992, 66–75.

25. W. Deming, "The Roots of Quality Control in Japan," *Pacific Basin Quarterly* (Spring 1985): 3–4.

26. D. Garvin, *Managing Quality* (New York: Free Press, 1988).

27. This study was conducted over a 3-year period by Ernst & Young and the American Quality Foundation. Five hundred and eight firms participated. The findings reported here are taken from two secondary sources: *Business Week,* November 30, 1992, and *The Wall Street Journal,* October 1, 1992.

28. S. Birley and P. Westhead, "Growth and Performance Contrasts Between 'Types' of Small Firms," *Strategic Management Journal* 11 (1990): 535–557.

29. For example, the production function or product life cycle curve.

30. M. Porter, *Competitive Strategy* (New York: Free Press, 1980). See Chapter 10.

31. Drucker, 1985. The following examples are from Chapter 19.

32. C. Schoonhoven, E. Eisenhardt, and K. Lyon, "Speeding Products to Market: Waiting Time and First Product Introductions in New Firms," *Administrative Science Quarterly* 35 (1990): 177–207; L. Bourgeois and K. Eisenhardt, "Strategic Decision Processes in High-Velocity Environment: Four Cases in the Microcomputer Industry," *Management Science* 34 (1988): 816–835.

33. M. Werner, "Planning for Uncertain Futures: Building Commitment Through Scenario Planning," *Business Horizons* (May–June, 1990): 55–58.

34. In the short run, firms can survive if price is less than average *variable* cost, but in the long run, negative contribution margins cannot be sustained. In the long run, price must be sufficient to cover average *total* costs.

35. J. Martin, M. Feldman, M. Hatch, and S. Sitkin, "The Uniqueness Paradox in Organizational Stories," *Administrative Science Quarterly* 28 (1983): 438–453.

36. C. Baden-Fuller and J. Stopford, *Rejuvenating the Mature Business* (London: Routledge, 1992).

37. Porter, 1980.

38. Adapted from W. Bulkeley, "Maturing Market: Computer Startups Grow Increasingly Rare," *The Wall Street Journal,* September 8, 1989, 1, 16.

39. Bulkeley, 1989.

40. M. Porter, "How to Attack the Industry Leader," *Fortune,* April 29, 1985, 153–166.

41. M. Selz, "Small Companies Thrive by Taking Over Some Specialized Tasks for Big Concerns," *The Wall Street Journal,* September 11, 1992, B1–2.

42. Porter, 1980, Chapter 12.

43. E. Welles, "Least Likely to Succeed," *Inc.,* December 1992, 74–86.

44. Porter, 1980, Chapter 9.

45. These examples are from Porter, 1980.

46. S. Galante, "Venture Firms Are Foraying into Fragmented Industries," *The Wall Street Journal,* October 6, 1986.

47. R. Grant, "The Resource-Based Theory of Competitive Advantage: Implications for Strategy Formulation," *California Management Review* 34 (Spring, 1991): 114–135.

48. These capabilities have, at various times, been described as "distinctive competencies" or "core competencies" by other authors. See C. Snow and L. Hrebiniak, "Strategy, Distinctive Competence and Organizational Performance," *Administrative Science Quarterly* 25 (1990): 317–336; C. Prahalad and G. Hamel, "The Core Competence of the Corporation," *Harvard Business Review,* May–June (1990): 79–91.

49. R. Rumelt, "Evaluation of Strategy," *Strategic Management,* D. Schendel and C. Hofer, ed. (Boston: Little, Brown, 1979), pp. 196–210.

Chapter 5

1. Of course, the formulation of a new venture plan and the implementation of that plan frequently do not proceed consecutively. There usually is considerable overlap. Just the act of collecting information often puts the prospective entrepreneur in contact with other businesspeople, creating the network for the new venture, a process that could be

considered implementation. Thus it is merely a simplifying convenience to divide analysis from action.

2. N. Carter, W. Gartner, and P. Reynolds, "Exploring Start-Up Event Sequences," *Frontiers of Entrepreneurial Research,* 1995 abstracts; online at www/babson.edu/entrep/fer.

3. R. Hisrich and M. Peters, *Entrepreneurship* (Homewood, IL: Irwin, 1992). Chapter 5.

4. K. Andrews, *The Concept of Corporate Strategy* (Upper Saddle River, NJ: Prentice Hall, 1980).

5. A. Cooper, C. Woo, and W. Dunkelberg, "Entrepreneur Perceived Chances for Success," *Journal of Business Venturing* 3 (Spring 1989): 97–108.

6. The concept of "full material disclosure" is a legal one. It means that, since others rely on the document for information regarding the business's prospects, these others are entitled to the full facts as they are known to the entrepreneur, or as they should be known to a reasonable person.

7. C. Bamford, T. Dean, and P. McDougall, "Initial Strategies and New Venture Growth: An Examination of the Effectiveness of Broad Versus Narrow Breadth Strategies," *Frontiers of Entrepreneurial Research,* 1997; online at www.babson.edu/entrep/fer/papers97/bamford/bam.htm. G. Hills, and R. Schrader, "Successful Entrepreneurial Insights into Opportunity Recognition," *Frontiers of Entrepreneurial Research,* 1998; online at www.babson.edu/entrep/fer.

8. C. Schwenk and C. Shrader, "The Effects of Formal Strategic Planning on Financial Performance in Small Firms: A Meta-analysis," *Entrepreneurship: Theory and Practice* 17 (Spring 1993): 53–64. A meta-analysis is a statistical analysis of a group of other research reports. It is, therefore, a study of studies. Also, a recent study showed that for young, new firms, planning that involves financial projections was positively related to both profits and financial strength. G. Lumpkin, R. Schrader, and G. Hills, "Does Formal Planning Enhance the Performance of New Ventures?" *Frontiers of Entrepreneurial Research,* 1998; online at www.babson.edu/entrep/fer.

9. K. Vesper, *New Venture Mechanics* (Upper Saddle River, NJ: Prentice Hall, 1993), 330.

10. D. Shepard, "New Venture Entry Strategy: An Analysis of Venture Capital Decision Making," *Frontiers of Entrepreneurial Research,* 1997; online at www.babson.edu/entrep/fer.

11. For a book-length treatment of the essentials of the business plan, see S. Rich and D. Gumpert, *Business Plans That Win $$$* (New York: Harper and Row, 1987); and David Gladstone, *Venture Capital Handbook* (Upper Saddle River, NJ: Prentice Hall, 1988). For a detailed outline in article form, see W. K. Schilit, "How to Write a Winning Business Plan," *Business Horizons* (July–August, 1987): 13–22.

12. See Chapter 10 of Vesper, 1993.

13. Vesper, 1993.

14. The summary outline presented here is adapted from Gladstone, 1988, 26–27.

15. When talking about an accounting concept like gross margin, we need to remember that the terms *high* and *low* are relative to what is achieved (and achievable) by the other firms in the industry.

16. Total quality management is a system of organizing that emphasizes benchmarking (determining the ideal levels of achievable quality), teamwork and participation, and the dedication of the company to continuous and ceaseless improvement of product and service quality. It is embodied in the work of W. Edwards Deming, the American productivity expert who introduced the system to Japanese industry after World War II. See Chapter 4.

17. Some venture capitalists believe that the deal structure is their particular field of expertise and that the business plan should not contain a specific structure. If the venture capitalist is interested in the proposal, they will offer the deal they want. It can be argued that the entrepreneur is the one who has something to sell (equity in the new venture) and, as the seller, has the obligation to set the initial price.

18. The term *unit* is used because sometimes shares are combined with various other rights, such as warrants or options.

19. Dilution refers to the phenomenon that occurs immediately after the financing. The new investor's shares are diluted after the offering when the new investor has paid more than the average price paid by the founders. This is the usual case. Dilution will be covered in Chapter 8.
20. Adapted from Schilit, 1987, 13–22.
21. See Chapter 4 of Gladstone, 1988.

22. Rich and Gumpert, 1987.
23. Vesper, 1993.
24. Excerpted from E. Roberts, "Business Planning in the Start-up High-Tech Enterprise," in *Frontiers of Entrepreneurship Research,* ed. R. Hornaday (Wellesley, MA: Babson College, 1983), 107.
25. Roberts, 1983.

Chapter 6

1. D. K. Berman, "Get Me Rewrite," *Business Week e.biz,* November 20, 2000, EB 12.
2. *Computer Industry Almanac,* published in *The Wall Street Journal, Special Section on World Business,* September 25, 2000, R 6.
3. *Ibid.*
4. *Ibid.*
5. M. Mandel and R. Hof, "Rethinking the Internet," *Business Week,* March 26, 2001, 117–122.
6. Data reported in *Business Week e.biz,* April 16, 2001, 4.
7. A. Harmon, "C.E.O. ROUND TABLE; When That Corner Office Is Also a Dorm Room," *The New York Times Business Section,* October 22, 2000, 1, 12–14.
8. "After the Party," *The Economist,* October 14, 2000, 82.
9. "The E.Biz 25," *Business Week e.biz,* May 14, 2001, 24–60.
10. T. Mullaney, "Gone But Not Forgotten," *Business Week e.biz,* January 22, 2001, 14–16.
11. "Fallen Stars," *The Wall Street Journal,* April 15, 2001, 11.
12. For example, *Fortune,* January 22, 2001, 33.
13. A. Weintraub, "Dead Letter?" *Business Week e.biz,* October 23, 2000, 82, 84; Web sites for the two companies are www.stamps.com and www.e-stamp.com.
14. M. Schrage, "Getting Beyond the Innovation Fetish," *Fortune,* November 13, 2000, 225–232.
15. D. Little, "Incubator—or Incinerator?" *Business Week e.biz,* October 23, 2000, 112–116.
16. F. Keenan, "Warehouse Trouble," *Business Week e.biz,* November 20, 2000, 124–126.
17. Primus. September 2000 survey of 502 online shoppers. Reported in *Business Week e.biz,* October 23, 2000, 50.

18. D. Berman, "What's the Trick," *Business Week e.biz,* July 24, 2000, 87–90.
19. J. Hechinger, "Campus Venture Capitalists Learn About Hubris," *The Wall Street Journal,* April 30, 2001, C 1.
20. R. Ho, "Online Auction Start-Up Auctiva Stirs eBay's Wrath," *The Wall Street Journal,* October 24, 2000, B2.
21. T. Weber, "Intangibles Are Tough to Value, But the Payoff Matters in the Dot-Com Era," *The Wall Street Journal,* May 14, 2001, B1; the Web site is www.pl-x.com.
22. A. Weintraub, "E-Assets for Sale—Dirt Cheap," *Business Week e.biz,* May 14, 2001, 20–22.
23. C. Shapiro and H. Varian, *Information Rules: A Strategic Guide to the Network Economy* (Harvard Business School Press, Boston, Mass.: 1999); a Web site with chapter summaries and PowerPoint slides is available at www.inforules.com.
24. For more see "Market for Ideas," *The Economist,* April 14, 2001, 72.
25. Shapero and Varian, *Information Rules,* 102.
26. *Ibid.,* 117.
27. E. Neuborne, "Bridging the Loyalty Gap," *Business Week e.biz,* January 22, 2001, 10.
28. Shapero and Varian, *Information Rules,* 174.
29. R. O. Crocket, "Penny Pincher's Paradise," *Business Week e.biz,* January 22, 2001, 12.
30. E. Neuborne, "No Buy? Then Bye-Bye," *Business Week e.biz,* April 16, 2001, 6.
31. C. Fox, "E-Commerce Business Models." Online paper presented at www.chrisfoxinc.com/eCommerceBusinessModels.htm.
32. P. Elstrom, "It Ain't Over 'Til It's Over," *Business Week e.biz,* November 20, 2000, 108–110.

33. These numbers are estimates from the following sources: *Business Week e.biz,* October 23, 2000, 106 (data from Goldman Sachs), Chris Fox, "E-Commerce Business Models." Online paper presented at www.chrisfoxinc.com/eCommerceBusiness Models.htm, and D. Blackmon, "Where the Money Is," *The Wall Street Journal,* April 17, 2000, R30.

34. D. Leonhardt, "Business Links on the Web Raise Antitrust Issues," *The New York Times,* July 7, 2000, online article.

35. J. Anders, "Yesterday's Darlings," *The Wall Street Journal,* October 23, 2000, R8.

36. J. Kerstetter, "A Fruitful Relationship," *Business Week e.biz,* November 20, 2000, 93–96.

37. D. Rocks, "Maitre d' Online," *Business Week e.biz,* July 24, 2000, 59–60.

38. A. Weintraub, "Getting You Out of Gridlock," *Business Week e.biz,* November 20, 2000, 73–76.

39. R. Hof, "Those Mighty Mini-Dots," *Business Week e.biz,* February 19, 2001, 56.

40. *Ibid.*

41. M. Williams, "A New Chapter," *The Wall Street Journal,* February 12, 2001, R32.

42. S. Hwang, "Clicks and Bricks," *The Wall Street Journal,* April 17, 2000, R 8.

43. *Ibid.*

44. B. Tedeschi, "E-Commerce Report: An Online Vintage, Still Unproved," *The New York Times,* May 7, 2001; www.nytimes.com/2001/05/07/technology/07ecommerce.html.

45. N. Wingfield, "Webzines Join Forces to Survive Net Shakeout," *The Wall Street Journal,* July 10, 2000, B 1.

46. H. Green and B. Elgin, "Do E-Ads Have a Future?" *Business Week e.biz,* January 22, 2001, 46–51.

47. "Banner Ad Blues," *The Economist,* February 24, 2001, 63–64.

48. *Ibid.*

49. Green and Elgin, 48–49.

50. R. J. Samuelson, "The Internet Predicament," *Newsweek,* February 26, 2001, 49.

51. "Web Sites Going Free-to-Fee," CNNfn Online, May 7, 2000. Web site not archived.

52. *Ibid.*

53. *Ibid.*

54. "Easy.Com, Easy.Go," *The Economist,* April 14, 2001, 61.

55. J. Useem, "Dot-Coms: What Have We Learned?" *Fortune,* October 30, 2000, 82–104.

Chapter 7

1. *The Wall Street Journal,* October 16, 1992, R7.

2. For example, the lessons of portfolio theory require a portfolio to exist. For many entrepreneurs, their business is their major, if not only, asset. Similarly, many of the assumptions of the capital asset pricing model do not hold for small, new, privately held firms.

3. This is for firms with total investments under $10 million. U.S. Bureau of the Census, *Quarterly Financial Report: Manufacturing, Mining and Trade Corporations, 4th Quarter, 1983,* 65, 130, 135 (Washington, DC: Government Printing Office, 1984).

4. This section follows Chapter 6 of E. Walker and J. Petty, *Financial Management of the Small Firm,* 2nd ed. (Upper Saddle River, NJ: Prentice Hall, 1986).

5. Adapted from R. Owen, D. Garner, and D. Bonder, *Arthur Young Guide to Financing for Growth* (New York: John Wiley, 1986), 231–233.

6. In addition to the previously mentioned books by Walker and Petty, 1986; and Owen, Garner, and Bonder, 1986; see B. Mavrovitis, *Cashflow, Credit and Collection* (Chicago: Probus, 1990); L. Masonson, *Cash, Cash, Cash* (New York: Harper, 1990); and Chapter 5 of B. Blechman and J. Levinson, *Guerrilla Financing* (New York: Houghton-Mifflin, 1991).

7. This refers to the relationship of short-term rates to long-term rates. A "normal" structure has short-term rates lower than long-term rates to account for the extra risk of distant time. Sometimes short-term rates are higher than long term, indicating a severe contraction in the money supply in the economy. In this case, borrowers will prefer

long-term money. Sometimes the gap between the long-term and short-term rates is
too large. In this case no one will want to
borrow long-term money, preferring a series
of short-term loans.

8. Jill Andresky Fraser, "Capital Steps," *Inc.,*
February, 1996, 42–47.

9. J. Timmons and H. Sapienza, "Venture
Capital: The Decade Ahead," in *The State of
the Art of Entrepreneurship,* eds. D. Sexton
and J. Kasarda (Boston: PWS-Kent, 1992),
pp. 402–437.

10. The state laws are known as blue sky laws.
The federal laws are primarily those of the
U.S. Securities and Exchange Commission
(SEC) that regulate private offerings. It is
imperative that any entrepreneur navigate
these waters with the aid of experienced
legal counsel.

11. Freear and Wetzel, 1992.

12. H. Stevenson, M. Roberts, and I. Grousbeck,
New Business Ventures and the Entrepreneur
(Homewood, IL: Irwin, 1989).

13. W. Bygrave, "Venture Capital Returns in the
1980s," in *The State of the Art of Entrepreneurship,* eds. D. Sexton and J. Kasarda
(Boston: PWS-Kent, 1992), pp. 438–461.

14. Timmons and Sapienza, 1992. An excellent
analysis of the venture capital industry.

15. Venture Capital Survey, Fourth Quarter
2000; online at wwwdyn.mercurycenter.com/
business/moneytree/report1.cfm.

16. Thus the epithet "vulture capitalist" when
the investors leave only bare bones of the
firm for the original entrepreneurs.

17. J. Emory, "The Value of Marketability as Illustrated in Initial Public Offerings of Common Stock," *Business Valuation Review*
(December 1990), 114–116.

18. E. Carlson, "SBA Introduces Its 'Micro
loan' Program," *The Wall Street Journal,*
June 6, 1992, B2.

19. L. Touby, "The New Bankrolls Behind
Women's Businesses," *Business Week,* September 21, 1992.

20. Adapted from J. Timmons, *New Venture
Creation,* 3rd ed. (Homewood, IL: Irwin,
1990).

21. Adapted from Robert A. Mamis, "Can Your
Bank Do This?" *Inc.,* March 1996, pp. 29–38.

22. L. Berton, "Asset-Backed Loans Aid Cash-
strapped Entrepreneurs," *The Wall Street
Journal,* November 28, 1989, B2.

23. In Chapter 5, we suggested that unless there
were good business reasons, a valuation
could be calculated at the end of a 5-year
period of projections.

24. They may also be bargaining over a host of
other issues. These will be discussed in the
next chapter.

25. Of course, historical returns are no indication of future returns. This is boilerplate language that all who solicit investments must
use. However, statistically, the best prediction of future returns is past returns. This
may be a misuse of statistics, however.

26. The government (taxes) is paid first, then
employees. Creditors are paid next, followed by equity investors, first preferred
stockholders, then common stockholders.

27. Arbitrage occurs when an asset (or business) has different prices in different markets. For example, a stock can be selling, for
a very short period of time because of the
speed of information, more in Tokyo than in
London. Why? Because news affecting earnings (in this case positively) is released in
Tokyo first (because of the time difference).
An arbitrageur can profit briefly by buying
the stock in London and selling it in Tokyo.
Because the price difference will be small
and the window of opportunity brief, in order to make money only very large transactions make sense.

28. This discussion follows Stevenson, Roberts,
Grousbeck, 1989.

29. This is how Thomas Parkinson of Northwestern University's entrepreneurship program describes it to his students.

30. A "pure play" is a firm that is undiversified
and operates in a single line of business. Because most new ventures operate as pure
plays, but few ongoing larger firms do, it is
difficult to get comparable capitalization
rates.

31. Of course, the actual amount of equity the
investor will own is subject to negotiation
and many other variables. These will be discussed in the next chapter. This example is
simplified for computation purposes.

Chapter 8

1. H. Stevenson, M. Roberts, and I. Grosbeck, *New Business Ventures and the Entrepreneur,* 3rd ed. (Homewood, IL: Irwin, 1989). See Chapter 6.

2. This follows Stevenson et al., 1989.

3. This follows J. Timmons, *New Venture Creation* (Homewood, IL: Irwin, 1990).

4. N. Heikens, "Software Firm Bets Future on Artificial Intelligence," *Indianapolis Business Journal,* October 11–18, 1993 and A. J. Schneider, "CID Cashes In Again; New Firm Goes Public," *Indianapolis Business Journal,* March 27–April 2, 1995.

5. Data from "Venture Economics," *Business-Week e.biz,* February 19, 2001, 28

6. These are based on the research of T. Tyebjee and A. Bruno, "A Model of Venture Capitalist Investment Activity," *Management Science* 30, no. 9 (1984): 1051–1066. Others have confirmed these findings, most notably: I. Macmillan, R. Siegal, and P. N. Subba-Narasimha, "Criteria Used by Venture Capitalists to Evaluate New Venture Proposals," *Journal of Business Venturing* 1 (1985): 119–128; W. Sandberg, D. Schweiger, and C. Hofer, "The Use of Verbal Protocols in Determining Venture Capitalists' Decision Processes," *Entrepreneurship: Theory and Practice* 13, no. 2 (1988): 8–20; R. Hisrich and A. Jankowicz, "Intuition in Venture Capital Decisions: An Exploratory Study," *Journal of Business Venturing* 5 (1990): 49–62.

7. R. Hisrich and A. Jankowicz, 1990. In a study employing a small sample, it was found that management was the most important of three factors. The others were opportunity and return.

8. See Chapter 3 of R. Alterowitz and J. Zonderman, *New Corporate Ventures* (New York: John Wiley, 1988).

9. Timmons, 1990.

10. Adapted from V. Fried and R. Hisrich, "Venture Capital Research: Past, Present and Future," *Entrepreneurship: Theory and Practice* 13, no. 1 (1988): 15–28.

11. L. Bransten, "Venture Capitalists Find Cash, But Few Great Ideas," *The Wall Street Journal,* October 22, 2000, C 18.

12. The most comprehensive directory is *Pratt's Guide to Venture Capital Sources* 13th ed., J. Morris and S. Isenstein, eds. (Needham, MA: Venture Economics, 1989).

13. Timmons, 1990.

14. This section follows H. Hoffman and J. Blakey, "You Can Negotiate with Venture Capitalists," *Harvard Business Review* 65, no. 2 (1987): 7–11.

15. H. Landstron, S. W. Manigart, C. Mason, and H. Sapienza, "Contracts Between Entrepreneurs and Investors: Terms and Negotiation Processes," *Frontiers of Entrepreneurship Research 1998;* online at: www.babson.edu/entrep/fer/papers98/XX/XX_C/XX_C.html.

16. This example was suggested by Stevenson et al., 1989.

17. Bank lending on cash flow is improbable without collateral, a guarantor, or a relative on the bank's board of directors. Therefore, this example should be considered hypothetical.

18. D. Moesel, J. Fiet, L. Busenitz, and J. Barney, "Factors Underlying Changes in Risk Perceptions of New Ventures by Venture Capitalists," *Frontiers of Entrepreneurship Research 1996;* online at www.babson.edu/entrep/fer/papers96/moesel/.

19. To see this, discount the total cash flow line by 50 percent. This figure is approximately $2,510,000. Divide the $2 million needed by this figure for 79.9 percent.

20. The source of this example is W. Sahlman, "Aspects of Financial Contracting," *Journal of Applied Corporate Finance* (1988): 25–36.

21. This example follows the one provided in the Duncan Field case (9-392-137) by R. O. von Werssosetz and H. I. Grousbeck, and accompanying Teaching Note (5-385-074) by M. Roberts, 1982 (Cambridge, MA: Harvard Business School).

22. R. Hisrich and M. Peters, *Entrepreneurship,* 2nd ed. (Homewood, IL: Irwin, 1992).

23. Adapted from www.hia.com/llcweb/ll-struc.html. "LLC vs. Corporation vs. Partnership vs. Sole Proprietorship; What Are They and How Do They Differ?" April 3, 1997.

24. Stevenson, et al., 1989.

25. As used in Section 2(15)(ii) of the Securities Act of 1933 shall include the following persons:

    (a) Any savings and loan association or other institution specified in Section 3(a)(5)(A) of the Act whether acting in its individual or fiduciary capacity; any broker or dealer registered pursuant to Section 15 of the Securities and Exchange Act of 1934; any plan established and maintained by a state or its political subdivisions, or any agency or instrumentality of a state or its political subdivisions, for the benefit of its employees, if such plan has total assets in excess of $5 million; any employee benefit plan within the meaning of Title I of the Employee Retirement Income Security Act of 1974, if the investment decision is made by a plan fiduciary, as defined in Section 3(21) of such Act, which is a savings and loan association, or if the employee benefit plan has assets in excess of $5 million or, if a self-directed plan, with investment decisions made solely by persons that are accredited investors;

    (b) Any private business development company as defined in Section 202(a)(22) of the Investment Advisers Act of 1940;

    (c) Any organization described in Section 501(c)(3) of the Internal Revenue Code, corporation, Massachusetts or similar business trust, or partnership not formed for the specific purpose of acquiring the securities offered, with total assets in excess of $5 million;

    (d) Any director, executive officer, or general partner if the issuer of the securities being offered or sold, or any director, executive officer, or general partner of the issuer;

    (e) Any natural person whose individual net worth, or joint net worth with that person's spouse, at the time of the purchase exceeds $1 million;

    (f) Any natural person who had an individual income in excess of $200,000 in each of the two most recent years or joint income with that person's spouse in excess of $300,000 in each of those years and has a reasonable expectation of reaching the same income level on the current year;

    (g) Any trust, with total assets in excess of $5 million, not formed for the specific purpose of acquiring the securities offered, whose purchase is directed by a sophisticated person as described in Rule 506(b)(2)(ii); and

    (h) Any entity in which all of the equity owners are accredited investors.

26. These observations are from comments made by Stephen J. Hackman, Esq. in a talk entitled, "Financing Entrepreneurial Ventures," at the Indiana Entrepreneurial Educational Conference, Indianapolis, Indiana, March 1, 1991.

27. See E. Altman, R. Haldeman, and P. Narayanan, "ZETA-Analysis: A New Model to Identify Bankruptcy Risk," *Journal of Banking and Finance* (June 1977): 29–54.

Chapter 9

1. J. C. Collins and J. I. Porras, *Built to Last: Successful Habits of Visionary Companies* (HarperBusiness: New York, 1997).

2. R. S. Kaplan and D. P. Norton, *The Balanced Scorecard: Translating Strategy into Action* (Harvard Business School Press: Boston, 1996).

3. B. Virany and M. Tushman, "Top Management Teams and Corporate Success in an Emerging Industry," *Journal of Business Venturing* 1 (1986): 261–274.

4. T. Tyebjee and A. Bruno, "A Model of Venture Capitalist Investment Activity," *Management Science* 30, no. 9 (September 1984): 1051–1066.

5. B. Bird, *Entrepreneurial Behavior* (Glenview, IL: Scott, Foresman, 1989).

6. A. McCarthy, D. Krueger, and T. Schoenecker, "Changes in Time Allocation Patterns of Entrepreneurs," *Entrepreneurship: Theory and Practice* 15 (1990): 7–18.

7. D. Norburn and S. Birley, "The Top Management Team and Corporate Performance," *Strategic Management Journal* 9 (1988): 225–237.

8. K. Andrews. *The Concept of Corporate Strategy* (Upper Saddle River, NJ: Prentice Hall, 1980).

9. J. Katzenbach and D. Smith, "The Discipline of Teams," *Harvard Business Review* (March–April 1993): 111–120.

10. Katzenbach and Smith, 1993.

11. J. Kamm and A. Nurick, "The Stages of Team Venture Formation: A Decision-Making Model," *Entrepreneurship: Theory and Practice* 17 (1993): 17–27.

12. See M. Wiersema and K. Bantel, "Top Management Team Demography and Corporate Strategic Change," *Academy of Management Journal* 35 (1992): 91–121; and K. Bantel and S. Jackson, "Top Management and Innovations in Banking: Does Composition of the Top Team Make a Difference?" *Strategic Management Journal* 10 (1989): 107–124.

13. S. Finkelstein and D. Hambrick, "Top Management Team Tenure and Organizational Outcomes: The Moderating Role of Managerial Discretion," *Administrative Science Quarterly* 35 (1990): 484–503.

14. Kamm and Nurick, 1993.

15. A. Murray, "Top Management Group Heterogeneity and Firm Performance," *Strategic Management Journal* 10 (1989): 125–141.

16. "The Melting Pot Bubbles Less," *The Economist,* August 7, 1993, 69.

17. W. Watson, K. Kumar, and L. Michaelsen, "Cultural Diversity's Impact on Interaction Process and Performance Comparing Homogeneous and Diverse Task Groups," *Academy of Management Journal* 36 (1993): 590–602.

18. "The Melting Pot Bubbles Less," *The Economist.*

19. *Ibid.*

20. J. Timmons, *New Venture Creation,* 3rd ed. (Homewood, IL: Irwin, 1990).

21. J. Carey and J. Hamilton, "Gene Hunters Go for the Big Score," *Business Week,* August 16, 1993, 44.

22. Timmons, 1990.

23. For in-depth treatments of the research on groups in general and work groups in particular, see J. R. Hackman, ed., *Groups That Work (and Those That Don't)* (San Francisco: Jossey-Bass, 1990); M. Shaw, *Group Dynamics: The Psychology of Small Group Behavior,* 3rd ed. (New York: McGraw-Hill, 1981); S. Worchel, W. Wood, and J. Simpson, eds., *Group Processes and Productivity* (Newbury Park, CA: Sage, 1991).

24. G. Dees, "Consensus on Strategy Formulation and Organizational Performance: Competitors in a Fragmented Industry," *Strategic Management Journal* 8 (1987): 259–277.

25. D. Slevin and J. Covin, "Creating and Maintaining High Performance Teams," in *The State of the Art of Entrepreneurship,* ed. D. Sexton and J. Kasarda (Boston: PWS-Kent, 1992): 358–386.

26. Timmons, 1990.

27. G. Parker, *Team Players and Teamwork: The New Competitive Business Strategy* (San Francisco: Jossey-Bass, 1990).

28. L. Michaelson, W. Watson, and R. Black, "A Realistic Test of Individual versus Group Consensus Decision Making," *Journal of Applied Psychology* 74 (1989): 834–839.

29. See S. Robbins, *Organizational Behavior,* 6th ed. (Upper Saddle River, NJ: Prentice Hall, 1993), Chapter 10.

30. Bird, 1989.

31. Timmons, 1990.

32. Robbins, 1993.

33. See C. Leanea, "A Partial Test of Janis' Groupthink Model: Effects of Group Cohesiveness and Leader Behaviour on Defective Decision Making," *Journal of Management,* Spring 1985, 5–17; and G. Morehead and J. Montanari, "An Empirical Investigation into the Groupthink Phenomenon," *Human Relations,* May 1986, 339–410.

34. See N. Kogen and M. Wallach, "Risk Taking as a Function of the Situation, the Person and the Group," *New Directions in Psychology,* vol. 3 (New York: Holt, Reinhart and Winston, 1967).

35. C. McCabe, "Entrepreneur's Notebook: The Value of Expert Advice," *Nation's Business,* November 1992, 9.

36. J. Rothstein, A. Bruno, W. Bygrave, and N. Taylor, "The CEO, Venture Capitalists and the Board," *Journal of Business Venturing,* March 1993, 99–113.

37. Collins and Porras, *Built to Last.* This section will apply the book's results to new venture issues and rely on the Collins and Porras text.
38. B. Schlender and L. Ellison, "Oracle at Web Speed," *Fortune,* May 1999; article online at www.ecompany.com/articles/mag/1,1640,4974,00.html.
39. M. Meyer, "Here's a 'Virtual' Model for America's Industrial Giants," *Newsweek,* August 23, 1993, 32.
40. John A. Byrne, "The Virtual Corporation," *Business Week,* February 8, 1993, 98–102.
41. "Virtual Corporations: Fast and Focused," *Business Week,* February 8, 1993, 134.
42. M. Casson, *Enterprise and Competitiveness* (Oxford, UK: Clarendon Press, 1990).
43. A. Chandler, *Strategy and Structure: Chapters in the History of American Industrial Enterprise* (Cambridge, MA: MIT Press, 1962.)
44. Chandler, 1962.
45. Kaplan and Norton, *The Balanced Scorecard.* This section will draw upon the concepts of the balanced scorecard and apply these concepts to entrepreneurial ventures.
46. J. Cornwall and B. Perlman, *Organizational Entrepreneurship* (Homewood, IL: Irwin). See Chapter 5.
47. B. Marsh, "Dance, Damn It," *The Wall Street Journal,* special small business report, November 22, 1991, R4.
48. B. Bowers, "Ommmmmmmmmmmm," *The Wall Street Journal,* special small business report, November 22, 1991, R4.
49. E. Carlson, "What If You Just Ate a Pizza?" *The Wall Street Journal,* special small business report, November 22, 1991, R4.
50. It is only with the passing of history and the noticeable philanthropy of these families that we think positively about their wealth and fortunes.
51. J. Dees and J. Starr, "Entrepreneurship Through an Ethical Lens: Dilemmas and Issues for Research and Practice," in *The State of the Art of Entrepreneurship,* D. Sexton and J. Kasarda, eds. (Boston: PWS-Kent, 1992), 89–116.
52. For standard treatments of human resource theory and personnel practice, see the following texts: G. Milkovitch and J. Boudreau, *Human Resource Management,* 6th ed. (Homewood, IL: Irwin, 1991); W. Cascio, *Applied Psychology and Personnel Management,* 4th ed. (Upper Saddle River, NJ: Prentice Hall, 1991); W. Werther and K. Davis, *Human Resources and Personnel Management,* 4th ed (New York: McGraw-Hill, 1993).
53. These examples are drawn from *Inc.* magazine's July 1993 issue on the best small businesses to work for.

Chapter 10

1. The word was coined by G. Pinchot in his book, *Intrapreneurship* (New York: Harper & Row, 1985).
2. B. Dumaine, "Closing the Innovation Gap," *Fortune,* December 2, 1991, 56–62.
3. J. Pierce and A. Delbecq, "Organizational Structure, Individual Attitudes and Innovation," *Academy of Management Review* 2 (1976): 27–37.
4. Adapted from R. Nielsen, M. Peters, and R. Hisrich, "Intrapreneurship Strategy for Internal Markets: Corporate, Nonprofit and Government Institution Cases," *Strategic Management Journal* 6 (April/June 1985): 181–189.
5. R. Burgelman, "Corporate Entrepreneurship and Strategic Management: Insights from a Process Study," *Management Science* 29 (December 1983): 1349–1364.
6. S. Zahra, "Predictors and Financial Outcomes of Corporate Entrepreneurship: An Exploratory Study," *Journal of Business Venturing* 6 (July 1991): 259–285.
7. E. Neuborne, "Pepsi's Aim Is True," *Business Week e.biz,* January 22, 2001, 52.
8. The information on 3M is extracted from P. Drucker, *Innovation and Entrepreneurship* (New York: Harper & Row, 1985).
9. This discussion follows G. Pinchot, 1985.
10. I. Hill, "An Intrapreneur-Turned-Entrepreneur Compares Both Worlds," *Research Management* 30 (May/June 1987): 33–37.

11. R. Knight, "Technological Innovation in Canada: A Comparison of Independent Entrepreneurs and Corporate Innovators," *Journal of Business Venturing* 4 (1989): 281–288.

12. G. Jones and J. Butler, "Managing Internal Corporate Entrepreneurship: An Agency Theory Perspective," *Journal of Management* 18 (1992): 733–749.

13. J. Cornwall and B. Perlman, *Organizational Entrepreneurship* (Homewood, IL: Irwin, 1990).

14. These sources are suggested in P. Drucker, *Innovation and Entrepreneurship.*

15. *Ibid.*

16. *Ibid.*

17. R. Burgelman, "Strategy Making as a Social Learning Process: The Case of Internal Corporate Venturing," *Interfaces* 18 (May/June 1988): 74–85.

18. R. Garud and A. Van de Ven, "An Empirical Evaluation of the Internal Corporate Venturing Process," *Strategic Management Journal* 13 (Summer 1992): 93–109.

19. D. Garvin, "Spinoffs and the New Firm Formulation Process," *California Management Review* 25 (1983): 3–20.

20. This discussion follows Pinchot, 1985.

21. T. Heller, "Loosely Coupled Systems for Corporate Entrepreneurship: Imagining and Managing the Innovation Project/Host Organization Interface," *Entrepreneurship: Theory and Practice,* Winter 1999, 24, 2, 25–31.

22. H. Sykes and Z. Block, "Corporate Venturing Obstacles: Sources and Solutions," *Journal of Business Venturing* 4 (May 1989): 159–167.

23. *Ibid.*

24. H. Geneen, "Why Intrapreneurship Doesn't Work," *Venture* 7 (January 1985): 46–52.

25. R. Kanter, "The New Workforce Meets the Changing Workplace: Strains, Dilemmas, and the Contradictions in Attempts to Implement Participative and Entrepreneurial Management," *Human Resource Management* 25 (Winter 1986): 515–537.

26. J. Duncan, P. Ginter, A. Rucks, and T. Jacobs, "Intrapreneurship and the Reinvention of the Corporation," *Business Horizons* 31 (May/June 1988): 16–21.

27. I. MacMillan, Z. Block, and P. Narasimha, "Corporate Venturing: Alternatives, Obstacles Encountered and Experienced Effects," *Journal of Business Venturing* 1 (Spring 1986): 177–191.

28. J. Quinn, "Managing Innovation: Controlled Chaos," Reprinted in *Entrepreneurship: Creativity at Work* (Cambridge, MA: Harvard Business Press, 1985).

29. Adapted from G. Pinchot, *Intrapreneurship,* pp. 198–199.

30. "Q & A: The *Inc.* Interview—Flashes of Genius" (George Gendron interviews Peter Drucker). The State of Small Business, 1996. *Inc.* Special Issue, p. 38.

31. M. Granovetter, "Economic Action and Social Structure: The Problem of Embeddedness," *American Journal of Sociology* 91 (1985): 481–510.

32. P. Dubini and H. Aldrich, "Personal and Extended Networks Are Central to the Entrepreneurial Process," *Journal of Business Venturing* 6 (1991): 305–313.

33. We use the terms *networking, partnering, joint ventures,* and *alliances* interchangeably to make the text more readable. Sometimes distinctions are made between these different forms based on ownership, control, number of participants, and other factors.

34. K. Harrigan, *Managing for Joint Venture Success* (Lexington, MA: Lexington Books, 1986).

35. B. Wysocki, "U.S. Incubators Help Japan Hatch Ideas," *The Wall Street Journal,* June 12, 2000, A1.

36. Quoted in U. Gupta, "A Shared Commitment," *The Wall Street Journal,* November 22, 1991, B2.

37. Dubini and Aldrich, 1991.

38. *Ibid.*

39. A. Hirschman, *Exit, Voice, and Loyalty* (Cambridge, MA: Harvard University Press, 1972).

40. M. Granovetter, "The Strength of Weak Ties," *American Journal of Sociology* 78 (1973): 1360–1380.

41. S. Birley, "The Role of Networks in the Entrepreneurial Process," *Journal of Business Venturing* 1 (1985): 107–117; B. Johannison, "New Venture Creation: A Network Approach,"

Frontiers of Entrepreneurial Research (Wellesley, MA: Babson College, 1986).

42. Dubini and Aldrich, 1991.

43. M. Dollinger, "Environmental Boundary Spanning and Information Processing Effects on Organizational Performance," *Academy of Management Journal* 27 (1984): 351–368.

44. Granovetter, 1973.

45. From E. Carlson, "Outside Directors Are an Asset Inside Small Companies," *The Wall Street Journal,* October 30, 1992.

46. Quoted in J. Saddler, "Electronic Bulletin Boards Help Businesses Post Success," *The Wall Street Journal,* October 29, 1992.

47. A. McCarthy, D. Krueger, and T. Schoenecker, "Changes in the Time Allocation Patterns of Entrepreneurs," *Entrepreneurship: Theory and Practice* 15 (1990): 7–18.

48. G. Astley and C. Fombrun, "Collective Strategy: Social Ecology of Organizational Environments," *Academy of Management Review* 8 (1983): 576–587.

49. M. Dollinger, "The Evolution of Collective Strategies in Fragmented Industries," *Academy of Management Review* 15 (1990): 266–285.

50. P. Coy, "Two Cheers for Corporate Collaboration," *Business Week,* May 3, 1993, 34.

51. M. Selz, "Networks Help Small Companies Think and Act Big," *The Wall Street Journal,* November 12, 1992, B2.

52. M. Geringer, *Joint Venture Partner Selection* (New York: Quorum Books, 1988).

53. J. Starr and I. Macmillan, "Resource Cooption via Social Contracting: Resource Acquisition Strategies for New Ventures," *Strategic Management Journal* 11 (1990): 79–92.

54. Geringer, 1988.

55. *Ibid.*

56. Starr and Macmillan, 1990.

57. F. Fry, *Entrepreneurship: A Planning Approach* (Minneapolis/St. Paul: West, 1993).

58. *A Profile of Franchising: Volume III.* A statistical abstract of the 1998 UFOC data. (IFA Educational Foundation: Washington, DC: February, 2000).

59. C. Hill and G. Jones, *Strategic Management: An Integrated Approach* (Boston: Houghton-Mifflin, 1992).

60. M. Carney and E. Gedajlovic, "Vertical Integration in Franchise Systems: Agency Theory and Resource Explanations," *Strategic Management Journal* 12 (1991): 607–629.

61. M. Jensen and W. Meckling, "Theory of the Firm: Managerial Behavior, Agency Costs, and Ownership Structure," *Journal of Financial Economics* 3 (1976): 305–360.

62. S. Norton, "Franchising, Brand Name Capital, and the Entrepreneurial Capacity Problem," *Strategic Management Journal* 9 (1988): 105–114.

63. J. Brickley and F. Dark, "The Choice of Organizational Form: The Case of Franchising," *Journal of Financial Economics* 18 (1987): 401–420.

64. This is somewhat problematic when a company like McDonald's considers the trading area for one of its locations to be a 4-minute drive.

65. J. Tannenbaum, "Angry Franchisees Turn Spotlight to FTC Enforcement," *The Wall Street Journal,* October 13, 1992, B2.

66. A. Sherman, "Franchiser Checklist," *Inc.,* January 1992, 89–90.

67. J. Emshwiller, "Investors Claim Ventures Meant No Opportunity," *The Wall Street Journal,* June 8, 1992, B1.

68. J. Tannenbaum and L. Valeriano. "Nutri/System Franchisees Live Franchiser's Nightmare," *The Wall Street Journal,* May 3, 1993, B1.

69. U.S. Department of Commerce, *Franchise Opportunity Handbook* (Washington, DC: Government Printing Office, 1984).

70. FTC Rule at 436.2(n).

Name Index

A

Abodeely, Paul A., 238
Abramson, Patty, 221
Ader, Jason N., 261
Adkins, Dinah, 30
Ala-Pietila, Pekka, 187
Aldelson, Sheldon G., 261
Argiris, Lisa, 237
Arguelles, Jesus, 237
Armony, Izhar, 275
Asseily, Henri, 11

B

Babbage, Charles, 70
Baldwin, James, 480
Ball, Andrew J., 216–217
Ball, Tony, 186
Barksdale, Jim, 400, 401
Barnard, Kurt, 88
Barrett, Craig, 311
Bartoli, Diane, 478–488
Barton, James, 466, 475
Bascomb, Neal, 478–488
Bedbury, Scott, 400
Beebee, Andrew, 8
Belluzzo, Rick, 186
Berg, Paul, 299–300
Bernstein, Ed, 212
Bezos, Jeff, 188
Bierman, Pamela, 499–510
Bingham, Bob, 94
Biondi, Frank, Jr., 192
Bisharat, Jaleh, 400
Block, Lawrence, 480

Blohm, David, 88
Blum, Scott, 30
Boissevain, Ben, 307
Boroian, Patrick J., 307
Bourke, Paul, 187
Boyle, T. C., 480
Branson, Richard C. N., 334, 336
Bresnick, Paul, 480
Brink, Greg, 496
Brockhaus, 41
Brooks, Bonnie J., 412
Brummett, Tom, 347–348
Buba, Crisanne, 234
Bullwinkle, Richard, 466, 470
Burns, Gary, 208
Burns, Robin, 97
Burton, Tim, 192

C

Calleja, Jay, 81
Carlisle, Michael, 479
Carter, Linda Kelleher, 420–434
Case, Steve, 186
Cassidy, Mike, 147
Change, Yi-Hsin, 394–405
Chappell, Tom, 43
Chen, Ping, 406–419
Chu, Quyen, 394–405
Cihra, Robert, 39
Cohen, Ben, 344
Cohen, Sheryl, 499–510
Coleman, Bill, 186
Collins, J. C., 18, 294, 306, 308, 311
Cooperstein, David, 12
Cooper, Tim, 480

Subject Index

Underutilized resource, 96
Unexpected opportunity, 67, 68
Unfamiliars, 297
United Ad Label, 321
"Up selling", 103
U.S. bankruptcy laws, 280
 Bankruptcy Reform Act of 1978
  Chapter 7 bankruptcy, 282–283
  Chapter 11 bankruptcy, 283
  Chapter 13 bankruptcy, 283
 BeFree Inc. example, 285
 options and bargaining power,
  283–284
 predictive model of bankruptcy (table),
  282
 warning signs/predictive models,
  281–282
User-based quality, 17
Utilitarian rule, 325
Utility, 107
Utility patents, 59

V

Valuable resources, 27–28
Value-based quality, 17
Value capture, 190–191, 192
Value creating, 27, 107
Value creation, 190
Value pricing, 197–198
Values, 65–66, 301
Venture capital, 229–230, 231, 256
Venture completion, 339
Venture plan, 127
Veriad, 321
Versioning, 198–199
Vertical niche, 208
Virgin Group Ltd., 334, 336
Virtual organization, 294, 312–313, 314

VirtualVineyard, 210
Vision, 54–55
Visionary companies, 294, 306, 309–310
Voice, 345

W

Wabash National, 115–116
Walden Paddlers, 313
Walker Digital Corporation, 103
Wal-Mart, 14–15, 25, 197, 310
Warrant, 272–273
Weak ties, 345–346
Webcor Builders, Inc., 216–217
"Wetware", 200
Wine.com, 210
winetasting.com, 210
Winner's Curse, 333
WomenAngels.net, 221
Women-focused venture capital firms,
 221–222
Women's Growth Capital Fund, 221
Women's Technology Cluster, 221
Woolco, 14
Workability test, 121
Working capital, 220, 222
Working group, 295
Work-in-process inventory, 225
Workplace 2000, 3

Y

Youth, entrepreneurship and, 2–5
Yoyodyne, Inc., 22–23

Z

Zara, 49
Zoots, 81